ENCYCLOPÉDIE NOIRE

Encyclopédie noire

The Making of
Moreau de Saint-Méry's
Intellectual World

SARA E. JOHNSON

Published by the
OMOHUNDRO INSTITUTE OF
EARLY AMERICAN HISTORY AND CULTURE,
Williamsburg, Virginia,
and the
UNIVERSITY OF NORTH CAROLINA PRESS,
Chapel Hill

The Omohundro Institute of Early American History and Culture (OI) is an independent research organization sponsored by William & Mary and the Colonial Williamsburg Foundation. On November 15, 1996, the OI adopted the present name in honor of a bequest from Malvern H. Omohundro, Jr., and Elizabeth Omohundro.

Cover art: Detail from *Moreau dévoilé: A Portrait Collage, Part II.* By Luz Sandoval and Sara E. Johnson. Adapted from Aménaïde Moreau de Saint-Méry, *Conte Moreau de Saint Méry,* circa 1800–1805, licensed by Ministero della Cultura—Complesso Monumentale della Pilotta-Galleria Nazionale di Parma.

Parts of this book draw on previously published work: "Your Mother Gave Birth to a Pig: Power, Abuse, and Planter Linguistics in Baudry des Lozière's *Vocabulaire Congo,*" *Early American Studies,* XVI (2018), 7–40, © 2018 The McNeil Center for Early American Studies, all rights reserved; "Moreau de Saint-Méry: Itinerant Bibliophile," *Library and Information History,* XXXI (2015), 171–197, © CILIP 2015, reproduced with permission of Edinburgh University Press Limited through PLSclear.

Library of Congress Cataloging-in-Publication Data
Names: Johnson, Sara E. (Sara Elizabeth), author.
Title: Encyclopédie noire : the making of Moreau de Saint-Méry's intellectual world / Sara E. Johnson.
Other titles: Making of Moreau de Saint-Méry's intellectual world
Description: Williamsburg, Virginia : Omohundro Institute of Early American History and Culture ; Chapel Hill : University of North Carolina Press, [2023] | Includes bibliographical references and index. | Text in English with extensive quotations in French, with translation into English. Also with quotations in Kreyòl, Kikongo, Spanish, Italian, and other languages, with translations into English.
Identifiers: LCCN 2023020762 | ISBN 9781469676913 (cloth ; alk. paper) | ISBN 9781469676920 (ebook)
Subjects: LCSH: Moreau de Saint-Méry, M. L. E. (Médéric Louis Elie), 1750–1819. | Moreau de Saint-Méry, M. L. E. (Médéric Louis Elie), 1750–1819—Criticism and interpretation—History. | Black people—Haiti—History. | Enslaved persons—Haiti—History. | Language and culture—Caribbean Area. | Enlightenment—Caribbean Area. | BISAC: HISTORY / United States / Colonial Period (1600–1775) | SOCIAL SCIENCE / Ethnic Studies / American / African American & Black Studies | LCGFT: Biographies.
Classification: LCC F1923 .J64 2023 | DDC 972.94/030922—dc23/eng/20230517
LC record available at https://lccn.loc.gov/2023020762

For my parents
For my Egún
For Julián, Amaya, and Carolina

CONTENTS

ILLUSTRATIONS

TABLE

NOTE ON TRANSLATION

I have chosen to include the original language of my sources in the body of the text whenever possible. The languages in which we think, speak, and write craft our worldview. The people whose lives and ideas are documented in this book did not use English as their primary language, if at all, and the prominent inclusion of other languages on the main page serves as a reminder of this reality. Many of these people would not have considered French their primary language either, although the sources about them were often written in French and other European idioms. I call attention to the non-European languages circulating in the orbit of Moreau de Saint-Méry and his interlocutors throughout the book. My hope is that readers will consult the source languages and make their own interpretations when possible.

The decision about how to translate *nègre* and *négresse* was a complicated one. In eighteenth-century Saint-Domingue, the terms denoted a Black man or a Black woman. In numerous sources, however, the word *nègre,* when unmodified by an adjective, carried the understanding of slave—blackness and the condition of enslavement conjoined—although the term was also used to refer to freed or free people. I translate the words as "Black." I have also elected to translate *esclave* as "enslaved" in many instances, especially when referring to specific people. This decision recognizes that a person was enslaved in addition to being other things (tall, musically gifted, shy, a mother, a sailor, a farmer): a complex person, not a commodity, even when legally defined as such. I retain the French terms *mulâtre* and *mulâtresse* in my English translations.

Unless otherwise specified, all translations from the French, Spanish, and Italian are my own. I have relied on Baudry des Lozières's admittedly suspect translations of Kikongo-continuum languages into French to pivot my own translations from his French into English. I have also tried to maintain the sentence structure and diction of the original languages, sometimes at the expense of somewhat clunky English prose, in order to preserve a sense of the original cadence and, often, the long-windedness of the original texts. When a single word in a foreign language appears for the first time in a chapter, it is italicized. The eighteenth-century convention of printing *ai* as *oi* (Français as François, as in Cap Français, for example) has been updated for modern readers.

ENCYCLOPÉDIE NOIRE

Introduction

Notes toward a Communal Biography
of Moreau de Saint-Méry

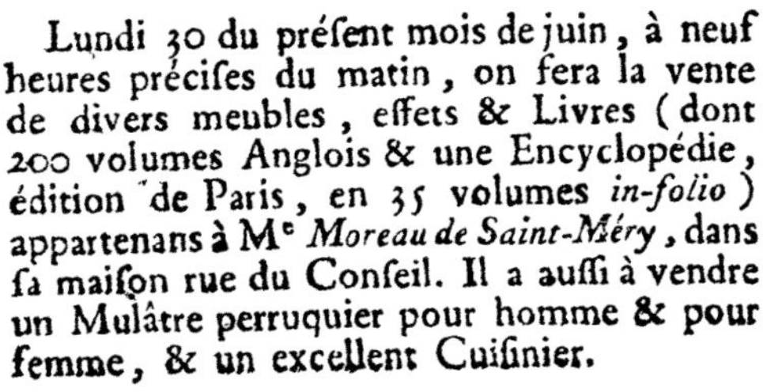

Lundi 30 du préfent mois de juin, à neuf
heures précifes du matin, on fera la vente
de divers meubles, effets & Livres (dont
200 volumes Anglois & une Encyclopédie,
édition ˜de Paris, en 35 volumes *in-folio*)
appartenans à Mᵉ *Moreau de Saint-Méry*, dans
fa maifon rue du Confeil. Il a auffi à vendre
un Mulâtre perruquier pour homme & pour
femme, & un excellent Cuifinier.

FIGURE I. "Biens et effets à vendre: Lundi 30 du présent mois de juin,"
Affiches américaines (Cap Français, Saint-Domingue), June 18, 1783, [4]. The
advertisement reads, "To be sold, Monday, the 30th of the present month
of June, at exactly nine o'clock in the morning, various furniture, effects
and books (including 200 volumes in English and an *Encyclopédie*, Parisian
edition, in 35 volumes *in folio*) belonging to M. Moreau de Saint-Méry, at his
house on Conseil Street. He is also selling a mulâtre wigmaker for men and
women, and an excellent cook."

In 1783, Médéric Louis Élie Moreau de Saint-Méry (1750–1819) was headed to
France from Cap Français. Born in Martinique, he had been living in Saint-
Domingue since 1775, where he dedicated much of his time to documenting
Caribbean social customs. The notice above is one of several advertisements
that appeared in the local newspaper announcing his imminent departure for
Europe. In some of these announcements, he advertised two thousand books for
sale. Part of a large library by standards throughout the colonial Americas, this
collection and its sale presaged his life as a bibliophile who would own thousands
of books and manuscripts, many rare, by the time of his death. In other ads,
he announced the publication of the first volume of his *Loix et constitutions,* the
printing of which was the motivation behind this particular trip to France. The

June 1783 advertisement announced the sale of his furniture, various effects, and
more books, two hundred of them in English (Figure 1). In addition, he mentioned the sale of his large-format, thirty-five-volume set of a Parisian edition
of the *Encyclopédie,* the eighteenth-century Enlightenment text par excellence.
Following these objects, he casually listed the sale of two men. One was a skilled
wigmaker. The other was an excellent cook. The books and the people Moreau
owned were moving in related transactional circuits: people, books, books,
people. His ability to fund his trip to Paris and the printing of a volume that has
sealed his legacy as a canonical source in Caribbean studies required the sale of
enslaved members of his household.[1]

   This advertisement captures the central concerns of this book. Moreau was
a multilingual philosophe with multigenerational ties to the Caribbean, his
self-proclaimed *patrie.* He was a slaveholding intellectual of the Jeffersonian
model, a man who thought and wrote about the much-discussed ideas of liberty
and equality even as he bought and sold human beings alongside furnishings,
books, and maps.[2] This book embraces the challenge of contrasting the capa-
ciousness of Moreau's intellect with the extreme violence that undergirded the
colonial system to which he devoted his life. Over the course of his career—as
a lawyer and judge, ethnographer, printer and bookseller, editor and translator,
official historiographer of the French Ministry of the Navy and Colonies, diplomat, and participant in a host of intellectual academies on both sides of the
Atlantic—Moreau's livelihood depended upon the study of and profits generated
from slaveholding societies. The book moves beyond the conundrum prevalent
when studying men of his ilk: "yes, he was a slaveholder / bigot, *but* he was a
genius / founding father / skilled writer / man of his times." Moreau was these
things because of, not despite, his investment in slavery. His work teaches us
much about the intellectual projects and biases of slaveholding elites anxious to
acquire political autonomy and scholarly status for their American homelands.
It likewise provides a wealth of information, much of it fragmentary, about the
people he studied and how they negotiated the legal customs and personal relationships designed to commodify them.

   While making notes on the practice of slavery in the United States during
his 1790s exile in Philadelphia, Moreau remarked that "the American people,
so excited about their own liberty, do not consider the liberty of others unless it
suits their political convenience" (le peuple américain si enflammé pour sa liberté
écoute la politique lorsqu'il s'agit de celle des autres). Moreau could have been
holding up a mirror to himself and the French colonial state he represented. For
example, as president of the Paris Commune electors in 1789, he worked enthu-
siastically for government reform even while he represented the planter lobby

and argued vociferously against the abolition of slavery and reforms that would have granted increased rights to free people of color in the colonies. An ideologue of white superiority who left copious descriptions of the alleged seductive voluptuousness *(volupté)* of free women of color, "priestesses of Venus" (prêtresses de Vénus) designed for pleasure, he personally raised and educated his beloved mixed-race daughter Aménaïde, his child with his freed Black housekeeper *(menagère)* Marie-Louise Laplaine. Their father-daughter relationship is captured in dozens of letters that provide a fascinating intertext to his published work. These double standards about the meaning of liberty and who was "deserving" of it would have been clear to a man who was deeply familiar with arguments spanning the whole spectrum of anti- to proslavery thought in the revolutionary Atlantic world. It is not anachronistic to evaluate his work according to the ideologies that he himself was instrumental in creating, evaluating, and disseminating. He was indeed a man of his times.[3]

All roads in French Caribbean historiography intersect with Moreau's work. His infamous explanation of the differences between Black and white racial groups has likewise made him a primary source on theories of racialization in the eighteenth-century Americas. His two seminal texts, the six-volume *Loix et constitutions* (1784–1790) and two-volume *Description topographique, physique, civile, politique et historique de la partie française de l'isle Saint-Domingue* (1797–1798), document the legal, social, cultural, and scientific customs of the French Antilles. The former was a compendium commissioned by the French court, with Moreau benefiting from the patronage networks of the "colonial machine." The latter, a classic in the genre of natural history, was read widely in the years after its publication and even used by former planters to justify their claims following the Haitian state's 1825 agreement to indemnify former French planters for their losses during the Haitian Revolution. The *Description* is now consulted widely by academics, fiction writers, and genealogists.[4]

Given the vast scope of Moreau's work, many roads through Latin American natural history, translation studies, 1790s Philadelphia print culture, and early American visual culture should lead to Moreau as well. He is a figure best understood beyond storylines that assume only a French colonial / nationalist framework as a point of departure or ending. He surfaced repeatedly at flash point historical moments in the revolutionary Atlantic world and as a doyen of historical memory of the hemispheric Americas: presiding over events in the aftermath of the storming of the Bastille in 1789; claiming to have found Christopher Columbus's remains while doing research in Spanish Santo Domingo; witnessing political and bibliographic practices in the early U.S. Republic; compiling, circulating, and archiving legal codices for the global French empire. This book positions Moreau at the center of a web whose skeins encompass stories that are geographically diverse (intra-American, transatlantic, and transpacific), linguistically rich, and deeply mired in the racial and class fault lines of the Age of Revolutions.

Moreau's achievements were, at every turn, predicated upon his extraction of labor, physical and intellectual, from enslaved people and free people of color. Enslaved women, men, and children took care of him; their work afforded him the leisure to write and contributed to the wealth he needed to amass his research collection. He litigated and tried cases within a legal system grounded in slave codes. He once even proposed that he be allowed to use money from the *caisse des libertés*—a fund containing the fees slaveholders paid to emancipate enslaved laborers—to cover the travel expenses he would incur collecting more information for the ensemble of work he called his *Ouvrage*.[5] Much as the wealth generated from slaveholding scaffolded the material possibilities of his life, his intellectual pursuits were similarly grounded in the institution of slavery. He wrote about the customs of people of African descent: their languages, dances, religious practices. He entertained learned audiences at the American Philosophical Society in Philadelphia and elsewhere with lectures about the ingenuity of the wooden locks used by the enslaved in Saint-Domingue (lectures accompanied by the objects themselves). Although images of the Enlightenment era showcase white men and women conversing in their salons and laboring in their workshops, whose intellectual activity was on display in Moreau's work? He preyed on Black knowledge, not only Black labor.

Even as he serves as the glue that binds together the stories that follow, Moreau acts as an unreliable center whose interpretations I question throughout. The structure of the book, along with a recasting of the stories of the people who made his life's work possible, turn the biographical approach inside out.[6] The core challenge and commitment of this book is to keep multiple groups in the same frame: the extended Moreau family; the enslaved, both those the family owned and the thousands who formed the bulwark of their communities; and the free people of color who were also the subject of his work.

The project is thus a communal biography, one that foregrounds Moreau's multiple households and professional relationships. To the extent that the biographical genre works on behalf of an individual subject, communal biography extends a reader's focus to the lives of others. These others, so often lost or known only through fragments, are critical interlocutors. Communal biography concentrates attention on what and whom we know and do not know historically. It is a creative, interdisciplinary enterprise that explores the lives of historical actors through prose narrative and close readings of archival documents. It functions through the accumulated weight of serialized anecdotes, both textual and graphic. Just as important, it experiments with the *way* the words and images are presented—the way of crafting a page, as it were—so that readers have to ingest and process information differently than they ordinarily might. At times, it provokes readerly discomfort, prioritizing the act of wondering that stretches what can be seen and understood. In some instances, it is a life-making endeavor—a pushback against "slaves" or even "enslaved" as the dominant category for studying people. Instead, people are encountered as language innovators; as members of kinship networks; as world travelers; as figures, often unwilling, in transatlantic scientific and moral debates; as brokers of their own social and political lives.

Communal biography, then, has allowed me to explore Moreau's legacy by re-archiving it to different ends that rebut the worst of the inheritance he and other planter intellectuals have bequeathed us. It showcases how Moreau's capacity to create and institutionalize knowledge—including knowledge about himself as a man who believed in his own biographical worthiness—was dependent on stolen labor. Every beautiful book he crafted contains an embedded story of hidden violence. We cannot evaluate Moreau simply as a legal scholar, bookseller, printer, arbiter of culture, and diplomat. His life and his work reveal how structures of violence, even evil, proliferated through the law, bookselling, printing, cultural history, and diplomacy. The narrative trope of dismemberment that haunts his ethnographic and legal descriptions of colonial life, for instance, existed alongside physical dismemberment of human beings. I use his life and work to expose violence in the social practices that were as quotidian as they were powerful. I repudiate the values of the system he defended while arguing that his work remains of vital importance.

And his work is indeed fundamental to understanding how the economic gains from slavery undergirded myriad, sometimes seemingly unrelated, cultural practices. An apologist for slavery, Moreau nonetheless left some of the most detailed accounts of the social customs of enslaved women and men, recounted amid the prosaic details of life in what many, including Moreau, considered a war zone. From these narratives, we also know that men and women set type, dried paper and folded pages, and fashioned elegant books in Moreau's printshop, providing a French and French Caribbean expertise to the early North American book trade that is often ignored. Meanwhile, Moreau's diligent translations of Spanish-language manuscripts, essays on Chinese culture, and exhaustive compilation of French jurisprudence evince the vitality of American intellectual debates in an age that prided itself on informed investigations into the forces that made the world go round. His mind contained an evolving index of information. A jurist, he was also a cultural historian with strong literary tendencies, concerned not only with what the laws were but how they were related to *mentalité* and behavior. An engagement with his work repulses and interests me on many levels: for the depths of its casual sadism; for Moreau's keen eye and almost obsessive fixation with punishment techniques and the particulars of typesetting styles; for his vibrant descriptions of a wide swathe of eighteenth-century life.

I use Moreau's work as a platform to explore how and to what ends he, and in turn we, craft stories and generate knowledge. I am interested in why stories are created, weaponized for profit or professional accolade, rejected, translated, consumed. The disciplinary divisions between fields such as natural history, literary criticism, and linguistics had not hardened in Moreau's time, and I have built my study of this late-eighteenth- and early-nineteenth-century world on the premise that these different categories of knowledge did, and still do, inform one another. Many of Moreau's interdisciplinary research methods are embedded into the content and format of this book. I repurpose the master's tools to dismantle his house and ideology, in part by showing that these tools were never solely his in the first place.[7]

Four methodological convictions explain Moreau's enduring legacy to scholars of slavery, print, and popular culture: a deep reliance on archival evidence; a commitment to multilingual research; mobilization of visual evidence; and work that cuts across the European imperial borders of the slaveholding Americas. Each chapter explicitly engages the value of these techniques to relate different, perhaps unexpected, accounts about the circulation of people and ideas during the upheavals of multiple revolutions. Devotion to amassing and circulating knowledge for practical use was a cornerstone of American and European Enlightenment projects. Moreau was heavily shaped by these ideals, particularly the desire to be useful. His prolific production, like that of many of his contemporaries, was peppered with the word *utilité,* what Shannon Lee Dawdy has called "the third leg of the Enlightenment."[8] Moreau, however, has himself proved useful to present-day scholars in ways he might not have imagined. This project erects an alternate world of knowledge production around a figure who defined himself as a producer of useful knowledge.[9]

The stakes of this project are inseparable from present-day international conversations about the legacies of slavery that address questions of documentation, memorialization, and the possibility of reparations.[10] My goal is to account for the active suppression and careless disregard of the voices of people who were both direct actors in shaping Moreau's intellectual trajectory and recipients of his "enlightened" ideas. This objective extends long-standing discussions in the historiography of slavery and its afterlives that argue "that incomplete history

Inability to associate
culture, ignorance, death
& evil

INTRODUCTION   7

remains a worthy pursuit" and that "theorizing what we might call the counter-fact, . . . the fact the archive is seeking to ignore, marginalize and disavow," be-comes a way of producing scholarship that is "accountable to the enslaved."[11] Scholarship, particularly within a Black feminist intellectual tradition, explor-ing methods such as "critical fabulation," "poetics of fragmentation," and "wake work," offers interpretive frameworks and formal experimentation with hybrid narrative genres that push the bounds of storytelling scholarship about unfree, unacknowledged labor and its material and psychological conditions. There is a groundswell of research in this field, much of it inspired by Saidiya Hartman, whose influential research probes the "protocols and limits" at work when trying to write narratives based on "listening for the unsaid, translating misconstrued words, and refashioning disfigured lives—and intent on achieving an impossible goal: redressing the violence that produced numbers, ciphers, and fragments of discourse, which is as close as we come to a biography of the captive and the en-slaved." Her most enduring contribution is addressing what she calls the "fictions of history"—its foundational "truths" and the discipline itself—in a context where "history pledges to be faithful to the limits of fact, evidence, and archive, even as those dead certainties are produced by terror."[12]

Creative writers have also done much of this work in the genres of poetry, speculative fiction, historical fiction, and the critical paratextual apparatus of scholarly essays and interviews about their writing. In her prose poems and es-says, the Trinidadian-Canadian writer M. NourbeSe Philip wonders how one can produce different kinds of knowledge against the odds outlined above: "It's as if we're moving towards an understanding that there's a built-in limit to how much those tools, including the archive, have helped us to this point. And this limit requires new approaches to engage the task at hand, to tell the stories of our time. . . . I feel that we are coming back to the same story—that is trying to tell itself—by 'untelling'; the same questions, but with different resources, different understandings." As both a project and a method, "untelling" involves an open-ness to unraveling/fracturing what we (think we) know and the accumulated layers of discourse that have allowed us to understand how and why we know it.[13]

This book takes seriously the call to explore "untelling" as a means of retell-ing to uncover stories about the past that historicism per se cannot. The study of slavery demands creativity and risk taking. It also requires attention to the idea that the worldviews of the dominated and the dominant (living in inter-connected, but not synonymous, worlds) require distinct and sometimes di-vergent sensitivities to evaluate. I believe in an ethical code to our scholarship that calls things out for what they were ("enslaved laborers," not "domestics";

"brutality," not "management principles"; "kidnapping," not "trade"; "children," not generic "slaves"); it rejects the euphemisms that make palatable the horrors through which our present world was built.

Communal biography assumes the value of informed speculation as one way to theorize the scarcity of written testimony left by what were millions of historical actors.[14] As such, this book attempts to think creatively about truth claims, what we consider evidence, and the value of wondering about what remains unknowable. This approach is particularly helpful when considering questions of subjectivity and interior life worlds, the "no man's land" of historical scholarship that sometimes evaluates such speculation as problematic when not tied to precise written documentation.[15] I consider subjectivity and interiority along a spectrum of thought—from calculated analysis, intention, and motivation to the more affective and emotional realm. They are states of mind that are communicative and self-reflexive, collective and individualized. Foregrounding what "could" have been for largely anonymous or little-known people centers human beings as a bundle of lived experience rather than ciphers. To capture what people living in disparate gendered, raced, and class-stratified environments might have thought and felt is one of the fundamental contributions of Black feminist scholarship to the study of slavery.

The four above-mentioned methods intersect with informed speculation to build this communal biographical study. First, the archival. The archives of slavery are textual. They are visual. They reside in many languages and the study thereof. They have metaphorical significance as guardians of epistemes and power. They are also repositories of millions of pieces of paper. A project with Moreau at its center recognizes that he was an archivist himself, over and above his work as author, printer, translator. His labor self-consciously generated a vast trove of information about slaveholding societies, and much of our understanding of what it means to be an Enlightenment-era bibliophile and record keeper is evident in Moreau's pursuits. He trafficked in manuscripts; a paper hoarder, he began his interactions with documents at the age of ten, when he worked in the record office in Martinique. Copying texts and purloining many original documents, he was extremely proud of his "immense collection that required twenty-four years of research, of work, of travel, enormous expense, etc., and that the destruction of several public record depositories in the colonies during the revolutionary storms renders original in several parts" (collection immense qui a exigé vingt-quatre années de recherches, de travaux, de voyages, une dépense énorme, etc., et que la destruction de plusieurs dépôts publics des colonies, pendant les orages révolutionnaires, rend désormais originale dans plusieurs parties). This "immense collection" was used to substantiate the regime of white supremacy.[16]

Moreau's archival imprint is scattered across Europe, the Caribbean, and North America. For example, in 1817, Louis XVIII purchased Moreau's corpus of print material, and it is now institutionalized as one of the cornerstones of the French colonial archives.[17] The F3 series that bears his name in Aix is almost inexhaustible in the scope of its diversity: handwritten snippets of transcribed Kreyòl satirical poetry by free women of color, newspaper clippings, voluminous correspondence, legal codices, manuscript witness accounts of heinous torture interrogations upon the enslaved. Alongside his personal library of books, maps, and periodicals sit planter pamphlet and essay screeds about why Saint-Domingue had been lost and how it might recover its former wealth. Moreau not only collected but organized his research: grouping colonies and topics together, often duplicating documents that were relevant to both for cross-referencing. Then there are his own voluminous works now housed in private and state archives and museums in Parma, Italy, as well as repositories including the French Bibliothèque nationale, the Library Company of Philadelphia, and the John Carter Brown Library. An extant copy of his bookstore's catalog is housed at the American Philosophical Society.

I followed the path of these materials. Like other scholars, I use them for purposes that exceed nationalist French historiography, challenge slaveholders' interpretations of events, pay attention to their materiality, and prioritize the ideas of diverse historical actors. There is no question that archives are repositories of power, filled in equal measure with the silences and the assumptions of the powerful. Despite this, they hold information that cannot be dismissed any more than it can be read uncritically. This project uses archival information in myriad ways: it reassembles it; it plays with and amends it in discomforting or unfamiliar fashion; it forces us to see gaps and fill them (or not) in ways that produce other ways of knowing.

With regard to languages, this book operates under the premise that a focus on linguistic specificity reveals ideological and interpersonal power dynamics critical to understanding the colonial world. Hierarchies within and between languages and those who speak, write, and transcribe them; glimpses of worldviews that manifest clearly through the particular word of choice (for example, *vika* versus *esclave* versus *slave*)—these are some of the stakes revealed when language is prioritized as a framework of analysis. My sources, especially in non-European languages such as Kikongo and Guaraní, challenge the continued Eurocentric balkanization of the study of the Americas into the dominant triumvirate of English-, French-, and Spanish-speaking communities. They dispute the dominance of these three languages and the related tendency to falsely equate one empire / nation to one language.[18] I approach language for what it teaches us about how words shape the horizons of our understanding, concurring with Christopher Ehret's contention that "every language is an archive. Its documents are the thousands of words that make up its lexicon."[19]

Moreau's commitment to achieving a working knowledge, if not fluency, in various languages provides an important intellectual model in the present. He worked in at least seven—French, English, Spanish, Dutch, Italian, Kreyòl, and Latin—and published scholarship concerning Chinese and Guaraní.[20] His engagement with these languages happened on multiple levels: performing diligent translations, negotiating oral and written business opportunities, reading and writing about materials produced in these languages, selling multilingual publications in his Philadelphia bookstore, amassing an extensive personal collection about the Americas in more than nine idioms, and publishing full-length monographs in French and English with type specially imported from London.[21]

In his capacity as author, editor, and printer, Moreau's attention to typography—the art of putting words and visual elements on a page, including letters and decorative reading stimulants—is a narrative strategy with continued resonance. The way in which stories were displayed and interpreted, through engravings, fancy fonts, and often literally on Black bodies, is a prime focus and theoretical tool of this book. The poet and typographer Robert Bringhurst notes that typography is "an essential act of interpretation," and I rely on it to make meaning. As was the case with Moreau's publications, this book uses visual imagery as illustration, as evidence, as mnemonic cue, as organizational guide. Each chapter is embellished with ornamental pieces that Moreau used in his own printshop, a reminder of his deep investment in the mechanical and artistic elements of the printing trade. My use of these graphics is meant to be discordant, evocative of the affective dissonance of his publications that were designed to please the eye, even as the words they inscribed were discursively violent.[22]

My communal biography entailed a communal, collaborative process that demanded artistic expertise. I have worked with a graphic artist, Luz Sandoval, to create and modify eighteenth-century and contemporary visual stimulants as a means of engaging with their storytelling possibilities. I collaborated with the University of North Carolina Press design team to nail down the correct typefaces and formatting. These sources picture a method of untelling and retelling, in dialogue with the rich scholarship demonstrating that "the visual *matters* to the rewiring of slavery's imaginary." For example, we adapted paintings to see below the surface level of Moreau's self-fashioning as a benevolent statesman; we made drawings to suggest collective biographies that explore household dynamics as much as they exist as representations of what people might have looked like. I experiment with the visual as a way of capturing sound and Black interiority. Taken together, these examples may force a reader to pause, find their expectation of certainty and clarity stymied, or feel entangled in a re-archiving process that does not always allow for an easy extraction of information.[23]

Finally, this project continues my own commitment to work that foregrounds the connection of people, ideas, and goods across imperial American frontiers. The following pages sketch the movement of enslaved people in the Moreau orbit between New Orleans, Martinique, Saint-Domingue, and the United States. They trace how a book Moreau published about China required laborers from all over the globe, Saint-Domingue and Batavia included, to gather in Philadelphia. Moreau was an important practitioner of hemispheric American historiography and letters. I take this to mean an orientation that prioritizes seeing "from" the Americas (Moreau resolutely identified as a man from the Caribbean despite living in Europe for much of his life); this perspective assumes the relevance of connections pursued across porous imperial and early national borders. His command of a dense body of work about the circum-Caribbean, including parts of North and South America, informed his belief that the Caribbean belonged to a circuit of ideas, commodities, and societies that were mutually interdependent. Moreau's work decisively illustrates that the "turn" toward extranational and comparative approaches to the study of the early Americas is in fact a return to the way many scholars of the period assessed their own worlds. His conviction that what was happening in Saint-Domingue could be useful to understanding events and ideas in Santo Domingo, Jamaica, Puerto Rico, or Philadelphia (and vice versa) was formed by his interest in the French state and its current and potential overseas territories.[24]

This communal biography is thus geographically expansive and grounded in numerous archives as well as several languages. It mines the possibilities of visual storytelling. I evaluate a multiplicity of sources that range from notarial records to newspaper advertisements to portraiture. Four print genres dominate the discussion: encyclopedias, natural histories, autobiographies in the form of legalistic memoirs and journals, and vocabularies / phrase books. I evaluate the content, format, and materiality of these texts, highlighting the "unnaturalness" of order presented in the genres that characterize eighteenth-century knowledge production. My work challenges us to see what happens when we view Moreau as a scholar who made ample use of speculation and was involved in "fiction writing" in his own right. His—and by extension other white metropolitan and creole—fantasies of dominance and submission are disputed.[25]

Moreau is the unreliable center from which these stories begin, and it is important to establish from the outset a sense of his life trajectory, particularly his material interests and intellectual beliefs. He was born in 1750 to a French family that had been living in Martinique for "more than 150 years" (plus de 150 ans) and boasted many high-ranking colonial administrators, particularly in the judiciary.[26] After spending five years studying law (as well as astronomy, math, and Latin) in Paris, he was admitted to the bar, and in 1775 he returned to settle in France's most prosperous American colonial city, Cap Français. He had an active law practice and served on the Superior Council (Conseil Supérieur). It was during these years that he cofounded the Cercle des Philadelphes, a group of planters and professionals interested in the natural sciences, art, and literature. He also continued his research on legal, cultural, and social issues. During one of his return research trips to France in 1788, he became very involved with metropolitan politics. He was a prominent city elector, represented Martinique in the National Assembly, and served as a public voice for the interests of the Club Massiac, a planter lobby in Paris known for its virulent proslavery views.[27] In 1790, he claimed he also received notice that he might be given the job of intendant of Saint-Domingue, the highest civil governing post in a French colony.[28]

After five years amid the tumult of revolutionary France, Moreau fled the country in 1793. He penned a swashbuckling story of his last-minute escape from Robespierre's agents onto the brig *Sophie,* a ship that carried him and his family to the United States. Upon arrival, he visited many Eastern Seaboard cities before settling in Philadelphia. Any intention of returning to Saint-Domingue was foiled by the events we now know as the Haitian Revolution, which changed the course of his life; he would never reside in the Caribbean again. The comte de Moré, in his memoir of this period, recalls Moreau lamenting, "You do not suspect who I am and what I was in days gone by? . . . I, who speak to you now, such as I am, was once king of Paris for three days and today I am forced to earn my bread by selling ink and pens and paper at Philadelphia." Far from limiting his exertions to peddling writing supplies, contraceptives, and hosiery, Moreau opened a multilingual bookshop that became a gathering center for fellow refugees from Caribbean and French revolutions. The shop housed a printing press, on which he published an assortment of pamphlets, periodicals, and work of his own that he had been researching, editing, and translating for years. His printing business, manned by itinerant fellow exiles in addition to his immediate family, published some of the most artistically sophisticated volumes emerging in the early U.S. Republic.[29]

Following passage of the Alien and Sedition Acts in 1798, Moreau returned to France.[30] He served briefly as historiographer of the French Ministry of the Navy and Colonies (Ministre de la Marine et des Colonies), then joined the French diplomatic corps at the invitation of his close friend Charles-Maurice de Talleyrand-Périgord.[31] He became the chief administrator of the strategically vital northern Italian duchies of Parma, Piacenza, and Guastalla. In 1805, he was recalled to Paris in disgrace for failing to put down a rebellion with what Napoleon Bonaparte deemed sufficient force and lived for the next fourteen years in "noble pauvreté," what one eulogist called "a state bordering on indigence" (un état voisin de l'indigence). Although "reduced to selling his silverware to survive" (réduit à vendre son argenterie pour subsister), he did, however, still employ servants; manage to direct and attend regular meetings at a variety of literary, economic, and agricultural societies; continue his editing and translation work; and acquire a large collection of expensive books. He also maintained his lifelong, multicontinental engagement with Masonic fraternities, serving as an officer in the Parisian Loge des Neuf Soeurs, a group whose membership rolls provide a who's who of elite political and philosophical circles. He died suddenly of a urinary tract infection in 1819.[32]

When cataloguing his virtues, Moreau wrote that he was a "good son, good husband, good father, good friend, good relative, good colleague, good master, good citizen" (bon fils, bon mari, bon père, bon ami, bon parent, bon confrère, bon maître, bon citoyen). "Good master" was one of the many societal roles that he aspired to, and his self-image was tied to seeing himself as not only charitable but beloved. This conviction in his goodness and, by extension, the benevolence that his fellow slaveowners were capable of, exemplifies the professed attitude that many colonial philosophes held in their ability to allegedly save Africans through their exposure to French civilization and proper management. He modeled a paternalistic worldview and belief in "enlightened" slaveholding.[33]

The sense of stature and authority that slaveholding gave Moreau is evident in a remark he made upon first arriving in the United States in 1794, after a difficult, 189-day Atlantic crossing:

[In Norfolk] I saw several colonists from Cap Français of my acquaintance. None of them seemed to me to be as courageous as I in enduring our common fall, and I could not help smiling scornfully when I heard a European settler lamenting the fate that had reduced him to being served by only two

Black servants (although his father had never had servants, either white or
Black), while thinking that I had seventeen when I left Cap Français, and
now had none left at all.

Je vis des Colons du Cap de ma connaissance. Nul d'entre eux ne me parut
aussi courageux que moi dans notre chute commune, et je ne pus m'empêcher
de sourire de dédain en entendant un Européen Colon déplorer le sort qui
l'avait réduit à n'être plus servi que par 2 Nègres à lui (quoique M. Son Père
n'eût jamais eu de domestique ni blanc ni noir), en pensant que j'en avais 17
en quittant le Cap et que je n'en avais plus du tout.

At the time he wrote this recollection, Moreau had most recently left Cap
Français in June 1788, at which point he owned enslaved people in both Saint-
Domingue and Martinique. It is not clear what happened to them between
1788 and 1794; based on his testimony elsewhere, he still owned people in 1790.
Subsequent chapters follow their traces, and it is worth remembering that the
seventeen individuals he mentioned here did not include people he enslaved
during earlier periods of his life: the wigmaker, cook, and laundress he advertised
for sale in 1783, for example. In addition to the material assets (including people)
that he owned in Martinique and in the north of Saint-Domingue, Moreau also
inherited a portion of a coffee plantation from his father's sister in the southern
parish of Torbeck, an area known for its wealthy free planter families of color.
Although revolutionary events in France and its Caribbean colonies resulted in
his losing some of the capital he had invested in human beings, their labor was
still reflected in the monetized value of the print material he anxiously shipped
from port to port and in his very existence as a learned man whose education and
lifestyle had long depended on their labor and sale.[34]

Such an appraisal of himself as a "good master," like his conviction that slaveholding could be beneficent, is an obvious strain on modern-day credulity. The
philosopher Charles W. Mills provides a helpful way of understanding Moreau's
worldview when he suggests that the Enlightenment "social contract" was
guaranteed—or rather secured—by a "racial contract." What Mills terms the
racial contract in turn demanded that "one has an agreement to *mis*interpret the
world. One has to learn to see the world wrongly, but with the assurance that
this set of mistaken perceptions will be validated by white epistemic authority,
whether religious or secular." Mills's formulation illuminates how the extraordinary violence of slavery could come to seem "ordinary," even mundane. Yet it is
clear that Moreau himself had doubts about the veracity of the lessons designed
to allow him to "see the world wrongly." In a 1785 speech to a Parisian learned
society that he once presided over, Moreau unequivocally stated that colonial life

necessitated inhabiting a war zone: "Servitude being nothing less than a veritable state of war, the enslaved are and must be the enemies of their masters and the noise of their chains constantly warns the latter that vengeance watches and stirs around them" (La servitude n'étant qu'un véritable état de guerre, les esclaves sont et doivent être les ennemis de leurs maîtres et le bruit de leurs chaînes avertit sans cesse cet dernier que la vengeance veille et s'agite autour d'eux). This book uses his and his contemporaries' own work to surface the hard realities of these conflicts at the level of language use among the islands' inhabitants, in chronicles of torture and resistance, via stories of forced migration, and through the study of print culture itself as documented in pamphlet wars, ethnographic scholarship, and the amassing of legal codes that were put to use for surveillance and management.[35]

My narration reprioritizes different actors, often at the micro-level of diction and sentence organization. A straightforward close-reading example demonstrates how one may undercut Moreau's interpretative observations to glimpse other worldviews. Consider Castor, a young man from the West African region commonly labeled as "Mandingue" in colonial sources. He died in 1782 while working for Moreau. We do not know the cause of his death nor how long and in what capacity he lived in Saint-Domingue. Moreau mentioned him in passing:

> I had the misfortune of losing a young Black Mandingo man named Castor, the 29th of November 1782, and the Blacks held his service on December 25th. I even contributed to the meal, which many masters do. . . . The mourning of the Blacks consists of dressing in white for several days and of folding the head scarf in half, put on carelessly, with the two ends hanging behind.

> J'eus le malheur de perdre un jeune nègre Mondongue, nommé Castor, le 29 Novembre 1782, et les nègres firent son service le 25 Décembre. Je contribuai même pour le repas, ce que font beaucoup de maîtres. . . . Le deuil des nègres consiste à se vêtir de blanc durant plusieurs jours, et à avoir le mouchoir de tête plié en demi-mouchoir, mis sans aucun soin, et avec les deux bouts pendans par derrière.

Moreau's construction of the first sentence is revealing—"I" had the misfortune to lose a young Mandingo man named Castor. Moreau is the subject herein: it was his loss and "misfortune." Although he did not specify how Castor's death affected him adversely, one can fathom that Moreau was most bothered by Castor's lost labor and market value. Likewise, it is Moreau's largesse that is highlighted in this anecdote; he was the generous benefactor who contributed to the cost of providing a meal at Castor's funeral.[36]

By reconfiguring whom Moreau designated as the subject and direct object of his sentence (a person, not a chattel), we experience a reorientation of focus. *Castor, a young man from West Africa, died in 1782 while he was owned by a man named Moreau.* It was Castor who suffered the calamity in this anecdote, having passed away as a young, enslaved man far from the place of his birth. We do not know anything about his life. Perhaps Castor was admired and loved; the community around him took the time to memorialize his death despite laboring for a relentless machine of colonial crop production. Moreau's self-referential and self-congratulatory tone notwithstanding, the entry provides grounds for speculation about the material and spiritual beliefs of the enslaved. We get a contemporaneous account of mourning rituals. People dressed in white and tied their headscarves in particular styles, sartorial choices that had their own meanings. There was a waiting period between Castor's death and the funeral. Food consumption was an element of the funerary service, and the enslaved managed to negotiate their owners' material support for these practices. Details such as these draw scholars to Moreau's work as they afford a glimpse, however brief and limited in its own understanding, of other priorities and cultural spaces.[37]

Moreau's life and scholarly trajectory were thus inseparable from his reliance on slavery. As such, a study of his work is one way of reading the Enlightenment with slavery at its center, neither as an unfortunate exception nor an unintended consequence. The labor and kinship relationships of Moreau's extended households form the conceptual and contextual backbone of this book. These networks foreground the many women in his circle, and each chapter reorients Moreau's family circles within a wider consideration of the nonwhite and international worlds in which they lived and worked. Many of the people enslaved by the Moreau family were owned across different households. For example, Marie-Louise Laplaine, a formerly enslaved woman, lived with Moreau as his housekeeper for five years. She had disposition over several enslaved people Moreau bequeathed to their daughter Jeanne-Louise "Aménaïde" Moreau de Saint-Méry, who eventually became the Contessa Dall'Asta; they collaborated about Aménaïde's inheritance for many years after their separation.[38]

Moreau also moved throughout the Atlantic world alongside Louise-Catherine Milhet, his legal wife and partner of thirty-eight years. She was the youngest daughter of a prominent slaveholding Louisiana merchant family. Her father, Jean Milhet, was imprisoned in the El Morro fortress in Havana, Cuba, after participating in the ill-fated French rebellion against the Spanish takeover of the Louisiana colony in 1768. He died shortly after the family relocated to Saint-Domingue. Louise-Catherine's mother, Louise Cheval Milhet, had been taken prisoner by the Choctaws as a child in the late 1740s, living among them

until British traders returned her to Louisiana. The most canonical of settler colonial tropes (fighting for one's crown in the face of great danger from competing
European empires) and of colonial genres (the early captivity narrative among
Native Americans) were rolled into the lived experiences of Moreau's closest relations. They informed his expansive perspective about the colonial American
world—across the Windward and Leeward Islands, mainland North America,
and Black and Indigenous communities. Louise-Catherine had two sisters, each
married to prominent men who collaborated on business and intellectual projects with Moreau: the physician Charles Arthaud and the lawyer and planter
Louis Narcisse Baudry des Lozières.[39]

The latter deserves special mention. Baudry des Lozières was Moreau's constant companion over the course of several decades—they worked together as
lawyers, and their two families often lived together in exile. Moreau named his
son after Baudry; the moniker Narcisse is an excellent summation of Baudry's
personality. Baudry succeeded Moreau as historiographer of the French Ministry
of the Navy and Colonies when Moreau assumed his administrative post in Italy.
Most important, Moreau trusted Baudry to act as the Moreaus' power of attorney and distributor of his publications from the 1780s to the years just before his
death. Baudry literally stood in for Moreau when necessary. I have grown to see
them as conjoined twins, lifetime interlocuters: wherever one finds Moreau, Baudry is not far behind. Though less well known outside French Atlantic historiography than his brother-in-law, Baudry has the deserved reputation as a strident
ideologue of white racial superiority. His work shared none of Moreau's nuance,
although the truth behind the adage about knowing someone by the company
they keep does cast them as more intellectually sympathetic doppelgängers than
one might suppose.[40]

Moreau and Baudry produced and advocated an Americas-centered articulation of knowledge. Moreau penned ecstatic paeans to his fellow intellectuals,
his "brotherhood" (peuple de frères) of savants, and relished his role as part of
a transatlantic and inter-American republic of letters. "Brotherhood" is an important indication of his main interlocuters. This book pays careful attention to
what both men were reading, and I have seen little to suggest that either Moreau
or Baudry actively engaged with women and their scholarship.[41] Regarding how
best to promote an Americas-centered knowledge base—what Jorge Cañizares
Esguerra has memorably termed a "patriotic epistemology"—Moreau wrote,
"But where are those who know the Colonies? By that I mean not those who
have seen them, or have even lived in them, but those who have studied them in
some way and who are in a position to shed light on that which concerns them"
(Mais où sont ceux qui connaissent les Colonies? J'entends par là non pas ceux

qui les ont vues, qui même les ont habitées, mais ceux qui les ont étudiées sous un rapport quelconque et qui sont en état d'éclairer sur ce qui les concerne). He, like other philosophes of his time, was a person who cared about the movement of stars and the best plant remedies for fever. He was an informed humanist acutely attuned to the world around him and curious about what made it work. After years of working on this book, I still marvel at Moreau's capacity to tune out close-quarter human suffering and be inured to the abuses he witnessed, caused, and depended upon. His work exemplifies the "dark side" of Enlightenment-era ideologies so ably critiqued by a range of postcolonial and revolutionary-era scholars.[42] Under what standards do these lived experiences and their discursive quantification qualify as enlightenment?[43]

Just as this book departs from traditional biography, what follows eschews the normative narrative structure of academic writing. Indeed, this introduction and the endnotes are the most conventional pieces of the project. Chapters 1, 4, and 8 form a three-part alphabetical *Encyclopédie noire*. As is the case with the spine of a book, the place where the pages are gathered and bound, these chapters set the foundational tone and politics of the work at the points of opening, regrouping, and closing. The *Encyclopédie noire* is modeled on Moreau's unfinished colonial American encyclopedia manuscript, his "Répertoire des notions coloniales," which was "a long work undertaken to show, under each word of a colonial dictionary, all the knowledge that this word is useful to know, and to make it possible to compare the various colonies with each other" (un long travail entrepris pour montrer, sous chaque mot d'un dictionnaire colonial, toutes les connaissances que ce mot rend utiles à savoir, et pour mettre à portée de comparer les diverses colonies entre elles). His project was itself loosely modeled on the French *Encyclopédie*. The *Encyclopédie noire* serves as a counter-text to Moreau's archive, even as it draws on that archive to achieve its aims. The format functions as a productive method for working with fragments of archival information. Long a source of inspiration and frustration to historians and literary scholars alike, fragments accrue in these chapters to open up vistas into occluded lives. Although the entries are discrete, they have an internal logic when read together, and the people and ideas contained throughout are often cross-referenced in other chapters.[44]

The entries fall into two broad categories. First, they document the people whom Moreau bought, sold, and manumitted. Scholarship on Moreau has made scant mention of his personal relationships with those he enslaved, although he claimed that he had "possessed slaves since [his] birth" (possède des Esclaves depuis [ma] naissance). As evident in the opening advertisement he placed in the *Affiches américaines,* he owned people who combed his hair, made his wigs, and cooked and served his food. They also managed his household, nursed his children, and washed the family's laundry. Women, those he nonchalantly referred to as "his" *mulâtresses* and *négresses,* make repeated appearances in the *Encyclopédie noire* as they traveled in intercolonial and transatlantic spaces with their owners. Though the information about them is insufficient to produce life stories, their inclusion provides a way of exploring how gendered and racialized forced labor sits at the heart of how women experienced the upheavals caused by the Haitian and French Revolutions, an approach that differs from the male-dominated and nationalistic stories of the era. Second, much as people from Africa and of African descent served him, they were also sources of information and objects of study. Moreau's reputation as a lawyer and a scholar was predicated on his professed expertise about them, and the entries demonstrate how he mobilized this knowledge. A creole, he saw himself as an interpretive voice and mediator between Europe and Africans in the Americas. Readers should approach this *Encyclopédie* prepared to use their imagination: to visualize people as interlocutors with their own thoughts and perspectives.[45]

Chapter 2 interprets a series of interimages, pictures about pictures, which I juxtapose with the popular and widely disseminated scenes of Caribbean life in the volume of engravings that accompanied Moreau's *Loix et constitutions.* *Recueil de vues des lieux principaux de la colonie française de Saint-Domingue,* based on the work of the painters and engravers Agostino Brunias and Nicolas Ponce, is well known for its depictions of luxuriously dressed (and partially nude) enslaved female and male figures and *gens de couleur.* I read portraiture of and produced in the Moreau-Brunias-Ponce collaboration against two pieces by the contemporary Caribbean artists Edouard Duval-Carrié and Marielle Plaisir. In addition, I have cocreated my own iconography—two portrait collages of Moreau and a re-creation of his household—as a way of juxtaposing self-representations of slaveholders as respectable paragons of virtue and intellect with the sadistic underbelly of the economic and social systems that invested Moreau with his authority. When read alongside the textual *Encyclopédie noire,* the images continue to strip Moreau down so that he and other colonists are linked to the violence underpinning their wealth and social status. Some of the images also foreground alternative community ties that existed within these structures of power.[46]

Chapter 3 also combines visual and textual analysis, setting Moreau's printing expertise squarely alongside polemical debates about the future of slavery,

possibilities of French imperial expansion, and questions of aesthetics. I argue
that Moreau narrated his work as much through its presentation—the mechanics of type, collaborations with engravers, extensive paratexts—as through its
form and content. He used print to secure a place in a particular knowledge
market that was also a human labor market. A book history approach juxtaposes
the mutually informing aspects of material culture, artisanship, and the migra-
tions (often forced) of the people who made Moreau's print work possible. Close
readings of two texts ground the discussion: Moreau's melodramatic and autobiographical *Mémoire justificatif* (1790) and *Voyage de l'ambassade de la Compagnie des Indes orientales hollandaises, vers l'empereur de la Chine* (1797–1798),
an account of the Dutch trade mission to the Qing court that Moreau printed,
edited, and translated.

After a return to the *Encyclopédie noire* in Chapter 4, Chapter 5 examines
Moreau's lesser-known natural history projects. I position translation, zoology,
and sexual coercion alongside one another—the need to understand and catego-
rize, to dissect, to use words as a way to exert control over discourse and people.
Eighteenth-century natural history's toxic taxonomic conflations between non-
European human beings and animals reveal the need to consider Moreau's
zoological scholarship alongside his better-known studies of the sexual mores of
Saint-Domingue. His Spanish-French translations of Félix de Azara's *Essais sur
l'histoire naturelle des quadrupèdes de la province du Paraguay* (1801) and Fray
Iñigo Abbad y Lasierra's *Historia geográfica, civil y natural de la Isla de San Juan
Bautista de Puerto-Rico* (1788) demonstrate how Moreau brought discussions of
Latin America and the hispanophone Caribbean into French natural history
circles. My attention to his translation of Spanish-language manuscripts also
brings Moreau's scholarship on Indigenous communities into focus, particularly
his curious work sounding out Guaraní, an Indigenous language of current-day
Paraguay, Argentina, and Bolivia.

Chapter 6 continues the discussion of the relationship between language and
power. It focuses on the gendered dimensions of sexual assault and the role that
print culture played in regimes of physical and psychic terror. I examine Baudry
des Lozières's Kikongo-French "Dictionnaire ou Vocabulaire Congo," where
commands such as "kneel down," "get undressed," and "sweep" were coupled
with phrases such as "your mother gave birth to a pig," "your milk is good," and
"do you love me?" Teaching allegedly useful phrases to colonists for extracting
the maximum labor out of men and women arriving directly from West Central Africa, this rare phrase book from 1803 demonstrates how language was
a weapon of war. Its *utilité* for combatants of African descent conflicted with
planter attempts to contain it. The chapter demonstrates that we must commit

to the study of African languages as American ones, especially given that the vast majority of Saint-Domingue's population on the eve of the revolution was African-born and non–French speaking.[47]

Chapter 7 experiments with form and narrative voice. It serves as a meditation on the role that illustrative storytelling can play in exploring the interior lives of people who are marginal in the archives. I use graphics to imagine a listening and reading puzzle that considers Kikongo from the perspective of its native speakers; to examine scribal and literacy practices of branding as performed on Black bodies and interpreted by people who were marked; and to create a short, natural history–style "description" from multiple points of view. Making use of runaway advertisements placed by Baudry des Lozières and others, the chapter advances its argument through reference to historical antagonists. Chapter 8 concludes the *Encyclopédie noire* with a discussion of Moreau's *Ouvrage* and its poisonous legacy.

The narrative arc of the book is such that chapters can be read consecutively or through pairings of source chapters and an intertext. The three installments of the *Encyclopédie noire* may be read alongside Chapter 2, an explicitly visualized presentation of some of the same historical figures and ideas. Those interested in the Kikongo "Vocabulaire" may wish to ruminate more about how it might have been heard when its phrases were brought to life through speech (Chapter 6 alongside 7). Experiments with typography and the visual occur throughout, especially in Chapters 2, 3, 7, and 8. The politics of language use are foregrounded in Chapters 5, 6, and 7. Key arguments are thus further developed and reinterpreted in these combinations through additional sources or alternate methodologies.

CHAPTER ONE

Encyclopédie noire

— Part I —

I begin with an image: a crowd peopled with thousands of Black faces and intermittent white ones. The setting is late-eighteenth-century Saint-Domingue. Moreau de Saint-Méry conjured this scene, claiming that "to see so many Black faces *[and the small proportion of white ones]*" (d'y voir autant de figures noires *[et à proportion aussi peu de visages blancs]*) had a startling effect on Europeans newly arrived in the Caribbean. In his words, so much blackness seemed to "melt away" (se fondre) white faces. He remarked that it took whites a long time before they could distinguish one Black person from another, going on to confess "that every time I returned from France to the colonies, I somewhat experienced this embarrassment" (toutes les fois que je suis revenu de France aux Colonies, j'ai eprouvé un peu cet embarrass). Moreau was quick to note that he soon acclimated to his surroundings, however, recovering his ability to differentiate Black people from one another, with all of their nuances of expression. The *ombres* that surrounded him—shadows, darkness, obscurity—became gradually legible. The passage is an important reminder of the demographics in Saint-Domingue, where the enslaved and free Black population exceeded that of the white more than tenfold. The imagery of Black faces surrounding white ones is literal. It is also an appropriate metaphor for one of the methodological and narrative through lines of this book.[1]

This chapter is the first part of an *Encyclopédie noire.* It is modeled on Moreau's unpublished hemispheric American *encyclopédie,* his "Répertoire des notions coloniales," which was in turn modeled on the French *Encyclopédie* and other colonial dictionaries. An experiment with form allows me to work with fragments of information concerning the people of African descent who undergirded Moreau's work on both personal and professional levels. When the fragments are serialized, they emerge as a collection of anecdotal narratives with their own logic as an ensemble. Historian Sarah Knott persuasively argues that "anecdote is a way of recasting . . . shards and nuggets of evidence, of turning absence into presence, what's mentioned *en passant* into the main drama," concluding that "historical interpretation can reside in the slow accumulation of a trellis of detail." There is an urgency to keeping Moreau and his Black interlocuters in the same frame and to seeing the people whose lives he passed through, disrupted, controlled, and narrativized. By doing so, the undifferentiated faces from Moreau's opening quote, his unknown laborers, and the "types" so prevalent in his work—the Congolese slave, the seductive *mulâtresse*—become discernable individuals.[2]

The encyclopedia format places slavery at the heart of the French Enlightenment's literary genre par excellence. The sheer quantity of information juxtaposed demands a format that balances contextualization, ease of retrieval, and focused analysis. Yet this *Encyclopédie noire* is inherently incomplete. I end the third installment with the letter *P* by design; Moreau himself stopped with *E*. The goal is not to walk a reader from *A* to *Z* but to disrupt the expectations of coherence, rational "objectivity," and comprehensiveness associated with this genre. Each entry opens in Bodoni type, a typographical tribute to Moreau's collaborations with the celebrated eighteenth-century Italian printer Giambattista Bodoni. The entries consist of Moreau's own words or are drawn from historical documents such as notary records directly tied to his activities. My interpretation follows these remarks, putting them into dialogue with a broader body of his work, historical events, and primary and secondary sources.

A

Aménaïde (Jeanne-Louise Moreau de Saint-Méry, Contessa Dall'Asta)

Aménaïde ("Jeanne-Louise, called Aménaïde, born May 21, 1778," "quadroon," "natural daughter [a child born outside of marriage] of an unknown father" and Marie-Louise Laplaine, a "free mulâtresse").

Aménaïde ("Jeanne-Louise, dite Aménaïde, née le 21 mai 1778," "quarteronne," "fille naturelle. . . . de père inconnu" et Marie-Louise Laplaine, "mulâtresse libre").[3]

See also Laplaine, Marie-Louise (Part II).

Aménaïde, Moreau's beloved daughter, embodies the long-term intimate connections Moreau had with people of African descent. The words above provide a glimpse into Moreau's most important affective and financial ties. He compensated the child's mother, a freed mulâtresse named Marie-Louise Laplaine, for her work as his housekeeper *(ménagère)* over the period of five years. This compensation awarded Jeanne-Louise / Aménaïde two enslaved women and two thousand livres to purchase an additional woman.[4] Why would Moreau bequeath such a large sum in human beings to his housekeeper's daughter? Aménaïde's baptismal record, dating from 1778, noted that the father was "unknown" (inconnu). In 1997, Michel Camus published a short research note suggesting that Moreau's generosity and the timing of Aménaïde's birth made it likely that she was Moreau's daughter. Corroborating evidence confirms this conclusion.[5]

A multi-year correspondence between Moreau and Aménaïde documents the close relationship between the two and provides many clues about their family lives. It is unclear where she passed the majority of her childhood, although in one letter Moreau lamented leaving her in Belleville, Paris, upon a return trip to the Caribbean; a 1788 notarial transaction between Marie-Louise Laplaine and Moreau demonstrates that Aménaïde was living in France by the age of ten. By the time she was fifteen, she had fled with the Moreau family from France to the United States.[6] When the family returned to Europe in 1798, Aménaïde accompanied them and subsequently moved with them to Parma, Italy, in 1801, where her father was appointed as an adviser to Ferdinand I, the duke of Parma, and eventually served as the administrator general of the duchies of Parma, Piacenza, and Guastalla. She married an Italian nobleman, Pompeo Dall'Asta, a marriage that would have increased the family's social capital in the city they had come to rule.

Aménaïde received a certificate of merit from the Parma Academy of Painting, Sculpture, and Architecture in 1802 and became a well-known painter (Figure 2), publicly exhibiting "Five Miniatures" (Cinque minature) (portraits) in an 1818 show. This certificate lists her surname as "Moreau de Saint-Méry," demonstrating that Moreau's "illegitimate" quadroon daughter did in fact carry Moreau's family name by the time she was in her twenties. As president of the Academy, Moreau affixed his name as well. Notice of her 1818 exhibit in a Parma newspaper appeared alongside news of conflict between the president of the Haitian Republic in the south, Jean-Pierre Boyer, and King Henry I (Henry Christophe) of the Kingdom of Hayti in the northern part of the island. The pages of Aménaïde's local newspaper thus kept political news from her island home in circulation. Over the course of her life, she served on the board of distinguished fine arts societies, earning an entry in a dictionary of notable residents of that city. A small formal portrait she painted of her father is now owned by Parma's National Gallery.[7]

"Chère, chère Aménaïde" was Moreau's constant correspondent; indeed, he felt her absence when more than a few days went by between missives. "You have promised us news by each post and we receive it with a lively impatience" (tu nous promets des Nouvelles par chaque courrier et nous les recevons avec une vive impatience).[8] When these letters are read alongside a personal journal Moreau kept while in Italy, a representative account of their interactions emerges and a sketch of the young woman Aménaïde takes shape. She was literate and a talented artist.

FIGURE 2. Aménaïde Moreau de Saint-Méry's certificate of merit from the Accademia Parmense di Pittura, Scultura, ed Architettura, Nov. 13, 1802. Fondo Carte Moreau de Saint-Méry, Dono Monza, box 6, Materiali per la biografia di M. Moreau de Saint-Méry, "Diplomi accademi," Archivio di Stato di Parma.

He noted that she sang beautifully at local entertainments among their friends, sometimes accompanied by her brother, Médéric Moreau de Saint-Méry *fils*. Entries recorded that Moreau bought her paint and took her on outings to see local artwork. In 1809, he sent the portraits she did of her son to well-known artists affiliated with the Parisian Société académique des Enfants d'Apollon and took the time to report their assessments to her. One such mentor suggested she make her "half [paint strokes] less red" (demi peintes moins rouges).[9]

A list of these intimacies continues. When Aménaïde married, Moreau took her bedroom as his home office.[10] The dynamics of a shared household in which she physically occupied a central space thus come to life. We see chronicled his anxiety about Aménaïde's ill health (her "nervous attack[s]" [attaque(s) de nerfs] and ailing eyesight) and what medicines he eagerly counseled her to take.[11] When she delivered a baby girl that he himself named Célestine (Titine / Titinette), he carefully recorded the onset and length of Aménaïde's labor. The day that Moreau noted Napoleon's coronation as emperor of France, he also recorded that this same granddaughter had a mouth sickness that had become worrisome.[12] His parental concern is nowhere more evident than when his letters sadly told her of his regrets that her husband was a philanderer and too fond of gaming. "I see unhappiness and sorrow fall upon me, my daughter and my little ones [his grandchildren] due to the foolish conduct of my son-in-law. . . . His horrible remarks and disgusting behavior are the horrible consequences of his principles" (Je vois fondre le Malheur et les chagrins sur moi et sur ma fille et sur mes petits par la conduite insensée de mon gendre. . . . Ses propos horribles, sa conduite dégoûtante sont les conséquences horribles de ses principes).[13] Moreau even remarked that one day he found a lock of Aménaïde's hair, cut twenty years earlier, that he had incredibly managed to save despite his many physical displacements throughout Europe and the Americas. What emerges is a deeply personal portrait of family relations, one in which adieus were made in French and Kreyòl: "Adieu chers amis, des baisers, en pile, en pile, joui" (Goodbye dear friends [his children], lots of kisses, joy). These *tendresses* contextualize continued relationships with their former homes in the Caribbean, ties captured in their excitement to be eating a special treat one evening thousands of miles away in Paris: callaloo, a typical creole stew.[14]

Prosaic details of Aménaïde's routines and her more intimate thoughts are revealed through this correspondence. Frustratingly, her letters have not come to light. Moreau's internal thought processes and affections provide a glimpse of hers: her distress about a difficult marriage, her pride in her children and her artistic accomplishments. Without letters in her own hand describing her state of mind, we are forced to wonder. As a child, when was she separated from her birth mother, Marie-Louise Laplaine? Did they stay in touch? Did she know that her mother was a mixed-race Black woman, once enslaved, or anything else about Laplaine's personal family history or of her mother's entrepreneurship? Was Laplaine's biological parentage a source of anxiety, a secret? According to letters, Aménaïde called Moreau's legal wife, Louise-Catherine Milhet, *"mère."* It is intriguing to consider at what point she might have started to refer and think of her as such.[15]

In the tripartite racial hierarchies that predominated in Saint-Domingue, such questions would have been important. Moreau left traces suggesting that Aménaïde was openly known as his daughter. In a 1790 publication, he mentioned "a young female child who owes her life to me, for whom my deep tenderness is known" (une jeune enfant qui me doit le jour, et pour laquelle ma vive tendresse est connue).[16] Were details of her mixed-race background passed through networks of rumor in the various places she resettled, or did Aménaïde pass as white when living in Paris, the United States, and Parma? During the family's time in Philadelphia, a city full of exiled planters from the colonies, many people knew the Moreau family well, and *on dits* about interracial couplings were certainly bandied about. For example, rumors circulated that Charles-Maurice de Talleyrand-Périgord, the "spider" of European politics for decades and Moreau's close confidant during their years of exile in the United States, had an elegant woman of color as a mistress. In Italy, the family entertained regular visitors whom they had known in the Caribbean. It is unlikely that Aménaïde would have been able to keep her parentage a secret. "Passing" in the conventional sense of the word would have been difficult and potentially risky. Was Aménaïde shunned or treated as second class? Nothing suggests that this was the case within the household. On the contrary, she was well loved. The phenotypical whiteness that "melted" into blackness in the opening image occurs here in reverse: her blackness could have been subsumed in a performance of white-ish identity and its privileges. Or, if she was openly known to have been of mixed racial ancestry, perhaps she adopted this identity freely in Europe. In France and Italy, for example, there were contemporaneous figures of African descent with public profiles. As someone who spent most of her life living away from the immediacy of large-scale slaveholding societies, the question of her blackness might have been less important to her social acceptance than her middle-class upbringing, social standing as the daughter of an influential citizen / intellectual, and eventual noble title.

For a man obsessively concerned with racial mixture and curtailing the rights of free people of color, Moreau's devoted relationship to this woman reveals the gap between public writings and private life. The person who had one of his closest long-term relationships with a mixed-race daughter is best remembered as the author of elaborate tables and commentary concerning the alleged differences between white and Black people that claimed the latter were inferior. In his description of the "20 manners of producing a quadroon" (Les Quarterons sont produits de vingt manières), he singled out this supposed type as follows: "white skin, but tarnished with a nuance of a very weak yellow" (la peau blanche, mais ternie par une nuance d'un jaune très-affaibli). Hair long and curly. "There are some quadroon women whose whiteness is such that it requires very well-trained eyes to distinguish them from white women" (Il est des Quarteronnes dont la blancheur est telle, qu'il faut des yeux bien exercés pour les distinguer des Blanches). The "well-trained" ability of his own eyes to ferret out racial admixture was implicitly suggested. He wrote and self-published these words about the importance of distinguishing people of even remote African ancestry from whites as an explicit caution against allowing them full economic and social privileges while his daughter played the piano, one he had shipped for her from France, in the rooms above their bookstore and while she worked side by side with her family doing manual labor in their printshop.[17]

When considered in a transatlantic sphere of prominent intellectuals with familial ties to slavery and the slave trade, Aménaïde Moreau de Saint-Méry's history is compelling for the extent of its textual and visual evidentiary traces and the ways it undercuts the legitimacy of what Marlene L. Daut identifies as Moreau's "pseudoscientific claims about 'interracial' degeneracy." Thomas Jefferson's relationship with Sally Hemings and that of William Murray, first earl of Mansfield with his beloved relative Dido Elizabeth Belle are two well-known, if different, points of comparison that test the limits of eighteenth-century taxonomies of racial difference as they intersected with intimate family life. Daut, in the only work devoted to an extended discussion of the relationship between Moreau and his daughter, wrote of how she found herself "endlessly wondering how Aménaïde might have read and responded to the passages in which her father paints such an unflattering portrait of women of color." "Would she have agreed that she was the exception rather than the rule or might she have loudly objected to her father's portrayals of women like her, offering herself . . . as the incontrovertible proof that women of color were capable of virtue by eighteenth- and nineteenth-century standards?" I, too, wonder, much as I wonder if she would have self-identified and been accepted as a woman of color either in the United States or Europe. Aménaïde's life provides an account of diaspora from Saint-Domingue different from the more commonly documented one of former male planters who spent years discursively fighting to recuperate their land, enslaved laborers, and wealth.[18]

Yet she was part of their inner circle. The printers' type ornament that introduces this entry and others where Aménaïde appears symbolizes Moreau's idea of his own beneficence in my mind: the smiling central face, the rich plumage, the sun-like rays that evoke Louis XIV's nobility and rank. It is an ornament that Moreau used widely in his publications, including on the title page of his *Description de la partie espagnole de l'isle Saint-Domingue*. The figure spreads its wing-like plumes in protection, in embrace. Moreau, the self-professed "good father" (bon père), safeguarded his daughter and raised her with material security and love; this was possible in large part because of their ownership of other people.[19]

Angélique

In 1783, [I freed] a Black woman and her two children, because she had nursed, in 1778, a young female child who owes me her life, and for whom my deep tenderness is known.

En 1783, [j'ai affranchi] une Négresse, et ses deux enfans, parce qu'elle avait allaitée, en 1778, une jeune enfant qui me doit le jour, et pour laquelle ma vive tendresse est connue.[20]

See also Nourrices (Part II).

When Aménaïde was an infant, she suckled at the breasts of a woman named Angélique. Marie-Louise Laplaine, while working as Moreau's ménagère, thus would have had the services of a wet nurse *(nourrice)* for her daughter. An act of *liberté* five years later, in March 1783 (Figure 3), identifies Angélique as a "Black creole woman, around thirty years old" (une négresse créole agée d'énviron trente ans). She was born in the Americas, perhaps Saint-Domingue, and was about the same age as Moreau. Angélique was the mother of two children, an eight-year-old daughter named Sophie and an anonymous four-month-old boy. These two children were manumitted alongside their mother. As is the case with many of the entries herein, I have extracted information embedded in various narratives (visual, notarial, periodical, natural historical) and given them a new context, a methodology that Caribbean literature scholar Nicole N. Aljoe dubs remixing. Such an approach highlights the life stories of other subjects, often knowable only through fragments, "refocusing on what had only seemed to recede into silence in comparison to what was going on in the foreground."[21]

Several investigative paths yield details of this woman's life. The first involves milk. Angélique worked as a wet nurse, and it is through this labor that traces of her life story can be discerned. In order for her to have been able to nurse Aménaïde, she must have been lactating, possibly after giving birth to her own child months or even a few years before Aménaïde's birth. The manumission record makes no mention of a child close in age to five (Aménaïde's age at the time). Had this child died? Had she or he been sold before 1783, or simply not included in Moreau's decision to free Angélique and her other two children? The very presence of Angélique's milk and the subsequent textual absence of a five- or six-year-old child in 1783 hint of an undocumented story of loss. Or perhaps there was no missing child but rather Sophie (eight at the time of manumission) had been nursed by her mother for at least three years; perhaps Angélique had been continuously performing the labor of nursing for any number of children in the interim.

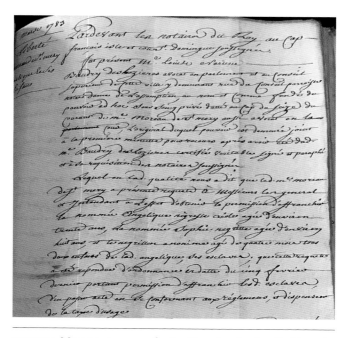

FIGURE 3. Manumission papers for Angélique, her daughter Sophie, and her four-month-old son. Moreau's brother-in-law, Louis Narcisse Baudry des Lozières, acted on his behalf. "Acte de liberté, Mar. 17, 1783, Archives nationales d'outre mer, Aix-en-Provence, Notariat Saint-Domingue, 542, Grimperel, acting notary.

    There is evidence that Angélique nursed others after Aménaïde. Moreau wrote that she "rendered the same service to the son of Don Bernardo de Gálvez, who died as the Vice-Roy of Mexico" (rendait le même service au fils de Don Bernard de Galvez, mort Vie-roi du Mexique). Gálvez, for whom Galveston, Texas, is named, supported the patriot cause during the American Revolution and lived in Cap Français in the early 1780s to take general command "of the combined armies of France and Spain" (des armées combinées de France et d'Espagne).[22] Moreau noted that Gálvez was popular with local residents, perhaps because, as Matthew Pratt Guterl suggests in another context, they spoke the mutually intelligible "language of slaveholding." While in Cap Français, Gálvez was involved in transactions with multiple people to buy enslaved men, women, and children. For instance, records from Moreau's own notary, Eloi-Michel Grimperel, document that Gálvez purchased a twenty-eight-year-old woman from Curaçao named Catherine, an eighteen-year-old African man named Koyo, a ten-year-old girl named Hariette, a twelve-year-old girl named Oursêne, and a twenty-year-old man named Pierre Louis Bonhomme. In addition to profiting from their stolen labor, Gálvez benefited from the work of a lactating woman Moreau enslaved. One of the many enslaved people whose labor cut across competing colonial regimes, Angélique was thus a Black woman who fed Moreau's daughter and Gálvez's son. These two influential men, a French creole functionary and a Spanish military officer, cemented their friendship through her milk. This deeply personal interaction is an example of what Lisa Lowe describes as the forced "intimacies" of many empires.[23]

While following the trace of Angélique's work as a nourrice, I also searched for a name that would allow Moreau's "négresse" to shed her anonymity. It is satisfying to imagine her moving about the Moreau household inhabiting a moniker: *Angélique, Angélique, Angélique.* It is evocative to imagine not just any child, but a girl named Sophie and her infant brother interacting with their mother or possibly Aménaïde, their *soeur de lait.* Because the law required people of color to be given new surnames in some approximation of an "African idiom" (L'idiôme Africain) upon their manumission, however, this knowledge is transient. At the moment when archival evidence changed them from anonymous people to Angélique and Sophie, they acquired the new names Mirza and Zilia; the little boy became Azor. The unstableness of naming as practice and search technique is a literal reminder that "in the archive of slavery, to be found is to remain undiscovered." Naming people, buying people, freeing people; being named and renamed, maimed, bought, and freed; advocating for one's freedom and that of one's children; having the children of others, some strangers, be entitled to one's breasts. Angélique negotiated a world where these behaviors were quotidian.[24]

Aradas

Arada women, eternal conversationalists, are rarely employed as domestic servants, given that of all the Africans, the Arada are those who are the least able to speak French; and it is by hearing it in their mouths that one has the greatest test for those who flatter themselves that they possess the Creole language. These women are grumbling and quarrelsome; one can recognize Arada women from the outside by their hips and butts, the amplitude of which has become the measure of all such comparisons of this type.

Les femmes Aradas, causeuses éternelles, sont rarement employées comme domestiques, attendu que de tous les Africains les Aradas sont ceux qui parviennent le moins à parler le français et que c'est à l'entendre dans leur bouche qu'on peut faire consister la plus grande épreuve de ceux qui se flattent de posséder le langage Créol. Ces femmes sont aussi accariâtres et querelleuses; on les reconnaît [les femmes Aradas] extérieurement à des hanches et à des fesses dont l'amplitude est devenue le dernier terme de toute comparaison de ce genre.[25]

Moreau's *Description* of the French part of Hispaniola detailed the social customs of the colony's population, including comments on at least fifteen groups that he designated as distinct African ethnicities. As in many Enlightenment-era texts, he attempted to classify knowledge by establishing categories. In this case, he attributed physical and cultural characteristics to different African-born enslaved communities. His goal: to make "all of these blacks better understood by the colonists" (tous ces nègres . . . mieux entendus des Colons). As Gérard Barthelemy has noted, Moreau's desire to classify different African-born communities on the island was in large part motivated by an interest in supplying colonists with the "knowledge indispensable for running a work group composed of numerous nations" (connaissances indispensables à la gestion de l'atelier en function des nombreuses nations qui le composent). Ethnographic knowledge was useful for maximized extraction of women's labor for agricultural profit.[26]

Moreau's remarks demonstrate how the study of eighteenth-century labor management intersected with the study of science and sexuality. The bold assertion that classificatory information could be derived from generalizations about butt and hip size says nothing about these women—and much about their observer. In this moment we catch Moreau looking: a voyeuristic, sexualized evaluation of body parts associated with reproductive capacity and sexual pleasure seamlessly accompanied comments on women's supposed personalities. One can imagine him making a series of mental diagrams or physical sketches of hips and butts, an anticipation of how measurements of head size were similarly mobilized as alleged evidence of personality traits such as intelligence in the following century. This entry is typical of the kinds of "facts" that Moreau deemed empirical observations of value. His misogynist anecdote—women as talkative, quarrelsome, cantankerous—also carried a subtext of deliberate recalcitrance.

Moreau's portrait of Arada women was accompanied by an evaluation of their perceived inability to speak French. "Of all the Africans," he claimed, they were the least likely to learn it, making them less desirable for domestic work in proximity to their owners. Language was thus an important marker for Moreau. In this example, it helped to explain who was supposedly suitable for what kinds of labor. Moreau's negative assessment of their French was combined

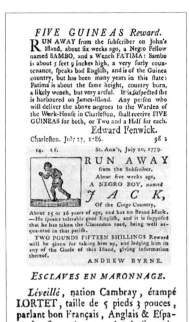

FIGURE 4. Newspaper advertisements highlighting the linguisitic skills of enslaved people in South Carolina, Jamaica, and Saint-Domingue. "Five Guineas Reward," *Columbian Herald, or the Independent Courier of North-America* (Charleston, S.C.), July 31, 1786, [3]; "Run Away," *Supplement to the Jamaica Mercury* (Kingston), July 24–July 31, 1779, 173; "Esclaves en Maronage," *Affiches américaines* (Cap Français, Saint-Domingue), Sept. 9, 1777, [1].

with admiration for their Kreyòl dexterity. He believed that Arada women set a standard that made other speakers realize their own linguistic inadequacy. Reading between the lines, Moreau's commentary thus provides a glimpse of women behaving on their own terms. They evinced a remarkable level of second- (or third- or fourth-) language acquisition, adapting to their circumstances by learning to dominate Kreyòl, one of Saint-Domingue's lingua francas. Refusal to learn (or display any mastery) of French while speaking fine Kreyòl suggests the community connections these women preferred to enable.

A broad swathe of late-eighteenth-century newspapers from the circum-Caribbean contextualizes Moreau's comments, demonstrating that language skills were noted by buyers, sellers, and owners searching for their escaped laborers (Figure 4). Advertisements reveal the cacophonous, yet intellectually and socially generative assortment of languages surrounding inhabitants of the early Americas. Daily life entailed negotiating complicated linguistic terrain. For example, on John's Island outside Charleston, South Carolina, in 1786, a man called Sambo, with a "surly" countenance, spoke "bad English." Jack, in 1779 Saint Ann's Bay, Jamaica, spoke "tolerable good English." What languages would these men have spoken well? Hailing from the wide expanse of West African lands commonly referred to in the Americas as Guinea and Kongo, Sambo and Jack would have been able to communicate in a variety of languages: perhaps Fula, Malinke, or Kikongo. Of course, plenty of notices document that enslaved people, both African and American-born, spoke, not one, but several European languages, in addition to their native African ones. For instance, a 1777 advertisement in Saint-Domingue for a runaway named Léveillé, from the Cambray nation, noted that he spoke "good French, English and Spanish." Moreau's multiple households provide ample evidence of the veracity of historian Philip D. Morgan's claim that "without a doubt blacks were the most linguistically polyglot and proficient ethnic group in the Americas." When trying to recover the experiences of enslaved people of African descent who did not leave copious written records, we must move beyond both monolingual and solely European frames of linguistic reference as we speculate about the languages in which they would have been thinking, speaking, bragging, joking, and dreaming.[27]

As a scholar, Moreau wrote about communities in which he was embedded. He circulated in at least two overlapping households, and the languages spoken within and between them evoke sound, scales of intelligibility, power. The Mandingo man Castor who worked for Moreau, the Senegalese adolescent Rosine who worked for Marie-Louise Laplaine and Aménaïde, several men from the Gold Coast—they could have known Wolof, maybe Bambara or Ewe. As a native Kreyòl speaker, Moreau would have engaged with people—Europeans, Africans, and creoles of all colors—who had different degrees of Kreyòl fluency. And of course, there was French, a language that the enslaved who worked for him might have had occasion to speak while living in the Caribbean and France. Each of these languages and the choice of when to use which one and with whom is a reminder that linguistic competence or the lack thereof could facilitate and impede everyday life opportunities.

Auba, Etienne (1683–1781)

It is in Trou where one witnessed the death, in 1781, of Etienne Auba, born in the Morin Quartier in 1683. A slave of M. Le Long, he went with him to the siege of Cartagena and was manumitted upon returning from that campaign, like all of the Black men who served there. . . .

He always appeared in public in a coat and with a sword. He spoke with good sense about the interesting things that he had seen. I had a long conversation with him in June 1779, and I found him to still be full of energy.

C'est encore au Trou qu'on a vu mourir, en 1781, Étienne Auba, né au Quartier-Morin en 1683. Esclave de M. Le Long qui le mena au siège de Carthagène, il fut affranchi au retour de cette campagne, comme tous les nègres qui y avaient marché. . . .

Il paraissait toujours en public en habit et en épée. Il parlait avec bon sens et avec intérêt de ce qu'il avait vu. J'eus avec lui une longue conversation au mois de Juin 1779, et je le trouvai encore plein d'énergie.[28]

Etienne Auba was just shy of one hundred years old when Moreau interviewed him, living on a small state pension granted in recognition of his military service. The participation of people of African descent in transnational armed struggles was embedded in the histories Moreau chose to include about notables of Saint-Domingue: both those who fought for European armies and those who fought against them, such as the Maroon fighters living in the mountainous regions of Spanish Hispaniola. Auba's interactions with Moreau reveal how Auba mobilized his dress and sword as a way of claiming his dignity and a small measure of respect in a society that did everything to preclude the healthy aging of people of African descent.[29]

When culling information from Moreau's work, one must acknowledge his sources and information-gathering processes. He was an avid reader of archival material and the scholarship of his contemporaries. He augmented these sources by soliciting his own information in written and oral form. An announcement in the *Affiches américaines,* for instance, thanked his fellow colonists for sending him "memoirs, maps and observations" (mémoires, des plans et des observations) about the different *quartiers* in the colony that would be of interest to local readers. Similarly, in his study of musical performances in Saint-Domingue, Bernard Camier found that Moreau used a written questionnaire to ask a local theater director about "material aspects" (aspects matériels) of how the business was run in order to complete his *Description de la partie française de l'isle de Saint-Domingue.* The anecdote about Etienne Auba also highlights Moreau's use of oral interviews.[30]

His "long conversation" with Auba is in keeping with other such in-person interactions he had with free people of color and the enslaved. Moreau used the stories gleaned from these conversations as generalizable evidence to make authoritative pronouncements. In another example, he claimed that African-born women preferred Black men as sexual partners. As he put it, "I have heard several black women avow it" (j'ai entendu plusieurs négresses l'avouer). Under what circumstances did he hear women avow it? Did he ask them directly or overhear snippets of conversation? He suggested that this preference was in part because of "the advantage which nature or the use of palm wine has given to Black men in what constitutes the physical agent of love . . . to which a white man is but a puny competitor" (l'avantage que la nature, ou l'usage du vin de palme a donné aux nègres sur les autres hommes dans ce qui constitue l'agent physique de l'amour . . . pour lequel le Blanc n'est qu'un chétif concurrent). This passage's deliberately titillating qualities are similar to Moreau's descriptions of the Vodou religion and the power of its "mysterious cult" (culte mystérieux). Despite being a white man *(blan)* with a profane eye, he performed his supposed expertise for readers who did not have access to this genre of information.[31]

Importantly, Moreau also recognized that there was a world of meaning that he could not penetrate despite his professed interpretive authority. Moreau's imagery of a crowd of Black faces becoming gradually distinguishable suggested that along with their faces he was also able to understand *them:* their customs and thoughts had a degree of legibility that a seasoned, native-born observer could ascertain. Although some people Moreau interviewed might have divulged information willingly, he noted that African-born enslaved people refused "quite obstinately, to give details of the customs of their countries. . . . It is only those who arrived when already old who entertain themselves speaking about it or who speak of it to white children" (qu'il refusent assez obstinément de donner des details sur les moeurs de leur pays. . . . Il n'y a guères que ceux venus déjà vieux qui s'en entretiennent quelquefois ou qui en parlent aux enfans blancs). *Quite obstinately refused.* Moreau proposed that this refusal stemmed from a fear of ridicule, by both whites and American-born creole enslaved people. But from the perspective of the enslaved, all forms of knowledge were potentially repositories of power and weapons of the oppressed. Moreau's observation suggests that the enslaved received outsiders' inquiries about African customs skeptically, even with hostility. In these circumstances, silence was thus a meaningful choice. The challenge of conveying the viewpoints of those who refused to engage is one pitfall of relying on planter sources.[32]

In another instance, Moreau noted that when enslaved people identified as Mina would recognize one of the "princes of their country" (des princes de leur pays), they would prostrate themselves at the princes' feet and make "bizarre signs" (signes bisarres) that were unintelligible to Moreau. When his comments are paired with recurring phrases from runaway slave advertisements that obliquely recorded the voices of the enslaved, ample evidence corroborates that the enslaved would dissemble, invent stories, outright lie, or choose silence. Local papers in Saint-Domingue contained news of Michau, a Congo, "not able to say the name of his master" (ne pouvant dire le nom de son maître). Or "an old Black man of the Coromantee nation" (un vieux Nègre, nation Cramanty), "not able to say *his* name *or* that of his master" (ne pouvant dire son nom, ni celui de son maître). In September 1790, two newly arrived young women from Africa were jailed in Port-au-Prince who were "branded BARRAS, below SARD, having their country marks on their faces, not able to say their names, or that of their master" (deux négresses nouvelles, étampées BARRAS, au-dessous SARD, ayant des marques de leur pays sur la figure, ne pouvant dire leurs noms, ni celui de leur maître). Of course these women knew their African names; they did not reveal if they recognized the names that were imposed upon them once they were forced into slavery in Saint-Domingue. Many other announcements recorded a person as saying that "[she/he] belonged" (se disant appartenir): Were these truthful attestations on their part? The master class and their employees acknowledged that an enslaved person's not being able to do, nor to say, nor to tell could be an exercise in subterfuge. Unintelligibility and illegibility were intentional.[33]

B

Blanchisseuse

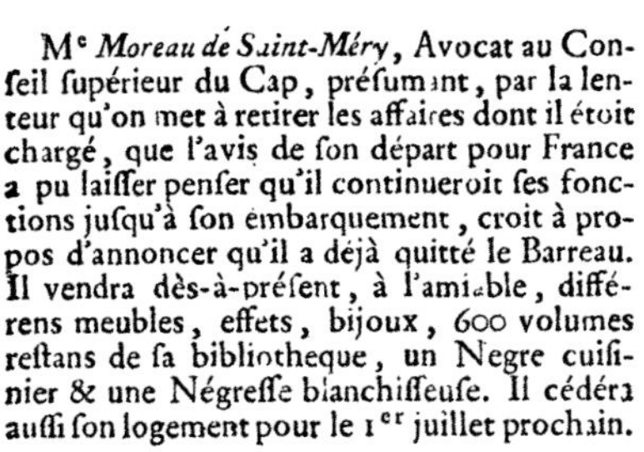

Me *Moreau de Saint-Méry*, Avocat au Conseil supérieur du Cap, présumant, par la lenteur qu'on met à retirer les affaires dont il étoit chargé, que l'avis de son départ pour France a pu laisser penser qu'il continueroit ses fonctions jusqu'à son embarquement, croit à propos d'annoncer qu'il a déjà quitté le Barreau. Il vendra dès-à-présent, à l'amiable, différens meubles, effets, bijoux, 600 volumes restans de sa bibliotheque, un Negre cuisinier & une Négreffe blanchiffeufe. Il cédéra auffi fon logement pour le 1er juillet prochain.

FIGURE 5. Advertisement for the sale of a woman working as Moreau's laundress. "Avis Divers: M. *Moreau de Saint-Méry,* Avocat au Conseil supérieur," *Affiches américaines,* May 14, 1783, [3].

Monsieur *Moreau de Saint-Méry,* lawyer at the Superior Council of Cap Français, presumes, due to the slowness of people removing the affairs with which he was charged, that the announcement of his departure for France has left people to think that he would continue his work after his departure; he believes it necessary to announce that he has already left the Bar. He is selling, from the present moment, different furniture, effects, jewels, the 600 volumes remaining in his library, a Black cook and a Black laundress. He will also be ceding his lodgings as of the first of next July.[34]

In May 1783, Moreau advertised the sale of his Black laundress (une négresse blanchisseuse) (Figure 5). The same advertisement also offered his Black cook for public sale, perhaps the same man that he tried to sell the month previously along with an enslaved wigmaker. It appears that this woman was purchased, as subsequent advertisements for the sale of Moreau's belongings did not mention her. The inventory itself highlights how Moreau's personal inanimate effects were placed on par with the human beings he owned. The books and the enslaved were linked, a confirmation that the power to travel, work, and purchase the reading material he needed for his livelihood as a lawyer and public intellectual was inseparably connected to his buying and selling of people. This anonymous woman also demonstrates that Moreau's achievements were predicated upon his masterly extraction of surplus value, intellectual as well as physical, from people of African descent. Indeed, Moreau made a point of turning her job into fodder for publication, composing an essay about "the washing of laundry in the Antilles" (le lessivage du linge dans les Antilles). Given that he was unlikely to have been washing his own laundry regularly, he probably consulted with her and others who worked for him, hovering in their work spaces, perhaps getting in their way, in a bid to discover the secrets of the trade so that he could write about them convincingly for Parisian agricultural journals.[35]

I have found no record of the laundress's purchase, either in 1783 or when Moreau's family might have originally added her to their household. In fact, for all of his diligent documentation of his own work and life accomplishments—archival manuscripts, rare printed material, and personal effects such as diplomas that he carefully preserved for a future biographer—I have seen no inventories listing the people he enslaved, no bills of sale or purchase, no invoices that might hint at expenses dedicated to food rations or the cost of clothing them in his voluminous piles of paper. That genre of documentation, itself limited, is mainly kept in archival sources such as notarial logbooks or newspaper columns. As people they shared the same living spaces. However, sources about the enslaved are housed in separate physical spaces from Moreau's own personal papers, with the exception of passing textual references that formed part of his self-narratives.

Although this woman remains anonymous in the present, she and her enslaved peers were indispensable domestic laborers in the Moreau home. At the time, Moreau had an infant son. Some group of women would have had to change and wash soiled diapers, nurse young Médéric, clean the dresses worn by Madame and the heavy court robes worn by Moreau. Laundresses, like wet nurses and more generalized child care workers, were usually women, and their labor was essential to social reproduction. Advertisements for their sale and recapture when they escaped peppered the colony's newspapers, and the figure herself is a common one in Caribbean literature.³⁶ Was the woman who belonged to the Moreaus tall, young, shy, bold, relieved to be changing households? Did she have a lover? Were her hands calloused? Could she swim, or did she stick close to the river's edge as she washed?

Boudacan

The Prince of Ouaire spent some time in Saint-Domingue, where the government accorded him the respect that the motive of his trip was sufficient to earn him. Arriving in France, he was received by Their Majesties with an infinitely flattering welcome; and chance has allowed, in this Assembly in Europe's most famous capital, for an American mouth to express to an African Prince the desire that we all have to be worthy of the high opinion that he has conceived for the French nation.

Le Prince de Ouaire a séjourné pendant quelque-tems à Saint-Domingue, où le Gouvernement lui a accordé des égards que le motif même de son voyage aurait suffi pour lui attirer. Arrivé en France, il a reçu de leurs Majestés un accueil infiniment flatteur, enfin il vient ajouter en ce moment à l'intérêt de cette Assemblée, où le hasard veut que dans la Capitale la plus célèbre de l'Europe, ce fait une bouche Américaine qui exprime à un Prince Africain le voeu que nous formons tous de justifier la haute opinion qu'il a conçue de la Nation Française.³⁷

In 1784, Boudacan-Marc, a twenty-year-old prince of the Kingdom of Warri / Iwere, came to Paris. According to Moreau, he also visited Saint-Domingue, where he was welcomed by the government in light of the future slave-trading alliances his kingdom and France might develop. Details about Boudacan's sojourn in the Parisian capital and the story of how he came to be there were detailed in a lecture that Moreau read to the Musée de Paris called "Observations sur le Royaume de Ouaire, à la Côte-d'Or en Afrique." The talk, published as a pamphlet, was full of information about Boudacan's home and noted that the French ship captain Jean-François Landolphe planned to open a slave-trading post there. Landolphe did in fact work with the *Olu / Oba* of Warri to establish a short-lived settlement in what is now modern-day Nigeria, close to the former kingdom of Benin. Boudacan, an Itsekiri man, met with the French monarchs and had his portrait painted at the request of the French court (Figure 6). Why he was dressed in feathers and leopard skin is unclear. These accoutrements might have resulted from a European artist's expectations rather than any

FIGURE 6. *Portrait of Prince Boudakan.* By Joseph Piazza. Oil on canvas.
Musée Bonaparte, Ville d'Auxonne, in. 2010.0.61, Photo Bruno François.

representation of his own clothing choices. Moreau lamented that during this
visit Boudacan often appeared in European dress rather than "an outfit that was
his own" (un costume qui lui fût propre). As one of his hosts, Moreau was proud
that "an American mouth" (une bouche Américain) was there to introduce this
African prince to French society. As a Caribbean intellectual, he believed in the
appropriateness of his role as a mediator between Europe and Africa.[38]

The text provided a detailed discussion of the Kingdom of Warri, including
specifics that could only have come from eyewitness accounts Moreau garnered
from Landolphe. Landolphe, who spent four months living at the Olu / Oba's
court, described greeting customs, architecture, the coral beads and clothing
worn by dignitaries, the legal system, the role of women, the use of cowries

for currency, facial scarification, a few words in "la langue Ouairienne," and a history of the ruling king's descent from a long-running Benin dynasty. This 1784 speech made it clear that Boudacan came from a community full of metal workers, artists, magistrates, and those who practiced a variety of religions, from Islam to traditional African religions. Moreau even went so far as to critique the kingdom's reliance on the slave trade as a source of public wealth, stating, "It is thus that Europe augments the crimes of Africa in order to procure for itself, in some way at the cost of human blood, the riches of the New World" (C'est ainsi que l'Europe augmente les crimes de l'Afrique pour se procurer, en quelque sorte au prix du sang humain, les richesses du Nouveau-Monde). Moreau's comments to his Parisian audience, though full of prejudices about the superiority of European customs, differed from his later invective that decried the alleged barbarism and violence of a generic African continent in order to justify the slavery of its inhabitants. In other words, his actual knowledge of and familiarity with a West African society contemporaneous to his own fell to the wayside when it was politically convenient to instead propagate stereotypes that denied African accomplishments in the arts, jurisprudence, and other social forms.[39]

C

Caraïbes and *crâne*

Among them [the enslaved people of Saint-Domingue] are found mixed in the descendants of some Caribs, of some Indians from Guyana, the Fox Indians of Canada, and some Natchez of Louisiana that the government, or men, violators of the Rights of Man, judged necessary or lucrative to reduce to slavery.

Parmi ceux-ci [les esclaves de Saint-Domingue], se trouve mêlée la descendance de quelques Caraïbes, de quelques Indiens de la Guyane, de Sauvages Renards du Canada, de Natchez de la Louisiane, que le gouvernement ou des hommes violateurs du Droit des Gens, jugeaient nécessaire ou lucratif de réduire à la servitude.[40]

A skull. A skull sitting in a curiosity cabinet, occasionally taken out for study or to be passed around from hand to hand. A head disinterred and blanched from exposure. A community's ancestral remains. Alongside his two brothers-in-law and other prominent men in Cap Français, Moreau cofounded the Cercle des

Philadelphes, one of the most active literary and scientific societies in the late-eighteenth-century Americas. In a discussion of the library and material artifacts collected by this learned society, he mentioned "the head of a former inhabitant of the island" (la tête d'un ancien habitant de l'Isle). Many colonists enjoyed archeological speculation, collecting clues about the island as they cleared the land for cultivation and published natural history accounts of their findings. This skull moved Moreau to pity. He noted that "these unfortunate ones would still exist had the first conquerors had the peaceful taste for study and the soul of the Philadelphes" (ces malheureux, dont la race existerait encore, si les premiers conquerans avaient eu le goût paisible de l'étude et l'âme des Philadelphes). A group including the most prominent slaveholders and functionaries in Saint-Domingue sat in a library, holding an Indigenous person's remains as they decried the Spanish colonizers for not being as inclined to "peaceful" study as they were. Such a posture infuriates; the irony is plain.[41]

Even as Moreau declared these "former" inhabitants of Hispaniola extinct, his opening commentary cited above acknowledged that Native communities of the larger hemispheric Americas were still being enslaved on the island, particularly those from other parts of the French empire in North and South America. The Fox, the Natchez, the Caribs, each engaged in their own histories of warfare, were interspersed among the larger enslaved population in Saint-Domingue. Moreau's elaborate tables of racial intermixture made specific mention of the "combinational mixtures of Black people with the Caribs or Indians or Western Indians" (combinaisons du mélange des . . . Nègres avec les Caraïbes ou Sauvages ou Indiens Occidentaux). He was interested in how the children resulting from relationships between Black and Indigenous people resulted in particular skin tones and hair that was more or less long, straight, or frizzy *(crépus)*. Native genocide and enslavement were thus not events of the past; they were ongoing processes by his own admission.[42]

Créole

I must now speak of the language that is used by all of the Blacks who live in the French colony of Saint-Domingue. It is a corrupted French, to which has been mixed many Frenchified Spanish words and where many maritime terms have also found a place. One can easily conceive that this language, which is nothing more than a true jargon, is often unintelligible in the mouth of an old African, and that one speaks it better the younger one learns it. . . . And one sure fact is that a European, however much he uses it, however long his residence has been in the islands, can never possess its subtleties. . . .

. . . I call upon the seductive creole women, who have adopted this expressive patois to paint their tenderness! . . .

There are a thousand nothings that one would not dare to say in French, a thousand voluptuous images that one could not succeed in painting in French and that Creole expresses or renders with infinite grace. It never says more than when it uses inarticulate sounds, of which entire sentences are made.

J'ai à parler maintenant du langage qui sert à tous les nègres qui habitent la colonie française de Saint-Domingue. C'est un français corrompu, auquel on a mêlé plusieurs mots espagnols francisés, et où les termes marins ont aussi trouvé leur place. On concevra aisément que ce langage, qui n'est qu'un vrai jargon, est souvent inintelligible dans la bouche d'un vieil Africain, et qu'on le parle d'autant mieux, qu'on l'a appris plus jeune. . . . et un fait très-sur, c'est qu'un Européen, quelque habitude qu'il en ait, quelque longue qu'ait été sa résidence aux Isles, n'en possède jamais les finesses. . . .

. . . J'en appelle aux séduisantes Créoles, qui ont adopté ce patois expressif pour peindre leur tendresse! . . .

Il est mille riens que l'on n'oserait dire en français, mille images voluptueuses, que l'on ne réussirait pas à peindre avec le français, et que le créol exprime ou rend avec une grace infinie. Il ne dit jamais plus que quand il emploie les sons inarticulés, dont il a fait des phrases entières.[43]

The above quotations, coupled with Moreau's discussion of the text of a Kreyòl-language song about estranged Black lovers ("Lissette quitté la plaine"), are the most well-cited and studied excerpts concerning Kreyòl in Moreau's work, indeed in much of the work on Kreyòl in the eighteenth- and early-nineteenth-century Caribbean.[44] The sexual dimension to his description of Kreyòl's beauty and functionality is evident. Literary scholar Deborah Jenson has made excellent use of other Kreyòl-language fragments, mostly of the vibrant tradition of popular songs she labels "courtesan poetry," found in Moreau's manuscript collection "Notes historiques." She has found ample evidence in these song fragments of the rarely recorded voices of nonwhite women who provide a "literary inscription of the process of unbecoming slaves, of discovering a public space of choice and power negotiations around the politics not of colony or nation, but shared bodies and affect." She transcribes and translates multiple versions of one song Moreau collected, "Na rien qui dous," an example of what she terms "indigo blues" because of how it portrays a discussion between two female indigo workers about the possibilities of sexualized labor. It contains the lyrics:

Comment toi vlé gagner cote?	How do you expect to gain status?
Si tos pas gagner largent	If you don't earn money
Yo vas dit, femme la li sotte	They will say that woman there is an idiot
Li pas connait fair paiyer blanc	She doesn't know how to make whites pay
Femme qui sote cé comme sa yo fair	Women who are idiots, that's what they do
Yo rauséyo, sa fait nou piquié	They [men] beat them, which makes us pity them
Comment toi vlé gagner côte	How do you expect to gain status
Si tos pas gagne[r] largent?	If you don't earn money?
Yo vas dis femme la li sôte	They will say that woman there is an idiot
Li pas connait fai paiye[r] blanc	She doesn't know how to make whites pay.

Jenson notes Moreau's comments about the "celebrity status" of well-known courtesans in Saint-Domingue, and her work illustrates how Moreau—eager to listen to, collect, and archive popular cultural forms—facilitated the ability of many generations of scholars to read with and against his analyses.[45]

Other Kreyòl transcriptions allow the aural worlds of the enslaved to be heard, even as Moreau perhaps missed the point of the utterances he collected. For instance, he documented that Black people used to ring the bells of the church in Cap Français with "deafening peals" (carillons assourdissans *[sic]*). The "sepulchral sound" (son sèpulcral) of the bells announcing a funeral occasioned the bell ringers and other enslaved people to say: a *"Bon blanc mouri: mauvé rété."* Moreau translated this saying as: "Un bon blanc est mort: les méchans restent" (A good white is dead. The mean ones remain). The double entendre here suggests that in sum the best white was a dead white. This short expression provides a view into the enslaved's world of satire and humor.[46] Moreau's use of it is in keeping with other instances when he discussed Kreyòl as a way to explain that "Blacks love proverbs and sentences. They even have some that are very moral" (les nègres aiment les proverbes et les sentences. Ils en ont même de très-moraux). When Moreau wished to add another layer of authority to his statements, he included

Kreyòl to show that local inhabitants, often the enslaved, would have agreed with his assessment. In the aforementioned entry on the Aradas, for example, he further noted that they were reputed to be "greedy" (avare) and "dog eaters" (mangeur de chiens). He remarked that other enslaved people developed the proverbial expressions "Rada mangé chien" and "Varichié tan com' Rada." The insertion of Kreyòl in his written work thus sometimes allowed Moreau to mobilize the opinions of the enslaved as back-up evidence supposedly demonstrating the accuracy of his own opinions, a technique of co-option.[47]

The opening remarks of this entry exemplify Moreau's incorporation of historically inaccurate and biased information. Eighteenth-century Kreyòl was not a "jargon," and it consisted of more than Frenchified Spanish words and mariner terms combined with "corrupted" French. In this case, the complete absence of any allusions to the African languages that formed both the substrate and lexical sources of Kreyòl is curious. Furthermore, while stating that it was a language that "creoles of all colors loved to entertain themselves in" (Créols *[de toutes les couleurs]* aiment à s'entretenir), Moreau suggested that it was the *only* language Blacks shared among themselves (les nègres n'en ont pas d'autre entr'eux). This statement is patently inaccurate given how many African-born slaves lived in Saint-Domingue and spoke mutually intelligible languages. The very existence of the Kikongo "Dictionnaire ou Vocabulaire Congo" (discussed in Chapter 6), a text published by his own brother-in-law, Louis Narcisse Baudry des Lozières, negates Moreau's claim.[48]

Moreau himself documented the presence of African languages in Saint-Domingue in a story about the Jesuit priest Pierre-Louis Boutin. During Boutin's long residence on the island from 1705 until his death in 1742, he made "the study of the numerous African languages and the morals / customs of those who lived in that part of the world his principle study" (l'étude des nombreux idiomes de l'Afrique, celle des moeurs des hommes qui habitent cette partie du monde, était la principale application du père Boutin). In the first decades of the eighteenth century, there was thus a precedent for studying African languages, made possible by what Moreau characterized as Boutin's close attention to the physical and spiritual health of the Black population of Cap Français. He noted that although some thought that the priest's "zeal . . . sometimes went too far" (zèle . . . avait été quelquefois trop loin), the local community mourned his death. Implying in one part of his work that people of African descent spoke only Kreyòl among themselves and using other commentary to present anecdotal evidence about the presence of African languages on the island exemplifies the contradictory information and misinterpretations in Moreau's work about the customs surrounding him.[49]

D

Domestique

I have freed five [of my slaves]. . . . In 1788, my Domestic, who, for 16 years, preferred to be mine as opposed to owning himself, who would have followed me to France, who would attach himself to me again if I returned to Saint-Domingue.

J'en ai affranchi cinq [de mes esclaves]. . . . En 1788, mon Domestique, qui avait préféré, pendant 16 ans, d'être à moi plutôt qu'à lui-même, qui aurait voulu me suivre en France, et qui s'attacherait encore à moi, si je retournais à Saint-Domingue.[50]

Moreau enslaved a man who worked as his domestic servant for sixteen years. According to Moreau's dates, this man would have entered his service in 1772, when Moreau was twenty-two. At the time, Moreau was completing a law degree in France, and he returned briefly to Martinique in 1774, where he visited his family before moving to Saint-Domingue in May 1775. While in Fort Royal, he took possession of some belongings, including "un domestique," some furnishings, a personal library he valued at four thousand French francs, and enough cash that he was able to temporarily loan his new legal mentor in Cap Français, Monsieur d'Augy, fifty Portuguese gold coins to purchase a man named Pierre, a *mulâtre* cook who arrived on the same boat from Martinique that carried some of Moreau's other possessions. This was no insignificant sum of money and assets. Again, Moreau's books and the people he owned circulated together. This male domestique from Martinique could very well have been the same man he freed in 1788. As recorded in both the *Mémoire justificatif* and his marriage contract, Moreau owned "several slaves" (plusieurs esclaves) in Martinique, many left there for "the usage of the lady, his mother" (l'usage à la dame, sa mère).[51]

This man is just the type of interlocutor a reader should keep in mind. He is now a silent figure in the shadows, one who lived and labored alongside Moreau for virtually Moreau's entire adult life in the colonies. What gossip might he have heard about notable locals as he attended to his master? What details could he share about the life of a man whom he served at such close quarters? Perhaps he cared for his clothing and helped him dress; during bouts of Moreau's gout, maybe he brought him diluted beer (acquired from Bristol in England), as Moreau himself suggested was a helpful remedy when feverish. At the time he appeared briefly in the printed record, Moreau and his family could no doubt have related countless details about what this anonymous man looked like, the timbre of his voice, and how he interacted with other members of the household and the neighbors living nearby on Rue de Conseil. They might have known where he decided to live and how he was able to earn a living after being freed.[52]

As was the case when Moreau discussed his "young Mandingo man named Castor" (jeune nègre Mondongue, nommé Castor), Moreau's choice of words when describing his relationship with his enslaved domestic is instructive: "preferred to be mine," "followed me," "attach himself." The verbs imply desire and free will on the part of this man, although he did not have the legal right to make decisions about his own welfare. The content of Moreau's comments is entirely self-referential. Can a modern-day audience believe that this man cared for him so much that he would rather belong to Moreau than "owning himself" and that he would willingly have returned to his service again after being manumitted? There is a delusional quality to such claims. It is possible that the two men developed a closeness despite the forced nature of their relationship. It is possible that this man might have wanted to continue in Moreau's employ as a paid servant following manumission given the difficulties he could have faced finding paid employment as a free man of color. It is also probable that Moreau saw what he wanted to see and heard professions of devotion that he wanted to hear.[53]

Moreau's interpretations, here and in other examples, claimed access to the interior lives of the enslaved. He presumed no conflict of opinion or interest when assessing their motivations, feelings, or beliefs. For instance, while positing that the tears of the enslaved were mostly insincere, he claimed: "I am not so unjust as to pretend that the tears of the Blacks are always feigned. There are some Blacks who cry because their hearts are broken, whose eyes tear up for a long time afterward when they speak of objects that were dear to them, such as their masters whom they have loved and served with estimable fidelity" (Je ne suis pas assez injuste pour prétendre que les larmes des nègres sont toujours étudiées; il est des nègres qui pleurent parce que leur coeur est déchiré, dont les yeux se mouillent lorsque long-tems encore après, ils parlent de quelques objets qui leur étaient chers, et parmi lesquels ils comptent des maîtres qu'ils ont aimés et servis avec une estimable fidélité). In a context that would have given enslaved people many reasons for despair, the example Moreau provided of their sincere grief was occasioned by sadness to be separated from the very people who held them in bondage. Moreau's account of mutual respect and care between his class and the people of African descent around him offers textbook examples of how what Toni Morrison calls an "Africanist presence" enabled white conceptions of selfhood.[54]

At one point in his life, Moreau mentioned having seventeen "domestics." We know of others: Castor, the laundress, the cook, the wigmaker, Angélique, Sophie, Myrtile, and Rosine. Would this anonymous man have known these other people well? Enslaved women named Martonne, Agathe, and Sylvie also lived with Moreau. "Seventeen and counting" has served as a mantra as I have endeavored to track them down, knowing full well that the number is an inaccurate guide to how many women, children, and men Moreau and his immediate family might have owned over the course of his life. These pages serve to gather the people living in his multiple households. Their names and their anonymity claim space.

E

Encyclopédie

Among his manuscripts, is a long work undertaken to show, under each word of a colonial dictionary, all of the knowledge that this word makes it useful to know, and to make it possible to compare diverse colonies. This work has gotten to the letter *E*.

Parmi ses manuscrits, est un long travail entrepris pour montrer, sous chaque mot d'un dictionnaire colonial, toutes les connaissances que ce mot rend utiles à savoir, et pour mettre à portée de comparer les diverses colonies entre elles. Ce travail est parvenu à la letter *E*.[55]

In a 1799 publication outlining all of his scholarship and publications, Moreau (referring to himself in the third person) mentioned his comparative colonial encyclopedia, the "Répertoire des notions coloniales." It remained unpublished at the time of his death. Referring to it as a "dictionary" in this announcement, much as the French *Encyclopédie* was a *Dictionnaire raisonné des sciences, des arts et des métiers,* its entries documented concepts related to everyday life: suggestions about a public works project for human waste in Cap Français, documentation about burial customs, notes on festival traditions. Many entries defined legal concepts and institutions. Moreau also included numerous entries for material objects and living creatures that described their uses: chestnuts, cider, holy water, bees. Nouns appeared more often than people as organizational categories. Of Saint-Domingue, he wrote that "the Encyclopedia, that work admired even by those who accuse it of insufficiency, only accorded [the colony] three or four lines" (l'Encyclopédie, cet Ouvrage admiré par ceux-mêmes qui accusent son insuffisance, n'a accordé que trois ou quartre lignes). He aimed to remedy this lack, not only for Saint-Domingue but for French and foreign colonies throughout the globe: Île Bourbon (present-day Réunion), Saint Lucia, Tobago, Guyana, Trinidad, Tobago, Cuba, all appear in his files. Despite a working draft covering only the first five letters of the alphabet, the scaffolding supporting it was voluminous. Thousands of documents, contained in almost three hundred folios, contextualized his entries and provide a sense of the subjects he would likely have included in the future had he finished this project.[56]

Dance / Danse. Abortion / Avortement. Abolition / Abolition. Cruelty / Cruauté. This last entry was left blank in the manuscript, but one can wonder what anecdotes Moreau might have thought fit to discuss. His descriptions of the first three terms and others relied on frequent reference to the enslaved and free people of color. His repertory of colonial notions made people of African descent and their customs central to a discussion of colonial life. In this sense, it shares common content with the *Encyclopédie noire,* even if Moreau's priorities were vastly different from my own. While encyclopedias synthesize knowledge, providing extractable information that can be recycled, mine does not contain entries that synthesize or provide closure. My entries documenting people expose Moreau's reliance on slavery. More important, however, these entries—glimpses into people's lives—ultimately aim to move beyond a central narrative that centers Moreau or that assimilates these people's stories to his. Rather than allowing his life and work to serve as the main points of connection, I ask a reader to embrace disconnection and to wonder about people as individuals and members of communities apart from the lives of their owners.

Esclavage

A large part of Africa is, so to speak, dependent on America, to which she gives her cultivators. Saint-Domingue alone possesses at least three-fifths of the slaves in the French islands of America. ~~It is not relevant to this description that concerns me to examine in and of itself the question of slavery and to verify whether a state of affairs to which it is difficult for humanity and philosophy not to sigh is a subject of accusation against the colonies; if the abolition of slavery in the colonies is necessary, useful or even possible, if slavery produces the evils that some attribute to it.... Never perhaps has a thing been stirred up with more important consequences.... it is not by a wish that moral sores can be closed; the deeper they are, the more their cure requires talent, precaution, slowness.... it would have been desirable~~

that the conviction of the impossibility of putting an end to slavery would have demanded that one think only of softening it, of putting an end to its rigor by means that even the interest of the masters would support. But I realize that I have gone on, almost despite myself, about that which I want to avoid; I return, thus, to the customs of the slaves in the French colony.

Une grande partie de l'Afrique est, pour ainsi dire, tributaire de l'Amérique à qui elle donne des cultivateurs. Saint-Domingue possède, à lui seul, au moins les trois cinquièmes des esclaves des îles françaises de l'Amérique. Il n'est pas relatif à la description qui m'occupe d'examiner en soi la question de l'esclavage et de vérifier si un état de choses auquel il est difficile que l'humanité et la philosophie ne donnent pas un soupir est un sujet d'accusation contre les colonies; si l'abolition de l'esclavage dans les colonies est nécessaire, utile ou même possible, si l'esclavage produit tous les maux que les-uns lui attribuent. . . . Jamais peut-être il n'a été rien agité de plus important dans ses conséquences. . . . ce n'est point par un voeu que les plaies morales peuvent être fermées, plus elles sont profondes, plus leur guérison exige de talens, de précautions, de lenteur. . . . qu'il eut été à désirer que la conviction de l'impossibilité de faire cesser l'esclavage eut exigé qu'on ne songeât qu'à l'adoucir, qu'à faire cesser sa rigueur par des moyens qui eussent trouvé l'intérêt même des maîtres pour appui. Mais je m'aperçois que je me livre presque malgré moi à ce que je veux éviter, je reviens donc aux moeurs des esclaves de la colonie française.[57]

This is one of the most insightful and maddening passages that Moreau penned about slavery. He crossed out the manuscript text above and excised it from his 1797 published version of the *Description de la partie française de l'isle Saint-Domingue*. It provides a stream of consciousness commentary, an unfiltered look at his thoughts. "Despite" himself (malgré moi), Moreau was compelled to comment upon the very issue that he most desired to "avoid" (éviter), one he believed had enormous consequences for the future of the colonial world. Slavery. Could and should it be ended, and if so, how? His equation of slavery to a deep "moral sore" (plaie morale) requiring profound thought to "cure" guardedly critiques the institution. He claimed that slavery festered beneath the surface, indeed at the core, of his society. He averred it to be justifiably indicted by moral philosophy and humanity writ large. Moreau's way of healing such a wound demanded slowness, deliberation, perhaps an amelioration of the living and working conditions of the enslaved rather than an end to the practice itself. Here is a glimpse

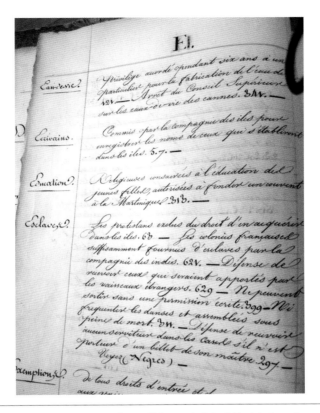

FIGURE 7. Manuscript copy of one of Moreau de Saint-Méry's indexes, letter *E*, including the entry for "esclavage" (slavery). Archives nationales d'outre-mer, Aix-en-Provence, France, Collection Moreau de Saint-Méry (Ser. F3).

of Moreau trying to straddle an impossible divide in a moment of intense social upheavals in France and in the colonies. The words were published during what was year six of the uprising among the enslaved and free people of color in Saint-Domingue that had begun in 1791. The time lapse between when he felt compelled to comment on slavery despite himself and when he revised and published his book saw the French temporarily abolish the institution with the Law of 4 February 1794 (16 pluviôse, An II).

Of course, it is easy to see how he could be carried away despite himself. While Figure 7 shows a neatly scripted entry for "esclavage" that appeared in a manuscript of his notes on the colonies, its short references to the topic could not hold. How could slavery and its future *not* be relevant to his *Description?* Africa was the birth continent for the vast majority of the inhabitants of the Caribbean. Some aspect of living in a slaveholding region informed almost every page of Moreau's work, even as subtext. It defined his tomes of legal codes and descriptions of dance. "Esclavage" in this example was cross-referenced as "voyez nègres." Slavery here corresponded to "Blacks," hence the institution itself was racialized. Even whiteness was understood in relation to what it supposedly was not. When Moreau wrote about the personalities of white men born in the colonies, for instance, he detailed their domineering personalities that resulted from having always attempted to bend the will of the enslaved to their own. White women imitated the fashion styles of people of color. Fully avoiding a discussion of slavery, either in the abstract or in the nitty-gritty details of daily life, would have fundamentally changed the nature of his professional career.[58]

In a neighboring context, Thomas Jefferson's determination to document the excisions that contained a condemnation of slavery in his earlier drafts of the Declaration of Independence by drawing a black line beneath them in his autobiography is a reminder that what Moreau deliberately deleted from his most famous work is instructive. Jefferson wrote: "The sentiments of men are known not only by what they receive but what they reject also. . . . The clause . . . reprobating the enslaving inhabitants of Africa, was struck out in complaisance to South Carolina and Georgia, who had never attempted to restrain the importation of slaves, and who on the contrary still wished to continue it. Our Northern brethren also I believe felt a little tender under those censures; for tho' their people have very few slaves themselves yet they have been pretty considerable carriers of them to others." Moreau's waffling about his alleged benevolent proslavery mindset is a bankrupt position. He abandoned his professed desire for reform and amelioration of the institution when revolutionary events in France and the Caribbean placed it into acute jeopardy.[59]

What this entry does not say is what the enslaved felt about esclavage. Yet there is an internal tension in the stories Moreau told. For example, he once wrote that Black people required less sustenance and fewer material things than most people. He then stated that when enslaved men and women ate, especially in situations where food was plentiful, they ate to the point of gorging themselves.[60] The reality of an enslaved person suffering from chronic hunger suffuses the image painted of her / him in the act of eating. It directly contradicts the very point Moreau has just tried to prove about their need for less food despite their grueling work conditions. He was not stupid, and he was not divorced from reality. Rather, he actively worked toward building and perpetuating the lies designed to maintain the status quo, all while being at the center of metropolitan and colonial debates about what the future might hold for the right to liberty, fraternity, and equality for men of all colors.

Esclavage is thus an umbrella term and concept.
Herein it signifies all of the people without whom Moreau _____.
would not have worn clean clothes.
would not have been able to subsidize his book collecting.
would have had less leisure time to think and study.
would have compiled a completely different legal code.
would not have eaten the same appetizing meals.
would not have been able to produce his scholarship.
These are the people whose stories require assembling.

I

Ibo

One places a high value on Blacks from the Gold Coast for agriculture, but in general their haughty character makes it difficult to lead them and demands that masters know how to study them. It is principally with regard to the Ibos that great surveillance is necessary, because chagrin or the slightest discontent causes them to commit suicide, the idea of which, far from terrifying them, seems to have some appeal to them because they adopt the dogma of the transmigration of souls. When no longer able to absolutely prevent this Pythagorean voyage, one has the head of the first one who kills himself cut off, or only his nose and ears, and kept at the top of a perch; then the others, convinced that this one will never dare to reappear in his native land thus dishonored in the opinion of his compatriots, and fearing the same treatment, renounce this dreadful emigration plan.

This disposition of the soul resulted in the Ibos being designated by these creole words: Ibos pend'cor à yo, (Ibos hang themselves).

On estime les nègres de la Côte d'Or pour la culture, mais en général leur caractère altier en rend le conduit difficile et elle exige des maîtres qui sachent les étudier. C'est principalement à l'égard des Ibos qu'une grande surveillance est nécessaire, puisque le chagrin ou le mécontentement le plus léger les porte au suicide dont l'idée loin de les épouvanter semble avoir quelque chose de séduisant pour eux, parce qu'ils adoptent le dogme de la transmigration des âmes. . . . lorsqu'on n'a pu prévenir absolument ce voyage pythagoricien, on fait couper la tête du premier qui se tue, ou seulement son nez et les oreilles que l'on conserve au haut d'une perche; alors les autres convaincus que celui-là n'osera jamais reparaître dans sa terre natale ainsi déshonoré dans l'opinion de ses compatriotes et redoutant le même traitement, renoncent à cet affreux plan d'émigration.

Cette disposition de l'âme qui fait désigner les Ibos par ces mots Créols: Ibos pend'cor à yo, (les Ibos se pendent).[61]

The suicide patterns of enslaved Africans in the Americas have received a fair amount of scholarly attention. Moreau's comments about the Igbo and their religious convictions echo beliefs documented in extant slave and planter narratives from Cuba, the French Caribbean, and the United States. In particular, the 1803 mass suicide of the Igbo enslaved near Savannah, Georgia, has entered the public imagination as an iteration of the Flying African tale.[62]

Moreau had a response to this problem as seen from the perspective of slaveholders; they needed to "know how to study" their laborers. Academic investigation was directly linked to surveillance and control. His offhand dismissal of some Igbos' decision to resist enslavement by taking their lives, claiming their motivations grew from the "slightest discontent," is in keeping with the affective flatness of recounting their beheading and public facial disfigurement. Importantly, although he believed that the spectacle of this torture had the desired effect of diminishing acts of suicide, a glimpse of Igbo reasoning also emerges in his comments. Despite their biases, Moreau's observations provide an informative glimpse of West African philosophical and practical responses to slavery. In some context, Moreau learned that the Igbo themselves might not want to return to their native country dishonored by missing body parts. The fear of the kind of reception they might receive at home, not solely the fear of retribution in their American circumstances, was a determining factor in their behavioral choices.

J

Jean-Baptiste

A Black man named *Jean-Baptiste*, hating agricultural work and wanting to get out of it, conceives of cutting, using the dimensions of his right arm, an arm of fairly hard wood, and for several months, he used his left hand to cut the wrist of his wooden arm with his sickle. When he finally had confidence in his cut, he put his true right hand in place but could not amputate it before the fourth blow.

Un nègre nommé *Jean-Baptiste*, détestant le travail de la culture, imagine pour s'en débarrasser, de tailler sur les dimensions de son bras droit, un bras de bois assez dur, et pendant plusieurs mois, il exerce sa main gauche à couper le poignet du bras de bois avec sa serpe. Lorsqu'enfin il se croit assez sûr de son coup, il place la vraie main droite qu'il ne pût cependant amputer qu'au quatrième coup.[63]

Jean-Baptiste entered the historical record when Moreau used him as an example of how the enslaved allegedly felt about their circumstances. His story appears as a brief anecdote mobilized to explain how the enslaved supposedly experienced chagrin, were able to endure physical pain, were bothered by the monotony and "constraint" (contrainte) of their existences, and, finally, had been known to hurt themselves for "frivolous motives" (la frivolité des motifs). Moreau felt qualified to assess Jean-Baptiste's thoughts, relating this tale for its evidentiary value about the interior life of the enslaved.[64]

The tale is striking. Jean-Baptiste's resourcefulness and sheer desperation are both palpable. In an age of enlightenment that prized empiricism and ingenuity, all of Jean-Baptiste's inventiveness and experimentation were put to destructive rather than creative use. He employed this ingenuity to create a wooden arm extension, a prosthetic, so that through a process of trial and error he could determine how to effectively maim himself. Prosthetic use among the enslaved was not unheard of. One contemporary observer even noted that a colonist in Gonaïves was nicknamed Master Wooden Legs (Maitre à jambes de bois) by the people forced to work on his behalf because of his habit of cutting off their legs below the knees. As a price for their perceived disobedience, he replaced their limbs with wooden peg legs.[65]

Although Moreau was interested enough to note that it took four hacks for Jean-Baptiste to sever his hand, there is no indication that he recognized or empathized with the terror that must have accompanied that bloody scene. There is no indication that he shared the repulsion with which we might respond to his words. A reader is not told if Jean-Baptiste survived. If he did, we could not trust Moreau's gloss on what Jean-Baptiste might have thought about having taken such a life-changing course of action.

Jean-Baptiste's story is immediately followed by information on another man, this time anonymous. He worked on the Duboisson estate, a sugar plantation that Moreau cited as a model of good management *(sage administration)* throughout Saint-Domingue. After stating that this man was known to have run away in the past and that he suffered from venereal disease, Moreau included his story as a continuation of his evidence for the enslaved's supposed ability to endure extreme physical pain. The man was in such great distress that he sharpened a knife and "with one cut he rendered himself a eunuch" (d'un seul coup il se rend eunuque). When his fellow enslaved women allegedly reproached him for his *"barbarity" (barbarité),* he reportedly replied, *"Look see . . . , my flesh, is it not mine!" (Hé bien . . . , ma chair, n'est-elle pas à moi!)*[66]

This example is chilling. First, the event: an enslaved man made the decision to cut off his own penis to escape the pain of venereal disease. Poor medical care resulted in a situation so egregious that he risked bleeding to death, or, if he survived, being left without a penis. These deterrents were not strong enough for him to abstain from such an act. His alleged response, *"my flesh, is it not mine!"* is also a present-day reader's chance to hear his voice, however mediated. By law, his flesh was not his. Yet he flouted the law via self-mutilation. He declared that his flesh *was* his. Moreau did not condemn the barbarity of slavery here; he condemned this man's response to it. The two examples are their own counter-testimonies to the very lesson that Moreau was trying to make about the alleged "frivolité" motivating the behavior of the enslaved.

Moreau's interpretive response to the incidents above, including his comments on managing the Igbo inclination for suicide, confirm his work's reputation as the "epicenter of studies of colonial racism." It is not anachronistic to judge him thusly. Michel-René Hilliard d'Auberteuil, another eighteenth-century natural historian, wrote that "in Saint-Domingue, whoever is white mistreats blacks with impunity." "The habit of being obeyed," he noted, "renders the master proud, tough, unfair, cruel, and makes him lose all moral virtues."[67] To evaluate Moreau's assessments as understandable from a man of his times is logically faulty. His times ran the spectrum from reactionary to revolutionary with regard to slave trading and slaveholding, and he was more well versed than most in anti- and proslavery arguments. Moreau did not experience the functioning of the institutions that enabled slavery in the abstract. He knew all about these tortures and abuses, including those that the enslaved inflicted upon themselves. He saw severed heads placed on pikes as warnings; he smelled burning flesh; he heard screams. Yet his scholarly voice is notably casual about violence and the desperation of his fellow human beings. He had a propensity to discuss extreme abuse in a lively and anecdotal yet detached and inhumane way. Although his sadism and lack of empathy were conditioned by his upbringing around such cruelties, it was not the only intellectual or moral path available to him. His affective dissonance is particularly remarkable when his discussion of frivolousness is based in examples of dismemberment and a system in which self-mutilation became a viable life (and death) choice for people.

"Autonomy, authority, newness and difference, absolute power"—Toni Morrison suggests that meditations on these matters were indelibly linked to the development of U.S. literature. They are equally resonant in the elaboration of Caribbean cultural production, particularly the body of planter literature (memoirs, how-to manuals, political tracts, natural histories) produced by Moreau and his contemporaries. This urge toward domination is embedded adjectivally in Moreau's prose: headless, suicidal, one-armed, castrated. The resulting contestation over absolute power and authority are likewise evident adjectivally: one-armed, suicidal, *altier*, castrated, cantankerous, *querelleuses.*[68]

END OF PART I

FIGURE 8. (*Facing page*) *Portrait Collage of Moreau de Saint-Méry, Part I.* By Luz Sandoval and Sara E. Johnson. The portraits, from top left to right: Detail from Wilbrode Magloire Nicolas Courbe and Charles Toussaint Labadye, *Médéric Louis Élie Moreau de St. Mery: Présid[en]t des elect[eur]s de Paris au mois de j[uil]let 1789 né à la Martinique le 13 j[anvi]er 1750, député de cette colonie au Etats génér[au]x de 1789,* 1789, Bibliothèque nationale de France; James Sharples, *Médéric-Louis-Élie Moreau de Saint-Méry,* 1798, pastel and black chalk on toned wove paper, Bequest of Charles Allen Munn, 1924, Metropolitan Museum of Art; Ostervald L'Ainé, *Ritratto de Moreau de Saint-Méry,* undated watercolor in private collection, Archivio di Stato di Parma; Anonymous [attributed to Jean Baptiste Isabey], *Ritratto dell'amministratore general degli Stati di Parma, Piacenza e Guastalla Médéric Louis-Elie Moreau de Saint-Méry,* n.d., Glauco Lombardi Museum—Parma; Aménaïde Moreau de Saint-Méry, *Conte Moreau de Saint Méry,* circa 1800–1805, licensed by Ministero della Cultura—Complesso Monumentale della Pilotta-Galleria Nazionale di Parma; Marielle Plaisir, detail from *Variation on Lámina 23,* from *The Book of Life,* 2017, inks, gold pigment, and pencils on paper, presented at the exhibition *Visionary Aponte: Art and Black Freedom,* Little Haiti Cultural Center, New York University, and Duke University, 2017–2018.

CHAPTER TWO

Unflattering Portraits

A Visual Critique

Paris Elector

Printer and Bookseller

Ambassador

Ambassador

Father

Cipher

Moreau de Saint-Méry sat for multiple portraits across two decades. In scholarly work, these images appear principally as illustrations that provide background biographical context, free of analysis or comment. Yet, as visual records, there is much they can reveal. In the collage, I have placed them in a novel representational field to move past the idea of them as illustrations of what Moreau looked like (Figure 8). This chapter recasts the representation of Moreau's figure, literal and ideological, and renews focus on the lives of the enslaved to reveal the fictions, visual and textual, erected by colonial slaveholders.[1]

Five of these portraits formally depict Moreau when he was living in France, the United States, and Italy; the sixth is a faceless cipher. The cipher appears as a figure onto which we can further project our own knowledge, a placeholder for other historically grounded visions of Moreau and his class. The upper left portrait is in profile, an image made into a commissioned seal to commemorate Moreau's role as president of the city electors of Paris during July 1789. Witnesses lauded Moreau's leadership of the de facto governing body in Paris during the first moments of revolutionary upheaval and his sangfroid as he issued more than three thousand orders over the course of days with no sleep. An ebullient song was even dedicated to his zeal and service to what would become the new French Republic: "His saintly foresight, unfurls today; the salvation of France, is due to none other than him" (sa sainte prévoyance, se dévoile aujourd'hui; Le salut de la France, ne sera dû qu'à lui). In the other portraits, Moreau faces forward, eyes looking out at the viewer. He is depicted with a double chin and a paunchy stomach; these features denote affluence and good living, although the diet that contributed to his girth also caused him painful gout. His dress indicates social status: lace cuffs and cravats, ornate embroidery, the trappings of authority such as sashes, braided epaulettes, lapel pins, and a sword at his side. This authority is likewise captured in the object he holds opposite the sword in the portrait by Jean Baptiste Isabey: a paper that reads "Conseil d'... Section d'... Legislation ... Rapport. . . . " It represents his work as a prolific functionary who wielded power with his pen.[2]

Here, then, was a man engaged in a particular mode of self-fashioning and concerned about how he might be remembered by posterity; a man who was intent upon projecting an image of philanthropic reputation, accomplishment, refinement, and power. His hagiographic biographers painted rosy pictures of a young man who was the apple of his widowed mother's eye, a child who "found many occasions to rescue the miserable Black slaves in the islands; he eloquently pled their cause with their masters" (il trouva maintes occasions de secourir les misérables esclaves noirs de l'île; il plaidait éloquemment leur cause auprès de leurs maîtres). Of course, he was himself a master and promoted the idea of himself as a "good" one. In a February 1809 letter he wrote to his daughter Aménaïde, he admonished her for getting his titles wrong in his granddaughter's baptism records, telling her that the document would need to be redone: "I have been noted as a simple counselor as opposed to a counselor of state" (on m'a indiqué comme un simple conseiller au lieu de conseiller d'État). All of his publications took care to list his accomplishments on the front cover, varying over the years to include those he felt were most important: administrator general of the duchies of Parma, Piacenza, and Guastalla, vice president of the Musée de Paris, lawyer in parliament, member of many scientific and literary societies in France, the United States, Italy, etc. He was a man who professed to live simply and put his studies and "usefulness" to the colonies ahead of his material interests, yet he was not immune to the lure of pomp and circumstance. As a member of the prestigious Superior Council (Conseil Supérieur) court in Cap Français, he would have worn "black robes trimmed with ermine" and sat on "gold-studded black leather chairs." Later, when in exile in Philadelphia and denied an invitation to a dance held by George Washington, he related that his social stature had fallen so much that he "begged Mr. Vaughan, my near neighbor, and my colleague in the Philosophical Society, to buy me one of the tickets of admission. But he replied that since I was a *shopkeeper* I could not aspire to this honor. . . . And what did I say to him? 'Don't you know that I have never been more your equal than now, when I am nothing?'"[3]

Médéric Louis Elie Moreau de Saint-Méry: self-important, vain, a believer in the status of public intellectual figures. There is a static quality to the portraits when viewed relationally: the sedentary, half-length poses, the consistently coiffed gray hair / wig, the tight-lipped facial expressions, the unremarkable background settings. Although they cover an epoch of his life that included tremendous ups and downs of wealth and position, the images hide these changes. This chapter considers Moreau and his relationships, professional and personal, through a variety of visual material that obfuscates and reveals. I take Moreau's interest in cultivating a public-facing persona as a challenge to engage the act of visual perception itself.

This opening portrait collage is one in a series of images that destabilize the edifice upon which Moreau's self-preferred legacy was built, subverting his cover story of respectability. Iconography in this chapter—of eighteenth-century Caribbean life that Moreau helped to popularize, of the contemporary Caribbean artists Edouard Duval-Carrié and Marielle Plaisir, and of my own cocreation concerning Moreau and his household—probes a straightforward concern. Unfreedom correlates to the planter class's experience of freedom. This cannot be said, or *seen,* enough. The visuals act as interconnected vignettes—short-form narratives that frame how Moreau and his work become the object through which we see the subject of slavery and its deep penetration into the lives of both individual people and larger institutions. The *Encyclopédie noire* creates a textual bridge between Moreau and the ways in which he was propped up, in a quotidian and philosophical sense, by the subjecthood of people of African descent. I have collaborated with artist Luz Sandoval to substantiate this line of argumentation graphically—through manipulation of eighteenth-century images; original figurative drawing based on the historical record; and attention to color, placement, and shape.[4]

Just as we may apply theory to a body of work or discuss how written works serve as intertexts, I use images as theory. This is in line with a branch of art history scholarship that W. J. T. Mitchell describes as "picture theory," as opposed to a "theory of pictures." Of particular interest is how image juxtaposition—the ways in which images are read alongside and against each other—produces meaning. Mitchell's concept of a metapicture, loosely defined as a picture about a picture, is helpful because it acknowledges the self-referential nature of works in dialogue. Although the interplay between eighteenth-century and contemporary images may at first seem an odd pairing for an early Americanist project, the interpretive power of images is as important as other contemporary frameworks for historical work. When placed into dialogue, these visuals redirect our focus to other ideas and perspectives, picturing an argument that Moreau's self-fashioned idea of the benign slaveholding statesman and intellectual is a myth.[5]

Let us return to Moreau. As Agnes Lugo-Ortiz and Angela Rosenthal remark in their excellent commentary on portraiture of the enslaved, it is important to remember that "the period marked by an expanding trade in human bodies coincided with the emergence of portraiture as a major field of representation in Western art."[6] In addition to portraits of himself, Moreau generated a record that has been undeniably important in constituting the iconography of the slaveholding Americas. He accrued intellectual capital through his mobilization of the visual in his historiographies: from geographic maps of various islands to detailed city plans, to illustrations of people and customs in places including China and the Caribbean. His work's status as an invaluable primary source in Caribbean studies is built on its textual as well as visual value. Moreau is most

AFFRANCHIS DES COLONIES.

COSTUMES
DES AFFRANCHIES ET DES ESCLAVES.
des Colonies.

FIGURE 9. *Affranchis des colonies* and *Costumes des affranchies et des esclaves des colonies*. Engraved by Nicolas Ponce, after Agostino Brunias. From Nicolas Ponce, *Recueil de vues des lieux principaux de la colonie française de Saint-Domingue* (Paris, 1791), nos. 25, 26. Courtesy of the John Carter Brown Library.

associated with the set of engravings commissioned to appear alongside his law and history compilation of the French Caribbean colonies. Engraved by the celebrated French artist Nicolas Ponce, they were published in Paris as *Recueil de vues des lieux principaux de la colonie française de Saint-Domingue* (1791). The compendium of eighty-two images is famous for its stylized depictions of Black subjects that were in turn based on engravings by Agostino Brunias.[7]

Although Brunias painted and engraved most of these images to depict the inhabitants of the Leeward Islands, especially Dominica and Saint Vincent, they have become synonymous with Old Regime society in the French Caribbean. They are what art historian Mia L. Bagneris has termed "pan-Caribbean" iconography. In her excellent work on the Italian painter (who lived for many years in the Caribbean), Bagneris contends that "in spite of the association of the artist's work with traditions of natural history or ethnography, suggesting the images as visual transcriptions of reality 'drawn from life,' Brunias's adaptation of so-called 'Old Master' precedents to fit the colonial context indicates that his paintings must be understood as fabricated representations of colonial fantasy filtered through a particularly selective vision and meant to appeal to planters and potential settlers."[8]

FIGURE 10. Original ensemble view of engravings, *Blanchisseuses, Affranchis des colonies, Danse de nègres*, and *Nègres jouant au bâton*. Engraved by Nicolas Ponce, after Agostino Brunias. From Nicolas Ponce, *Recueil de vues des lieux principaux de la colonie française de Saint-Domingue* (Paris, 1791), no. 26. Courtesy of the John Carter Brown Library.

The details in Brunias's *Affranchis des colonies* and *Costumes des affranchies et des esclaves des colonies* (Figure 9) highlight the figures' finery and depict free people of color and the enslaved in relaxed poses as they gossip and buy and sell wares. The idleness or recreational release portrayed in the dancing and stick-fighting scenes that accompanied these two engravings (Figure 10) suggests that free, unsurveilled, and pleasurable time was constitutive, even representative, of a typical day in the life of the enslaved and free people of color in the colonies.

FIGURE 11. *Blanchisseuses.* Engraved by Nicolas Ponce, after Agostino Brunias. From Nicolas Ponce, *Recueil de vues des lieux principaux de la colonie française de Saint-Domingue* (Paris, 1791), no. 26. Courtesy of the John Carter Brown Library.

No one is dressed plainly; even the figure of the topless woman presumably representing *l'esclave* wears two layers of striped clothing.

In the *Blanchisseuses* portrait in Ponce's compilation, the Black and mixed-race laundresses are depicted enjoying conversations with other women in provocative, seminaked poses along a scenic riverbed (Figure 11). The physically demanding, labor-intensive work of bending, scrubbing, pounding, and bleaching hand-washed items is idealized to such a degree that it is unrecognizable. Instead, a sexualized portrait of pornographic titillation takes precedence over a documentation of manual labor.[9]

Importantly, Moreau's use of these images as a companion piece to his work was part of illustrating certain "types." A dominant characteristic of his oeuvre is its organization around presenting different subgroups of the population—"the Africans," "free women of color," "creole white women," and so forth. He believed that these sketches of local life informed his work "as an observer, as a historian" (comme Observateur, comme Historien). He placed value in his own eyewitness ability. For example, his oft-cited portrait of mixed-race *mulâtresse* women noted:

> The entire being of a mulâtresse is given up to love, and the fire of this goddess burns in her heart, to be extinguished only with her life. This cult is her whole code, all of her votive offerings, her entire happiness. There is nothing that the most inflamed imagination can conceive of that she has not offered, guessed, or accomplished. Captivating all the senses, surrendering them to the most delicious ecstasies, holding them in suspense by the most seductive raptures: those are her whole study. Nature, in some way the accessory to pleasure, has given her charms, appeal, and sensibility.

> L'être entier d'une Mulâtresse est livré à la volupté, et le feu de cette Déesse brûle dans son coeur pour ne s'y éteindre qu'avec la vie. Ce culte, voilà tout son code, tous ses voeux, tout son bonheur. Il n'est rien que l'imaginaison la plus enflammée puisse concevoir, qu'elle n'ait pressenti, deviné, accompli. Charmer tous les sens, les livrer aux plus délicieuses extases, les suspendre par les plus séduisans ravissemens: voilà son unique étude; et la nature, en quelque sorte, complice du plaisir, lui a donné charmes, appas, sensibilité.

As is the case with Moreau's textual description, the accompanying iconography of these women functioned less as individualized portraiture than as a way of representing people grouped together as classes and his ideas about them—concerning hierarchy, sexual and manual labor availability, cultural attributes. Types, in stereo, amplified and circulated to project a worldview of domination in which the dominated were content with their condition.[10]

The portraits in the opening collage creation (Figure 8) are intended to be read alongside one another as well as the *Recueil de vues*. I arranged them in order to make meaning in part through other pictures. Haitian-born artist Edouard Duval-Carrié's *Colons et châtiments* (2004) is a series of interimages that likewise offer pictorial commentary on Brunias / Ponce / Moreau's collaboration and Figure 8. The work provides a productive theorization of power, capital, and violence.[11] In the eight-paneled piece (Figure 12), the planters / colonists depicted are linked with an unambiguous scene of punishment. The richly dressed colonists below and the Black woman and man being punished above exist together unequivocally. The latter are represented with arms splayed, bare feet, simple body coverings. They engage in no carefree recreational time. They wear no expensive linen or towering headwraps, no jewels, no shoes. The symbolic cues used in idealized portrayals of the enslaved are absent. The man is being crucified, intensely vulnerable and exposed; he is staked to the ground in such a way that the very center of the image, the part most illumined, falls at his groin, his manhood and personhood imperiled. The woman literally and metaphorically bears the weight of the colonial system; her movement is stilled, even as her muscled arms hint of a clenched struggle against such imprisonment.

Duval-Carrié created golden frame vignettes that are decorated with delicate flowers, beads, and ridges. A large shell ornament, echoes of the French framing tradition of *rocaille,* connects the two frames vertically. The linkage makes clear that, without the squared-off scene above, the scene in the round would be different, even impossible. Indeed, the framing here is crucial: the rounded shapes of the lower images are reminiscent of Ponce's *Recueil de vues.* Ponce's circular designs, set off against the larger white backdrop of the page, help direct and focus a viewer's gaze on the figures. The effect in both works is similar to peering through a lens to bridge a distance, to hone the eye. Duval-Carrié is adept at integrating colonial-era iconography into his work, demonstrating how "the 'politeness' of artifice not only veils but also engenders and enables the horrific production and consumption of refinement." The individualized faces of the *colons* (colonists) in their westernized portrait poses contrast with the depictions of the enslaved in poses more "typical" and constitutive of their environments than anything found in the Ponce / Brunias / Moreau referent that Duval-Carrié seems to deliberately reenvision and redraw. *Colons et châtiments* pictures Lugo-Ortiz and Rosenthal's reminder to link the development of an art form—portraiture—with the escalation of the transatlantic slave trade.[12]

Duval-Carrié collaborated with Haitian artist Sylva Joseph to have his original four painted portraits reinterpreted as sequined art. The color variance between the oil and sequined paintings is powerful. In the first, there is a range of bright green vegetation and a brocaded chair, yellow fancy dress, brown earth, and blue sky and sea. The colors evoke the vibrancy of a Caribbean landscape. In the sequined version, the tone and value of the color are somber. A lighted daytime scene is transformed to night: the dark side of enlightenment, a subtext of an underworld that haunts. If one were to see inside of a scene, to get to its heart, this might be the result. The colors of mourning predominate—purple, black, crimson, the hue of spilled blood. Combined with the deadened eye sockets of the masters' portraits, a ghostly, eerie effect emerges. The artists' color palettes across the painted and sequined versions suggest a causational correlation between societal respectability, wealth, and corporeal torture.[13]

Duval-Carrié's colons are both man and woman, and his oil portraits racialize them. The man could be white or mixed race, and the female colonist appears to be a mixed-race woman. Their phenotypes are inconclusive in the sequined version. *Colons et châtiments* is an indictment of a system, one in which a small

FIGURE 12. *Colons et châtiments.* By Edouard Duval-Carrié. Sequined versions by
Sylva Joseph. 2004.

percentage of people of African descent also profited alongside their white counterparts. The Milhet-Moreau women owned people; Marie-Louise Laplaine and
Aménaïde Dall'Asta owned enslaved women, as well.[14]

Baron de Vastey's *Le systeme colonial devoilé (The Colonial System Unveiled)*
(1814) is a vivid prose intertext to the picture theory that places this chapter's images into dialogue. As is the case with Moreau's work, the power of Vastey's prose
lies partly in the painterly richness of his descriptions: words create stark, damning portraits in the mind. Marlene L. Daut and Chris Bongie have done much
to establish Vastey as a key figure in a Black Atlantic humanist tradition that deliberately and meticulously "unveiled" the limits of Enlightenment-era thought
and colonial violence.[15] Vastey, also a creole historian of Saint-Domingue, ably
dissected Moreau's work for its grotesqueness in defending a legal structure that

equated people with mules and swine. His oeuvre is an invaluable refutation of Moreau's scholarship. In one of the most repugnant and damning sections of *The Colonial System Unveiled,* Vastey narrates a geographic tour of Saint-Domingue's parishes to document local inhabitants' customs, echoing Moreau's method in *Description topographique, physique, civile, politique et historique de la partie française de l'isle Saint-Domingue.* The text is a natural history of French-controlled Hispaniola that prioritized a vastly different body of observations and anecdotes, however. Vastey named distinguished families and the tortures they inflicted upon the enslaved—what Daut describes as a campaign of public shaming in print, because, as Vastey put it, "not a single one of the[se] monsters . . . has suffered the penalty that his foul deeds merit; not a single one has experienced even the slightest punishment for his crimes."[16]

Similar to the violence depicted in the coupled images of Duval-Carrié's work, Vastey's writing corrects the fantasy-like aura of the Brunias / Ponce prints. It also challenges the distance Moreau's portraits put between himself and his background as a slaveholder, along with the violence this ownership supposed. Many of Vastey's claims indicted Moreau's colleagues, the men who worked as lawyers and magistrates in the courtrooms of Saint-Domingue. For example, Moreau appeared as a lawyer in a case decided by the below-mentioned Magistrate Pourcheresse, a man who refused to provide clothing to the people he enslaved. Like Vastey and Duval-Carrié, I study the island's so-called distinguished and worthy citizens by placing them into the same stop-motion frames as those who served them in flesh and blood. We must remember that torture in Saint-Domingue "occupied a prominent niche in the set of techniques by which masters sought to discipline and terrorize their slaves." Vastey wrote:

> Bichot, master-builder, resident of Port-de-Paix, in an outburst of jealousy tore away the privates of his black mistress with a razor, and then had boiling oil spread over that part of her body.... Lombard, one of the magistrates for the Superior Council of the Cape, entertained himself by cutting off the ears of his unfortunate blacks; having reduced them to this cruel state, he would then burst into a fit of unrestrained laughter....
>
> Pourcheresse from Vertières, one of the magistrates for the Superior Council of the Cape, and Charrier [the co-owner of small provision grounds] . . . were so cruel toward their slaves that they forbade them to wear any clothing, even if it was bought at their own expense; they forced those poor blacks to go naked, with nothing more than a little rag about the waist, or what in this country is called a *tanga*....
>
> Bauduy, retired magistrate for the Superior Council of Port-au-Prince, resident of the district of Bellevue, one afternoon had his confectioner flogged to death for having offered him sweetmeats that were, according to him, poorly made....
>
> . . . Another fury of a woman, by the name of Siouaret Ducoudrai, would administer two to three hundred lashes, after which she would take newly melted sealing wax and slowly pour it over the wound, one drop at a time....
>
> Whenever a child died, Latour Duroc, settler, resident of Bas-Limbé, would put the disconsolate mother in an iron collar until such time as she produced a new one. He had a black woman confined in an underground dungeon that was a foot deep in water, despite the fact that he had fathered three children with the woman.

In this mode of reportage, there is no polite distance from the punishments, no respite from the accumulated tension and disgust generated by more than fifteen pages of names, locations, and atrocities. A reader cannot lose sight of the human beings mangled, mutilated, and executed. Claiming that he spoke to survivors, viewed their wounds, even "awaken[ed] the remains of the numerous victims you [the colonists] thrust into the grave," Vastey offered what Daut has termed a "proto-*testimonio*" of colonial savagery. His pointed condemnation was bold and subversive. One can imagine Moreau jumping out of his portrait frame, gasping in outrage, rushing to the defense of his indicted colleagues.[17]

Returning to the collage of Moreau's portraits, colorizing and stacking them is meant to turn the observer into the observed; to turn the racialized white subject into the racialized white object; to objectify Moreau as an ideologue of white supremacy as he objectified free people of color and the enslaved in his fanciful portraits of life in the tropics. He is typecast, standing in for an economic class and a white supremacist ideology. *Moreau dévoilé: A Portrait Collage, Part II* is an interimage to *Portrait Collage of Moreau de Saint-Méry, Part I,* Ponce's compilation, and Duval-Carrié's work. It also seeks to visually represent the heart of Vastey's critique. This negative rendition of the collage (Figure 13) signifies an incisive, X-ray–like underbelly: of violence, of unrighteousness, of opulence made possible by extreme deprivation. In each image, Moreau's eyes emit a disconcerting glow. In *Colons et châtiments,* the eyes of the colonists are blacked out. The collage denotes predatory monsters—the zombified undead, vampires, ghoulish specters, Marx's description of capital accumulation made possible through leeching the lifeblood of once-living workers. This collage directs our eyes to see through the staid conventional portraits; instead of from the outside in, we see from the inside out. Color saturations in part 2 tell a different story than in part 1—the lightest areas appear darkest (literally and metaphorically); the darkest take on different shades. *We will completely unveil this colonist. Nous dévoilerons complètement ce colon.* These were the words that Moreau's antagonists used when they accused him of actively working against the interests of free people of color; of slave trading in the Parisian capital; of being of African descent himself.[18] Unveil, unmask. These were Vastey's verbs of choice to publicly expose the lie of colonial respectability. The zombified images also unmask. The portraits "Elector," "Printer and Bookseller," and "Ambassador," in particular, have darkened Moreau's facial contours to the edge so that his luminous eyes peer through a veneer, a façade, a mask (Figure 14). These visual prompts cannot be unseen. Moreau's projection of himself across time is spoiled, and the rot shines through.

The static quality of Moreau's portraits across time mirrors the scarcity of empirical data available regarding his own personal and scholarly evolution. As

Elector

Printer and Bookseller

Ambassador

Ambassador

Father

Cipher

FIGURE 13. (*Facing page*) *Moreau dévoilé: A Portrait Collage, Part II.* By Luz Sandoval and Sara E. Johnson. Adapted from the portraits, from top left to right: Detail from Wilbrode Magloire Nicolas Courbe and Charles Toussaint Labadye, *Médéric Louis Élie Moreau de St. Mery: Présid[en]t des elect[eur]s de Paris au mois de j[uil]let 1789 né à la Martinique le 13 j[anvi]er 1750, député de cette colonie au Etats génér[au]x de 1789,* 1789, Bibliothèque nationale de France; James Sharples, *Médéric-Louis-Élie Moreau de Saint-Méry,* 1798, pastel and black chalk on toned wove paper, Bequest of Charles Allen Munn, 1924, Metropolitan Museum of Art; Ostervald L'Ainé, *Ritratto de Moreau de Saint-Méry,* undated watercolor in private collection, Archivio di Stato di Parma; Anonymous [attributed to Jean Baptiste Isabey], *Ritratto dell'amministratore general degli Stati di Parma, Piacenza e Guastalla Médéric Louis-Elie Moreau de Saint-Méry,* n.d., Glauco Lombardi Museum—Parma; Aménaïde Moreau de Saint-Méry, *Conte Moreau de Saint Méry,* circa 1800–1805, licensed by Ministero della Cultura—Complesso Monumentale della Pilotta-Galleria Nazionale di Parma; Marielle Plaisir, detail from *Variation on Lámina 23,* from *The Book of Life,* 2017, inks, gold pigment, and pencils on paper, presented at the exhibition *Visionary Aponte: Art and Black Freedom,* Little Haiti Cultural Center, New York University, and Duke University, 2017–2018.

FIGURE 14. Detail of *Moreau dévoilé: A Portrait Collage, Part II.* By Luz Sandoval and Sara E. Johnson. Adapted from the portraits, from left to right: James Sharples, *Médéric-Louis-Élie Moreau de Saint-Méry,* 1798, pastel and black chalk on toned wove paper, Bequest of Charles Allen Munn, 1924, Metropolitan Museum of Art; Ostervald L'Ainé, *Ritratto de Moreau de Saint-Méry,* undated watercolor in private collection, Archivio di Stato di Parma; Anonymous [attributed to Jean Baptiste Isabey], *Ritratto dell'amministratore general degli Stati di Parma, Piacenza e Guastalla Médéric Louis-Elie Moreau de Saint-Méry,* n.d., Glauco Lombardi Museum—Parma.

a witness of, a participant in, and an unwilling refugee from two revolutions that upended the politics and social realities of his Saint-Domingan and French homelands, Moreau left a curious lack of documentation concerning how these experiences might have changed him. Although he continued to edit his manuscripts until the time of his death in 1819, he did not publish a major work after 1805. His personal letters contain little detailed discussion of politics, although he kept abreast of events in the Caribbean. I cannot say whether his experiences alienated or entrenched his confidence in chattel slavery as a fundamental principle of economic development and social order. As he lived alongside his daughter and grandchildren, did he come to believe in the potential racial equality of people regardless of their genealogy? Mixed in among his papers is news about postrevolutionary Haiti that shows his knowledge of a king, a president, statesmen, and authors of African descent whose proclamations and writings were circulating in the public sphere. In his letters, he mentions his desire for an audience with Emperor Napoleon to request payment for his services after being summarily dismissed from his post in Italy. Yet his analyses of these postrevolutionary worlds on both sides of the Atlantic are conspicuously absent.

The surfeit of visual documentation of Moreau's appearance contrasts with the lack of visual documentation about his household circles. Let us return to the idea of pairing and juxtaposition as a form of critique, seen through Moreau's household, particularly the women in his life. Moreau's most constant companion was his wife, Louise-Catherine Milhet Moreau de Saint-Méry. In a hundred-plus-page memoir documenting his proslavery credentials, Moreau praised his wife in passing and noted how fortunate he had been in his choice of partner. He wrote that she had been "formed at the school of misfortune" (formée à l'école du malheur). This school of "malheur" refers to the Milhet family history of forced exile from Louisiana to Saint-Domingue with the Spanish takeover of the Louisiana colony in 1768. In addition to the enslaved woman Martonne and the two children that Louise-Catherine and Moreau inherited from her mother upon their marriage, his new wife also owned other tangible property: furniture, clothing, and even some diamonds. Thus, although Moreau suggested that his wife's past made thriftiness a key part of her "patrimony," she was not without material assets. Extant copies of letters she penned hint at a woman full of energy. Her French orthography had an orality to it, suggesting that she might have had a limited formal education.[19]

FIGURE 15. *Ritratto di Louise-Catherine Milhet, moglie dell'amministratore Moreau de Saint-Méry* (rounded frame mine). Anonymous. N.d. Glauco Lombardi Museum—Parma.

In a watercolor portrait, Madame Louise-Catherine Moreau de Saint-Méry is shown while the family was resident in Italy (Figure 15). Her softly draped clothing, coupled with her turban, were in vogue at the opening of the nine-teenth century. Her gaze is candid and direct. In Italy and back in France for the final fourteen years of his life, Moreau regularly noted her companionship in daily social activities, her knee problems, and her great affection for their family. During an 1809 visit to Paris by their son and grandchildren (Aménaïde's son and daughter), Moreau remarked, "Grandmama is like the hen that has re-found her chick" (est comme la poule qui a retrouvé son poussin).[20] A doting grand-mother ruling the household roost: this message of domesticity can be dated backward. In Philadelphia, she entered Moreau's journal as a scold, making her husband desist his late-night conversations with friends since he had to work the next day. Louise-Catherine Moreau might also have needed to rest because she too labored in their bookstore and printing business, handling printed pages and folding them alongside Aménaïde while her son and nephew set type.[21]

Art historian Floriana Cioccolo has suggested that this is not a painting of Moreau's wife, however, but that it could be a self-portrait of his daughter, Aménaïde. The possibility is intriguing. In addition to providing another extant example of Aménaïde's work, it would document what she looked like. Is it possible that the face resembles Moreau's, particularly around the set of the eyes? Can one discern what Moreau himself called a phenotypical "trace" of the quadroon classification with which she was legally designated upon birth? Such an effort reinscribes the absurdist logic of a system that felt the need to classify human beings according to their "nth degree" of whiteness in the first place. There is no doubt that her appearance would have affected how easily she would have been able to integrate into French, North American, and Italian societies. A portrait of her, especially one that she might have created herself, would further whet my curiosity about a woman who could have told her own unique stories: of life in multiple Saint-Domingue exile communities in Europe and the Americas; of trying to work as a female painter in the male-dominated social and artistic circles in which she traveled; of the complex family life she shared with an ideologue of Caribbean proslavery and racialist thought.[22]

Although the subject and artist of the above portrait are uncertain, Aménaïde did paint a portrait of her father (Figure 16). One can imagine her reflection in Moreau's eyes as he gazed upon her fondly while she worked. Moreau was proud of his daughter's artistic accomplishments and encouraged her mentorship by professional artists. Like the portrait attributed to Jean Baptiste Isabey (middle row, right portrait in Figure 8), her work depicts Moreau in an ornately embroidered dress coat with lace sleeves and cravat. Rather than holding a piece of paper as in the former, he sits beside a single volume on a desk. The book's marbled leather binding and gold leaf–tinged spine suggest that it is a precious book, and the ribbon protruding from its pages suggests that it has been read and remarked upon. This tome resembles Moreau's imprints and the hundreds of pages of manuscripts and notes that he bound in just such a manner. Small details such as the reddish nose and cheeks and the lines under his eyes and around the mouth hint at wrinkles from age and laughter. Aménaïde's depiction of her father, although warmer than the Isabey, Ostervald, and Parisian elector portraits, also has mistakes in proportion—the enormous head and strangely large hand, for example. The huge face draws further attention to the same porcine features depicted in other portraits: upturned nose, sagging jowls, weak chin. For a trained painter, these artistic choices that distort perspective could be intentional, a commentary on Moreau's character.[23]

Portraiture depicting the master class thus emerges: Moreau and his wife or, potentially, his daughter. During his years in exile and after moving back to

FIGURE 16. *Conte Moreau de Saint Méry.* By Aménaïde Moreau de Saint-Méry. Circa 1800–1805. Licensed by Ministero della Cultura—Complesso Monumentale della Pilotta-Galleria Nazionale di Parma.

Europe, he regularly lived with his sister (a slaveowner in Martinique), sisters-in-law, and several nieces. A web of household relationships would have also included women such as the enslaved Martonne, who lived with the family in the Caribbean and France; Rosine, a young girl he gifted to his daughter; Angélique, mother to her own children and the wet nurse of Moreau's son; or the family's anonymous laundress. Of these women, there are no extant physical descriptions or visual documentation.

However, I can depict them in a way that visualizes freedom's parasitical reliance on unfreedom and leisure's requirement of someone else's labor. The vignette frame, traditionally designed to be clearer in the center with a faded periphery, can be dispensed with altogether. A step outside the proverbial circle allows an exploration of that same "periphery" as central. The work I have cocreated does not represent violence as overtly as Duval-Carrié's; yet threat, menace, and appropriation of a group's labor for the benefit of others underpins the pairings we could make to the Moreau portraits above. To think beyond the point of saturation that has familiarized a characterization such as that of the available nubile seductresses depicted in Brunias / Ponce's oeuvre, we can visualize Moreau's actual blanchisseuse differently (paired with Madame Moreau de Saint-Méry, for example). Here she is not selling sex via a riverine laundering scene in nature's boudoir but carrying heavy loads (Figure 17). Moreau's writing about her provided no individualization: she was a Black woman à vendre, a washerwoman to be sold. Her life as we know it was tied to the violence contained in the casual wording of her being liquidated alongside his other, nonliving possessions: furniture, jewels, and the six hundred volumes remaining in his library. The iconicity of the sexualized type in the engraving is contrasted with the concreteness of what she might have experienced in May 1783. To perceive her is to know that much of her time that spring would likely have been spent thinking about her new living and labor arrangements; using her own networks of friends and kin to ascertain information; perhaps trying to assert her own will into the selling and buying process.

A different set of narrative possibilities emerges when people are depicted in community. Figure 18 is a figurative re-creation of Moreau's household. Rather than portraits of bourgeois individual slaveholders as (il)liberal subjects (Figures 15 and 16), this is a drawing of the Moreaus among their workers. Each person pictured is documented in archival records. They are in motion, not static. Their vital presence is constituted in the children's chubby toes that beg to be tickled; the concentration with which the wigmaker adjusts a curl; the sturdiness of their bodily contours; the brightness of their white linen headwraps and rough osnaburg shifts; and the blueness of clothing materials meant to signal servitude. After searching for these individuals for so many years, assembling dramatized depictions of them in one frame felt surprisingly compelling. A collective biography emerged from fragments visualized into narrative.[24]

The household is crowded and alive with competing emotions, desires, intentions. The people whom James H. Sweet describes, in a larger context of the transatlantic and inter-American trade in people, as "refugee strangers" come together with their knowledge of lives lived in Louisiana, experiences of the Parisian capital, native-tongue thoughts in the languages of Senegal or the different Kreyòls they spoke in Martinique and Saint-Domingue. I am as interested in the relationships they had with one another as those they had with their owners—conversations between Martonne (3) (conspicuously not the Martonne stereo-

FIGURE 17. *Blanchisseuse X.* By Luz Sandoval. 2020.

typed and sexualized in Figure 34) and Angélique (6) as they cared for Black and white children together; the jokes shared, or perhaps competition felt, between Moreau's valet (1) and hairdresser (2). In this rendering, do the blanchisseuse and the cook (5 and 4) know that they will shortly be sold off? Historical fragments of information tie these people to their masters (as people for sale or manumitted, as travel companions and unfree laborers). How did they interact when alone with one another, when walking through the streets or visiting friends? Their faces in Figure 18 are deliberately turned aside or rendered without detailed features since we cannot know how they looked. Angélique and the children she cared for are the exception. They present an invitation to consider the fullness of personalities in community, an invitation that suspends the need to claim

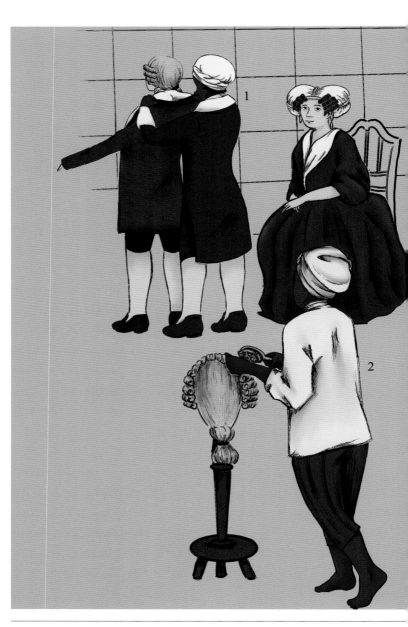

FIGURE 18. *The Household*. By Luz Sandoval and Sara E. Johnson. 2020. (1) An anonymous manservant aids Moreau as Madame Moreau sits nearby; (2) Anonymous wigmaker; (3) Martonne; (4) Anonymous cook; (5) Anonymous washerwoman; (6) Angélique holds anonymous child and Aménaïde with Sophie to the side. The monkey Coco is also on the prowl.

Alteration
in font
of - portings

historical accuracy. These figures take up room; they claim space. The ensemble cast is a Caribbean-centric adaptation of the "upstairs / downstairs" motif of British great houses; the portrayal reveals how those in (chattel) service form the backbone of domestic life.[25]

※ ※※※※※※※※※※※※※※※※※※※※※※※※※※※※※※※※※※※※※ ※
※ ××××××××××××××××××××××××××××××××××× ×
※ ※※※※※※※※※※※※※※※※※※※※※※※※※※※※※※※※※※※※※ ※

An evocative drawing from the series *The Book of Life* by the French Caribbean artist Marielle Plaisir provides a fitting conclusion (Figure 19). It is a variation on *Aponte Lámina 23,* one of the drawings included in the *Visionary Aponte: Art and Black Freedom* exhibit that sought to re-create the famed and missing *libro de pinturas* of the Cuban free Black carpenter and revolutionary José Antonio Aponte. He was executed in 1812 as part of what came to be known as the Aponte conspiracy in Cuba, and all that remains of his lost book are records from the three-day interrogation conducted between him and Spanish colonial officials detailing the content and significance of the images therein. Plaisir suggests that her drawings are intended to "evoke the way Aponte escapes from the world by deconstructing his time and place, moving through mythology, religion, death, war, love. . . . Aponte's 'Book of Paintings' represents a kind of beautiful exile, his process of dreaming about a better world." Plaisir depicts a seated, crowned Black figure, a rendering of the portraits of messianic Black kings that peopled the pages of Aponte's mixed-media book. Though smaller than the two human figures that surround it, the "king's" face is flesh, its warm brown hues contrasting to the whiteness of the others.[26]

The piece is vibrantly colored—from the tendrils of delicately floating sargasso in aqua and red to the center splash of granite-like browns offset by the deep orange and yellows of the skeletal figure's chest cavity. One is reminded of a Caribbean coral reef in motion; the king sits atop a stack of coral while marine life floats by. The pinpricks of finely drawn white dots evoke both crystal chandeliers and the spot pattern of tropical fish; the droplets of red—bubbles, blood—also foreground connections between man-made luxuries and the natural world. It is a pictograph of the detailed portraits of flora and fauna that form the centerpiece of most natural histories, including some of Moreau's work.

Like Duval-Carrié and Joseph's collaboration, the image exquisitely renders both life and death / dying simultaneously. A skull and skeletal torso topped by an elegantly coiffed and towering colonial-era wig are depicted just below the brown figure. The head and its wig are set in relief by their black and white

FIGURE 19. *Variation on Lámina 23*. From *The Book of Life*. By Marielle Plaisir. 2017. Inks, gold pigment, and pencils on paper. Presented at the exhibition *Visionary Aponte: Art and Black Freedom,* Little Haiti Cultural Center, New York University, and Duke University, 2017–2018.

delineation among bursts of primary colors. Elsewhere, I have written of how Plaisir's image evokes Cuban author Alejo Carpentier's classic novel of the Haitian Revolution, *El reino de este mundo (The Kingdom of This World),* which opens with white waxen and bewigged heads displayed in a shop window. The heads presage the guillotine, uprisings of the enslaved, and other revolutionary events to be witnessed by the novel's enslaved protagonist, Ti-Noel. Plaisir's figurative rendition of skeletal remains allows for infinite interpretations of the relationship between dreams of Black freedom and the destruction of the tropical colonial regime.[27]

Although this piece was imagined as commentary on 1810s Cuba, it pictures the same pan-Caribbean interpretative possibilities of Brunias's work. I wish to draw attention to the figure in the top left corner. A man in black fancy dress observes the scene, surrounded by red dots reminiscent of blood splatters. His head is an empty silhouette, less detailed than the folds on his collar. He is faceless, a stand-in for generalized, cloaked (and menacing) authority. He is Moreau's cipher from the opening portrait collage. This faceless Moreau surveils the scene "as a historian" (comme Historien) and offers pithy, authoritative anecdotes about a world that he sees and one that contains depths he cannot or does not wish to fathom. Alternately, he perceives these depths of feeling and knowledge but ruthlessly suppresses them.

The well-elaborated details of Moreau's facial features across the opening five portraits of the chapter—close-set eyes, aquiline nose, prominent forehead beneath a receding hairline—are vacated. This erasure places Moreau and the fellow colons he speaks for on par with the anonymous, interchangeable faces of the Black masses conjured in the portrait Moreau drew of them at the opening of my *Encyclopédie noire.* Plaisir's work pictures my method; it anonymizes Moreau as I bring both anonymous and little-known figures to the forefront of my discussion. These figures move in the same world and are indeed interdependent. This chapter reminds us to perceive and evaluate them as such, particularly the structures of physical, psychological, and ideological violence that knitted them together.

The national portrait galleries of imperial centers are filled with smug depictions of important men. They are sedate and poised, in contrast to the anxiety Moreau and other slaveholders described in their speeches about living in a "state of war." They are individuals, separated from those who coiffed and slept with them, provided the teeth for their dentures, soldiered in their wars, and otherwise contributed to their stature. Thomas Jefferson, George Washington, Bernardo de Gálvez—whose lives would a visual communal biography of these men reveal?

CHAPTER THREE

Print Culture and the Empires of Slavery

Moreau de Saint-Méry sold people to buy books and books to buy people. Books and human beings circulated in related transactional circuits. He used print to secure his social and professional status in a transatlantic and inter-American knowledge market that was also a human labor market. Print was not neutral; it was mobilized, as it had long been in the French colonies, to enable the acquisition of people and to buttress proslavery ideological claims and imperial ambitions. "Untelling" histories of slavery in order to retell them requires attention to books as material objects.

Moreau's relationship to print culture should be evaluated beyond the content of his published, circulating texts. His expertise was also technical and artistic, key elements of his scholarly persona and narrative voice that are rarely discussed. He was unusual, a prolific scholar who gained enough knowledge as an adult to assist in the printing of his own work, eventually on his own printing press. He narrated his work through its print mechanics as well as through its generic form and content. The more collaborative and potentially attractive the project, the more it appealed to him. This chapter demonstrates that what we have been taught to appreciate as a beautiful book is also to understand what Simon Gikandi has so eloquently argued: that "the institution of slavery and the culture of taste were fundamental in the shaping of modern identity, and that they did so not apart but as nonidentical twins, similar yet different. . . . In this dialectic of identity and difference, slavery and taste came to be intimately connected even when they were structurally construed to be radical opposites." Moreau repeatedly called a reader's attention to the aesthetic dimensions of printing. And the aesthetic is an inherently political process of choosing what to make visible or invisible. While a ship manifest, law tome, or plantation ledger is easily associated with the brutality of slavery, we must also consider how Moreau's sophisticated printed volumes, including those that did not touch on slavery at all, were made possible by his slaveholding investments.[1]

Typographical visualization was an integral part of how Moreau composed his work, as both an author and occasional compositor. As he wrote, he also planned how his pieces would appear. The visuality of his scholarship was not limited to illustrations. At a time when every piece of type and every engraving was placed by hand and inked on paper, Moreau deliberately chose to engage design complexity across the many pages of his oeuvre—mixed typefaces and sizes, printers' type ornaments, specially commissioned illustrations, precise layouts.

This understanding of Moreau's creative scholarly process echoes my own method for telling stories about slavery. My visual-narrative choices aim to draw attention to the labor of the people who have been sidelined by his work. This chapter is a communal biography that emerges around and through the printed page; the page is a conduit, and I close read it as such. Analyzing Moreau as a book technician allows for an entrée into another world of his collaborators, one beyond his household. The cast of characters contains people alongside a book professional's case of metal type. Indeed, the Garamond typeface in which this book is printed mimics the appearance of Moreau's self-published imprints, including the smashed-looking aperture in the lowercase a. This chapter is printed in Bodoni for contrast. The typefaces serve as a reminder to glean meaning from the design of the words and the material conditions that made their production possible, not simply from the words themselves.

The material underpinnings of two understudied texts in Moreau's oeuvre make clear the connections between the meticulous artisanship of his publications and the historical ugliness they documented on the page at different points in Moreau's career. First, I consider the Paris moment in the late 1780s and early 1790s, a time when Moreau was a well-known public intellectual who had compiled a multivolume colonial legal code. This endeavor gained him printing expertise and brought him new political power in the capital that coincided with his appointment as a city elector and eventual representative of Martinique in the French National Assembly. In 1790, he published *Mémoire justificatif,* an autobiographical screed intended to defend his proslavery credentials in the face of accusations that he had promoted the abolition of slavery. This publication provides a wealth of information about Moreau's direct involvement in slavery—as master, as compiler of legal codes for the French state, as intellectual interested in print culture, as spokesperson and member of the patronage system operated by the white Caribbean *colon* communities at home and abroad. It is a critical source when tracing the shift in Moreau's public persona from self-styled moderate proponent of reforming the conditions under which the enslaved labored to increasingly hard-line opponent of any reforms that would allegedly compromise the vise-like grip that slaveowners used to manage their labor force. By the 1790s, he was ardently articulating his belief that "if our slaves can suspect . . . if they are convinced that they are no longer in absolute dependence in respect to us, if they see that without our participation, the *mulâtres* have become or will become our equals, there is no longer any hope that France can retain her colonies" (si nos esclaves peuvent soupçonner . . . s'ils sont convaincus qu'ils ne sont plus à notre égard dans une dépendance absolue; s'ils voient enfin que sans notre participation, les mulâtres sont devenus ou doivent devenir nos égaux, il n'est plus d'espoir pour la France de conserver ses colonies). When asked if it "would do for a man to be the property of another man" (un homme ne faurait être la propriété d'un autre homme), he replied that one could not "command massacres under the pretext of effecting purely philosophical hypotheses" (commander les massacres sous le prétexte de réaliser des hypothèses purement philosophiques).[2]

The question of whether a person had the right to own another person was anything but an abstract philosophical concern in Moreau's life. After fleeing revolutionary France in the fall of 1793, Moreau and his family found themselves unable to return to Saint-Domingue. Cap Français, their former home, had been burned to the ground months previously. Revolutionary events in the Caribbean made it impossible for the Moreaus to ever resume the life they had known. The people they had enslaved in Martinique and Saint-Domingue were beyond their control.[3] Newly deprived of enslaved laborers and their wealth, the Moreau family settled in Philadelphia, where they operated a multilingual bookstore and printshop between 1794 and 1798. It was during these years that Moreau worked on many of his most influential publications.[4]

The second text under consideration, Moreau's two-volume *Voyage de l'ambassade de la Compagnie des Indes orientales hollandaises, vers l'empereur de la Chine, dans les années 1794 et 1795* (1797–1798), was a translated and extensively edited account of businessman Andreas Everardus van Braam Houckgeest's diplomatic journey with the Dutch embassy to meet the emperor of Qing China, Qianlong.[5] It is the most beautiful imprint made at Moreau's Philadelphia shop, a work of art that he completed in his final years as a book professional before returning to France. The text's production required collaborations between Chinese, Caribbean, European, and North American artists, technicians, and authors. Moreau's work as a printer, translator, and editor highlights the underacknowledged international expertise contributing to the technical accomplishments of the early United States book trade. Information about how Dutch merchants had capitalized on Asian markets was potentially highly lucrative to both a U.S. audience that was just entering the "China trade" and the French government, whose revolutionary army had invaded the Netherlands and helped to establish an allied state. As France's richest colonies in the Caribbean were in danger of being lost owing to rebellions by the formerly enslaved and free people of color in addition to invasions from competing European armies, access to recent data about the well-established Dutch colonies in the east was well timed.[6] My discussion of Moreau's involvement with this publication also sheds light on his interactions with Van Braam at his self-titled "Chinese Retreat" (La retraite chinoise), a mansion in the Pennsylvania woods where Moreau not only was surrounded by precious artwork from China but also experienced his first encounters with Asian laborers.

Both of these moments bear out the essential truth that Moreau had an ability to extract labor, intellectual as well as physical, from people of non-European descent in order to elevate himself. As different as they are in subject matter and generic form, these texts make clear that Moreau's printing practice—and its corollary practices of authorship, editing, spelling, illustrating, designing—was fundamentally about mastery, ownership, and extraction. Moreau was driven to acquire printing expertise as a tool to reproduce his own knowledge and world order. Aesthetic projects and slaveholding practices must be read as mutually informing.

MÉMOIRE JUSTIFICATIF

FIGURE 20. Frontispiece from Moreau de Saint-Méry, *Mémoire justificatif* ([Paris, 1790]). Courtesy of the John Carter Brown Library.

Waging War via Typography

Moreau's *Mémoire justificatif* was published in the midst of multiple crises fought across the pages of pamphlets and periodicals circulating in France and its colonies in the 1790s. The first was the call by French colonial planters to have representation in the new National Assembly. Another concerned disagreements between these white colons, aligned with the Club Massiac, and a group of *gens de couleur*, who called themselves the *colons améri-caines*. The latter claimed that they should also benefit from the rights discourses emerging out of the French Revolution. The playful flower pattern of the pamphlet's title page belies the seriousness of its content because, for Moreau, this publication was a direct rebuttal of the "infamy that the most atrocious calumny had called down on [his] head" (l'infamie que la plus atroce calomnie a appellée sur ma tête). This infamy resulted when he was falsely accused of having made a motion for the abolition of slavery on the floor of the National Assembly. He expressed his motivation thusly: "Amid the sentiments that shred my heart, there is one that dominates them all: it is that of my innocence. . . . It is my *duty* to say all, to show my whole life" (au milieu des sentimens qui déchirent mon coeur, il en est un qui les domine tous, c'est celui de mon innocence . . . c'est pour moi *un devoir* de tout dire et de montrer ma vie toute entière). Autobiographical impulse was motivated by self-preservation. Moreau's "innocence" depended on protecting his reputation as a bastion of white power and privilege. His tone was indignant, angry, combative, self-pitying, self-aggrandizing, and zealous.[7]

Moreau chose a generic convention of his legal trade to mount an ardent defense. The *mémoire justificatif* was a standard eighteenth-century genre, a hybrid form in which life writing was mixed with personal expository prose, depositions, and other evidence to make a "justifying" case on behalf of its subject. Moreau's text contained fifty-six pages of call-and-response between Moreau, his readers, and his detractors. An additional ninety-six pages consisted of supporting documents to buttress his claims, most in the form of reprinted correspondence.[8] This memoir is an immensely informative document for biographical purposes, providing a summary of his upbringing and career path along with valuable primary sources that flesh out his life narrative until 1790. It is likewise invaluable as a source of information about the women, men, and children who lived, worked, suffered, and were sold as Moreau's property—the fugitive subjects of my *Encyclopédie noire*.

Mémoire justificatif reads like a melodrama: a courtroom placed on a stage. It documents intrigue, death wishes, criminal complaints, and community

rancor that showcase characters who appear as everything from "investiga-
tors" to those who risked hanging by bloodthirsty mobs. Moreau cast himself
in the role of the tragic protagonist, his honor and livelihood at stake. In
June 1789, Louis Charton published *Observation de M. Charton à la motion
de M. Moreau de Saint-Méry,* an eight-page report accusing Moreau of making a motion to abolish slavery. Charton had approximately six hundred of
these pamphlets printed and distributed throughout Paris. When he first
found out about this pamphlet, Moreau noted that he paid it little heed, remarking, *in italics,* "*some people were above suspicion*" *(il y'avait des hommes
au-dessus du soupçon).* "Some people are above suspicion" is a common refrain in the text. Moreau believed that his proslavery credentials spoke for
themselves. His allies among the colonists begged him to publicly refute the
claims, and in one farcical scene groups of them traveled from house to house
in Paris interviewing the other delegates that Charton claimed as witnesses to
Moreau's motion. They sought thirty people in total, and twelve—including
a banker, several lawyers, an apothecary, a bookshop owner, and a baker—
replied that they had not heard Moreau lobby in favor of abolition. Moreau
likewise had more than one hundred people sign declarations of support that
refuted Charton's claims, declarations that Moreau then reproduced. He and
his friends even waylaid Charton at his own residence and made him publicly
claim authorship of the pamphlet, recording a written and signed testimonial
of their interrogation session. His Parisian colleagues concluded that Charton fabricated the story, and Moreau was not only cleared in the eyes of his
fellow colons but also secured a position as a deputy from Martinique in the
National Assembly. Charton, scorned as a mere *"Sheet manufacturer" (Fabri-
quant de draps),* was summarily dismissed. To add insult to injury, Moreau
drew attention to Charton's orthographical faults by reproducing them in full:
Moraux de Saint-Méry, Collons, demender, généralse, Consitoyens, i *étaient.*[9]

   Why did Moreau feel the need to publicly justify his devotion to slavery?
Why did a Parisian tradesman with no easily discernible colonial holdings
start a nasty political rumor? Was he hired to do so? Moreau provided no
motive behind such an attack, although he hinted that professional jealousy,
even economic competition with an unnamed party back in Saint-Domingue,
might have been the cause. The text's very existence proves that he had
enemies. To call someone an abolitionist and to accuse him of making a
binding legal motion in the halls of government was the kiss of death in the
proslavery communities in which Moreau traveled.[10]

   The stakes of the drama only increased once word arrived in Saint-
Domingue about Moreau's alleged motion. Significantly, he carefully
framed his account of how he heard about its impact there as a moment

that connected his proslavery credentials with print culture. He maintained that he was busy correcting the proofs for his pamphlet attacking the Abbé (Henri) Grégoire's recently published work in favor of the rights of free people of color when he received word that his brother-in-law, the physician Charles Arthaud, had been dragged from his home in view of his very pregnant wife.[11] Members of the extended Moreau-Milhet family came close to being lynched by a "furious mob" (Peuple en fureur) because they were related to him. They went from well-regarded citizens to "fugitives" (fugitifs) in hiding for six weeks. Moreau, who had planned to shortly return to Saint-Domingue, potentially as its new intendant, the highest civil authority on the island, claimed that if he had not been waylaid by pressing political concerns in Paris, he would have been lynched himself. As he pointed out, the earth of his adoptive home would have been "watered with his blood" (arros[é] de [s]on sang) after he had the pleasure of "enjoying the spectacle of [his beloved wife and son] having their throats slit" (pour jouir du spectacle de les voir égorger). His martyrdom—as a hardworking intellectual, as a defender of the colonies—would have been complete.[12]

The text, then, is saturated with angst and anger. This sensationalist energy emerges in the graphic elements of the page as well as through the words themselves. A close reading of two exemplary pages surfaces his intellectual and emotional state of mind (Figure 21 and Figure 22). These pages clearly connect Moreau's self-worth to his knowledge of printing. Extrapolated outward, the mechanics of print culture—including decisions about formatting choices and familiarity with printing, binding, and other professional circuits—was how Moreau and others associated with colon communities waged a war to preserve their very livelihoods.

I present these examples as page proofs, reading above and below the footnote line. Moreau made extensive use of paratexts in his work: editor's prefaces, translation notes, and footnotes that offered both parallel and divergent commentary about what was happening in the principal narration. Although the single black line separating the top and bottom of the page is deceptively simple, it marks a sleight of hand. It is a contrived cordon between the laborers needed

to maintain Moreau's life as an intellectual; it falsely marks a clear break between the person picking coffee on his Torbeck estate and the engraver hired to illustrate his maps. The proofs (preuves) here represent the material dimension of his "proof" and draw attention to Moreau as both a wordsmith and a producer of physical books.

The footnote pictured on pages 105–106 begins on page 104, continuing across three pages. It dominates the page layout. The smaller type size and narrower line spacing are eye-catching because of the sheer length of the entries. The text highlighted in blue is drawn from the minutes of a meeting of the Superior Council (Conseil Supérieur) in Saint-Domingue during which the court laid out its charges against Moreau for fomenting the radical idea of abolition. He published this report to communicate his sense of betrayal at being convicted in the court of opinion by his fellow magistrates. Comments highlighted in purple provide a glimpse of Moreau's own research and printing operations before he became owner of a bookshop and printing house in Philadelphia. They detail his self-described "expense accounting" (comptes), and I read these accounts as both narrative description and economic statements of cost. His commentary constitutes a book historian's dream. Moreau's publications, the final products, coexist on the same page with his transaction ledger detailing behind-the-scenes rationales for how and why his work was printed the way that it was.[13]

Above the line, the text concerns the enslaved majority of the population, and it purports to predict their intentions and behavior. Moreau was called a "monster of *ingratitude* and ferocity" (un monstre *d'ingratitude* et de férocité). Who, his fellow magistrates asked, knew better than Moreau that abolition would (allegedly) lead to the massacre of the white population and also to the mutual self-destruction of different African nations, who were "mortal enemies" (mortellement enemies)? Abolition would be a murderous endeavor and destroy the French economy. The Council's declaration was a strident pushback against the metropolitan Society of the Friends of the Blacks (Société des Amis des noirs) and what colons considered this group's false portraits of the misery of enslaved laborers. Who knew better than Moreau that efforts to abolish slavery would have a devastating effect on white AND Black survival? *Personne.* No one. Again, Moreau believed himself to be a member of a group "of *men above suspicion*" *(des hommes au-dessus du soupçon)*. Despite his lifetime of work supporting the status quo, however, he was labeled a traitor. Anyone who has spent any time reading colon invective is familiar with the contradictory declarations of good will this sort claimed for their enslaved workers and the dire warnings they issued against the threat of white massacre. Considered as part of a narrative trope, Moreau's assertion that the call for abolition would indeed constitute a great "crime" against the public good (and thus that the enslaved did not have a right to their freedom) is nothing new.[14]

Below the line, the content is more unexpected and interesting. Moreau's footnotes detour into a print minutiae discussion that relates print culture

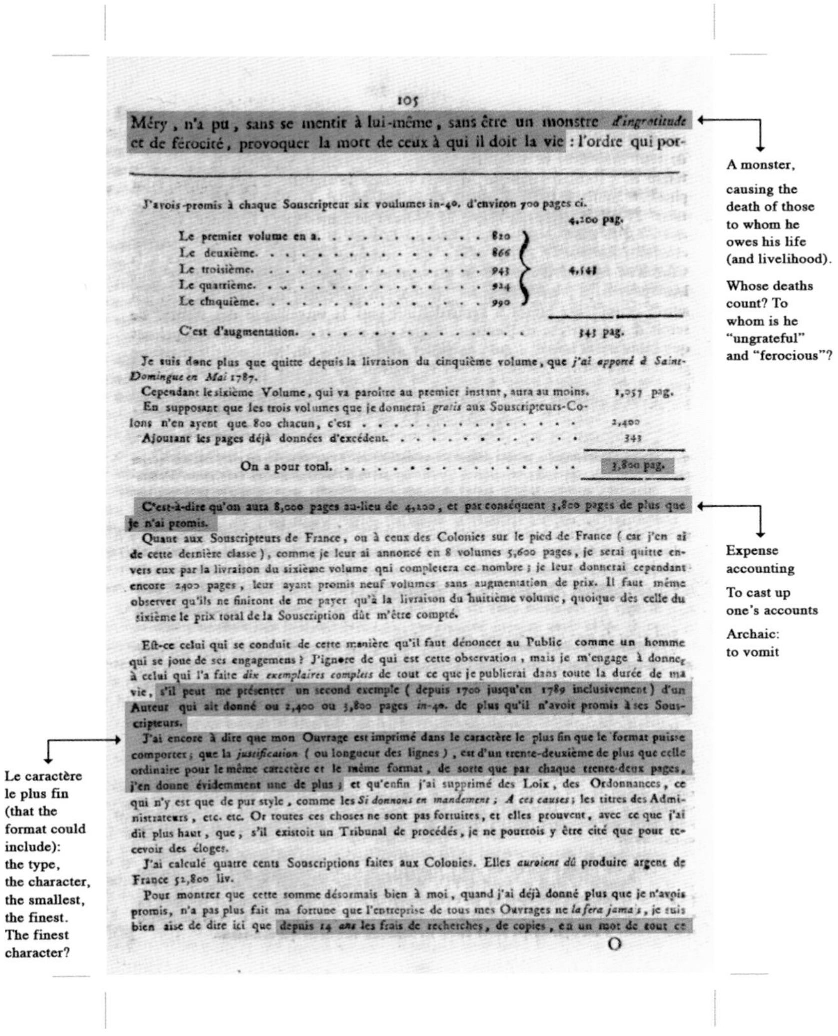

105

Méry, n'a pu, sans se mentir à lui-même, sans être un monstre *d'ingratitude* et de férocité, provoquer la mort de ceux à qui il doit la vie : l'ordre qui por-

J'avois promis à chaque Souscripteur six voulumes in-4º. d'environ 700 pages ci.

4,100 pag.

Le premier volume en a 810
Le deuxième 866
Le troisième 943   } 4,141
Le quatrième 534
Le cinquième 990

C'est d'augmentation . . . .   541 pag.

Je suis donc plus que quitte depuis la livraison du cinquième volume, que j'ai apporté à Saint-Domingue en Mai 1787.
Cependant le sixième Volume, qui va paroître au premier instant, aura au moins .   1,057 pag.
En supposant que les trois volumes que je donnerai *gratis* aux Souscripteurs-Colons n'en ayent que 800 chacun, c'est   2,400
Ajoutant les pages déjà données d'excédent   541

On a pour total . . . .   3,800 pag.

C'est-à-dire qu'on aura 8,000 pages au-lieu de 4,100, et par conséquent 3,800 pages de plus que je n'ai promis.
Quant aux Souscripteurs de France, ou ceux des Colonies sur le pied de France (car j'en ai de cette dernière classe), comme je leur ai annoncé en 8 volumes 5,600 pages, je serai quitte envers eux par la livraison du sixième volume qui complétera ce nombre ; je leur donnerai cependant encore 2400 pages, leur ayant promis neuf volumes sans augmentation de prix. Il faut même observer qu'ils ne finiront de me payer qu'à la livraison du huitième volume, quoique dès celle du sixième le prix total de la Souscription dût m'être compté.

Est-ce celui qui se conduit de cette manière qu'il faut dénoncer au Public comme un homme qui se joue de ses engagemens ? J'ignore de qui est cette observation, mais je m'engage à donner à celui qui l'a faite *dix exemplaires complets* de tout ce que je publierai dans toute la durée de ma vie, s'il peut me présenter un second exemple (depuis 1700 jusqu'en 1789 inclusivement) d'un Auteur qui ait donné ou 2,400 ou 3,800 pages *in-4º.* de plus qu'il n'avoit promis à ses Souscripteurs.

J'ai encore à dire que mon Ouvrage est imprimé dans le caractère le plus fin que le format puisse comporter; que la *justification* (ou longueur des lignes) est d'un trente-deuxième de plus que celle ordinaire pour le même caractère et le même format, de sorte que par chaque trente-deux pages, j'en donne évidemment une de plus ; et qu'enfin j'ai supprimé des Loix, des Ordonnances, ce qui n'y est que de pur style, comme les *Si donnons en mandement ; A ces causes;* les titres des Administrateurs, etc. etc. Or toutes ces choses ne sont pas fortuites, et elles prouvent, avec ce que j'ai dit plus haut, que, s'il existoit un Tribunal de procédés, je ne pourrois y être cité que pour recevoir des éloges.

J'ai calculé quatre cents Souscriptions faites aux Colonies. Elles *auroient dû* produire argent de France 52,800 liv.
Pour montrer que cette somme désormais bien à moi, quand j'ai déjà donné plus que je n'avois promis, n'a pas plus fait ma fortune que l'entreprise de tous mes Ouvrages ne *la fera jamais*, je suis bien aise de dire ici que *depuis 14 ans* les frais de recherches, de copies, en un mot de tout ce

O

Annotations (right margin):

A monster,

causing the death of those to whom he owes his life (and livelihood).

Whose deaths count? To whom is he "ungrateful" and "ferocious"?

Expense accounting

To cast up one's accounts

Archaic: to vomit

Annotation (left margin):

Le caractère le plus fin (that the format could include): the type, the character, the smallest, the finest. The finest character?

FIGURE 21. Sample page proof adapted from Moreau de Saint-Méry, *Mémoire justificatif* ([Paris, 1790]), 105. By Luz Sandoval and Sara E. Johnson. Original courtesy of the John Carter Brown Library.

teroit à Saint-Domingue l'abolition de l'esclavage, y seroit le signal du massacre de tous ses Habitans, la perte de toutes ses Manufactures, la cessation de tout commerce et navigation, et par conséquent le signal de la subversion totale de la fortune publique, dans la balance de laquelle il faut compter pour plusieurs milliards la Province de Saint-Domingue, sans parler des autres Antilles. Et qui sait cela mieux que M. Moreau de Saint-Méry ? Personne. *Comment donc a-t-il pa consigner dans les cahiers des Electeurs de Paris sa Motion pour l'affranchissement des Noirs ?* Il sait mieux que personne que les Nègres achetés à la Côte d'Afrique se divisent et se distinguent à Saint-Domingue, comme dans leur pays natal, en différentes Nations mortellement ennemies les unes des autres et toujours prêtes à s'entredétruire sans la surveillance des Blancs. Ce seroit donc pour ces malheureux Nègres eux-mêmes un funeste et cruel présent que celui de la liberté, qui, après les avoir réunis un jour pour le massacre général des Blancs, leur laisseroit le pouvoir de tourner leurs armes contre eux, et de se massacrer à leur tour, jusqu'à ce que les plus forts réduisissent les autres à l'esclavage dans lequel et pour lequel ils semblent nés, et fissent.

Moreau as an authority of colonial race relations (who could usually tell black people apart)

qui tient au Manuscrit, ne se sont jamais élevés moins haut qu'en ce moment où j'emploie quatre personnes, qui me coûtent au moins 4,000 l. de France par an. (J'en ai eu jusqu'à onze à Saint-Domingue, travaillant en même temps ou chez moi, ou dans les Gieffes et autres dépôts publics.)

C'est donc pour le Manuscrit environ (tournois) . . . . 60,000 liv.
L'impression de mes six volumes, le brochage, pliage, magasinage, etc.
passent 48,000
Les Gravures (*elles ne sont pas comprises dans la Souscription*) vont déjà au moins à 20,000

J'ai donc dépensé en ce moment (calcul fait au plus bas). . . . . 128,000 liv.

Slavery of Africans as a positive good: "in which and for which they seem to be born"

Sans parler de mon temps, qui vaut quelque chose.
Voilà mes comptes. Si quelqu'un est curieux, d'après cela, de venir s'associer dans mes bénéfices, il peut paroître. La seule chose que je veux me réserver, ce sont les sentimens qu'un jour la justice des Colons m'assurera, et dont je jouis d'avance (quelque chose qu'on fasse) par la persuasion que je l'ai méritée à cause de mon attachement pour eux, et de mon désintéressement, dont ma femme et mes enfans n'auront peut-être pas à se féliciter un jour.
Mais, comme je ne veux pas être exposé à de pareilles explications à l'avenir, je déclare ici formellement : 1°. que désormais je ne dépends plus que de mon zèle pour les époques et les circonstances des livraisons qui seront évidemment à l'avenir de puis dans jusqu'au neuvième volume, lorsque celle du sixième volume sera faite ; 2°. que je ne veux plus de Souscription, et qu'on payera chaque volume le prix que j'y mettrai ; 3°. et enfin, que si mes matériaux fournissent plus de 9 volumes in-4. sur Saint Domingue, j'entends que ceux que je publierai au-delà de ce nombre me soient payés par quiconque jugera à propos de se les procurer, anciens Souscripteurs et autres indistinctement.

Qu'il me soit permis d'ajouter un mot à tout ceci, pour faire remarquer quel langage on fait parler au Comité de la partie du Nord de l'Isle Saint Domingue contre moi dans les deux Arrêtés !.... (Celui-ci et celui du N°. 62). Si un Comité pouvoit être mû par des sentimens personnels on croiroit... Je n'ai pas pris la plume pour me plaindre de l'ironie et du sarcasme (ils ne m'auroient pas atteint) ; mais d'une injustice qui blesse autant les Membres du Comité que moi-même.

Expense accounting: Manuscript preparation, print production and engraving costs.

Labor (including His uncompensated TIME) is central to the value of his calculations, although the unpaid labor needed to subsidize the cost of these professional expenses is not a line item. How did he afford the cost of the laborers he did pay? The line between the main body and the footnote artificially separates the labor force necessary for his work.

FIGURE 22. Sample page proof adapted from Moreau de Saint-Méry, *Mémoire justificatif* ([Paris, 1790]), 106. By Luz Sandoval and Sara E. Johnson. Original courtesy of the John Carter Brown Library.

to honor: honor among thieves (in this case his slaveholding readers). For instance, pages 105–106 documented Moreau's tremendous offense at being accused of not fulfilling his authorial duties to his paying subscribers. This was an attack on his probity! Not only did he angrily refute the accusation of being an abolitionist, he wanted to show that he was not a cheat. He justified his honesty by documenting the cost of the expenses he accumulated, including labor, in his role as a published public intellectual.

His counterattack is rich in information about his research and print operations. For example, in 1789 he employed four people in Paris to help him publish his work, and he employed as many as eleven in Saint-Domingue. These collaborators labored in his private home, in clerks' offices, and in other public archives at his command. Colleagues sent him information: private correspondence from fellow colons, official files from bureaucrats working in places such as Guadeloupe and Cayenne. The footnotes also include a detailed accounting of the page count for his *Loix et constitutions.* He ranted, Who "can show me . . . (between 1700–1789) . . . an author who has provided between 2,400 and 3,800 pages, in quarto, more than that which was promised to his subscribers?" He included the specific financial costs of employee salaries, printing, folding, storage, and engravings, as well as his investment of time. For those determined to believe that page count and significant book-producing expenses were not proof that he put his subscribers' satisfaction above his own personal interest, he added, "I must also say that my Work is printed in the smallest type that the format could support; that the *justification* (or the length of the lines), is a thirty-secondth greater in size to that which is normally used for the same type size and format, such that for every thirty-two pages, I obviously am providing one extra" (J'ai encore à dire que mon Ouvrage est imprimé dans le caractère le plus fin que le format puisse comporter; que la *justification* [ou longueur des lignes], est d'un trente-deuxième de plus que celle ordinaire pour le même caractère et le même format, de sorte que par chaque trente-deux pages, j'en donne évidemment une de plus). What the page lost in terms of legibility because of the significantly smaller letter size and spacing it gained in its communicative performance of anger, proof of economy, and precision.[15]

This accounting bridges Moreau's preoccupation with type and page margins to my own argument about the connection between print and blood spilled in the fields. This statement is not meant to be hyperbolic; my concern is with linking bibliographic history to physical violence. The information missing from his accounting—narrative and economic—is considerable. Where are the enslaved? Although I have no evidence that he used enslaved labor in his own printshop, the connections between slavery, the enslaved, and his publications are everywhere. The volumes he defended here *(Loix et constitutions)* documented French Antillean case law: how many lashes were appropriate for an offense committed by an enslaved person guilty of *X*, *Y*, or *Z*, or what was the punishment for a free person of color considered too "insolent" (*insolente*). This work counted the French Ministry of the Navy as a subscriber, and this same ministry subsidized his research and granted him access to its archives. The extra thirty-third page that his expertise allowed to be produced was thus designed to benefit an audience whose job it was to create, publicize, and enforce white supremacist policies and politics. The people whose lives were circumscribed by these laws paid a direct price for these publications. For instance, who might Moreau have sold to pay a printer's fees or to acquire an engraver's expertise? Figure 1 demonstrates that he sold two men to help pay for his return trip to France to print this legal compilation. The unpaid laborers provided capital to compensate the paid ones. Those who were legally disposable were indispensable. His accounting is grossly incomplete.[16]

Alongside manipulation of margin size and careful consideration of typeface as a means of purveying information across his oeuvre, this particular work included a preponderance of other typographical elements used as communication tools that shouted out their emphaticness: to showcase dismay, sarcasm, irony, vanity. He used italics, boldface, dark lines. The text is littered with exclamation points ("hélas!" "Hé bien! ce scélérat, ce fou, cet homme execrable, c'est moi" [alas! Well! This villain, this crazy man, this execrable man, it is me]), an example of what Jennifer DeVere Brody describes as how "punctuation marks mediate, express, (re)present, and perform—the interactions between the stage of the page and the work of the mind." This piece stages Moreau's open declaration of his alliance with the most reactionary colonists associated with the Club Massiac.[17]

Period . . .

Moreau was enamored with the mechanical art of typography, and I take his interest seriously. In the opening advertisement to his classic two-volume *Manuel typographique, utile aux gens de lettres, et à ceux qui exercent les différents parties de l'Art de l'Imprimerie* (1764, 1766), the celebrated eighteenth-century printer and typefounder Pierre-Simon Fournier wrote, "This part of the typographic art, that enters into the order of knowledge analogous to that of men of letters, is commonly strongly neglected; even those among them who most take pride in knowing books, are often very embarrassed when it comes to giving an accurate idea of the character [type style] with which they are printed." Moreau did not neglect this knowledge. His formation as an Enlightenment man of letters led him to actively acquire an education from experts in bookshops and printshops in Saint-Domingue, France, Philadelphia, and, eventually, northern Italy. At the time of his death in 1819, his personal library still contained many volumes concerning the history, art, and technical aspects of the printing profession. When critiquing his rivals for attacking his honor, Moreau focused not only on their biases but their lack of "knowledge in Typography" (connaissances en Typographie). His scorn echoed the words of Lawrence Wroth, author of a classic text on North American colonial printing, who wrote that it was difficult "to repress the feeling of superiority that the lover of books must experience when he thinks of the mere reader of books. . . . To love the contents of a book and to know and care nothing about the volume itself, to love the treasure and to be unmindful of the earthen vessel that loyally holds and preserves it, is to be only a half lover." Moreau's professed sensitivity to and love of the printed "vessel" in which proslavery diatribes appeared is manifest in his public commentary and in the material objects he worked on—what type styles best mobilized emotions, how to procure engravings of contented en- slaved laborers, what bindery offered the best services. The sense of superi- ority this knowledge afforded him is evident every time he slighted Charton's profession and lack of spelling knowledge or accused his critics of ignorance about the basics of the printing business.[18]

Moreau's reputation as a source of knowledge about the logistics of the print trade was in place before he made a professional occupation of such knowledge in Philadelphia. For example, in a further effort to document his proslavery credentials, his *Mémoire justificatif* noted that in 1785 and 1789 he helped a fellow colon, David Duval de Sanadon, publish and distribute his work critiquing the idea of abolition: "He gives me his manuscript for consul- tation. It is I who refer him to a printer, a binder, who corrects the proofs, and who distributes and helps sell it" (Il me communique son Manuscrit en me consultant. C'est moi qui lui donne un Imprimeur, un Relieur, que corrige les épreuves, que distribute et fait vendre). If Moreau is to be believed, he occupied a pivotal role in expat colonial circles in Paris by connecting the different pieces of what Robert Darnton has referred to as a print "communi- cations circuit" that consisted of authors, printers, distributers, and readers.[19] Moreau was particularly adamant that people from the Caribbean who were familiar with French Caribbean linguistic expressions should be involved in the proofreading of texts about the region, believing that printers in France were often unequipped to correctly print this content and prone to making errors. This was a logical desire: the quality of a printed text improves when typeset by someone familiar with the language(s) in which it is written. Just as elite colons lobbied for the right to determine the laws regarding slavery and freedom that were most applicable to their homelands, the mechanics of printing work about the colonies demanded finesse and expertise that only a local such as himself could provide. Proofreading was an exercise in slaveholding patriotism. Moreau laid claim to and asserted mastery over knowledge and the colonial societies that produced it.[20]

Direct links between proslavery interests and print are well documented.[21] State-employed printers and the private printer businesses that emerged en force after 1789 were tied to the maintenance of slavery, and, as Jeremy D. Popkin writes, journalists in Saint-Domingue "knew full well that they were running enterprises that helped maintain slavery. . . . freedom of the press did not always mean an expansion of freedom for all members of society." Moreau used periodical culture for the same reasons that his society always had— to place advertisements selling and trying to recover enslaved people, for culling information, for promoting his work and reputation. If the practice of slavery was the practice of living in a state of war, print and its attendant mechanics were weapons in a slaveholder's arsenal.[22]

Moreau's relationship to print culture is thus more complex and interesting when seen beyond the connections one might draw between him and his published, circulating texts. His scholarly persona exceeds the meaning of the words on the page. It can be found in his ability to manifest his "usefulness" (utilité) to the colonialist regime by determining how those words were laid out and in what typeface. It is evident in his collaborations with other colonial authors as a go-between with the professional world of a printshop. His technical expertise grew exponentially between the mid-1780s and 1790s, and he developed an aesthetics that combined economic considerations of production costs with an interest in producing texts that pleased the eye and stimulated the brain. In order for his scholarly taste to emerge on the page, he relied on a network of laborers, paid and unpaid.[23]

Moreau's palpable anger and disappointment at being accused of holding abolitionist beliefs—accusations publicized at the same time that he was also accused of being a slaveholding reactionary—is inseperable from his self-professed zèle (zeal). Near the opening of his Mémoire justificatif, he wrote:

It is useless for me to speak of the pains that this Work [his multi-volume law compilation] has given me, the disappointments I have had to swallow, the obstacles that my lack of fortune has created to my zeal, the privations that I have endured in order to accomplish a design/ project that I dare call vast; in short, everything that proves that my personal interest is always sacrificed for the public interest, and most particularly for the interest of the colonies. I call on those familiar with my private life and the interior of my home [as witness to this].

Il est inutile que je parle des peines que cet Ouvrage m'a données, des dégoûts qu'il a fallu dévorer, des obstacles que mon défaut de fortune a suscités à mon zèle, des privations que j'ai endurées, pour accomplir un dessein que j'ose appeler vaste; enfin, de tout ce qui prouve que ce qui m'est personnel est toujours sacrifié à l'intérêt de la chose publique, et plus particulièrement à celui des Colonies. J'en appelle à ceux qui connaissent ma vie privée et l'intérieur de ma maison.

The *O* in "Ouvrage" is capitalized here and elsewhere to indicate Moreau's sense of its scope and perceived value to the French state and a wider transatlantic and inter-American reading public. Further claiming his martyrdom to the public good despite being branded a traitor by some of his peers, he continued: "I defy anyone to name a millionaire landowning colonist who serves the colonies more and better than me. If I had put as much money into buying land as I have into producing my useful work, my fortune would be worth more, but not my sentiments" (Je défie qu'on me cite un Colon propriétaire-millionaire qui serve plus et mieux les Colonies que moi. Si j'avois employé à y acheter du terrein ce que j'ai mis à faire des ouvrages pour leur utilité, ma fortune vaudrait mieux, mais non pas mes sentimens). Of course, it is not the "millionaire landowning colonist[s]" who first come to mind when imagining those who worked without respite to serve the colonies "more and better" than him. This is a masterful statement of how Moreau ignored the genocidal human labor toll around him.[24]

Moreau's involvement in the Parisian and French colonial print sphere was thus indelibly connected to his public role as a proslavery champion. This persona was most in evidence during the debates he had with members of the Amis des noirs and prominent men of color between 1789 and 1792, the colons américains, who were also living in Paris. These pamphlet and periodical wars, with men such as Pierre Antoine Monneron, a delegate from the Île de France, and Julien Raimond and Vincent Ogé, free men of color from Saint-Domingue who accused him of slave trading in the Parisian capital, sedimented his position as a zealot. His very appearance in the 1791 caricature *Discussion sur les hommes de couleur*, discussed in Chapter 4, demonstrates how central he was in these debates. Although Moreau liked to consider himself among the "enlightened" slaveholders who wished to ameliorate the conditions under which the enslaved labored—a *"bon maître"* (good master)—there is no moderation or restraint in his 1790s Parisian publications. What are now the Collection Moreau de Saint-Méry and the Bibliothèque Moreau de Saint-Méry in the French colonial archives contain hundreds of hateful screeds regarding how to return Saint-Domingue to slaveholder control, works that Moreau determinedly collected from the 1790s until the time of his death. His zealousness and zealotry are on perpetual display as collector, author, publisher, archivist, and propagandist.[25]

Moreau as a Print Professional

In 1794, four years after the publication of *Mémoire justificatif,* Moreau and his extended family had settled in Philadelphia after fleeing France. Moreau's interest in printing blossomed into a full-time occupation that generated enough money alongside his bookselling business for a livelihood.[26] During his forced exile in the United States, he self-published much of his work. Although Moreau was dismayed that life circumstances had reduced him to the occupation of "shopkeeper" (boutiquier), his temperament—simultaneously gregarious and studious—was well suited to negotiating a business whose primary concern was books. He was already known as a man who kept a large library, and he developed a lifelong practice of collecting books, including fine and rare ones.[27] His conviction that the technical and philosophical arts involved with book production—from writing to engraving to printing—were a way of "making eternal" (d'éterniser) human accomplishment and leaving a legacy for posterity would have had particular resonance at this juncture of his career when his life was at a crossroads.[28]

The choice of location was strategic. Scholarship has done an excellent job documenting how "la famosa Filadelfia" was the center of a vibrant, hemispheric American and transatlantic print community between 1790 and 1820. Bookshops, including Moreau's own, sold multilingual materials, and printers published texts in languages including French, Spanish, German, and English.[29] As François Furstenberg demonstrates, Philadelphia was "an American capital city . . . awash with French people, French goods, and

French culture." Much of this French culture was Caribbean-centric, and "wares from Saint Domingue permeated [the] marketplace; the island was a vital part of the city's trade network in the early 1790s."[30] Eighteenth-century observers acknowledged the importance of Moreau's bookshop as a center of French life for people fleeing revolution in France and the Americas. Patrons viewed the store as a vital information hub and psychic refuge; it had a piece of the Bastille on display and sold contraceptives alongside quite a large selection of printed materials and sundry goods.[31] The diplomat and power broker Charles-Maurice de Talleyrand-Périgord, arguably the most famous of the regular visitors to the shop, gratefully remarked that "here [New York] we know nothing about France. All our news comes from your house." Moreau wrote of how his fellow exiles would get together, and "we opened our hearts to one another, we poured out our feelings; and each of us knew the other's most intimate thoughts" (nous nous ouvrions nos coeurs, nous en épanchions les sentimens, et nos pensées les plus intimes devenaient communes à l'un et à l'autre). Scholars describe the store as a "rendezvous of all the notable French exiles then in Philadelphia," a "magnet for exiles," and "a re-creation of an enlightened French salon bravely weathering uncontrollable events, a small piece of the Republic of Letters in exile."[32]

Although Moreau was a fixture in French and French Caribbean social and print circles, I now turn to his important work concerning a part of the world that does not first come to mind when assessing his oeuvre: China. Moreau's publication of Van Braam's two-volume *Voyage de l'ambassade* exposes the connection between violence and print aesthetics. The intellectual rigor of the imprint is embedded in the volumes' content and craftsmanship; they inspire a book history and social history approach that generates stories about hemispheric American, transatlantic, and Dutch-Sino-French-American knowledge exchange. These were not just any books; they were beautiful, highly sophisticated volumes in the context of the early North American book trade. *Voyage de l'ambassade* required collaborations between francophone Caribbean, Chinese, European, and North American authors, technicians, and artists to publish. An analysis of the publication models a communal biography of Moreau through material print culture.[33]

Even as the volumes were encased in beautiful bindings and content was narrated in part through commissioned engravings, Moreau's aesthetic interest in documenting Chinese culture was grounded in economic concerns. He set himself the task of translating foreign cultures into commodities: through his literal translations from Dutch to French (and occasionally from the Chinese supplied by Van Braam) and figuratively through his mobilization of visual imagery and typography. The etymological roots of *translate*, meaning "to carry across," showcase how his work carried meaning and knowledge across cultural divides. The project was explicitly imperial and had a number of prospective audiences. In the early United States, direct trade with China had begun ten years previously, a commerce that would make fortunes for merchants in cities such as Salem, New York, and Philadelphia.[34] This book would have appealed to Moreau's local clients. In addition, the Dutch had a lucrative trade with Qing China, and the Netherlands had just been forced into an alliance with France after the republican French victory during the Flanders Campaign. Information about and access to Dutch-established Chinese partnerships was potentially of increased interest to a wider French audience that had been eagerly reading about China since seventeenth-century Jesuit missionaries had been sending reports back to Europe.[35]

I juxtapose three versions of the book's title page in this chapter as a reminder to read from the page; this method centers the usefulness of visual prompts and demonstrates how print materiality embeds valuable socio-historical stories. The original title page promoted novelty—details about parts of China that were unknown to Europeans (Figure 23). Title, subject, and publication specifics were presented in clean lines composed in varied point sizes, and the first word was printed in darker ink to claim a reader's attention. The roman type style gave way to italics showcasing Moreau's name (bigger even than Van Braam's). Moreau proudly announced his credentials: "Editor, Printer-Bookseller." The Philadelphia imprint was placed in close relation with a larger web of circulation via the "Principal Bookstores" of the United States and those in the "principal Cities" of Europe. The intended takeaway? This was a valuable publication worthy of the public's attention.

My adaptation of the title page includes some of the text's interior plates, highlighting the array of international artisans who produced the visual material that suffused the work (Figure 24). The illustrations were based on work produced by Chinese artists. The two scholars–state functionaries depicted in this rendition originally appeared as a full-page plate of four figures. The figurative representations of people in China would have been part of the book's appeal at a time when there was an enormous appetite for knowledge about the country. The intricate details captured in the engravers' delicate shading showcase cloth decorated with cranes and the shape of buttons that highlighted these men's ranks. In the lower left corner, I have integrated an additional illustration from the text: a pot tinker, whose depiction bleeds into an image of a bridge. Like much natural history, these

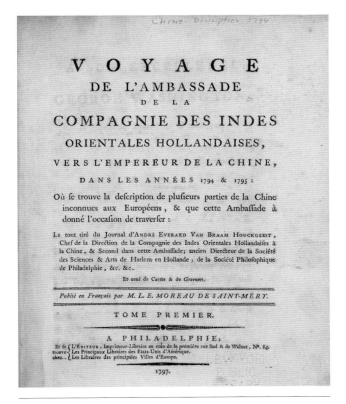

FIGURE 23. Title page of M. L. E. Moreau de Saint-Méry, ed. and
trans., *Voyage de l'ambassade de la Compagnie des Indes orientales
hollandaises, vers l'empereur de la Chine, dans les années 1794 et
1795 . . . Le tout tiré du journal d'André Everard van Braam Houckgeest . . .*, I (Philadelphia, 1797). Courtesy of HathiTrust.

volumes promised descriptions of people, industry, and natural and man-
made wonders.

I have also reproduced three words in a horizontal top banner in Figure
24—ESCLAVES, GOMGOM, COULIS—that Moreau included in his editorial appendix, "Notes and Explanations, in Alphabetical Order, Serving to Explain Several Chinese Words, and Some Important Details Contained in This
Work." These words focus our attention on Moreau's interpretative process.
They speak to labor hierarchies and linguistic concepts that connected Moreau's scholarship on China to his work on Africans in the Americas. For a

FIGURE 24. Composite title page I adapted from M. L. E. Moreau de Saint-Méry, ed. and trans., *Voyage de l'ambassade de la Compagnie des Indes orientales hollandaises, vers l'empereur de la Chine, dans les années 1794 et 1795 . . . Le tout tiré du journal d'André Everard van Braam Houckgeest . . .*, I (Philadelphia, 1797). By Luz Sandoval and Sara E. Johnson. Original courtesy of the Library Company of Philadelphia.

man trained in Enlightenment ideals of acquiring encyclopedic knowledge, this project would have been a sheer editorial delight for Moreau. It demanded that he catalog documents, read extensively, and add explanatory notes—geographical, cultural, linguistic, and historical.[36] Again, his formation as a master living in a slaveholding society provided the framework through which he could understand other parts of the world, even ones that ostensibly had nothing to do with his own. Moreau's involvement with Van Braam might have also suggested new labor practices precisely when revolutionary upheavals upended the conventional practice of African chattel slavery in the French Caribbean.

Expanding the hands-on knowledge he had acquired before his arrival in Philadelphia, Moreau took an active role in the printing side of his business. In an age when the printing profession was still very much a skilled, labor-intensive trade learned through family affiliations or long years of apprenticeship, Moreau seemed to enjoy this work despite his lack of formal training. He bought a new press and a set of type, imported from England; he purchased metal cast ornaments.[37] He used these to publish several newspapers and approximately twenty-four other pieces, in both French and English. Some were broadsides, and others included long volumes numbering upward of one thousand pages and filled with engravings.[38] One of the newspapers, the *Courrier de la France et des colonies*, was a collaboration with the French editor Louis François Roger Armand Gatereau, another exile from Saint-Domingue. The newspaper's six-day-a-week run between 1795 and 1796 placed Moreau squarely at the heart of providing written information that was essential to the local community.[39]

Moreau had expert assistance that enabled him to produce publications of such high artistic quality. A posthumously published journal that Moreau kept about his time in the United States, *Voyage aux États-Unis de l'Amérique, 1793–1798*, provides a unique entrée into Moreau's time as a book professional. Like his *Mémoire justificatif*, the volume is autobiographical, organized around daily notes and insertions of correspondence written to and from him. It is simultaneously a diary and a natural history, chronicling the customs of the United States in a format reminiscent of his other works: the mores of the population, the architecture of several urban centers, comments on slavery. From it we learn that he and the male members of his family worked the shop's typecase. Moreau's wife, Louise-Catherine Milhet, and Aménaïde seem to have labored in the store, in addition to being involved in the post-presswork stages of hanging pages to dry and folding them for insertion into books.

Just as Moreau employed people to research and print his *ouvrage* before life in exile, he took advantage of the large number of fellow Saint-Domingue refugees in Philadelphia to hire his paid workers. Journeymen printers were always in demand, and Moreau was fortunate enough to employ several professionals. His journal notes that he hired "as head workman of my printing press La Grange, a Parisian who had been a printer in Paris and gone from there to Cap Français to follow his trade. The fire and the disasters brought him to Philadelphia. I also took Despioux, a young compositor from Bordeaux, driven from Cap Français for the same reasons" (Je pris pour maître ouvrier de mon Imprimerie La Grange Parisien qui avait imprimé à Paris, qui était passé comme Imprimeur au Cap d'où l'incendie et les désastres l'avaient conduit à Philadelphie. Je pris aussi Despioux jeune compositeur Bordelais chassé du Cap par les mêmes causes).[40] Because of the expertise of these workers, Moreau's publications appeared with the type accurately laid out and evenly spaced **sothatitdidnotlookl ikethis**. His shop could also produce more creative, nonalphabetic print. Consider this sentence from the first volume of Van Braam's work:

A deux heures nous avons paſſé ſur un pont extrêmement long, qui offre cette forme ⁓. Il eſt au-deſſus d'une rivière d'une grande largeur, conſtruit partie en pierres de taille ,

FIGURE 25. Design element in M. L. E. Moreau de Saint-Méry, ed. and trans., *Voyage de l'ambassade de la Compagnie des Indes orientales hollandaises, vers l'empereur de la Chine, dans les années 1794 et 1795 . . . Le tout tiré du journal d'André Everard van Braam Houckgeest. . . , I* (Philadelphia, 1797), 106. Courtesy of HathiTrust.

The flow of the Chinese bridge, its long, graceful shape, was communicated visually through an image (Figure 25). The drawing in Van Braam's manuscript journal flowed into the typeset page, giving it life and character.[41]

Another of Moreau's journal entries, dated October 21, 1794, noted: "[Gabriel] De Combatz suggested that he be my clerk for six months for a hundred and fifty dollars. He had been employed in the bookshop in Geneva, and had had a fine shop in Cap Français. I accepted his offer the next day" (Descombatz me proposa d'être mon commis pendant six mois pour 150 dollars. Il avait été employé dans la librairie à Genève, et en avait eu un beau magasin au Cap Français. J'acceptai sa proposition le lendemain).[42] These were the years when Moreau brought to press his canonical *Description* volumes of the Spanish and French sides of Hispaniola. For these and other publications that centered on life in the colonies, the in-house knowledge shared by him and his workers about local Caribbean idiomatic expressions would have made his shop an ideal publisher. Decombaz himself had been a fellow member of the Cercle des Philadelphes in Cap Français, and his own bookstore there housed a popular lending library and reading room (*cabinet littéraire*). Modern-day readers are aware of Decombaz in part because Moreau's *Description de la partie française de l'isle Saint-Domingue* has been heavily used to cement our knowledge of reading habits, intellectual circles, and print culture in Saint-Domingue. His story illuminates the material logistics of the labor arrangments in Moreau's shop that made the very publication of *Description* possible. That Decombaz temporarily worked in Moreau's store before going on to open a competing one in Philadelphia provides a window into print culture networks both on the island and among its practitioners once in exile. The published version of his *Description* sealed Moreau's canonical status as a go-to for information about these same practitioners and the longer history of the press in Saint-Domingue. Decombaz's labor in Moreau's shop unknowingly contributed to Decombaz's own legacy.[43]

Moreau's web of collaborators thus illustrates the undervalued impact that the French and Haitian Revolutions had on the emerging U.S. print industry. The books printed in Moreau's shop were expertly crafted. Technically and aesthetically speaking, the Van Braam volumes show the most involved workmanship, and their artistic touches far exceeded those present in most books published in the United States at the time. The Van Braam volumes were printed in quarto, a luxury, large-size format, and totaled more than 650 pages with 15 leaves of plates. Extant copies show paper boards with a leather spine, gold leaf, and hand-lettering of the title. The cords were recessed. In keeping with much of his production, Moreau (and his printer employees) used copious visual stimulants. For example, year and date markers appear in the margins as signposts to the text. Ornaments were placed throughout: head- and tailpieces of objects such as musical instruments and roses, in addition to stacked lines and borders. In short, the books were handsome to look at and to handle.[44]

The material characteristics of the text elucidate labor relations. I again invoke Lawrence Wroth's comments about true book aficionados. He contended that "the booklover, more richly endowed [than a reader], broods over the hand that fashioned the volume he reads." Such unabashed fetishism of the book notwithstanding, the hands that fashioned Moreau's imprints enabled his visual storytelling methodology. In addition to French and French Caribbean–based artisans and technicians, Moreau worked with John Vallance, who engraved the *Plan of the City of Macao in China Possessed by the Portuguese 1795 (Plan de la ville de Macao à la Chine possédée par les portugais 1795)* as well as the maps in Moreau's *Description de la partie française de l'isle Saint-Domingue.* Vallance, originally from Scotland, worked for several firms in Philadelphia for more than thirty years. Maps were critical to visualizing the topography detailed in Moreau's publications, from the Dutch embassy's trip between Canton and the Forbidden Palace in China in the Van Braam collaboration to the various provinces of Saint-Domingue in *Description*. A. P. Folie, another engraver, did at least four leaves of images that depict carts, plows, and people transporting merchandise in *Voyage de l'ambassade*. These engravings might have been commissioned because of Moreau's enthusiastic assessment that "on going through this collection [the larger ensemble of Van Braam's illustrations brought back from China], one is convinced how much agriculture and commerce, the two grand moving agents of politics, are active in China" (en parcourant cette Collection de vues, on peut se convaincre combien l'agriculture et le commerce, ces deux grands agens du mouvement dans le corps politique, ont d'activité à la Chine). Agriculture and commerce were the dominant concerns of European colonial politics as well. Moreau also collaborated on the Van Braam volumes with Seymour, probably either Joseph or Samuel Seymour, a family of engravers known for its association with the renowned printer Isaiah Thomas in Massachusetts and for Samuel's work on the earliest trips to the Rocky Mountains and Upper Mississippi in the 1820s. Seymour is credited with engraving several outdoor scenes, including one demonstrating the architecture of several bridges (Figure 26). Moreau had direct contact with these artisans; they would have appeared in his expense accounting as paid collaborators.[45]

There were other artists, however, arguably the most vital for bringing to life the graphic, nontypographical component of this publication about China. Although uncredited, the work of Chinese artisans was thoroughly integrated into the imprint. Disappointingly, there is no source noted for at least five of the engravings, including the illustrations of local Chinese dress (see Figure 24). Yet evidence suggests that Pu Qua, an artisan known for producing images of the working-class professions in Qing China, largely for the export trade, was likely the source of many of Moreau's illustrations.[46] The figure on the left third of the Moreau–Van Braam engraving in Figure 24 helps to make this connection. It clearly resembles the watercolor of a tinker that was included in George Henry Mason's *Costume of China* (1804) (Figure 27 and Figure 28).[47] This engraving would have appeared in a reverse perspective once it was imprinted on paper. The clear correspondence between the images suggests that Van Braam must have had examples of Pu Qua's art in his personal collection and that he made them available to Seymour to engrave. In addition to Pu Qua's work, the designs of other artisans who worked closely with Van Braam while he was living in China might also have been reproduced in this imprint. Moreau noted that Van Braam "had constantly employed, during five years, two Chinese illustrators" (a employé

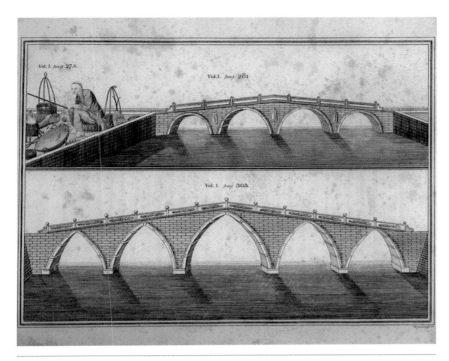

FIGURE 26. Chinese bridges. Engraving by Seymour. From M. L. E. Moreau de Saint-Méry, ed. and trans., *Voyage de l'ambassade de la Compagnie des Indes orientales hollandaises, vers l'empereur de la Chine, dans les années 1794 et 1795 . . . Le tout tiré du journal d'André Everard van Braam Houckgeest . . .*, I (Philadelphia, 1797), plate opposite page 280. Courtesy of HathiTrust.

constamment, durant cinq années, deux dessinateurs Chinois). He also noted that Van Braam "conceived of sending Chinese painters to travel at his expense throughout the whole of China, in order that they might collect views of every thing curious and picturesque which that country contains." The resulting art was in Van Braam's possession and could have been chosen by Moreau and Van Braam to appear in the book.[48]

Voyage de l'ambassade was thus an imprint that required Chinese illustrators, refugee Parisian/Saint-Domingan master printers and compositors, Scottish and North American engravers, a Dutch businessman and collector, and an exiled Martinican lawyer to bring to press. One must add Moreau's wife and children, who did various jobs in the book and printshop, to this communal book biography as well. The comingling of international aesthetic

FIGURE 27. (*Left*) *A Tinker (Un Chaudronnier).* Attributed to Pu Qua. From George Henry Mason, *The Costume of China, Illustrated by Sixty Engravings: With Explanations in English and French* (London, 1800), plate 37. Courtesy of the Wellcome Collection.

FIGURE 28. (*Below*) Detail of composite title page 1 adapted from M. L. E. Moreau de Saint-Méry, ed. and trans., *Voyage de l'ambassade de la Compagnie des Indes orientales hollandaises, vers l'empereur de la Chine, dans les années 1794 et 1795* ... *Le tout tiré du journal d'André Everard van Braam Houckgeest* . . ., I (Philadelphia, 1797). By Luz Sandoval and Sara E. Johnson. Original courtesy of HathiTrust.

print cultural traditions made these books into a museum on the page, a textual and visual artifact that complemented the stately mansion that Van Braam built for himself outside Philadelphia. Histories of revolution, forced migration, and imperial jockeying for access to new mercantile and labor markets were all documented in *Voyage de l'ambassade*'s craftsmanship. Moreau's use of print technologies and those who understood them allowed him to narrate these stories at multiple embedded levels.

✳✳✳✳✳✳✳✳✳✳✳

"La retraite chinoise":
A Colonialist Outpost in 1790s Philadelphia

Moreau's collaboration with Van Braam began while the former was living in a residence that Van Braam styled "the Chinese Retreat."[49] Moreau provided much of the information about Van Braam's biography and earlier travels in the extended editorial preface to the book. *Voyage de l'ambassade* recounts a trip taken by Andreas Everardus van Braam Houckgeest at the behest of the Dutch East India Company (Vereenigde Oost-Indische Compagnie, or VOC) between 1794 and 1795. Van Braam had worked for the company in China and Macao during the 1770s, and he rejoined the Dutch East India Company as director of the factory in Canton (Guangzhou) in 1788. While in Canton he managed to procure an official visit on behalf of the Dutch East India Company to Emperor Qianlong's imperial palace in Beijing in honor of the emperor's sixtieth year in power.[50] *Voyage de l'ambassade* is a detailed diary of the round-trip voyage.[51]

Van Braam was also a slaveholder, a fact that has gone unremarked in scholarship on his life. He is a historical figure about whom information is readily available, yet those who made him his money are not so easy to trace. A self-described enthusiast of the American Revolution, Van Braam became a U.S. citizen during a four-year sojourn between residences in China, and he promptly invested his money in Charleston, S.C., long the hub of the Atlantic slave trade into the southern states. A merchant, he also ran a plantation near the Stono public landing. Van Braam seems to have imported some of his knowledge about rice production from processes he witnessed in China.[52] Maryann, her fourteen-year-old daughter Lucy, and Sylvia "of

ABSENTED from the fubfcriber, on Thurfday evening, the 8th inftant, a Negro Wom₂n named *Maryann*, alfo her daughter named *Lucy*, about 14 years of age, well known, both had on when they went away, a blue cloth jacket and petticoat; they were formerly the property of Mrs. Delahowe, and are well known in this City.—A reward of *Five Dollars* will be given for each to any perfon who will apprehend the faid negroes, and deliver them to the Warden of the Work houfe.—All perfons are hereby forbid from harbouring or carrying the faid negroes out of this State, as they may depend on having the law put in force.—A genteel reward will be given to any perfon who will give information where they are harboured, on conviction of the offender.

A. E. Van Braam Houckgueft.
April 15th, 1784.

RUN AWAY
FROM the Subfcriber the third inft. a Negro Wench named SYLVIA, formerly the property of Arthur Graham, late Waggon Conductor of the Southern Army: She is about five feet eight inches high, of the Guinea country, and has the marks on both cheeks, alfo a deep hollow in the left one; She is of a very dark complexion, and had on when fhe went away a white woollen wrapper, green coat, and a check handkerchief round her head.—As fhe has lately been feen a few miles out of town, it is fuppofed fhe will attempt to conceal herfelf in the country, therefore all perfons are hereby cautioned from harbouring or employing the faid Negro, under the penalty of being profecuted as the law directs. A reward of *Three Guineas* will be paid to whoever takes up and delivers the faid Wench to me at No. 51, Tradd-ftreet.

A. E. VAN BRAAM HOUCKGEEST.
Charlefton, March ae.   (61

FOR SALE,
On FRIDAY;
The 15th auguft,
At the plantation now occupied by Mr.
Van Braam, near Stono public landing,
Two Negro Carpenters
WHO are good workmen; a fmart waiting boy about 16 years old; a com .leat wafher and ir ner, who is likewife an excellent cook, & acquainted with making paftry, with her female child 6 years old.
ALSO,
Several articles of valuable houfhold and kitchen furniture, fundry dry goods, viz. broad cloths, blankets, li nens. checks, handkerch efs, nankee , ftripes, &c.
LIKEWISE,
Two valuable forrel horfes, Virginia bred 4 years old, fir for either fadkle of chair; a phæ on and chair, with harnefs compleat, feveral faddles, and f me plantation tools; hogs, cattle, and a Philadelphia built boat, with oars and awning compleat.

FIGURE 29. Advertisements announcing the escape and sale of people enslaved by Van Braam. From *South-Carolina Gazette, and Public Advertiser* (Charleston), Apr. 14–Apr. 17, 1784, [3]; *South-Carolina Gazette, and General Advertiser* (Charleston), Apr. 1–Apr. 3, 1784, [3]; *City Gazette, or the Daily Advertiser* (Charleston), July 30, 1788, [2].

the Guinea country" ran away from him in the spring of 1784. When he left South Carolina in 1788, he sold five women, men, and children: two carpenters, a sixteen-year-old "waiting boy," a washerwoman who was also a pastry chef, and her six-year-old daughter (Figure 29). These are some of the uncredited, unaccounted for individuals whose skilled hands labored on Van Braam's behalf.[53]

Van Braam's primary employer, the Dutch East India Company, operated a centuries-long global trade business, strongest in the islands now part of Indonesia and Japan. With a monopoly on the spice trade (cinnamon, nutmeg, and cloves) and the introduction of cash crops such as coffee, tea, rubber, and sugar, the company yielded tremendous profits for European investors, a profit garnered at great human cost, particularly in Batavia/Indonesia, capital of the Dutch East Indies.[54] Van Braam's wife, Catharina Cornelia van Braam, was the daughter of Baron Pieter van Reede van Oudtshoorn, the

FIGURE 30. *Portrait of A. E. van Braam Houckgeest.* Anonymous. Circa 1795. Courtesy of RKD—Netherlands Institute for Art History.

deputy governor of the Cape Colony, a Dutch settler colony in what is now Cape Town, South Africa. Van Braam's extended family thus worked as high functionaries of the global Dutch empire at the sites of its most violent appropriations of land and labor. The production of crops and the luxury items valued by a global market depended on the exploitation of forced laborers.[55]

Van Braam displayed his collection of objects from China to visitors at the Chinese Retreat, and Moreau was enraptured with the novelty of his collection (Figure 30). He recorded his first encounter with Van Braam on May 8, 1796, noting, "I saw the Chinese brought by M. Van Braam" (Je vis les Chinois amenés par M. Vanbraam). By the seventeenth of the same month, Moreau had agreed "to edit his account of his voyage as Dutch Ambassador to Canton and Pekin [sic], and to print and publish it" (d'être l'Editeur de son voyage de l'Ambassade hollandaise de Canton à Pekin et de la publier imprimé). He was in fact the translator of the volume as well; it is unclear when and how Moreau learned Dutch, but Van Braam was fluent in French and closely inspected Moreau's work. When Moreau referred to seeing "the Chinese brought by M. Van Braam," he was referring to people, not things. In the editorial preface to *Voyage de l'ambassade*, Moreau stated: "He had brought with him several Chinese men. . . . One believes oneself truly transported to China when surrounded by these living Chinese people and by the drawings of their morals, their practices, their monuments and their arts" (Il a amené plusieurs Chinois. . . . On se croit donc vraiment transporté à la Chine quand on est environné de ces Chinois vivans et de ces images de leur moeurs, de leurs usages, de leurs monumens et de leurs arts).[56] The five Chinese workers who accompanied Van Braam when he sailed from China to Philadelphia in 1796 were objects of fetishization alongside the porcelain, silks, and other fine objects destined to become so popular in the West under the guise of *chinoiserie*. Art collector Charles Carpenter, who spent many years reassembling Van Braam's art and furniture collection in the 1970s, noted: "Wherever he went crowds followed his coach with its Chinese coachman and Chinese footman. Van Braam was a flamboyant man and he obviously enjoyed the spectacle he created." Western exhibitions of nonwhite others—Africans, Native Americans, Asians—reveal the connections between Atlantic slavery and settler colonialist and orientalist discourses.[57]

Van Braam had every intention of making an ostentatious splash in his new home. It was situated on 360 acres on the banks of the Delaware River, and from its roof allegedly hung "silvery-toned bells . . . which tinkled merrily in every high wind." One visitor, Julian Niemcewicz, called Van Braam "at once a Dutch Baron and a Chinese Mandarin," decrying Van Braam's overspending on land and labor, expenses that earned him a stint in debtors' prison. Niemcewicz wrote that the house was "immense, surmounted with a cupola and decorated with golden serpents in the Chinese manner. . . . We entered a hall filled with different objects from China, more curious than useful. . . . All this, very precious here, very pretty, was made in China at a very low price; labor is considered as nothing there.[58] These observations, full of racialized ideas about cheap Chinese labor, suggest how the idea of mobilizing that supply of labor in order to maintain a luxurious lifestyle, conspicuous in its material ostentation, went hand in hand. The mansion was still known as "China Hall" in the twentieth century despite a long succession of owners. One sensationalist 1950s newspaper article remarked on the "eerie tales" that surrounded it; the residence was the source of endless rumors, including that it was a "former slave market" and an "illegal port of entry" for unspecified Asian immigrants. It was a Civil War hospital and eventually a school for the orphans of Black soldiers. Its continued place in the lore of Bristol County, Pennsylvania, is related as much to the former inhabitants of the place as the building itself.[59]

Another contemporary eyewitness account of life at the Chinese Retreat was recorded by Van Braam's grandson, Lucius Quintius Cincinnatus Roberts, who lived there as a child. In addition to the five Chinese workers mentioned above, apparently Van Braam had a "Malay woman" as a "housekeeper"; Roberts claimed her name was Madam Lana. How did this woman, perhaps from Indonesia, come to be in Van Braam's employ?[60] The intimacy in this household arrangement corresponds to Van Braam's time working for the VOC and the local labor that functionaries such as Van Braam would have commanded in both domestic and factory settings. Madam Lana played a prominent role in the home—disciplining children and running its daily operations. Roberts described how his grandfather "was possessed of the most ungovernable temper I ever witnessed in any person, and would exercise it occasionally upon his servants and family to the astonishment of all present. He would utter . . . such sudden peals of roarings as resembled thunder more than that of a human voice." That his own family noted Van Braam's difficult, raging personality is a stark reminder that Van Braam's servants were forced to negotiate a volatile working environment.[61]

Under what circumstances did these female and male workers accompany Van Braam to the United States? Did they leave Batavia and China voluntarily? Were they paid for their labor? Were they effectively captives, isolated on this property in the remote Pennsylvania woods that would have been difficult to reach without access to a horse or boat? Did they accompany Van Braam to London and eventually to Holland when he left Philadelphia? Unfortunately, I have been unable to trace any notice of them farther than the Chinese Retreat. As was the case with Moreau's households, these domestic laborers were central to the functioning of the home; their presence provided evidence of social status and legitimacy in hierarchical colonial and early U.S. societies; and they might have provided information (cultural, linguistic) that was mobilized in their masters' intellectual circles. They now move in the margins of archival records.

Empire transferred itself through books, but books were also a way that empire hid its own self-perpetuation under the guise of aesthetic choices and beautiful things. By attending to the social history of the Moreau–Van Braam volumes, we see the chilling outline of an East Asian labor market in the Americas that was already beginning in Van Braam's Philadelphia home. Imagine a tableau vivant, but, rather than living actors recreating a piece of art in silent and static poses, visualize exoticized people moving around and serving Van Braam's guests, surrounded by all manner of precious art. When the elite of Philadelphia visited, their coats might have been taken by a Chinese man, their dinner and port served by another, their meals planned by a housekeeper from the Indonesian archipelago, and their tour of Van Braam's extensive Chinese art and furniture collection given by the very individuals who had accompanied the collection from Canton/Guangzhou. These men were those Moreau blithely claimed "seem to have come purposely to attest the truth of what he [Van Braam] has related concerning their country, or has represented in his collection of drawings" (semblent être venus pour attester les faits que ce Voyageur a pris chez eux, et consignés dans sa colletion de dessins).[62]

What ideas might have occurred to Moreau as he wined, dined, and worked on this manuscript while conversing about China and the ever-evolving revolutionary and mercantile world? After losing control over his own enslaved laborers, did he imagine the possibility of new workers that might be taken from foreign ports to Atlantic sites? Contemplating Van Braam's staff, he could have seen in them possible replacements for his own society's labor force. Caribbean planters were at the vanguard of schemes decades later to recruit or impress people from India and China for labor in places such as Guyana, Guadeloupe, Jamaica, Cuba, Martinique, and Trinidad. In the transition of African to Asian labor, Asian bodies often emerged as a fantasy for slaveholders confronting the inevitability of abolition.[63]

Moreau was a product of the eighteenth-century Caribbean, and he used his worldview as a slaveholder to interpret his world and others. This preoccupation is evident in a discussion of labor practices included in a set of editorial notes that Moreau coauthored containing information on "many Chinese words" (plusieurs mots chinois) and concepts to accompany his translation and publication of Van Braam's work (Figure 31).[64] Moreau's paratexts are as critical to understanding his work as the translations they were meant to augment. They positioned him as an expert, as a connoisseur, as the framer of the story.[65]

His preferred expository mode when working on a piece he did not author solely was the incorporation of explanatory notes: sometimes done via footnotes, other times in essays, glossaries, and even highly elaborated indexes and tables of contents. The table of contents in this publication alone was more than seventy pages. Moreau wrote, "Persuaded that several

NOTES ET EXPLICATIONS

PAR ORDRE ALPHABÉTIQUE,

*Pour ſervir à l'intelligence de pluſieurs mots Chinois, & de quelques
détails contenus dans cet Ouvrage, & former, en quelque ſorte, un
ſupplément à la Table générale des Matières miſe à la fin du ſecond
volume.*

FIGURE 31. Title page of "Notes et explications par ordre alphabétique...."
From M. L. E. Moreau de Saint-Méry, ed. and trans., *Voyage de l'ambassade
de la Compagnie des Indes orientales hollandaises, vers l'empereur de la
Chine, dans les années 1794 et 1795 ... Le tout tiré du journal d'André Everard van Braam Houckgeest ...*, I (Philadelphia, 1797), lxvii–lxxx. Courtesy
of the Library Company of Philadelphia.

explicatory notes would add to the interest of the work, the author and editor have placed them at the beginning of each of the two volumes to which
they belong. The same motive has inspired everything, the desire to please
the public" (Persuadé que quelques notes explicatives ajouteraient encore à
l'intérêt de l'ouvrage, l'Auteur et l'Éditeur en ont placé à la tête de chacun
des deux volumes auquel elles appartiennent plus particulièrement. Le même
motif les a inspirées toutes, le désir de plaire au public).[66] This desire to
please his reading public had a direct impact on the physical characteristics
of his imprints: illustrations to linger over, maps for reference, easily readable
typefaces, decorative type ornaments, and the large quarto format in this
publication and others, such as his canonical publication *Description de la
partie française de l'isle Saint-Domingue.*

Moreau added an entry for ESCLAVES to his "Notes" and to his index. To
be clear, there was no discussion of "slaves" or "slavery" in Van Braam's
account. Moreau's economic and personal interest in the institution of slavery
in the Americas made the question of its existence in China a logical topic
of commentary, a term to place in the notes even though it did not appear in
the book at hand. Moreau noted: "There [were] not precisely slaves in China,

but indentured servants. They are, so to speak, part of the family" (il n'y a pas précisément d'esclaves à la Chine, mais des espèces d'engagés à tems. Ils sont, pour ainsi dire, partie de la famille). "Not precisely slaves" (pas précisément d'esclaves): this phrase is such a euphemistic and alarmingly unstable evaluation of labor dynamics. Were people somewhat, though not exactly, forced to work against their will? Was this labor a result of an inherited condition? His paternalistic choice to understand slavery as a matter of reciprocal familial relationships mimicked his comments about the great love and devotion his own enslaved felt for him. It corresponded to a broader tradition in slaveholding societies in which benign terms were used to characterize involuntary servitude, be it under indenture or other forms of excruciatingly poor wages.[67]

There were, however, laborers who appeared repeatedly in the body of the text and earned a corresponding entry in Moreau's editorial notes. These were the men, hundreds of them, who physically carried the embassy on their shoulders in palanquins supported by poles of bamboo, moving through arduous terrain in the dead of winter: COULIS. Moreau defined this term as "a name that came from India, [and] is given to men who do all sorts of work, but principally to those who carry persons, merchandise, etc. This occupation is considered as the lowest of all, because it is that of such individuals who cannot find another. Almost all of them go with their head and feet naked" (Ce nom qui vient de l'Inde est donné aux hommes appliqués à toutes sortes de travaux, mais principalement à ceux qui portent les personnes, les marchandises, etc. Cette occupation est considérée comme la dernière de toutes, parce qu'elle est celle des individus qui n'en trouvent pas d'autre. Ils vont presque tous la tête et les pieds nus). A term from India, imported by the British, it became current among the international traders assembled in Canton, and Van Braam referenced these people constantly, talking of "changing" them along the way as one would a horse. The difficulty of procuring their labor resulted in numerous delays and frustrations. On one occasion, upon discovering that twenty-seven of their forty-eight bottles of liquor had been broken during transport, Van Braam wrote: "Those cursed *Coulis* frequently let the cases fall violently upon the ground hardened by the frost, on purpose that the bottles might break and the liquor run out, which rendered their burden so much the lighter. I[t] would have been impossible for our conductors to attend to every *Couli*, since they were sometimes spread over a space of more than two leagues. Besides, I have repeatedly said that no Mandarin is able to controul that class of men, the very refuse of the Chinese nation. There is then no remedy but patience." On another occasion he noted:

"I stopped there half an hour in order to get four *Coulis*, which were procured for me by the Mandarin. He sent also one of his servants with me on horseback, to keep an eye over those scoundrels, and prevent their desertion. . . . The roads were so exceedingly bad that the *Coulis* were constantly half way up their legs in mud; and it was so slippery that they were every moment in danger of falling." Desertion, fugitivity, violence. Although Van Braam might not have mentioned slavery as an institution, he described being carried around by laborers who sought to flee and worked under life-threatening conditions. Eight of these men died of exhaustion during the trip. Moreau thus wrote about new and unfamiliar contexts by calling upon familiar ones. Van Braam, too, proved equally adaptable at expropriating people's labor to advance his own interests, moving between the familiar world of labor in VOC circles of power and privilege and the new horizons of Chinese diplomatic arrangements and then quickly integrating the system of African chattel slavery in the Americas into his repertoire of forced labor practices.[68]

One final example, the word GOMGOM from Moreau's glossary, reveals how much his understanding of slavery and its attendant cultural practices informed his understanding of Chinese cultural traditions. Moreau wrote that a "GOMGOM" (*gum-gum* or *gom-gom*) was a suspended copper basin that resounded like a bell when hit by a large stick; it was seemingly a gong. He then made the astonishing claim that it was not a Chinese word at all! According to his logic, in African countries the word "GOMGOM," similar to the word *tam-tam*, was the name used for a drum. The entry highlights how his experiential knowledge about the Caribbean, knowledge heavily influenced by African cultural forms, made him feel qualified to offer interpretative gestures about other parts of the world.[69] Black cultural practices, in this case the naming of musical instruments, grounded his comparative worldview. Although he might not have consciously realized this tendency in his own intellectual formation and analytical work, it seeped through much of his commentary. His personal contact with the enslaved and free people of color in his social circles provided the framework—alongside his knowledge of French jurisprudence—to make his own sense of things as disparate as Chinese social hierarchies and plantation organization or Chinese musical traditions and those in Africa and the Caribbean.

A second composite and amended title page further visualizes this publication as a communal book biography (Figure 32). It brings individuals to the surface as an overlay, accounting for the labor on the physical book and the labor of those who worked in its real-world margins. The *Voyage* is not only Van Braam's but also Madam Lana's; that of 無名氏之二 (anonymous man two) and his four fellow companions at the Chinese Retreat; and that of hundreds of cold and exhausted porters. The title-page announcement of a description—"où se trouve" (where is found)—expands to acknowledge, if not find, two male "Domestiques Malais," a young enslaved boy, a pastry chef, and Sylvia "of the Guinea Country" as part of the networks circulating around Van Braam who fattened his purse and put him on a life and publishing trajectory toward Moreau. Pu Qua is credited for work that was likely his and that of his associates in Guangzhou. Seymour, one of the few artisans with a signature byline, appears alongside his printshop associates La Grange and Despioux.

The Price of Good Taste and the "Dark" Side of Print History

This chapter responds to Simon Gikandi's call to "read these two spheres of social life—one rooted in the realm of the aesthetic, civility, and taste, and the other in the political economy of slavery—in the same register."[70] In these examples, print technology gave structure and substance to the epistemology that guided Moreau's personal and intellectual life, allowing him to disseminate proslavery ideological claims and imperial ambitions as he fussed over type, read the most scintillating scholarship, or conversed with engravers about their craft. The slave trade was intertwined with the emergence of books as bourgeois luxury items, as museum-like, as encyclopedic in breadth of knowledge. In Moreau's case, the "superiority" of the lover, of the owner, and the *producer* of a beautiful book did not mark a clear separation from ownership and control over a human body. The former depended on the latter.

A closing example brings people, slavery, and (racial) revolution together around actual printed pages in production and transit. Moreau wrote about dance, a topic that he found of great ethnographic interest. He evaluated it as a manifestation of national and transatlantic high and popular culture, including among African diasporic communities in the Caribbean. Moreau worked on this piece, originally conceived of as an article in his "Répertoire des notions coloniales," in the late 1780s, and it was published in three

FIGURE 32. Composite title page 2 adapted from M. L. E. Moreau de Saint-Méry, ed. and trans., *Voyage de l'ambassade de la Compagnie des Indes orientales hollandaises, vers l'empereur de la Chine, dans les années 1794 et 1795 . . . Le tout tiré du journal d'André Everard van Braam Houckgeest. . . ,* I (Philadelphia, 1797). By Luz Sandoval and Sara E. Johnson. Original courtesy of the Library Company of Philadelphia.

different editions, once in Philadelphia at his own printing house under the title *Danse* (1796) and twice in Parma under the title *De la Danse* (1801 and 1803). The Italian editions were made by Giambattista Bodoni, arguably the most celebrated of eighteenth-century European printers and a man who became a close associate of Moreau's when Moreau was the administrator general of the duchies of Parma, Piacenza, and Guastalla. The vanity of having his own work appear with a Bodoni imprint epitomizes Moreau's desire to act as patron, as a man of good taste. The people collected around the page proofs and editions of the piece over the course of a decade formed a web of artisanal knowledge, print circuits, and power. In its production stage, Talleyrand read the volume and corrected the proofs in Moreau's bookshop when he kept regular company with Moreau during their joint exile. Moreau's young son, "whom [he] had made into an excellent compositor" (dont j'avais fait un excellent compositeur), had learned enough of the print trade by then to help set the type as he worked alongside his father and other print professionals. Once he had published the work, Moreau sent it to his friend in Saint-Domingue. This friend, no other than the military commander Donatien Marie Joseph de Vimeur, vicomte de Rochambeau, replied in a letter from Cap Français:

> You depict the dance of the creoles in such pleasing colors that I couldn't resist making a close examination of the different dances which you describe so well. Until now I had never had time to see them, during my stormy mission in this part of the world.
>
> . . . The dance is certainly lively in the tropics!
>
> How right you are in saying that the time is still pregnant with great events, particularly here! You are wise in your decision to philosophize for some time to come at the corner of Walnut Street [his bookshop location], and I promise faithfully to send you word if I think a sojourn on this land could be pleasing to you. But no, remain where you are! We'll hope the troubles in this colony are almost over, but nobody can possibly say for certain.
>
> Do you wish to know in two words how things stand? Here it is: The Men of Color wish to seize the property of the proprietors, and are giving bad advice to the Africans, who are becoming openly defiant. The Africans haven't yet dared to think about wholesale freedom, but they prefer soldiering to farming. The small group of whites not in the army is irritated and humiliated. The colony is still divided among head-men like Rigaud, Beauvais, Villatte, who administer their sections for personal gain, and among those like Toussaint and Laveaux, who work for the Republic. Everything has taken on a military aspect; those who make sugar do so with sabres at their sides and guns on their shoulders.
>
> Do you wish to know where we are going, or rather where we will be going? I know nothing about that, but what I am sure of is that I am in a hellhole![71]

I quote this letter at length to establish the stakes that emerge by pairing the ostensibly "light" topic of performance taste with both politics and Moreau's work as a writer and printer. The brutal Rochambeau—famed for importing attack dogs into Saint-Domingue trained to eat Black insurgents, during the same years that the Bodoni reprints of *De la Danse* were published (1801–1803)—was a friend of Moreau's who conferred with him about the advisability of returning to Cap Français. He was a source of up-to-date commentary about events on the ground, particularly as they were inflected by shifting racial and class alliances. Rochambeau—son of the American Revolutionary hero and soon to be infamous for stringing people up or drowning them en masse during the unfolding of the Haitian Revolution— took time while working in a "hellhole" partially of his own making to discuss Moreau's thoughts about culture. It would be hard to name a more controversial and reviled figure in Haitian revolutionary studies than Rochambeau, Moreau's confidante and book pen pal. It would be hard to name a figure more critical to the unfolding of Napoleonic foreign policy, including in Saint-Domingue and Louisiana, than Talleyrand, another of Moreau's confidantes and book collaborators.[72]

This letter from Rochambeau was dated July 15, 1796. Just two months before, in May 1796, Moreau was at Van Braam's for the first time. The timing is coincidental, yet suggestive. Rochambeau effectively told Moreau that he had made the right decision to stay away from Saint-Domingue, that his days of masterly leisure were over, and that he had better hope for the best with his bookshop. But Moreau already knew that change was in the air; even in 1790 he had been forced to defend his proslavery credentials and the institution itself in Parisian halls of power. As he dallied with Van Braam, he had his literal eye on alternative labor possibilities, his sights exposed to other racialized bodies who could be extracted from their (colonized) homes if the need arose. As evidence that other Caribbean planters would later follow his example in the quest for new laborers after the abolition of chattel slavery, "coolie" eventually became a derogatory term to refer to indentured servants from India and China in his Martinican homeland (and elsewhere in the Caribbean). The losses that resulted in his Philadelphia exile (of the people he enslaved, of his properties in Saint-Domignue, of his life as a lawyer) resulted in increased opportunities to channel discursive violence onto the page. Moreau's zèle was productive, calculating, and a source of direct and indirect danger to many. It drowned out other perspectives and consigned people to servitude, marginality, and expendability in real life and on the page. I have analyzed Moreau's increasingly sophisticated printing practice and reanimated it with my own visual choices in order to reckon with and to partially account for the presence of these people, many forced migrants themselves. At whose expense was Moreau's accounting done? Lingering memories of Black, Chinese, and "Malay" inhabitants of a Pennsylvania house in ruins. The sound of bells—silver ones tinkling from Van Braam's cupola or gongs whose names sounded like words that Africans used to designate their drums. The page has surfaced these connections.

CHAPTER FOUR

Encyclopédie noire

— Part II —

INDEX OF ENTRIES

Racial undermining

J

Jeanne and Sylvie

New York, May 28, 1794

We learned that Jeanne, my mother-in-law's *mulâtresse*, was dead. I presented my compliments to Chancellor Livingston, then went to the Custom House for our luggage.

Nous apprîmes que Jeanne, mulâtresse de ma belle-mère était morte. J'allai saluer M. le chancelier Livingston, ensuite à la douane pour nos effets.[1]

This entry appeared in a journal Moreau de Saint Méry kept while in exile in the United States between 1794 and 1798. As his immediate family traveled from city to city on the Eastern Seaboard looking for a place to settle, so, too, did his fellow colonists from the revolutionary Caribbean and France. A month before this entry was recorded, Moreau mentioned that his mother-in-law had arrived in Philadelphia. He wrote, "With [her] was . . . her griffon Sylvie" (Avec ma belle-mère était . . . sa griffonne Sylvie). Madame Louise Cheval Milhet, referred to as the widow Milhet (la Veuve Milhet) in official documents, had affective and financial ties that closely connected her to homes in Saint-Domingue and Louisiana. Once held captive by the Choctaw as a child, she eventually accumulated capital at the expense of others' dispossession, demonstrating the coercive intersection of settler colonialism and chattel slavery on a hemispheric scale. By 1794, she traveled in the company of at least two enslaved women after fleeing Saint-Domingue. This travel occurred even though the French National Convention had outlawed slavery on the island months previously. Although it is unknown when they all left Saint-Domingue, Sylvie and Jeanne could very well have been legally freed women *(affranchies).* Their arrival in the United States ensured continued bondage.[2]

Jeanne's death was important enough for Moreau to record, but it was included in a list of other seemingly meaningful and mundane activities, such as a visit to Robert Livingston, the future American negotiator of the Louisiana Purchase. The casualness of the announcement is jarring; that he would take note of the death of a domestic servant suggests that she had some value, affective or monetary, to the family. Nowhere in the journal is a reader told the cause of Jeanne's death or how long she might have been ill. Sylvie is likewise invisible apart from when she was listed as a companion for a young child that also accompanied the widow Milhet. However, they were there in the flesh working alongside their well-documented owners. They were shipboard, calming and soothing adults and children alike, despite what must have been their own fears; they formed part of a network of forced migrants heading into the unknown. Sparse fragments combined with conjecture make details about their kinship and community ties as new Caribbean transplants in the City of Brotherly Love possible to visualize.

For example, Jeanne had a daughter. "A little quadroon girl named Sophie, age 1, daughter of the mulâtresse named Jeanne" (une petite carteronne nommé Sophie agée d'un an, fille de la mulâtresse nommée Jeanne), was bequeathed by Moreau's mother-in-law to Moreau and his new bride, Louise-Catherine Milhet, on the occasion of their marriage in 1781. When Moreau recorded Jeanne's death in 1794, Jeanne's daughter Sophie would have been a teenager; he had once owned her. Moreau stated that he no longer had any enslaved people by 1794, although it is unclear what happened to the people he still owned in Martinique and Saint-Domingue between the outbreak of the revolt in Saint-Domingue in 1791 and his arrival in the United States in 1794. If Sophie were still alive, would word of her mother's death in Philadelphia have reached her? Madame Milhet also died in Philadelphia and was denied burial by several Catholic churches because she had not received last rites. Where would Jeanne have been buried in this foreign land, and would she have had a close community there to witness her final hours? Moreau suggested that the widow Milhet regularly attended Catholic services with her children and "all those over whom she had any authority" (tous ceux sur lesquels elle avait quelque autorité). Perhaps Jeanne was one of these people, an observant Catholic herself.[3]

In Sylvie's case, it is unclear what happened to her once her mistress died in 1795. Perhaps she entered Moreau's household. She would have been seen as a valuable commodity when his family arrived with little capital in the United States. My hunch is that Sylvie was in fact "inherited" by Moreau and his wife.

In Moreau's correspondence with his daughter, a woman named Sylvie appeared several times as a domestic servant in Paris. She was marked as different from the other servants. For example, Aménaïde's son teased her. In a letter to his daughter, Moreau wrote that Edouard was "always droll with Sylvie. He applies himself mostly to a critique of her language. He malignantly asks grandmama [a fellow Kreyòl speaker] from which country is this expression" (toujours drôle avec Sylvie. C'est surtout à la critique de son langage qu'il s'applique. Il demande malignement à grand maman de quel pays est cette expression). It is possible that this was the same Sylvie who migrated from Saint-Domingue to the United States with Madame Milhet; perhaps she had also moved from Louisiana to Saint-Domingue before that with the widow Milhet and Milhet's other enslaved workers. She lived with Moreau and his family in various parts of Europe, and there is no way of knowing if she did so as an enslaved person, as someone receiving wages, or in a nebulous situation as the family's dependent.[4]

Moreau and Louise-Catherine's marriage contract offers clues about Jeanne and her daughter Sophie; it also contains other important information. Recorded on April 9, 1781, the contract was witnessed by the notary Eloi-Michel Grimperel the day after Moreau had been to the same office to make his bequests to Marie-Louise Laplaine and Aménaïde (see Figure 33). As he legally made a settlement on his mixed-race *ménagère* and daughter (even as they had continued ties), he entered into another with his white wife. There is an almost party-like quality about the crowded signature page—a gathering of the Moreau-Milhet relational web as witnesses to the union: men and women, important colonists and functionaries. These signatures flourish, scrawled freely and with individual character across a white page with no justified margins. I juxtapose the people represented by their own signatures with the people whose presence was also contained on another page of this contract, albeit *without* their signatures and involved in a transaction that surely felt distinctly unfestive: Sophie, Marthonne, and Myrtile were "gifts" at this party. They appear listed in closely written, hard-edged text. Notarial records shrink important events in people's lives to words on a page. These words—the styles in which they were written and the format in which they appear—are instructive. Enslaved people of African descent appeared in such contracts in lists and entries that commodified their whole existences into age (most often approximate), market value, and perhaps bodily markings and geographic points of origin. Similar to plantation records, these documents identified people as things, belying a spectrum of relationships between them and the people around them that would consequently be broken, shifted, and reconstituted as they exchanged owners.

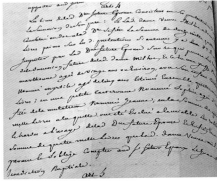

FIGURE 33. Sample pages from the marriage contract of Moreau de Saint-Méry and Louise-Catherine Milhet. "Mariage de Moreau de Saint-Méry et Louise-Catherine Milhet," Apr. 9, 1781, Archives nationales d'outre-mer, Aix-en-Provence, France, Notariat Saint-Domingue, 861, Grimperel, acting notary.

Articles 3 and 4 of the contract listed the goods Moreau and his bride brought to the marriage. Moreau's property was valued at sixty thousand livres (including human property), in addition to "several" (plusieurs) slaves in Fort Royal, Martinique. These enslaved people were not listed by name. The widow Milhet played a direct role in the Moreau family's fortunes, particularly in augmenting the workforce that served them. Although Moreau described her as poor and destitute as a result of her multiple moves between mainland North America and the Caribbean, notarial records show that after Milhet first arrived in Saint-Domingue with her three daughters, she had many assets, including enslaved men and women. She continued doing business in New Orleans, and there is a record of her interactions with people of African descent. In 1781, she gave the couple three people as part of Louise-Catherine's dowry. Jeanne's quadroon daughter Sophie was deeded along with Marthonne, *"une griffe"* in her twenties, and Marthonne's quadroon five-year-old son Myrtile ("avec son enfans carteron *[sic]* nommé Myrtile age de cinq ans").[5]

Importantly, the widow Milhet's assets were also bestowed upon Moreau's close friend, brother-in-law, and collaborator Louis Narcisse Baudry des Lozières when he married Milhet's oldest daughter Catherine in 1777. Their marriage contract included three people as part of Catherine's dowry: an eighteen-year-old mulâtresse named Catherine, a twelve-year old mulâtre named Jean-Baptiste, and Fary [unclear], a nine-month-old girl. Catherine and Jean-Baptiste were born in Louisiana and had likely moved to Saint-Domingue with the Milhet family.

These three people might have eventually shared living and working spaces with the many other people that Baudry and his wife owned, people whose lives I discuss in Chapters 6 and 7.[6]

In contrast to the brevity of the news that "Jeanne, my mother-in-law's mulâtresse, was dead," this entry expands Jeanne's world. It provides a glimpse of the enslaved women, men, and children (infant to adolescent) who migrated and shared households with the Moreaus and their in-laws in Louisiana, Saint-Domingue, Martinique, Philadelphia, and likely Paris and Parma.

K

Kinson, Aloou (a.k.a. Jean Jasmin)

ALOOU KINSON, *born on the Gold Coast of Africa in 1714*, was purchased there by Captain Bertrand and sold in Le Cap. M. Thoumaseau, a mason, bought him and taught him his trade. He was baptized . . . and received the name *Jean Jasmin*. . . . Jasmin . . . because of his intelligence and his conduct, [was] freed [by Thoumaseau] on November 10, 1741. . . .

Filled with a profound veneration for Jasmin, in 1788 I dared to promise him that I would obtain express authorization for his hospice from the minister. I cannot remember, without tears of tenderness still close to escaping from my eyes, the joy that he felt.

ALOOU KINSON, *né à la Côte d'Or, en Afrique, en 1714*, y fut acheté par le capitaine Bertrand et vendu au Cap. M. Thoumaseau, maçon, l'acheta et lui enseigna son métier. Il fut baptisé . . . et reçut le nom de *Jean Jasmin*. . . . Jasmin. . . . mérita par son intelligence et sa conduite, que celui-ci l'affranchit dès le 10 Novembre 1741. . . .

Rempli d'une vénération profonde pour Jasmin, j'osai lui promettre, en 1788, que j'obtiendrais du ministère une autorisation expresse pour son hospice. Je ne puis me rappeler, sans que des larmes d'attendrissement en soient encore près de s'échapper de mes yeux, de la joie qu'il en eut.[7]

This commentary documents the efforts made by free people of color to support their community. Many adults and children, *"destitute free people of color" (les pauvres gens de couleur libres)*, were sheltered and fed owing to the care of Jasmin and his wife Catherine, a "négresse de Foeda." The work done at the hospice was in part provided by enslaved labor; Jean-Louis, one of Jasmin Thoumaseau's laborers, ran away from them. Moreau and the Cercle des Philadelphes publicly sponsored Jasmin's hospice, but their attempts to have it officially authorized ultimately caused an uproar. Decrying public prejudice, Moreau addressed himself directly to "Virtuous Jasmin!" (Vertueux Jasmin!), telling him not to lose hope. He wrote: "Console yourself; a voice consecrated to truth, to the panegyric of the good and the blame of the wicked will have published your virtues. This voice will be heard; and a thousand others will become its echo" (console-toi; une voix consacrée à la vérité, au panégyrique des bons et au blâme des méchans aura publié tes vertus. Elle sera entendue cette voix; et mille autres en deviendront les échos).[8]

The proposed ventriloquism of these interactions is ear-catching. Moreau, public bard untouched by prejudice and a "voice consecrated to truth," would speak *for* Jasmin. The very laws that Moreau helped to enforce to keep this man's word and deeds undervalued, even criminalized, resulted in a situation where Jasmin had few choices but to allow Moreau to serve as intercessor. His narrative about Jasmin served as a reflection about Moreau's own good deed. Ultimately, it was not solely the memory of Jasmin's virtues that brought tears to Moreau's eyes years later; it was the recollection of Jasmin's gratitude toward him for proposing that the hospice receive official recognition. His sponsorship of Jasmin allowed Moreau to see himself not only as a benefactor of free people of color but also as a benefactor for this African man whose "intelligence and conduct" earned him his freedom.

Laplaine, Marie-Louise

To compensate Marie-Louise, called La Plaine, a free mulâtresse, "for her care of the home of the benefactor, during the span of five years that she resided in his home," as well as to her daughter, the quadroon Jeanne-Louise, called Aménaïde, Moreau de Saint-Méry leaves the following gifts:

    —a Black woman, Félicité, 25 years old;

    —a young Black girl, Rosine, 12 years old, Senegalese;

    —and the sum of 2,000 livres that should be used to buy another
       Black woman.

The ownership of the three slaves is attributed to the daughter, Jeanne-Louise, but it is the mother Marie-Louise who will have the usufruct, that is to say that she will be able to use them without, however, being able to sell them.

Pour récompenser Marie-Louise, dite La Plaine, mulâtresse libre, "de ses soins pour le ménage du donateur [Moreau de Saint Mery] pendant l'espace de cinq ans qu'elle a résidée chez lui," Moreau lui fait, ainsi qu'à sa fille, la quarteronne Jeanne-Louise, dite Aménaïde, les dons suivants:

—une négresse, Félicite, 25 ans;

—une négrite, Rosine, 12 ans, sénégalaise;

—et une somme de 2,000 livres qui doit être employée à l'achat
d'une autre négresse.

La propriété des trois esclaves est attribuée à la fille, Jeanne-Louise, mais c'est la mère Marie-Louise qui en aura l'usufruit, c'est-à-dire qu'elle pourra les utilizer sans cependant pouvoir les vendre.[9]

In a 1781 notarial record, a Black enslaved woman named Felicité and an adolescent child named Rosine were bequeathed to Marie-Louise Laplaine and her quadroon daughter Aménaïde. Laplaine worked as Moreau's housekeeper *(ménagère)* for five years. In addition, Moreau pledged money toward the purchase of another person, whom he specified must also be a woman. Archives are full of outright silences, but they also hold countless pieces of illegible information and bad penmanship. This bequest alone included five stipulations about the management of the gifts that would no doubt shed more light on how Moreau assessed his relationship with Laplaine; they are difficult to decipher. Another record shows that Laplaine had herself been enslaved until 1766.[10]

Marie-Louise Laplaine began living with Moreau in 1776. A contemporary observer noted that it was "quite the fashion here for everyone to have one of these princess[e]s to live with as housekeepers or nurses," and one of the most well-known published accounts of such a relationship is chronicled in John Gabriel Stedman's relationship with the Black woman Joanna in 1770s Surinam.[11] Ménagères, notes historian Stewart R. King, "were often free blacks and generally came from the lower social and economic ranks of free colored society."[12] In addition to employing Laplaine beginning in 1776, Moreau also purchased "two Black men from the merchant house Stanislaus Foache and Company" (deux Nègres que j'ai achetés de la Maison Stanislaus Foache et Compagnie) with the first profits from his legal practice that year. A year after his arrival in Saint-Domingue, he was thus living with a mixed-race woman and was the owner of several enslaved people who would have been in Laplaine's orbit, potentially working under her command. She would presumably have exercised some contractual economic rights to act on his behalf, particularly during a period in 1779 when Moreau was ill and close to death and she oversaw his care.[13]

Under what circumstances did Laplaine become free? What did she think of Moreau as an employer and lover? Did she maintain a relationship (physical, affective) with him after his marriage to Louise-Catherine Milhet? They were certainly involved in transactions concerning future arrangements for Aménaïde. In a 1788 bequest, Laplaine gave her daughter "a roughly eighteen-year-old creole Black woman named Agathe, Martinican" (une négresse créole nomée Agathe Martiniquaise agée d'environ dix-huit ans). Moreau accepted this gift in his capacity as "guardian" (tuteur) for Aménaïde, an arrangement that was reached in 1782, when Aménaïde was four. Because Agathe was born in Martinique, it is possible that at some earlier time Moreau had transferred ownership of her to Marie-Louise Laplaine; he owned women and men in his native Martinique. Three months after this bequest, Laplaine moved into a new lodging: a multi-room apartment with a kitchen and a courtyard. The contract lists her as the renter. Were Aménaïde and her mother close? Aménaïde did bear her mother's middle name, Louise, a reminder of their connection. Once Aménaïde went to Europe as a young child, what eventually became of Laplaine? Did she survive the course of the Haitian Revolution? Did she ever see her daughter again?[14]

These questions demand answers that may never be forthcoming. A biographical trajectory would be more satisfying than the isolated scraps and glimpses of her life that were preserved in state records. What we do know is that in 1781 Laplaine was relatively well set up. Not only did she have control, through her three-year-old daughter, of two enslaved women, she might have already been commanding the labor of others. In the near future, she would own Agathe and another unidentified enslaved woman. Laplaine's domestic space thus included many women and girls of African descent. Moreau's various households did as well. There are at least nine that we know of, two of whom he helped acquire their own human property.

Little Girl (Petite fille)

[I freed] in 1780, a little girl, who died shortly thereafter. In doing this, I satisfied my heart.

[J'ai affranchi] en 1780, une petite fille, morte presque aussi-tôt. J'ai en cela acquitté mon Coeur.[15]

This anonymous little girl died free. She did not live long enough to enjoy her freedom. Her existence in Moreau's orbit is only documented through two sentences. The fragment is equal parts an opening and a foreclosure. What circumstances surrounding this acquittal of the "heart" would have compelled him to free her? Could she have been his daughter, born to an enslaved woman with whom he had a relationship while involved with Marie-Louise Laplaine in Saint-Domingue? What was his obligation to this child and perhaps to one of the child's still-living loved ones whose good opinion he desired to maintain? Ten years after her death she was on his mind, enough that he claimed the justness of his act in a publication proclaiming his proslavery credentials. She was mourned.

M

Maison de Santé

Ever since Africa has given cultivators to the American colonies, the hearts of those who have not suffocated their natural sentiments, have been upset to see the abandoned state in which the sick Africans brought by the ships were left. Crammed into tiny storerooms, kept in the middle of the city where the air is not calculated to restore them, only too often made into the scene of cruel epidemics, they offered the heartbreaking spectacle of humanity disregarded by greed. A young surgeon conceived the project of a hospice, where careful care would save these precious beings, and he set out to enrich himself by doing good. . . .

The setting of this hospital, called the *House of Health,* is fortunate in its elevation. . . .

When one reflects that without this House of Health, thousands of beings would have died from the sea scurvy with which they were attacked, when they only needed pure air and healthy food, one blesses M. Durand's idea, one applauds his zeal and his sensibility, and upon contemplating his hospice and the pretty garden which forms part of it, the heart feels tender and sings his praise.

Depuis que l'Afrique donne des cultivateurs aux colonies américaines, les coeurs, où l'on n'avait pas étouffé les sentimens de la nature, étaient soulevés de voir l'état d'abandon où étaient laissés les Africains malades, apportés par les navires. Entassés dans des magasins très-resserrés, gardés au sein de la ville, dont l'air n'était pas propre à les rétablir, et qu'ils n'ont rendue que trop souvent le théâtre d'épidémies cruelles, ils y offraient le spectacle déchirant de l'humanité méconnue par la cupidité. Un jeune chirurgien. . . . conçut le projet d'un hospice, ou des soins assidus pourraient conserver des êtres précieux, et il entreprit de s'enrichir en faisant le bien. . . .

L'exposition de cet hôpital, appelé *Maison de Santé*, est heureuse par son élévation. . . .

Quand on réfléchit que sans cette maison de santé, il aurait péri plu-sieurs milliers d'êtres, qui pour être sauvés du scorbut de mer dont ils sont attaqués, n'ont eu besoin que d'un air pur et d'une nourriture saine, on bénit l'idée de M. Durand, on applaudit à son zèle, à sa sensibilité, et en contemplant son hospice et le joli jardin quie en fait partie, le coer s'atten-drit et prononce son éloge.[16]

If one were to read this entry alone, it would be possible to imagine a philan-thropic and compassionate aspect to Moreau's beliefs. His comments suggest an attunement to the suffering of others and highlight his self-presentation as a man of sensibility, an enlightened and paternalistic slaveholder. What he termed "nat-ural sentiments," those that should not be "suffocated" by commercial interests, included sympathy for one's fellow human beings. The lives of these sick women, children, and men were valued, even "precious" (précieux), and their abject con-dition was to be pitied. In this entry, they were imagined as people, however mute, rather than property marks in an account book or a captain's log. Moreau admired the savvy M. Durand, who devised a way to serve the public good while still turning a profit through their care. Durand's solution to the problem of how to address the plight of the thousands of people who came to be known callously as "refuse" slaves was presented as a prime example of how fellow feeling and entrepreneurial spirit could benefit society. Refuse—leftover, unwanted, too ill to be purchased, left for dead—transformed into worth.[17]

Of course, whose public good was being served? I am struck by the dead end of Moreau's sentimentalist logic, seen clearly in his spatialist imagery. He imagined enclosed, airless urban rooms (a corollary to the suffocation of morality) versus a garden setting in breezy, mountainous surroundings. The "precious beings" held in the former had access to poor-quality food and were surrounded by fetidness and rampant disease. His comparison of the prison to the hospice (each, in fact, a form of prison) eschewed the logical comparison of the airless storeroom in town to what had until recently been the dungeons of a slave fort or the hold of a ship. People were sickened precisely because of the conditions under which they were captive before and during the Middle Passage. Moreau knew this, yet he rejoiced that these people could be "saved." Durand attempted to keep them alive so that they could die at a more allegedly convenient time, once they were fit for purchase and had made someone a profit. If one believes that Moreau might have cared for their plight, even sincerely, he also knew the hardships awaiting them in the event of their recovery. His public performance of sentiment is derisory and offers no way of assessing the feelings and trauma of the enslaved themselves.[18]

Marguerite Rebecca

I want to speak of Albinos, or White-Blacks as they are called in the colony. . . .

Marguerite Rebecca [born in 1767] is sweet and hard-working. She reads, writes (I have saved some of her writing), does calculations well, and has in her speech and her countenance the assurance of a person of her status. She sews beautifully (I have worn shirts made by her), she is gay and seems to be different from other Blacks only due to her physical features. . . .

. . . Her skin, animated by the great heat, also blushes due to the embarrassment she experiences when she is observed. . . .

. . . Her hair is a kind of curly wool, agreeable enough when touched.

Je veux parler des *Albinos* ou *Nègres-blancs*, comme on les nomme dans la Colonie. . . .

Marguerite Rebecca est douce et laborieuse. Elle lit, écrit (je conserve de son écriture), et chiffre bien, et a dans ses discours et dans sa contenance, l'assurance d'une personne de son état. Elle cout à merveille (j'ai porté des chemises faites par elle), elle est gaie, et paraît ne différer des autres nègres que par les traits physiques. . . .

. . . Sa peau que la grande chaleur anime, se colore aussi par l'effet d'une espèce de honte qu'elle éprouve lorsqu'elle est considérée. . . .

. . . Ses cheveux sont une espèce de laine d'un blond roux, assez agréable au toucher.[19]

Marguerite Rebecca was a sixteen-year-old Black albino woman. Interviewing her in 1783, Moreau documented that she could read, write, cipher, and sew. What did Marguerite like to read, and to what use did she put her ability to do mathematics? What things did she write about, and for what reason might Moreau have kept her handwriting? This detailed discussion of her skin, eyes, stature, and "gay" personality also included observations about the hair on her head. He was sure to mention that her eyebrows and pubic and armpit hair were of the same texture and color, in addition to providing the information that she had recently started menstruating and had survived both smallpox and measles. Moreau's scientific inquiries required having complete access to Marguerite and united his reading knowledge of albinism with empirical knowledge gained by touch, sight, and sound. The intimacy of wearing her handiwork, touching her hair, reading her writing, and being close enough to see her "blush" (se colore) when examined is indicative of how Moreau studied Black bodies, often at close quarters, as a means of advancing his intellectual career. And it is clear that these examinations brought him pleasure.

The details about his interactions with Marguerite are saturated in prurience; one does not have to look hard to see this side of Moreau and his fellow *colons'* work. Allusions to the sexualized nature of the labor of enslaved women, free women of color, and white women is a through line in Moreau's anecdotes, whether discussing issues such as concubinage, prostitution, or marriage in Spanish Santo Domingo, Philadelphia, Cap Français, or Italy.

Moreau de Saint-Méry

We will completely reveal this colonist, whose facial features and skin color raise suspicion of a double betrayal: that of the rights of man and of his brothers *properly speaking.*

*If African blood does not run in *M. Moreau*'s veins, which is problematic, we can only assume that he landed in the colonies, in the middle of the prejudice he wants to defend, and not being known to anyone, judged the rank to which he would be forced to descend; for by what external signs did he come from an origin other than that common to all mulâtres?

Nous dévoilerons complètement ce colon, dont les traits du visage et la couleur de la peau font soupçonner une double trahison: celle des droits de l'homme et de ses frères *proprement dits.*

*Si le sang africain ne coule pas dans les veines de *M. Moreau*, ce qui est problématique, il ne faut que le supposer débarqué dans les colonies,

au milieu du préjugé qu'il veut défendre, et n'étant connu de personne,
pour juger du rang où on le forcerait de descendre; car par quels signes
extérieurs provenait-il une autre origine que celle commune à tous les
mulâtres?[20]

Moreau, revealed. Moreau, unveiled. Was he of African descent? While commentators often cite his familial ties to Joséphine de Beauharnais, the Martinican-born wife of Napoleon Bonaparte, they rarely assert that an enslaved or free Black ancestor might have been part of the family tree. Moreau's propensity to "read" physiognomy for hidden traces of Black ancestry is echoed in these accusations about his own supposed skin color and facial traits. I have seen no documentation of how he responded to such claims. Yet he must have known of them. The accusations, born of orally disseminated rumors and circulated in print in France for all to see, would undoubtedly have gotten under his skin, disturbed his state of mind.

The work of historian Florence Gauthier, which chronicles the 1789–1791 debates in the French National Assembly concerning the granting of rights to free people of color in the French colonies, is an exception to the lack of scholarly commentary on Moreau's racial ancestry. Comments such as "Moreau, mixed race himself" (Moreau métissé lui-même) or "Moreau was able to hide his mixed ancestry, which evidently was not visible" (Moreau a pu cacher son métissage que se trouvait être peu visible) assume that he was indeed of African descent. She categorizes him as a "néo-blanc," literally, a "new white." Jean Casimir concurs, referring to him as "of African descent" and a "mixed-race colonist who lived as a white person by hiding his *métissage.*" Gauthier does not speculate about the possible source of this ancestry or provide corroborating evidence. However, her claims are likely based on accusations such as those she cites above by several men of color *(gens de couleur)* who were involved in a vitriolic pamphlet war in Paris about the feasibility of enforcing the Declaration of the Rights of Man in the colonies. Gauthier sets up Moreau and the mixed-race Julien Raimond as the principal antagonists in this public debate. Raimond, from Aquin, in the southern part of Saint-Domingue, was a wealthy mixed-race planter and slaveowner himself. He and his other self-styled *colons américains* collaborated with the Society of the Friends of the Blacks (Société des Amis des noirs), led by French revolutionaries such as Jacques-Pierre Brissot de Warville and Henri Grégoire (Abbé Grégoire), to fight for civil and economic rights on behalf of free people of color.[21]

These rumors offer unverifiable commentary, both gossip and an indication of an important moment when Caribbean-based local knowledge of family relations and on-the-ground suspicions traveled to the French metropole, where they were disseminated in writing. At stake in considering this commentary is that multiple contemporaries identified him as one of their own, a fellow slave-owner of African descent, "brothers properly speaking." Evidence and recorded testimony concerning how people of African descent responded to Moreau and his work is invaluable, even if its truth value is difficult to confirm. What might they have known that modern-day historians do not? Was this a case of what Moreau would have considered invented slander for political gain or a strategic surfacing of facts? In his time, the intimation of his blackness was wielded as a stick by both Blacks and whites who distrusted him and opposed his politics. In Moreau's prolific autobiographical accounts of his life (the *Mémoire justificatif,* correspondence, personal diaries), there is a gap, an absence, a predictable silence in the archive about any African ancestry. He self-identified as white, with all of the attendant privileges that his own professional career made sure whiteness would continue to afford.

Would this book read differently if Moreau were indeed of remote African descent? Would a reader find his public and private persona more disturbing? Such a reading would force a discussion of class to the fore, a reminder not to essentialize blackness as inherently oppositional in the colonial regime. That we still wonder if Moreau had African ancestors, that we cannot dismiss the relative value of his racial identity in light of his unmistakable reactionary politics, shows how beholden we remain to the racist world that he helped to create and defend. In Moreau's era, some people of African descent belonged to the master class, even though they were discriminated against for their ancestry. Whether or not Moreau was himself part of this group, his oeuvre prioritized a discussion of color over class that continued to orient discussions of postrevolutionary Haiti. Casimir notes: "Moreau de Saint-Méry left another sad legacy in Haitian society, through the mediation of the historians of Pétion's republic. His work obscured the interpretation of social relations before and after 1804 by pointing it in the direction of the color question. This maneuver obfuscates the much more serious damage caused by the monopolization of private property and the tacit acceptance of the right of conquest on the part of the colonizers and their direct descendants." The struggle to destroy slavery was a class war as well as a racial war. In the aftermath of French defeat in Saint-Domingue, this struggle spoke to the manifestion of color ideologies that surfaced in conflicts between the northern Kingdom of Hayti and the Republic to the south. These struggles continued to prioritize the interests of the few rather than to create true economic and social equality for the masses of the formerly enslaved.[22]

Mulâtresses and Martonne

Paris, February 1787

I left Paris the 9th with my wife, my son, my *mulâtresse* and her daughter.

Je quittai Paris le 9 avec ma femme, mon fils, ma mulâtresse et sa fille.[23]

This entry confirms that Moreau lived in France with people of African descent; it is not clear how many might have come and gone with him during his multiple sojourns in the metropole. On a brief return research trip to the Caribbean in 1787–1788, this anonymous mixed-race woman and her daughter returned with his immediate family. They were likely enslaved. Who and how old were they, and how might they have integrated into the Parisian capital? Who was the father of this mulâtresse's daughter? Was she conceived in France or the Caribbean? The fragment invites conjecture.

It is possible that this woman's name was Martonne. She entered into the public record in a remarkable way. As we have seen, from 1789 to 1792 Moreau was engaged in a strident pamphlet war with several people of color residing in France. Writing on behalf of the planter lobby interest group called the Club Massiac, Moreau defended the rights of colonists to make their own laws and publicly advocated against free people of color having equal rights. Two of his publications, *Considérations présentées aux vrais amis du repos . . . à l'occasion des nouveaux mouvemens de quelques soi-disant Amis-des-noirs* (1791) and *Observations d'un habitant des colonies, sur le mémoire en faveur des gens de couleur . . . adressé à l'Assemblée nationale* (1789), epitomize the sarcastic invective he directed against his political enemies. This invective included supposedly horrifying accusations that the Société des citoyens de couleur even counted a "woman . . . some minors, some domestics, [and] some enslaved people" (une femme . . . des mineurs, des domestiques, des esclaves) among its membership. In a response to allegations published in the Parisian papers in April 1790, Moreau wrote:

Those who have printed, for example, that I was engaged in slave trafficking in France, ask Marton, my mulâtresse, who left my home on April 14, 1789, if I sold her to someone. She lives at No. 59 Cléri Street. If one were to go to the Vendôme, one would find a declaration, dated November 16th, that proves if I am a hated master and if people of color prefer to live in France rather than the colonies.

Que ceux qui ont imprimé, par exemple, que je faisais en France, un trafic d'esclaves, demandent à Marton, ma mulâtresse, sortie de chez moi le

14 avril 1789, si je l'ai vendue à quelqu'un. Elle loge rue de Cléri, no. 59.
Qu'on aille à la section de Vendôme, on y trouvera, à la date du 16 novembre, une déclaration qui prouve, et si je suis un maître haï, et si les gens
de c[o]uleur préfèrent la France aux Colonies.

The "ceux" in this case was none other than Vincent Ogé, the free man of color
who went on to lead an armed revolt against white planters in Saint-Domingue
just months after he published this allegation. The story of Ogé, who was tor-
tured at the wheel and publicly executed, is one that most scholars, from the eighteenth century to the present, highlight as a formative moment in what would
become the Haitian Revolution.[24]

Ogé's accusation is worth citing in its entirety. In a pro-revolutionary periodical called *Le Patriote français,* he wrote:

> I denounce a fact that will revolt you, Mr. Patriot, you who defend the
> cause of the Blacks, and that will doubtless revolt all good patriots and
> enlightened men. M. Moreau de Saint-Méry has sold in these last days,
> to the Chevalier de Rodouin, a mulâtresse, who has lived for the last two
> and a half years in Paris. This sale, contrary to all of the rules that prohibit
> this infamous traffic in France . . . will appear even more frightful when
> considering the moment in which it was done and the man who did it. If
> the sale was not consummated, it is because M. Redouin could not pay.
> *Signed,* OGÉ jeune.

> Je vous dénonce, monsieur le Patriote, un fait qui vous révoltera, vous qui
> défendez la cause des noirs, et qui révoltera sans doute tous les bons pa-
> triotes et les hommes éclairés. M. Moreau de Saint-Méry a vendu ces jours
> derniers, à M. le chevalier de Rodouin, une mulâtresse, qui vit depuis deux
> ans et demi à Paris. Cette vente, contraire à tous les réglemens qui prohi-
> baient en France ce trafic infâme . . . vous paraîtra sans doute encore plus
> affreuse, en considèrant le moment où elle est faite, et l'homme qui l'a fait.
> Si le marché n'a pas été consommé, c'est que M. de Redouin n'a pas pu payer.
> *Signé,* OGÉ jeune.

The information contained herein is detailed and personal: the length of the stay
of the woman who was sold or almost sold, the buyer's name, and the state of
his finances. Moreau was very active in the early days of the French Revolution,
serving as a delegate for Martinique in the National Assembly and gaining fame
as president of the electors of Paris in the days immediately following the July 14
attack on the Bastille. Suggestions that he was an advocate of liberty, while trafficking people in the nation's capital, were newsworthy.[25]

Ogé's claims about Moreau's bad character, based on his alleged transactions in human flesh, were corroborated by other free people of color, including the aforementioned colons américains. Moreau attacked them anonymously in his *Observations;* they determined his identity and decried his role as part of the white colonists' "criminal coalition" (coalition criminelle) against them. They wrote: "A Colonist who we have seen glorified among you during the most perilous moments of the revolution," a colonist for whom "the principles of liberty that he appeared to profess have given way to principles of scorn and the most absolute despotism," that colonist "must be revealed; he is Moreau de Saint-Méry." This revelation, far from damaging his credentials with his fellow colonists in Paris, would have solidified his position as their ally.[26]

Martonne appeared in the guise of a satirical print regarding these same debates about the rights of free people of color (Figure 34). Part of a much larger tableau that included many well-known figures, this detail of the left portion of the image depicts Moreau reading a long scroll. One of the captions explaining the unfolding farce (no. 9) quotes Moreau, "Demandez à ma mulatresse rue de Clery No 22 *[sic],*" a direct reference to the public print conflict. A caricatured Black woman, presumably his "mulâtresse," leans over a barrel in front of him, her posterior close to his genitals in a sexualized posture as she gazes on the scene wonderingly. Clothed, but barefoot and well-muscled, she is in less obvious distress than the bound and crouching enslaved person being manhandled to her right. It is telling that Moreau's public image was tethered to this Black woman's presence. Even in the metropole, his stature was connected—propped up and undercut—by assumptions about Black people's bodies and minds.[27]

This story, presented both textually and visually, has Moreau and other male planters of color and politicians as the protagonists. What of Martonne, the anonymous woman who was evoked as a pawn in this debate? Moreau claimed that he did not sell her but that she was living nearby, at No. 59 Rue de Cléri to be exact. The circumstances under which she was making a living are unknown. On April 4, 1789, however, Moreau's wife petitioned the Table de Marbre for Martonne's freedom, acknowledging the principle that there were no slaves in France. The court passed a sentence of freedom on April 6, 1789. Documents list Martonne as a thirty-four-year-old mulâtresse from Louisiana and state that she "arrived in France with Mr. and Mrs. Moreau de Saint-Méry on July 2, 1788 . . . in Havre de Grace, although they did not make a declaration of her presence" as required by the 1777 Police des Noirs. Was her manumission in part inspired by the publicity attached to her presence and potential sale in Paris? Ten months had elapsed since her arrival in France. Did Moreau's involvement in

FIGURE 34. Depiction of Martonne and Moreau de Saint-Méry. Detail
from *Discussion sur les hommes de couleur.* Circa 1791. Courtesy of the
Bibliothèque nationale de France.

metropolitan debates about the rights of free people of color have the unexpected
result of helping Martonne manage her own path as a freed woman?[28]

This Martonne could have been the same woman who had previously left
France in 1787 with Moreau's family and her own daughter. The daughter's
whereabouts by 1789 are uncertain; she could have remained in the Caribbean
(Martinique or Saint-Domingue) when Moreau and his family returned to both
islands. It is possible that she is the same Mart(h)onne that Moreau's mother-
in-law gave to him and his new bride as a wedding dower.[29] The Milhet family's
long residence in Louisiana suggests that Mart(h)onne could have accompanied the family when they left Louisiana for Saint-Domingue. At the time she
was gifted to the newlyweds, she had a five-year-old son named Myrtile. His

whereabouts and the whereabouts of her daughter, if Martonne was indeed the same mulâtresse who left Paris with the Moreau family in 1787, are unknown. These absences suggest that even though she was eventually freed, her children might not have been.

Moreau directed his readers to a depot where Martonne's testimony could be found. *Look there to see if I am really a hated master! Look there to see if slaves really prefer life in Europe to that in the colonies!* This firsthand testimony would be valuable, of course, as it would ostensibly present the perspective of the person most directly affected by these transactions. But that Moreau insisted people read Martonne's statement suggests, in part, what we might find. Certainly it did not complain about him, decry his inhumanity, accuse him of unwanted sexual advances. He might have very well been innocent of all of these aggressions. However, it would be a stretch to believe Moreau each time he claimed that people he enslaved loved him more than they loved themselves. While he counted being a "bon maître" as one of his many virtues, I have no corroborating evidence.[30]

I linger on this example because it goes to the heart of the shadow relationships that this *Encyclopédie noire* attempts to illuminate. Martonne and the other mulâtresses and négresses that Moreau enslaved have offered no corroborations or accusations of any nature in these pages. They were real women, appearing in a few lines in Moreau's massive oeuvre. Moreau could have been a kind, even generous master so far as masters go. Undoubtedly, these women themselves would have been able to tell many stories that differentiated between the "good" and the "bad" owners that they and their families and acquaintances had to deal with while enslaved. I am not collapsing all owners together, and which owner one had could absolutely mean the difference between life and death, a modicum of independence, or constant harassment.[31] I cannot say with any certitude whether Moreau would have seen Martonne and the others, many very young, as humans with their own needs, rights, and convictions. Neither the law nor social customs in Moreau's world would have made this customary. We can acknowledge, as Lisa Lowe suggests, that "the concept of freedom is not self-evident; it was and is both fragile and contested in relation to the varieties of communities it affirms, disciplines, and divides." I believe it likely that, from the perspective of those enslaved, the best master was no master at all. The search for their own words, their own opinions, their own thoughts is destined to yield more questions than answers.[32]

Yet these fragments about Martonne place her in a Parisian neighborhood during the unfolding of the French Revolution. Friends would likely have told her that she was mentioned in local newspapers; if she could read, she might have discovered this herself. She would have been an adolescent when the Spanish arrived to take over her Louisiana place of birth and had memories of the resulting forced migration to Saint-Domingue. She eventually would have had a community in Saint-Domingue, too, and moved with or without them between there and France. She might have stayed in Paris during the Terror once freed from the Moreau-Milhet family. Or perhaps she was eventually anxious to return to the French colonies if she knew that the Law of February 4, 1794, coupled with a sustained fight for freedom on the ground at "home," had resulted in the manumission of her loved ones.

A story about the Age of Revolutions with Martonne as its focus centers women. It centers transatlantic and inter-American movement, forced migration, and separation from kin. Her view of the upheavals of the eighteenth century was based in the Black communities of Paris who contended with their former and current masters and the Police des Noirs, a law designed to surveil and impede their movement in France. Her perspective would undercut nation-bound stories of how revolution was experienced. Had she not lived through the *longue durée* of multiple revolutions unfolding in Louisiana, Saint-Domingue, Paris?

Mulâtresses, part II

FIGURE 35. *Mulâtresse écriteau.* By Luz Sandoval. 2020.

Moreau compiled another source that vividly recorded the voices and behavior of mixed-race women. Herein is a record of people talking back, of their listening and not liking what was being said, of their being impudent and combative in words and deeds. An entry in his compendium *Loix et constitutions* documented a legal decision from June 9, 1780, in which Marie-Anne and Françoise, two *mulâtresses libres,* were convicted in absentia for verbally insulting and getting into a physical altercation with a white woman. The judgment made note of at least some of their alleged words. Françoise cried "Houra" at Madame Castillon, and when challenged—*are you talking to me?*—Françoise replied, *"Oui, femme à soldat,"* at which point Castillon threw rocks at her, and a brawl ensued. The underlying cause for this altercation went unremarked.[33]

Marie-Anne and Françoise were sentenced to be attached to a post bearing a signboard with the words "MULATRESSE INSOLENTE ENVERS LES FEMMES BLANCHES" in Cap Français's busy Place de Clugny market (Figure 35). It would have been someone's job to fashion signboards, or *écriteaux,* such as these, a material product underpinning the legal codes of white rule. In addition, the women were fined, and the court specified that Marie-Anne would even be forced "to sell her own male and female slaves" to cover the cost if necessary. Different in tenor than the scripted affirmations that were likely in Martonne's declaration, these unpredictable, uncontrolled words demanded physical, psychological, and economic punishment.[34]

N

Négresses

The day before yesterday Praxelle [Moreau's house servant in Paris] brought in two Black women from Martinique with whom I played during my childhood. Great joy on all our parts. They are very amazed by my memory of things and people from my country.

Praxelle m'a amené avant hier deux négresses de la Martinique avec lesquelles je jouais dans mon enfance. Grande joie de part et d'autre. Elles sont bien étonnées de mon ressouvenir et des choses et personnes de mon pays.[35]

At the time his two childhood playmates visited him in August 1809, Moreau had settled in Paris permanently. The circumstances under which they left Martinique and traveled to France are intriguing. Had they been enslaved when Moreau played with them as a child? What might have been the substance of their conversation that warm summer day after they chose to locate and visit Moreau after almost fifty years? Did his memory of them require prompting? Were they in search of financial aid or a job reference? Did this encounter meet their expectations, and was it ever repeated? The record of these two women is fleeting. Yet they inhabited common physical and psychological space with Moreau. Their lives overlapped as childhood playmates and as adults, briefly, as they met far from home in a Parisian neighborhood. Though they remain un-named, they would have had a *longue durée* impression of the man.

This entry is a short one. Much like the French *Encyclopédie,* Moreau's "Réper-toire des notions colonials" and my own contain entries of varied lengths. Yet the word *négresse* appeared hundreds, if not thousands, of times in Moreau's oeuvre. *Négresses* is a term, a category, an epistemological worldview that undergirded a significant percentage of Moreau's work. Black women: actual people, a trope, persons subject to legal codes, the focus of unwanted advances, entrepreneurs, ex-pert planners. The brevity of the entry belies the expansiveness of their presence.

Nourrices

Among the slaves that belong to me in this moment [1790], there is one whom I render the continual object of my good deeds. She is the wet nurse of my son. And if I ever had any cause to complain about her, I would free her to punish her.

Parmi les Esclaves qui m'appartiennent en ce moment, il en est une que je rends l'objet continuel de mes bienfaits, c'est la nourrice de mon Fils; et s'il était possible que j'eusse jamais à m'en plaindre, je l'affranchirais pour la punir.[36]

An anonymous enslaved woman nursed Moreau's son, just as a woman named Angélique nursed his daughter. In Moreau's eyes, the former was so devoted to the family that she would never desire her own freedom. Moreau in fact inter-preted the very idea of emancipating her as equivalent—importantly in his mind and in her mind—to punishment. The unnamed "good deeds" he rendered her—extra food, a comfortable place to sleep, time with her own nursing child?—were imagined as providing such favorable circumstances that freedom would be un-desirable. As was the case with the example of his male domestique of sixteen years, Moreau saw himself as a benevolent master who inspired deep loyalty and affection. The existence of this supposed affection was used not only as evidence of his own good character but also as proof that the people serving him, and by ex-tension the enslaved more generally, did not wish for liberty when treated "well."

Elsewhere Moreau noted that although white women should ideally nurse their own children, their "weak" (faibles) constitutions made it much more com-mon for them to be "reduced to soliciting from an enslaved woman the sacrifice of her blood in order to preserve the being to whom they could only give life. But their children are nourished before their eyes, and they dispute their caresses with the wet nurse" (réduites à solliciter d'une esclave le sacrifice de son sang pour conserver l'être à qui elles n'ont pu donner que la vie. Mais leurs enfants sont nourris sous leurs yeux, elles disputent leurs caresses à la nourrice). The subject herein is white women and their parenting choices (or lack thereof), and Moreau was entering into a lively debate about the desirability of breast-feeding one's own children; he implied that though they perhaps wished to feed their children, they often could not.[37] Moreau conjured an image of white and Black women almost fighting over the affections of the infants in question. This was not the first time he entered into conversations about breast-feeding. When in Philadelphia, for example, he offered his services as a lactation consultant to an ailing, but reluctant, neighbor suffering from painful cracked nipples. This woman was so embarrassed by the encounters that she never spoke to him again.[38]

Extensive scholarship concerning the use of wet nurses, however, shows that "of all enslaved people, wetnurses probably experienced the most direct forms of control of their mobility and social relations, and slaveholders often prevented them from living with their own families and caring for their own children during this crucial phase of their lives."[39] Baron de Vastey, chronicler of the savage practices of white colonists, included many tales of nourrices who found themselves in physical danger, their proximity to their masters a liability.[40] Who were this anonymous woman's children, children who might also have belonged to Moreau because the condition of enslavement was passed through the mother's status? If she did indeed have children who survived and lived in her care, would they have been playmates of Moreau de Saint-Méry *fils*?

When speaking in the abstract about white motherhood, Moreau suggested that a wet nurse was "almost always freed for the price of this good deed" ([la nourrice] qu'on affranchit presque toujours pour prix de ce bienfait). At the time he wrote of this anonymous woman, his son would have been eight years old, and the custom of freeing a woman for these services had still not led him to do so. I do not know any circumstances about her life after 1790. Moreau might have freed, sold, or perhaps lost track of her during the convulsions that would soon rack the island. Or, put differently, she could have taken advantage of his permanent absence from Cap Français after 1788 to try to negotiate her own future in what would have been the dangerous, ever-shifting political and social dynamics of northern Saint-Domingue.[41]

An eighteenth-century French portrait of another anonymous nourrice from Saint-Domingue—although we do not know who she was or her decisions and thoughts about her life circumstances—is instructive (Figure 36).[42] She is depicted holding and offering food to the curiously adult-looking yet miniature Marie-Anne Grellier, the putative subject of the work. But it is the nourrice who

FIGURE 36. *Chanteloup, Portrait de Marie-Anne Grellier dans les bras de sa nourrice.* After 1718. Portrait commissioned by a family from Saint-Domingue, resident in France, of their daughter and her wet nurse. Musée du Noveau Monde La Rochelle, https://commons.wikimedia.org/wiki/File:Chanteloub,_Portrait_de _Marie-Anne_Grellier_dans_les_bras_de_sa_nourrice.png

sits center stage. Her face captures the attention: her direct gaze, slightly flushed cheeks, youth, individuality. What might she have been thinking during the long hours that she sat for a portrait that was hers as much as that of her charge? Although nursing and child care would no doubt have occupied much of her time, the portrait makes apparent that she would have had private thoughts, feelings, and ambitions as well. When speculating about the women who served the Moreau family as wet nurses, this visual artifact is valuable precisely because it so clearly captures this woman's individuality. Esteemed enough by the family to be painted (as Moreau publicly vaunted his own esteem for his enslaved women's care of his children), the woman shown here, much as Angélique and the anonymous wet nurse, was her own person.[43]

I close this entry on wet nursing by considering how white women in Moreau's family circle also served as wet nurses to the babies they enslaved. In 1791, he suggested that a woman living with them in Paris had been nursed by her mistress when her own mother had died. He wrote, "I have at home, in Paris, a mulâtresse from Martinique, who has never had any other wet nurse than her mistress" (J'ai chez moi, à Paris, une mulâtresse de la Martinique, que n'a jamais eu d'autre nourrice que sa maîtresse).[44] Moreau mentions several of his mulâtresses, and it is impossible to confirm to whom he referred. As a result, the mistress he referred to is likewise unclear. Again, several mixed-race women lived with the family in Paris during the 1780s and early 1790s, most likely enslaved but perhaps as wage laborers after the publicity surrounding Martonne's case. This woman could have been nursed by a mistress/owner outside the family before being brought into the Moreaus' home. Or did Moreau mean that his own wife had provided this care? Moreau and Louise-Catherine's son was born in 1782; if the person he alluded to as living at home with the family in Paris shared Louise-Catherine's milk with Moreau's son, she would have been a young child in 1791. Of course, "tracking" a woman's milk is an imperfect, futile endeavor because of the private, often undocumented nature of reproductive labor. Louise-Catherine could have been pregnant and suffered a miscarriage or stillbirth that would have allowed her to lactate at other times. Although deducing even the age of the woman Moreau refers to here as living in his household is thus difficult, a more evocative question is whether particular and mutual affective ties might have resulted from this relationship between mistress and child.

END OF PART II

CHAPTER FIVE

Unnatural History

Translation, Coercion, and the Limits of Colonialist Knowledge

FIGURE 37. *Simia trepida Linn.* By G. F. Edwards. 1764. From Johann
Christian Daniel, Georg August Goldfuss, and J. A. Wagner, *Die Säugthiere
in Abbildungen nach der Nature, mit Beschreibungen* (Erlangen, Germany,
1774), Plate XXVII. Courtesy of the John Carter Brown Library.

In 1777, two years after settling in Saint-Domingue, Moreau de Saint-Méry
adopted a monkey. It was a capuchin, similar to Karl Linnaeus's *Simia trepida*
pictured in Figure 37. In 1780, he acquired another. When re-creating Moreau's
households, I did not foresee that loud, rambunctious monkeys often held court.
The first, whom he named Faquin (Rascal), was apparently intelligent and so
attached to Moreau that he shed literal tears when they were separated and threw

things at him when he wanted more attention. As Moreau strode through the streets of Cap Français, Faquin rode on his shoulder, tail wrapped around his neck. This monkey terrorized Moreau's "domestics" (domestiques), who were forced to chase him when he got loose, although Moreau recounts that some of the people he enslaved, those he referred to casually as his "nègres," loved to have Faquin remove lice from their hair. Of great sentimental value to his owner, the monkey was also a specimen, an animal whose behavior he closely observed. In fact, Moreau chronicled Faquin's sexual proclivities, including his habit of satisfying his "brutal passion with young cats of both sexes" (passion brutale sur de jeunes chats de deux sexes). Moreau likewise recorded Faquin's reactions to a young West African monkey of a different species that Moreau deliberately brought home for that purpose. In Moreau's words, Faquin made an "assault" (assaut) on her. Although the female monkey was initially "indifferent" (indifférente) to Faquin's attentions, things took a violent turn when "he became ardent enough to employ force" (il fut assez ardent pour vouloir employer la force), at which point "she resisted" (elle résista), causing "him to only grow more imperious" (il n'en devint que plus impérieux). Faquin died after several years, and Moreau suspected his (enslaved) servants of poisoning him. Their innocence was only established after Moreau dissected Faquin and found copious quantities of hot, stolen rice pudding in his throat.[1]

Moreau replaced Faquin with Coco, a monkey of the same species. These animals were part of the regional animal trade occurring in the markets of Cap Français. Less intelligent and "sweet" (doux), Coco nonetheless loved to sleep with Moreau's son; he behaved more aggressively toward Moreau's daughter Aménaïde, not allowing her to touch him unless Moreau was nearby. Moreau brought Coco with him and his family to Paris, and the monkey died there in 1784, victim of the cold weather. Moreau cut him open as well, only to discover that his vessels were deprived of blood.[2]

Moreau's anecdotes are arresting. His interest in zoology and in natural history writ large was both bookish and experimental. Did he take notes as he dissected and removed the organs of these animals that had shared his homes on two continents? Did he ever intervene to protect the cats? Faquin's vicious "assault" on a captive, unwilling female is just as unnerving as Moreau standing by to watch, even instigate, this aggression. It is impossible to ignore the echoes of analogous master-enslaved behavior such an attack suggests; there is an undertone to Moreau's words that implies he was likewise thinking of human behavior as he watched and narrated this violent spectacle of natural history unfolding in real time. The simultaneity of intimacy and detachment— physical, psychological, and intellectual—is an unsettling undercurrent in much of Moreau's *ouvrage*. That he recorded Faquin's and Coco's names for posterity only highlights the absence of the names of most of the anonymous domestic laborers who cared for these monkeys and their masters.

We know of Moreau's monkeys and the behavioral lessons they taught him because he inserted their stories into a two-volume publication by Félix de Azara, *Essais sur l'histoire naturelle des quadrupèdes de la province du Paraguay* (1801), that he edited and translated from Spanish to French. Moreau's compilation, printing, and editorial practice was about showing mastery: of other texts, of their contexts, of people, of places. This is abundantly clear in his paratextual work—notes and appendices to volumes that he did not author. He did not just sell a story and its content. Rather, his editing and translation projects helped him to secure a place in a particular knowledge market that was simultaneously a market for unpaid human labor.[3]

This chapter explores the link between the field of natural history and language. In doing so, it draws attention to three themes present throughout this book: the study of language as a means of asserting power over colonized people, the pilfering of knowledge created by non-European others as a means for white intellectuals to accrue social position, and the omnipresence of violence. Translation, dissection, and sexual coercion existed alongside one another—the need to understand and categorize, to open up, to use words to exert control over discourse and bodies. Foreign languages were vital data for Moreau, similar to animal and human anatomy or the sociological information he gathered. His study of language, including pronunciation, functioned as a form of self-fashioning, allowing him to insert himself at the apex of eighteenth- and early-nineteenth-century international natural history hierarchies. Attention to Moreau's translation of Spanish-language manuscripts shows how he helped to bring discussions of Latin America into the intellectual ambit of French Enlightenment circles. Moreau, icon of French Caribbean thought, also belongs in discussions of Latin America and the hispanophone Caribbean. His acumen in multiple European languages and attempts to engage with non-European ones, specifically his work on Guaraní, an Indigenous language of Paraguay, models an important strand of eighteenth-century comparative American scholarship of continued contemporary relevance. Any history of the Americas cannot be told through European languages alone.

Discourses of domestication and creole ways of knowing, long important in studies of the Spanish American Enlightenment, focus attention on the disturbing overlap between Moreau's natural history research on people and animals. His work on the projects examined herein brought Moreau directly into collaboration with Georges Cuvier, a scion of comparative anatomy. A link between monkeys and men was an important one for turn-of-the-century French scientists, Cuvier in particular, and very much a topic of conversation as it related to

Africans and their descendants. Moreau's experiments with his own monkeys in the 1780s foreshadowed the evolution of scientific racism. Although he does not seem to have engaged in an empirical attempt to prove the soundness of his infamous theory describing the physical characteristics and personality traits that resulted when the blood of Europeans, Africans, and Indigenous Americans mixed (I have found no evidence that he physically experimented on people), the logic behind his taxonomy ultimately relied on characterizing some people as dangerously subhuman in ways that made them expendable apart from their capacity to work or have sex. In the blurring of the human-animal boundary, mobilization of unacknowledged or sublimated Indigenous and Black knowledge, and development of scholarship that depended on intimate encounters, Moreau repeatedly demonstrated that claims to universal and enlightened truths were designed to buttress the ideological and governing power of people and institutions invested in slavery. Even when his work was not ostensibly about slavery, his status as a logician of slavery informed it.

In keeping with a communal biographical approach, this chapter brings into focus the contributions of the largely anonymous people around Moreau and the authors of Moreau's source texts. The human stakes of doing so are clear in the oft-cited words of the poet Elizabeth Alexander, who uses the figure of Sara / Saartjie Baartman to succinctly link violence, racism, and misogyny to the field of natural history. In the verses below, she imagines how Baartman, infamously marketed as the Venus Hottentot, would have responded to her tormentors in Paris as she lay dead on an examination table.

Monsieur Cuvier investigates
between my legs, poking, prodding,
sure of his hypothesis.
. . . .
. . . He complains
at my scent and does not think
I comprehend, but I speak
English. I speak Dutch.

I speak a little French as well, and
languages Monsieur Cuvier
will never know have names.
. . . .
I have not forgotten my Xhosa
clicks. My flexible tongue
and healthy mouth bewilder

FIGURE 38. Detail of *Guenon patas*. Circa 1850–1861. Nash Collection of Primates in Art and Illustration, University of Wisconsin–Madison Libraries.

this man with his rotting teeth.
If he were to let me rise up

from this table, I'd spirit
his knives and cut out his black heart,
seal it with science fluid inside
a bell jar, place it on a low
shelf in a white man's museum
so the whole world could see
it was shriveled and hard,
geometric, deformed, unnatural.

Baartman was sold to an animal trader in Paris and placed on display during late 1814 and early 1815, living in squalid conditions near the Palais Royal and being forced to perform as the public ogled what was billed as her large posterior. She died at the age of twenty-six and was dissected by Cuvier, her labia and brain placed on display. Alexander's poem converts Cuvier into a specimen in his own museum of curiosities acquired from the colonial world. The vaunted scientist was Moreau's collaborator; they traveled in the same natural history circles. At the center of these circles were animals: winged, ferocious or meek, four-legged, some quite valuable for their market potential. These intellectual circles also hemmed in people they sought to classify as some variation of animals: *indien (non) soumis,* nègre, Hottentot. These people functioned as fantasies of unnaturalness in the service of unnatural history.[4]

Did Moreau go to see Baartman in Paris during the last years of his life? A resident of the city, he surely would have known of her visit. During these years, he was an active member of many scientific and literary societies, including the Musée de Paris and the Société royale d'agriculture. He would have read about her in Parisian periodicals or seen the caricatures of her posted in shop windows. Given his connections with Cuvier, he could have received a personal invitation to visit her: Was not Moreau himself counted an expert on colonial taxonomy? Had he not already published his own work on African women's buttocks and their evidentiary value? Recall his work on Arada women. Or there was Marguerite Rebecca, put on display, her private areas subject to examination as part of Moreau's research into albinism. Moreau had spent more than forty years collecting, studying, sometimes dissecting his own specimens—monkeys, manuscripts, stories about the enslaved. It is difficult to imagine that he would not have gone to see Baartman. She was meant to be understood by the so-called great men of these institutions and the general public as a step in the evolutionary scale—a missing link, supposedly closer to ape than to man.[5]

The inclusion of Alexander's poem signals how the discursive and physical violence of natural history work might have been experienced by those who paid a steep price for their involuntary involvement with scientific inquiry, for those who spoke "languages [African and Indigenous ones] Monsieur Cuvier / [would] never know [had] names." The capuchin monkeys visually mark an ironic chapter framing and orientation function: from Linnaeus's docile, smiling, almost human-like depiction with its prominent nipples (Figure 37) to a visibly aggressive and potentially dangerous creature showing no interest in being domesticated (Figure 38). Again, the human stakes of the natural history paradigms set by slaveowners and their colleagues are also made perfectly clear in the biting commentary of Moreau's intellectual nemesis, the mixed-race Baron de Vastey. In 1814, Vastey noted, "Even as I write this down, I cannot stop myself from laughing at the thought of all those absurdities. . . . Learned writers and clever anatomists have spent their lives arguing over facts that are as clear as daylight, while others have spent them dissecting the bodies of humans and animals in order to prove that *I,* who am now writing, belong to the race of Ourang-Outangs. Still laughing (for who would not laugh at such nonsense)" (Moi-même en écrivant ceci, je ne puis m'empêcher de rire de tant d'absurdités. . . . des docteurs écrivains et de savans anatomistes ont passé leurs vies les uns à discuter sur des faits qui sont clairs comme le jour, les autres à disséquer des corps humains et d'animaux, pour prouver que *moi,* que écrit maintenant, je suis de de la race de l'Orang-Outang. Je me demande toujours en riant [car qui ne rirait pas de pareilles bêtises]). This chapter never loses sight of the experience of a Baartman or the truths penned by Vastey. It documents Moreau's engagement in intellectual conversations concerning natural history—from his collaborative work with peers to his glosses on publications, including Jesuit manuals and the work of Inca Garcilaso de la Vega—and foregrounds the named and unnamed stakeholders in these debates.[6]

Moreau's Translation of the Spanish Imperial Archive

After returning to France in 1798 following his exile in the United States, Moreau renewed his contacts in Parisian intellectual circles before assuming his diplomatic post in Italy. He came into possession of several Spanish-language texts via his friendship with José Nicolás de Azara, the career Spanish diplomat and antiquary who worked for many years in Rome and then in Paris, where he died after helping to negotiate the treaty that would see the Spanish beholden to Napoleon Bonaparte. José's brother, Félix de Azara, a soldier, military engineer, and amateur naturalist who had spent almost twenty years stationed in Paraguay, sent him many manuscripts about the region for safekeeping. José Nicolás de Azara entrusted some of these to Moreau for translation, apparently against his brother's wish to publish them himself. He also lent Moreau a copy of Fray Iñigo Abbad y Lasierra's *Historia geográfica, civil y natural de la Isla de San Juan Bautista de Puerto-Rico* (1788). The content of these texts corresponded very closely with the type of information Moreau was determined to document regarding French Caribbean society. His excitement about gaining access to them reflected his interest in natural histories from throughout the Americas, as evinced in his Philadelphia bookstore's stock of volumes from Hernando de Soto's work on the Floridas to those by J. Hector St. John de Crèvecoeur and Thomas Jefferson on what would become the United States.[7]

Moreau and José Nicolás de Azara were introduced in October 1798 by Charles-Maurice de Talleyrand-Périgord, who also helped Moreau secure a post as historian of the French Ministry of the Navy and Colonies as well as his prime position as administrator general in the duchies of Parma, Piacenza, and Guastalla. Though it is unknown whether Moreau had specific instructions about the utility of a connection with the Spanish diplomat, he and Napoleon's future spymaster would likely have been thrilled to make inroads with a man so closely connected to ongoing foreign relations negotiations at the Spanish court. At this moment, France was engaged in complicated geopolitical discussions about territorial claims in South America, the Caribbean, North America, and northern Italy. By 1800, for example, secret treaty negotiations had transferred the enormous Louisiana territory from Spain back to France. Acquiring Félix de Azara's manuscripts was a French and French-creole run on the Spanish imperial archive. For Moreau, these projects allowed him to exercise translation as an act of imperial acquisition over knowledge at a moment when the literal expansion of the French empire into parts of the Spanish Americas was a possibility. Although the authors of these texts were loyalists of competing European empires, Moreau evinced an intellectual affinity for his fellow colonial masters. I take the word *master (maître)* literally to mean owners of other people and their labor. He identified with the power they exerted.[8]

A few words about the discipline of natural history establish the context of Moreau's work. Natural history refers to both a field of study that reached its height in the eighteenth and early nineteenth centuries and the literary genres that accompanied it. The natural history milieu in which Moreau labored was one in which many prominent European theorists decried the supposed inferiority of American specimens—plants, animals, and people—while anxiously seeking out knowledge about the potential commercial value of new commodities. From patronizing scholars who philosophized about specimens collected from abroad to financing expeditions outfitted to search for, document, and monetize said specimens, the French, Spanish, and British crowns sponsored much of this evolving field of inquiry about the colonized world. Christopher P. Iannini argues that the "culture of natural history was dominated by individuals with a direct material interest in the stability of colonial slavery." Moreau's fascination with the discipline should be considered as part of his personal formation as a colonial subject who proudly self-identified simultaneously as an American and as a master. Indeed, the core criterion of his Americanness was indelibly related to how his place of birth, a slaveholding society, allowed him to own other people as a marker of social rank, with all of its attendant privileges.[9]

Like many creole intellectuals, Moreau engaged in what Jorge Cañizares-Esguerra has memorably termed a "patriotic epistemology," fighting back against characterizations of New World inferiority. Moreau sought recognition for the value of a localized, Antillean knowledge base, one generated to serve the interests of the elite—planters, merchants, and those with an investment in a hierarchical status quo. When describing one of the goals of his own research, he wrote, "We hope that local knowledge, so necessary and so difficult to acquire, will be drawn from this source" (Nous espérons qu'on puisera dans cette source les connaisances locales, si nécessaires et si difficiles à acquérir). He wrote, edited, translated, and published several genres of natural history that strove to establish taxonomies about the world. In addition to his work on a comparative colonial encyclopedia, Moreau had experience with other short-form essay writing about natural history topics: an overview of horses in Saint-Domingue, the merits of different kinds of potatoes and sugarcane varieties, how to make wine from oranges, the types of wooden locks employed by the enslaved. Accounts of people, animals, and plants in his work were coupled with stories that evoke a sense of what his world sounded like and looked like as well as how it was experienced, right down to its everyday nuisances—from flies to bedbugs to mosquitos—all described in vivid prose that inspires a present-day reader with the desire to swat.[10]

Moreau is best known for his work in the popular genres of the *description* (topographic, political, cultural) and the *voyage* (travel narratives), the latter often compiled in the form of a personal journal. His self-published *Description topographique, physique, civile, politique et historique de la partie française de l'isle de Saint-Domingue* is a classic of the former genre, as is his *Description topographique et politique de la partie espagnole de l'isle Saint-Domingue* about the Spanish-governed side of Hispaniola. Moreau's journal about life in the United

States, *Voyage aux États-Unis de l'Amérique,* in addition to his translation of *Voyage de l'ambassade de la Compagnie des Indes orientales hollandaises, vers l'empereur de la Chine dans les années 1794 et 1795* exemplify the latter. Although it would be a mistake to see his investment in natural history in purely instrumentalist terms—his attention to extracting, creating, and transmitting knowledge was born from a deep-seated and palpable curiosity—his work served a larger colonialist project while garnering him personal benefits such as job opportunities and professional esteem. By his own account in his *Note des travaux du c[itoy]en Moreau-St.-Méry,* he had also completed a two-volume "description of Jamaica, translated from the English" (une description de la Jamaïque, traduite de l'anglais). In addition, he wrote a short essay on the West African Kingdom of Ouaire (the Warri Kingdom), "Observations sur le Royaume de Ouaire, à la Côte-d'Or en Afrique," and thousands of pages about Italy. Moreau's contributions to natural history writing were extensive in terms of geographic scope, subject matter, and linguistic competence.[11]

The French Caribbean was thus just one focus of Moreau's engagement with natural history. His commitment to disseminating knowledge about the Spanish-occupied Americas that first appeared in his work on Santo Domingo resurfaced in translations of what would become two canonical texts. The first was the aforementioned history of the quadrupeds of Paraguay. Its author, Félix de Azara, would go on to become well known for his natural histories of Latin American Indigenous populations as well as animals, particularly birds; he was painted by Francisco de Goya, cited by Charles Darwin and John James Audubon, and remains well known in scholarship about the Río de la Plata and Paraguay. Moreau's translation was published in Paris in 1801, a year before the original Spanish version appeared in Madrid as *Apuntamientos para la historia natural de los quadrúpedos del Paragüay y Rio de la Plata* (1802).[12]

Moreau, then, first introduced Félix de Azara's work to the public, effectively scooping him and claiming this Spanish American material as part of a French intellectual tradition. Although natural historians shared a common set of principles across national and imperial lines—whom they should be reading, how to present and ship specimens, how to illustrate their findings—the world of natural history was competitive, and individuals and those they worked with (on expeditions or while associated with particular institutions) strove to have their own discoveries published first and credit accrued to their names. Moreau's published translation placed him into direct communication with leading figures at the Institut national des sciences et arts, a powerful Parisian institution that was embedded into the new patronage systems emerging in postrevolutionary France. Moreau directly sought approval of the work from three leading scientists, Cuvier; Bernard-Germain-Étienne de La Ville-sur-Illon, comte de Lacépède; and Claude Richard, and their endorsement signaled a triumph for Moreau as he sought to exhibit his intellectual credentials on his return to France.[13]

Moreau's other Spanish-French translation, dated 1798 and incomplete, was of Fray Iñigo Abbad y Lasierra's *Historia geográfica, civil y natural de la Isla de San Juan Bautista de Puerto-Rico,* previously published by Abbad y Lasierra in Madrid. Much as Moreau's *Description de la partie française de l'isle Saint-Domingue* is an obligatory text for those studying Saint-Domingue and the French Caribbean more generally, Abbad y Lasierra's *Historia geográfica* serves an equally important role in the historiography of Puerto Rico. Abbad y Lasierra, a Benedictine priest, spent ten years living on the island. His history is replete with accounts of the war between the Spanish and local Indigenous populations, natural disasters and crop growing advice, descriptions of local animals, accounts of the contemporary inhabitants, and, famously, some of the earliest documentation of cultural artifacts such as the *guiro,* a fabled instrument in Puerto Rican music. As was the case with Moreau's publication *Danse* (1796), the people involved with the various editions of Abbad y Lasierra's text were a who's who of seminal figures in Caribbean history and literature. Despite a notation by Moreau in 1799 that he was going to send it "to press" (va mettre sous presse), his translation was never published. Yet that he had already determined it would be one octavo-sized volume suggests that he was in the process of doing so. Although describing the work as a translation, he observed that it was "augmented by his own research" (traduite par lui de l'espagnol, et augmentée par ses propres recherches). This claim is in keeping with the copious investigative research he completed on other texts, although the extant manuscript unfortunately does not contain many of these notes.[14]

Where and when did Moreau learn Spanish? The value of his intellectual legacy is in part attributable to his dedication to studying the Americas as an interrelated whole, a task made possible because he could work in its many languages. His proficiency in Spanish was well beyond an introductory level. It is possible that he practiced speaking it with dignitaries such as the aforementioned Bernardo de Gálvez, the man to whom he lent his son's wet nurse Angélique when Gálvez was stationed in Saint-Domingue. He could have learned some from the enslaved people in his extended households; many people laboring in Saint-Domingue had previously worked in Santo Domingo, and newspapers of the time demonstrate their linguistic proficiencies in Spanish. Moreau's posthumously sold book collection contained multiple Spanish-French dictionaries, and he learned to read Spanish well. This is circumstantial evidence and not a satisfying explanation for his skills, however.

By the 1790s, he was able to translate very challenging texts, in terms of both their length and advanced vocabulary and phrasing. Indeed, both Félix de Azara and Abbad y Lasierra's texts struggled to document cultures and animals that were unfamiliar to the authors themselves. That is, they needed to describe Indigenous communities, African and African-descended free and enslaved people, and the names of plants and living creatures that would have been new to them and their reading publics. Azara, for example, did not have a Spanish word that corresponded to a capybara. Abbad y Lasierra's text was dense with descriptions of fruits such as guanabanas, beds called *barbacoas,* and flying cucubanos. Moreau likewise struggled to translate the Spanish and Indigenous names for these terms into French. For example, when trying to document the word *barrero,* he characterized it as a nitrate-rich soil but confessed that "[he] had not been able to inform [himself] more precisely about the true nature of this earth" (Je n'ai pu parvenir à m'instruire plus précisément de la vraie nature de cette terre). When defining the word *chacarra* as a Native American garden, Moreau resorted to comparing it to the marshland cultivated by "the vegetable-growers on the outskirts of Paris" (les Maraichers aux environs de Paris). He had to use language and, importantly, his study of the context in which it lived to make comparisons that would have resonated with readers in France and its colonies.[15]

Although he was ostensibly the translator, not a full-fledged editor of Azara's manuscripts, Moreau did not stay marginalized in his translation. As was the case with the volumes on China discussed in Chapter 3, Moreau's erudition and personality surfaced all over the book, most often in the paratexts. When he thought Azara had made an error, he said so, repeatedly. It is common to find comments such as "one could think that this opinion of [Azara's] is wrong" (on peut penser que cette opinion [Azara] est hasardée). When Azara said he was not sure that Black people could have albino children, Moreau quickly responded, "Everyone knows that Black people have albino children. I have seen several in the Antilles, and I described one albino Black woman born in Saint-Domingue (see my Description of that island, tome 1, p. 56 and following, quarto edition)" (Tout le monde sait que les Nègres ont des enfans albinos. J'en ai vu plusieurs dans les différentes Antilles, et j'ai décrit une Négresse albinos née à Saint-Domingue [voyez ma Description de cette île, t. 1.er, p. 56 et suivantes, édit. in-4°]). This citation refers to the woman Marguerite Rebecca, documented in Chapter 4. Moreau's close inspection of her body resulted in his ability to produce a written record (published in a large folio size) that circulated across languages, colonies, and empires. Moreau's opening comments to Azara's texts were extensive, and he even cited himself in the index every time he offered a translator's note, thereby putting himself on equal footing with other content in the book. Except for a few occasions, his "Note[s] du Traducteur" (Translator's Notes) were editorial additions, as opposed to comments on his translation choices themselves.[16]

Moreau was thus hypervisible in the text. Modern-day translation studies have argued for the importance of recognizing the translator as part of the creative process, the translation act as important as the final product itself. By being the first to disseminate Azara's work, Moreau positioned himself as a collaborative coauthor; he made it his own. This process of claiming ownership over the project was accomplished typographically as well. For example, the discussion on the capuchin monkey, the cay, became an avenue for him to make his own personal observations. His commentary took over the text, in font size not much smaller than the main body, moving out of the footnotes for a full six and a half pages over which he narrated much of the opening anecdotes about his monkeys' behavior. Moreau similarly had much to say about the Taytétou, a wild pig (Figure 39). He took advantage of the opportunity to interject his own discussion concerning the history of imported pig (and bird) settlement in Saint-Domingue, citing his French *Description* as an intertext. The note even acknowledged the revolutionary-era name changes in Saint-Domingue: Port-au-Prince to Port-Republican, a correction made between the manuscript and print editions.

Moreau used this translation project to demonstrate his (comparative) natural history chops. He ensured that every single animal Azara identified contained an initial translation into contemporary scientific nomenclatures of the day: those of Linné (Linnaeus), Georges-Louis Leclerc, comte de Buffon, and the aforementioned Lacépède and Cuvier. For example, the catlike animal Azara claimed the Guaraní called either chibigouazou or *mbaracaya,* Moreau also listed as the Linnaean *Felis pardalis,* Buffon's *Ocelot,* and Lacépède's *Felis ocelot.* In a text organized around entries for four-legged animals, the opening of every entry began with a display of Moreau's own knowledge. He also invited Cuvier to add a few of his own footnotes about several animals, establishing the two as intellectual peers and collaborators. Cuvier's influence was on the rise, and Moreau benefited from this connection.[17]

Moreau's copious "Note[s] du Traducteur" thus made him an active textual interlocutor, of both the authors whose work he translated and his future readers. He noted that his own notes were often designed to

> lead to a citation of several hundred passages in Buffon. These, as he noted in his preface, Don Félix d'Azara pulled from the first twelve volumes of

(41)

obscure ou plus noire que le reste, et les soies plus rudes dans les espèces qui sont sauvages.

Aussi n'ayant point de confiance dans ces assertions de la Borde, mon opinion est-elle que le Patira est mon Taytétou adulte, qui a la ligne blanche en travers sur le garrot, et point en long comme le suppose la Borde, lequel se trompe pareillement lorsqu'il lui donne des soies douces, et qui peut-être altère le nom même en écrivant Patira au lieu de Pécari.

Il est aisé de se convaincre, d'après cette description du Taytétou par M. d'Azara, que le Pécari que d'Aubenton a décrit dans l'ouvrage qui lui est commun avec Buffon, est réellement un Taytétou; et c'est une preuve de plus de la justesse du reproche que fait M. d'Azara à ceux qui ont confondu le Tagnicati et le Taytétou en un seul animal, sous le nom de Pécari.

J'ai vu en 1787, au Port-au-Prince, aujourd'hui Port-Républicain, chez le gouverneur général la Luzerne, l'un des Pécaris qu'il avoit fait venir de la province de Carthagène dans l'Amérique méridionale, et par le port du même nom, avec le dessein de les multiplier dans l'île de la Gonave, dépendante de Saint-Domingue. Cet animal étoit aussi un vrai Taytétou, d'après la description de M. d'Azara.

(42)

Les autres Pécaris venoient d'être envoyés à la Gonave, comme je l'ai dit dans ma Description de Saint-Domingue (t. 2, p. 529, in-4.°); et en 1788, ils paroissoient y avoir déjà multiplié.

Ce Pécari étant indiqué comme une espèce de cochon marron ou sauvage, le gouverneur général la Luzerne avoit pensé, d'après plusieurs rapports, que la multiplication en seroit utile, et offriroit un moyen de subsistance de plus dans un pays où l'on fait beaucoup de cas de la chair du cochon marron.

Je ne sais quel est, en ce moment, le résultat de cette expérience, ainsi que de celle faite à la même époque et dans la même petite île de la Gonave, en y lâchant des oiseaux de plusieurs espèces; des Agamis de Cayenne, des Tourterelles et deux oiseaux Martins, venus de l'île de France, etc. etc. (*Note du Traducteur*).

the Spanish translation [of Buffon's *Histoire naturelle*] done by Don Joseph Clavijo and from the 1775 French version, in 12mo. I thought I should keep them all, adding first to the citation to be found in Clavijo, that of the 1775 French volume; then, to all of these citations, the citations corresponding to the Louvre edition in quarto, the only one that Buffon authorized and whose typographical beauty places it above all others.

amène la citation de plusieurs centaines d'endroits de Buffon. Celles-ci, comme l'annonce la préface de Don Félix d'Azara, ont été tirées par lui des douze premiers volumes de la traduction espagnole de Don Joseph Clavijo, et de l'édition française de 1775, in - 12. J'ai cru devoir les conserver toutes, en ajoutant d'abord à la citation à chercher dans Clavijo, celle du volume

français de 1775; puis à la totalité de ces citations, les citations correspon-
dantes de l'édition in – 4.⁰ du Louvre, la seule que Buffon ait avouée, et que
sa beauté typographique place au-dessus de toutes les autres.

Buffon had been head of the Jardin du roi and author of the most widely read
and cited natural history in Europe. José Clavijo y Fajardo, director of the corresponding Real Gabinete de Historia Natural in Madrid, translated Buffon's
bestseller as the *Diccionario de la historia natural,* thereby introducing it to
Spanish-speaking publics on both sides of the Atlantic. Moreau was deeply familiar with the content of both Buffon and Clavijo's work and had strong opinions not only about the research itself but about which editions were the most
important for typographical, artistic, and scientific purposes. We have seen his
obsession with the bibliographic value of different print editions of texts, from
his personal copy of the large-format edition of the *Encyclopédie* that he sold to
raise cash to the octavo version he marketed in his bookstore. Moreau found that
Clavijo's translation of Buffon's work was "very highly esteemed" (extrêmement
estimée) among Spanish speakers, conserving "all of the stylistic beauties" (toutes
les beautés du style) of the original "transported into their own language" (trans-
portées dans leur propre langue). Clavijo dedicated years of research to the project, and Moreau was particularly drawn to a Spanish-Latin-French dictionary
Clavijo had developed but never published. Moreau lamented this fact, saying
that such a volume would have made his own work significantly easier and that
its publication would be "a veritable service to natural history" (un veritable service à l'histoire naturelle).[18]

A dictionary is a critical tool in any translator's labor, and the use of Latin as
an interlanguage, or pivot language, between Spanish and French would have
greatly facilitated the translation process. Latin served as a Rosetta Stone, helping speakers of either the source or target language. Moreau learned Latin when
he was sent to France to be educated as a young adult, becoming very proficient.
Latin had in fact become less of a lingua franca in European scientific circles by
Moreau's time, losing much of its intellectual heft as a source and target language
to French itself. By translating Azara's work from Spanish into French, Moreau
was placing it into a potentially bigger readership pool in the international scientific world, whose members relied increasingly on translations of scholarly work
and possessed French fluency regardless of national origin. French had become
a new lingua franca in eighteenth-century European natural history circles.[19]

Claiming that he had "the constant desire to render the original with fidelity"
(le desir constant de rendre l'original avec fidelité), Moreau's intent to use the mot
juste indicates a belief in precision and exactitude as an underlying translation

theory. Not only did he want to ensure that the animals Azara documented in Latin America correctly entered the pantheon of known quadrupeds; he also wanted to make sure that the language itself used to describe them to French readers was accurate. Although this obligation to an original may seem commonplace now, Moreau was working during a moment that witnessed a move away from free-form interpretation and paraphrasing that privileged readability and cultural sensitivity to the host language toward a word-to-word correspondence that valued "loyalty to the original text in matters of vocabulary, style, and ideas." Again, this goal of exactitude proved difficult when searching for words and concepts that had no corresponding terms in Europe and European languages. Exactitude was also a philosophically slippery slope when Azara's original work was often openly scornful of the local knowledge on which it was based.[20]

Moreau's personal beliefs, like Félix de Azara's, were related to his choice of projects, his decisions about diction, and the tenor of his editorial work. Translation studies scholar Susan Bassnett asserts that the practice of translation "involves much more than language. Translations are always embedded in cultural and political systems and in history. For too long, translation was seen as purely an aesthetic act, and ideological problems were disregarded." Antoine Berman has shown that "there is no translator without translating position." *Essais sur l'histoire naturelle des quadrupèdes* provides an opportunity to foreground how Moreau's positionality linked his linguistic work to the violence of religious conversion, land appropriation, sexual exploitation, and a centuries-old Spanish conquest of Paraguay and the Río de la Plata region.[21]

Unsound(ing) Natural History Hierarchies

Moreau's work on *Essais sur l'histoire naturelle des quadrupèdes* involved much more than a mediation between Spanish (including Paraguayan regional Spanish) and French. The original manuscript and the translated publication used Guaraní, both the people and their language, as a framing device. At the close of the eighteenth century, the Guaraní were one of several Indigenous groups, including the Mbaya and the Payaguá, living in what is now Paraguay, Brazil, and parts of Argentina. They had an extended relationship with the Jesuits, who began settling there in the 1580s; before their expulsion in 1767, the Jesuits established

more than thirty mission settlements, or *reducciones,* among the Guaraní.
Guaraní, a Tupi language and longtime lingua franca in Paraguay, currently has
more non-Indigenous speakers than Indigenous ones. Additionally, Moreau had
access to several more of Félix de Azara's manuscripts, including an unedited
"Descripción histórica, phísica, política, y geográfica de la Provincia del Paraguay"
that he was also planning to translate. He claimed that this other volume contained "research about several tribes, or nations of non-submissive Indians, of
which he had studied and learned the languages and about which he provides
a multitude of details unknown in Europe" (recherches sur plusieurs tribus ou
nations d'Indiens sauvages, dont il a etudié et appris les langues et sur lesquels il
donne une multitude de détails inconnus en Europe).[22]

Moreau's translation and Azara's Spanish edition of his work on quadrupeds
were suffused with Guaraní linguistic nomenclature of animal names. Although
language has the potential to provide access to Native epistemologies, Azara's
texts explored a Guaraní worldview in a deliberately limited way. That is, although some information about these animals was embedded in their Guaraní
names, Azara rarely recorded information about how they might have figured in
medical, religious, or other knowledge produced about them. Azara frequently
undercut Guaraní assessments of their natural surroundings. For example, he
wrote, "Some people told me that this species was called *Angouya-y-bigoui* (Rat
that lives under the ground) because they are sure that it never leaves its burrow,
. . . but I don't believe this at all, because I have seen the remains of this rat more
than 30 inches from its hole" (Quelques personnes m'ont dit que cette espèce
s'appelait *Angouya-y-bigoui* [Rat qui habite sous terre], parce qu'on assure qu'il ne
sort jamais de son réduit, . . . mais je ne le crois point, attendu que j'ai vu des restes
de ce Rat à plus de 30 pouces [81 centimètres 1 tiers] du trou). Or, "I was also told
that this rat caused a lot of damage to manioc roots; but I don't believe this particular [detail]" (On m'a dit aussi qu'il causait beaucoup de dommage aux racines
du manioc; mais je ne crois pas que cette particularité). The Guaraní's familiarity
with animal behavior was invalidated, although Azara was often dependent on
Indigenous and enslaved informants for information and specimen collection.
Azara peppered his text with possessive pronouns, presenting the animals with
Guaraní names yet describing them, for instance, as "my *Tayazous*" (mes *Tayazous*). In Moreau's translation, then, there is a work of double claiming. Azara asserted authority over Guaraní terms and information, often undercutting them;
Moreau then translated Azara and preempted Azara's ability to be the first to
publish decades of his work on his own terms.[23]

Although Azara did not employ language as a means of deeply engaging and
appreciating the value of Guaraní worldviews, both he and Moreau had a fixation

with pronouncing Guaraní correctly. Moreau even made a guide for syllabic pronunciation that he included as an appendix to his translation: "Prononciation syllabique des mots Guaranis qu'on trouve dans cet ouvrage." A few possibilities might explain this desire on Moreau's part. He was deeply influenced by Buffon, who argued that the correct pronunciation of species names was important. Moreau was also likely aware of how other scholars, including the Jesuit Francisco Clavigiero, author of several histories of pre-Columbian Mesoamerica, had rebuked Buffon for not knowing Indigenous languages. His development of a pronunciation guide was potentially a way of deflecting this critique of his own work: if he did not know Indigenous languages, he could at least present the appearance of knowing *about* them.[24]

Moreau was also formed in an intellectual milieu of eighteenth-century French and British scholarship about Native North and South American languages that, as Sean P. Harvey has observed, increasingly associated "impressions of Native sounds . . . with negative views of the developmental progress of Native minds." In his work on Native North American language politics, Harvey reminds us that "in an era when dozens of vernaculars competed in Europe, and when exploration and imperialism led Europeans to encounter a 'language of birds' in China and one ostensibly nearer to 'Apes, than men' in Africa, Europeans were prepared for diverse languages." He concludes that they were "accustomed to encountering linguistic difference and making invidious comparisons." As Pierre François Xavier de Charlevoix, a French Jesuit priest, observed, "The Sioux Indian hisses rather than speaks. The Huron . . . speaks thro' the throat," and "the Algonquin pronounces with a softer tone, and speaks more naturally." Similarly, John Heckewelder, a retired missionary active with the American Philosophical Society in Philadelphia, opined that he was unable to "well give" his correspondent "an idea on paper" of a *"whistled* sound" in Delaware. This linking of how a language sounded and how the physical formation of human organs such as the throat and the mouth producing these sounds might differ across cultures marked a confluence of European natural history and philology in the service of colonial domination. Like examinations of heads and genitalia, body parts associated with speech were examined to promote ideas of difference and hierarchy.[25]

How language sounded to its auditors was thus politicized and fed into evolving dogmas of cultural superiority. For Azara, Guaraní was "very difficult" (très-difficile), and he claimed that it took "more than a year to achieve it" (il faut plus d'une année pour en venir à bout). Like the speakers cited above, Azara had clear prejudices about languages, scornfully declaring that Guaraní, for example, "lacked a ton of terms" (il manque d'une foule de termes), supposedly including numbers more than four. He seemed to have appreciated Native languages based on how "guttural" (gutturale) and "nasal" (nasale) they were; the less of either the better. Despite his prejudices, Azara asserted his knowledge of the language repeatedly in his descriptions. Speaking of the "*Sarigoué*" (opossum), Azara insisted that this word be "pronounced like I have said and how the Guaraní language demands" (prononcé comme je l'ai dit et comme l'exige l'idiome Guarani). He likewise claimed that "the Guaraní pronounce the *z* like a sound somewhere between the *z* and the *s*. Thus one can equally write Tayazou or Tayasou" (les Guaranis prononcent le *z* comme un son qui tient le milieu entre le *z* et l's. Ainsi l'on peut écrire également Tayazou ou Tayasou). His interest in pronouncing the language was matched by his interest in transcribing the sounds accurately. As a result, in his preface to *Essais sur l'histoire naturelle des quadrupèdes,* Azara claimed that "the proper names are written with a *Guaraní* orthography" (le noms propres sont écrits avec l'orthographe *Guaranique*). This orthography was different from seventeenth-century and present-day transcriptions of the language, which make use of extensive diacritics to indicate nasal sounds.[26]

Moreau and Azara certainly knew about and had access to written texts published in Europe both about and in the Guaraní language. Azara commented that he was familiar with Father Luis de Bolaños's famous Guaraní catechism as well as other Jesuit dictionaries and grammars. Monastic scholastic traditions, particularly Jesuit ones, were very important to Moreau's work as well, with regard to both these volumes and his translation of the ambassador's voyage to China. For example, Charlevoix, most well known for his work *Histoire et description générale de la Nouvelle France* (1744) (which included sections on Saint-Domingue, Canada, and what is now the U.S. South) also wrote a book on Paraguay, *Histoire du Paraguay,* in 1757. Moreau owned this volume, in addition to several others, including *Relations des missions du Paraguay* (1757). Moreau also read and cited non-European authorities about Latin America. For example, he annotated Azara's comments on the *mborebi* (tapir) by citing a 1632 French translation of Garcilaso de la Vega's *Histoire des Incas* for comparison of species in Paraguay and Peru (Figure 40). He was thus familiar with a range of extant sources about this particular Latin American geographic region and discussions about how to transcribe Indigenous languages.[27]

With regard to sound, Moreau made the aforementioned appendix to his translation of Azara's work in order to incorporate the "*Guaraní* orthography" to which Azara referred (Figure 41). The appendix is curious and evocative. First, it demonstrates how Moreau used visual prompts for the study of sound. He made a guide with specific instructions about how a selection of words should be uniformly pronounced by French speakers. Eight pages in length and containing

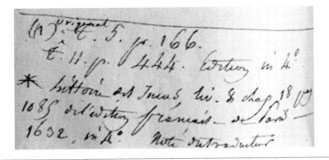

FIGURE 40. Handwritten translator's note showing Moreau de Saint-Méry's citation of Garcilaso de la Vega's commentary on the *mborebi* in the manuscript copy of "Essais sur l'histoire naturelle des quadrupèdes . . . de la province du Paraguay." This is a working draft of his translation. Archives nationales d'outre-mer, Aix-en-Provence, France, Collection Moreau de Saint-Méry (Ser. F3), 118.

more than ninety entries, it appears near the beginning of the book, just before a separate appendix containing an "Explication of Latin American Terms, Employed in This Work" (Explication des termes de l'Amérique méridionale, employés dans cet ouvrage). It is unclear what oral and written sources Moreau relied on for guidance; although Azara did discuss pronunciation, he did not always comment on how precise syllables should be emphasized, as Moreau did here. For example, Moreau claimed *Agouaragouazou* was pronounced "A-GOU-a-RA-gou-a-ZOU," the capital letters representing the long sounds indicated in Moreau's instructions. Strangely, Moreau's pronunciation guide did not include a definition of the words or any indication about why certain ones were included and others were not. What was an *Agouaragouazou* (fox)? Why struggle to capture the right way of reproducing, in this case through syllabic transcription, Guaraní sounds? Was it an academic enterprise unmoored from judgment, or did Moreau share Azara's belief that the supposed inferiority of certain sounds indicated a corresponding inferiority of Indigenous intellect? He did not provide enough commentary for me to assess his motivations. Indeed, the guide lacks substantive depth.[28]

The appendix does, however, point to the potential dead end of Moreau's sound prompt. Although this guide was expressly about sound, it stopped short of serving an analytic purpose that linked sound to particular knowledge. For a reader, these syllables meant little outside the way they were pronounced; the guide could not be mobilized for actual conversation about these animals, for example. Revisiting Garcilaso de la Vega's comments on language and

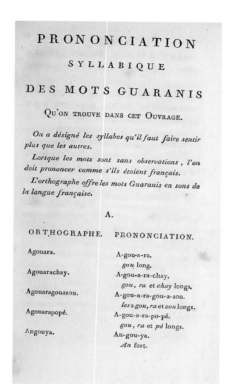

FIGURE 41. Title page of "Prononciation syllabique des mots Guaranis qu'on trouve dans cet ouvrage." From Félix d'Azara, *Essais sur l'histoire naturelle des quadrupèdes de la province du Paraguay . . .*, trans. M. L. E. Moreau-Saint-Méry, 2 vols. (Paris, 1801), I, lix. Courtesy of the John Carter Brown Library.

mistranslation as related to sound is instructive. Citing the work of Margarita Zamora, Anna Brickhouse notes what Zamora calls Garcilaso's "reenactment of the first verbal encounter" between the Spanish and a man whom they captured in order to find out the name of the land where they had arrived. In the same work that Moreau cited above, Garcilaso wrote:

> The Indian, by the gesticulations and movements of the hands and face [the Spaniards] were making at him (as if to a mute) understood that they were asking him [something] but did not understand what they were asking, and to what he understood [the question to be], he responded quickly (before they did him some harm) and named his own name, saying Berú, and added another and said Pelú. He meant to say: If you're asking me my name, I'm called Berú; and if you're asking me where I was, I'm saying that I was in the river. . . . The Christians understood according to their desire,

imagining that the Indian had understood them and had responded pur- posefully, as if he and they had been speaking in castilian, and since that time, which was the year 1515 or 16, they have called that richest and grand empire Perú, corrupting both names, as the Spaniards corrupt almost all the words that they take from the language of the Indians of that land.

Zamora interprets Garcilaso's conclusion as "the Europeans are incompetent interpreters of the language of the Indians." European attempts to hear and say words correctly had no communicative value, or a value quite unlike the intended purpose of the source language. As Moreau strove for exactitude—in word pronunciation, definitions, and translations between Guaraní, French, and Spanish—faithfulness to an original did not mean that he or Azara apprehended the situational meaning or essence of a term or idea in a way that the Guaraní, producers of this zoological knowledge in their naming practices, would have recognized. But perhaps this was the point. After all, misunderstanding Berú did not forestall Spanish violence.[29]

This idea of corruption and failed interpretations leads to a third point about Moreau's appendix. By reducing a complex linguistic tradition into sounds va- cated of corresponding meaning and importance, Moreau (and Azara) also re- duced the Guaraní's value as a knowledge source. Literary critic Karen Stolley has convincingly written about ideological attempts to "domesticate" empire in the context of the eighteenth-century Spanish American Enlightenment. This involved the need for "a different kind of storytelling," a discourse that required authors "to bring into domestic life, to adapt (an animal or plant) to intimate association with and to the advantage of people in a process directed toward pragmatic or utilitarian ends." In her compelling work on Félix de Azara, she documents how he attempted to domesticate nature, his zoological and survey- ing work along the Brazilian border serving the interests of the Spanish crown. Azara's and Moreau's linguistic feints represent attempts to domesticate lan- guage for their own utilitarian ends. Azara's biases caused him to deliberately demean or misapprehend Guaraní. Moreau, as a non-Guaraní speaker, would have depended on Azara's interpretations.

Even as sound was vacated of meaning, however, Moreau told a story through his appendix. He declared his own supposed competence and grounding in the linguistic complexities of the Río de la Plata region, a competence that his French- reading audiences would not have had. He became an inexpert expert, an expert in appearance only. Stolley's connection of this domesticating narrative practice to its "intimate association with" and for "the advantage of" its practitioners related both to languages and to the people who spoke them. The contexts under which these spoken linguistic interactions were occurring is critical; the forced adaptation of people, as opposed to animals and plants, to intimacy and domestication was coercive and violent.[30]

Intimate Epistemology and the Unnatural Histories of the Americas

As is the case when close reading Moreau's work, other voices and stories become evident when reading Félix de Azara's. Moreau's and Azara's positionality as authors and translators should be studied alongside the communities in which they lived. Intimate informants were foundational to the content generation of their work, and the likelihood of exploitation was highest for the people deemed expendable in Azara's and Moreau's worldviews. For example, who was pronouncing these words that Azara and Moreau took care to record? Who taught Azara Guaraní? A reader occasionally gets a sense of marginal figures nearby, people authoritatively determining the best places for Azara's traveling party to set up a dry campsite or explaining how they could prevent being bitten by snakes. Azara's quadruped volume and his other supplemental texts are full of expressions such as "he / she told me" (on m'a dit) or "they told me" (ils m'ont dit). He recorded several incidents of Indigenous community members bringing him animals, including different kinds of rats that they found in the environs of their dwellings. "Francisco [his] black" (Mon nègre Francisque) also brought him rat specimens.[31]

The geographies Azara traversed were peopled by Indigenous and African and African-descended laborers, both in the cities and in the Jesuit missions. Azara was himself a slaveowner, and his claim to be an "untaught naturalist" (un naturalista original), isolated and far from people of knowledge, is inaccurate. He lived alongside and within communities with their own learned traditions, including the people he enslaved. Kathleen S. Murphy asserts that although some "colonials acknowledged the authority of their black and indigenous informants as experts about American nature, they represented such expertise as merely the raw materials out of which they fashioned new natural knowledge." This assessment applies to Azara and Moreau; they relied on informants even as they dismissed their expertise as unworthy. They laid claim.[32]

These informants also included the women in Azara's circles. They, too, would have been able to provide linguistic training, information about local conditions, and domestic work. This domestic work could have included caring for Azara's animals; as one scholar notes, he often "kept live animals caged or free in his room." These women certainly seemed to have been engaged for sex. Charles A. Walckenaer, a personal acquaintance of Azara from the time the latter worked for several years in Paris at the Musée national d'Histoire naturelle (Natural History Museum), made the following remarks about Azara in *Voyages dans l'Amérique méridionale*, his French edition of Azara's manuscript:

> However, born under a burning climate, full of strength, vigor and health, at the age when the blood circulates by bubbling in the veins, raised in camps, could he have the power and even the will to defeat this impulse that leads one sex toward another? No, without a doubt. But, perfectly educated on the character and of the manner of living of the women in these regions, he avoided, as much as he could, the Christianized Indian women, and preferred above all others the light-skinned *mulâtresses*.

> Cependant né sous un climat brûlant, plein de force, de vigueur et de santé, dans cet âge ou le sang circule en bouillonnant dans les veines, élevé dans les camps, pouvait-il avoir la puissance et même la volonté de vaincre cette impulsion qui entraîne un sexe vers l'autre? Non sans doute; mais parfaitement instruit du caractère et la manière de vivre des femmes de ces contrées, il esquivait, autant qu'il le pouvait, les indiennes chrétiennes, et préférait à toute autre les mulâtresses un peu claires.

In Walckenaer's editorial estimation, why would a virile young man deny himself the pleasures of the flesh, especially when living among women from "these" regions? When determining who exactly was designated by the term *mulâtresses,* Azara's own words provide clarification. Azara dedicated a whole chapter to "people of color" (gens de couleur) in his work. He claimed that all people of African mixed-race descent were designated as *mulâtre;* those of mixed Indigenous heritage were *métis.* Whether this was an accurate picture of on-the-ground usage in the region, Azara signaled that he preferred to sleep with Black women, although Christian and non-Christian Indigenous women also satisfied his needs. He declared that

> connoisseurs prefer *mulâtresses* to Spanish women. They also claim that they experience with them a particular pleasure that other women do not make them experience. For the rest, these *mulâtresses* do not suffer either

from chastity or resistance; it is very rare that they keep their virginity past the age of nine or ten years old; they have spirit, finesse and aptitude in everything; they are clean, generous, and even magnificent.

les connaisseurs préfèrent les mulâtresses aux femmes espagnoles: il préten- dent de plus, qu'ils goûtent avec elles un plaisir particulier que les autres ne leur font pas éprouver. Du reste, ces mulâtresses ne si piquent ni de chasteté, ni de résistance; il est bien rare qu'elles conservent leur virginité jusqu'à l'âge de neuf ou dix ans: elles ont de l'esprit, de la finesse et de l'aptitude à tout; ... elles sont propres, généreuses, et même magnifiques.

This is who he was. Azara slept with these women, sometimes children, and he shared stories about this aspect of his time in South America with his peers and collaborators. It is only too easy to imagine Walckenaer's prurient interest in these anecdotes as he and Azara conversed. Sex with racialized female bodies, those supposedly the most appreciated by "connoisseurs," became another ob- ject of study. To know, that is, *connâitre,* in the biblical sense, involved sexual encounters deemed appropriate evidence for taxonomic descriptors that included ruminations about the "mediocre size of male [Guaraní] sex organs" (les parties sexuelles des hommes ne sont jamais que d'une grandeur médiocre) in contrast to the "very large" (très-larges) ones of Guaraní women (who he reported also had excessively large lips and very fat buttocks). Indeed, Azara claimed that this "singularity" (singularité) was "common to all the other nations" (commune avec toutes les autres nations).[33]

Such information indicts natural history in these sites and is part of a centuries- old tradition that explicitly linked sexual domination, colonial violence, and co- lonial science. As Elizabeth Polcha has argued in her work on Azara's contempo- rary, the soldier and popular amateur natural historian John Gabriel Stedman, "We must confront the disciplines of study that prospered from the exploitation of women." "Women of color," Polcha observes, "were infrastructural within the knowledge economy of the eighteenth century, rather than marginal." Though Azara wrote about these issues in a casual, almost banal, manner, an underlying history of coercion, likely rape, is entrenched in these firsthand experiences re- corded as knowledge production about Latin America. The commodification of this knowledge required a double extraction—of the body and of the stories.[34]

In this expression of possession, control, and mastery, Azara echoed Moreau. The hypersexualized mulâtresse served a particular function in Moreau's work as well, allowing him to purportedly evaluate an array of other cultural and economic practices that he deemed relevant to understand societies in places including Saint-Domingue and Philadelphia: sexual partnerships across and within racialized groups, hygiene and bathing rituals, sumptuary practices, lack of educational opportunities, venereal diseases, the mentality of the white men and women who could coerce obedience from those they enslaved or free people they simply wished to put in their place. In addition to lauding these mixed-race women as "priestesses of Venus" (prêtresses de Vénus), Moreau also appeared conflicted about the way the reputation of the skills they supposedly possessed made them prematurely "precocious" (précoces). Moreau observed that "it would be afflicting to see the point to which . . . the time that separates childhood from puberty is barely respected" (On serait affligé de voir jusqu'à quel point . . . le terme qui sépare l'enfance de la puberté . . . est à peine respecté). The physical labor (sex included) of these women afforded natural historians their domestic comforts, leisure time for academic pursuits, and access to information. The "pleasures of taxonomy" were physical and intellectual for these men. As we have seen, Marie-Louise Laplaine, Moreau's *ménagère* and a *mulâtresse libre,* provided Moreau with the services above, in addition to giving him a family. She was the mother of his beloved daughter.[35]

In working with Azara's text, Moreau recognized homologous life experiences and intellectual tendencies. The two authors shared an intimate epistemology despite their different national loyalties. In an act of intellectual narcissism, Moreau could see aspects of his own lived experiences and interests as he translated Azara's manuscripts. They were both driven to exercise control over bodies—people, monkeys, rats. Their privilege was marked by their ability to cut open animals, to have people at their command to care for both them and their specimens. Dissection could be considered the most intimate act of natural science. Likewise, Gayatri Chakravorty Spivak has observed that "translation is the most intimate act of reading." These intimacies were physical and intellectual. In Azara's work, Moreau found a compatriot—a man of letters for whom natural history was inextricable not just from empire and slavery but from sexual mastery in particular. It would be too much to call Moreau's translation of this work—with its interjections, amplifications, and adamant taming of the original text—a work of pornography. But his entire body of scholarship most certainly sits uncomfortably on that line of "ethnopornography," what one volume has elaborated as a "merging [of] the ethno-, the porno-, and the -graphos." The authors "presen[t] us with the disturbing theory that all ethnography relates to a deep-seated desire to penetrate the other."[36]

Questions of lust and penetration bring us back to Moreau's monkey business. Moreau inserted his observations about his own household animal-human dynamics as a commentary on Azara's work on the titi monkey. Moreau's anecdotes about Faquin and Coco also included the story of a family in Martinique that owned a baboon. This animal, Moreau observed, conceived "such a violent passion for the daughter of its master, a young person whose beauty reigned over all, including brute animals, that he could not see her without showing off his frenzy in all sorts of ways. To this frantic love was joined a furious jealousy for all men who came close to her" (une passion si violente pour la fille de son maître, jeune personne que sa beauté faisait sans doute régner, même sur les brutes, qu'il ne pouvait l'apercevoir sans étaler sa frénésie de toutes les manières. A cet amour effréné se joignait une jalousie furieuse pour tous les hommes qui approchaient d'elle). Moreau was sure to note that he personally "saw" (j'ai vu) this animal demonstrating "frantic," "frenz[ied]" "LOVE" and "PASSION" and "JEALOUSY" (capitalization mine) for a human being; his empirical eye was a witness to inter-species lust, and his discussion of animals and humans crossed in this example. Monkeys desired humans—what did this observation say about evolutionary scales? Did Moreau witness this baboon with an erection as he "show[ed] off" his frenzy? Cay monkeys and baboons are not only quadrupeds, the subject of Azara's work, but facultative bipeds. This means that they are capable of moving both on four legs and also on two legs when necessary. By the logic of interpolation, perhaps humans are more facultative bipeds than obligate ones in certain sex positions when they cease being upright and get on all fours. Moreau clearly had sex on his mind, seemingly of a coercive nature, as he inserted himself and his monkey prosthesis into his translation of a scientific tome on South America. It is especially distasteful to imagine him textually ejaculating his own memories of his and other *colons'* pre-Haitian revolutionary life of sexual predation into the pages of this translation.[37]

I conclude this discussion of intimate coercion with an imagined interior monologue written in Guaraní: the voice of an anonymous Indigenous woman, perhaps living as a Christian on a Jesuit reduction, or a mixed-race African woman clearing fields in the Pampas. She studies the natural historian, thinking her own thoughts about multiple exploitative animals: avian, feline, and human.

Kuae mbia, ia ikañimaä vae, oparandu urubure
This man with the strange hair asks questions about the *iribus:* vulture
Oipota oikuaa aechara vae jou yagua vae; ani, oimera yagua reta kuae rupi
He wishes to know if I have seen it feed on the *jaguarete,* and if the *jaguarete* lives near here
Amope, jae oguata chendive kaa rupi
He sometimes travels in the woods with my kinfolk
Che aikuaa jae cherekata vae pitu ovaë yave
I know he will seek me out come nightfall.[38]

The Mot Juste, However *Injuste* and Unjust

Just as Moreau shared an (intimate) epistemology about American geographies with Félix de Azara, he would have considered Iñigo Abbad y Lasierra a kindred intellectual spirit as well. His translation of Abbad y Lasierra's work included no randy monkey tales and no moments when the collaborators commented on their own libidinous desires for racialized women. However, *Historia geográfica, civil y natural de la Isla de San Juan Bautista de Puerto-Rico* shared many common themes with Moreau's compilations about French Caribbean law and social customs. The text echoed the ambitious desire of Moreau's work to capture the uniqueness of island life. No subject was too small to broach, and the coverage was capacious. Abbad y Lasierra's narration worked in two temporalities: sixteenth- and seventeenth-century Puerto Rico as a battleground between the Indigenous population and the Spanish conquistadores and contemporary depictions of late-eighteenth-century mores and the natural environment. Moreau's extant manuscript translation "Histoire geographique, civile et politique de l'isle de St. Jean-Baptiste de Porto-Rico" is close to four hundred pages and follows Abbad y Lasierra's text closely. It was a working draft—footnote numeration was inserted but not completed, and translations are missing or in progress, as is clear in the crossed-out words and marginal markups in Figure 42. The research notes promised about Puerto Rico from his "augmented" translation (augmentée par ses propres recherches) are largely absent.[39]

A discussion of the imbrication between natural history and language would not be complete without attending to the finer details of word choice as the primary means of conveying signification. It is fortunate that Moreau's work exists in draft, complete with all of its messiness and queries. In Figure 42, there are two *x*'s in the left margins near the middle of the page. These marked words for which Moreau was seeking exactitude. In this case, how to translate *maracas* and *guitarillo*? Ideas mattered, precision mattered. Although Moreau eagerly courted the favor of European-based natural historians, he contributed to the vitality of Americas-focused conversations through a desire, even an anxiety, to develop local, informed knowledge that only a creole, or long-term inhabitant of the Americas, could claim. Immediately to the left of the marginal *x*'s are three words punctuated with an exclamation mark. His note, "est un banza!" radiates excitement. Even as a guitarillo was quite literally a "petite guitarre," as

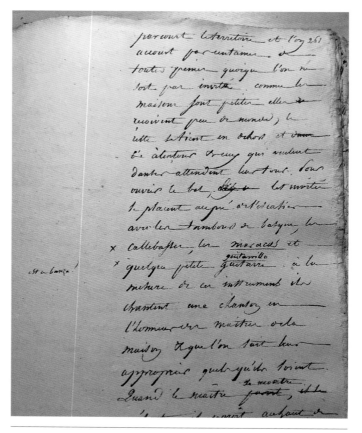

FIGURE 42. Moreau's translator's note on the "banza." From Iñigo Abbad y Lasierra, "Histoire geographique, civile et politique de l'isle de St. Jean-Baptiste de Porto-Rico," trans. Moreau de Saint-Méry, Manuscript 116, Service historique de la Défense, Château de Vincennes.

he noted in his translation, Moreau believed it to be more precisely something else: a banza. French language (in a French translation) was not the ideal way to capture a Puerto Rican instrument. A Santo Domingan word, itself perhaps derived from the West Central African Kimbundu word for a stringed instrument called an *mbanza,* was more precise. A Caribbean theory of translational *fidelité,* of choosing just the right word when carrying meaning across cultural fields, meant being able to pinpoint the linguistic, semantic richness of the Caribbean itself. The contemporaneous metropolitan move toward valuing more word-for-word correspondence suited Moreau, the proud *antillais.*

The banza was a precursor to the banjo, made from a gourd covered with animal skin to which were usually added a neck and four strings. Moreau devoted many pages to descriptions of the music and dance traditions produced by the enslaved in his *Description de la partie française de l'isle de Saint-Domingue,* including a short description of the banza. The instrument was also the subject of scornful descriptions by some white colonists and visitors to the island. For example, Richard de Tussac wrote:

> As for the guitars, which the Blacks call *banzas*, this is what they consist of: they cut lengthwise, through the middle, a fresh calabash. . . . The[y] stretch across it the skin of a goat, which they fasten around the edges with small nails; they make two little holes on this surface, then a kind of slat or roughly flattened piece of wood constitutes the neck of the guitar; they stretch over it three strings made of pitre (a kind of string taken from *the agave plant,* commonly known as *pitre*). . . . On this instrument they play airs composed of three or four notes, which they repeat incessantly. This is what the Abbé Grégoire calls sentimental, melancholy music, and what we call the music of savages.

> Quant aux guitares, que les nègres nomment *banza,* voici en quoi elles consistent: Ils coupent dans sa longueur, et par le milieu, une callebasse franche. . . . Ils étendent dessus une peau de cabrit, qu'ils assujettissent autour des bords avec des petits cloux; ils font deux petits trous sur cette surface, ensuite une espèce de latte ou morceau de bois grossièrement aplati, constitue le manche de la guittarre; ils tendent dessus trois cordes de pitre (espèce de filasse tirée de *l'agave,* vulgairement *pitre*). . . . Ils jouent sur cet instrument des airs composés de trois ou quatre notes, qu'ils répètent sans cesse; voici ce que l'évêque Grégoire appelle une musique sentimentale, mélancolique; et ce que nous appelons une musique de sauvages.

Although these comments were ostensibly about music, they were also about biology and racial difference. Rather than the disparaging and dismissive attitude captured above, Moreau took a certain pride in extolling local traditions. They were critical to making Saint-Domingan culture Saint-Domingan. This might have been one of the few things about which he and the Abbé (Henri) Grégoire, a reformer with whom Moreau disagreed in print regarding the morality of slavery, might have concurred: the banza itself should not be discounted as the instrument of "savages." Moreau's annotation captures his excitement to have found a musicological equivalent to the banza in a Spanish-controlled Caribbean island. This pan-Caribbean musical link was understood to be a result of traditions

based in common African origins, origins that he wrote about in other publications. Elsewhere I have argued for understanding interisland musical performance traditions—deliberate choices about the construction of instruments,
fashion styles, rhythmic signatures—as examples of African diasporic aestheticized political consciousness. Here we see Moreau noticing this as well, even if
he did not understand the depth of the shared knowledge he was witnessing.
Like the Chinese *gom-gom / tam-tam* discussed in Chapter 3, Moreau created
associations about other parts of the world based on his experience with African-
derived cultural forms. And he gained this experience by being raised as a slaveholder in a slaveholding society.[40]

Inasmuch as both Abbad y Lasierra and Moreau relied on natural history
genres to categorize people based on their behaviors, they looked to musical
instrumentation as a data point. The stakes of using this information become evident here as we witness Moreau's act of translation. The right kind of
slaveowner—the empiricist, detail-oriented type who had local expertise in local
languages—needed only to observe, record, and pronounce words correctly to
prove his entitlement to command. Moreau's intellectual enthusiasm and curiosity exceeded pure instrumentalism, but instrumentalism was a determining factor in his zeal *(zèle)*. The historian Santa Arias reminds us that Abbad y Lasierra's
"choices in historical writing clearly followed trends of Enlightenment historiography and advocacy for the rational management of slaves and the liberalization
of commerce to revitalize the empire." Moreau was similarly convinced that if
managed properly, the enslaved could continue to grow the coffers of Caribbean
slaveholders, their metropolitan allies, and the French state. Commerce, and the
labor required to keep it moving, could be effectively restored to pre-1794 paradigms of control if local Caribbean intellectuals could regain their right to own
their labor supply. By the time Moreau worked on this manuscript, the French
National Convention had abolished slavery in the colonies. It was still legal in
Puerto Rico.[41]

The year 1798 was in fact a momentous moment of flux for Moreau to be working on his translation of Abbad y Lasierra's *Historia geográfica* (Figure 43). In his
preface, Moreau noted that it was vital for French readers to know about Puerto
Rico, given that the island was "a neighbor" (une voisine) of Saint-Domingue.
He stated:

> The Spanish colonies of the New World are generally very little known, and
> that of Puerto Rico, despite the importance of its location and several other
> advantages, is perhaps the most ignored of all. I even confess that despite
> the research that has occupied me for twenty-five years, I had barely a few

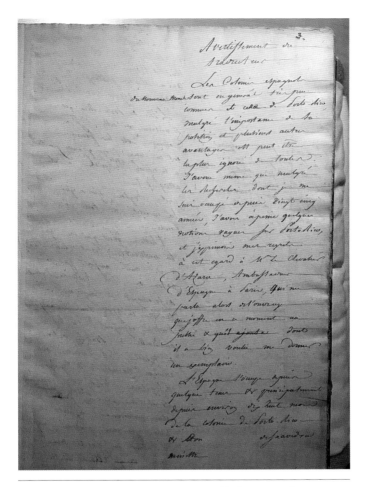

FIGURE 43. "Avertissement. . . ." From Iñigo Abbad y Lasierra, "Histoire geographique, civile et politique de l'isle de St. Jean-Baptiste de Porto-Rico," trans. Moreau de Saint-Méry, Manuscript 116, Service historique de la Défense, Château de Vincennes.

vague notions about Puerto Rico, and I expressed my regrets on this matter to the Chevalier Azara, the Spanish ambassador in Paris, who then spoke to me about the work that I now offer to the public, of which he kindly gave me a copy.

Les colonies espagnoles du Nouveau Monde sont en général très peu connues et celle de Porto Rico, malgré l'importance de sa position et plusieurs autres

avantages, est peut-être la plus ignorée de toutes. J'avoue même que malgré les recherches dont je me suis occupé depuis vingt-cinq années, j'avais à
peine quelques notions vagues sur Porto Rico, et j'ai exprimé mes regrets à
cet égard à M. le Chevalier d'Azara, ambassadeur d'Espagne à Paris, qui me
parla alors d'ouvrage que j'offre en ce moment au public dont il a bien voulu
me donner un exemplaire.

The 1790s marked a period of British aggression toward Spanish and French
colonies in the Caribbean reminiscent of 1762, when the British occupied both
French Martinique and Spanish Havana. In 1797, the British invaded Puerto
Rico, only to be repelled by the Spanish with the assistance of French residents
on the island. In 1793, the British also invaded western and southern Saint-
Domingue, which they succeeded in occupying for the next five years during
what became the Haitian Revolution. Moreau's interest in Puerto Rico is in part
explicable as a moment of shared crisis. With his close friend Talleyrand soon to
take over as Napoleon's foreign minister, there was reason to hope that discussions about the reestablishment of slavery in French domains might be on the
horizon.[42]

I close by bringing Indigenous populations, in this case Caribbean ones, back
into the discussion of Moreau's natural history work. Although most discussions
of his ouvrage focus on the categories of whiteness vis-à-vis blackness (and all of
the complexions he described in between), Moreau had a long-standing interest in Indigenous histories. For example, his research has been used as a source
of information on the Natchez relocation from Louisiana to Saint-Domingue;
he documented the enslavement of five hundred people sent from Louisiana in
the 1730s, in addition to more people from Louisiana and Canada who were
sold there in the years afterward. Moreau told stories of the Indigenous caciques
of Hispaniola at the time of the conquest, recounted the locations of stores of
earthenware pottery, and even made etchings of copper Spanish coins he claimed
to have found in a burial site close to Columbus's settlement of Natividad, in
Moreau's time a sugar plantation outside Limonade, Saint-Domingue.[43] Gonzalo
Fernández de Oviedo y Valdés, Antonio de Herrera y Tordesillas, Juan de Castellanos—in short, many narrators of classic accounts of the conquest appear across
Moreau's work on Hispaniola and again as he expanded his knowledge of Puerto
Rico when translating Abbad y Lasierra's *Historia geográfica*.

Moreau's knowledge was also derived from embodied sources, not just contained in books and objects. He developed it through evidence found in bodily
human remains and in stories about the living. We must not forget the Taino
skull that was stored in the Cercle des Philadelphes building, passed around for

Moreau and his fellow members to hold. Or the "human bones" (ossemens humains) Moreau claimed to have seen in the coastal caverns outside Jérémie, not
far from where he reported there were once buried "Indian bodies, all placed
parallel facing the same direction" (des corps d'Indiens placés tous parallèlement
dans la même direction).[44]

There were also enslaved Indigenous people that circulated in Moreau's orbit;
he condemned their enslavement while simultaneously claiming that they were
largely extinct. Yet he told of contemporaneous Indigenous Carib and Taino
women, a "very small number" (très-petit nombre), who "were turned into domestics [in Saint-Domingue], because [he] did not know of them being employed
any other way" (on fait des domestiques, car je ne sache pas qu'on les ait employés
à d'autres usages). Domestic labor, with all of its possible sexual dangers, again
emerges as a way that Indigenous women experienced enslavement. Indigenous
populations also appear in Moreau's taxonomic study of racial admixture in the
colonies. When they "mixed with Blacks or whites, or any of the different types
of mixtures of these two colors" (mêlés aux nègres ou aux blancs, ou aux divers
résultats du mélange de ces deux couleurs), he observed, "there is no longer any
difference between their descendants and that of mulâtres except that their hair
is blacker and straighter for longer" (il n'y a plus de différence entre leur descendance et celle des mulâtres, si ce n'est que les cheveux sont plus long-tems noirs,
plus long-tems plats). Moreau's natural history claims around Native history
were bookish, eyewitness, and sometimes hands-on. He categorized and classified people by making lists of features: hair, the size of hands and feet, skin
complexion, supposed sexual availability. Combinations of these traits were used
by him and Azara to classify quadrupeds as well. Although natural history takes
the study of life as its focus of inquiry, Moreau's and Azara's investigations into
people, places, and animal life are everywhere about violence, dispossession, and
death. In the case of language, the desire to capture and control people is equally
clear, as the following investigation into the Kongolese dictionary produced by
Moreau's brother-in-law, Louis Narcisse Baudry des Lozières, also shows.[45]

❋❋❋❋❋❋❋❋❋❋❋❋❋❋❋❋❋❋ ❋❋❋❋❋❋❋❋❋❋❋❋❋❋❋❋❋❋

CHAPTER SIX

"You Are a Poisoner"

Planter Linguistics in Baudry des Lozière's "Dictionnaire ou Vocabulaire Congo"

P H R A S E S.

donne-moi ton bras.	toalam mioko.
tu es une bête.	gnéi ïoba.
balaye la chambre.	kombazo.
fils de femme dé-bauchée.	kounou goua kou.

FIGURE 44. Excerpt from "Dictionnaire ou Vocabulaire Congo," in [Louis Narcisse] Baudry des Lozières, *Second voyage à la Louisiane, faisant suite au premier de l'auteur de 1794 à 1798 . . .*, 2 vols. (Paris, 1803), II, 115.

"Give me your arm." "You are a beast." "Sweep the room." "Son of a debauched woman." These are English translations of four phrases that appeared in succession in a "Congo" language learning tool published in 1803 by Louis Narcisse Baudry des Lozières (Figure 44). A planter, amateur linguist, and Moreau's brother-in-law, Baudry included many such incongruous terms and phrases in his "Dictionnaire ou Vocabulaire Congo," a project he imagined as a useful guide for American colonists. Taken out of context, "give me your arm" (*donne-moi ton bras / toalam mioko*) is an innocuous request, perhaps an offer of assistance. The next line, "you are a beast" *(tu es une bête / gnéi ïoba)*, is less subtle in its implied insult, and the pronoun *tu* suggests familiarity. The command to "sweep the room" *(balaye la chambre / kombazo)* has an authoritative, even confrontational tone when read after the previous entry. The final phrase, "son of a debauched woman" *(fils de femme débauchée / kounou goua kou)*, is inexplicable. Who is being addressed, and why would such an expression appear in a phrase book? Other examples are more disturbing and graphic. The progression of the phrases in this small excerpt has a metaphoric quality that stands in for the whole. It underlies the process of colonization from the perspective of the colonizer—"give me your arm," "come with me," "under my tutelage you shall learn about civilization." When seen as an analogy of the colonial process, the excerpt relates an overture of friendship belied by the forced labor and abuse that is to come.[1]

This chapter draws on Baudry's work to continue the discussion of how the study of language and print culture exposes the quotidian violence and sexual coercion structuring Moreau and Baudry's world. My focus is the mobilization of the Kongo family of languages across the French colonial empire during the Age of Revolutions, and I make a threefold argument. First, Baudry's "Vocabulaire" provides a critical reminder of the need to more systematically consider African languages as American ones. The "Congo" Baudry documented is Kikongo, an important Bantu cluster language in West Central Africa. At a decisive historical juncture, it was a key vector of communication for those who participated in the Haitian Revolution. People from West Central Africa, a region that stretched from the Loango Coast south to Luanda, formed a substantial percentage of the African-born population in Saint-Domingue and North America, especially in South Carolina, Georgia, and Louisiana. John Thornton, whose scholarship has done much to document the importance of Central African culture in the Americas, particularly African political formation in the Haitian Revolution, notes, "Slaves from this region made up the majority of those imported into Saint-Domingue for the last twenty years before the Revolution. . . . They were common enough among the rebels that Congo became a generic term for the rank and file of the slave insurgents." By setting Baudry's expertise alongside expanding scholarship on the "Kongolese Atlantic," I wish to restore our sense of Kikongo as one of the lingua francas of Saint-Domingue.[2]

Second, the "Vocabulaire" was undertaken as a project to maximize labor extraction and to create a psychological instrument of abuse, even as it purported "to soften" (adoucir) the lives of the enslaved people it addressed. Words project power, and the study of languages in the extended Americas was frequently occasioned by the desire to conquer land, people, and consciousness. The terms of the "Vocabulaire" and the paratext surrounding them highlight the fantastical self-fashioning of the planters who violently exploited men, women, and children yet envisaged themselves as benefactors and enlightened owners. A close reading affords a glimpse of the intimacy of person-to-person contact in colonial zones, particularly its sexual dimensions. My purpose is to imagine the printed words on the page as utterances within a sociohistorical context. This entails exploring the motivations and scholarship (social interactions and source material) of those attempting to speak and codify the world of Kikongo that surrounded them. It also requires informed speculation to include the perspective of those who heard some approximation of Kikongo shouted at them in anger or whispered to them in the slave quarters by those to whom the language did not belong.

Third, the turn toward supranational concerns in the study of the early Americas—be it vast, comparative American, or transatlantic—marks a *retour* to how many scholars of the period assessed their own worlds. Foreign-language study—including concerns with mutual intelligibility, control over others, and the possibility of transcribing oral speech so that it could be used in both scholarly environments and tense on-the-ground situations—was a fundamental method by which late-eighteenth- and early-nineteenth-century American scholars engaged their global business concerns and extended household networks. Indeed, restoring an analytic framework marked by transcolonial itineraries, linguistic interactions, and contingent politics more aptly reflects the world as it was experienced by those living, conducting their research, and disseminating their findings in the time before the nation-state became geopolitically dominant.[3] In the Caribbean, such a perspective was turned at once locally and outward, be it in transatlantic, African diasporic, or hemispheric and archipelagic directions. Baudry's "Vocabulaire" documents an assertion of power that extended its hopeful reach from West Africa to large swathes of North America to the *plaines* and *mornes* of Saint-Domingue.

Although the "Vocabulaire Congo" provides a window into what was most of interest to colonists, it also provides modern-day readers with filtered access into the parallel yet divergent worlds that the enslaved inhabited and how they might have interacted with their masters. An analysis of the text and the ideas it contains reveals a communal biographical approach that centers other people in the Baudry and Moreau households. These people were key interlocutors, informants without whom the "Vocabulaire" could not have existed. It is critical to understand that the Kikongo language in Saint-Domingue was shaped by a dialectical process in which the term Congo increasingly became synonymous with the most determined and efficacious resistance on the part of the enslaved. Put simply, Baudry's "Vocabulaire" offers an implicit recognition that a principal language of communication was also a local threat that eluded planter control. At the time of its publication, during the massive Napoleonic expedition sent to restore control over the French Caribbean colonies, the "Vocabulaire" exemplified the hope of transforming a tool of revolutionary exchange back into one of attempted domination. As an invaluable literary artifact of this moment, the "Vocabulaire" illustrates what it means to speak of language as a weapon of war. The combatants are revealed in an archive of words.

No Slaves, No Colonies: That Is an Incontestable Fact
for Those Familiar with Colonial Matters

Baudry des Lozières (Figure 45), the author of this "Vocabulaire Congo" and the inscriber of the heading above, is not as well known outside French Atlantic historiography as Moreau. Whereas Moreau was a French creole, Baudry was born in France. He claimed, however, to speak with authority about the colonies because of his "stay of twenty-five years." (séjour de vingt-cinq ans). The two met while practicing law in Cap Français, and they married two sisters. They spent long periods of their adult lives in each other's company, and Baudry described them as "linked by blood and by friendship, for close to thirty years" (liés par le sang et par l'amitié, depuis près de trente ans). Baudry acted as Moreau's power of attorney for transactions ranging from manumissions of the enslaved to inquiries about his book publications; he was the one who handled the manumission of Angélique, Moreau's wet nurse, and her children. They were active Masons and shared intellectual pursuits: Baudry hoped to write an *Encyclopédie coloniale,* and Moreau researched and published excerpts of his colonial encyclopedia. Both helped establish the Cercle des Philadelphes in Saint-Domingue, an important scientific and cultural society in the early Americas. Over the course of these decades, they lived abroad together as they fled the French and Haitian Revolutions and eventually took government jobs under Napoleon. Baudry in fact succeeded Moreau as historiographer of the French Ministry of the Navy and Colonies when the latter assumed his diplomatic post in northern Italy.[4]

Like Moreau, Baudry has a reputation as a strident ideologue of white racial superiority. He is best known for his invective against *"nigrophiles."* I translate the term as "n—— lovers," rather than "lovers of Black people," since the pejorative, hate-filled sense of the former more closely coincides with how he invoked the word. Dedicated to "all of the honest colonists, victims of the revolution of the n[——] lovers" (tous les Colons honnêtes, victimes de la révolution des Nigrophiles), the "Vocabulaire" positioned itself as a proslavery tract. Much like his book *Les égaremens du nigrophilisme* (1802), it justified the transatlantic African slave trade as both a "civilizing" mission and a necessity for colonial agriculture. Advancing the belief that merchants and planters were "liberators" (libérateurs) of the people they purchased, he suggested French enslavement of Africans saved those who would "perish from hunger" (périraient de faim) and from the dangers of bad governance among so-called brutes and barbarians. His self-serving sophistry led him to assert that slavery as practiced in the colonies was only slavery "in name" (que par le nom), not as "odious" (odieux) as fanatical philosophes exaggerated it to be. In fact, echoing Moreau's contentions about slavery

L. N. Baudry Deslozières.
Comm.d.t des Montagnes de Léogane et Colonel
Insp.r.teur de Crète Dragons. 1790.

FIGURE 45. Portrait of Louis Narcisse Baudry des Lozières. 1790. Frontispiece
from G[abriel] C[hastenet-]d'Esterre, *Précis historique sur le régiment de Crète,
dragons; suivi d'une notice sur la vie militaire, politique et privée de M. Baudry-
Deslozières, colonel-inspecteur dudit régiment,* 3d ed. ([Paris?], 1804). Courtesy of
the John Carter Brown Library.

in *Mémoire justificatif* and *Considérations présentes aux vrais amis du repos et du
bonheur de la France; à l'occasion des nouveaux mouvemens de quelques soi-disant
Amis-des-noirs,* Baudry gave metropolitan actors and their allegedly ill-formed,
abstract policies more acerbic attention and causal responsibility for the Haitian
Revolution than he afforded the enslaved and free people of color themselves. He
boldly claimed that planters loved Black people since they knew how to pursue
their desire to improve the lives of their laborers without risking the public interest. This seeming contradiction—a policy of enslaving people as a way of caring
for them—underscores the structure of sentiment he created to undergird his
proslavery propaganda.[5]

Baudry's material motivations underpinning his claims are discernable. In
addition to practicing law in Saint-Domingue, he was a landowner who had

firsthand knowledge of forced labor practices on his coffee plantation in the
mountains outside Léogâne. A 1789 letter that his wife wrote to Moreau demonstrates the Baudry family's reliance on slavery for economic profit. She bemoaned
the fact that they did not own more people because a bigger labor pool would
have yielded a larger harvest. With seeming resignation, however, she noted, "But
I have new Blacks, who need a lot of care, and as a consequence, I go very slowly.
You know that the first law of a settler is to take care of his property, and I assure you that the Blacks are very happy with my presence" (mais j'ai des Nègres
nouveaux, qui ont besoin de beaucoup de ménagement, et en conséquence je vais
bien doucement. Vous savez que la première loi d'un Habitant est de ménager son
mobilier, et je vous assure que les Nègres sont bien contens [sic] de ma présence).
One must wonder how "happy" Madame Baudry's enslaved workers were about
her purportedly benign oversight of their lives. Her comments are a reminder
that a genocidal regime of labor extraction made Saint-Domingue a major coffee
producer as well as "Europe's most profitable colony and the world's largest producer of sugar" at the end of the eighteenth century.[6]

In his scattered recollections of events of the Haitian Revolution, Baudry
lamented that his subsequent oeuvre was colored by "melancholy" (mélancolie).
This was due to the memory of losing "all of his fortune in a day" (la perte qu'il
fit en un seul jour de sa fortune), the lingering physical injuries inflicted by insur-
gent enslaved people and lower-class whites *(petits blancs),* and his being forced to
live in exile with his family in "frightful misery" (la misère affreuse). The tone of
his work is more hostile and delusional than melancholic, and a barely contained
bile outweighs the feigned bonhomie of the kind, paternalistic planter he hoped
to portray. This range of affective stances brings into focus the artifice and fic-
tionality of narratives written by the planter elite across the Americas: they vac-
illated from implying that all their enslaved adored them to categorically stating
that all Black people were inherently dangerous enemies and inferior beings who
deserved to be enslaved.[7]

Baudry spent four years of this "frightful misery" in Philadelphia, living with
the Moreaus and later in a cottage in Germantown. He was a regular visitor to
Moreau's bookstore, probably consulting many of the texts he used as source
material for his work and trading notes about his own research with other exiled
colonists. Members of these circles tended to read their work aloud to one another, creating an atmosphere of nostalgic reverie that indulged their intellectual
pretensions. Baudry's career, and by extension those of other exiled Caribbean
planters in the early North American republic, is important for centering race,
language, and colonialism in discussions of Philadelphia's print culture community. In part because Baudry's unspecified business interests produced "only a

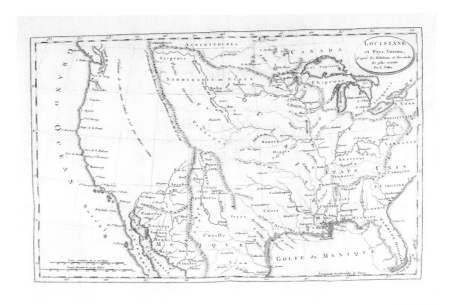

FIGURE 46. *Louisiane et pays voisins, d'après les relations et les cartes les plus recentes.* This map demonstrates the combined size of the upper and lower Louisiana colony and includes Indigenous nations. Frontispiece from [Louis Narcisse] Baudry des Lozières, *Second voyage à la Louisiane, faisant suite au premier de l'auteur de 1794 à 1798 . . .* , 2 vols. (Paris, 1803), I. Courtesy of the John Carter Brown Library.

trifling profit," Moreau purchased return tickets to France for both families in 1798, when they became personae non gratae in the United States following the Alien and Sedition Acts.[8]

"Dictionnaire ou Vocabulaire Congo" appeared as an appendix to Baudry's *Second voyage à la Louisiane* (1803), which was a follow-up to the account of his first trip. Both texts were poorly organized anecdotal narratives of eighteenth-century political and natural history in Louisiana (the lower territories of *la Nouvelle France,* which stretched from the Ohio Valley through Saint Louis, Mobile, and New Orleans) and Saint-Domingue. Figure 46 is a reproduction of the map Baudry included in his work on Louisiana and shows the immense territory claimed by the French in North America. Discussion of the imbrication of Louisiana and Saint-Domingue within the nostalgic context of a lost but recoverable empire reflected Baudry's and other exiled planters' optimism that the Napoleonic expedition would return their American properties (both land and the enslaved) to French control. Many scholars have debated whether a military victory in Saint-Domingue would have been followed by an increased French presence in the Lower Mississippi, as opposed to what resulted: the selling of remaining French lands to the United States as part of the Louisiana Purchase. Baudry's "Vocabulaire Congo" was meant to be used, and its inclusion in a volume about Louisiana suggests that he expected this crash course in Kikongo to be of practical importance both in the Caribbean and on the North American mainland.[9]

The seventy-four-page "Vocabulaire Congo" contains a list of more than 650 words and 120 phrases that provide French-to-"Congo" translations. The project was compiled in the last decade of the eighteenth century, when the study of linguistics and philology was popular in France and gaining steam in the new United States among scholars such as Thomas Jefferson and Peter S. Du Ponceau. Unlike earlier missionary linguistic undertakings, Baudry's text was a very secular project, not evangelical in purpose. Nor was it a treatise interested in detailed theories of the origins, hierarchies, or relationships among language groups.[10] Although it contained a long description of the slave trade in the Central African coastal communities of Ambriz, Cabinda, and Loango, it was not an ethnographic project that used language to study Kongo communities in the Americas and speculate about a Kongolese worldview. Rather, it was a project motivated by a desire to be "useful," whose core defining principle was maximizing trade profit and labor extraction in direct-encounter situations.

Baudry envisioned this publication as a guidebook for planters, especially those new to the Americas. Ironically, the same revolution that Baudry repeatedly reviled became a potential selling point for the book, as he suggested that the large number of planter deaths would occasion the arrival of inexperienced people needing language training. Similar to a modern-day Berlitz language and phrase book, this guide would ideally give planters a means of communicating with the enslaved in their language. Baudry fancied that, by having this capability, a planter would be able to form a bond of trust with his labor force:

The majority [of planters] buy Blacks, and they do not know their language. . . . Being a planter myself, I understood the utility of this type of science and dedicated myself to it during my moments of leisure. I tried to learn only enough to understand my newly arrived slaves [bossals] and to make myself understood. Nothing is sadder than the Black person taken on board. . . . Accustomed to dealing only with cruel people in his own country, he arrives in a country he does not know, among men whom he naturally compares to the executioners and cannibals of his country of birth. . . . But knowing how to talk to him, you cheer him up, you inspire him with confidence. His hope born, you allay the memory of his hut, of his sad family, and soon he will see you as nothing but a man superior to him, a benefactor who tears him away from death, misery, and the degradation of man.

La plupart [des planteurs] achètent des nègres, et ils n'en connaissent pas le langage. . . . Étant planteur moi-même, j'ai senti l'utilité de cette espèce de science, et dans mes momens de loisir je m'y suis livré. Je n'ai cherché qu'à en savoir assez pour entendre mes esclaves *bossals* et en être entendu. Rien n'est plus triste que le nègre pris à bord. . . . Accoutumé dans sa patrie à n'avoir affaire qu'à des hommes cruels, il arrive dans un pays qu'il ne connaît pas, parmi des hommes qu'il compare naturellement aux bourreaux et aux anthropophages de son pays natal . . . mais sachez lui parler, vous l'égayez, vous lui inspirez de la confiance. Son espérance naît, vous lui adoucissez le souvenir de sa cahute, de sa triste famille, et bientôt il ne voit plus en vous qu'un homme supérieur à lui, qu'un bienfaiteur qui l'arrache à la mort, à la misère et à la dégradation d'homme.

There was no intentional irony in Baudry's claims. Again, his assertions exemplify how he imagined a world in which he had saved Africans from the dangers of their native land. The horrors of the Middle Passage and forced labor in the colonies allegedly did not compare to the misery they would have suffered on the African continent.[11]

Most crucially, Baudry posited language as playing an essential role in the acclimation, or "seasoning," process. He believed that competence in an African language among the master class could be a soothing, friendly gesture of goodwill, a skill worth acquiring for very practical reasons. Observing that "these unhappy slaves often perish soon after their arrival because they cannot make themselves understood" (Ces malheureux esclaves périssent souvent peu de temps après leur arrivée, parce qu'ils ne peuvent pas se faire comprendre), Baudry hoped that this guide would improve their chances of survival, a presumed benefit for both the enslaved and their owners. Baudry noted that his work would "also be very useful to doctors and surgeons who can only treat newly arrived Africans poorly if they are not able to ask them questions" (est encore d'une grande utilité pour les médécins, pour les chirurgiens que ne peuvent que traiter mal les nègres nouveaux, s'ils ne sont pas en état de leur faire des questions). Many of the phrases were included with this audience in mind. Terms such as "dysentery" *(dyssenterie / minga)* and phrases such as "is your stomach okay?" *(ton estomach est-il bon? / miévésé ptima tiak ou?)* and "do you have a hernia?" *(as-tu une hernie? / guëië madongou bakzi?)* are easy to take at face value in the context of poor living and working conditions. Others, such as "are you blind?" *(es-tu aveugle? / guéie m'pofo?)* and "do your ears hurt / are you hard of hearing?" *(as-tu mal aux oreilles? / béla koutou?),* also carry insulting connotations in the context of forced labor and possible resistance to it.[12]

Baudry's endeavor to "understand" the enslaved was no doubt also motivated by a desire to recognize potential sedition and to rupture the secrecy afforded to the enslaved by their knowledge of a language outside their masters' purview. A planter's ability to understand and "listen in" on the Kongolese enemy was a valuable skill, both in everyday conflicts between members of a slave society and during "official" war. If we remember these two social groups as locked in combat rather than coexisting peacefully, we understand that acquiring some level of proficiency in an enemy's tongue had varied strategic uses. Baudry's text embodies the tensions that would have been seething just below the surface in Saint-Domingue during the last decades of the eighteenth century; speakers used Kikongo for a range of purposes, often in opposition to one another.

Baudry understood the practical applications of learning African languages, and he maintained that this linguistic work was part of a much longer research project. He informed readers that he had "united [all the jargons of Africa] with exactitude after ten years of hard work" (avais réunis [tous les jargons de l'Afrique] avec assez d'exactitude, et après dix ans d'un travail assidu). It is unclear if "jargons" referred to languages from multiple regions—say, Kikongo and Wolof—or if he was referring to the multiple Bantu languages that would have been spoken by people from West Central Africa—Kikongo, Kimbundu, Kituba, and the coastal variant of Kikongo known as Kisolongo. He lamented that events of the Haitian Revolution, however, left him with only "some notes on the language of the Kongos" (quelques notes sur le langage des Congos), a far cry from the encyclopedic "twenty-four- or twenty-five-volume work" he was hoping to publish on the colonies. In addition to on-the-ground practical uses, this kind of linguistic "science" production was integral to accruing social and intellectual capital. Baudry reaped the benefits of his human chattels' physical labor and their intellectual knowledge. For example, familiarity with colonial customs afforded job opportunities and membership invitations to the various learned societies and academies that Baudry and Moreau held dear, from the Cercle des Philadelphes in Cap Français to the American Philosophical Society in Philadelphia to French salons. Baudry's "Congo dictionary" seems to have been particularly impressive to the Académie de Marseille, which counted him as a member owing in part to this publication.[13]

Within the context of Baudry's study of African languages, the aforementioned demographics in Saint-Domingue are indispensable to understanding his investment in such a project. James E. McClellan III notes that "ninety-nine slave ships arrived in Saint-Domingue in 1789 alone, and crammed into their [holds] breathed 27,000 slaves." He cites sources that number the total enslaved population between 500,000 and 700,000. When we remember that, in the three decades before the publication of Baudry's text (1770–1799), 232,530 people were estimated to have been boarded by French merchants specifically from Central Africa, it is clear that knowledge of Kikongo would have been enormously helpful for those buying and selling their fellow human beings both along the African coast and in the Americas. In her work on the Haitian Revolution, Carolyn E. Fick asserts, "The Congolese were certainly among the most numerous of the ethnic groupings composing the African-born slave population, and although reputedly well-adjusted to slavery, they constituted the predominant nation among the maroons." Moreau himself, the source for much subsequent scholarship on the Kongolese, extolled their physical attractiveness, virtues in the arts, and good qualities as workers, concluding that they had "a sweetness and gaiety that makes them sought after" (d'une douceur et d'une gaieté qui les fait rechercher). Kongolese women in particular were "sought after" for sexual reasons. Moreau blithely blamed these women for white male desire, stating, "In a country where the values are not of exemplary purity, Congolese women's penchant for libertinage has increased ours for them" (dans un pays où les moeurs n'ont pas une pureté exemplaire, le penchant des négresses Congos pour le libertinage a-t-il augmenté celui qu'on a pour elles). Language study was a vehicle of sexual aggression then as it functions as a window into that aggression now. Concluding with comments that only call attention to the false portrait of the carefree, happy enslaved that he had just painted, Moreau said, "One could reproach them for being a little inclined to flight" (On peut leur reprocher d'être un peu enclins à la fuite).[14]

An increasing amount of scholarship is dedicated to the "Kongolese Atlantic," in which places such as Saint-Domingue, Brazil, Cuba, and the South Carolina–Georgia Lowcountry form crucial nodes of connection. The presence of words from Bantu languages in religious rituals and medicinal practices (Vodou, Palo Mayombe) is one way that scholars trace the continued importance of Central African cultures in the Americas. As one of the most creative and indispensable of human inventions, language gives form to social interactions. Its study elucidates these relations and is crucial to understanding how people of different backgrounds negotiate their contact with one another. A study of the vocabulary of the enslaved, both for Baudry's generation and in the present, is thus an important view into multiple markers of belonging in the Atlantic world, from social relationships involving labor to spiritual practices showing how people interacted with their natural environments, ancestors, and gods.[15]

Conversations with scholars of the Bantu language region and my own comparison of Baudry's text with other French-Kongo dictionaries from the period show enough correspondence to confirm that Baudry did in fact record actual Kikongo words. Christina Frances Mobley's study of Bantu words used in eighteenth-century Saint-Domingue concludes that Baudry's dictionary uses "western varieties" of Kikongo. The terms in the "Vocabulaire" were not invented. Baudry claimed to have interviewed native speakers, and he probably had access to written documents as well. Equally important is the actual use of these terms in day-to-day personal conversations. How syntactically correct were the phrases when it came to the conjugation of verbs or appropriate word order? How would they have sounded to the people being addressed? Did his transcriptions account for intonation? Although many of the terms might have been accurate, the linguistic value of Baudry's combination of them into "usable" phrases is more difficult to gauge.[16]

Issues of accuracy and usability in Baudry's "Vocabulaire" are intriguing. Its very existence also pushes us to think more imaginatively, both about how language was used then and about how we classify and interpret its use now. Although official written documents may give the impression that Saint-Domingue was largely French speaking, the reality was far different. By the late eighteenth century, more than two-thirds of the population was African-born, and many of its residents were not conversant in French. What do we learn if we think about the majority of the colony as non-French-speaking? Other languages predominated in quotidian life, including a variety of Bantu-family languages, various West African idioms, and Haitian Kreyòl. The creation and perceived demand for a text like Baudry's illustrates the limits of European languages for fully telling the stories of these sites. Given the demographic statistics mentioned above, it is implausible to think of Haitian Kreyòl and French as the sole, even the predominant, languages in Saint-Domingue just before the revolution. A more expansive approach is needed to account for the vast linguistic diversity of the early American geographies we tend to study as mono- or bilingual. An approach that includes the perspectives of those who spoke these languages is likewise essential.[17]

A firsthand example makes this point eloquently. In correspondence between the French republican commissioners and two former leaders of the Haitian Revolution's early years, Jean-François Papillon and Georges Biassou, the latter two complained that they could not control some of their fellow insurgents, "a multitude of *nègres* of the coast [of Africa] who for the most part can scarcely make out two words of French but who above all were accustomed to fighting [à guerroyer] in their country." Jean-François and Biassou might have been referring to Kongolese rebels, and their non-mastery of French clearly had no effect on their desire or ability to fight. In fact, if we refer to the latter stages of the Haitian Revolution, when the leader Jean-Jacques Dessalines warned his troops in 1804 against becoming victims of the "artful eloquence of the proclamations of their [the French army's] agents," then scarcely making out "two words of French" could provide a distinct advantage to combatants tempted to believe in the false promises emerging from the French state.[18]

Jean-François and Biassou understood the French language's limitations. Baudry did, as well. Navigating the many idioms on the island, they recognized the need to expand their linguistic horizons in the quest for power over those whose labor they hoped to command. In the late eighteenth century, then, at the pinnacle of French control, we see an open acknowledgment of the importance of multiple languages and global geopolitical contexts to an understanding of local conditions. We might productively ask: At what point and why did we lose sight of Kikongo as a Saint-Domingan and American language? In the present moment, Haitian Kreyòl studies continue to be outnumbered by the francophone and anglophone ones of the island. The study of Kikongo as a Haitian language is even less well documented. Michael A. Gomez, in his discussion of "talking half African" as part of the "transformation" of African identities in the U.S. South, provides a succinct answer to why such questions matter. He states, "Within the context of a political struggle, which is exactly what slavery was, it ceased to matter whether specific cultural forms could be maintained over increasing spans of time and space. What mattered instead was achieving a self-view in opposition to the one prescribed by power and authority."[19]

The Kongo language continuum was one such cultural mode of self-fashioning for the enslaved population in Saint-Domingue. Far from the American "legacy" language it has become today, Kikongo was a living, vibrant language that tens of thousands of women, men, and children thought in, dreamed in, plotted in, and used to comfort or confront each other. Although it gave way to Haitian Kreyòl or French (or English, Spanish, or Portuguese in other territories), its relative longevity in a particular location is only one pertinent research concern. As a key communication tool for those who participated in one of the modern world's most extraordinary political and social struggles, Kikongo is of paramount importance. If we think of Saint-Domingue as a predominantly non-French-speaking space, we must explore the avenues of inquiry that appear when we consider Kikongo (and by extension other African idioms) as an American language.[20]

In a world where it was less costly to continuously import African men, women, and children to work than to ensure their survival for more than a few years, there was no foreseeable end to the need to study African languages.

Mastery might not have been the ultimate goal of this second-language learning, but the capacity to utter spontaneous phrases that were lexically and gram-
matically intelligible would have been vital. One way to do so was by means of
the *vocabulaire,* a genre that highlights contact. In her excellent work on Native North American vocabularies, Laura J. Murray argues, "The vocabulary is a
more idiosyncratic and culturally evocative linguistic genre than the dictionary
or the grammar." Suggesting, much as I do here, that it is a textual display of
colonial power relations rendered linguistically, she goes on to state, "Sudden
tonal switches from friendship to hostility are quite typical. . . . Vocabularies
tend to present speakers who trust neither their interlocutors, their interlocutors'
language, nor their own grasp of their interlocutors' language." These comments
ring true for Baudry's text, as well. A seemingly kind question such as "do you
have an appetite?" *(as-tu de l'appétit? / guéie bakzi zala?)* was quickly followed by
the slurs "son of a debauched woman" *(fils de femme débauchée / kounou goua kou)*
and "my, aren't you ugly!" *(que tu es laid! / guéïé manbéné m'bi!).* That the phrase
book section of the text provided such colorful language and insults, however,
suggests free rein of the imagination—whether or not the students of Kikongo
were comfortable with their grasp of the language, their relative lack of fluency did not prevent them from finding the proper epithets to hurl at their
newly acquired "property." Though Baudry called this text both a vocabulaire
and a *dictionnaire,* it was really the former, given that there were no accompanying definitions of the included words. Definitions would have provided ethnographic background for how people in either Saint-Domingue or Louisiana
might have used these words. Many of the terms and phrases, however, are so
graphic that, by imagining them as utterances, I can theorize about the context
of their use.[21]

"Chagrin: Banbou i kelé andi"

—Entry under *C* in "Vocabulaire Congo"

Arranged in loose alphabetical order in French, each letter in the header section of the "Vocabulaire" included a list of words and then phrases using some
of the corresponding terms (Figure 47). A listing for "we" *(nous / béfo)* was followed by the phrase "we are good" *(nous sommes bons / béfo miévésé).* One can
imagine the surreal, even disorienting impression such a comforting assurance
of goodness uttered by a planter or other slave driver must have made. "To finish" *(achever / sonpouka / salakomaka)* was followed by the expression "go finish
your work" *(allez achever votre ouvrage / guéïé koinda sala sonpouka).* The format,
then, was designed to make terms usable and intelligible in the context of day-
to-day interactions. It was not a format that encouraged grammatical and lexical

(130)

est-il là.	likoko ?
il y est.	kéléka likoko.
je suis fâché.	mang'zi.
ta mère a mis au monde un cochon.	mamakou oli outa goulonbou.
tu es empoisonneur.	guéïé n'doki.

L.

Lᴀ.	Ovo.
là-bas.	konan.
lâcher.	lazika. — bika.
laid.	m'bi.
lait.	dévouaman. — man-vouiman. — kiali. mayéné.
lance.	léonga.
langage.	binbon.
langue	loudémi. — louloumi.
languette.	kolo.
langousse. (espèce d'homar ou arai-gnée de mer.).	kosa magnan.
largeur.	ïanguil.
laver.	soukoula.
léger.	linguézé. — linga.
lever quelque chose.	nangouna. — téléma.

FIGURE 47. Words and phrases for *L* in "Dictionnaire ou Vocabulaire Congo." From [Louis Narcisse] Baudry des Lozières, *Second voyage à la Louisiane, faisant suite au premier de l'auteur de 1794 à 1798 . . .*, 2 vols. (Paris, 1803), II, 130.

proficiency, however. That is, information was not presented in an order that built on previous information: there were no lists of pronouns, no examples of how to conjugate verbs or vary verb tenses—not even a list of consecutive numbers, one of the first things that most new language students encounter.[22]

A textual analysis of a few words establishes the geopolitical context of the "Vocabulaire." These terms set the stage for real-life interactions in the enslaved's new environment. Baudry included entries for "my country" *(mon pays/sia-ménon)* and the "country of the whites" *(pays des blancs/poutou-mondélé),* as distinguished from what life might have been like in "your country" *(ton pays/sia-kou),* the "country of the Blacks" *(pays des nègres/poutou-fioté).* There were in fact several entries for "white" that distinguished the color from the man. An assortment of trade items *(merchandise),* many of them fabrics, provides a glimpse into the local economy and its global reach—*indienne/songui pinba* was a popular cloth manufactured in Europe to imitate Indian textile printing. In the "country of the whites," with its different social structures and expectations, labor hierarchies were documented. Entries for "master" *(maître/foumou/bakala)*, "mistress" *(maîtresse/foumou kinto)*, "slave" *(esclave/vika)* and "big house/plantation" *(habitation/botta)* demonstrated vital terms to understanding the plantation complex of a slaveholding society. Activities in the field found their apogee in the seemingly benign phrase "the sugar is very good" *(le sucre est bien bon/sukidi boté manbéne)*. This is one of the phrases a reader can indeed imagine being used frequently in late-eighteenth-century Saint-Domingue or in nineteenth-century Louisiana. Worldwide economic systems put into place over centuries, systems that occasioned massive population flows, movement of goods, and untold human grief, culminated in the ability to mouth these seemingly simple words with such complicated underpinnings. The global dimensions of American agriculture, migration, and linguistic patterns were embedded in the research that allowed Baudry to publish such a sentence.[23]

Although Baudry provided relatively little ethnographic description of the Kongolese once they disembarked in the Americas, he echoed Moreau's comments that they "had a sweet, humane, and hospitable character" (ont un caractère doux, humain, et hospitalier). They allegedly "spread joy throughout the workplace with their silliness, and are among their equals, what our superficial personalities are in our societies" (répandent la joie avec leurs folies dans les ateliers, et sont parmi leurs semblables, ce que nos esprits superficiels sont dans nos sociétés). This amiability made them "popular for domestic needs" (recherchés pour les besoins domestiques). Household activities were thus well represented in Baudry's "Vocabulaire." The "go finish your work" entry could have applied to a litany of tasks he suggested a new planter might wish to have performed: lighting a light, attending to a child, taking someone water or a plate, wiping this or that. The presence of a noun such as "laundry" *(linge)* made perfect sense when combined with the presence of the verb "scrub" *(frotter)*.[24]

An examination of verbs, both their meaning and their grammatical presentation, is particularly instructive. Though there was an assortment of questions included as helpful phrases, the "Vocabulaire" did not have a primarily dialogic function. Rather, imperative phrases documented commands as opposed to conversations. These commands used both the formal *vous* and more personal *tu*. "Go look for my needle" *(allez chercher mon aiguille/miakou koinda vouka)*, "sweep the room" *(balaye la chambre/kombazo)*, and "hurry up" *(dépêche-toi/ïenga nana)* are representative examples. In a guidebook for planters, the imperative mood is not surprising. What, then, should be made of the *utilité* of planters' mastering some of the other verbs he documented, especially if we imagine them as commands? "To kneel," "to love," "to kiss," "to tickle," or "to embrace"? Under what situations would a planter or physician need to know how to say these words in Kikongo?[25]

Baudry's "Vocabulaire" provides a direct indication of interpersonal, close-quarter coercion, often of a sexual nature. Nowhere is this more evident than in some of the entries for helpful phrases. From the banal yet supplicant "Yes sir" *(oui monsieur/guété moenné),* one moves to more insidious snippets of inter-action. Commands to "open your mouth" *(ouvre ta bouche/zibla monnoé)* or "go to bed" *(allez-vous coucher/ïenda léka koinda)* combine with the micromanage-ment indicated by sentences such as "don't put too much salt on what you eat" *(ne sales pas beaucoup ce que tu manges/katata sia m'salou bakanako dia tiakou).* These phrases suggest that, even when engaged in self-care rituals such as eating or sleeping, the enslaved were supervised and intimidated. A cringeworthy phrase such as "do you love me?" *(m'aimes-tu?/menou zozé guëïé?)* indicates how a mas-ter might have required admiration, respect, and amorous affection in addition to physical labor. And what should be made of a phrase such as "your milk is good" *(votre lait est bon/miévézé kiali tiakou)?* Perhaps Baudry envisioned it as a useful phrase for a wet nurse. We have seen two of these women circulating in Moreau's and Baudry's circles—Angélique and a woman who remains anonymous.[26]

Coupled with verbs such as "to kiss" *(baiser/zibika)* and "to embrace" *(em-brasser/fifa),* these terms are an ominous reminder of what a gendered analysis of the abuses of slavery adds to our understanding of life in the most profitable slave society in the Americas. Certain phrases such as "are you pregnant?" *(es-tu grosse?/guëïé oïémito mayemita?),* "get undressed" *(va te déshabiller/guëïé koinda bolola m'lélé tiakou),* and "do your testicles hurt?" *(as-tu mal aux testicules?/makata etia koué béla?)* could be understood in a medical context. Such a limited interpretation, however, runs counter to the well-documented record of sexualized violence and harassment suffered by the enslaved. A rich bibliography documents this topic, and as Wilma King puts it succinctly, "Vul-nerability to sexual exploitation by Europeans began before African women were removed from their homeland, and the practice continued in the Americas." Men were victims of this sexual harassment, as well. In a comment that recog-nized this practice as abusive, yet simultaneously excused it, Moreau wrote, "One might even be authorized to say that the heat of the climate that irritates de-sire, and the *ease of satisfying it,* will always render the legislative precautions one would like to take against this abuse useless, because the law remains silent where nature speaks imperiously" (italics mine) (On est même en quelque sorte autorisé à dire, que la chaleur du climat qui irrite les désirs, et la facilité de les satisfaire,

rendront toujours inutiles les précautions législatives qu'on voudrait prendre contre cet abus, parce que la loi se tait où la nature parle impérieusement). As we
have seen, in Moreau's estimation, Kongolese women were particularly marked as
willing sexual partners because of their alleged libidinous nature. Of course, the
publication of the "Vocabulaire" and the account of such attitudes in Moreau's
famed *Description de la partie française de l'isle Saint-Domingue* occurred in the
literal midst of revolutionary pushback against the violence made possible in a
context in which a planter's authority was virtually unchecked.[27]

This history of conflict and resistance on the part of the enslaved is embedded in many words and phrases. Verbs such as "to lie," in the sense of telling an
untruth *(mentir / louvounou),* were provided along with nouns such as "homi-
cide" *(vonda montou)* and "thief" *(voleur / moévi).* The phrase "if you don't work
I will beat you" *(si tu ne travailles pas je te battrai / guëïé salako filam singa akona
matakou tiakou)* suggests work stoppage or outright refusal to labor. The term for
"brigand" used the same term, *n'doki,* as in the phrase "you are a poisoner" *(tu es
empoisonneur / guëïé n'doki). N'doki,* a word that refers to a witch / sorcerer, indicates that Baudry was equating troublemakers, poisoners, and witches: they all
posed both spiritual and real-world threats. The "Vocabulaire" provides linguistic evidence of the anxiety slaveholders felt about enslaved women and men seeking retribution. A phrase like "what ship brought you?" *(quel navire t'a porté? / kia
kombi nata guëïé?)* also hints at the ties forged during the horrors of the Middle
Passage; the formation of shipmate kinship networks was key to surviving and
resisting the alienation of people's new lives in the Americas.[28]

The reality of a landscape in Saint-Domingue, where the death rate for the
enslaved was "higher than anywhere else in the western hemisphere," is brought
home by the violence emanating from these words (Table 1). Planters were
taught to curse and denigrate their laborers. For a perceived infraction, the enslaved might have insults directed against their progenitors in what amounted
to a Kikongo game of "yo mama" with a drastically lopsided power differential
in which one person had the power of life or death over another. Baudry imagined phrases such as "your mother gave birth to a pig" and "son of a debauched
woman" as helpful conversational knowledge. I'd like to emphasize that Baudry
also provided multiple translations for various words directly related to punishment. In an indication that different Kongo dialects were spoken around
him, he noted, "Every group has words that are particular to it. When a group
doesn't understand one word, they comprehend another" (Chaque cahute a
des mots qui lui sont particuliers. Quand elle n'entend pas l'un, elle comprend
l'autre). His choice of which terms were important enough to include in tripli-
cate is instructive. Three expressions were provided for "whip" *(fouet): m'singa,*

singa gombé, and *motamis.* In addition to knowledge of the three phrases for the object itself, a planter was taught how to threaten, "Be careful of the whip" *(prends garde au fouet / bika m'singa lakota).* An instrument of torture and an example of how to use it in a "practical" sentence were thus foregrounded. Three words were also listed for "fear" *(peur): boman, ouili,* and *bamoën.* This was an emotion that a planter or driver would need to provoke constantly to enforce discipline and compliance. In addition to providing concrete words that incited fear of violence ("whip"), Baudry ensured that conversationalists would know that they were talking about fear; hence the need for the abstract words that referred to the emotion itself. Finally, three words were given for the verb "to cry" *(pleurer): lila, dila,* and *mazanga.* "Cry" was an important enough con-cept that a planter needed to master the expression "do not cry" *(ne pleurez pas / lila bakanako).* Like many of the terms contained in the book, this one was polyvalent. Provided in the imperative, the phrase implies a range of emotions from strict command to an attempt at comforting a suffering person / people. Baudry's avowed politics—rabidly proslavery but "kindly" so—makes both ex-planations possible.[29]

The psychological dimensions of linguistic violence on display here are deeply disturbing; there is a sadistic element to the text's pedagogical intent. In other words, the "Vocabulaire" was not simply a manual with instructive phrases for directing tasks. It is clear that, in addition to providing words for the jobs them-selves, the text was designed to teach the abusive language that one needed to compel people to perform these jobs. "Whip." "Fear." "Cry." Although Baudry told his readers that speaking Kikongo would persuade the enslaved that they were fortunate to be owned by such a "superior benefactor," the very words he bothered to document blatantly chronicled force and derision. The enslaved were beaten down with the tongue as well as the whip. They could be forced to undress, compelled to tickle or be tickled, have their milk supply inspected, all in some approximation of their "native language" and while being asked if they "loved" their oppressors. Baudry casually sketched situations that entailed provoking pain (kidnappings and sales, miserable labor conditions, and a lit-any of other physical and psychological abuse) and suggested that planters and their agents had the right to assuage that same pain. There was a collective and narcissistic pathology at work that normalized such antisocial and inhumane behavior. Not only did the text normalize this delusional orientation toward others' feelings; it also cloaked its sadism in a language of emotions that included so-called compassion.

The darkness of this source, its inherently disturbing nature, is belied by Baudry's upbeat conclusion after years of contact with Kikongo; he claimed that

TABLE I. Sample Terms and Phrases from the "Dictionnaire ou Vocabulaire Congo"

FRENCH	KIKONGO	ENGLISH
canne à sucre	mousinga	sugarcane
singe	kiman	monkey
antropophage	lianga bantou	cannibal
chaine	panga	chain
sang	minga	blood
agenouiller	foukaman	to kneel
baiser	sounga	to kiss
jouer du violon	sika sanbi	to play the violin
frottez cela	kiafiona	to scrub that
allez achever votre ouvrage	guéïé koinda sala sonpouka	Go finish your work.
allez chercher mon aiguille	miakou koinda vouka	Go look for my needle.
prends garde au fouet	bika m'singa lakota	Be careful of the whip.
oui monsieur	guété moenné	Yes sir.
je suis fâché	mang'zi	I am angry.
ta mère a mis au monde un cochon	mamakou oli outa goulonbou	Your mother gave birth to a pig.
tu es empoisonneur	guéïé n'doki	You are a poisoner.
quel navire t'a porté?	kia kombi nata guéïé?	What ship brought you?
m'aimes-tu?	menou zozé guéïé?	Do you love me?
es-tu grosse?	guéïé oïémito? –mayemita?	Are you pregnant?
votre lait est bon	miévézé kiali tiakou	Your milk is good.
que tu es laid!	guéïé manbéné m'bi!	My, aren't you ugly!*

*The exclamation point appears in the original.

Source: "Dictionnaire ou Vocabulaire Congo," in [Louis Narcisse] Baudry des Lozières, *Second voyage à la Louisiane, faisant suite au premier de l'auteur de 1794 à 1798 . . . ,* 2 vols. (Paris, 1803), II, 108–146.

it was "the most pleasant language, and often it greatly helps one understand other African languages. Its sweetness is seductive, and I do not think that even the Italian language beats it" (c'est d'ailleurs la langue la plus aisée, et souvent elle aide beacoup à concevoir les autres de l'Afrique. D'un autre côté, sa douceur est séduisante, et je ne crois pas que la langue italienne même l'emporte sur elle). His adjective of choice, "seductive" (séduisante), carries a sexual innuendo when we recall that Kongolese women were marked as desirable and available sexual partners. Although Baudry repeatedly described African intellect as inferior, he did not use language as "proof" of this belief. In this, he differed from natural historians such as Félix de Azara, whom we have seen associating the sounds of different Indigenous Latin American languages to their speakers' alleged inferior cultures. Baudry's assertions, however, are a further example of how Americanist scholars used their language skills to ostensibly foster good relationships (between "heathens" and the "true" God, between slavers and the enslaved) while bringing the full force of violence to bear on their antagonists.[30]

A Note on Sources, Methods, and Delusion

Michael A. Gomez eloquently describes language as "the bridge and the void over which it extends. . . . A weapon of war. . . . A primary theater of conflict, a principal site of contention." He states: "The real question is not, how difficult was it for Africans to learn English [or, I might add, French, Spanish, Kreyòl, Dutch, or Portuguese] words? Rather, the truly important queries are, what did it mean to the African to hear and at some point repeat words associated with his captors? What did it signify to the African to be expected to learn and embrace concepts which further concretized his condition of social death?" In the context of Baudry's linguistic work, what of the men and women beaten down in some approximation of their "own" languages when they arrived from Africa? An antagonist could have wielded an enslaved person's own language, or, again, some version of it, as an undeniably strong weapon.[31]

It is critical to see (and hear) this material from the vantage point of the enslaved and to hypothesize about how eighteenth-century Kikongo speakers might have assessed the content and nuances of their language when it came from the mouths of strangers. We can visualize Baudry's scholarship "at work" in the fields or in closer quarters. What would it have been like to stand in the sun listening to commands shouted in what sounded nothing like an enslaved person's actual language? To be told to "go get undressed"? The next chapter attempts just such a visualization. This orientation accounts for the active suppression and careless disregard of the opinions of people who both were direct actors in determining Baudry's intellectual trajectory and found themselves the de facto recipients of his "enlightened" ideas. Though the source itself was written by and about a planter, we can reinsert the silent interlocutors of these exchanges. The newly enslaved were processing and negotiating their environments through experiences gleaned from their homelands, the transatlantic voyage, and a new landscape where they were surrounded by a cacophony of languages and the cultures that spoke through them. The study of language (whether Haitian Kreyòl, French, or Kikongo) and its relation to power and personhood was multidirectional. Like Baudry, the enslaved were also thinking about multilingualism as a route toward control over their lives. Multilingual Americanist scholarship provides a method for studying the subjectivities of the enslaved as well as white colonial identities in formation.

Work in comparative African historical linguistics provides a similarly rich methodology for assessing these subjectivities. Kathryn M. de Luna suggests that when studying orally based knowledge production, "Words are as much historical sources as political treatises or court testimony because language is a product of the history of its speakers and words bear the content of that contested history." In his analysis of Baudry's "Vocabulaire," James Sweet demonstrates this approach through a close reading of four terms that appear within—*mvika, macoute, ndoki,* and *mpoutou.* By studying the words used by the enslaved themselves and their history in West Central Africa, he shows that an understanding of how those same words were employed in the Americas, particularly Saint-Domingue, allows for a reorientation of history from the perspectives of the enslaved. And the stakes of doing so are high. As he puts it:

> To shrug our shoulders and concede to the futility of excavating African ideas in the Haitian Revolution is to reify those European intellectual strands that are familiar and accessible. Such a move forecloses *any* African intellectual history of the Haitian Revolution and leaves us with the same old "Enlightenment" and "Age of Revolution" approaches that are far more ahistorical (and essentialist) than those that try to center on the majority-African rebels. Bringing the Africanist's methodological toolbox to bear on Haitian sources challenges the way we understand "slavery" and "revolution" in Haitian history and memory.

Sweet's extended exegesis of the term *mvika* is evocative. He writes: "For Baudry, *esclave* translated as *vika* in Kikongo. The ambiguity of this term begins to come into view when we also recognize that Baudry also translated *captif* as *m'vika.* As we know, all slaves were captives, but not all captives were slaves." Sweet then posits that *vika* and *mvika* were fundamentally the same word in Kikongo (the *m* "a singular noun prefix for the root *-vika*") and that its root was *-pika / -bika*. He cites the work of several Africanist linguists and historians, including Wyatt MacGaffey, Marcos Abreu Leitão de Almeida, and Jan Vansina, to conclude:

> **pika (-bika, -vika)* did not imply chattel slavery at all: rather, the essence of these terms was "master exchange." . . . In St. Domingue at least, the Kikongo words *vika, m'vika,* and *bika* operated side-by-side, opening onto a field of meaning that might explain the prevalence of *petit marronage* and French colonists' seeming tolerance of slave gatherings at markets, provision grounds, and weekend festivals. . . . They [the people who used the term *mvika*] were "slaves" who had "left or parted," or "abandoned," and were now "waiting for someone" who might serve as a new protector / patron.

Rather than understand themselves as chattel, legally bound, along with their descendants, to an owner, the people who shared these words with Baudry had other understandings of what slavery could mean. As "dependents" of a master, they had some rights, including the right to look for other people who might better "protect" their interests. Baudry's "Vocabulaire," when assessed by linguists of Kikongo, has the capacity to reorient our understanding of life on the ground in the literal words of those who formed the backbone of the population. For example, a word as central as "slave" and how it was understood by the people capitalized and commodified as such is fundamental to any discussion of slaveholding societies where we might trace its use.[32]

Baudry noted that personal familiarity with Kikongo enabled him to re-create his project from the notes he salvaged when fleeing Saint-Domingue. He asserted that he gleaned information about Africa through "the interrogation of a crowd of Africans" (l'interrogation d'une foule d'Africains) among the "bossals," and his word choice to describe his research method implies questioning under duress. He made no mention of reticence to share information, although it is probable that his ego or ignorance prevented him from recognizing that information was being held back or deliberately misfed to him. With regard to the information-seeking process, a few phrases indicate the method used in this search to pin down and codify language equivalents—the presence of an interlocutor and someone looking for information. Consider the prompt "what do you call this thing?" (*comment nommez-vous telle chose? / dezina liandi nandi?*). The breakdown in communication potential is evident in the phrases, supplied in both the past and present tenses, "did you understand?" (*as-tu entendu? / ouadi kélé?*) and "do you understand?" (*entends-tu? / ouadzoué?*). This breakdown was inevitable, given that there were probably massive mispronunciations and missing

words projected by those speaking what were already only written approxima-
tions of lived speech. Baudry recorded the word for "cannibal" *(antropophage)*
as *lianga bantou*. The literary scholar Elisabeth Boyi presumes that the accurate
term would have been *liaka bantu*. The exchange of one consonant would have
rendered this word inaccurate. This example suggests that Baudry was listening
to what he heard but hearing it incompletely. His informants were likely misleading him as well, and I concur with de Luna's assessment that "Baudry's teachers
fitted his mouth with words so that he would sound dumb." Finally, Kikongo is
a tonal language, and it is unlikely that he could have adequately captured these
sound nuances on the page.[33]

Baudry appreciated the challenge posed by transcription, however. A few
notes in his work indicate that he ruminated about how to capture sounds in
writing in such a way that they could be brought back to life when read out loud.
In the context of his linguistic work on Kikongo, it is important to note that it
was one of three vocabularies included in the appendixes of his books on Louisiana. The other two were shorter works on the Native American languages Dakota ("Langage des Naoudoouessis") and Ojibwa ("Langage des Chipouais"). He
made almost verbatim scholarly orthographic claims in all three, explaining that
he "attempted to write as one pronounces [the languages], and consequently, it is
necessary to read all of the letters and sound them out" (j'ai tâché d'écrire comme
on prononce; en conséquence, il faut lire toutes les lettres et les faire sonner).
In this attempt to transcribe sound, he echoed Moreau's discussion of Guaraní.
However, the "usefulness" of Baudry's work for a projected audience depended
on making these languages available in written form that could then be reproduced orally. The stakes were higher and less theoretical than in Moreau's work.
Baudry was thus actively engaged with the prime goals of foreign-language learning: the physical act of forming one's tongue, throat, and breath into speakable
terms; developing a good ear for listening and hearing foreign sounds manifest
as coherent words; and recording those same terms in writing.[34]

Although Baudry might have indeed known how to speak some Kikongo and
must have heard it regularly, it is not far-fetched that he might have also verified terms, perhaps even copied them, from written sources. There were several
missionary dictionaries of French-Kikongo, but I do not know if he had access
to them. In addition, I suspect that much of Baudry's work on this "Vocabulaire" might have been stolen. In a statement asserting that he liked to give credit
where credit was due, Baudry wrote: "We owe part of the present chapter to
M. Landophe, the ship captain, who spent a lot of time on the coasts of Africa.
He reminded us of some of the information that we had lost due to the events in

Saint-Domingue.... He is well known in Saint-Domingue and all of the colonies for his long and important services" (Nous devons quelques parties du présent chapitre, à M. Landolphe, capitaine de vaisseaux, qui a beaucoup fréquenté les côtes d'Afrique. Il nous a rappelé quelques-uns des renseignemens que nous avons perdus dans les événemens de Saint-Domingue. . . . Il est bien connu à Saint-Domingue et dans toutes les Colonies, par ses longs et importans services).[35] This is the same Jean-François Landolphe who spent time living in the Warri King-dom, brokered an arrangement for a slave-trading *comptoir* there, and hosted Prince Boudacan in France; Moreau hosted both Landolphe and Boudacan at the Musée de Paris in 1784. As Baudry suggested above, and as is apparent in Landolphe's many appearances in the pages of *Affiches américaines,* his "import-ant services" to Saint-Domingue included making the trade in people between the island and West Central Africa profitable. He appears to have studied many African languages during his years working as a slave trader. An anonymous manuscript copy of the "Vocabulaire" in the Bibliothèque nationale de France, whether the original property of Landolphe, Baudry, or someone else, is suspi-ciously similar to Baudry's published version.[36]

Whether Baudry created or copied some of this manuscript, he was likely familiar with the slave trader Louis de Grandpré's *Voyage à la côte occidentale d'Afrique* (1801). Grandpré's volume contained an appendix of "Congo" words that he believed would be helpful for trade situations along the coast and on shipboard; many of the words and their translations are identical to Baudry's. The same Parisian publisher, Jean Gabriel Dentu, published both books within a year of each other. While Grandpré's appendix did not contain phrases, it did record some extremely striking words mixed in alongside common verbs and nouns. These include "testicle" (*testicule / macata*), "sexual parts of a man" (*parties sexuelles de l'homme / seté ou soutou*), "sexual parts of a woman" (*parties sexuelles de la femme / neno*), and "another sexual part" (*autre partie sexuelle / didy*). The possible referent for this last term is in itself striking—anus? clitoris? Again, the inferences that can be drawn from the inclusion of such terms suggest abhorrent practices. If one is inclined to suppose that traders needed these words purely to determine the health and reproductive capacity of their captives, the phrase "junction of the two sexes" (*junction des deux sexes / songai*) suggests that viola-tion of the enslaved was simultaneously mercenary and sexual. I mention this dimension of Grandpré's vocabulaire to highlight the recurrent mention of sex-ual organs coupled with verbs that invoke physical intimacy, whether coerced or consensual. The two vocabulaires expose how sexual abuse was endemic to colo-nial domination. Although "sexual parts of a woman" is euphemistic in French, perhaps more direct in the Kongo translation provided, a euphemistic veiling (through silence) of this dimension of violence would be a misleading scholarly choice in and of itself.[37]

I close by considering two other texts that could have served as Baudry's linguistic models in the geographic sphere of influence Christopher Miller terms the "French Atlantic triangle." His text shares many common characteristics with the vocabulary genre, but it also reads as a how-to planter manual. This genre of instructional guide was published in the Caribbean and South and North America to share ideas concerning management techniques for enslaved people, crop rotation guidelines, and information about botanical science. *De-bow's Review* in a later North American context was one of the most well known. Though these manuals did not often include linguistic work, there were elaborate language studies in Jean Antoine Brûletout de Préfontaine's *Maison rustique, à l'usage des habitans de la partie de la France equinoxiale, connue sous le nom de Cayenne* (1763) and S. J. Ducoeurjoly's *Manuel des habitans de Saint-Domingue* (1802). The first contained an appendix with an extensive Galibi-French word list, alphabetized first in French and then again in the Indigenous Carib language Galibi. Conceived as a manual for how new settlers might "succeed" in French Guiana, the volume had detailed information about how to manage labor relations with Indigenous and Black workers. Moreau sold this book in his Philadelphia bookshop, so it is likely that both he and Baudry, given their interest in languages and French overseas settlements, would have been familiar with it. Ducoeurjoly's *Manuel des habitans* was a detailed look at life in Saint-Domingue for would-be planters and other new arrivals. It had a French–Haitian Kreyòl dictionary, one of the earliest. Like Baudry's work, it included phrases and even staged imaginary conversations between French and Kreyòl speakers ranging from ship captains to planters to the enslaved. In a posthumous 1819 book sale of Moreau's personal library, all three of these books—Grandpré's, Ducoeurjoly's, and Brûletout de Préfontaine's—were listed in the catalog.[38]

The three publications underscore two observations. First, their presence in two catalogs documenting the contents of Moreau's bookstore and library is circumstantial evidence that they might have exercised some influence over both Baudry's and Moreau's scholarship. They were grounded in firsthand knowledge of the African coast, the French Caribbean, and South America, and all three works would have confirmed the value of doing linguistic work in non-European languages. Like Baudry's Kikongo study, they emphasized the practical skills necessary for labor management without validating the target listeners' thoughts about their own circumstances. However, that these same studies needed to include threats, such as the aforementioned "if you don't work I will beat you," allows us to visualize an uncooperative enslaved interlocutor. Second, the content of the books corroborates the indelible connections between colonial violence and language study. Kikongo, Galibi, and Haitian Kreyòl were all necessary, perhaps as much as French or English or Spanish, to the day-to-day workings of the colonial machine. Along with the whip, they were the gas that powered the engine (commanding cane to be cut, coffee to be harvested, specimens to be collected, or crying babies to be soothed). It is easy to see languages such as Galibi and Haitian Kreyòl, which were "born" in the Americas, as American ones. The "Vocabulaire Congo," specifically designed for use in the extended French Americas, also reminds us that, at certain historical moments, African languages were American too.

To conclude, I wish to return to the "melancholy" that Baudry used to center his own experience and, by extension, that of all the other "honest colonists" who lost their lands, their enslaved workers, and their research, "victims of the revolution of the n[——] lovers." Planter melancholy must be placed alongside a Kikongo entry that Baudry alphabetized under the letter *C:* "chagrin," or *banbou i kelé andi.* Though it is not clear whose humiliation, distress, and embarrassment Baudry was concerned about and why such a word would be necessary, let us ground this emotion in the perspective of an enslaved person. Baudry viewed himself as a benefactor and his "Vocabulaire" as a public service not just for planters but for the enslaved as well. Yet, as we have seen, it was rife with contradictions. How do we reconcile claims of Kongo gaiety with the need for phrases such as "do not cry" or "chagrin"? A state of mind that Baudry saw or heard in front of him (tears, crying) or that he was able to intuit (distress, sadness, anger) mandated the inclusion of corresponding Kikongo words. Yet the very causes of this distress (separation from loved ones, nonstop work, illness, torture) were not recognized as such, nor did he take responsibility for them. Backbreaking labor was acknowledged in the phrase "does your back hurt?" *(ton dos te-fait-il mal? / nima tiakou bèla?),* but that pain became acceptable when it was displaced with the "knowledge" that these same laborers would have been "worse off" in Africa.[39]

The imagination called on to create this delusional interpretation of the world is considerable. In an 1803 issue of the *Edinburgh Review,* a critic of Baudry's work on Louisiana commented on its oddities. He derisively noted that "the only uniformity which it possesses, is the perpetual egotism of the author. . . . The childishness of Citizen Baudry is indeed so excessive, and so various, as to become amusing; and the entertainment is from time to time heightened by the reflection, that this singular creature is actually Historiographer of the French colony department." Another contemporary review called Baudry's language "fantastical" and suggested that his *"reflections,* as they are termed, are evidently opinions or ideas adopted *without* reflection." What read as entertaining and childish to early-nineteenth-century European readers also registers as malevolent. To return to Charles W. Mills, his assertion about colonialist philosophy is extremely cogent and valuable. He suggested that "the Enlightenment . . . 'social contract' is underwritten by a 'racial contract'" and that this racial contract demanded that "one has an agreement to misinterpret the world. One has to learn to see the world wrongly, but with the assurance that this set of mistaken perceptions will be validated by white epistemic authority, whether religious or secular." Baudry and Moreau's work epitomize this contract. Their jobs as Napoleon's historiographers of the French overseas colonies required just such a profession of colonialism's "civilizing" mission, a belief in themselves as "good masters." Competence in Kikongo was imagined as part of this mission. The gross misinterpretations of the world endure.[40]

Ultimately, the tenor of Baudry's proslavery claims should be expected from someone who, as Marlene L. Daut has suggested, believed it necessary to wage "a war of annihilation" on people of African descent in the final years of the Haitian Revolution. Baudry, however, understood that African (and Native American) language acquisition was vital to understanding the late-eighteenth-century Americas. His work serves an important function in the present and brings me full circle to my opening assertions. The study of the Americas has been self-consciously "global" for several hundred years now. More to the point, when did we lose sight of Kikongo as one of the many languages of the Americas? The domination of English in much of the scholarship about the global South or extended Caribbean seems shortsighted to those who work primarily in languages such as Kreyòl, Spanish, Dutch, Portuguese, and French. But to quote Craig Womack in the context of scholarship on Native American literatures, there are "vast, and vastly understudied" repositories awaiting our attention. Much as late-eighteenth-century Americanists saw the need to give priority to the study of non-European languages, there is a continued need to do so today. This is one way to decenter white planter intellectuals and their legacy. The next chapter offers another.[41]

CHAPTER SEVEN

B.DRY LOZ

Illustrative Storytelling

Scholars of the enslaved are confronted with the evidence of things not seen. Unrecorded experiences. Unvoiced motivations. These silences constitute the recessed corners of the past.[1] The graphics in this chapter engage the impasse created by a lack of historical documentation concerning the thoughts of those who left few written records. Illustrative storytelling in its literal sense is one method of imagining the experiences of people desperate to figure things out in a world where so many new and ongoing experiences would not have made sense: masters who thought they were fluent in Kikongo shouting gibberish, people burning unintelligible symbols into one's skin. Misunderstanding could have violent consequences. In these three visual examples, incomprehension and meaning vie with each other, much as creating understanding in a world of incomprehension was a vital intellectual and affective task for enslaved people intent on survival.

✳✳✳✳✳✳✳✳✳✳✳✳✳✳✳ ✳✳✳✳✳✳✳✳✳✳✳✳✳✳✳✳✳

A Listening Puzzle

In the presence of the unintelligible, one still heard sound. It could communicate threat, invitation, promise. It beckoned in shouts or whispers, repelled via tone or pitch. It was augmented and made meaningful through the body praxis of gesture. Listening to the sound of the human voice and converting that which was incoherent into meaningful words and eventually language (imbued with direct consequences) took time. This process was a fundamental challenge for the children, women, and men enslaved and transported across the Atlantic Ocean, from island to island and across and within the North and South American mainland empires. It was knowledge acquired with difficulty, and ingesting these letters, reading them not as words but as sounds, is also meant to be.

Vikamoklav

Ndndndndndndndndndndndndndndndndndndndndndnd n d n d

Soosutamaka ta zambi weri mousiinga ndo nkosomaitrepitutatasingaa ban

gwaigwaygue anduvo malikakubipumazibizi

lila dila fiotefiotaympofofifaaaaaa

msingaaawetemundmborimakata

mbouloukakata GOULONBOU

kio mbi mousinga mou si

nwavika kombazo nd mp mb ndookii Vonda montou

e mangzi klav mb pamba, msinga MO AY VI

moévi, ioba ka **motamis** mondele mbi ioba bacala

kosondokiinotoswomopoisonawo

ndmsndmsingusingadezina iandinandi

kiman menoozozaigwaigway fioteyangaMFou singe!

sucrefamosingawiramdimakatanakawo dakwofa yandi ouili

mvikavika fakunle mbi nw lakoda iobakimanmingapangamakatavika

lakota?

Would the African-born, Bantu-language continuum speakers serving as interlocutors in Louis Narcisse Baudry des Lozière's linguistic research have understood the terms and phrases that Baudry carefully studied, copied, and published in his "Dictionnaire ou Vocabulaire Congo"? Would these utterances have sounded like nonsense, initially as foreign in meaning as the other languages circulating on the island of Hispaniola such as Kreyòl, French, Spanish, or Fon? Would speakers and listeners have been involved in what Wyatt MacGaffey has memorably called "dialogues of the deaf?"[2] Perhaps listeners found some sounds vaguely intelligible as isolated words. Or perhaps the sounds that they heard were decipherable and acquired meaning when joined into phrases and sentences. We can imagine that people stood in angry disbelief, reflecting, "I think this man is trying to tell me my mother is a pig." We can picture the dismay and fear of a woman or man being touched against her or his will while listening to some iteration of *menou zozé guéïé* or *mang'zi*.

mbimotamissingalakota mangziloudémi ludemi
potou mondelemondélémondaylaymondailai mond/eɪ/leɪ.   panga   minga
mousingalakota
paysdesblancschaine**SANG**fouet
countryofwhiteschainebloodwhip

potou mundele mondele **mondélémondaylaymondailai**   panga   minga msi
lakota
paysdesblancs   payee day blan   mbi   chaine   sang   fouet
countryofwhites   ugly   chain   blood

sukidi botémanbéne

kia kombi nata guéïé

singemponok kiman

menoozozaigwaieaiastula**chaudepissegonorrheamboulou**sucre

NDOKI mingomingaguaaiaaaguayiaygwaiiaiguéiéguéiéguéiéguéié

brigandbloodbloodyouyouyouyouyouyouyouyouyouuglyuglyuglyuglyugly
uglywhiphurryup!!!!!!!!!!!![3]
**poisonerbloodbloodyouyouyouyouyouyouyouyouuglyuglyuglyuglyugly
uglyunintelligible
hurryup!!!!!!!!!!!**   *Do you understand?*   *Did you understand?*

sound chaos babble
letter disorder gibberish
parede de   incomprehension
frustration
grief rage disbelief
recognition?   *Oudzoué?*   *Oudi kéle?*

The act of listening re-created through this puzzle converts what one might have heard into that which is seen and must be decoded as written signs. Sound is visualized, speaking converted to typed characters. In reading the puzzle, the eye jumps, searching for meaning, perhaps impatient, caring only for the words that are recognizable. As is the case when listening to the unfamiliar, one searches for signification that might be pinned down as a way of feeling grounded. The puzzle is a mix of nonsense and words in multiple languages. I wrote it to be wrestled with aloud, notating what would be long and short vowel sounds in English with the consonant blends that simulate those found in attempts to notate eighteenth-century Kikongo. Punctuation serves as conventional shorthand to communicate the intention of an utterance by marking shifts in tone and emphasis. Debates surrounding the best written forms for a host of traditionally oral languages, from French-based Kreyòl to Indigenous idioms, work as a subtext as I move between phonetic or etymological inscriptions. Consider the diacritic *accent aigu* on each *é* sound that Baudry used: two examples are found in the noun *mondélé* (country) and the critical pronoun *guéïé* (you). Phonetically, Baudry's choice of the French *é* could be transcribed "ay," "ai," or "ei" for an anglophone reader or as the International Phonetic Alphabet symbol /eɪ/.[4] With no "you" to command, there would be little point in his phrase book. When spoken at and to someone, the word would need to resonate as familiar.

My musings about transcription and typographical presentation mimic trying to pin down the ephemeral: to capture baffling speech as writing is an attempt to illuminate the occluded inner functioning of the mind. Outright confusion, gradual recognition, a refusal to engage: each signals the perception, sentiment, and intentionality of Baudry's interlocutors. Robert Bringhurst explains that, although legibility is a foundational principle of typography, there is "something more than legibility: some earned or unearned interest that gives its living energy to the page." That living, kinetic energy of letters arranged in jarring positions and to form words that may or may not make sense is intended to provoke readerly discomfort. One can describe the confusion that the enslaved might have felt, but is the recognition of such *felt* and *understood* in a different way when shared, however briefly? That discomfort and frustration is meant to come full circle to acknowledge the tremendous intellectual energy of those forced to exist physically, spiritually, and linguistically in a world controlled by predatory strangers.[5]

As we saw in previous chapters, Moreau and Baudry both appreciated the difficulties posed by transcription of spoken sounds to print. When trying to capture the South American Indigenous language Guaraní so that French readers and speakers would be able to pronounce the words in his translated natural history of Paraguay, Moreau wrote that he had "designated the syllables that it was necessary to emphasize more than others" (On a désigné les syllabes qu'il faut faire sentir plus que les autres). One of the ninety-three examples he provided was the word *gou-a-zou-pou-cou*, noting that the *"gou, zou* and *cou"* should be "long." In his work on the West African Warri Kingdom, Moreau observed, "The sound of the syllable *ou,* in the pronunciation of the word *Ouaire,* being very strong in the mouth of the natives of the country, I believed it necessary not to elide this syllable so that its pronunciation would be better appreciated in French" (le son de la syllabe *ou,* dans la prononciation y mot *Ouaire,* étant très-fort dans la bouche des naturels du pays, on a cru ne devoir pas élider cette syllabe, afin que sa prononciation fût mieux sentie en Français). When discussing Kikongo and the Native American languages Dakota and Ojibwa, Baudry explained that, in the case of Dakota, "the letters with a circumflex should be pronounced long. For example, *ouâ âtô,* ou *ichinaoubâ"* (les lettres où il y a un accent circonflèxe doivent être prononcées longuement. Par exemple, *ouâ âtô,* ou *ichinaoubâ*). In the case of *gu é Ï é,* was the *tréma (i)* Baudry added between the *És* his way of documenting that the vowel should be pronounced distinctly? Actual Kikongo could require a variance in tone across the length of the breath that held that sound. Textual Kikongo in the "Vocabulaire" is flat. ——————————— Kikongo cluster languages are not. ⌁ Discernible tonal variation, within words and within word combinations, would require rising and falling sounds.[6]

How might *gu é Ï é* have sounded to the eighteenth-century listeners Baudry imagined? They would have had to make allowances for inadequate tonal accuracy, in addition to vocabulary and syntax that were likely to be unclear. The likelihood of miscomprehension was enormous, as was the possibility that listeners might have engaged in what Anna Brickhouse calls "motivated mistranslation," the strategic process of deliberately misunderstanding what they heard or providing false information when queried so as to "unsettle" colonial projects.[7]

Thus far, the listeners and sources of Baudry's "Vocabulaire" have been abstracted, albeit actual, human beings. Thousands of people from the West Central African region labeled the Kongo appeared across the pages of Saint-Domingue's newspapers and in notarial records; they inhabited the same urban and rural household work spaces as the Baudry and Moreau families. These people formed a significant subset of the enslaved population. One was a man renamed Louis. He was five feet, two inches tall, quite powerful and broad shouldered. He sported a beard and had "healthy legs" despite his "small feet." His speech was slow, although we do not know if the language he spoke slowly was his native one or the one(s) he learned upon arrival in Saint-Domingue. He had filed teeth that served as their own indicator of community belonging in his homeland and "reddened eyes," perhaps due to exhaustion or disease (Figure 48).[8]

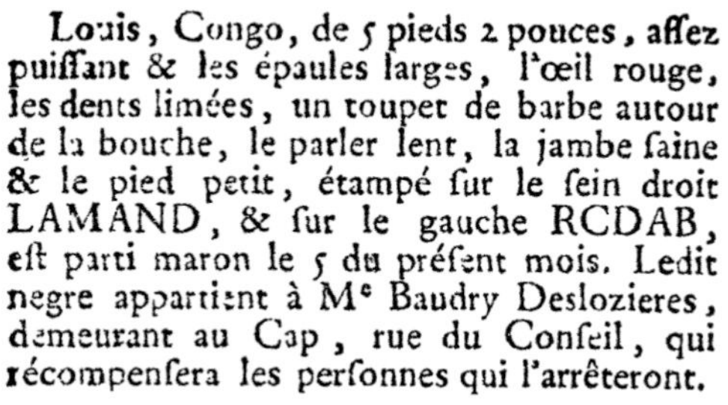

Louis, Congo, de 5 pieds 2 pouces, affez
puiffant & les épaules larges, l'œil rouge,
les dents limées, un toupet de barbe autour
de la bouche, le parler lent, la jambe faine
& le pied petit, étampé fur le fein droit
LAMAND, & fur le gauche RCDAB,
eft parti maron le 5 du préfent mois. Ledit
negre appartient à Me Baudry Deslozieres,
demeurant au Cap, rue du Confeil, qui
récompenfera les perfonnes qui l'arrêteront.

FIGURE 48. Runaway advertisement seeking the return of Louis to Baudry des Lozières. From "Esclaves en maronage," *Supplément aux Affiches américains* (Cap Français, Saint-Domingue), Aug. 4, 1784, [4].

Louis ran away from Baudry in 1784, when they were both living in Cap Français. By fleeing, he defied Baudry's assertion of ownership. Louis and Baudry were thus real-life historical antagonists, engaged in a battle of wills and contested authority. Would Louis have understood Baudry's Kikongo—the insults, threats, possible queries about his health, or invective against his (Louis's) mother? **Zi. I. Sia.** *Not.* **Ouad.** *Understand. I not understand.* This is my nonsensical piecing together of isolated parts of speech. Louis did not understand or accept the logic and intent behind the words in the "Vocabulaire." He did not view Baudry as a benefactor entitled to his labor and life.

Consider another scene peopled with historical actors, although the circumstances are abstract and fantastical in their own way. The setting is a mountaintop outside Léogâne, in the western province of Saint-Domingue. Planted with coffee and including an array of outbuildings, the site was originally purchased by Baudry in 1788 and named Crete. In this Caribbean Crete, a frequent visitor described how Baudry gave its quarters Western classical names such as Mount Ida, the attributed birthplace of the Greek god Zeus. According to the same eyewitness account, "His famous ornamental gardens that one called Greek-style gardens, and that were suspended on the side of the high mountain, excited the curiosity of guests who went to visit and who left there with the memory of Semiramis's gardens [the Hanging Gardens of Babylon]" (ses fameux jardins d'agrémens qu'on appelait jardins à la grecque, et qui, suspendus sur le côté d'une haute montagne, excitaient la curiosité des arrivans qui allaient les visiter, et en sortaient avec le souvenir des jardins de SÉMIRAMIS). The property was bought "naked [bare], meaning without Blacks, without tools and almost uncultivated" (toute nue, c'est-à-dire, sans nègres, sans ustensiles, et presque sans culture). The cultivation of coffee plants and landscaped gardens required hard manual labor, and Baudry reportedly effected these changes because his wealth allowed him to "cover his habitation with arms and to render it flourishing from the point of view of utility and pleasure" (couvre son habitation de bras et la rend florissante sous les points de vue d'utilité et d'agrémens).[9]

This literal "covering" of a space with "arms"—people who tamed the wilderness by cutting, removing, collecting, digging, harvesting—mandated the labor of at least "50 . . . *bossals,*" who worked the land in the late 1780s. They could also have served as domestic servants in Baudry's home at Crete or his houses in Port-au-Prince or Cap Français. Some of these African-born enslaved were no doubt West Central Africans. Louis would not have been linguistically or culturally isolated in the Baudry households. These Kongolese laborers would have included some of the people Baudry questioned for details about their language. These workers were supervised, a neutral verb hiding a raft of coercive practices, by a manager, a doctor, two overseers, and Baudry's secretary. And of course we have seen that Madame Baudry herself was intimately involved in the day-to-day operations of the estate, particularly with her "new Blacks."[10]

If the man called Louis was recaptured, *if* he survived his work regimen, and *if* he continued in Baudry's service, he could very well have been sent to labor on this coffee plantation in subsequent years. Would Baudry, or the managers he employed and perhaps instructed in a few Kikongo phrases, have successfully communicated their meaning to the enslaved laborers? I suspect that physical coercion was the most widely practiced communication strategy between these groups. Although inhabiting the same spaces, they likely had a radically different understanding of their immediate surroundings. Would Louis and the other newly arrived people living on the plantation have referred to this mountaintop idyll as Crete, a place not in the least bit idyllic in their own experience? According to local newspapers and visitors, some of the terrain in the vicinity of Baudry's land had other names: one area was known as Moussambé / Massembé / Mozambé, and another was called "le Gris-Gris." These names were grounded in African-derived words and cultural practices, likely attributable to the large numbers of Kongo-identified people living there and working the land. Visions of ancient Greece and West Central Africa coexisted. This coexistence was not harmonious.[11]

esssssssssskkkkkkkkkkkkkkkkllllllllllllavvvvvv (short *e* in an English context)
esklav = vika? Esklav ≠ vika? Esklav = mvika?[12]
esklav = esclave
esclave = slave
esclave = enslaved = vika
esclave = enslaved = mvika = me?
Esclave = slave = vika = me? him? my child? your mother?
Esclave = motamis = whip
Esclave = chagrin = banbou ikelé andi
Esclave = nègre
Esclave = nègre = nèg = black

Keyword violence was inherent to unbecoming and becoming. Sound and speech—aurality and orality—were converted to meaning in an uneven, distinctly personal yet also communal manner. I now move from sound to the embodied sensation of touch. The enslaved negotiated unfamiliar languages (in the example above, a language that might have been just barely familiar) and unfamiliar scriptural practices. The latter were also experienced as brutal exercises in power that marked new, often contested meanings about who they were and what was expected of them.

⁎⁎⁎⁎⁎⁎⁎⁎⁎⁎⁎⁎⁎⁎⁎⁎ ⁎⁎⁎⁎⁎⁎⁎⁎⁎⁎⁎⁎⁎⁎⁎⁎⁎

Flesh Wounds

The soundscape of the spoken languages of slavery was polyglot. Likewise, the print cultures of slavery had multiple registers and canvases: periodicals, natural histories, law codes, flesh. I am attentive to the multiple textualities that the enslaved would have been forced to negotiate. Consider the brand that two women, Thérèse and Magdeleine, both identified as Nago, had on their bodies:

B.DRY LOZ

Both women ran away from Baudry des Lozières in 1791. They were captured and jailed in Port-au-Prince in May of that year. I do not know if the print notice announcing their imprisonment resulted in their forced return to their owners.[13]

Power was projected in markings / letters in what amounted to a fleshy public sphere. As people moved, their bodies were read. Letters declaring belonging / nonownership of self were inscribed on the skin, such that the skin limited one's ability to effectively disappear. No matter how people ran, walked, hid, or disguised themselves, these brands increased their vulnerability. What did Thérèse and Magdeleine see when they looked down at their own disfigured flesh? If they were burned on their chests, did the marks deform their breasts and change how they viewed themselves (as women, as sexual partners, as mothers)? The dot / period holding the place of the "au" in Baudry's name suggests an iron typeface forged of just a single shape: a punctuation mark in the abstract, a potential keloid in the material world. Some group of artisans in Saint-Domingue would have had a business forging metal letters for livestock and human branding. From these women's vantage point, a brand across their chests would have appeared like this:

ZOꓵ ⅄ꓤꓷ˙B

Though registered as upside down and reversed according to the left-to-right reading pattern of Romance- and English-language readers, these marks would not necessarily have registered thusly to Thérèse and Magdeleine. Probably Yoruba speakers, they might have been untrained to read or write in their native or adoptive languages, although Yoruba itself has a written tradition dating back to Ajami script in the seventeenth century. However, conceiving of these two women, and by extension other African-born enslaved peoples, as "illiterate" obscures the reality that they might have been well versed in reading other bodily markings—what came to be called country marks in the Americas—a reference to scriptural body practices employed in Africa. Scarification rituals served "aesthetic, religious, and social" purposes and were "widely used by many West African tribes to mark milestone stages in both men and women's lives, such as puberty and marriage. [Scarification] is also used to transmit complex messages about identity; such permanent body markings may emphasize social, political and religious roles. . . . [They are] ways of showing a person's autobiography on the surface of the body to the world." In other words, the links between marks on the body and questions of belonging, identity, and community would have been a familiar concept for these women—in a different context.[14]

The physicality of a branding wound would have had psychological ramifications. The curves and straight lines that corresponded to shapes—unfamiliar letters—had symbolic and real-world associations. If those lettered names were not in a language / sound pattern one recognized, the internal calculations explaining such disfigurement could have ranged from bewilderment to anger to shame. Slavery as an institution led to the development of multilingual, multimedia (if flesh can be deemed a medium) reading and scriptural practices that converted flesh wounds to letters, then letters to names. The length of time it would have taken each African-born person to know that the figures / names impressed into her / his flesh were synonymous with de facto authority over her / his body would have been an intensely personal and individual experience. In this example, internal thought processes linked script to terror.[15]

PAIN 1. the terror of being pinned in place and waiting for a heated branding iron to sear through one's skin 2. the branding's aftereffects: discoloration, chapping, possible infection, necrosis, shock, nightmares, nervousness; the lingering smell of burning and charred flesh its own source of anxiety and repugnance.

On a scale measuring the effects of the personal desecration of one's flesh for someone else's purpose, did someone stamped **TIBO** consider him- or herself more fortunate than someone branded **JEAN CASTELBON** or **L G DE BRETIGNI-BOISSEAU ST M**? Or consider the aforementioned Louis, Baudry's Kongolese enslaved man who had **LAMAND** branded on the right breast and **RCDAB** on the left. His entire chest was marked with letters indicating a succession of owners. A shorter name or set of initials would have resulted in less burned skin, which in turn would potentially have taken less time to heal. The Dominican missionary Jean-Baptiste Labat, casually commenting on how brands were applied in early-eighteenth-century Saint-Domingue, noted that a person "who had been sold and resold several times would appear in the end as covered with characters as the Egyptian obelisks."[16]

Regardless of the name or initials used, the scarring was intended to be permanent, and marks were burned onto prominent places such as the chest, cheeks, stomach, and back. Over the course of multiple owners (multiple brands across an ever-increasing body area) or even in the event of manumission, one exhibited the letters forever as one cooked, cleaned, made love, planted cane, picked coffee beans, harvested indigo, or shared a meal with friends. Even when those who were "stamped" (étampé[e]) bore marks that were "illegible" (illisible), their scarred bodies were witness to their humiliation and commodification. That such illegibility is a characteristic noted in hundreds of advertisements for people who ran away suggests that these same people attempted to deface their brands as a strategy of deliberate obfuscation.

The series of signs in the pictures **ZOJ YЯD.B** and **BADƆЯ DИAMA⅃**, perhaps more than the *colon*-sponsored violence captured in **B.DRY LOZ** and **LAMAND RCDAB**, reminds us of the thought and affective process imposed on a person becoming someone different as a result of enslavement. Understanding these signs entailed an embodied, painfully acquired literacy. This interpretation process underscores a series of upside-down inversions—of the scriptural markings, of the subject, of the logic of print, of the world. We (contemporary readers are implicated in this process, as well) can read for knowledge embedded in and beneath the surface.[17]

✳✳✳✳✳✳✳✳✳✳✳✳✳✳✳✳✳✳ ✳✳✳✳✳✳✳✳✳✳✳✳✳✳✳✳✳✳

Interiorized Natural History

Spring 1783

The air was dry, and there was no shade to be had for miles. No cover apart from the tall cane stalks that stretched as far as she could see. She knew that she must steer clear of them; the harvest was in process. X——, just shy of her twentieth birthday, struggled to walk the few remaining feet to a ravine where she could hide. If she could just make it to Morne Pelé . . . Y——, her father, would be there, waiting to help her. He might come with food. The promise of his presence kept her moving. She had heard *blan* calling this region the *"terre promise"*; the quality of the sugarcane growing around her was a constant topic of conversation when they gathered. The conversations she heard most often in snatched conversations with friends concerned sleepless nights due to the *mòde moustik*, overcrowding, the meanness of the *commandeur* at the Chatenoye plantation, or the sudden furies of the *maître* at Habitation Portelance.[18]

The open air and green of the fields contrasted to the oppressiveness of her lodging in Le Cap. The building where she cooked meals and occasionally sorted supplies for M. Curet, the medical practitioner from whom she had escaped again, was not her home, and she dreaded being forced to return. This time she had fled once more to the outskirts of Le Cap, heading to the Quartier Morin. She knew she could not risk returning to the vicinity of Habitation Gravé to find her sister. But these roads were of good quality and well traveled; it was dangerous to come this way.

Rosette—he had insisted on that name. His clumsy flirtations always began with compliments about her beauty before he became aggressive. His little flower. The *r* sound was hard to form her mouth around, and it sounded flat and unimaginative. Her mother had been born across the sea where names indicated when one was born and how one was connected to one's *egun*. She had been named accordingly within her community.

I must keep going. The river is close, murmuring. How to cross? Hide the knife. Hide the knife. If they find it, I will be condemned. Its weight is comforting; I am condemned already. His expression as I shoved it in his face . . . his shock as I slashed at his arms.

I begged him to sell me. He always comes after me, each time I run, whatever I do. I will not live with the dread—him catching me by the latrines or on my palette come dark. Why won't he sell me? If not to the Gravé habitation, somewhere anywhere somewhere. If I can make it to the next morne, Y—— will hide me.

ESCLAVES EN MARONAGE.

Une Négreſſe nommée *Roſette*, âgée d'environ 19 ans, de moyenne taille, rouge de
peau, étampée CURET, eſt partie marone
depuis trois mois : on ſoupçonne qu'elle eſt
ſur l'habitation *Gravé*, où elle a des relations.
Ceux qui la reconnoîtront, ſont priés de la
faire arrêter & d'en donner avis à M. *Curet*,
Maître en Chirurgie au Cap : ceux qui la ra-
meneront auront 66 l. de récompenſe.

October 16, 1782

Une Négreſſe nommée *Roſette*, rouge de
peau, de moyenne taille, ayant un enfoncement au front, ſérieuſe, parlant peu, eſt partie
marone le 8 de ce mois pour la centieme fois.
On avertit de ſe méfier d'elle, volant & menaçant du couteau ; en un mot, c'eſt un ſujet
rempli de vices. Elle a emporté pour ſix por-
tugaiſes de marchandiſes. M. *Curet*, Mᵉ en
Chirurgie au Cap, récompenſera ceux qui
auront occaſion de lui ramener ladite Négreſſe.

March 26, 1783

Roſette, de moyenne taille, jolie de figure,
rouge de peau, ayant au milieu du front un
trou très-remarquable & qu'elle a ſoin de
cacher, eſt partie marronne depuis un mois,
on dit l'avoir vue ſur l'habitation de M. *de
Charite*, au Quartier-Morin. Ceux qui en
auront connoiſſance, ſont priés de la faire
arrêter, & d'en donner avis à M. *Curet*,
rue Conflans. Il y aura récompenſe.

October 27, 1784

A Black woman named *Rosette,*
around 19 years old, of medium size,
reddish skin, stamped CURET, ran
away three months ago: it is supposed
that she is on the *Gravé* habitation,
where she has family. Those who
know her are asked to arrest her and
to give notice to M. *Curet,* Master of
Surgery in Le Cap; those who bring
her back will have a 66-pound reward.

A Black woman named *Rosette,* reddish skin, medium build, having an
indentation on her forehead, serious,
speaking little, ran away on the 8th
of this month for the hundredth
time. One is warned to beware of her,
stealing and menacing [people] with
a knife; in a word, she is a subject full
of vices. She left with six *portugaises'*
worth of merchandise. Mr. *Curet,*
Master of Surgery in Le Cap, will
award those who have the opportunity to bring back the said négresse.

Rosette, of medium build, pretty face,
reddish skin, having a very remarkable hole in the middle of her forehead that she takes care to hide, ran
away a month ago. She has been spot-
ted on the habitation of Mr. *Charite,*
in Quartier-Morin. Those who have
knowledge about the situation are
asked to arrest her and to give news to
Mr. *Curet,* Conflans Street. There is a
reward.[19]

In hurricane season, Rosette ran away from her owner, a surgeon in Le Cap. She was gone for at least several months. Networks of family and friends in the vicinity likely helped to hide her.

He has caught me. I will not return to his control. I will run again and again and again (one hundred times if need be). Next time he comes close I will take his knife and kill him.

Curet captured Rosette again, despite his assertion that she was "full of vices": a thief, an enslaved woman who dared assault her master. However, two years after he advertised for her return in 1782 and after an unknown number of times she had run away and been recaptured in the subsequent interval, she went missing yet again.

Twou modi sa a sou fwon mwen fè li enposib pou mwen kache. *This damn hole on my forehead makes it impossible to hide.* **Tout moun konnen mwen isit la.** *Everyone knows me here. I will not go back to that house willingly.*

FIGURE 49. *Rosette.* By Sara E. Johnson and Luz Sandoval. 2020.

A phrase catches my attention: *elle est partie marone . . . pour la centième fois.*
On avertit de se méfier d'elle, *volant et menaçant du couteau; en un mot, c'est
un sujet rempli de vices. One is warned to beware of her, stealing and menacing
[people] with a knife; in a word, she is a subject full of vices.* The "she" in question
was called Rosette. Could her master's phrasing of "the hundredth time" be hy-
perbole? What would give a woman cause to escape so often? Rosette's force of
character and resilience must have been formidable as she set off each time despite the punishment that was likely inflicted upon her when she was recaptured.
The logistics of pulling off such a series of escapes required ingenuity and determination. Absolute determination. She welcomed waywardness, to use Saidiya
Hartman's formulation, engaging in a "practice of possibility at a time when all
roads, except the ones created by *smashing out,* are foreclosed."[20]

We can imagine the anxiety that Rosette must have felt to disguise herself
given what seems to have been the "very remarkable hole" on her forehead.
How might she have acquired such a hole, what Curet earlier described as an
indentation? Was the change in semantics—"enfoncement" (1783) to "trou
très-remarquable" (1784)—a sign of escalation through injury? Curet was a
surgeon—did he experiment on her? Trepanning? Was there an assault involved?
Was the hole open and subject to infection? Did the "care" she took "to hide" it
necessitate a headcloth, inventive hairstyles? She must have employed various
modes of self-reinvention to override this remarkable physical trait. Here we have
a description of Rosette's forehead: it has entered the historical written record.
Yet I do not know what such a description means, let alone what the hole would
have meant to her.[21]

Curet pursued Rosette relentlessly over a number of years, despite her obvious
determination to steal away. Why not sell her? The announcements he placed
in the local newspaper hint at obsessiveness; he desperately wanted to have this
woman, as "full of vices" as he claimed her to have been, under his direct control.
What conditions existed / festered / typified their shared living space?

Rosette was reserved. If we take some of Curet's description at face value, she
was quiet and serious in his presence, planning for a future without him in it.
Mention of her ties to friends and family in local communities points to the
strength of relationships that were beyond the purview of her owner. That she
was recaptured many times suggests that she never went too far; someone or

some set of people must have kept her from fleeing due east from Le Cap "à l'es-pagnol," for example, across the Spanish border that served as refuge for many escapees.

Unlike the people in the first two examples, Rosette had no direct relationship with either Moreau or Baudry. Like Louis, Thérèse, and Magdeleine, she also escaped and lived for an unknown period of time *en marronage*. As was the case for others like her, she would have had her own rationale and opinions motivat-ing her behavior. These thoughts could have included self-interest, pain, despera-tion, anger, hope. I presume no uniformity of thought between Rosette's motiva-tions and those of others, but I search for logical subtexts that could explain life choices. It is a truism in the field of slavery studies that information about what people were thinking and feeling is not readily available in the historical record; this is especially the case for those who left few written records of their own.

This lacuna of information does not preclude the need to reconstruct the pos-sible intentions of the protagonists we write about. The stakes in these examples are high. For students of slavery writ large—its print cultures, languages, and psychotic, psychological, and material legacies—Moreau, Baudry, and Curet cannot have undisputed narrative authority. Informed speculation can disrupt this legacy of dominance, in part through an exploration of interior life worlds. I take interiority to cover a wide spectrum of thought: from calculated analysis, intention, and motivation to the realm of emotions. Rather than being impassive ciphers who are acted upon, people with their own will emerge. Mediated text and images offer hints of subjectivity; in these cases, sensory input from hearing, seeing, and bodily touch is plumbed for how it might have stimulated a person's understanding of themselves and the world. Close attention to grammar and diction—who is designated as the subject of sentences, what words are used to describe people and their environment—is facilitated when the "what if" for these historical actors is centered. The process of surfacing these possibilities, the practice of wondering, is itself a method of inquiry that serves as a compass to ground a type of scholarship that demands accountability to those we study. This type of critical creative exercise need not always make it into the final drafts of our work in order for a reorientation of perspective to occur.

Speculation thrives in the graphic, from every word cluster in M. NourbeSe Philip's poetry collection *Zong!* to Kyle Baker's retelling of Nat Turner's story to John Jennings's and Damian Duffy's deliberation about the appropriate color palette to illustrate Octavia Butler's work. My attempts herein function along-side other mobilizations of the visual to creatively flush out alternative stories and interpretations. The reality imposed upon the world by those who treated Louis,

Magdeleine, Thérèse, and Rosette as objects requires multiple narrative modes to circumvent and subvert. Visual interpretations of inner thought processes are one such mode of excavating lies as well as other potential "truths."[22]

Speculation also thrives in anecdote. Moreau's widely cited natural histories relied on anecdotal observation as a form of evidence, and it is a defining characteristic of his narrative style. Some of his anecdotes—describing the geographic boundaries of a neighborhood, its number of churches or local personalities—seem harmless enough. Others are much less so. A formula emerges, although there are exceptions: in such and such year, in such and such place, an enslaved woman or man named A did B, and this is *why* they did so and *how* they felt. The man at the "center" of this book was a serial embellisher, someone who operated in a world of planter fantasies about enlightened slaveholding and "bon maîtres." We must question, refuse, take back his assumed authority to speak on the enslaved's behalf. My own use of anecdotal information, most common in the book's more experimental chapters, is a necessary counterweight to Moreau's invocation of anecdote as "documentation" of the motivations, thoughts, ideas, and sentiments of the enslaved. Unlike him, I eschew pronouncements and generalizations. I claim no authority over their thoughts.

This chapter's third example of interiorized natural history crosses the line between fact and fiction most directly. My rendition of Rosette's story is fictional, however much its creation is based on inference and some verifiable context; the feelings and ideas I project onto her are likely anachronistic. Writing about her and others throughout this book in the third person—a mode that involves extensive use of the conditional verb tense (what might she or he think or do) and using diction such as "perhaps," "maybe," "it is possible"—is infinitely easier than evoking/imposing the first person. A blatant eruption into the headspace of an imaginary "I" is a mode that literary historians, as much as "Historians" with a capital *H*, shy away from. However, this brief but methodologically intentional "I" and the clearly speculative "she" have a potential benefit. My hope is that they signal the need for a critical interpretive process that sifts and weighs the veracity of truth claims and that spots the discordant and discomforting. I aim to draw a parallel between my quite obvious conjecture and Moreau's and Baudry's. They, too, were involved in "critical fabulation," in "speculation," in "fiction writing." Their work is replete with outright lies.

✳✳✳✳✳✳✳✳✳✳✳✳✳✳✳✳ ✳✳✳✳✳✳✳✳✳✳✳✳✳✳✳✳

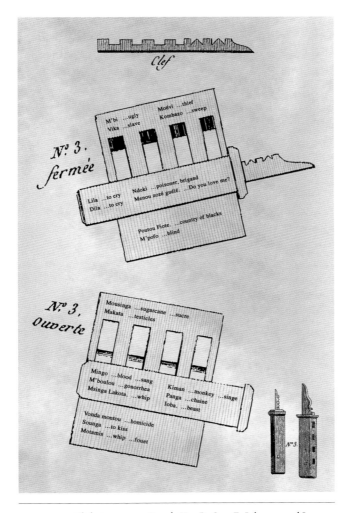

FIGURE 50. *Clefs et serrure, a Puzzle Key.* By Sara E. Johnson and Luz Sandoval. 2020. Adapted from images in Moreau de Saint-Méry, "Note sur les serrures de bois, dont les nègres se servent aux Antilles," *Mémoires d'agriculture, d'économie rurale et domestique,* I (Winter 1789), 24.

The three keys shown in Figure 50 fit into a wooden lock "employed by Blacks in the Antilles" (dont les nègres se servent aux Antilles). The idea of the enslaved using locks on their doors feels generative, a fact of material culture that upends some of my hitherto subconscious assumptions about privacy and security (of oneself, of one's belongings). In this example, locks were employed to secure the entrances to people's living quarters when they were away at work. When considering the existence, perhaps commonness, of these locks in Saint-Domingue, I wondered if they were only fastened to the outside of a building and used when people were absent. In other words, could people enter a space and affix them from *inside* their lodgings to lock people (masters, others) out? Was there a mechanism for them to create an interior space that they could control to their satisfaction?

Moreau wrote a 1789 essay and supplement for an agricultural periodical that described these wooden locks and keys, and he included detailed drawings of four different sets with their interior and external spring mechanisms. I reproduce and modify the keys and lock "number three" in its "open" and "closed" forms. On "well-ordered plantations" (les habitations bien ordonnées), masters had their carpenters provide these locks so that "the unhappy" (ces malheureux) would be able to safeguard their "meagre belongings" (les chétifs objets). As he put it, this was a necessary precaution because "once a workgroup contracted the habit of theft, this penchant did not limit itself to things that belonged to the enslaved; masters and neighbors would feel the effects soon enough" (Lorsqu'un atelier contracte l'habitude du vol, ce penchant ne se borne pas aux choses qui appartiennent aux esclaves, le maître et les voisins s'en ressentent bientôt). According to Moreau's logic, it would evidently not do to have those whose lives were stolen from them try to steal from the system.[23]

I have altered Moreau's diagrams so that these keys and lock could visually serve as a key to words contained in the listening puzzle that opened this chapter. The people considered herein would not have had the benefit of an accessible cheat sheet explaining rough word correspondence between languages. They learned through trial and error, close attention, or deliberate attempts *not* to show what they might have comprehended in the new idioms and rituals of slavery that surrounded them. The drawings also function as a visualized metaphor underpinned by material culture. Closed-off space (keeping some parts of the mind and of the body off-limits) contrasts with decisions to allow comprehension and access. This negotiation of one's surroundings is mirrored by the wooden mechanisms that closed or opened access to the locks and what they guarded.

CHAPTER EIGHT

Encyclopédie noire

— Part III —

O

Ouvrage

We do not say here how much this Work has cost us. In a devouring climate, where one in some way has to compete with insects over papers, what fatigues, what expenses on trips it was necessary to undertake in order to discover what one desires! What research and what time to find things in public depots where they are badly ordered!

Nous ne disons point ici combien cet Ouvrage a dû nous coûter. Dans un climat dévorant, ou l'on dispute en quelque sorte les Papiers aux Insectes, quelles fatigues, quelles dépenses dans les Voyages qu'il faut entreprendre pour découvrir ceux qu'on désire! Quelles Recherches et quel temps pour les trouver dans les Dépôts publics où ils sont mal en ordre![1]

One encounters the adjective "monumental" repeatedly in discussions of Moreau de Saint-Méry and his *Ouvrage*. His work and corresponding stature were and remain significant in studies of the Caribbean, particularly the francophone Caribbean.[2] For good reason, he is one of *the* primary sources that generations of scholars have relied on. His literal and ideological imprint is everywhere: from the extant books and periodicals produced in his Philadelphia bookstore to his framing of *colon* and Caribbean-centered knowledge about the hemispheric Americas to the catalogues of archives worldwide that house the print culture he collected and produced during his lifetime. His stamp, perhaps physical, was certainly imprinted on the lives of the people whom he enslaved and employed.

Let us take Moreau's monumental canonicity literally. The proposed public works project at the top of Figure 51 was an 1802 design by the Italian architect Ferdinando Cossetti for an "arco di trionfo" commemorating Moreau's service to the duchy of Parma. Below it is the 1789 French revolutionary engraving of Moreau as a city elector, his portrait above a stone plinth. Both the Italian and French monuments signal power and honor, bestowing on Moreau a legacy of societal appreciation and permanence in the face of human mortality. Moreau would have seen these actual and projected monuments to himself and sat for the portraits that likewise helped to cement his legacy. Preoccupied with his reputation while alive, he was also concerned with how he might be evaluated by future intellectuals. In the opening comments to his *Description topographique et politique de la partie espagnole de l'isle Saint-Domingue,* Moreau wrote:

> It is in tracing this history that I recollect, almost at every line, that the historian exercises the power of a real magistracy, and that he ought to throw down his pen with affright, if he forgets, for a single moment, that, at a future day, posterity may have no other testimony than his to direct its judgment, on facts and individuals; and that, if this testimony deceives, he is chargeable with irreparable injustice; unless, indeed, posterity detecting the partiality of the historian, cites him, in his turn, before its awful tribunal, and stigmatizes his name, by placing him among the perjured witnesses.

> C'est en la traçant, cette histoire, que je me rappelle, presque à chaque ligne, que l'historien remplit une vraie magistrature, et qu'il doit jeter sa plume avec effroi, s'il a oublié, un seul instant, qu'un jour la postérité voulant porter un jugement sur un fait ou sur un individu, pourrait n'avoir d'autre témoignage à invoquer que le sien, et que si son jugement la trompe, il se rend coupable d'injustices irréparables; à moins que reconnaissant la partialité de l'historien, la postérité le citant lui-même à son redoutable tribunal, ne le flétrisse en le plaçant au nombre des juges corrompus.

Perjured witnesses, deceitful testimony, irreparable injustices committed by historians serving as judges and interpreters—this is forceful language, and I meet Moreau with his own words. I have indeed "detect[ed] the partiality" of Moreau

FIGURE 51. Italian and French monuments to Moreau de Saint-Méry. Ferdinando Cossetti, "Progetto di arco di trionfo dedicato a Moreau de Saint-Méry," [1802], Archivio di Stato di Parma, Raccolta Mappe e Disegni, vol. IX, no. 45, vol. 12, nn. 54a–b; Wilbrode Magloire Nicolas Courbe and Charles Toussaint Labadye, *Médéric Louis Élie Moreau de St. Mery: Présid[en]t des elect[eur]s de Paris au mois de j[uil]let 1789 né à la Martinique le 13 j[anvi]er 1750, député de cette colonie au Etats génér[au]x de 1789,* 1789, Bibliothèque nationale de France.

as a historian and "stigmatize[d]" his name and Ouvrage when such critique was warranted.[3]

This book is not a monument to Moreau. I started it well over a decade ago, and I have felt a profound ambivalence about devoting considerable intellectual energy to such a repugnant man and his work. Many times I have been tempted to leave it unfinished owing to the violence, prurience, bigotry, sadism, and casual disregard for Moreau's fellow human beings regularly on display. Immersion in the writings of Moreau and his fellow planters, the seemingly endless archive that he collected of his contemporaries, and their blueprints on how to recover Saint-Domingue, sometimes through open calls of genocide, is nauseating. "We do not say here how much this Work has cost us." Moreau's words are melodramatic, yet they resonate with my own scholarly experience writing this book.

As time progressed, this project became less about Moreau and more about how to use him as a platform to see other things. Moreau's profound commitment to the potential "utility" of his work calls to mind Imani Perry's comment that "historians are always asking what parts of the past we need in order to imagine our future. African American historians are particularly focused on rethinking what we need to understand about our past. How do we build archives of information to help us make history useful?" I have found that experimental writing modes have enabled me to process the past differently, to query why this man who admitted that sometimes he could not even tell one Black person from another is still regularly cited as an authority on hemispheric slavery two hundred years later. It has been generative and exciting to look beyond monuments and archives meant, in Kim F. Hall's words, "to celebrate white achievement."[4]

Monuments dedicated to Moreau, for example, led to other stone memorials. Consider two funeral pillars composing the visual *Aménaïde's Pillars* (Figure 52). The first is a photograph of the marble monument erected in honor of Aménaïde Dall'Asta and located in the Dall'Asta family crypt in the Cimitero della Villetta outside Parma's city center. The inscription on the pillar, chiseled below emblems of nobility and a wreath of ever-blooming flowers, reads:

QUI RIPOSA
AMENAIDE MARIA DE SAINT MERY
VEDOVA DI POMPEO DALL'ASTA
MORÌ ALLI 19 MAGGIO
1839

HERE RESTS
AMENAIDE MARIE DE SAINT MERY
WIDOW OF POMPEO DALL'ASTA
DECEASED MAY 19
1839

The drawing next to the photograph of her actual stone memorial reimagines the pillar. The verticality of both monuments physically and metaphorically

FIGURE 52. *Aménaïde's Pillars*. By Luz Sandoval and Sara E. Johnson. 2020. Photograph by Sara E. Johnson.

represents Aménaïde's almost fantastical story of social ascent in the hierarchical world of the Old Regime: from a mixed-race child born out of wedlock to a formerly enslaved woman in the French colonies to society countess and accomplished painter in Italy. The distance in social circumstances between her birth and death was partially made possible because of the sale of the bodies and exploitation of the labor of others; the marble marker in Parma represents a celebration of one person's ascent—a memorialization of her life and death— that was procured by other peoples' involuntary sacrifices.[5]

Martinique-born Agathe, African-born Rosine, Sénégalaise girl X, African-born X, Sylvie: so many women were bound to Aménaïde in order to ensure her prosperity. The possibilities of these actual lives foreclosed are represented by skulls instead of ornate flowers. I reenvision her pillar as an unfulfilled tree of life. Foundational, subterranean roots blossom into mortuary stone producing only one aboveground trajectory instead of many branches; the pillar, or trunk, has consumed rather than nurtured. This is an indictment of both Aménaïde's individual position as a slaveholder as well as the global system in which she thrived that rewarded moral failing. Of course, these people would have made lives for themselves in the shadow of Aménaïde's, her mother's, and her father's remote, sometimes absentee ownership. The act of naming them, even in claiming their anonymity, is its own memorialization. Although Père Jean-Baptiste Labat casually compared the bodies of enslaved and freed peoples to Egyptian obelisks owing to their branded flesh, bodies made into unwilling monuments and transcripts of commodification, these images picture a sharp refutation of monumentalizing ideologies that prospered as a result of the exploitation of racialized capital in the form of human beings.[6]

In the course of conversations with fellow scholars over the years about how the slaveholding activities of prominent public figures often go unremarked, I have more than once been told some version of "it is not surprising how many people were involved—everyone did it." I have deliberated about how to make the lamented prevalence of such activity understandable in concrete and intimate ways, to make what has come to be understood as the historically "normal" and "ordinary" practices of enslavement clearly resonate as abnormal, as sadistic, as extraordinary. To once again borrow Baron de Vastey's terminology, how does one "rend the veil" on crimes against humanity that will never be punished?[7]

One way to do so has been to directly link Moreau's immersion in print culture—his books and publications—to people, including, importantly, people of African descent. To return to the refrain: people, books, books, people. They moved in the same circuits, sometimes within the same transactions, on board the same ships, within the same households. When writing of the state of colonial libraries for the entry "bibliothèque" in his colonial encyclopedia, Moreau wrote:

> It is very difficult to preserve books [unreadable in the manuscript] where the insects devour them with a furor and rapidity truly distressing for the learned man who loves to find in books the surest friends, the most wise counsel, the most useful knowledge, consolers.

> Il est très difficile de conserver des livres [unreadable] où les insectes les dévorent avec une fureur et une rapidité vraiment affligeantes pour l'homme instruit qui aime à trouver dans les livres les amis les plus sûrs, les conseils les plus sages, les connaissances les plus utiles, les consolateurs.[8]

Books were depicted as friends, as sources of comfort and wisdom. They were anthropomorphized and lifelike, capable of achieving true intimacy with their readers. As fellow scholars, we can no doubt identify with some of these sentiments. During Moreau's 1793 flight from France to the United States, he wrote:

> I wasn't a stranger to liquor, and if I had been fond of it I could have borne the distress of finding a chest filled with my literary works (which had arrived on board too late to be put in the hold and so had been put between decks) exposed and soaked to the point of damaging all my papers, engravings and drawings. One must have the soul of an author to understand the agonizing despair that comes with such a discovery. . . . I salvaged my materials as well as I could; but some of them will forever bear witness to how greatly they suffered.

> Je ne fus pas étranger à la liqueur et si je l'avais aimée j'aurais pu me consoler avec elle du chagrin de voir une caisse qui renfermait des matériaux de mes ouvrages, et qui arrivée trop tard à bord pour entrer dans la cale, avait été mise dans l'entrepont gâtée et mouillée au point d'endommager mes papiers, des gravures et des dessins. Il faut avoir des entrailles d'auteur pour savoir tout ce qu'une pareille vue a de désolant. . . . Je recueillis mes matériaux comme je pus et il en est qui attesteront toujours combien ils ont souffert.[9]

Moreau's materials in the second excerpt were also anthropomorphized, capable of bearing witness, of suffering. In the logic of Moreau's worldview, books could be alive, even though he knew they were not. They could have feelings, even though he knew they did not. The ocean spray that wet, molded, and ruined printed material onboard could be *felt* by those very inanimate materials themselves just as its effects could be lamented by their owners. This same worldview, in striking contrast, effectively held that the human beings on boats crossing the Atlantic who suffered from exposure, fetid conditions, and the loss of their lives and freedom could not feel, or, rather, *they did not feel in ways that mattered*. Living people could be legalized as valuable objects, civilly dead in critical ways, although Moreau knew, objectively and viscerally, that they were not so. They could exist without feelings for kin that approximated his own, even though he knew that this was not true. They could exist as *parts* of themselves—the parts that cooked, carried, cleaned, dusted off bookshelves, or existed as cash assets. In short, they could be *arms*, severed from rational, feeling selves connected to whole bodies.

Moreau's household depicted as a collection of dismembered arms shows how these arms transformed the space into a home, an organized library, a private scientific menagerie, profit (Figure 53). The pineapple, floating midair near the

FIGURE 53. *The Household, Redux*. By Luz Sandoval and Sara E. Johnson. 2020.

center of the room, concretizes whose labor was actually creating the vaunted hospitality that Moreau extolled as a cornerstone of creole life. The effect is horrific, creepy, exposing the lie that a person could ever exist solely as labor: *mains d'œuvres, manos de obra,* workhands. The legal system that Moreau defended and described with such dedication effectively defined their labor (including their reproductive labor) as their raison d'être, their existential purpose. Yet the labor they performed demanded patience, artistry, technical knowledge, kindness, good judgment—skill sets unique to living, thinking, feeling beings.

Many arms have appeared in this book's pages—the severed limb of Jean-Baptiste, a man who chose to dismember himself as a way to change the conditions of his existence as an enslaved man; *les bras qui couvrent* (the arms that covered), a euphemistic expression for the workers who converted the rugged lands of Louis Narcisse Baudry des Lozières's coffee plantation into terraced gardens; the portrait of a young girl named Marie-Anne Grellier *dans les bras de sa nourrice* (in the arms of her wet nurse); the arms and hands that set type, served tea in imported Chinese porcelain cups, washed clothes, handled animal specimens. This book *is* meant as a monument to the people connected to those arms. They appear, often in passing, to insist on their personhood in toto. What I cannot say about them produces its own space. That space is not blank but assumes an outline, working as a placeholder that awaits further elaboration. The project is built on the work of generations of scholars in Black intellectual traditions who acknowledge that "the impossibility of recovery is inextricable from the moral imperative to attempt it."[10]

My ouvrage suggests a communal biographical mode that matches Moreau's sea of faces: people that Moreau could not always differentiate but who we are determined to perceive. I have mustered scattered historical fragments of information into one cognitive frame so that those who stood in Moreau's, Baudry's, Van Braam's, Azara's, Aménaïde Dall 'Asta's, and other anonymous slaveholders' shadows would be woven into the narrative cloth. In so doing, I echo Anna Brickhouse's call for a "reparative approach to a written colonial archive that we think we already know—an approach that seeks imaginative or speculative possibilities and their consequences rather than the mere exposure of flawed ideological positions." Moreau's utility to scholars in subsequent generations is that alongside the chronicles of self-satisfied, vindictive, or coldly calculating slaveowners, we notice other lives and hear, however faintly and often through the amplification of speculation, other stories. We contemplate who and what we know and do not know historically and undermine the veracity of the accounts that Moreau and others have left us.[11]

P

Poison

But it is unfortunately too certain that old Africans in Saint-Domingue profess the odious art of poisoning; I say profess because there are some who have a school to which hate and vengeance send more than one disciple.

Mais il est malheureusement trop certain que de vieux Africains professent à Saint-Domingue l'art odieux d'empoisonner; je dis professent, car il en est qui y ont une école où la haine et la vengeance envoyent plus d'un disciple.[12]

I opened this *Encyclopédie* with "Aménaïde," an example of the personal relationship that breached the color line Moreau actively worked to enforce. I close with "poison," a substance with which to end one life or multiple lives, abuse, or textual experiments. One of the first entries in Moreau's "Répertoire des notions coloniales" was for arsenic. The idea of danger and threat would thus have been immediately encountered by those moving alphabetically through his projected compendium about colonial society. He claimed that it was "to this mineral substance that one owes almost all of the poisonings done in S[aint]-D[omingue]. Most colonists are persuaded that their Blacks, especially those from [illegible] Africa, are familiar with the poisons taken from the plant kingdom" (à cette substance minerale qu'on doit presque tous les empoisonnments qui se font à SD. Le plus grand nombre des colons sont persuadés que leur nègres, sur tous ceux [illegible], côte d'Afrique, connaissent des poisons pris dans le règne vegetal). When combined with comments indicating that a "school" of resistance run by Africans would have a regular supply of new "disciple[s]," Moreau's fluctuation between the idea of slavery as a benevolent, familial institution and slavery as a state of warfare is palpable.[13]

A for "arsenic," *P* for "poison": both are terms germane to a primer on colonial life. The entries encapsulate metaphorically the relationship between scientific knowledge collection, encyclopedic publishing, and violence. Poison had effects that were empirically observable and clinically knowable. Yet it left devastation and chaos in its wake, feeding planter paranoia and torturous legal regimes of control over those determined to resist their commodification. Attempts to gather knowledge and to project order, coherence, and rational objectivity onto a topic could not silence the inherently personal and conflictual brutality of slavery.

In a similar vein, *P* could likewise have introduced an entry for Polydor, a man who led an armed rebellion in the 1730s. Though Polydor was killed, Moreau informed his readers that there was a savanna named after him in the sugar-producing region of Trou, close to the Spanish border with Santo Domingo. Other "sanguinary brigand[s]" (brigand[s] sanguinaire) succeeded Polydor in this same region: Canga in 1777 and Gillot Yaya in 1787. The topography was imbued with the memories of those who had their own visions of an alternate present and future. Even as Moreau's natural histories depicted landscapes— the plantations, the people who lived on them, the natural resources—these same landscapes contained subterranean voices belonging to the people working the land and living a life apart from discursive proclamations of so-called good masters and barbarous brigands.[14]

Poison also leaves a long intellectual trail. It has seeped into much of what we know and how we approach our study of the extended Caribbean when we use Moreau as a guide. A communal biography of Moreau seeks to act as antidote to this poison. Its unfolding dismantles the planter intellectual inheritance that Moreau has left us by deliberately connecting knowledge production and storage to institutions reliant on slavery, by embracing the multilingual richness of the archives of slavery in ways that do not exploit languages for utilitarian goals of labor and natural resource extraction, by showing how good taste and sophisticated aesthetic choices about art and print culture are embedded in power relations and extensive networks of people whose contributions are often sidelined. It has allowed women's stories of intercolonial and transatlantic migration and loss, stories often surviving as fragments, to be centered in accounts of the Age of Revolutions that are usually male dominated and nationalistic. It has focused less on what Moreau thought about a particular issue (one need only consult his prolific publications to find this information) and more on the people around him as these publications were being written.

Moreau interjected himself confidently into his writing, often switching to the first person when recounting an anecdote, assuming his opinions mattered, that his worldview was shared. His *I* left voluminous narrative and documentary records to control how he would be perceived, as demonstrated in his many extant personal papers in French archives and a folio labeled "Material for the Biography of Mr. Moreau de Saint-Méry" (Materiali per la biografia di M. Moreau de Saint-Méry) that contains diplomas and honors that he saved and were eventually donated by the family to the Archivio di Stato di Parma. However, we cannot tell the story of this single white male subject without actively engaging the violence that enabled him to see himself as biographical, as worthy of having his story told.[15]

In the process of writing this book, another *I* has surfaced frequently in the prose. This *I* is my own. The first line of the *Encyclopédie noire* states, "I begin with an image: a crowd peopled with thousands of Black faces and intermittent white ones. . . . Moreau de Saint-Méry conjured this scene. . . ." My *I* emerged as a method to counterbalance Moreau's legacy, to frame it on my own terms. This *I* assumed a presence, not to draw attention to myself, but to wrestle with the force of Moreau's outsized ego. My *I* is a multilingual researcher, a curator of visuals, a manipulator of type. When the manuscript was almost complete, I came across Marian Bantjes's discussion of print design. She noted, "Where others might look at measurable results, I tend to be interested in more ethereal qualities, like 'Does it bring joy?' 'Is there a sense of wonder?' and 'Does it invoke curiosity?'" "I'm mystified," she continued, "as to why visual wealth is not more commonly used to enhance intellectual wealth." Curiosity, wonder, discomfort, distaste, intentional invocation of the uncertain—these thoughts have inspired my bridging of the textual and the visual in the book's typography.[16]

A communal biographical approach thus emerged from slow research, experimentation, and personal experience. Annette Gordon-Reed opens her Pulitzer Prize–winning book on the Hemings family with an account of what it felt like to sit in the archives and hold the original copy of Thomas Jefferson's Farm Book for the first time. She had studied it for years, but she notes the power of sitting in front of and touching the actual pages that had once been in Jefferson's hands, the book that entered observations and minutiae about the daily workings of Jefferson's properties and "his" people: the Hemings and other enslaved children, women, and men. She writes, "When I opened the pages to see that very familiar hand and the neatly written entries, many of which I knew by heart, I was completely overwhelmed." "It was wrenching to hold the original," she goes on, "and to know that Jefferson's actual hand had dipped into the inkwell and touched these pages to create what was to me a record of human oppression. It took my breath away." I likewise experience astonishment and anger when working directly with bibliographical materials, many once belonging to Moreau, which have managed to survive the ravages of climate, revolutions, benign neglect. I am aware that they have been preserved with more attention and care than was devoted to many of the people whose lives are chronicled within them.[17]

What Gordon-Reed does not say, but what can be read between the lines, is how she felt as a Black woman historian as she held that book, knowing that her choice of profession would not have been open to her in Jefferson's America, that he would have objectified her as a human with gendered monetary value. When I consider Moreau's comments on the abstract idea of posterity as judge, I cannot help but imagine his surprise to find me playing that professional role.

Long ago at a conference I discussed Moreau and his well-known accounts of "seductive" women of color and African and African-descended peoples' alleged lasciviousness with other scholars of the French Atlantic. I commented that it would no doubt have felt as curious and incongruous to Moreau to know I was chronicling his life as I felt ambivalent about being one of the many to have done so. I can say with the conviction born of many years of study that Moreau would have objectified me, as was his wont. Matter-of-factly, it is impossible *not* to feel and know this. I was told by a colleague in wary and surprised tones that I needed to take a step back, to preserve my objectivity.

What precisely would this mean? My colleague's discomfort with such an admission—of a subject under study likely having strong opinions about the legitimacy of his or her biographer and said biographer bringing this up as a legitimate part of the research process—is a mark of privilege. Though my preferred academic voice rarely leads to personal rumination, seeing myself as Moreau's interlocuter has at times felt intimately distasteful. I believe that this connection strengthens my work. My research has a situated, embodied politics. To quote Saidiya Hartman, "This story is told from inside the circle." Slavery is not an abstract institution of the past for me but one that is embedded in family history shared by my elders for as long as I can remember. It throws a shadow over the present. I chose to take a step forward, to engage, to turn to art and experimentation because it was the only way to write this book.[18]

ACKNOWLEDGMENTS

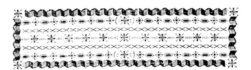

One of the greatest pleasures of finishing any book is the opportunity to acknowledge the people and institutions that supported its creation over the course of many years. Fellowships from the Library Company of Philadelphia, the American Council of Learned Societies, the Ford Foundation, the University of California Consortium for Black Studies in California, the Bibliographical Society of America, the Society of Hellman Fellows, and the University of California, San Diego, enabled archival visits and facilitated dedicated writing time. Archivists at the Archives nationales d'outre-mer in Aix-en-Provence, the Archivio di Stato and Biblioteca Palatina in Parma, the John Carter Brown Library, and the Library Company of Philadelphia have been particularly helpful with sharing their knowledge about some of the largest collections of personal papers and extant print material concerning Moreau de Saint-Méry.

Special thanks are due to the transamerican reading group that formed in the aftermath of the Translation and Transmission in the Early Americas SEA Summit. This book benefited immeasurably from the astute commentary offered by Jesse Alemán, Rodrigo Lazo, and Kirsten Silva Gruesz. Our workshops made me write when I would not otherwise have found the time, and I have so enjoyed the close readings of one another's manuscripts over the years. Abrazotes. Kirsten, you have modeled so much of how to do this job with grace.

I thank Luz Sandoval, who was always ready for an artistic challenge and who took my designs and sketches and brought them to life. Marlene Daut, James E. McClellan III, Sue Peabody, and Bernard Camier were generous in sharing concrete information about archival sources. My thanks to Edouard Duval-Carrié and Marielle Plaisir for letting me reproduce their provocative and inspiring art.

I owe a huge thanks to everyone who read the full manuscript and shared their expertise and invaluable advice: Anna Brickhouse, Ada Ferrer, Cathy Kelly, Sarah Knott, Jennifer Morgan, Josh Piker, and Nick Popper. Anna Brickhouse helped me get unstuck, and her discernment as a reader is unparalleled. Ada

Ferrer has been a long-term interlocutor, and her own work, including the re-markable *Visionary Aponte: Art and Black Freedom* collaborative project, has been an inspiration. Sarah Knott served as a regular sounding board, and I am so grateful for her attention to both the big picture and sentence-level aesthetics. Many colleagues and friends have read and discussed pieces along the way, and I thank Leslie Alexander, Marlene Daut, Fatima El-Tayeb, Zaire Dinzey-Flores, Meta DuEwa Jones, and Lisa Ze Winters for their generosity and intellectual camaraderie.

I also wish to acknowledge what a gift it has been to work with the Books program at the Omohundro Institute of Early American History and Culture. Cathy Kelly has been a champion of this project for many years. She has been open to every imaginative foray and critical intervention that I have wanted to make, staying committed to my vision and voice. Thank you for your expert readerly eye, encouragement, and patience. It has been a pleasure to work to-gether. Thanks as well to all of the anonymous reviewers who pushed me to connect the dots and provided corrections and helpful suggestions. Emily Suth's enthusiasm about the project, expertise with permissions, coding of a very com-plex manuscript, and general advice about every aspect of book production have been immensely valuable. This book has undergone a copyediting and source-checking process offered by a group of editorial experts *sans pareil*. I wish every scholar could have the experience of having their work receive such close, skilled reading. My profound gratitude to the remarkable Virginia Montijo Chew. Your expertise and your dedication to this project—making sure each detail was just right at every stage of production—have made this a true collaboration. Thanks also to her team members Kathryn Burdette and Kaylan M. Stevenson. And to the OI editorial apprentices who checked every single citation and then some, thank you! Mark Simpson-Vos at the University of North Carolina Press has been a pleasure to work with, and I thank everyone in UNCP's Editing, Design, and Production department for bringing my work to life. Thanks also to Joseph Stuart for compiling the index.

This project has benefited tremendously from invitations to present differ-ent pieces at seminars and conferences over the years. Thank you to the orga-nizers and to the engaged audiences that have provided energetic feedback and encouragement. I wish to acknowledge the Rocky Mountain Seminar in Early American History sponsored by Brigham Young University and the University of Utah. Special thanks to Chris Hodson for his ongoing advice and sense of humor. Thanks also to the Early Modern Studies Institute Age of Revolutions virtual workshop hosted by Nathan Perl-Rosenthal and Clément Thibaud; Robin Derby, who hosted me at the University of California, Los Angeles, Atlantic

History Colloquium; Rachel Sarah O'Toole for the invitation to join her Latin American Studies seminar at the University of California, Irvine; David Bell for the lively session at the Shelby Cullom Davis Center for Historical Studies at Princeton University; and Kristen Block for the opportunity to present at the Transatlantic Enlightenment seminar at the Humanities Center at the University of Tennessee. The intellectual spaces offered at conferences sponsored by the Association for the Study of the Worldwide African Diaspora (ASWAD), the American Studies Association (ASA), the Association for Caribbean Historians (ACH), the Society of Early Americanists (SEA), the Society of Nineteenth-Century Americanists (C19), and the Omohundro Institute of Early American History and Culture have been productive and stimulating. I have exchanged ideas with many colleagues in these and related venues, and Rosanne Adderley, Allison Bigelow, Christian Crouch, Rashauna Johnson, Nathalie Pierre, Grégory Pierrot, Dixa Ramírez-D'Oleo, Gordon Sayre, Alyssa Sepinwall, and Sophie White deserve special mention. Doris Garraway has lent an ear and been a source of knowledge for all things Moreau-related. Jean Casimir has helped me orient my study of Haiti since I was fortunate enough to work with him while still a graduate student.

I have worked alongside wonderful colleagues at UCSD and am privileged to be in a Literature Department that is truly multilingual and interdisciplinary. My ongoing thanks to Kazim Ali, Jody Blanco, Dennis Childs, Page duBois, Amelia Glaser, Stephanie Jed, Misha Kokotovic, Lisa Lampert, Lisa Lowe, Nicole Miller, Rosaura Sánchez, Shelley Streeby, Nicole Tonkovich, Katie Walkiewicz, Meg Wesling, and Nina Zhiri, many of whom I have consulted with about different aspects of the book and who have invited me to classes or conferences to share material. Special cheers to Nancy Kwak and Katie Walkiewicz for the shared meals and inspiration as I came through the very final stretch. Nancy Ho-Wu and Heather Zion have always advocated on my behalf, and I thank them for their friendship. I also thank Nancy for her help with the Chinese translations that appear in Chapter 3. Props are due as well to the wonderful intellectual community of UCSD's Black Studies Project, and I am so grateful to Angela Booker, Jessica Graham, Cecilia Ozkan, and Lorraine Makone for making it such a vibrant, fun, and thriving place to collaborate.

Mark B. Kelley, Eunice Sang Lee, Andrea Zelaya, and Joanmarie Bañez provided their assistance over the past decade as graduate student researchers and have provided immense bibiliographic help. I am particularly thankful to Eunice for her positivity and excellent organizational skills over the course of several years. I also wish to thank my thoughtful, fierce, and remarkable undergraduate and graduate students at UCSD. They have pushed me to think outside the box and to figure out the best ways to teach and learn from much of the material that informed this project. Finally, thanks to Marina Bezzati for her assistance in Parma, Italy, and to Natalino Tonghini for the enthusiastic tour he gave me of the Museo Bodoniano.

A sabbatical year at the University of Cambridge sponsored by a fellowship from the American Council of Learned Societies was hugely rewarding. Special thanks are due to Renaud Morieux, Philippine Charaud, Sarah Pearsall, Bronwen Everill and Mónica Moreno Figueroa for the warm welcome, for reading chapter drafts, and for many fruitful conversations over good food. Thanks to the Centre for Research in the Arts, Social Sciences and Humanities (CRASSH) and the CRASSH fellows during the 2018–2019 academic year for providing a wonderful intellectual community. A shout-out to the fun-loving and hospitable crew on North Terrace: Yolanda Bossini and Richard Warwick, Ted Meeks and Lee Bouchard. We could not have relocated and thrived without our York family: Judy Frost, who helped make England a home away from home and who also brought Richard Dobson and Mark Ormond into our lives. Many thanks to Emma Hunter and the wonderful group of interlocuters at the Centre for Global History seminars at the University of Edinburgh. I also thank the American Literature Research Seminar at the Rothermere American Institute, University of Oxford, and the exciting group of scholars that convened at Newcastle University for the 2019 Konesans conference, particularly its organizers, Hannah Durkin and Vanessa Mongey.

I also wish to recognize my fellow members of the "Archival Fragments, Experimental Modes" OI Coffeehouse table for our grounding conversations and collective close reading during the pandemic: Sharon Block, Sarah Eyerly, P. Gabrielle Foreman, Karen Graubart, Kirsten Silva Gruesz, Jennifer Morgan, Renaud Morieux, Mairin Odle, Lorelle Semley, Terri Snyder, Rachel Wheeler, and SJ Zhang. Sarah K, what fun to start this collaboration together. Thanks are due to Karin Wulf for her excellent idea to convene these tables and for giving scholars around the world an opportunity to find community in a time of isolation.

Friendship has sustained the writing of this book. Talking through ideas, sharing meals, sitting together in Zoom Rooms or cafés, mourning our collective losses over the past years, jointly raising children, and holding each other accountable for deadlines has kept me sane. My profound thanks to Zaire Dinzey-Flores and Eddie Paulino, Fatima El-Tayeb, Erin Gurney, Solange Jacobs Randolph, Tara Javidi, Meta DuEwa Jones, Sadia Najmi and Kip Walker, Nancy Kwak and Brian Byun, Rebekah Lugo, Luis Alvarez and Marilyn Espitia, Natalia Molina, Ingrid Banks, Robin Sinclaire, and Lisa Ze Winters. I also owe so much to Saige Walding and Julie Wynne, true friends and accomplished professionals who have helped me weather the uncertainties of living with multiple sclerosis for more than twenty years. You have literally kept me walking and writing.

In P. Gabrielle Foreman's moving essay about the ongoing political stakes of working in Black Studies, an essay that is also a homage to her own mentors, she writes, "I am standing in the fields, still, in mourning and in awe, with heirloom seeds in hand *("This deep, Barbara?" "Too shallow you say, Nellie?")* passed on by those who daily swallowed sacrifices too big, too tough, for me to chew, shaving years and family away to till and study, to peck others' young beaks, to plant in hard ground and harvest plenty. Come, let's tend to what they've planted, and water and till and travel toward justice together" (Foreman, "A Riff, a Call, and a Response: Reframing the Problem That Led to Our Being Tokens in Ethnic and Gender Studies; or, Where Are We Going Anyway and with Whom Will We Travel?" *Legacy: A Journal of American Women Writers,* XXX [2013], 316). I, too, am standing in fields watered by those who made many sacrifices with the hope that the next generation would thrive as people and scholars. *("This deep, VèVè?")* VèVè Clark's mentorship from the time I was an undergraduate on a visiting summer fellowship at University of California, Berkeley, to the year of her untimely death has profoundly shaped how I approach my work. My ongoing thanks to Ula Taylor for her friendship and for all she has done to keep VèVè's legacy alive. My debt to my mentors and friends in the field of Black Studies writ large is a huge one, and I have tried to repay it over the years. To the Black feminist writers and artists who have shaped my worldview, to fellow travelers in the fields of Haitian Revolutionary studies, Caribbean studies, and comparative literature, thank you for your groundbreaking and inspirational work.

This debt has also been incurred in the everyday world. It is an honor to acknowledge my grandmother Minnie Olivia Toney Johnson and grandfather Geylon Johnson, who raised eight children in rural Jim Crow Mississippi. I am forever obliged to Grandma Minnie for humoring me with hours of storytelling, inevitably while gardening, cooking, or generally keeping busy, until her 106th year. Boundless thanks to Sonia Wilmetta Jefferson, Iris Johnson, Gladys Hildreth, Lloyd Johnson, Henry Johnson, and Carol Lorraine Washington, beloved aunts and uncles who always made plenty of quality time to spend with me. Ava Johnson, Herticine Sweet, and Barbara Azeltine were also the best kind of aunties—funny, warm, sarcastic, and ready to lend an ear. Many thanks to Linda and Rob Paulsen for helping to introduce me to the excitement of studying history and for maintaining that excitement over the years. And a big shout-out to Carolyn Widener, who always says yes to helping out when we need to travel for work or just need an extra hand. Thanks to Michael and Edra Widener, who offer us infinite love. When finishing this book, I lost two of my first cousins to the pandemic: Professor Bertina Hildreth Combes and Mark Clarence Washington. You are missed so deeply. To the remaining group of eleven, may our friendship and love continue to flourish, even as we mourn their absence.

This book is dedicated to Ken and Carolyn Johnson, who have always been my rock and have set an example of what most matters in the world and why we must fight for it. Words cannot express how much you mean to me. Julián, Amaya, and Lina are daily sources of joy. Jennifer, Elias, Mia, and Benjie, I love you much. My final thanks go to Danny Widener, who has been the best of partners in every way. He has read every chapter, multiple times over. His infinite curiosity about and knowledge of African diaspora communities alongside his commitment to doing work that knows its own stakes are a true source of inspiration.

NOTES

Introduction

1. Classified advertisement placed by Moreau de Saint-Méry, "Biens et effets à vendre: Lundi 30 du présent mois de juin," *Affiches américaines* (Cap Français, Saint-Domingue), June 18, 1783, [4]. The announcement concerning the two thousand volumes Moreau was selling stated, "Une bibliotheque d'environ deux mille volumes choisis, à vendre par parties. Il faut s'adresser à M. *Moreau de Saint-Méry,* Avocat en Parlement et au Conseil supérieur au Cap, à qui elle appartient" (ibid., Jan. 15, 1783, [3]). Published over the course of six volumes, *Loix et constitutions des colonies françaises de l'Amérique sous le vent* . . . ([Paris], [1784–1790]) was collaborative and demanded several research trips to France and neighboring colonies. For his book collection at the time of his death, see the posthumous sale of materials advertised in the *Catalogue des livres et manuscrits de la bibliothèque de feu M. Moreau de Saint-Méry . . . dont la vente se fera le mercredi 15 décembre 1819* . . . (Paris, 1819).

2. Moreau should be included in wider conversations about various American enlightenments happening in the last decades of the eighteenth century. Conversant in European classical, historical, dramatic, and epic traditions, he also read widely in works about and by Latin American, Caribbean, and North American thinkers. David Brion Davis included him alongside a discussion of the prominent planters and intellectuals Thomas Jefferson and Bryan Edwards of Jamaica. See Davis, *The Problem of Slavery in the Age of Revolution, 1770–1823* (1975; rpt. New York, 1999), 184–195. William Max Nelson discusses Moreau in the context of a detailed analysis of "Atlantic Enlightenment," suggesting that if we know "more about figures like Moreau, the contours of the Atlantic Enlightenment will become significantly clearer." See Nelson, "The Atlantic Enlightenment," in D'Maris Coffman, Adrian Leonard, and William O'Reilly, eds., *The Atlantic World* (London, 2015), 657. Moreau's work is cited extensively in scholarship on the French colonial world.

3. Moreau de Saint-Méry, *Voyage aux États-Unis de l'Amérique, 1793–1798,* ed. Stewart L. Mims (New Haven, Conn., 1913) (hereafter cited as Mims, *Voyage*), 334 ("liberté"); see also the English translation of the diary, Kenneth Roberts and Anna M. Roberts, eds. and trans., *Moreau de Saint Méry's American Journey [1793–1798]* (Garden City, N.Y., 1947), 310 (hereafter cited as Roberts and Roberts, *American Journey*); Médéric Louis Élie Moreau de Saint-Méry, *La description topographique, physique, civile, politique et historique de la partie française de l'isle Saint-Domingue* . . . , ed. Blanche Maurel and Étienne Taillemite, new ed., 3 vols. (Saint-Denis, France, 2004), I, 104. This work was originally published as M. L. E. Moreau de Saint-Méry, *Description topographique, physique, civile, politique et historique de la partie française de l'isle Saint-Domingue* . . . , 2 vols. (Philadelphia, 1797–1798). Unless otherwise noted, all citations to Moreau's *Description* throughout are to the 2004 edition published by the Société française d'histoire d'outre-mer (hereafter cited as *Description de la partie française de l'isle Saint-Domingue*). A few scholars have documented Moreau's

relationship with Marie-Louise Laplaine. Aménaïde is discussed throughout this book, particularly in Chapters 1, 2, and 8.

4. See Moreau de Saint-Méry, *Description de la partie française de l'isle Saint-Domingue,* 86–102, for tables describing various racial combinations. For a fascinating interpretation of Moreau's racial descriptions, see Leah Gordon's "Caste Portraits," http://www.leahgordon.co.uk/index.php/project/caste/. For the "colonial machine," see James E. McClellan III and François Regourd, *The Colonial Machine: French Science and Overseas Expansion in the Old Regime* (Turnhout, Belgium, 2011). The Cuban novelist Alejo Carpentier obliquely references Moreau in *El Reino de este mundo* (1949) as that "ruddy, pleasure-loving lawyer of the Cap" (aquel rubicundo y voluptuoso abogado del Cabo). See Carpentier, *The Kingdom of This World,* trans. Harriet de Onís (New York, 1970), 78; *El reino de est mundo,* 6th ed. (Mexico City, 1991), 61. Carpentier's reference to Moreau in a novel that grounds his philosophy of "lo real maravilloso" in the events of the Haitian Revolution is a tribute from one preeminent archivist of the Americas to his predecessor. Sites such as genealogy.net often cite material contained in Moreau's work. During his lifetime, he was called upon to testify based on his "expert" knowledge. For example, while in exile, he testified in the Circuit Court of Philadelphia "concerning colonial regulations, and particularly concerning the legal rate of interest in San Domingo, where the affair took place." See Roberts and Roberts, *American Journey,* 213.

5. Charles Eugène Gabriel de la Croix, marquis de Castries, the secretary of state of the navy, wrote to Moreau, "Her Majesty has given you an honorable and useful proof of her satisfaction with your services, by granting you a gratuity of 12,000 French livres, to be taken from the Caisse des libertés in the colony [Saint-Domingue], to which you have more particularly devoted your work" (Sa Majesté vous a donné une preuve tout-à-la fois honorable et utile de la satisfaction qu'elle a de vos services, en vous accordant une gratification de 12,000 liv. de France, à prendre sur la Caisse des libertés de la Colonie [Saint-Domingue] *à laquelle vous avez plus particulièrement consacré vos travaux*). See "No. 78," in Moreau de Saint-Méry, *Mémoire justificatif* ([Paris, 1790]), 132.

6. There is an extensive bibliography on biography as historical form and life writing. Some texts that have been helpful include Annette Gordon-Reed, "Writing Early American Lives as Biography," *William and Mary Quarterly,* 3d Ser., LXXI (2014), 491–516; Jill Lepore, "Historians Who Love Too Much: Reflections on Microhistory and Biography," *Journal of American History,* LXXXVIII (2001), 129–144; Sue Peabody, "Microhistory, Biography, Fiction: The Politics of Narrating the Lives of People under Slavery," *Transatlantica,* II (2012), http://transatlantica.revues.org/6184; and the work on Black Atlantic biographical subjects in Lisa A. Lindsay and John Wood Sweet, eds., *Biography and the Black Atlantic* (Philadelphia, 2014).

7. See Audre Lorde's rightfully influential articulation in "The Master's Tools Will Never Dismantle the Master's House," included in the collection *Sister Outsider: Essays and Speeches* (Berkeley, Calif., 1984), 110–114.

8. Shannon Lee Dawdy, "Proper Caresses and Prudent Distance: A How-To Manual from Colonial Louisiana," in Ann Laura Stoler, ed., *Haunted by Empire: Geographies of Intimacy in North American History* (Durham, N.C., 2006), 141. Moreau claims that the primary lesson he learned from his mother was "The length of man's life is measured by its

utility" (la durée de la vie de l'homme se mesure sur son utilité) (*Mémoire justificatif*, 2). In her work on multiple American enlightenments, Caroline Winterer writes that, during the latter half of the eighteenth century, Americans "began to think of themselves as *enlightened* and of their era as an *enlightened age*. To these people, becoming enlightened meant using reason and empirical data as their guides rather than inherited tradition or biblical revelation. . . . Today . . . we wonder how they dared call themselves enlightened when they left so much misery and injustice in the world, and when some of the projects they put into motion appear to us to have yielded such ambiguous or even tragic results" (Winterer, *American Enlightenments: Pursuing Happiness in the Age of Reason* [New Haven, Conn., 2016], 1).

9. My last book explored the transcolonial intellectual histories of the enslaved and free people of color (*The Fear of French Negroes: Transcolonial Collaboration in the Revolutionary Americas* [Berkeley, Calif., 2012]). Here, my dominant concern to critically center blackness in its myriad, nonessentialist, and experientially diverse meanings during the late eighteenth century is still in place. My method approaches a biographical subject in creative, collective, and critical ways to tie a revolutionary-era historian to his slaveholding colonial investments.

10. There is an extensive literature on the legacy of slavery and reparations, including public history projects such as the 1619 Project in the *New York Times Magazine* (Aug. 14, 2019); city, state, and federal commissions and legislation tasked with investigating the possibility of reparations; and university-led commissions to investigate the legacy of slavery at institutions such as George Washington University, Cambridge University, Rutgers University, and the University of Virginia. For examples of well-discussed and important work in a U.S. and French context, see Daina Ramey Berry, *The Price for Their Pound of Flesh: The Value of the Enslaved, from Womb to Grave, in the Building of a Nation* (Boston, 2017); Ta-Nehisi Coates, "The Case for Reparations," *Atlantic,* June 2014, 54–71; Edward E. Baptist, *The Half Has Never Been Told: Slavery and the Making of American Capitalism* (New York, 2014); and Crystal Marie Fleming, *Resurrecting Slavery: Racial Legacies and White Supremacy in France* (Philadelphia, 2017).

11. Work on archives and the production of power is particularly indebted to Michel-Rolph Trouillot's seminal *Silencing the Past: Power and the Production of History* (Boston, 1995). See also Laura Helton et al., "The Question of Recovery: Slavery, Freedom, and the Archive," special issue of *Social Text,* XXXIII, no. 4 (125) (December 2015), esp. 7. Stephanie E. Smallwood's "Politics of the Archive and History's Accountability to the Enslaved" gives a succinct overview of these issues, rightly showing that "for as long as it has been a subject of professional scholarship, American slavery has exposed the methodological limits of the discipline of history. And for just as long, a prolific list of radical intellectuals has made a tradition of trying to write the enslaved into history by challenging received understandings of the archive" (*History of the Present,* VI, no. 2 [Fall 2016], esp. 120–121, 125). Marisa J. Fuentes's *Dispossessed Lives: Enslaved Women, Violence, and the Archive* (Philadelphia, 2016) has done much to draw critical attention to these issues. In dealing with the idea of how to tell stories about the revolutionary age more broadly, see David Scott's work, particularly "Antinomies of Slavery, Enlightenment, and Universal History," *Small Axe,* XIV, no. 3 (November 2010), 152–162 and *Omens of Adversity: Tragedy,*

Time, Memory, Justice (Durham, N.C., 2014). In the context of the Haitian Revolution specifically and the role that fiction plays in representing voices of the enslaved, see Régine Michelle Jean-Charles, *"Memwa se paswa:* Sifting the Slave Past in Haiti," in Soyica Diggs Colbert, Robert J. Patterson, and Aida Levy-Hussen, eds., *The Psychic Hold of Slavery: Legacies in American Expressive Culture* (New Brunswick, N.J., 2016), 86–106. Marlene L. Daut, Grégory Pierrot, and Marion C. Rohrleitner's edited volume *Haitian Revolutionary Fictions: An Anthology* (Charlottesville, Va., 2022) gathers fictions from across three continents.

12. The proliferation of names that define alternate methodologies indicates the ongoing need for and consequent richness of such work. On "critical fabulation," see Saidiya Hartman, "Venus in Two Acts," *Small Axe,* XII, no. 2 (June 2008), 1–14; on "protocols and limits," see ibid., 2–4, 9; on "poetics of fragmentation," see Nicole N. Aljoe, *Creole Testimonies: Slave Narratives from the British West Indies, 1709–1838* (New York, 2012), esp. chap. 1; on "wake work," see Christina E. Sharpe, *In the Wake: On Blackness and Being* (Durham, N.C., 2016). Jocelyn Fenton Stitt provides another excellent framing of what she terms "absence aesthetics" and the possibilities of life writing to "create a different feminist epistemological space from fiction, concerned with marking the limits of the archive and creating new forms of Caribbean historiography and aesthetics based on women's experiences." See Stitt, *Dreams of Archives Unfolded: Absence and Caribbean Life Writing* (New Brunswick, N.J., 2021), 8, 11.

13. Patricia Saunders, "Defending the Dead, Confronting the Archive: A Conversation with M. NourbeSe Philip," *Small Axe,* XII, no. 2 (June 2008), 71.

14. Sophie White has shown how mining French court records allows the voices of the enslaved to "spring to life," challenging notions of what written sources can count as autobiographical documentation of individual lives and communities in the eighteenth-century Atlantic world. See White, *Voices of the Enslaved: Love, Labor, and Longing in French Louisiana* (Williamsburg, Va., and Chapel Hill, N.C., 2019), 5.

15. Many scholars have explained the benefits of a robust interaction between the disciplines of literature and history. In the words of Doris Garraway, literary criticism has a unique role to play in considering "what cannot be verified; to posit what could never have been documented in any historical archive; to recover the fantasies, beliefs, mentalities, and silences in which the desires and anxieties of historical subjects may be lodged." See Garraway, *The Libertine Colony: Creolization in the Early French Caribbean* (Durham, N.C., 2005), xii. Her work on Moreau has been very influential on my own. I concur with Eric Slauter's belief that "attempting to reconstruct the perspectives of people described within texts, people who have left few other traces of their intellectual history, is an enterprise too important to be left to a single discipline." History and literature, both the study and writing thereof, are two disciplines with countless narrative modes that do the work I attempt here. See Slauter, "History, Literature, and the Atlantic World," *WMQ,* 3d Ser., LVI (2008), 158.

16. *Note des travaux du citoyen Moreau-St.-Méry* (Paris, 1799), 5. Anyone who has worked in his archives cannot fail to notice that he owned copies of what seem to be original government documents among his private papers. He was so attached to his research materials that he once wrote, "I fulfilled the formalities which were necessary in order to

have my boxes; and on July 23 I had the happiness of again setting eyes on these materials, which had cost me so much expense, worry, weariness and trouble. Of all the pleasant experiences of my life, this was the one that I enjoyed the most. I call to witness all authors, of whatever kind they may be." See Roberts and Roberts, *American Journey,* 194. Moreau combed various French and Spanish colonial archives, in addition to exploring a variety of institutions in the Americas such as local Catholic churches and the personal papers of friends and acquaintances. For example, people sent him information from London, Madrid, and Cayenne. He collected materials relevant to the new United States while he was living there. As further proof of how valuable his work was to him, he wrote about the fires that broke out in Philadelphia during his residency. He asked a reader to "judge, then, of my anxiety in these moments with a business that equally dreads water and fire, and me having my colonial collection with me" (qu'on juge de mon anxiété dans ces Momens avec un commerce qui rédouté également l'eau et le feu et moi ayant avec moi ma collection colonial). See ibid., 332; Mims, *Voyage,* 358.

17. See Archives nationales d'outre-mer, Aix-en-Provence, France (ANOM), Collection Moreau de Saint-Méry (Ser. F3). There are 297 registers *(registres)* containing hundreds of folders of his papers. These are filled with manuscripts of his own work, correspondence with and belonging to others, maps, and many other original and copied sources. ANOM also holds the remnants of his personal library of more than 3,000 items in the Bibliothèque de Moreau de Saint-Méry. Moreau himself remarked that he might have had one of the only full runs of *Affiches américaines,* a periodical source that is critical to anyone working on Saint-Domingue. With regard to maps, he collected, sold, and published them over the course of his career, and this interest resulted in the large map collection that is also part of the Collection Moreau de Saint-Méry. Dating from 1490 to the early 1800s, they range from hand-drawn maps to printed ones, some monochrome, others finely done in watercolors, many of large spatial conception and design and an equal number of depictions of local sites. In his Philadelphia bookstore catalog, he advertised more than 120 *cartes geographiques* of Europe, Africa, Asia, and the Americas, the latter comprising more than half of them. That Moreau carried the work of famed French cartographers Jacques-Nicolas Bellin, Louis Brion de la Tour, Guillaume de L'Isle, Jean-Nicolas Buache, and Jean-Claude Dezauche demonstrates his interest in and familiarity with some of the finest work in the eighteenth-century cartographic tradition. This knowledge facilitated his authorial and editing work, as he was producing his own maps for several of his imprints while living in Philadelphia. He also carried maps of U.S. states including Maine, Maryland, and Massachusetts, done by Samuel Lewis, the famed American cartographer, as well as important maps of the West Indies that were circulated by the British publisher Thomas Jefferys. He placed special emphasis on the Antilles, given the number of different maps he advertised for islands such as Antigua, Cuba, Martinique, Guadeloupe, Jamaica, Dominica, Grenada, and coastal Guyana.

18. In the Kikongo vocabulary discussed in Chapter 6, there is an entry for *vika,* translated by its compiler as "slave." In his work on Baudry des Lozières's same "Dictionnaire ou Vocabulaire Congo," James Sweet suggests that *vika* meant a person who was a kinless dependent with the right to potentially search for a better master. This person could even have periodic, expected times of *marronage;* critically, this was *not* a person who became

chattel with the expectation of enslaved posterity in perpetuity. Sweet's critique makes an excellent case for the importance of historical linguistic methodologies for the study of slavery. I comment on this term in both Chapters 6 and 7. See Sweet, "Research Note: New Perspectives on Kongo in Revolutionary Haiti," *Americas,* LXXIV (2017), 83–97. Susan Gillman's articulation of the limits of formulations that equate an empire with just one language is helpful for thinking of language spectrums in any given colonial situation (personal conversation, 2019). For example, French colonial rule obviously entailed fraught relationships between French, Kreyòl, Vietnamese, Kikongo, Bambara, etc. Even Moreau's work on Spanish and Italian sources has remained largely outside the purview of Caribbean-focused scholarship.

19. For a sustained analysis of the intersections between historiography and the study of language, see Christopher Ehret, *History and the Testimony of Language* (Berkeley, Calif., 2011), 3 (quotation). Many Italian publications (original works and translations) were about the early Americas. Francesco Saverio Clavigero's important book about early Mexico was first published as *Storia antica del Messico . . . ,* 4 vols. (Cesena, Italy, 1780–1781) and published in Spanish later. Once the Jesuit order was disbanded in the Americas, many relocated to Rome. See chap. 5 in Miguel de Asúa, *Science in the Vanished Arcadia: Knowledge of Nature in the Jesuit Missions of Paraguay and Río de la Plata* (Leiden, 2014). Some of the earliest Kikongo language manuals were also done by Italian scholars; see Jean de Dieu Nsondé, *Langues, culture et histoire Koongo aux XVIIe et XVIIIe siècles: À travers les documents linguistiques* (Paris, 1995).

20. I discuss Moreau's work in Spanish and Dutch in later chapters. Regarding English, an extant letter he wrote to Alexander Hamilton provides a sense of his linguistic abilities at the beginning of his stay in the United States. After meeting Hamilton in 1794, Moreau sent him a letter promoting his bookstore. In this unedited transcription of the letter, he wrote, "The Kind Reception I have been honoured with by your Excellency, Seems authorize me to hope that my Enterprize will not be intirely indifferent for your Goodness. Nobody feels more deeply than me the grief of Seing your Excellency Leaving a Department where his ability and his fondness of his country was so eminently perceived. But for the true Citizen the means of Serving his native land, may be meet with at every Step or at every Instant. I am with Respect, Sir, of your Excellency the most obedient and very humble servant. Moreau de st Méry." The letter contained a French postscriptum excusing his English: "I dare to expect that Your Excellency's complaisance will make up for what my incorrect English will not express to you well in relation to my respectful devotion" (J'ose attendre La complaisance de Votre Excellence qu'elle Suppléera à ce que mon Anglais incorrect ne lui exprimera pas bien par rapport à mon respectueux dévouement). See "To Alexander Hamilton from Médéric Louis Elie Moreau de St. Méry, 15 December 1794," *Founders Online,* National Archives, https://founders.archives.gov/documents /Hamilton/01-17-02-0433, orig. publ. in Harold C. Syrett, ed., *The Papers of Alexander Hamilton,* XVII, *August 1794–December 1794* (New York, 1972), 444–445. Moreau also wrote to George Washington and John Adams on the same day, advertising his new bookstore; Adams was a patron of his bookshop. For the letter to Adams, see https://founders .archives.gov/?q=Moreau%20de%20saint%20mery&s=1111311111&sa=&r=7&sr=. For the letter to Washington, see https://founders.archives.gov/?q=Moreau%20de%20saint%20mery

&s=111131111&sa=&r=8&sr=, orig. publ. as David R. Hoth and Carol S. Ebel, eds., *The Papers of George Washington,* Presidential Series, XVII, *1 October 1794–31 March 1795* (Charlottesville, Va., 2013), 274–275.

21. See [Moreau de Saint-Méry], *Catalogue of Books, Stationary* [sic], *Engravings, Mathematical Instruments, Maps, Charts, and Other Goods of Moreau de St. Mery, and Co's. Store, No. 84, South Front-Street, Corner of Walnut* (Philadelphia, 1795). Upon leaving Philadelphia, he advertised the sale of many of his personal belongings, including "a complete Printing office wherewith the publication of several works, whether in French, or in English may be undertaken at the same time." This advertisement is available as an unsourced newspaper clipping in "Historique de Saint-Domingue . . . ," 1797–1798, ANOM, F3, 201. It also appeared in the *Aurora General Advertiser* (Philadelphia), July 20, 1798, [4].

22. Robert Bringhurst, *The Elements of Typographic Style,* 3d ed. (Point Roberts, Wash., 2004), 19. All printers' type ornaments that appear in this book are ones that Moreau used in his own Philadelphia printshop, both in the work that he wrote, translated, and edited himself and in the jobs he printed on behalf of others. He imported his printing press and his type from London. Edmund Fry and Isaac Steele, "letter-founders to the Prince of Wales" in London, seem to have supplied some of the ornaments. The 1793 edition of their specimen book contains designs Moreau used regularly. See, for example, numbers 13 (rose), 21 (musical instruments), 32 (horizontal musical instruments), 74 (state home), 86 (the "Finis" plate found at the close of the *Encyclopédie noire*), in Fry and Steele, *Specimen of Metal Cast Ornaments, Curiously Adjusted to Paper . . .* (London, 1793). Publications in which Moreau used the printers' type ornaments found throughout this book include, for example, Moreau de Saint-Méry, *Description topographique, physique, civile, politique et historique de la partie française de l'isle Saint-Domingue* (1797–1798), I, 100 (single floral border), 745 (three stacked lines of floral and *X*-shapes border headpiece), II, 816 (arrow design dash); M[édéric] L[ouis] É[lie] Moreau de Saint-Méry, *Description topographique et politique de la partie espagnole de l'isle Saint-Domingue . . . ,* 2 vols. (Philadelphia, 1796), title page (crowned face with plumes); M. L. E. Moreau de Saint-Méry, ed. and trans., *Voyage de l'ambassade de la Compagnie des Indes orientales hollandaises, vers l'empereur de la Chine, dans les années 1794 et 1795 . . . Le tout tiré du journal d'André Everard van Braam Houckgeest . . . ,* 2 vols. (Philadelphia, 1797–1798), I, xxix (asterisk border), xlv (five stacked lines headpiece), II, 379 (rose head- or tailpiece), 439 (musical instruments central page ornament); C[laude] C[orentin] Tanguy de La Boissière, *Observations sur la dépêche écrite le 16 janvier 1797 par M. Pickering, secrétaire d'État des États-Unis de l'Amérique, à M. Pinkney, ministre plénipotentiaire des États-Unis près la République française* (Philadelphia, 1797), 3 (seven stacked borders headpiece), 50 ("Finis" tailpiece).

23. There is a large bibliography on the intersection between the visual and slavery; see, for example, Huey Copeland, Krista Thompson, and Darcy Grimaldo Grigsby, eds., "New World Slavery and the Matter of the Visual," special issue of *Representations,* CXIII, no. 1 (Winter 2011). The volume's excellent introduction by Copeland and Thompson reminds us, "Given that both word and image have long been experienced as sites of constraint for black populations, it makes a kind of sense that African diasporic practitioners have time and again worked to deform extant representational conventions in order to carve out spaces of subjective autonomy. . . . The visual *matters* to the rewiring of slavery's imaginary,

in examining the ways in which black subjects have appropriated widely available representational means only to undo their formal contours, to break apart their significatory logic, or to reduce them to their very substance" ("Perpetual Returns: New World Slavery and the Matter of the Visual," ibid., 10). See also the essays in Celeste-Marie Bernier and Hannah Durkin, eds., *Visualising Slavery: Art across the African Diaspora* (Liverpool, U.K., 2016), and chaps. 1 and 4 of Johnson, *Fear of French Negroes.*

24. In *Fear of French Negroes,* I examined transcolonial collaborations in great detail, arguing for the existence of competing inter-Americanist intellectual and material traditions, many of which existed along a pro- and antislavery continuum. For an overview of the phrase "transnational turn" as it is used much as "global turn" has been, see Donald E. Pease, "Introduction: Re-mapping the Transnational Turn," in Winfried Fluck, Pease, and John Carlos Rowe, eds., *Re-framing the Transnational Turn in American Studies* (Hanover, N.H., 2011), 1–46. A volume with many important essays that mapped out these connections is Caroline F. Levander and Robert S. Levine, eds., *Hemispheric American Studies* (New Brunswick, N.J., 2008).

25. Again, this observation about the fictional nature of much planter propaganda is a long-standing result of the excellent work of previous scholars. See, for example, Barbara Bush, "'Sable Venus,' 'She Devil,' or 'Drudge'? British Slavery and the 'Fabulous Fiction' of Black Women's Identities, c. 1650–1838," *Women's History Review,* IX (2000), 761–789. Joan [Colin] Dayan also expresses the fungibility of disciplines / writing practices widely taken to be completely distinct when she remarks, "To read the Black Code with *The Hundred and Twenty Days of Sodom* is to understand that the strategies for degrading a body into mere matter—whether called 'a novel' or 'the law'—are both fictions that must be read as histories" (Dayan, "Codes of Law and Bodies of Color," *New Literary History,* XXVI [1995], 293).

26. Moreau de Saint-Méry, *Mémoire justificatif,* 2 (quotation). Given his stature as a public intellectual figure, there is plenty of biographical information available about Moreau, much of it derived from the various journals and memoirs he wrote about his own life. See Anthony Louis Elicona, *Un colonial sous la Révolution en France et en Amérique: Moreau de Saint-Méry* (Paris, 1934). The introductory essay "Moreau de Saint-Méry," by Étienne Taillemite, to the 2004 edition of *Description de la partie française de l'isle Saint-Domingue,* vii–xxxvi, also contains a wealth of information, as does Monique Pouliquen's introduction to Médéric Louis Élie Moreau de Saint-Méry, *Voyage aux États-Unis de l'Amérique, 1793–1798,* new ed., ed. Pouliquen (Saint-Denis, France, 2007), 7–29. See also the extensive introductory materials in Carla Corradi Martini, ed., *Historique etats de Parme, 1749–1808* (Parma, Italy, 2003). There is also an excellent collection of essays in Dominique Taffin, ed., *Moreau de Saint-Méry; ou, Les ambiguïtés d'un créole des Lumières* ... ([Fort-de-France], Martinique, 2006). Finally, see Marcel Dorigny, Dominique Rogers, and Taillemite's catalog to the 2004 exhibition *Des constitutions à la description de Saint-Domingue: La colonie française en Haïti vue par Moreau de St-Méry* ([Fort-de-France?] Martinique, 2004). This collection centers Moreau as a means of discussing pressing colonial concerns.

27. Moreau de Saint-Méry, *Mémoire justificatif,* 2–4. The first French settlers arrived in Martinique in 1635, and Moreau placed his ancestors in this "founding" group of settler

colonialists. For an excellent study on French legal regimes, see Laurie M. Wood, *Archipelago of Justice: Law in France's Early Modern Empire* (New Haven, Conn., 2020). For his collaborations with the Cercle des Philadelphes, see James E. McClellan III, *Colonialism and Science: Saint Domingue in the Old Regime* (Baltimore, 1992). I thank him for his advice about consulting Moreau's manuscript translation of Fray Iñigo Abbad y Lasierra's work on Puerto Rico. Such was Moreau's fame that his friend Beaumetz, another French man living in exile in the United States, informed him that a play or pantomime called *The Bastille; or, Liberty Triumphant* was performed in New York on June 25, 1795, in which Moreau was the leading character. John Hodgkinson, the renowned British American actor, played Moreau. See Beaumetz to Moreau, June 26, 1795, cited in Roberts and Roberts, *American Journey*, 186–189. On the Club Massiac, see Gabriel Debien, *Les colons de Saint-Domingue et la Révolution: Essai sur le Club Massiac (août 1789–août 1792)* (Paris, 1953).

28. Moreau wrote, "October 23 a letter announced that I was named to the intendance of Saint-Domingue" (Le 23 octobre une lettre annonce que je suis nommé à l'Intendance de Saint-Domingue) (*Mémoire justificatif*, 32); I have not seen this confirmed anywhere but in Moreau's own words. His conflict with Louis Charton in 1790 seems to have led to the death of some of his political ambitions in the French American colonies; see Chapter 3. In a 1789 conversation with the marquis de Lafayette, when asked what position he aspired to, Moreau replied, "My ambition was to become Administrator of a colony; that having been born in America (which he did not yet know), that having given my life to the study of the legislation and the history of the colonies, I believed, even out of honesty, to belong to them more than anywhere else, and that after having served Paris with some success, I would die happy if I were useful to my true country [Martinique] or to the colony to which had received my care for fifteen years, at a time when I foresaw that they would not be free from trouble" (Mon ambition était de devenir Administrateur d'une Colonie; qu'étant né en Amérique, [ce qu'il ne savait pas encore], qu'ayant donné ma vie à l'étude de la Législation et de l'Histoire des Colonies, je croyais, même par probité, leur être plus propre qu'à toute autre chose, et qu'après avoir servi Paris avec quelque succès, je mourrais content si j'étais utile à ma véritable patrie ou à la Colonie, qui avait mes soins depuis près de quinze ans, à une époque où j'entrevoyais qu'elles ne seraient point exemptes de troubles) (ibid., 22).

29. *Mémoires du comte de Moré (1758–1837)* (Paris, 1898), quoted in Roberts and Roberts, *American Journey,* xix. Moreau took credit for introducing inhabitants of the newly independent United States to contraceptives, "certain small contrivances—ingenious things said to have been suggested by the stork. . . . I carried a complete assortment of them for four years; and while they were primarily intended for the use of French colonials, they were in great demand among Americans, in spite of the false shame so prevalent among the latter." He sold these in his Philadelphia bookstore alongside pornographic books. See Roberts and Roberts, *American Journey,* 177–178 (quotation), and Mims, *Voyage,* 193, for his descriptions of what he was selling at his store. For Moreau's swashbuckling story, see *Description de la partie espagnole de l'isle Saint-Domingue,* I, 1–3.

30. The Alien and Sedition Acts expelled many foreign residents from the United States, and the legislation set a precedent for anti-immigrant U.S. policy. The French were

one targeted group; when Moreau was given notice that he might be deported, his inquiries about the charges against him returned notification that John Adams, the Federalist president who had lobbied in favor of the legislation, said, "Nothing in particular, but he's too French" (Roberts and Roberts, *American Journey,* 253).

31. Talleyrand, one of the most important figures in European diplomatic history, was a close friend of Moreau's and intervened at many stages of his life to further Moreau's career. He subsidized *Description de la partie francaise de l'isle Saint-Domingue,* introduced him to powerful friends and future collaborators, and tried to "obtain for [Moreau] a position which will call you here [a return to France in 1797], and which gives you independence without too much work. I well know that you were never afraid of too much work; but I am lazy, take great pleasure in being so, and want my friends to have the same opportunity." See Talleyrand to Moreau, Feb. 17, 1797, in Roberts and Roberts, *American Journey,* 238–239. During their exiles in Philadelphia, Moreau said, "On every night we were together, without a single exception, Talleyrand and I discussed the condition of France in the past, her present lot, and finally what would happen to her in the future. The last part of the picture always made us think of Louisiana, and we found many reasons to make us wish to have a home there for ourselves. Then we would determine to devote all our thoughts and energies in this direction, and Talleyrand would decide that we would wind up by becoming its governors" (ibid., 215–216). By 1797, Talleyrand wrote, "I have made so little progress in getting support for our excellent ideas relative to the colonies that I have given up everything we planned together about that. Present-day diplomats are not at all impressed with the possibilities of Louisiana" (ibid., 239). He was instrumental in getting Moreau his subsequent post in Italy.

32. [Augustin-François de] Silvestre, *Discours prononcé le 30 janvier 1819, lors de l'inhumation de M. Moreau de Saint-Méry, membre de la Société* ([Paris], 1819), 4; [François] Fournier-Pescay, *Discours prononcé aux obsèques de M. Moreau de Saint-Méry, le 30 janvier 1819* ([Paris], 1819), 10. See also Louis Gabriel Michaud, *Biographie des hommes vivants; ou, Histoire par ordre alphabétique de la vie publique de tous les hommes qui se sont fait remarquer par leurs actions ou leurs écrits* (Paris, 1818), 502–503. For his time in Parma, see Emilia Carra's *Gli inediti di Moreau de Saint-Méry a Parma* (Parma, Italy, [1954]), 63–150; Carla Corradi Martini, "Aspetti inediti di vita parmigiana negli scritti di Moreau de Saint-Méry," *Aurea Parma,* LXIV, fasc. 2 (August 1980), 137–142; [Marzio Dall'Acqua], *L'ossessione della memoria: Parma settecentesca nei disegni del Conte Alessandro Sanseverini* (Parma, 1997); and Christine Peyrard, Francis Pomponi, and Michel Vovelle, eds., *L'administration napoléonienne en Europe: Adhésions et résistances* (Aix-en-Provence, France, 2008). For more on Moreau's Masonic ties, see Taillemite, "Moreau de Saint-Méry," in *Description de la partie française de l'isle Saint-Domingue,* xiv–xv, xxxii–xxxiv; and, more generally, Bernard Faÿ, *La Franc-maçonnerie et la révolution intellectuelle du XVIIIe siècle* (Paris, 1942).

33. Moreau de Saint-Méry, *Mémoire justificatif,* 34.

34. Mims, *Voyage,* 46–47 (English translation mine); Moreau de Saint-Méry, *Mémoire justificatif,* 34, 109. Although the passage does not specify how many of these seventeen "domestiques" were enslaved, it does establish that he had a household of servants. Since he and others routinely referred to their enslaved as "domestiques" after abolition in 1794, it is reasonable to surmise that the people he mentions here were mostly, if not all, enslaved

Black women and men. See John D. Garrigus, *Before Haiti: Race and Citizenship in French Saint-Domingue* (New York, 2006) for more on these wealthy families of color in the area. Moreau's father's sister Madame Hagard, wife of a former captain of the dragoons and chevalier de Saint-Louis, left him and his sister part of this estate. See Moreau de Saint-Méry, *Mémoire justificatif,* 104.

35. Charles W. Mills, *The Racial Contract* (Ithaca, N.Y., 1997), 18, quoted in John Ernest, *Liberation Historiography: African American Writers and the Challenge of History, 1794–1861* (Chapel Hill, N.C., 2004), 3; Moreau de Saint-Méry, "Discours de Moreau de Saint-Méry, sur les affranchis des colonies, prononcé par lui dans l'assemblée publique du Musée de Paris," Apr. 7, 1785, ANOM, F3, 156.

36. Moreau de Saint-Méry, *Description de la partie française de l'isle Saint-Domingue,* 80.

37. In African diasporic religions from Regla de Ocha to Vodun, practitioners still dress in white to mark a variety of ritual occasions. Details about the way that religion was practiced in the past, particularly among the enslaved, are gleaned through passages in archival sources such as these. Moreau provided many such descriptions of rituals, most famously of a Vodun ceremony. Whether he knew what he was seeing and understood its meaning has been the subject of much debate, including Stephan Palmié's discussion of the "Eh, Bomba" song in "Conventionalization, Distortion, and Plagiarism in the Historiography of Afro-Caribbean Religion in New Orleans," in Wolfgang Binder, ed., *Creoles and Cajuns: French Louisiana—La Louisiane française* (Frankfurt, Germany, 1998), 315–344. Remarking elsewhere that the choice of how to tie a scarf indicated a host of meanings, from a woman's being single to her being unavailable, Moreau showed he was clued into some knowledge about the epistemological codes inherent in sartorial choices.

38. See Julie Hardwick, Sarah M. S. Pearsall, and Karin Wulf, introduction to "Centering Families in Atlantic Histories," special issue of *WMQ,* 3d Ser., LXX (2013), 205–224. For more on Marie-Louise Laplaine, see Michel Camus, "Une fille naturelle de Moreau de Saint-Méry à Saint-Domingue," *Revue de la Société haïtienne d'histoire et de geographie,* XLVI, no. 162 (March 1989), 51–52, and Chapters 1 and 4, below. Camus notes her date of manumission as June 20, 1766.

39. Moreau de Saint-Méry, *Mémoire justificatif,* 6–7.

40. L[ou]is-N[arci]sse B[audr]y Deslozières, *Les égaremens du nigrophilisme* (Paris, 1802). A number of advertisements in the *Affiches américaines* announced that Baudry would be acting as Moreau's representative in Saint-Domingue while the latter was abroad. For one such announcement, including the information that Moreau was going to France and that "the printing [of his work] is the object of his trip" (l'impression [de son ouvrage] est l'objet de son voyage), see *Supplément aux Affiches américaines,* July 9, 1783, [1–10], esp. [1]; and see "Acte de liberté," Mar. 17, 1783, ANOM, Notariat Saint-Domingue, 542, Grimperel, acting notary, for an example of Baudry's legal power of attorney on Moreau's behalf.

41. Moreau wrote: "There is nevertheless in the human species a class that is friendly to all others, and which only truly rejoices when it shares the fruit of its labors; similar to the industrious bee, it prepares goods whose enjoyment is often unknown to it; its emulation is the wish to be useful; its sweetest reward is to know that it truly is. United by a common bond, all those who form this precious class love each other without knowing

one another and seek each other out with no other goal but the general advantage. . . . Yes, scholars form among themselves a brotherhood" (Il est néanmoins dans l'espèce humaine une classe amie de toutes les autres, et qui ne jouit vraiment que quand on partage le fruit de ses travaux; semblable à l'abeille industrieuse, elle prépare des biens dont la jouissance lui est souvent inconnue; son émulation, c'est le voeu d'être utile; sa plus douce récompense, de savoir qu'elle l'est véritablement. Unis d'un lien commun, tous ceux qui forment cette classe précieuse s'aiment sans se connaître et se recherchent mutuellement sans autre but que l'avantage général. . . . Oui, les savans forment entr'eux un peuple de frères). See Moreau de Saint-Méry, *Discours sur l'utilité du musée établi à Paris: Prononcé dans sa séance publique du 1er décembre 1784* (Parma, Italy, 1805), 4–6. I have not come across any extended intellectual conversations he had with women or references he made to their work. He argued for the inclusion of women in salons, such as events at the Musée de Paris, and he represented female clients in divorce proceedings in Saint-Domingue. The manuscripts and printed material documenting some of these cases and many more is mentioned in Victor Advielle, *L'odysée d'un normand à St. Domingue au dix-huitième siècle* (Paris, 1901), 267–283. Six volumes of Moreau's work were purchased in 1875 and given to the Fonds Advielle in Arras. My attempt to retrieve records of these cases was unsuccessful owing to the destruction of many of these records during the German bombing of the city in 1915. For more on women in Enlightenment-era intellectual circles, see Sarah Knott and Barbara Taylor, eds., *Women, Gender, and Enlightenment* (Basingstoke, U.K., 2005); and Dena Goodman, *The Republic of Letters: A Cultural History of the French Enlightenment* (Ithaca, N.Y., 1994).

42. Moreau de Saint-Méry, *Description de la partie française de l'isle Saint-Domingue*, 8 ("Colonies"). See also Jorge Cañizares Esguerra, *How to Write the History of the New World: Histories, Epistemologies, and Identities in the Eighteenth-Century Atlantic World* (Stanford, Calif., 2001), esp. chap. 4. Critiques that document the imbricated nature of eighteenth-century European scientific, political, and social thought with the infamous set of laws governing the enslaved and free people of color in the French colonies Enlightenment theory have done much to ask, "How should we read the Enlightenment?" and answer, "With the Code Noir in hand!" See Louis Sala-Molins's *Le code noir; ou, Le calvaire de Canaan* (Paris, 1987); and Michèle Duchet, *Anthropologie et histoire au siècle des Lumières: Buffon, Voltaire, Rousseau, Helvétius, Diderot* (Paris, 1971). Laurent Dubois's "Enslaved Enlightenment: Rethinking the Intellectual History of the French Atlantic" provides a succinct overview of the history and stakes inherent to Eurocentric and Americas-centered approaches to the study of the Haitian Revolution, with particular attention to incorporating the role of the enslaved into these discussions. See Dubois, *Social History*, XXXI (2006), 1–14. Toni Morrison writes, "As the sociologist Orlando Patterson has noted, we should not be surprised that the Enlightenment could accommodate slavery; we should be surprised if it had not. The concept of freedom did not emerge in a vacuum. Nothing highlighted freedom—if it did not in fact create it—like slavery." See Morrison, *Playing in the Dark: Whiteness and the Literary Imagination* (Cambridge, Mass., 1992), 38. There is a huge literature on the often-contentious readings of the Enlightenment via postcolonial critiques and an equally large body of research on the "global"

dimensions of eighteenth-century intellectual traditions done by scholars such as Felicity Nussbaum and Anthony Pagden.

43. In Toni Morrison's masterful reading of Bernard Bailyn's work on the planter William Dunbar, she probes how Dunbar, an educated man, lover of books and science, became immune to the suffering of those around him. "Once he is moved into that position, he is resurrected as a new man, a distinctive man—a different man. And whatever his social status in London, in the New World he is a gentleman. More gentle, more man. The site of his transformation is within rawness: he is backgrounded by savagery" (Bailyn, *Voyagers to the West: A Passage in the Peopling of America on the Eve of the Revolution* [New York, 1986], 488–492, quoted in Morrison, *Playing in the Dark,* 44). Morrison notes that Bailyn used William Faulkner's fictive Colonel Sutpen from *Absalom, Absalom!* (1936) for his comparison to Dunbar's experience in Mississippi, another example of the fruitful pairing of history and literature to explore slaveholding mentalities.

44. Moreau de Saint-Méry, *Note des travaux du c[itoy]en Moreau-St.-Méry* (Paris, 1799), 5 ("un long travail"). The explanation of the spine as the gathering space of a book comes from a printshop webpage. See https://www.formaxprinting.com/blog/2013/01/book-printing -lingo-what-is-the-spine-of-a-book. In one of the only articles that he published from "Répertoire," he wrote, "The adoption of the title *Répertoire de notions coloniales* was born from the conviction that a single man could not dare to promise an encyclopedic work and from the desire of the author to excite more scholarly pens to perfect and even to rectify that which would have come from his own" (L'adoption du titre de *Répertoire de notions coloniales* était né de la persuasion qu'un seul homme ne peut oser promettre un ouvrage encyclopédique et du désir qu'avait l'Auteur d'exciter des plumes plus savants à perfection- ner et même à rectifier ce qui serait sorti de la sienne) (Moreau de Saint-Méry, *Danse: Arti- cle extrait d'un ouvrage . . .* [Philadelphia, 1796], 8). He took great pleasure in reading aloud parts of his encyclopedia to fellow colonists, both when he was still living in the Caribbean and while in exile in the United States. It was a collective project of sorts. Moreau also had American sources as a model. See, for example, his mention of Fournier de Varenne's work on a "Supplément à L'Encyclopédie pour la partie des colonies," in Moreau de Saint-Méry, "Discours préliminaire," in *Loix et constitutions,* I, xxiii. Varenne apparently shared many of his entries with Moreau, who was very concerned that people living in the Caribbean should write and disseminate their own histories.

45. Moreau de Saint-Méry, *Mémoire justificatif,* 34. Most scholarship on Moreau does not study his daily contact with his and others' enslaved people nor his interactions with people of color. Several exceptions are studies of his vitriolic pamphlet debate with Julien Raimond and other *gens de couleur,* chronicled in Florence Gauthier, "Au coeur du *préjugé de couleur:* Médéric Moreau de Saint Méry contre Julien Raimond, 1789–91," *Cahiers des anneaux de la mémoire,* VI (2004), 43–68; and Gauthier, *L'aristocratie de l'épiderme: Le combat de la Société des citoyens de couleur 1789–1791* (Paris, 2007). See also Dominique Rog- ers's excellent "Entre 'Lumières' et préjugés: Moreau de Saint-Méry et les libres de couleur de la partie française de Saint-Domingue," in Taffin, ed., *Moreau de Saint-Méry,* 77–93.

46. Nicolas Ponce, *Recueil de vues des lieux principaux de la colonie française de Saint- Domingue* (Paris, 1791). These were based on Agostino Brunias's work on Dominica and

Saint Vincent, although they have been widely associated with Moreau for more than two centuries. See Chapter 2 for a discussion of this work.

47. [Louis Narcisse] Baudry des Lozières, *Second voyage à la Louisiane, faisant suite au premier de l'auteur de 1794 à 1798 . . .* , 2 vols. (Paris, 1803), II, 108 ("kneel" / *agenouiller*), 111 ("do you love me?" / *m'aimes-tu?*), 112 ("sweep" / *balayer*), 122 ("get undressed" / *va te déshabiller*), 130 ("your mother gave birth to a pig" / *ta mère a mis au monde un cochon*), 131 ("your milk is good" / *votre lait est bon*).

Chapter One

1. Médéric Louis Élie Moreau de Saint-Méry, *La description topographique, physique, civile, politique et historique de la partie française de l'isle Saint-Domingue . . .* , ed. Blanche Maurel and Étienne Taillemite, new ed., 3 vols. (Saint-Denis, France, 2004), I, 73 (hereafter cited as *Description de la partie française de l'isle Saint-Domingue*). After noting that he suffered from an initial inability to distinguish one Black person from another when he returned to the Caribbean from France, Moreau remarked that he eventually could and that "all of the affections, all of the passions are depicted there [on the face] with the character that is proper to each of them, and nothing is lost, even the blush that betrays innocence in favor of pleasure, although this expression may seem strange" (toutes les affections, toutes les passions s'y peignent avec un caractère que est propre à chacune d'elles, et rien n'y est perdu, pas même la rougeur qui trahit l'innocence en faveur du plaisir, quoique cette expression puisse paraître étrange). When speaking about the natural facial variation and expressive traits of the Black people around him, Moreau's prime example purports to document how a blush appears on the face of someone experiencing "pleasure" for the first time. The undercurrent of prurience and innuendo in so much of his prose is striking and disturbing. Population statistics on colonial Saint-Domingue vary, particularly concerning the number of enslaved people. One of the often-cited sources for the demographics of the island is Moreau de Saint-Méry himself. For example, see Laurent Dubois, *Avengers of the New World: The Story of the Haitian Revolution* (Cambridge, Mass., 2004), 30.

2. Sarah Knott, *Mother Is a Verb: An Unconventional History* (New York, 2019), 264–265. The manuscript of Moreau's "Répertoire des notions coloniales; par ordre alphabétique" is held at Archives nationales d'outre-mer, Aix-en-Provence, France (ANOM), Collection Moreau de Saint-Méry (Ser. F3), 73–77.

3. Baptismal record of Jeanne-Louise, dite Aménaïde, Dec. 10, 1778, Archives nationales, État civil du Cap-Français, cited in Michel Camus, "Une fille naturelle de Moreau de Saint-Méry?" *Généalogie et historie de la Caribe,* no. 93 (May 1997), 1960 n. 2.

4. "Donation," Apr. 8, June 13, 1781, ANOM, Notariat Saint-Domingue, 861, Grimperel, acting notary.

5. See Camus, "Une fille naturelle de Moreau de Saint-Méry?" *Généalogie et historie de la Caribe,* no. 93 (May 1997), 1960. Monique Pouliquen confirms that Moreau had a mixed-race family in the comprehensive biographical overview of him in Médéric Louis Élie Moreau de Saint-Méry, *Voyage aux États-Unis de l'Amérique, 1793–1798,* new ed., ed. Pouliquen (Saint-Denis, France, 2007), 27–28. Marlene L. Daut discusses this relationship in *Tropics of Haiti: Race and the Literary History of the Haitian Revolution in the Atlantic*

World, 1789–1865 (Liverpool, U.K., 2015), chap. 4 (220–252). Dominique Rogers, "Entre Lumières' et préjugés: Moreau de Saint-Méry et les libres de couleur de la partie française de Saint-Dominque," in Dominique Taffin, ed., *Moreau de Saint-Méry; ou, Les ambiguïtés d'un créole des Lumières . . .* ([Fort-de-France], Martinique, 2006), 87, also provides helpful archival information about Aménaïde Dall'Asta and Angélique.

6. Moreau de Saint-Méry to Aménaïde Dall'Asta, May 29, 1809, in "Moreau de Saint-Méry: Correspondance à sa famille, 1808–1809," transcribed by Cecilia Paini, under the supervision of Carminella Biondi (thesis, Università degli studi di Parma, 1986–1987), from the manuscript letters in Fondo Carte Moreau de Saint-Méry, Dono Monza, Archivio di Stato di Parma, Italy (hereafter cited as "Correspondance, 1808–1809"). The manuscript letters (1806–1813) are in four bound volumes and three additional folders and were given to the Archivio di Stato di Parma by the Countesses Aménaide and Clelia Monza, Moreau's granddaughters, known as the Monza sisters (sorelle Monza). See also "Donation," May 30, 1788, ANOM, Notariat Saint-Domingue, 869, Grimperel, acting notary. Moreau discusses his daughter frequently during the trip from France to the United States in his diary. See Moreau de Saint-Méry, *Voyage aux États-Unis de l'Amérique, 1793–1798,* ed. Stewart L. Mims (New Haven, Conn., 1913); and the English translation of the diary, Kenneth Roberts and Anna M. Roberts, eds. and trans., *Moreau de Saint Méry's American Journey [1793–1798]* (Garden City, N.Y., 1947).

7. Roberto Lasagni, *Dizionario biografico dei parmigiani,* III (Parma, Italy, 1999), 595. Various issues of the *Gazzetta di Parma* from 1800 through 1890 have turned up traces of Aménaïde's continued involvement in the Parma art scene and her descendants' efforts to keep her legacy alive. For "Five Miniatures" (Cinque miniature), see *Gazzetta di Parma,* Oct. 13, 1818, 330. For her formal portrait of Moreau (Aménaïde Moreau de Saint-Méry, *Conte Moreau de Saint Méry,* circa 1800–1805, Galleria Nazionale di Parma), see the discussion in Chapter 2. The Italian sojourns of Saint-Domingue and Haitian exiles is worthy of further attention. See, for example, LeGrace Benson, "A Queen in Diaspora: The Sorrowful Exile of Queen Marie-Louise Christophe (1778, Ouanaminth, Haiti–March 11, 1851, Pisa, Italy)," *Journal of Haitian Studies,* XX, no. 2 (Fall 2014), 90–101.

8. Moreau to Aménaïde Dall'Asta, Mar. 10, 1809, "Correspondance, 1808–1809" ("des Nouvelles"). Moreau addressed many of his letters to his daughter Aménaïde Dall'Asta with terms of affection. For example, on May 20, 1809, he wrote, "Yesterday was your birthday, my dear Aména [her nickname]. I made a thousand wishes for everything that could be useful for your happiness. There is not a single one that is new, but the feeling that repeats them at every annual return, despite the different nuances due to my age, yours, and the circumstances in which we find ourselves. It is always fatherly love that inspires me and if the expression varies the motive is always the same" (C'etait hier, ma chere Aména, ton anniversaire. J'ai fait mille voeux pour tout ce qui peut être utile à ton bonheur. Il n'est pas un seul qui soit nouveau, mais le sentiment qui les repete a chaque retour annuel, a cependant des nuances differentes relatives à mon age, au tien, et aux circonstonces où nous nous trouvons alors. C'est toujours l'amour paternel qui m'inspire et si l'expression varie le motif est constamment le même). Another, dated May 31, 1809, speaks of their shared adoration for Aménaïde's son, who was visiting Moreau in Paris. He wrote, "What a shame, my dear, that we could not enjoy him together!" (Quel dommage, chere

amie, que nous ne puissions pas en jouir ensemble!). In another example of the strong family bonds between Aménaïde and her family, her brother, Moreau de Saint-Méry, fils, wrote to her on June 21, 1809, "You make fun of me, my dear Aménaïde, with your thanks for the care I took of our dear Edouard" (Tu te moques de moi, ma chère Aménaïde, avec tes remerciemens [sic] des soins que j'ai pris de notre cher Edouard). See ibid. I have reproduced the French here as it appears in Moreau's letters, sometimes without accent marks.

9. Moreau to Aménaïde Dall'Asta, Sept. 6, 1809, ibid. ("demi peintes"). Moreau kept a detailed journal from 1801 to 1807 that includes their daily family rituals. See, for example, June 23, 1802: "Went to the concert with Count Bianchi where my daughter sang two pieces" (Été au concert du comte Bianchi où ma fille a chanté 2 morceaux); Apr. 12, 1802: "Aménaïde begins with oil on the sketch of Aeneas" (Aménaïde commence à l'huile sur l'ebauche d'Enée); Nov. 20, 1802: "My daughter receives her certificate as Academician from the Academy of Fine Arts of Parma" (Ma fille reçoit le brevet d'académicienne des Beaux Arts de Parme). See "Journal de Moreau de Saint-Méry," 5 vols., transcribed by A. Saccò, I (1801–1802), G. Quaquarelli, II (1803–1804), G. Tambini, III (1805), D. Faidherbe, IV (1806), and S. Zanardi, V (1807), under the supervision of Carminella Biondi (theses, Università degli studi di Parma, 1980–1986), from the manuscript "Journal de ma vie," in Fondo Carte Moreau de Saint-Méry, Dono Monza, Archivio di Stato di Parma, Italy. The five volumes of this manuscript journal were gifted to the Archivio di Stato di Parma by Moreau's granddaughters.

10. See "Journal de Moreau de Saint-Méry," Dec. 2, 1802: "Marriage of my daughter with the Count Pompeo Dall'Asta at eight o'clock in the morning. Lunch at 12. Had Charles Dall'Asta and his wife and Count Bianchi to dine. Took my daughter's room for an office" (Mariage de ma fille avec le comte Pompée Dall'Asta à 8 heures du matin. Dejeuner à 12. Eu Charles Dall'Asta, sa femme et le comte Bianchi à diner. Pris la chambre de ma fille pour cabinet).

11. See ibid., July 23, 1802: "Nervous attack; Aménaïde indisposed" (Attaque de nerfs; Aménaïde incommodée). See also Moreau to Aménaïde Dall'Asta, Oct. 17, 1809, "Correspondance, 1808–1809": "Your three letters speak of the poor state of your eyes, especially in the letter from the 5th. This causes me a lot of pain. Do not hesitate for a moment to stop your painting, it is an essential necessity. Do not play with this organ. An absolute cessation will work wonders, especially with rice water. I demand it of your friendship, your reason" (Tes 3 lettres parlent du mauvais état de tes yeux surtout celle du 5. Cela me cause beaucoup de peine. N'hésite pas un instant à suspender ta peinture, c'est une nécessité indispensable. Il ne faut pas jouer avec cet organe. Une cessation absolue fera merveille surtout avec l'eau de rice [sic]. Je l'exige de ton amitié, de ta raison).

12. After being awoken at 5:30 in the morning by his son-in-law, Moreau noted: "At 6:30 the pain became stronger and more frequent. . . . I believe that my daughter is about to give birth. She gets into the labor bed at 7:30. Ten minutes later and with three abdominal pushes she very happily gives birth at 7:45, to a very healthy girl whose name I chose: Célestine. . . . I received many visits and congratulations for the birth of my Célestine" (À 6 heures et demie les douleurs deviennent plus forts et plus fréquentes. . . . Je juge ma fille va accoucher. Elle passe au lit de douleurs à plus de 7 heures et demie. 10 minutes après et avec trois coliques elle accouche très heureusement à 7 heures trois quarts, d'une fille

très bien portante dont j'ai [faite] choisi le nom: Célestine. . . . Reçu plusieurs visites et des félicitations sur la naissance de ma Célestine). See "Journal de Moreau de Saint-Méry," Nov. 24, 1804. See also ibid., Dec. 2, 1804: "Célestine's sore mouth becomes worrisome. . . . Coronation of Napoleon I in Paris" (Le mal de bouche de Célestine devient inquiétant. . . . Couronnement de Napoléon Premier à Paris).

13. Moreau to Aménaïde Dall'Asta, Oct. 4, 1809, "Correspondance, 1808–1809." See also, for example, Moreau to Aménaïde Dall'Asta, Oct. 29, 1810: "What a picture for a father to see his daughter constantly treated with contempt by her husband who denies her everything!" (Quel tableau pour un père que de voir sa fille constamment traitée avec mépris par son mari que lui refuse tout!) (Paini, "Introduzione," ibid., xlvii).

14. Moreau to Aménaïde DAll'Asta, Feb. 6, 1809 ("Adieu"), July 3, 1809, both in "Correspondance, 1808–1809."

15. Ibid., Sept. 22, 1809 ("mère").

16. Moreau de Saint-Méry, *Mémoire justificatif* ([Paris, 1790]), 34.

17. Moreau de Saint-Méry, *Description de la partie française de l'isle Saint-Domingue,* 86–102 (quotation on 91). Moreau wrote that his "well-trained" eye, "accustomed from childhood," could differentiate between Africans from the Gold Coast and *mulâtres,* despite the similarity in their "yellowish tint" (teinte jaunâtre). He wrote, "One could take several of them for mulâtres, if marks more or less multiplied, more or less insignificant *for the eye which has not been accustomed to them from childhood,* did not show that they are Africans and Blacks" (On pourrait en prendre plusieurs pour des mulâtres, si des marques plus ou moins multipliées, plus ou moins ridicules *pour l'oeil qui n'y a pas été accoutumé dès l'enfance* ne montraient qu'ils sont Africains et nègres). See ibid., 50 (italics mine).

18. Daut, *Tropics of Haiti,* 224.

19. Moreau de Saint-Méry, *Mémoire justificatif,* 34 ("bon père"); M[édéric] L[ouis] É[lie] Moreau de Saint-Méry, *Description topographique et politique de la partie espagnole de l'isle Saint-Domingue . . .* 2 vols. (Philadelphia, 1796), title page.

20. Moreau de Saint-Méry, *Mémoire justificatif,* 34.

21. "Acte de liberté," Mar. 17, 1783, ANOM, Notariat Saint-Domingue, 542, Grimperel, acting notary. On remixing as a method and the importance of embedded testimony by and about the enslaved, see Nicole N. Aljoe, *Creole Testimonies: Slave Narratives from the British West Indies, 1709–1838* (New York, 2011), introduction and chap. 1, esp. 33 ("refocusing").

22. Moreau de Saint-Méry, *Mémoire justificatif,* 34 ("rendait"); Moreau de Saint-Méry, *Description de la partie française de l'isle Saint-Domingue,* 363 ("armées combinées"). Gálvez is the subject of a full-length biography by Gonzalo M. Quintero Saravia, *Bernardo de Gálvez: Spanish Hero of the American Revolution* (Chapel Hill, N.C., 2018).

23. Matthew Pratt Guterl, *American Mediterranean: Southern Slaveholders in the Age of Emancipation* (Cambridge, Mass., 2008), 17; Lisa Lowe, *The Intimacies of Four Continents* (Durham, N.C., 2015); "Vente de mulâtresse" (Catherine), Oct. 3, 1782, "Vente de nègre" (Koyo), May 7, 1783, "Vente de negritte" (Hariette), May 7, 1783, "Vente de negritte" (Oursêne), May 7, 1783, "Vente de mulâtre" (Pierre Louis Bonhomme), May 7, 1783, in ANOM, Notariat Saint-Domingue, 542, Grimperel, acting notary.

24. See "Reglement des administrateurs concernant les gens de couleur libres," June 24

and July 16, 1773, in Moreau de Saint-Méry, *Loix et constitutions des colonies françaises de l'Amérique sous le vent . . .*, 6 vols. (Paris, [1784–1790]), V, 448–449 (quotation on 449); and Stephen Best's provocative essay, "Neither Lost nor Found: Slavery and the Visual Archive," *Representations,* CXIII, no. 1 (Winter 2011), 155 ("archive").

25. Moreau de Saint-Méry, *Description de la partie française de l'isle Saint-Domingue,* 51.

26. Ibid., 51. See also Gérard Barthelemy's excellent article "Tentatives de description de l'Afrique et des Africains à partir des Amériques à la fin du XVIIIe siècle," in Taffin, ed., *Moreau de Saint-Méry,* 147–158 (quotation on 147).

27. "Five Guineas Reward," *Columbian Herald, or the Independent Courier of North-America* (Charleston, S.C.), July 31, 1786, [3]; "Run Away," *Supplement to the Jamaica Mercury* (Kingston), July 24–July 31, 1779, 173; "Esclaves en Maronage," *Affiches américaines* (Cap Français, Saint-Domingue), Sept. 9, 1777, [1]; Philip D. Morgan, "Life in the New World," in *Captive Passage: The Transatlantic Slave Trade and the Making of the Americas* (Washington, D.C., and Newport News, Va., 2002), 139. For an excellent discussion of African-language use in what would become the United States, see Michael A. Gomez, *Exchanging Our Country Marks: The Transformation of African Identities in the Colonial and Antebellum South* (Chapel Hill, N.C., 1998). See also Chapter 6.

28. Moreau de Saint-Méry, *Description de la partie française de l'isle Saint-Domingue,* 186–187.

29. Scholars such as Stewart R. King have shown how military service could sometimes lead to manumission, improve social status, and provide extended networks of personal and professional relationships in Saint-Domingue. See King, *Blue Coat or Powdered Wig: Free People of Color in Pre-revolutionary Saint Domingue* (Athens, Ga., 2001), 248.

30. *"M. Moreau de Saint-Méry* saisit avec empressement cette occasion," *Affiches américaines,* May 14, 1783, [3] ("mémoires"); Bernard Camier, "Moreau de Saint-Méry et la musique coloniale des Antilles françaises au XVIIIe siècle," in Taffin, ed., *Moreau de Saint-Méry,* 175–176 ("aspects matériels").

31. Moreau de Saint-Méry, *Description de la partie française de l'isle Saint-Domingue,* 58, 67–68 ("culte mystérieux," 68). Given what we know of Moreau's interests and research habits, he could very well have done some type of empirical study of Black male anatomy. Black bodies were on constant public display.

32. Ibid., 58. In the context of Cuba and British North America, for example, there is clear evidence that creole Africans also understood that knowledge was being withheld from them by those who were African-born. The Cuban artist and religious leader Felipe García Villamil discusses this withholding of information in the context of religion. In an interview he stated: "Those who came from Africa had another way of thinking, as well as another way of talking. . . . There in Cuba you can see how they tried to lay the foundations for their religion in spite of all the changes: the changes in climate, the change in plants. . . . So when we arrived at the religion, our ancestors took a long time to begin to teach us a little bit. Some of them refused to teach to us *criollos,* because they were afraid we would take over or misuse the knowledge." See María Teresa Vélez, *Drumming for the Gods: The Life and Times of Felipe García Villamil, Santero, Palero, and Abakuá* (Philadelphia, 2000), 24.

33. Moreau de Saint-Méry, *Description de la partie française de l'isle Saint-Domingue,*

51; "Nègres Marrons," *Supplément aux Affiches américaines,* Jan. 4, 1783, [1] ("ne pouvant dire"); "Nègres Marrons," *Supplément aux Affiches américaines,* June 29, 1782, [1] (ne pouvant dire son nom, ni celui de son maître") (italics mine); "Esclaves marrons entrés a la geôle," *Affiches américanes,* Oct. 7, 1790, [1] ("deux négresses nouvelles"); "Nègres Marrons," *Supplément aux Affiches américaines,* Mar. 6, 1784, [1] ("se disant appartenir").

34. "Avis divers: M. *Moreau de Saint-Méry,* Avocat au Conseil supérieur," *Affiches américaines,* May 14, 1783, [3].

35. *Note des travaux du c[itoy]en Moreau-St.-Méry* (Paris, 1799), 6.

36. For example, an advertisement from the *Affiches américaines* reads, "a Black woman, wetnurse, a good subject, a good enough laundress and ironer, passable seamstress and cook, and a good laundress of silk stockings, with her little Black child, about seven months old" (une Négresse nourrice, bon sujet, assez bonne blanchisseuse et repasseuse, couturiere et cuisiniere aussi passablement, et bonne blanchisseuse de bas de soie, avec sa Négritte âgée d'environ sept mois). See "Biens et effets à vendre," *Supplément aux Affiches américaines,* Feb. 19, 1783, [3]. The list of her skills suggests that she performed many household functions in what could not have been a situation affording much relief from labor. Mayotte Capécia [Lucette Ceranus], *Je suis Martiniquaise* (Paris, 1948), Joseph Zobel, *La Rue Cases–Nègres* (Paris, 1950), and Simon Schwarz-Bart, *Pluie et vent sur Télumée Miracle; roman* (Paris, 1972) all feature female characters in this role.

37. Moreau de Saint-Méry, "Observations sur le Royaume de Ouaire, à la Côte-d'Or en Afrique," in *Mémoires du Musée de Paris,* Belles lettres et arts, no. 1 (Paris, 1785), 43–72 (quotation on 68). I have found no contemporary accounts of Boudacan's visit to Saint-Domingue in the newspapers there. He was escorted by Jean-Francois Landolphe, a ship captain with extensive ties to Saint-Domingue (see Chapter 6). Notes on Boudacan's wearing European dress when Moreau and his other hosts hoped to see him in his own country's clothing are found on 70. Moreau described the crowns worn by Warri monarchs, and they were not feathered as depicted in the portrait. However, the importance of the coral-colored beaded necklace in the portrait to denote high status does appear in his description of the Warri Kingdom (48).

38. Ibid., 68 ("bouche"), 70 ("costume").

39. Ibid., 52. Moreau's comments (drawn from Landolphe's personal experiences) differ remarkably in tone and content from Thomas Jefferson's almost contemporary contention that Africans had produced no art, learned no trades, and had no genius, with the exception of the relatively good musical ear that he had witnessed among some enslaved Africans in the Americas.

40. Moreau de Saint-Méry, *Description de la partie française de l'isle Saint-Domingue,* 83.

41. Ibid., 349. See James E. McClellan III, *Colonialism and Science: Saint Domingue and the Old Regime* (Baltimore, 1992), esp. pt. 3. Charles Arthaud, Moreau's brother-in-law and president of the Cercle des Philadelphes, wrote a short treatise on the island's native inhabitants, borrowing heavily from Jesuit Pierre-François-Xavier de Charlevoix's work and citing Père Nicolson's as well. See *Recherches sur la constitution des naturels du pays, sur leurs arts, leur industrie, et les moyens de leur subsistance* (Cap Français, Saint-Domingue, 1786). In it, he remarks that Louis Narcisse Baudry des Lozières owned an Indigenous stone axe, found on the banks of the Massacre River and given to him by a businessman

in Cap Français (4). It was exhibited to members of the club and apparently looked much like one of the four printed in Père Nicolson's work, *Essai sur l'histoire naturelle de l'isle de Saint-Domingue, avec des figures en taille-douce* (Paris, 1776), plate 10.

42. Moreau de Saint-Méry, *Description de la partie française de l'isle Saint-Domingue,* 86 ("combinaisons"), 89 (crépus). Work by Brett Rushforth (*Bonds of Alliance: Indigenous and Atlantic Slaveries in New France* [Williamsburg, Va., and Chapel Hill, N.C., 2012]) and Andrés Reséndez (*The Other Slavery: The Uncovered Story of Indian Enslavement in America* [Boston, 2016]) and the work-in-progress by Noel Smyth on post-1730 Natchez communities discusses Native North American enslavement, including the movement of the enslaved between North America and the Caribbean. See also "Native American Slavery in the Seventeenth Century," ed. Arne Bialuschewski and Linford D. Fisher, special issue of *Ethnohistory,* LXIV (2017). A perusal of the *Affiches américaines* highlights that Native peoples were enslaved alongside their African and African-descended counterparts. Among a selection of runaways being held in jail, for example, there was a man "à l'Artibonite: le 28, un Indien, sans étampe, âgé d'environ 26 ans, ayant des marchandises dans un panier, et se disant appartenir à M. Trussel, au Port-de-Paix"; see "Nègres Marons," *Supplement aux Affiches américaines,* June 7, 1777, [1]. Indigenous Studies scholarship documents the long arc of discursive strategies that have declared Native populations in the Caribbean to be extinct, despite their continued fraught existences. See, for example, the edited volume by Maximillian C. Forte, *Indigenous Resurgence in the Contemporary Caribbean: Amerindian Survival and Revival* (New York, 2006).

43. Moreau de Saint-Méry, *Description de la partie française de l'isle Saint-Domingue,* 80–81.

44. For example, see the work of Marie-Christine Hazaël-Massieux, including *Textes anciens en créole Français de la Caraïbe: Histoire et analyse* (Paris, 2008).

45. See Deborah Jenson's discussion of Kreyòl language poetry, particularly chapters 7 and 8, in *Beyond the Slave Narrative: Politics, Sex, and Manuscripts in the Haitian Revolution* (Liverpool, U.K., 2011), esp. 279 ("courtesan"), 282 ("celebrity"), 289 ("indigo"). She writes that the different textual fragments of songs suggest that it's "as if Moreau had asked for a knowledgeable source to help in reconstituting a known song. These documents collectively point strongly to an oral tradition known by persons capable of helping Moreau to assemble notes on the corpus—and to potential imperfections in the accuracy of the transcriptions" (284). For "Na rien qui dous," see M. L. E. Moreau de Saint-Méry, "Chansons créoles," in "Notes historiques," ANOM, F3, 139, 21–22, cited in Jenson, *Beyond the Slave Narrative,* 286. Jenson notes the issues with transcription that are evident in this and other poems.

46. Moreau de Saint-Méry, *Description de la partie française de l'isle Saint-Domingue,* 340. This anecdote is reminiscent of a song recorded in 1927 in the United States, when John Scruggs, a formerly enslaved man in Virginia, sang a version of the song "Little Old Log Cabin in the Lane" about "mistress and master" "sleepin' side by side." The masters were most beloved when they were dead and buried next to each other. See *Times Ain't Like They Used to Be: Early American Rural and Popular American Music, 1928–1935,* produced by Sherwin Dunner and Richard Nevins (Shanachie Entertainment, 2000), videodisc (DVD), circa 70 min. The song was popular in the U.S. minstrel circuit. The first chapter

of Laurent Dubois's *Avengers of the New World* opens with an anecdote about Moreau and the importance of his *Description de la partie française de l'isle Saint-Domingue,* centering it as a primary source that generations of scholars have relied on to paint a portrait of the incredibly violent and fantastically wealthy colony of Saint-Domingue. He includes the anecdote on the church bells (11).

47. Moreau de Saint-Méry, *Description de la partie française de l'isle Saint-Domingue,* 51 ("avare," "mangeur de chiens," "Rada mange chien"), 56 ("proverbes").

48. Ibid., 82 ("Créols"), 83 ("pas d'autre entr'eux"). For more on Kreyòl, see Philip Baker, "Assessing the African Contribution to French-Based Creoles," in Salikoko S. Mufwene, ed., with the assistance of Nancy Condon, *Africanisms in Afro-American Language Varieties* (Athens, Ga., 1993), 123–155.

49. Moreau de Saint-Méry, *Description de la partie française de l'isle Saint-Domingue,* 525.

50. Moreau de Saint-Méry, *Mémoire justificatif,* 34.

51. Ibid., 103–104n; "Mariage de Moreau de Saint-Méry et Louise-Catherine Milhet," Apr. 9, 1781 (quotations), ANOM, Notariat Saint-Domingue, 861, Grimperel, acting notary.

52. See the entry for "bière" in Moreau's colonial dictionary, "Répertoire," ANOM, F3, 74. I am reminded of figures such as William Lee, George Washington's enslaved manservant, who often accompanied him and was famously captured by his side in the John Trumbull portrait. See Trumbull, *George Washington and William Lee,* 1780, oil on canvas, 36 × 28 in. (91.4 × 71.1 cm), Metropolitan Museum of Art, New York, https://www.metmuseum.org/art/collection/search/12822.

53. Moreau de Saint-Méry, *Description de la partie française de l'isle Saint-Domingue,* 80.

54. Ibid. On an "Africanist presence," see Toni Morrison, *Playing in the Dark: Whiteness and the Literary Imagination* (Cambridge, Mass., 1992).

55. *Note des travaux du c[itoy]en Moreau-St.-Méry,* 5.

56. See Moreau's commentary in "Variétiés," *Supplément aux Affiches américaines,* Sept. 15, 1787, [1].

57. Moreau de Saint-Méry, *Description de la partie française de l'isle Saint-Domingue,* 46. For the six-volume bound manuscript, see also ANOM, F3, 96–101.

58. See his descriptions of white men and women in *Description de la partie française de l'isle Saint-Domingue* (for example, 34–44). See Joan [Colin] Dayan's discussion of this phenomenon in "Codes of Law and Bodies of Color," *New Literary History,* XXVI (1995), 283–308, esp. 283–284; see also Jenson, *Beyond the Slave Narrative,* 280–281.

59. "Declaration of Independence: Thomas Jefferson's Draft with Congress's Changes (July 4, 1776)," in Thomas Jefferson, *Notes on the State of Virginia,* ed. David Waldstreicher (Boston, 2002), 47. Moreau echoed Jefferson's invective against the British for establishing slavery in its colonies and then inciting these same enslaved against him when he wrote, "I will add that the colonist never went looking for slaves in Africa; it was the Europeans who brought them to us and this trade was always favored and protected by the administration of the kingdom" (J'ajouterai que les Colons n'ont jamais été chercher des esclaves en Afrique; mais que ce sont les Européens qui nous les ont apportés & que ce commerce a toujours été favorisé & protégé par l'administration du royaume). See M. L. E. Moreau de

Saint-Méry, *Considérations présentées aux vrais amis du repos et du bonheur de la France; à l'occasion des nouveaux mouvemens de quelques soi-disant Amis-des-noirs* (Paris, 1791), 31.

60. Moreau de Saint-Méry, *Description de la partie française de l'isle Saint-Domingue*, 61.

61. Ibid., 51.

62. See Jason R. Young, "All God's Children Had Wings: The Flying African in History, Literature, and Lore," *Journal of Africana Religions*, V (2017), 50–70; and Terri L. Snyder, *The Power to Die: Slavery and Suicide in British North America* (Chicago, 2015).

63. Moreau de Saint-Méry, *Description de la partie française de l'isle Saint-Domingue*, 78.

64. Ibid.

65. [Pompée-Valentin], Baron de Vastey, *The Colonial System Unveiled*, ed. and trans. Chris Bongie (Liverpool, U.K., 2014), 114. He also provided an example of an enslaved woman who had to carry around a wooden baby when one of her children died (118).

66. Moreau de Saint-Méry, *Description de la partie française de l'isle Saint-Domingue*, 78.

67. Daut, *Tropics of Haiti*, 222 ("epicenter"), 82; [Michel-René] H[illiard] d'[Auberteuil], *Considérations sur l'état present de la colonie française de Saint-Domingue: Ouvrage politique et législatif; presenté au minister de la marine*, I (Paris, 1776), 136 ("habit"), 145 ("mistreats").

68. Morrison, *Playing in the Dark*, 44.

Chapter Two

1. This chapter is inspired by the visual material that suffused Moreau's work, in particular his collaborations with Nicolas Ponce, whose *Recueil de vues des lieux principaux de la colonie française de Saint-Domingue* (Paris, 1791) was intended to accompany Moreau's *Loix et constitutions des colonies françaises de l'Amérique sous le vent . . .* , 6 vols. (Paris, [1784–1790]).

2. *Chanson sur la prise des Invalides et de la Bastille, les lundi 13 et mardi 14 juillet 1789 . . .* ([Paris], 1789). The chevalier Pierre Jean Georges de Callières de l'Etang, an early supporter of the reforms promised by the French Revolution, composed this song about Jacques Necker and Moreau and dedicated it to "mon parent, Moreau de Saint Méry, President des 300 Electeurs de Paris." Thomas Carlyle wrote of him: "Moreau de Saint-Méry of tropical birth and heart, of coolest judgement. . . . What a head; comparable to Friar Bacon's Brass Head! Within it lies all Paris. Prompt must the answer be, right or wrong; in Paris is no other Authority extant. Seriously, a most cool clear head;—for which, also thou O brave Saint-Méry, in many capacities, from august Senator to Merchant's clerk, Bookdealer, Vice-King; in many places, from Virginia to Sardinia, shalt, ever as a brave man, find employment" (Carlyle, *The French Revolution: A History*, I [Paris, 1837], 278). On the three thousand orders, see Anthony Louis Elicona, *Un colonial sous la révolution en France et en Amérique: Moreau de Saint-Méry* (Paris, 1934), 42.

3. Elicona, *Un colonial sous la Révolution*, 10. For his comments to his daughter, see Moreau to Aménaïde Dall'Asta, Feb. 20, 1809, in "Moreau de Saint-Méry: Correspondance à sa famille, 1808–1809," transcribed by Cecilia Paini, under the supervision of Carminella Biondi (thesis, Università degli studi di Parma, 1986–1987), from the manuscript letters in Fondo Carte Moreau de Saint-Méry, Dono Monza, Archivio di Stato di Parma,

Italy (hereafter cited as "Correspondance, 1808–1809"). On the dress and physical setting of the Superior Council, see James E. McClellan III, *Colonialism and Science: Saint Domingue and the Old Regime* (Baltimore, 1992), 43. For his comments to Vaughan, see Moreau de Saint-Méry, *Voyage aux États-Unis de l'Amérique, 1793–1798,* ed. Stewart L. Mims (New Haven, Conn., 1913), 358–359; and the English translation of the diary, Kenneth Roberts and Anna M. Roberts, eds. and trans., *Moreau de Saint Méry's American Journey [1793–1798]* (Garden City, N.Y., 1947), 333 (hereafter cited as Roberts and Roberts, *American Journey*).

4. Inspiration for clothing and other details was drawn from a variety of eighteenth- and nineteenth-century sources. One example is the portraiture of George Washington and his Black servants, including John Trumbull's 1780 depiction of Washington and William Lee, his enslaved manservant and a spy for the patriot army, and the supposed portrait of Washington's chef, Hercules, which may not be a portrait of Hercules or a chef at all. See "George Washington's Enslaved Chef, Who Cooked in Philadelphia, Disappears from Painting, but May Have Reappeared in New York," *Philadelphia Inquirer,* Mar. 1, 2019, https://www.inquirer.com/food/craig-laban/george-washington-slave-chef -cook-hercules-gilbert-stuart-painting-wrong-20190301.html; Trumbull, *George Washington and William Lee,* 1780, oil on canvas, 36 × 28 in. (91.4 × 71.1 cm), Metropolitan Museum of Art, New York, https://www.metmuseum.org/art/collection/search/12822.

5. In his influential *Picture Theory: Essays on Verbal and Visual Representation* (Chicago, 1994), W. J. T. Mitchell writes: "The metapicture is a piece of moveable cultural apparatus, one which may serve a marginal role as illustrative device or a central role as a kind of summary image, what I have called a 'hypericon' that encapsulates an entire episteme, a theory of knowledge. . . . They are not merely epistemological models, but ethical, political, and aesthetic 'assemblages' that allow us to observe observers. In their strongest forms, they don't merely serve as illustrations to theory; they picture theory" (49). For more on portraiture in general, see T. H. Breen, "The Meaning of 'Likeness': American Portrait Painting in an Eighteenth-Century Consumer Society," *Word and Image,* VI (October–December 1990), 325–348. Caribbean art and literature have long provided interpretive commentary on historical subjects, engaging, questioning, and revising accounts of historical actors and events.

6. See Agnes Lugo-Ortiz and Angela Rosenthal's introduction in Lugo-Ortiz and Rosenthal, eds., *Slave Portraiture in the Atlantic World* (New York, 2013), 7. They continue: "Portraiture . . . insists on the face as a primary site of an imagined subjectivity, often at the expense of the rest of the body. Its metaphysical aura of transcendence has been conventionally understood as a privileged tool for the visualization of 'being,' and for the production of the subject as visuality. . . . However, in the logic of chattel slavery, it is the face that seems to be overcoded by the subjected body, and 'facelessness' the means by which the slave is theoretically rendered a nonsubject." For more on eighteenth-century portrait conventions, see the introduction and essays in Ellen G. Miles, ed., *The Portrait in Eighteenth-Century America* (Newark, Del., 1993).

7. Ponce belonged to many fine arts academies in France and produced a similarly elaborate set of engravings about French history at the same time he collaborated with Moreau. See Nicolas Ponce, *Les illustres français; ou, Tableaux historiques des grands hommes de*

la France . . . (Paris, [1790–1816]). *Recueil* contains geographic views of various cities in Saint-Domingue, local monuments, and a detailed map of Cap Français. According to the volume's front cover, Ponce worked with René Phelipeau, who engraved the maps and city plans. Moreau did believe that Brunias's prints were accurate representations of scenes he saw in Saint-Domingue. In his commentary on a martial arts practice among the Black residents of Saint-Domingue that involved the use of stick batons, he wrote, "This joust, that I have had engraved after an English design, has rules similar to those of fencing" (Cette joute, que j'ai fait graver aussi d'après un dessin anglais, a ses règles comme l'escrime). Presumably the "English design" referenced here is to Brunias's work. See Moreau, *La description topographique, physique, civile, politique et historique de la partie française de l'isle Saint-Domingue . . .* , ed. Blanche Maurel and Étienne Taillemite, new ed., 3 vols. (Saint-Denis, France, 2004), I, 71 (hereafter cited as *Description de la partie française de l'isle Saint-Domingue*).

8. See Mia L. Bagneris, *Colouring the Caribbean: Race and the Art of Agostino Brunias* (Manchester, U.K., 2018), esp. chap. 3, coda (quotations from 143 and 230). In regard to the Ponce volume, she notes, "A suite of beautiful stiple engravings made by Brunias himself in 1779–80, apparently during a brief return to London, served as the source of the images reproduced by Ponce for Moreau de Saint-Mery's project" (221). I concur with her sense that "more than simply uncomplicated examples of plantocratic propaganda, Brunias's paintings function as unique indices of a critically inchoate moment in the forging of modern understandings of race. At times, they offer the possibility of interpretations that seem contrary to the purposes for which they were created" (233). "The artist's pictures reflect a unique vision of the world in which he lived, demonstrating the broad spectrum of human diversity but also suggesting openings for questioning a hierarchy of value along the continuum of human difference" (236).

9. Bagneris continues, "Brunias's depiction of the nymph-like bathers in *Mulâtresses and Negro Woman Bathing* prefigures literary representations of mixed-race beauties as teeming with sexual appeal, often despite their desire to remain virtuous and chaste. Such treatments represent the sensual nature of mixed-race women as innate, the inevitable result of the transgressive circumstances of their birth; their bodies are born to sin because, originating in the illicit merger of black and white flesh that resulted from the colonial encounter, they are born of sin" (ibid., 149). "The image of the mixed-race Venus as depicted in the painting suggests the colonial Caribbean as a liminal world in which the pleasures of the flesh might be indulged without compromising one's Britishness; where in fact one's Britishness specifically *entitled* one to enjoy them" (163).

10. Moreau de Saint-Méry, *Mémoire justificatif* ([Paris, 1790]), 48; Moreau de Saint-Méry, *Description de la partie française de l'isle Saint-Domingue,* 104. The English translation is from Moreau de Saint-Méry, *A Civilization That Perished: The Last Years of White Colonial Rule in Haiti . . .* , ed. and trans. Ivor D. Spencer (Lanham, Md., 1985), 81–82.

11. See Edward J. Sullivan, ed., *Continental Shifts: The Art of Edouard Duval Carrié* (Miami, 2007). The power of visual art that uses juxtaposition to suggest the interdependence, rather than the disconnect, of objects rooted in violence and refinement is found across a wide swathe of African diasporic art. Fred Wilson's 1992 installation *Mining the Museum* at the Maryland Historical Society did this masterfully. As Huey

Copeland and Krista Thompson write, "In the section of the installation labeled 'Metalwork, 1793–1880,'" the artist famously paired a prized repoussé silver tea service with slave shackles lent to the MHS by a private collector; "in 'Cabinetmaking, 1820–1960,' he situated four beautifully preserved nineteenth-century chairs around a whipping post that had long been consigned to storage." See Copeland and Thompson, "Perpetual Returns: New World Slavery and the Matter of the Visual," special issue of *Representations*, CXIII, no. 1 (Winter 2011), 8–9.

12. For more on French framing traditions, see Bruno Pons, "Les cadres francais du XVIIIe siècle et leurs ornaments," *Revue de l'art,* LXXVI (1987), 41–50. A later work, *Sugar Conventions* (2013), integrates Brunias's prints directly. See Lesley A. Wolff, Michael D. Carrasco, and Paul B. Niell, "Rituals of Refinement: Edouard Duval-Carrié's Historical Pursuits," in the catalog for the Florida State University Museum of Fine Arts exhibition *Decolonizing Refinement: Contemporary Pursuits in the Art of Edouard Duval-Carrié* (Tallahassee, Fla., 2018), 7. They write: "In *Sugar Conventions,* [Duval-Carrié] thus glazes Brunias's 'saccharine' images with a coating of refined sugar crystals. Layered one over another, sugar becomes historicized and aestheticized, while Brunias's idyllic scenes are then inscribed with the urgency of contemporary industry. Duval-Carrié thus employs sweetness to subversive ends, drawing in and then enchanting the viewer, only to reveal upon closer examination how the object of desire, be it art or sugar, actually serves as a tool of destruction and violence." Duval-Carrié has long worked in portraiture, one of his most well-known pieces being the Jean-Claude Duvalier portrait *J. C. Duvalier en folle de marié* (1979); he also created many works that incorporate Haitian revolutionary-era figures such as Toussaint Louverture.

13. Many thanks to Edouard Duval-Carrié for providing background about the history of this piece. The original work was created for the traveling exhibit *Révolution française sous les tropiques* for the bicentennial of the French Revolution. He and Joseph re-created these images as sequined pieces. For more on the sequin arts tradition in Vodou, see Donald J. Cosentino, ed., *Sacred Arts of Haitian Vodou* (Los Angeles, 1995); and Nancy Josephson, "Artists on Artists: Nancy Josephson on Haitian Sequin Artists," in "The Americas Issue: Tribute to Haiti," special issue of *Bomb,* no. 90 (Winter 2004 / 2005), 14–17.

14. Scholarship has explored the practice of slavery within communities of African descent. Notarial records document business transactions across the Americas in which free people of color—female and male, black and mixed race—sold and bought children, women, and men. See, for example, Susan M. Socolow, "Economic Roles of the Free Women of Color of Cap Français," in David Barry Gaspar and Darlene Clark Hine, eds., *More than Chattel: Black Women and Slavery in the Americas* (Bloomington, Ind., 1996), 279–297. Marisa J. Fuentes's chapter on Rachael Polgreen in Fuentes, *Dispossessed Lives: Enslaved Women, Violence, and the Archive* (Philadelphia, 2016), 46–69, also argues that it is critical to acknowledge the intraracial and intragendered dimensions of violence against enslaved women. In 1789, gens de couleur "owned one-third of the plantation property, one-quarter of the slaves, and one-quarter of the real estate property in Saint-Domingue, as well as competing in commerce and trade" (quoted in Joan [Colin] Dayan, "Codes of Law and Bodies of Color," *New Literary History,* XXVI [1995], 297).

15. Marlene L. Daut, *Baron de Vastey and the Origins of Black Atlantic Humanism* (New

York, 2017); [Pompée-Valentin], Baron de Vastey, *The Colonial System Unveiled,* ed. and trans. Chris Bongie (Liverpool, U.K., 2014). Importantly, Vastey claimed that "the wives of these monsters proved equally proficient in the commission of such deeds: when it comes to debauched and indecent conduct, several of those furies—the shame and dishonour of their sex—equalled and even surpassed the men, committing the most abominable excesses, the most unimaginable crimes and unparalleled acts of cruelty" (ibid., 123).

16. Vastey, *Colonial System Unveiled,* ed. and trans. Bongie, 123. See also Daut, *Baron de Vastey,* 119. Vastey was a key critic of Moreau's, and his commentary appears throughout this book. In *Colonial System Unveiled,* Vastey cites a case showing that "in the public records, entered on the very same line, one finds slaves, horses, cattle, mules, hogs, etc., all one and the same thing: a man was sold with pigs, it made no difference. As proof of these assertions, we provide a word-for-word transcription of a decision of the Council of the Cape, which we have drawn from Moreau de Saint-Méry's compilation *[Loix et constitutions]*" (Vastey, *Colonial System Unveiled,* ed. and trans. Bongie, 126). The case in question is not only collected in Moreau's work, but Moreau himself was the lawyer for the defendant, who was ordered to sell off his assets to reimburse the plaintiff for the "two negroes, four mules" that died. The magistrate for the case was Monsieur de Pourcheresse de Vertiéres, the same man cited earlier in the text for his sadism; see ibid., 111–112.

17. Malick W. Ghachem, "Prosecuting Torture: The Strategic Ethics of Slavery in Prerevolutionary Saint-Domingue (Haiti)," *Law and History Review,* XXIX (2011), 985–1029, esp. 987 ("prominent"); Vastey, *Colonial System Unveiled,* ed. and trans. Bongie, 106 ("remains"), 111–113, 117, 118; Daut, *Baron de Vastey,* 116.

18. See Chapter 4 for a discussion of Moreau's public arguments with various mixed-race political antagonists.

19. Moreau wrote: "From the cradle she was surrounded by good examples, and I believed that the habit of thriftiness was her patrimony. I felt that my choice [of a spouse] would bring me honor, and every day, for close to nine years, I have become more and more convinced of it" (Elle avait été, dès le berceau, environée de bons exemples, je crus que l'habitude de l'économie était un patrimoine; je sentis que mon choix m'honorerait, et chaque jour, depuis près de neuf ans, m'en a de plus en plus convaincu) (Moreau de Saint-Méry, *Mémoire justificatif,* 8). See also the Introduction and Chapter 4, particularly the latter for the "Jeanne and Sylvie" and "Mulâtresses and Martonne" entries. The articles outlining Louise-Catherine's dowry and the stipulations of their marriage contract are found in "Mariage de Moreau de Saint-Méry et Louise-Catherine Milhet," Apr. 9, 1781, Archives nationales d'outre-mer, Aix-en-Provence, France (ANOM), Notariat Saint-Domingue, 861, Grimperel, acting notary. Examples of her writing, including its grammar and spelling errors, are found in her letters to Aménaïde in "Correspondance, 1808–1809." For instance, on May 29, 1809, she wrote, "Ils son arrivez samedi 27 a 4 heur de l'après diné ses chere enfans et tu te doute ma chere Amenaide du Plaisir que j'ai éprovez en embrassan mille fois ces enfans cheris" (They arrived Saturday the 27th at four in the afternoon these dear children and you cannot doubt, my dear Aménaïde, the pleasure I felt hugging these dear children one thousand times).

20. Moreau to Aménaïde Dall'Asta, May 29, 1809, in "Correspondance, 1808–1809." Moreau received a letter from his friend Jean Nicolas Demeunier describing Paris in

July 1797: "As for the sensible people, the true friends of liberty, their number has not decreased; but they are not seen at brilliant fêtes, where everyone shines in the splendor of Greek and Roman raiment: they busy themselves with more useful affairs" (Roberts and Roberts, *American Journey,* 234).

21. "My wife would have to urge the boisterous company to go home to bed. . . . 'Tomorrow you will play the sluggard in your bed until noon; but promptly at seven o'clock in the morning your friend must get up and open his shop'" (Roberts and Roberts, *American Journey,* 215). See the note written by Angelo Pezzana attached to a gifted copy of Moreau's *Description topographique, physique, civile, politique et historique de la partie française de l'isle Saint-Domingue . . .* (Philadelphia, 1797–1798) to the Parma library (la bibliothèque de Parme). Pezzana added three notes contextualizing the value of the work, details likely provided by Moreau himself. One of Pezzana's annotations stated that the library should congratulate itself *(se feliciter)* for owning copies of this rare work "because it was printed by himself in Philadelphia during the time that he [Moreau] was obligated to save himself [escape] there to remove his illustrious head from the axe of Robespierre's executioners. M[oreau] de Saint-Méry's son, the heir of his father's talents, then a child, worked with one of his cousins on the typographical composition, while his amiable mother and his charming sister were in charge of the hanging [to dry] and the folding of the printed pages" (parce qu'il a été imprime par lui-même à Philadelphie dans le temps qu'il fut obligé de se sauver là bas pour soustraire son illustre tète à la hache des bourreaux de Robespierre. M de Saint-Méry fils, l'héritier des talents de son père, alors enfant, travaillait avec un de ses cousins à la composition typographique, pendant que son aimable mère et sa charmante soeur étaient chargées de l'étendage et du pliage des feuilles imprimées). See Biblioteca Palatina, Parma, Italy, Z. IV. 22610/1. The manuscript donation slip is reproduced as figure 112 in [Marzio Dall'Acqua], *L'ossessione della Memoria: Parma settecentesca nei disegni del conte Alessandro Sanseverini* (Parma, Italy, 1997).

22. See Floriana Cioccolo's discussion of the uncertainties surrounding attribution of this painting in "Artiste a Parma e a Milano: La creatività femminile fra obbligo pedagogico e veto istituzionale," *Memorie della accademia delle scienze di Torino,* XXIV (2000), 345–347.

23. In his journal entry for Jan. 14, 1802, Moreau noted, "Aménaïde a achevé mon portrait." See "Journal de Moreau de Saint-Méry," I (1801–1802), transcribed by A. Saccò, under the supervision of Carminella Biondi (theses, Università degli studi di Parma, 1980–1981), from the manuscript "Journal de ma vie," in Fondo Carte Moreau de Saint-Méry, Dono Monza, Archivio di Stato di Parma, Italy. Many thanks to Catherine Kelly for our conversation about this image.

24. In working on this group portrait, I found myself thinking of William J. Wilson's "Afric-American Picture Gallery." Writing under the pseudonym "Ethiop," Wilson published a seven-part collection in the *Anglo-African Magazine* (1859) in which he imagined a gallery with paintings and sculptures of notable African-descended people as well as landscapes picturing scenes such as the slave trade. There were no actual images published alongside his descriptions. Rather, his prose imagined what such a gallery might include and how visitors might respond to it, an important way of performing what Ivy G. Wilson calls a "curatorial" practice for an antebellum Black public sphere. My household portrait

came together in color on the page after I pulled its members together in my mind and thought about them collectively. See Wilson, *Specters of Democracy: Blackness and the Aesthetics of Politics in the Antebellum U.S.* (New York, 2011).

25. James H. Sweet, "Reimagining the African-Atlantic Archive: Method, Concept, Epistemology, Ontology," *Journal of African History,* LV (2014), 147–159.

26. See the entry on Marielle Plaisir and her series of drawings, *The Book of Life,* in the catalog for the New York University exhibit *Visionary Aponte: Art and Black Freedom,* Feb. 23–May 4, 2018, 16. For more on José Antonio Aponte, see the work of Ada Ferrer, Matt D. Childs, Linda Rodriguez, Kris Minhae Choe, Eric Anderson, Sibylle M. Fischer, Agnes Lugo-Ortiz, Stephan Palmié, Jorge Pavez Ojeda, and the excellent digital humanities exhibition https://aponte.hosting.nyu.edu. The *Visionary Aponte* exhibit conceived jointly by Ferrer and Duval-Carrié proved very inspiring for my own work.

27. Sara E. Johnson, "'He Was a Lion, and He Would Destroy Much': A Speculative School of Revolutionary Politics," discussion of Ada Ferrer's *Freedom's Mirror: Cuba and Haiti in the Age of Revolution,* in *Small Axe,* XXIII, no. 1 (March 2019), 195–207.

Chapter Three

1. See Simon Gikandi's provocative and beautifully argued *Slavery and the Culture of Taste* (Princeton, N.J., 2011), xii.

2. M. L. E. Moreau de Saint-Méry, *Considérations présentées aux vrais amis du repos et du bonheur de la France; à l'occasion des nouveaux mouvemens de quelques soi-disant Amis-des-noirs* (Paris, 1791), 32 ("homme"), 48 ("esclaves"). An example of his self-proclaimed "moderate" stance, one that found fault with some of the practices of slavery, is the comment he made about a project for a law he wished to pass "to protect the enslaved from the misfortune of changing masters at every instant, by correcting, in several ways, the fiction of colonial law that would like them to be treated as if they were furniture" (pour garantir les esclaves du malheur de changer de maîtres à chaque instant, en corrigeant, à plusieurs égards, la fiction du droit colonial qui voulait qu'on les considérât comme des meubles). See Moreau de Saint-Méry, *Note des travaux du c[itoy]en Moreau-St.-Méry* (Paris, 1799), 2.

3. As noted in Chapter 1, the enslaved women who traveled with Madame Milhet, Moreau's mother-in-law, joined the family household in the United States, and it is unclear what happened to them after her death. At least one woman, Sylvie, seems to have remained with the family when they returned to Europe.

4. Anthony Louis Elicona devotes several chapters to Moreau's life in the United States in *Un colonial sous la Révolution en France et en Amérique: Moreau de Saint-Méry* (Paris, 1934). For more on Moreau and his time in Philadelphia, see Sara E. Johnson, "Moreau de Saint-Méry: Itinerant Bibliophile," *Library and Information History,* XXXI (2015), 171–197.

5. The complete title, which notes the presence of engravings and maps along with Van Braam's qualifications as author, is M. L. E. Moreau de Saint-Méry, ed. and trans., *Voyage de l'ambassade de la Compagnie des Indes orientales hollandaises, vers l'empereur de la Chine, dans les années 1794 et 1795: Où se trouve la description de plusieurs parties de la Chine inconnues aux Européens, et que cette ambassade à donné l'occasion de traverser: Le tout tiré*

du journal d'André Everard van Braam Houckgeest, chef de la direction de la Compagnie des Indes orientales hollandaises à la Chine, et second dans cette ambassade; ancien directeur de la Société des sciences et arts de Harlem en Hollande; de la Société philosophique de Philadelphie, etc. etc.; et orné de cartes et de gravures, 2 vols. (Philadelphia, 1797–1798) (hereafter cited as *Voyage de l'ambassade*). J. J. L. Duyvendak notes that Van Braam's three-volume original Dutch manuscript is at the Rijksarchief at The Hague, gifted to the institution by his grandson. The title is *Memoriaal wegens de ambassade der Nederlandsche Oost-Indische Compagnie voor den Kyzer van China in de Jaren 1794/5 benevens de beschrijving der reize bij die gelegenheid door Andreas Everardus van Braam Houckgeest, chef der Nederlandsche directie in China en Tweede in gemelde Ambassade.* See Duyvendak, "The Last Dutch Embassy to the Chinese Court (1794–1795)," *T'oung Pao*, 2d Ser., XXXIV (1938), 1–137, esp. 5, which includes Chinese and Dutch original documents about the embassy.

6. Moreau makes note of the French arrival in Holland in his diary on Apr. 1, 1795; see Moreau de Saint-Méry, *Voyage aux États-Unis de l'Amérique, 1793–1798,* ed. Stewart L. Mims (New Haven, Conn., 1913), 196 (hereafter cited as Mims, *Voyage*). The English translation of the diary was published as Kenneth Roberts and Anna M. Roberts, eds. and trans., *Moreau de St. Méry's American Journey [1793–1798]* (Garden City, N.Y., 1947) (hereafter cited as Roberts and Roberts, *American Journey*). This journal of Moreau's life from 1794 to 1799 is often cited for its rich depictions of French exile life and the early American Republic. For more on the relationship between revolutionary France and the Netherlands, see Simon Schama, *Patriots and Liberators: Revolution in the Netherlands, 1780–1813* (New York, 1977).

7. Moreau de Saint-Méry, *Mémoire justificatif* (Paris, 1790), 2. The Club Massiac was a political club composed mostly of those who had vested interests in the maintenance of slavery in the colonies (its members were often owners of enslaved laborers), and it actively lobbied against abolition and the implementation of the Declaration of the Rights of Man and of the Citizen in the colonies. Its name derived from its meeting place at the Hotel Massiac.

8. Moreau reproduced a great number of letters in his work, particularly in his *Voyage aux États-Unis* and his *Mémoire justificatif.* These primary sources included his own letters and those that he received from others.

9. Moreau de Saint-Méry, *Mémoire justificatif,* 23 ("soupçon"), 26–27, 37 ("Fabricant"), 93–96. He further showed his disdain for Charton when he wrote, "Although l'*Observation* to my alleged motion is not a model of eloquence, it is an enormous distance from what Charton knows how to do, as the spelling and the diction belonging to him in our Dialogue from September 5 prove" (Quoique l'*Observation* à ma prétendue motion ne soit pas un modèle d'éloquence, elle est à une distance énorme de ce que Charton sait faire, comme le prouve l'orthographe et la diction de ce qui lui appartient dans notre Dialogue du 5 Septembre) (ibid., 39). See Louis Charton, *Observation de M. Charton à la motion de M. Moreau de Saint-Méry* (Paris, 1789).

10. Moreau implied that there was intrigue against him—back in Saint-Domingue and in Paris—but did not name a culprit or explain the motivations for it.

11. Moreau de Saint-Méry, *Observations d'un habitant des colonies, sur le mémoire en faveur des gens de couleur, ou sang-mêlés, de St-Domingue et des autres isles françaises de*

l'Amérique, adressé à l'Assemblée nationale . . . (n.p., [1789]). This publication directly addressed [Henri] Grégoire, *Mémoire en faveur des gens de couleur ou sang-mêlés de St. Domingue, et des autres isles françaises de l'Amérique, adressé à l'Assemblée nationale* (Paris, 1789).

12. Moreau de Saint-Méry, *Mémoire justificatif,* 33 ("spectacle"), 51 ("Peuple"), 53 ("arros[é]"); Moreau de Saint-Méry, *Considérations,* 19. He wrote, "The public rage increased instead of extinguishing itself, and October 18, they treated my brother-in-law as I have said [he was, despite the supplications of his young wife, who was seven months pregnant, dragged out of his home, promenaded, hit and conducted to the place where they wanted to kill him, from which he only escaped owing to the pity of some people who pulled him away from the mob], and they went to look for Mr. Gauvin *(in order to hang him)* and afterward my unfortunate mother-in-law, her daughter, my brother-in-law, my cousin, were all wandering, fugitives, at the mercy of the first who might want to deprive them of their lives, which unhappiness and their fatigue had perhaps already ended" (La rage augmente dans le Public au-lieu de s'éteindre, et le 18 Octobre on traite mon beau-frère comme je l'ai dit [(il) a été, malgré les supplications de sa jeune femme, grosse de sept mois, traîné hors de chez lui, promené, frappé et conduit vers le lieu où l'on voulait lui donner la mort, à laquelle il n'échappe que par la pitié de quelques personnes qui l'arrachent aux furieux], l'on va chercher M. Gauvain *(pour le pendre),* et désormais ma malheureuse belle-mère, sa fille, son gendre, mon parent, tous sont errans, fugitifs, à la merci du premier qui voudra leur arracher une vie que la douleur et leurs fatigues ont peut-être déjà terminée). See Moreau de Saint-Méry, *Mémoire justificatif,* 31 ("[il] a été, malgre les supplications . . . furieux"), 32 ("La rage," "l'on va chercher").

13. Moreau de Saint-Méry, *Mémoire justificatif,* 106.

14. He wrote, "Yes, without a doubt, the crime that they impute to me is great, but that itself makes me less capable of it" (Oui, sans doute, le crime qu'on m'imputait était grand, mais par cela même j'en étais moins capable). See ibid., 54, 105–106.

15. Ibid., 105.

16. For "insolent," see, for example, Moreau de Saint-Méry, *Loix et constitutions des colonies françaises de l'Amérique sous le vent . . . ,* 6 vols. (Paris, [1784–1790]), VI, 32.

17. Moreau de Saint-Méry, *Mémoire justificatif,* esp. 33; Jennifer DeVere Brody, *Punctuation: Art, Politics, and Play* (Durham, N.C., 2008), 5. For an excellent example of how punctuation and typography more generally were mobilized in the African American print sphere, see Marcy J. Dinius, "'Look!! Look!!! at This!!!!': The Radical Typography of David Walker's *Appeal," PMLA,* CXXVI (2011), 55–72.

18. [Pierre-Simon] Fournier, le Jeune, *Manuel typographique, utile aux gens de lettres, et à ceux qui exercent les différents parties de l'Art de l'Imprimerie,* II (Paris, 1766), i–ii; Moreau de Saint-Méry, *Mémoire justificatif,* 104n; Lawrence C. Wroth, *The Colonial Printer* (1931; rpt. New York, 1994), xvii. An extant copy of the catalog prepared for the posthumous sale of Moreau's personal library in 1819 contained an array of literature related to the printing trade. See *Catalogue des livres et manuscrits de la bibliothèque de feu M. Moreau de Saint-Méry . . . dont la vente se fera le mercredi 15 décembre 1819 . . .* ([Paris], 1819). At the time of his death, Moreau owned copies of Fournier's classic *Traités historiques et critiques sur l'origine et le progrès de l'imprimerie* (Paris, 1763) and a reprint of *The Printer's*

Grammar, Containing a Concise History of the Origin of Printing . . . Chiefly Collected from Smith's Edition (London, 1787). He also owned copies of books printed after his return to Europe, such as A. G. Camus, *Histoire et procédés du polytypage et de la stéréotypie* (Paris, [1801]) and [Pierre-Claude-François] Daunou, *Analyse des opinions diverses sur l'origine de l'imprimerie* (Paris, [1802]). Of course, the *Encyclopédie,* which he offered for sale in his store, also had a detailed description of printing. Moreau was a neighbor in Paris of the printer and widow Marie-Rosalie Vallat-la-Chapelle Huzard, who held the auction of his print materials. The families seem to have been in communication about experiments around animal husbandry. Moreau's interest in animal research and natural history is explored in Chapter 5. For more on Huzard, see Scott Ellwood, "One Dynasty, Three Names," May 24, 2019, The Grolier Club, https://grolierclub.wordpress.com/2019/05/24/one-dynasty-three-names/.

19. Moreau de Saint-Méry, *Mémoire justificatif,* 35 ("communique"); Robert Darnton, "What Is the History of Books?" *Daedalus,* CXI, no. 3 (Summer 1982), 65–83 (quotation on 67). For David Duval de Sanadon's proslavery views, see [Duval de Sanadon], *Discours sur l'esclavage des nègres, et sur l'idée de leur affranchissement dans les colonies; par un colon de Saint-Domingue* (Amsterdam and Paris, 1786); and [Duval de Sanadon], *Réclamations et observations des colons, sur l'idée de l'abolition de la traite et de l'affranchissement des nègres* (Paris, 1789).

20. Moreau indicated how precision in language mattered and was a mark of creole authority, particularly concerning racial categories in the Caribbean. For instance, he criticized a publication that announced: "The Estates General *will take into consideration the status of the Black slaves,* or *the Men of color,* in the colonies as well as in France" (Les Etats-Généraux *prendront en considération* le sort *des Esclaves noirs,* ou *Hommes de couleur,* tant dans les Colonies qu'en France). Moreau added an editorial note saying that this notice must be the work of editors / censors / commissaire-redacteurs, as *"this redaction,* Black slaves, Men of color, *is not nor could not be that of a Creole and certainly not of a Creole who writes about the colonies, where there are no other Slaves than Black slaves and where one says People, not Men of color"* (*cette rédaction* Esclaves noirs, Hommes de couleur, *n'est pas et ne peut pas être celle d'un Créole et sur-tout d'un Créole qui écrit sur les Colonies, où il n'y a d'autres Esclaves que des Esclaves noirs, et où l'on dit Gens et non pas Hommes de couleur*). See *Mémoire justificatif,* 86. Moreau published *Mémoire justificatif* with one of the official printers of the French National Assembly. A year later, the same printer, François Jean Baudouin, now working as part of the Imprimerie nationale, issued Moreau's *Considérations.* For more on him, see Frédéric Barbier, Sabine Juratic, and Annick Mellerio, *Dictionnaire des imprimeurs, libraires et gens du livre à Paris, 1701–1789, A–C* (Geneva, Switzerland, 2007), s.v. "Baudouin, François Jean," 183–187.

21. See David Geggus, "Print Culture and the Haitian Revolution: The Written and the Spoken Word," American Antiquarian Society, *Proceedings,* CXVI, pt. 2 (2006), 299–316. For a comparative European context, see Paula E. Dumas, *Proslavery Britain: Fighting for Slavery in an Era of Abolition* (Houndmills, Basingstoke, U.K., 2016). Scholarship on antislavery connections to the material underpinnings of print culture is vast, and many of the most well-known nineteenth-century abolitionists in the United States and England worked as newspaper editors and printers. For example, see Sara E. Johnson, "'Sentinels

on the Watch-Tower of Freedom': The Black Press of the 1830s and 1840s," in Johnson, *The Fear of French Negroes: Transcolonial Collaboration in the Revolutionary Americas* (Berkeley, Calif., 2012), 157–187; Derrick R. Spires, *The Practice of Citizenship: Black Politics and Print Culture in the Early United States* (Philadelphia, 2019); Jeannine Marie DeLombard, *Slavery on Trial: Law, Abolitionism, and Print Culture* (Chapel Hill, N.C., 2007); Katharine Gerbner, "Antislavery in Print: The Germantown Protest, the 'Exhortation,' and the Seventeenth-Century Quaker Debate on Slavery," *Early American Studies,* IX (2011), 552–575; Lara Langer Cohen and Jordan Alexander Stein, eds., *Early African American Print Culture* (Philadelphia, 2012); Lawrence C. Jennings, "The Interaction of French and British Antislavery, 1789–1848," in Patricia Galloway and Philip P. Boucher, eds., *Proceedings of the Fifteenth Meeting of the French Colonial Historical Society Martinique and Guadeloupe, May 1989,* XV (1992), 81–91; Jennings, *French Anti-slavery: The Movement for the Abolition of Slavery in France, 1802–1848* (Cambridge, 2000); David Clover, "The British Abolitionist Movement and Print Culture: James Phillips, Activist, Printer, and Bookseller" (paper given at the Society for Caribbean Studies [UK] annual conference, 2013, Warwick University, Coventry, U.K.).

22. Jeremy D. Popkin, "A Colonial Media Revolution: The Press in Saint-Domingue, 1789–1793," *Americas,* LXXV (2018), 3–25 (quotation on 5). Patrick D. Tardieu writes of "the printing press, which came to Saint-Domingue to repress the runaways" (L'imprimerie, venue à Saint-Domingue pour réprimer les nègres marrons); see Tardieu, "Pierre Roux et Lémery: Imprimeurs de Saint-Domingue à Haïti," *Revue de la Société haïtienne d'histoire et de géographie,* LXXIX, no. 218 (April 2004), 1–30 (quotation on 10).

23. As Catherine E. Kelly has argued in the context of the contemporary early U.S. Republic, "Aesthetics, both as theory and praxis . . . served as a vehicle for people . . . to consolidate their social, cultural, and even economic power." See Kelly, *Republic of Taste: Art, Politics, and Everyday Life in Early America* (Philadelphia, 2016), 11.

24. Moreau de Saint-Méry, *Mémoire justificatif,* 9 ("inutile"), 109 ("défie"). *Zèle* was a word that Moreau employed routinely in relation to himself to highlight his industriousness and enthusiasm. As he put it, "I am known as a very hard-working man" (Je suis connu pour un homme très laborieux) (50). In a similar statement that praised his own zeal, Moreau noted in the prospectus for *Loix et constitutions:* "We will not speak of the pains and the fatigue that we have suffered in order to unite scattered and poorly ordered pieces in a country where the ravages of insects and upheavals of climate make research painful and costly. We will call upon those who know these places and these objects that our zeal has made us run after and pursue without respite; they alone can appreciate the disgust we have been forced to devour/swallow" (Nous ne parlons pas des peines et des fatigues que nous avons éprouvés pour parvenir à la réunion de pièces éparses et mal en ordre dans un pays où les ravages des insectes et les révolutions du climat rendent toutes les recherches pénibles et couteuses. Nous en appelons aux personnes qui connaissent les lieux et les objets que notre zèle nous a fait parcourir et poursuivre sans relâche; elles seules peuvent apprécier tous les dégoûts qu'il nous a fallu dévorer); see "Prospectus," in Moreau de Saint-Méry, *Loix et constitutions des colonies françaises de l'Amérique sous le vent . . . propose par souscription* (Paris, 1784), 5–6.

25. See, for example, Pierre Monneron, *Sur les gens de couleur: Observations sur une lettre*

de M. Moreau de Saint-Méry, député de la Martinique à l'Assemblée nationale . . . (Paris, 1791). For *"bon maître,"* see Moreau de Saint-Méry, *Mémoire justificatif,* 34. These debates between Moreau and the colons américains and Amis des noirs are documented in great detail in Florence Gauthier, *L'aristocratie de l'épiderme: Le combat de la Société des citoyens de couleur, 1789–1791* (Paris, 2007). For the debate more broadly, see Malick W. Ghachem, "The 'Trap' of Representation: Sovereignty, Slavery, and the Road to the Haitian Revolution," *Historical Reflections / Réflexions historiques,* XXIX (2003), 123–144; and David Geggus, "Racial Equality, Slavery, and Colonial Secession during the Constituent Assembly," *American Historical Review,* XCIV (1989), 1290–1308.

26. A forty-four-year-old refugee from both Saint-Domingue and France, Moreau was initially employed in the physically exhausting and psychologically demeaning job of merchant clerk in New York. A slaveholder from the tropics, he expressed no irony when he bitterly recounted how this job required him to be on the docks "exposed to the burning heat of the sun" (exposé aux ardeurs du soleil) doing "galley-slave labor" (condamnation aux galères). See Roberts and Roberts, *American Journey,* 127; Mims, *Voyage,* 141, 142. This clerkship ended when Moreau went into partnership with a German businessman, Baron Frederick Franck de la Roche, who provided the initial funds to open his bookstore in Philadelphia. The two eventually fell out and discontinued their partnership. Moreau arranged to keep the printing press and some of the other stock that La Roche had financed. His seventy-six-page catalog, published in 1795 in both French and English, contained the following advertisement: "MOREAU DE St. MERY, and CO. take the opportunity of their Catalogue to repeat that they are established in the general business of Stationers, Booksellers and Dealers in most fashionable and choice Engravings. They will also have connected therewith a Printing Office and Bookbindery, adding thereto a select collection of Music. They purchase French Books, and deal in every kind of business on commission. They will also continue to fulfill orders for Books (or other things) from several parts of Europe, on the most reasonable terms. In short, they will not spare any care in studying to accomplish their enterprize intended to propagate and diffuse knowledge." See [Moreau de Saint-Méry], *Catalogue of Books, Stationary* [sic], *Engravings, Mathematical Instruments, Maps, Charts, and Other Goods of Moreau de St. Mery, and Co's. Store, No. 84, South Front-Street, Corner of Walnut* (Philadelphia, 1795).

27. Mims, *Voyage,* 358 ("boutiquier"). Moreau's above-cited posthumous book sale provides a window into his collecting activities. An entry for "bibliothèque" in his "Répertoire des notions coloniales; par ordre alphabétique" also provides clues, albeit incomplete ones, about the size of his collection. He noted: "There are not, therefore, numerous libraries in the colonies and that of the editor of this work being composed of about [3? 9?] thousand volumes was noticed more for its number perhaps than for its choice [contents]" (Il n'existe donc point de bibliothèques nombreuses dans les colonies et celle du rédacteur de cet ouvrage qui étant composé d'environ [3 ? 9?] mille volumes était remarquée plus pour son nombre peut-être que par son choix). Unfortunately, the number he records in his own handwriting was illegible in the manuscript and microfilm. See Archives nationales d'outre-mer, Aix-en-Provence, France (ANOM), Collection Moreau de Saint-Méry (Ser. F3), 74.

28. In his edited volume *Idée générale ou abrégé des sciences et des arts à l'usage de la*

jeunesse (Philadelphia, 1796), Moreau noted the value of printing as follows: "It is thanks to this fine art that men express their thoughts in works that cannot be destroyed except by the upheaval of nature. He repeats them with promptitude, with elegance, with correction and almost ad infinitum" (C'est à la faveur de ce bel Art que les hommes expriment leurs pensées dans des ouvrages qui ne peuvent être détruits que par le bouleversement de la nature. Il les répète avec promptitude, avec élégance, avec correction et presque à l'infini) (143–144). Of engraving, he wrote, "With engraving, we prepare in advance for those who will follow us, an almost inexhaustible mass of truths, inventions, forms, the means to eternalize our sciences and our arts" (Par la Gravure, nous préparons d'avance à ceux qui nous suivront, un amas presqu'intarissable de vérités, d'inventions, de formes, de moyens d'éterniser nos sciences & nos arts) (146).

29. See Rodrigo Lazo, *Letters from Filadelfia: Early Latino Literature and the Trans-American Elite* (Charlottesville, Va., 2020) for "la famosa Filadelphia" and more on Spanish-language work. On German-language print culture in the early United States, see Patrick M. Erben's work, including *A Harmony of the Spirits: Translation and the Language of Community in Early Pennsylvania* (Williamsburg, Va., and Chapel Hill, N.C., 2012). For French imprints, see note 38.

30. François Furstenberg, *When the United States Spoke French: Five Refugees Who Shaped a Nation* (New York, 2014), 17; James Alexander Dun, "'What Avenues of Commerce, Will You, Americans, Not Explore!': Commercial Philadelphia's Vantage onto the Early Haitian Revolution," *William and Mary Quarterly*, 3d Ser., LXII (2005), 480. The 1790s Philadelphia French community was rife with conflicting factions informed by French revolutionary and colonial politics. To give a sense of the vitriol circulating and how commerce had to be conducted delicately so as not to offend possible customers or put one in danger, consider the advertisement below, contained in a clipping that Moreau pasted to a piece of paper he dated May 1806. It read: "A report has been in circulation that the subscriber had received an order for, and had manufactured a Crown for the pretended Emperor of Hayti—the report is false. It is true that the several tyrants, who have destroyed St Domingo, have reduced the subscriber to the necessity of applying to the resources of his own industry for the support of his family; but, it is as true, that he has still sufficient honor and firmness left, to exercise his feeble talents only for those whose patronage is desirable, and to refuse them to a BRIGAND covered with blood and crimes. S. Chaudron." Although this announcement is dated after Moreau's 1798 departure from the United States, it is indicative of the climate in Philadelphia during the following decade as well. That the merchant felt it necessary to make a public statement denying that he was providing merchandise to Henry Christophe, the king of Hayti, shows the networks of rumor and surveillance within which commerce had to be conducted. It also demonstrates Moreau's continued interest in events happening in the Kingdom of Hayti. See "Historique de Saint-Domingue, 1797–1798," ANOM, F3, 201.

31. Moreau carried a large inventory of domestic and imported books, the majority in French and English, although he also stocked titles in Latin, German, Dutch, Spanish, and Italian. He sold the classics of what Robert Darnton has famously termed "livres philosophiques," or the "forbidden best-sellers of Pre-revolutionary France," from Pierre Choderlos de Laclos's *Les liaisons dangereuses* (1782) to the "libertine" work of "Crébillon

fils" (Claude Prosper Jolyot de Crébillon) and Restif de la Bretonne (Nicolas-Edme Restif). See Darnton, *The Forbidden Best-Sellers of Pre-revolutionary France* (New York, 1996). Collections of John Milton's and Geoffrey Chaucer's poetry, William Shakespeare's plays, and a large assortment of novels, many of them female-authored texts, were stocked. For example, British narratives such as Henry Fielding's *History of the Adventures of Joseph Andrews and of His Friend Mr. Abraham Adams* (1742) and Tobias Smollett's *History and Adventures of an Atom* (1740) were available alongside best-selling moralizing tales of seduction such as Susanna Rowson's *Charlotte, a Tale of Truth* (1791), French translations of Phebe Gibbes's *Elfrida; or, Paternal Ambition* (1786), and Fanny Burney's *Cecilia, or Memoirs of an Heiress* (1782). Moreau's establishment also sold "the choicest engravings and drawings," several kinds of almanacs, manuals on subjects such as gardening and bookkeeping, spelling and grammar books in various languages, songsters, and several kinds of paper. Medical volumes included treatises on tropical diseases, midwifery, and "the Management of Female Complaints, and of Children in early Infancy." A philosophe, Moreau sold Montesquieu's *De l'esprit des loix* (1750), John Locke's *Essay concerning Human Understanding* (1689), Henry Pemberton's *View of Sir Isaac Newton's Philosophy* (1728), Voltaire's *Henriade* (1723) and *Voyages et aventures d'une princesse Babylonienne . . .* (1768), a nine-volume octavo edition of Georges-Louis Leclerc, comte de Buffon's *Histoire naturelle, générale et particulière* (1749–1804), and, of course, Denis Diderot and Jean Le Rond d'Alembert's *Encyclopédie, ou dictionnaire raisonné des sciences, des arts et des métiers* (1751–1780) (he sold an edition of thirty-six volumes in octavo, a less fancy one than his own personal copy). Religious titles graced his shelves as well, from different versions and sizes of the Bible to a French translation of the Koran. A freemason, Moreau also marketed several masonic items, including one listed as a "Free-Mason's Pocket Companion." See *Catalogue of Books,* 11 ("Free-Mason's"), 12 ("Management"), 76 ("choicest").

32. Roberts and Roberts, *American Journey,* 202 ("nothing"), 214 ("hearts"); Mims, *Voyage,* 223 ("coeurs"); Joseph G. Rosengarten, "Moreau de Saint Mery and His French Friends in the American Philosophical Society," American Philosophical Society (APS), *Proceedings,* L (1911), 170 ("rendezvous"); Ashli White, *Encountering Revolution: Haiti and the Making of the Early Republic* (Baltimore, 2010), 31 ("magnet"); Doina Pasca Harsanyi, *Lessons from America: Liberal French Nobles in Exile, 1793–1798* (University Park, Pa., 2010), 2 ("re-creation"). Victor Hugo provides a vivid nineteenth-century assessment of Talleyrand: "During thirty years, from the interior of his palace, from the interior of his thoughts, he had almost controlled Europe. He had permitted himself to be on terms of familiarity with the Revolution, and had smiled upon it: ironically, it is true, but the Revolution had not perceived this. He had come in contact with, known, observed, penetrated, influenced, set in motion, fathomed, bantered, inspired all the men of his time, all the ideas of his time, and there had been moments in his life when, holding in his hand the four or five great threads which moved the civilized universe, he had for his puppet Napoleon I., Emperor of the French, King of Italy, Protector of the Confederation of the Rhine, Mediator of the Swiss Confederation. That is the game which was played by this man." See Hugo, "Talleyrand" (1838), in Hugo, *Things Seen (Choses vues),* I (New York, 1887), 2. See also for Hugo's quotation Roberts and Roberts, *American Journey,* 216–217n.

33. There is an intriguing silence behind the financial arrangements that allowed

Moreau to produce such elaborate, expensive imprints. Some of his publications were subsidized through subscriptions, many to high-profile men such as the French consul in the United States or Talleyrand. His journal suggested that by the end of his sojourn in the United States, he was in straightened economic circumstances. He remarked, "I tried to sell everything that I could make into money, of which I was very short, since my business was no longer going on" (J'achevai de vendre tout ce dont je pus faire de l'argent dont j'étais fort léger, car mon commerce n'allait plus); see Roberts and Roberts, *American Journey*, 255; Mims, *Voyage*, 265. This included personal items such as his son's Renaudin violin, Aménaïde's pianoforte, and, as he noted in an advertisement in a local newspaper, he was "likewise willing to dispose of several works of his own library and some of his maps." This advertisement is an un-sourced newspaper clipping in "Historique de Saint-Domingue 1797–1798," ANOM, F3, 201. The advertisement also circulated in local papers, including several issues of the *Aurora General Advertiser* (Philadelphia); see, for example, July 20, 1798, [4].

34. Henry W. Kent wrote a summary of the Van Braam–Moreau collaboration; see Kent, "Van Braam Houckgeest, an Early American Collector," APS, *Proceedings*, XL, pt. 2 (1930), 159–174, esp. 168. See also Jean Gordon Lee, *Philadelphians and the China Trade, 1784–1844* (Philadelphia, 1984); A. Owen Aldridge, *The Dragon and the Eagle: The Presence of China in the American Enlightenment* (Detroit, 1993); and Caroline Frank, *Objectifying China, Imagining America: Chinese Commodities in Early America* (Chicago, 2011).

35. See Elizabeth Cross's informative "The Last French East India Company in the Revolutionary Atlantic," *WMQ*, 3d Ser., LXXVII (2020), 613–640. There is a very long bibliography of work on Jesuit tracts concerning China.

36. Moreau read widely when working on this project and included copious citations to particular editions and page numbers of previous work on China. Prominent Jesuit tracts such as Joseph Amiot's *Mémoires concernant l'histoire, les sciences, les arts, les moeurs, les usages, etc. des chinois . . .* (Paris, 1776–1789), Joseph-Anne-Marie de Moyriac de Mailla's *Histoire générale de la Chine . . .* (Paris, 1777–1783), and the popular series *Lettres édifiantes et curieuses . . .* (Paris, 1702–1766) dominated his editorial citations.

37. Antony Griffiths notes: "The printers in Paris were good. As members of the Communauté des Maîtres Imprimeurs en taille-douce, they had all completed a demanding apprenticeship of four years, followed by two years as a journeyman ('compagnon')." See Griffiths, "Proofs in Eighteenth-Century French Printmaking," *Print Quarterly*, XXI (2004), 3–17 (quotation on 17). Moreau's diary entry dated Apr. 4, 1795, stated, "The press ordered from London arrived by the American ship Adrienne" (L'imprimerie demandée à Londres arriva par le vaisseau américain L'Adrienne). On June 24, 1795, he noted that he "received news from London that they are sending the type for my printing press" (les caractères pour mon imprimerie) (Roberts and Roberts, *American Journey*, 180, 186; Mims, *Voyage*, 196, 202). The 1793 edition of the specimen book of metal cast ornaments issued by Edmund Fry and Isaac Steele contains ornaments that Moreau used throughout the work he published in Philadelphia (*Specimen of Metal Cast Ornaments, Curiously Adjusted to Paper . . .* [London, 1793]).

38. For more on French-language imprints in Philadelphia at the time, see Catherine Hébert, "French Publications in Philadelphia in the Age of the French Revolution: A

Bibliographical Essay," *Pennsylvania History,* LVIII (1991), 37–61. A discussion of the number of imprints is found on 38. Moreau maintained contact with many booksellers, both locally and in other cities. The subscription list for M[édéric] L[ouis] É[lie] Moreau de Saint-Méry, *Description topographique et politique de la partie espagnole de l'isle Saint-Domingue . . .* (Philadelphia, 1796) boasts not only figures such as Vice President John Adams but copies for well-known tradesmen such as Benjamin Franklin Bache, Mathew Carey, Thomas Bradford, Robert Campbell, Thomas Stephens, and H & P Rice, all listed as "Imprimeur" or "Libraire" ("Liste des souscripteurs, par ordre alphabétique," front matter). His journal indicates that he dined, corresponded, and marketed his goods via other booksellers. These include a Mr. Hunter, a British bookseller who had worked in Jamaica and reopened a store in Norfolk; General Henry Knox, a former Boston bookseller until he joined the Continental army and eventually served as secretary of war under George Washington; Paul Joseph Guérard de Nancrède, a bookseller in Boston who served as his "correspondent"; and an unnamed correspondent in Charleston, South Carolina, where he advertised his own publications. He maintained ties to booksellers abroad as well, specifically as outlets for distributing his own work. Several Saint-Domingue, Hamburg, and Paris bookstores and printers sold the volume, according to his notes. See Roberts and Roberts, *American Journey,* 181 (quotation), 238.

39. Roberts and Roberts, *American Journey,* 206; Mims, *Voyage,* 214. The Historical Society of Pennsylvania holds some of the extant issues. Moreau was elected as a member of the American Philosophical Society, and extant meeting records document his public lectures. Incidentally, Théodore-Charles Mozard, a well-regarded journalist and printer in Saint-Domingue, editor of the *Gazette de Saint-Domingue,* and later French consul in Boston, was inducted into the American Philosophical Society on the same day as Van Braam and C. F. Volney, Jan. 20, 1797. See *Early Proceedings of the American Philosophical Society for the Promotion of Useful Knowledge, Compiled by One of the Secretaries, from the Manuscript Minutes of Its Meetings from 1744 to 1838* (Philadelphia, 1884), 246.

40. Roberts and Roberts, *American Journey,* 203–204; Mims, *Voyage,* 212.

41. *Voyage de l'ambassade,* I, 106.

42. Roberts and Roberts, *American Journey,* 175; Mims, *Voyage,* 191. Moreau noted that Decombaz opened a competing establishment in Philadelphia the following year and wrote that "I dismissed Combatz *[sic]* from my service—regretfully, because of his knowledge of the details of my business, which long experience had given him to a superior degree" (Je renvoyai De Combaz de mon service. Il était à regretter par l'utilité dont il m'était dans les détails de mon Commerce qu'il possédait supérieurement comme acquis par une longue expérience). See Roberts and Roberts, *American Journey,* 203; Mims, *Voyage,* 212. Decombaz returned to Saint-Domingue within a few years. See the subscription list for Moreau's *Description topographique, physique, civile, politique et historique de la partie française de l'isle Saint-Domingue . . . ,* II (Philadelphia, 1798), iii (hereafter cited as *Description de la partie française de l'isle Saint-Domingue*). He was again a "libraire, au Cap-Français." Moreau also employed another clerk in 1796 but on September 11, 1797, recorded, "My young and interesting clerk, Jules, born in Paris, and belonging to one of the many families who trusted the wild promises of the Scioto Company and had been driven by poverty to take refuge in Philadelphia, died from yellow fever, although just two

days before he had helped me with my moving" (Mon jeune et intéressant commis nommé Jules, né à Paris, et d'une des familles qui s'étant livrées aux promesses chimériques de la Compagnie de Sciotto, avait été réduit par la misère à se réfugier à Philadelphie, mourut de la fièvre jaune, quoique l'avant-veille encore il aidât mon déménagement). See Roberts and Roberts, *American Journey,* 237; Mims, *Voyage,* 246. Indeed, the journal is full of the sudden deaths of his friends and acquaintances from yellow fever and the general furor that the outbreak caused in Philadelphia.

43. Jean Fouchard's work, including "Les joies de la lecture à Saint-Domingue," *Revue d'histoire des colonies,* XLI (1954), 103–111, cites Moreau's *Description de la partie française de l'isle Saint-Domingue* for this information about Decombaz's reading room and other observations about reading practices in colonial Saint-Domingue. The work of Father Adolphe Cabon on the early press in Saint-Domingue also relies heavily on Moreau's work. See *Cabon's History of Haiti Journalism,* with an introduction and notes by Clarence S. Brigham (Worcester, Mass., 1940), originally published as Adolphe Cabon, "Un siècle et demi de journalisme en Haïti," in *La petite revue hebdomadaire* (Port-au-Prince, Haiti), Apr. 12 –Nov. 14, 1919. For more on Haitian print culture, including during the colonial period, see Justin Emmanuel Castera, *Bref coup d'oeil sur les origins de la presse haïtienne (1764–1850)* (Port-au-Prince, Haiti, 1986).

44. A member of the Grolier Club did the most comprehensive work on the bibliographic dimensions of Moreau's work. See Henry W. Kent's excellent "Chez Moreau de Saint-Méry, Philadelphie . . . with a List of Imprints Enlarged by George Parker Winship," in *Bibliographical Essays: A Tribute to Wilberforce Eames* (Cambridge, Mass., 1924), 67–78; and Kent, "Encore Moreau de Saint-Méry," in [Deoch Fulton, ed.], *Bookmen's Holiday: Notes and Studies Written and Gathered in Tribute to Harry Miller Lydenberg* (New York, 1943), 239–247. He noted that the work from Moreau's printshop had "real, individual character" (ibid., 242).

45. Wroth, *The Colonial Printer,* xvii; *Voyage de l'ambassade,* I, xx (quotation), II, 219 (map); George C. Groce and David H. Wallace, *The New York Historical Society's Dictionary of Artists in America, 1564–1860* (New Haven, Conn., 1957), 570 (Seymour), 644 (Vallance).

46. The most elaborate engraving in the publication is a paint-like two-page foldout image of the Chinese court in which the Dutch ambassador is shown performing the traditional prostrated "kowtow" as a mark of respect before the Chinese emperor. For more on this image, in particular, see George R. Loehr, "A. E. van Braam Houckgeest: The First American at the Court of China," *Princeton University Library Chronicle,* XV (1954), 179–193. For more on Pu Qua, see Yeewan Koon, "Narrating the City: Pu Qua and the Depiction of Street Life in Canton," in Petra ten-Doesschate Chu and Ning Ding, eds., with Lidy Jane Chu, *Qing Encounters: Artistic Exchanges between China and the West* (Los Angeles, 2015), 217–231.

47. Mason was a solider stationed in Canton's British trading factory in the 1790s, and upon returning to London, he published what would become a famous collection of plates with English and French commentary. He noted that he had "obtained correct drawings of the Chinese in their respective habits and occupations" (Preface, [iii]), and each illustration is attributed to "Pu-Qùa, Cantòn, Delin." See George Henry Mason, *The Costume of*

China, Illustrated by Sixty Engravings: With Explanations in English and French (London, 1800). Mason confirmed that he had access to Van Braam's account, stating, "In order to render this purpose effectual, it was absolutely necessary to attach a few lines of explanatory letter-press to each plate, and wherever the recollection of the Editor is deficient, he has repaired it by careful selections from the narratives of almost every traveller, from Nieuhoff and Navarette to Staunton and Van Braam" (Preface, [iii]). Mason's plates contain an image labeled "A Mandarin of Distinction in His Habit of Ceremony," and although the portrait is not the same as any of the four figures that Moreau compiled into a plate in his publication (see two of them in Figure 24), it has distinctly the same style in terms of perspective and details about the clothing. Charles H. Carpenter, Jr., who spent years tracking down pieces that had been part of Van Braam's original ensemble of artwork, furniture, and porcelain, notes that the Moreau–Van Braam engraving, published before the Mason compilation, was modeled on Pu Qua's work. See Carpenter, "The Chinese Collection of A. E. van Braam Houckgeest," *Antiques,* CV (1974), 342 (Fig. 11). He notes that an album containing these original watercolors was located by Dr. George R. Loehr at the Biblioteca Nazionale Centrale di Firenze.

48. *Voyage de l'ambassade,* I, x–xi ("employé constamment," xiv); *An Authentic Account of the Embassy of the Dutch East-India Company, to the Court of the Emperor of China, in the Years 1794 and 1795 . . . Taken from the Journal of André Everard van Braam . . . Translated from the Original of M. L. E. Moreau de Saint-Mery . . . ,* 2 vols. (London, 1798), II, 298 ("conceived").

49. Roberts and Roberts, *American Journey,* 218; Mims, *Voyage,* 227.

50. Scholarship has outlined the details about this trip, using Chinese sources, the Dutch manuscript, and Moreau's translation of Van Braam's account. See, for example, Duyvendak, "The Last Dutch Embassy to the Chinese Court," *T'oung Pao,* 2d Ser., XXXIV (1938), 1–137; and Duyvendak, "Supplementary Documents on the Last Dutch Embassy to the Chinese Court," *T'oung Pao,* 2d Ser., XXXV (1940), 329–353. Van Braam has also been studied in the context of early American contact with China. As a naturalized citizen, Van Braam was the first American to visit the Forbidden City. An example of this work includes John Rogers Haddad, *The Romance of China: Excursions to China in U.S. Culture, 1776–1876* (New York, 2008). Haddad likewise makes note of the treatment of the laborers forced to carry the embassy from Canton to Peking in chapter 1.

51. Five hundred copies of the first volume of the imprint bound on an American ship to France were captured by French privateers in early 1798. They were sold in France and made into a two-volume work. This edition, only half complete, was in turn translated and sold in London, Germany, and Holland. When the book did make it back to Philadelphia, it was the English pirated edition. Mathew Carey sold it in his shop, as did Bache in his bookstore. English citations in this chapter are hereafter from this pirated edition, *Authentic Account of the Embassy.* Van Braam's traveling partner, the official ambassador, was no other than Isaac Titsingh, the father of modern Japanology in France, a man who Moreau was sure to note "resided a long time in Japan, and even employed himself in acquiring information concerning that interesting country, the language of which he understands" (I, 282).

52. A Philadelphia paper printed an article concerning news from Charleston that

stated: "It is said that Mr. Van Braam Houckgeest has invented a machine for pounding of rice, which, from the simplicity of its structure, and the easy manner in which it can be worked, possesses superior advantages to any other hitherto invented. It is an improvement on the rice machine already in use, but instead of six pestles, or pounders, works twelve: to do this one horse is sufficient, and will pound 40 barrels of rice in ten hours." See *Pennsylvania Packet, and Daily Advertiser* (Philadelphia), Apr. 27, 1786, [2].

53. I have not seen any scholarship documenting Van Braam's life as a slaveholder, although the for sale and runaway advertisements in local Charleston papers provide evidence that he did indeed profit from enslaved labor. Maryann appeared as a runaway in the *South-Carolina Gazette, and Public Advertiser* (Charleston), Apr. 14–Apr. 17, 1784, [3]. Sylvia appeared as a runaway in the *South-Carolina Gazette, and General Advertiser* (Charleston), Apr. 1–Apr. 3, 1784, [3]. The final announcement in which Van Braam sold multiple enslaved people was printed in the *City Gazette, or the Daily Advertiser* (Charleston), July 30, 1788, [2]. The sudden death of four of Van Braam's children from a diphtheria outbreak combined with straightened financial circumstances led to his decision to leave the United States and return to China. Information on Van Braam's life in Charleston is found in Mabel L. Webber, "Marriage and Death Notices from the South Carolina Weekly Gazette," *South Carolina Historical and Genealogical Magazine*, II (1918), 107–110; and Webber, "Marriage and Death Notices from the South Carolina Weekly Gazette," ibid., XIX (1918), 137.

54. For background on the VOC, see John E. Wills, Jr., *Pepper, Guns, and Parleys: The Dutch East India Company and China, 1662–1681* (Los Angeles, 2005); and Nick Robins, *The Corporation That Changed the World: How the East India Company Shaped the Modern Multinational*, 2d ed. (London, 2012).

55. Van Braam's trip occurred precisely when the VOC was mired in corruption and just after the British legation's first, now legendary, embassy to China in 1792–1794. Led by Lord George Macartney, a consummate representative of British colonial power who had previously been governor of the British West Indies and Madras, India, the trip, along with Van Braam's, became key points of contact between Europe and the Qing Dynasty. For an insightful analysis of Macartney's trip and its importance to historiography from the nineteenth century to the present, see historian James L. Hevia's *Cherishing Men from Afar: Qing Guest Ritual and the Macartney Embassy of 1793* (Durham, N.C., 1995). Macartney's trip also resulted in the publication of several multivolume accounts of China in the immediate aftermath of Moreau's publication of Van Braam's work. Within just a few years, there were already British, French, and German compilations of these two trips, some accompanied by sixty color plates, text, and other images pirated from the Van Braam–Moreau original. Moreau's text and its artwork thus entered into continental European print culture circuits about China. See, for example, [Joseph-François] Charpentier de Cossigny, *Voyage à Canton, capitale de la province de ce nom, à la Chine* . . . (Paris, 1799); and Jean Godefroi Grohmann, *Moeurs et coutumes des Chinois, et leurs costumes en couleur d'après les tableaux de Pu-Qùa peintre à Canton pour servier de suite aux Voyages de Macartney et de Van Braam; 60 planches avec le texte français et allemande/* Johann Gottfried Grohmann, *Gebräuche und Kleidungen der Chinesen dargestellt in bunten Gemälden von dem Mahler Pu-Qùa in Canton als Zusatz zu Macartneys und Van*

Braams Reisen; 60 Kupfer mit Erklärung in deutscher und französischer Sprache herausgegeben (Leipzig, Germany, 1800).

56. Roberts and Roberts, *American Journey,* 214; Mims, *Voyage,* 222; *Voyage de l'ambassade,* I, xiii.

57. Carpenter, "The Chinese Collection of A. E. van Braam Houckgeest," *Antiques,* CV (1974), 338–347 (quotation on 338). Carpenter comments on the sale of 114 lots of Van Braam's collection at a Christie's auction in 1799. In his work on Van Braam, Henry W. Kent points out, "It should not be forgotten that before this time no such opportunity [to see Chinese people] had ever been offered to Americans." See Kent, "Van Braam Houckgeest, An Early American Collector," APS, *Proceedings,* XL, pt. 2 (1930), 168. For references to the five Chinese immigrants on board, see the advertisement announcing the arrival of the *Lady Louisa* in *Claypoole's American Daily Advertiser* (Philadelphia), Apr. 28, 1796, [2]. This figure was repeated in subsequent scholarship, including the articles written by Edward R. Barnsley, a descendant of Van Braam, who noted that when Van Braam's ship docked in Philadelphia, there were "five native Chinese" with him. See "History of China's Retreat: Paper Read by Edward R. Barnsley before the Bucks County Historical Society at Doylestown, May 6, 1933," *Bristol Courier* (Pa.), May 10, 1933, 1. Barnsley's series of articles was published in the May 9, 10, 11, 1933, issues of the *Bristol Courier.* For more on chinoiserie, see the essays in Petra ten-Doesschate Chu and Jennifer Milam, eds., *Beyond Chinoiserie: Artistic Exchange between China and the West during the Late Qing Dynasty (1796–1911)* (Leiden, Netherlands, 2019); and Kiersten Larsen Davis, "Secondhand Chinoiserie and the Confucian Revolutionary: Colonial America's Decorative Arts 'After the Chinese Taste'" (Ph.D. diss., Brigham Young University, 2008). Lisa Lowe, *The Intimacies of Four Continents* (Durham, N.C., 2015) documents the connections between Caribbean and North American slavery, American and British consumerism, and the China trade. Also see Chi-ming Yang, *Performing China: Virtue, Commerce, and Orientalism in Eighteenth-Century England, 1660–1760* (Baltimore, 2011) for a discussion of this artistic trend in England. For the dangers of fetishization of actual people, see Michelle Smiley's work on a later period in the United States, "Daguerreotypes and Humbugs: Pwan-Ye-Koo, Racial Science, and the Circulation of Ethnographic Images around 1850," *Panorama: Journal of the Association of Historians of American Art,* VI, no. 2 (Fall 2020), https://doi.org/10.24926/24716839.10895.

58. The luxury of the former mansion, including its gold leaf wallpaper and silver bells, is described in "Old China Hall's 100 Years: Historic Buildings on the Banks of the Delaware," *Philadelphia Inquirer,* Nov. 5, 1891, 6. Niemcewicz continued: "What is most interesting in all this collection is about 60 notebooks of Chinese paintings representing with the greatest accuracy their techniques in arts and crafts, their sciences, their agriculture, ceremonies, criminal code, natural history, botany, geographical maps, etc." See Julian Ursyn Niemcewicz, *Under Their Vine and Fig Tree: Travels through America in 1797–1799, 1805 with Some Further Account of Life in New Jersey,* ed. and trans. Metchie J. E. Budka (Newark, N.J., 1965), 62–63.

59. See Muriel Wagner's "Eerie Tales Surround History of Croydon's 'China Hall': Old Mansion Rumored as Former Slave Market," *Bristol Daily Courier,* Sept. 20, 1956, 21. She opens her article by stating: "Since my early years the mention of China Hall in Croyden

by the Delaware has carried with it an aura of the mystical, half known past. It was often rumored to have contained a slave market within its great halls and grounds; sometimes reputed to have harbored colored slaves, and as often said to have been an illegal port of entry for orientals—complete with escape tunnel from the mansion to the river." Who these "orientals" were—language demonstrating the casual racism of 1950s America—and from what time period they became associated with the house as part of an alleged illegal immigration scheme is unclear. Of interest is the continued association of Black and Asian individuals with the property. The mansion was painted by William Russell Birch in 1809. See Birch, *China Retreat Pennsyla. the Seat of Mr. Manigault,* 1809, hand-colored engraving mounted on paper, 6 × 7.75 in. (16 × 20 cm), Library Company of Philadelphia, https://digital.librarycompany.org/islandora/object/islandora%3A323587. See also Birch, *Van Brant's* [sic] *Place on the Delaware River,* circa 1808, watercolor, 5.5 × 7.5 in. (15 × 20 cm), The Library Company of Philadelphia, https://digital.librarycompany.org/islandora/object/Islandora%3A13387?solr_nav%5Bid%5D=f609bb315566559d6cea&solr_nav%5Bpage%5D=0&solr_nav%5Boffset%5D=0.

60. "History of China's Retreat," *Bristol Courier,* May 10, 1933, 1–2 ("Malay"). Barnsley cites the memoirs of Lucius Quintius Cincinnatus Roberts, but he does not note if they were published or handed down in personal family papers. During the original embassy trip, Van Braam's cortege included a "Domestique Européen" and "Deux Domestiques Malais" along with Chinese servants. One of these men died during the trip owing to the poor traveling conditions. See *Voyage de l'ambassade,* I, 30.

61. "History of China's Retreat," *Bristol Courier,* May 11, 1933, 3 ("was possessed"). In addition to Madam Lana, the housekeeper, Barnsley notes that the passengers included "a young Malay man named Kinties whom van Braam sent to Holland where he was educated as a physician but was unfortunately drowned upon returning to his native country" (ibid., May 10, 1933, 2). On the eventual demise of the Chinese Retreat, Barnsley writes, in exoticizing language that echoes Muriel Wagner's "Eerie Tales," *Bristol Daily Courier,* Sept. 20, 1956, cited above: "Van Braam had come to Bucks County with the intention of staying here the remainder of his life. But circumstances did not permit; just what went wrong the writer has not been able to unravel. Perhaps it was because of his quick temperament, or perhaps his unique household with its Oriental environment was a little too much for the placid farming life of Bristol Township"; see "History of China's Retreat," *Bristol Courier,* May 11, 1933, 3.

62. "Avertissement de l'Éditeur," in *Voyage de l'ambassade,* I, xiii; "Advertisement of the Editor," in *Authentic Account of the Embassy,* I, xiii; Moreau's diary mentioned passing time there with Talleyrand, Volney, and other prominent French exiles. See Roberts and Roberts, *American Journey.* Van Braam was well connected in the city via his membership in the American Philosophical Society and access to the social circle that his daughter's marriage to the wealthy Morris merchant family assured.

63. For more on this labor transition, see Walton Look Lai, *Indentured Labor, Caribbean Sugar: Chinese and Indian Migrants to the British West Indies, 1838–1918* (Baltimore, 1993); Kathleen López, *Chinese Cubans: A Transnational History* (Chapel Hill, N.C., 2013); Moon-Ho Jung, *Coolies and Cane: Race, Labor, and Sugar in the Age of Emancipation* (Baltimore, 2006).

64. "Notes et explications par ordre alphabétique . . . ," in *Voyage de l'ambassade,* I, lxvii. Many of the Chinese words he compiled had a pragmatic, linguistically oriented dimension, including instructions on how a foreigner should pronounce them. "COHANG"—a group of merchants in Canton who had sole trading rights with Europeans—was a word in which "one must not pronounce the final g sound" (ibid., I, lxix). Confucius, "the first among all of Chinese philosophers," was a name Moreau opted to record as "CONFUCIUS" and *"Kong-fou-tsé,"* even though Van Braam insisted that the correct pronunciation of his name was *"Hong-fou-tsé"* (ibid., lxx). I return to the stakes Moreau and his brother-in-law Louis Narcisse Baudry des Lozières ascribed to the correct pronunciation of foreign words in subsequent chapters in this book. Moreau's notes also asserted mastery over knowledge about China through explanations that dealt with conceptual terms and ideas. For instance, he detailed the aphrodisiac properties of birds' nests ("NIDS D'OISEAU") (ibid., lxxvi), commented on "public women" ("FEMMES PUBLIQUES") and prostitution (ibid., lxxii), and explained weights and measures as used in China.

65. The first appendix in *Voyage de l'ambassade* provided running commentary on the art and material objects Van Braam brought to Philadelphia from China. Under the title "Notice of a Collection of Chinese Drawings, in the Possession of M. van Braam, Author of this Work" ("Notice des objets qui composent la Collection de dessins Chinois de M. van Braam, Auteur de cet Ouvrage"), Moreau catalogued them after consulting, indeed being admittedly awed by, a portfolio containing more than eighteen hundred illustrations, mostly watercolors (I, xvii–xliv). As noted, the volume's preliminary matter also included "Notes et explications," a list of key terms and concepts, which is similar to the appendixes in his publications about French and Spanish Santo Domingo and his work on the Río de la Plata region in current-day Paraguay. I address Moreau's paratexts further in Chapter 5. The actual Chinese terms in the book were written in roman type, not Chinese characters; his typecase would not have included them. At one point during his trip, Van Braam visited a temple dedicated to Confucius and spoke wonderingly of its craftsmanship. He mentioned a cupola with inscriptions in gold, and Moreau's publication left lines to print "the following characters" (les caractères suivans). The inscriptions are marked by three dotted lines and appear incomplete (I, 58). Was Moreau hoping to insert Chinese characters here? This is one of the many topics I believe that he and Giambattista Bodoni would have enjoyed discussing when Moreau lived in Parma because Bodoni cut Chinese letter punches, conserved at the Museo Bodoniano in Parma, Italy.

66. The original stated: "As to the work of the Editor, it has been done with the greatest care; and it has at least the merit of great fidelity, since there is not a single line that has not been submitted to the examination of the Author, to whom the French language is familiar enough that he can be an excellent judge" (Quant au travail de l'Éditeur, il a été fait avec le plus grand soin, et il a du moins le mérite d'une grande fidélité, parce qu'il n'en est pas une seule ligne qui n'ait été soumise à l'examen de l'Auteur, auquel la langue française est assez familière pour qu'il en soit un excellent juge). See "Avertissement de l'Éditeur," in *Voyage de l'ambassade,* I, xiv.

67. *Voyage de l'ambassade,* II, viii.

68. Ibid., I, lxx ("l'Inde"); *Authentic Account of the Embassy,* I, 118 ("stopped"), 211 ("cursed"). Van Braam spoke casually of "changing Coulis at noon" (134) or "this morning,

at six o'clock, I ordered my *Coulis* to be called" (104). Entries such as "breakfast and a change of *Coulis* were the occasion of this halt" abounded (168). Outright refusal to go forward is also noted several times. Van Braam wrote: "The *Coulis* set us down in the streets, refusing to carry us any farther unless they were better paid. Two hours were spent in disputes, which ended in an acquiescence in their demand. In the mean time the weather was become exceedingly bad, with wind and rain" (104). In another instance, "The *Coulis,* twelve of whom had been ordered for the Ambassador's palanquin, and as many for mine, set me down at half a league from the city, in the road and in the midst of the mud, because their number was reduced to five, the other seven having made off as soon as they had received their hire. After waiting an hour, four other Coulis came to my relief" (117). He concluded, "Perhaps he [the man in charge of hiring transport] was less blameable than we imagined, since it is so difficult to manage the *Coulis,* as we ourselves had but too well experienced" (208). For the eight men who died of exhaustion, see Duyvendak, "The Last Dutch Embassy to the Chinese Court," *T'oung Pao,* 2d Ser., XXXIV (1938), 43.

69. *Voyage de l'ambassade,* I, lxxiii; he then stated that the correct word for *drum* was "Lo," citing Jean Amiot, *Mémoires concernant l'histoire, les sciences, les arts, les moeurs, les usages, etc. des Chinois* . . . (1776–1791).

70. Gikandi, *Slavery and the Culture of Taste,* 3.

71. Roberts and Roberts, *American Journey,* 216 ("compositor"); Vicomte de Rochambeau to Moreau, July 15, 1796, quoted ibid., 218–219 (quotations on 219); Mims, *Voyage,* 225 ("compositeur"), 227–228.

72. See Sara E. Johnson, "'You Should Give Them Blacks to Eat': Waging Inter-American Wars of Torture and Terror," *American Quarterly,* LXI (2009), 65–92.

Chapter Four

1. Moreau de Saint-Méry, *Voyage aux États-Unis de l'Amérique, 1793–1798,* ed. Stewart L. Mims (New Haven, Conn., 1913), 137 (hereafter cited as Mims, *Voyage*). See also the English translation of the diary, Kenneth Roberts and Anna M. Roberts, eds. and trans., *Moreau de Saint Méry's American Journey [1793–1798]* (Garden City, N.Y., 1947), 123 (hereafter cited as Roberts and Roberts, *American Journey*). Moreau's designation of Sylvie's racial "category" is in keeping with his much-studied schema of racial groups and their personalities. According to him, a "griffonne" would be "from 24 to 32 parts white and to 104 to 96 parts black," whatever this would have meant; see Médéric Louis Élie Moreau de Saint-Méry, *La description topographique, physique, civile, politique et historique de la partie française de l'isle Saint-Domingue* . . . , ed. Blanche Maurel and Étienne Taillemite, new ed., 3 vols. (Saint-Denis, France, 2004), 96 (hereafter cited as *Description de la partie française de l'isle Saint-Domingue*). For an excellent study of household relations that cut across the enslaved-master divide in metropolitan France and Saint-Domingue through a series of microhistories, see Jennifer L. Palmer, *Intimate Bonds: Family and Slavery in the French Atlantic* (Philadelphia, 2016).

2. Roberts and Roberts, *American Journey,* 44; Mims, *Voyage,* 48. See the work on freedom suits by Rebecca J. Scott and Jean M. Hébrard, *Freedom Papers: An Atlantic Odyssey in the Age of Emancipation* (Cambridge, Mass., 2012); and Edlie L. Wong, *Neither*

Fugitive nor Free: Atlantic Slavery, Freedom Suits, and the Legal Culture of Travel (New York, 2009).

3. "Mariage de Moreau de Saint-Méry et Louise-Catherine Milhet," Apr. 9, 1781, Archives nationales d'outre-mer, Aix-en-Provence, France (ANOM), Notariat Saint-Domingue, 861, Grimperel, acting notary; Roberts and Roberts, *American Journey,* 193; Mims, *Voyage,* 206. Madame Milhet's priest as well as the German and Irish Catholic churches refused to bury her. Moreau notes that she was buried in the Anglican cemetery. One of the first things Moreau printed in his shop was a book of Catholic prayers in French, a publication that sold out immediately. Buyers among the faithful could have been of many races. For more on Philadelphia's African American and French Caribbean population, see Gary B. Nash, *Forging Freedom: The Formation of Philadelphia's Black Community, 1720–1840* (Cambridge, Mass., 1991).

4. Moreau de Saint-Méry to Aménaïde Dall'Asta, July 3, 1809, in "Moreau de Saint-Méry: Correspondance à sa famille, 1808–1809," transcribed by Cecilia Paini, under the supervision of Carminella Biondi (thesis, Università degli studi di Parma, 1986–1987), from the manuscript letters in Fondo Carte Moreau de Saint-Méry, Dono Monza, Archivio di Stato di Parma, Italy (hereafter cited as "Correspondance, 1808–1809"). In another letter from July 26, 1809, Moreau's grandson, Edouard Dall'Asta, wrote a letter to his parents Aménaïde and Pompeo (dictated and transcribed phonetically) stating, "Silvie te dit bonjour. Si tu savais comme elle même bien" (Silvie tells you hello. If you knew how much she loves me) (ibid.).

5. "Mariage de Moreau de Saint-Méry et Louise-Catherine Milhet," Apr. 9, 1781, ANOM, Notariat Saint-Domingue, 861, Grimperel, acting notary. In 1780, for example, the widow Milhet loaned the free Black man Jean-François, a mason, 1,540 livres in gold and silver coins from Spain and Portugal to purchase Marie, a Black hairdresser, so that the two could marry. See "Obligation," Sept. 23, 1780, ANOM, Notariat Saint-Domingue, 360, Casaumajour, acting notary.

6. "Mariage de Baudry des Lozières et Catherine Milhet," Aug. 3, 1777, ANOM, Notariat Saint-Domingue, 526, Doré, acting notary.

7. Moreau de Saint-Méry, *Description de la partie française de l'isle Saint-Domingue,* 411, 413.

8. Moreau de Saint-Méry, *Description de la partie française de l'isle Saint-Domingue,* 411 ("Foeda"), 414 *("pauvres"),* 415 ("Vertueux"), 416 ("console-toi"). For the advertisement that mentions Jean-Louis, see "Esclaves en maronage," *Supplement aux Affiches américaines* (Cap Français, Saint-Domingue), Feb. 5, 1783, [4].

9. Michel Camus, "Une fille naturelle de Moreau de Saint-Méry à Saint-Domingue," *Revue de la Société haïtienne d'histoire et de geographie,* XLVI, no. 162 (March 1989), 51. The original transfer of property is located in "Donation," Apr. 8, June 13, 1791, ANOM, Notariat Saint-Domingue, 861, Grimperel, acting notary. Marie-Louise's name is spelled "La Plaine" in this document.

10. Michel Camus, "Une fille naturelle de Moreau de Saint-Méry?" *Généalogie et historie de la Carïbe,* no. 93 (May 1997), 1960. Camus cites Archives nationales, État civil du Cap Français, Dec. 10, 1778, as the source of Laplaine's manumission papers.

11. Jean-Philippe E. Belleau, "Love in the Time of Hierarchy: Ethnographic Voices in

Eighteenth-Century Haiti," in Larry Wolff and Marco Cipolloni, eds., *The Anthropology of the Enlightenment* (Stanford, Calif., 2007), 217 (quotation); J[ohn] G[abriel] Stedman, *Narrative, of a Five Years' Expedition, against the Revolted Negroes of Surinam, in Guiana, on the Wild Coast of South America; from the Year 1772, to 1777* ..., 2 vols. (London, 1796). For an excellent discussion of the role of housekeepers within the U.S. slave-trading business, see Alexandra J. Finley, *An Intimate Economy: Enslaved Women, Work, and America's Domestic Slave Trade* (Chapel Hill, N.C., 2020), chap. 4. See also Emily Clark's work on the shift from *ménagère* to *placée* in chapter 2 of *The Strange History of the American Quadroon: Free Women of Color in the Revolutionary Atlantic World* (Chapel Hill, N.C., 2013).

12. Stewart R. King, *Blue Coat or Powdered Wig: Free People of Color in Pre-revolutionary Saint Domingue* (Athens, Ga., 2001), xxiii. King notes that "these women, and their children, often achieved remarkable economic success, and when they did, they very often adopted the values and behavior of the planter elite group" (xxiii). If Marie-Louise Laplaine had a notarized contract, she would have been able to "buy and sell on his behalf, exercise authority over his slaves, and, indeed, behave both as his junior business partner and as a member of his family"; in short, she would have been given "economic rights" as his "pseudo-kin" (93).

13. Moreau de Saint-Méry, *Mémoire justificatif* (Paris, 1790), 5 n. 1, 6 (quotation).

14. "Donation," May 30, 1788, ANOM, Notariat Saint-Domingue, 869, Grimperel, acting notary; "Bail d'appartement," Aug. 30, 1788, ANOM, Notariat Saint-Domingue, 870, Grimperel, acting notary. A short research note by Bernadette Rossignol and Philippe Rossignol notes "le décès de sa mère" when referring to Marie-Louise Laplaine. There is, unfortunately, no source cited for this information. See Rossignol and Rossignol, "Moreau de Saint-Méry," *Généalogie et Histoire de la Caraïbe*, no. 171 (June 2002), 4221.

15. Moreau de Saint-Méry, *Mémoire justificatif,* 34.

16. Moreau de Saint-Méry, *Description de la partie française de l'isle Saint-Domingue,* 409–410.

17. For a succinct overview of how sensibility was mobilized in the late eighteenth and early nineteenth century, see Sarah Knott, *Sensibility and the American Revolution* (Williamsburg, Va., and Chapel Hill, N.C., 2009), 4–15.

18. Moreau wrote, "I do not deny that the trade gives rise to abuses; and I desire, along with other good people, that these abuses should be prevented or punished" (Je n'ignore pas que la traite donne lieu à des abus; et je desire, avec les gens de bien, que ces abus soient prévenus ou punis). He also wrote, however, that the abuses suffered by the people who were sold into the trade, people alternately described as criminals or victims, were nothing compared to those they would have "suffered" in Africa. In fact, the trade "saved the lives of thousands of men" (en conservant la vie à des milliers d'hommes). See M. L. E. Moreau de Saint-Méry, *Considérations présentées aux vrais amis du repos et du bonheur de la France; à l'occasion des nouveaux mouvemens de quelques soi-disant Amis-des-noirs* (Paris, 1791), 49, 50.

19. Moreau de Saint-Méry, *Description de la partie française de l'isle Saint-Domingue,* 73, 74n, 75n. Moreau knew about Buffon's discussion of another Black albino woman and was interjecting his own thoughts into this debate. This woman appeared as Plate I in

[Georges-Louis] Leclerc, [comte] de Buffon, *Histoire naturelle, générale et particulière . . . ,* new ed., XX (Paris, An VIII [1799]), 346. For more on this woman, named Geneviève, see Alyssa Goldstein Sepinwall, "Whiteness, Gender, and Slavery in Enlightenment Le Havre: Marie Le Masson Le Golft's Self-Fashioning as a *Femme des Lettres," Journal of the Western Society for French History,* XLVIII (2022), 25–27. See also Andrew Curran's discussion of Buffon's use of the term "nègre-blanc," including Geneviève, in Curran, "Rethinking Race History: The Role of the Albino in the French Enlightenment Life Sciences," *History and Theory,* XLVIII (2009), 151–179.

20. Florence Gauthier, *L'aristocratie de l'épiderme: Le combat de la Société des citoyens de couleur, 1789–1791* (Paris, 2007), 280.

21. Ibid., 237 ("néo-blanc"), 280 ("lui-même"); Florence Gauthier, "Au coeur de préjugé de couleur dans la colonie de Saint-Domingue: Médéric Moreau de Saint Méry contre Julien Raimond, 1789–91," *Le canard républican,* June 10, 2010, https://lecanardrépublicain .net/spip.php?article356 ("cacher"); Jean Casimir, *The Haitians: A Decolonial History,* trans. Laurent Dubois (Chapel Hill, N.C., 2020), 54 ("descent"), 89 ("hiding"); John D. Garrigus, "Opportunist or Patriot? Julien Raimond (1744–1801) and the Haitian Revolution," *Slavery and Abolition,* XXVIII (2007), 1–21.

22. Casimir, *The Haitians,* 91.

23. Moreau de Saint-Méry, *Mémoire justificatif,* 13.

24. Moreau de Saint-Méry, *Considérations,* 9, 73. See also [Moreau de Saint-Méry], *Observations d'un habitant des colonies, sur le mémoire en faveur des gens de couleur, ou sang-mêlés, de St-Domingue et des autres isles françaises de l'Amérique, adressé à l'Assemblée nationale . . .* (n.p., [1789]).

25. Ogé jeune, letter, *Le Patriote français,* Apr. 18, 1790, 4.

26. Gauthier, *L'aristocratie de l'epiderme,* 118. Representatives of the colons américaines remarked: "Malgré leur coalition [les colons blancs] criminelle pour empêcher les Citoyens de couleur de sortir du royaume, de se rendre dans leur patrie, et même de correspondre avec elle; malgré leurs injures, leurs personnalités, malgré les mille et un libelles dont ils ont inondé la capitale; malgré les observations impolitiques et anonymes* d'un Colon que nous nous glorifierions d'avoir vu parmi vous, dans les moments les plus périlleux de la révolution, si les principes de liberté qu'il paraît avoir professé n'avaient fait place à ceux du mépris et du despotisme les plus absolus." [Note:] "*L'anonyme doit être dévoilé; c'est M. Moreau de S. Méry."

27. Gauthier examines this print in part 4, chapter 3 of *L'aristocratie de l'épiderme,* 308–321.

28. Érick Noël, ed., *Dictionnaire des gens de couleur dans la France moderne: Paris et son bassin; entrée par localités et par année (fin XVe siècle–1792), Paris suivi des provinces classées alphabétiquement,* I (Geneva, Switzerland, 2011), 264 (quotation). Many thanks to Sue Peabody for our discussion about the Police des Noirs. See Peabody, *"There Are No Slaves in France": The Political Culture of Race and Slavery in the Ancien Régime* (New York, 1996) for more on the 1777 legislation that attempted to bar the entry of Black people into France and created rules about those who were already resident in the country having to register their presence with the government.

29. Although one Mart(h)onne is listed as "griffe" in the marriage contract and the

other as a "mulâtresse" in the manumission papers issued in France, and the ages of the two women (around twenty in 1781 and thirty-four in 1789) show a gap of six years, her age in the marriage contract is listed as approximate, and the French authorities might have used a different description to characterize her skin color. See "Mariage de Moreau de Saint-Méry et Louise-Catherine Milhet," Apr. 9, 1781, ANOM, Notariat Saint-Domingue, 861, Grimperel, acting notary; Noël, ed., *Dictionnaire des gens de couleur,* I, 264.

30. Moreau de Saint-Méry, *Mémoire justificatif,* 34 ("bon maître").

31. This reality is explained beautifully in the last paragraphs of Toni Morrison's novel *A Mercy* (New York, 2008). As a mother reluctantly asks a male stranger to buy her child in order that she might escape the certainty of her current owner's depredations, she writes, "There is no protection but there is difference. . . . Because I saw the tall man see you as a human child, not pieces of eight" (166).

32. See Lisa Lowe's thoughtful critique of the liberal "genealogy of freedom" in "History Hesitant," *Social Text,* XXXIII, no. 4 (125) (December 2015), 89 (quotation). I also appreciate David Kazanjian's reminder that his sources provided "profound challenges to classically liberal conceptions of freedom, conceptions that often go unquestioned and thus are perpetuated in work that attends principally to the questions of who did what, where, and when. These include, for instance, meliorist conceptions like the idea that the movement from slavery to freedom is ideally progressive and developmental, the idea that subjects willfully desire and thus volitionally seek to be free, the idea of the individual will as such, the idea that subjects ought to have a desire they know and seek to realize." His idea that as scholars we do "not want to stop historicists from offering their speculative fiction as if it were realist" and that we should "read for the scenes of speculation in the archives we recover" is very akin to my own approach to Moreau's work. See Kazanjian, "Scenes of Speculation," ibid., 79–81. See also the entry for "Créole" in Chapter 1 for comments concerning the double entendre found in the expression "A good white is dead. The mean ones remain."

33. Moreau de Saint-Méry, *Loix et constitutions des colonies françaises de l'Amérique sous le vent . . . ,* 6 vols. (Paris, [1784–1790]), VI, 30–32 (quotations on 31). In another case from January 31, 1782, a man named Jean-Baptiste was convicted of being "insolent envers les Blancs" and, after wearing a sign proclaiming this insolence in the Clugny market, was sentenced "to be whipped, branded, and attached to a chain gang as a forced laborer for three years" (à être fouetté, marqué, et attaché à la Chaîne publique, comme Forçat, pendant 3 ans) (ibid., 225). Joan [Colin] Dayan mentions the case of the women, saying that "their punishment—its form and the place chosen for display [the Clugny market, the center of creole life]—demonstrated to such women where (and to whom) they belonged." See Dayan, "Codes of Law and Bodies of Color," *New Literary History,* XXVI (1995), 295.

34. Moreau, *Loix et constitutions,* VI, 32. The best example I can find of an écriteau is in Katherine Dauge-Roth's *Signing the Body: Marks on Skin in Early Modern France* (London, 2019), especially chapter 4, where she discusses signs as they were used to criminalize people. She notes: "Such placards, or *écritaux,* accompanied each sentence of branding. Wearing these texts contributed to the spectacle of degrading punishment in a society where honor and reputation were everything. . . . Consistently printed in all capitals,

probably to facilitate reading by the public and perhaps to make the executioner's task of copying it onto a placard easier, the text of the placard was personalized, containing the offender's name and specific crime" (231); see 232 and 233 for visual examples. The business behind these punishment practices would have included people who made the signs and people who made the effigies. In the case of Marie-Anne and Françoise, would these effigies have been racialized somehow?

35. Moreau de Saint-Méry to Aménaïde Dall'Asta, Aug. 4, 1809, in "Correspondance, 1808–1809."

36. Moreau de Saint-Méry, *Mémoire justificatif,* 34.

37. Moreau de Saint-Méry, *Description de la partie française de l'isle Saint-Domingue,* 42 (quotations). See Valerie Fildes, *Wet Nursing: A History from Antiquity to the Present* (Oxford, 1988).

38. Moreau wrote: "A young woman was nursing her first child. One of her breasts had a crack. She was suffering dreadfully from it. . . . A woman neighbor, seeing this woman fading away, questioned her. She told her the truth, and even went so far as to show her the ailing breast. But when her friend urged her to let the doctor see it, she was refused. Frightened by the danger, she spoke to me about it. I determined to speak to this woman about her condition, using all the discretion demanded by the most violent prejudice, and tell her of the risk she was running, and of the death with which her condition threatened her much-loved little boy. I argued that she was failing in the most sacred duties of nature and religion; and finally I told her that her obstinacy was truly suicide. Speaking as a husband and father, I used such eloquence that the patient was convinced, and promised to entrust herself to the enlightened care of a doctor. . . . although she knew that she owed me the saving of her life and that of her child, this young mother never spoke to me again and didn't even wish to acknowledge my existence." See Roberts and Roberts, *American Journey,* 288. In his state-by-state description of slavery in the United States, written years after his residence there, Moreau also noted the cruel treatment of a young enslaved woman in Charleston who was beaten by her mistress, was jailed, and suffered painful engorgement. He noted: "The unhappy creature, whose breasts, grown big with milk, had caused her severe pain, hastened to empty them so that they would fill with a more recent milk. Then, having washed them, she nursed her child, whom the mistress had made drunk with Madeira wine in order to stop the infant's cries during the six days of the mother's detention" (ibid., 307).

39. See the excellent essays in the special issue on motherhood coedited by Camillia Cowling, Maria Helena Pereira Toledo Machado, Diana Paton, and Emily West, "Mothering Slaves: Motherhood, Childlessness, and the Care of Children in Atlantic Slave Societies," *Slavery and Abolition,* XXXVIII (2017), esp. Cowling et al., "Mothering Slaves: Comparative Perspectives on Motherhood, Childlessness, and the Care of Children in Atlantic Slave Societies," 223–231 (quotation on 226), and Sasha Turner, "The Nameless and the Forgotten: Maternal Grief, Sacred Protection, and the Archive of Slavery," 232–250, which is particularly insightful. Sue Peabody also discusses wet nursing in her multigenerational story of slavery in the Indian Ocean, *Madeleine's Children: Family, Freedom, Secrets, and Lies in France's Indian Ocean Colonies* (New York, 2017).

40. See Vastey's indictment of the behavior of Saint-Domingue's colonists, cited in Chapter 2. As one of his examples of the vulnerability of wet nurses, he documented the horrendous treatment of a Martinican woman named Sophie, who served the Larchevesque-Thibaud family; the husband was an attorney alongside Moreau in Cap Français's Conseil Supérieur. "Having already nursed one of his children, she was nursing a second, when Madame Larchevesque-Thibaud became suspicious of this woman, jealously assuming she was involved with her husband. As proof to the contrary, she insisted that Larchevesque-Thibaud take a pistol and shoot the poor woman; the obliging husband carried out the orders of his fury of a wife." See [Pompée-Valentin], Baron de Vastey, *The Colonial System Unveiled,* ed. and trans. Chris Bongie (Liverpool, U.K., 2014), 111 (quotation), 160 n. 69. I will not continue to catalog the subsequent tortures that were inflicted on Sophie.

41. Moreau de Saint-Méry, *Description de la partie française de l'isle Saint-Domingue,* 42.

42. There is an increasingly extensive body of scholarship about portraiture of the enslaved. See, for example, the excellent collection of essays in Agnes Lugo-Ortiz and Angela Rosenthal, eds., *Slave Portraiture in the Atlantic World* (New York, 2013); as well as Simon Gikandi, *Slavery and the Culture of Taste* (Princeton, N.J., 2011); and Catherine Molineux, *Faces of Perfect Ebony: Encountering Atlantic Slavery in Imperial Britain* (Cambridge, Mass., 2012).

43. Jennifer L. Morgan's discussion of *Portrait of an African Woman Holding a Clock,* which appears on the cover of her book, captures precisely the intentionality and invitation that I see in the nourrice's face. She writes of the portrait: "Her visage conveys nothing if not knowing. She knows who she is in relation to the painter; she knows what she sees. She locks eyes with her viewers and comes close to dismissing us with the turn of her lip—dismissing, perhaps, our questions about who she is. When I look at her, I see someone who understands her own value." See Morgan, *Reckoning with Slavery: Gender, Kinship, and Capitalism in the Early Black Atlantic* (Durham, N.C., 2021), x.

44. Moreau, *Considérations,* 71 n. 1 (quotation). Emily West and R. J. Knight, "Mothers' Milk: Slavery, Wet-Nursing, and Black and White Women in the Antebellum South," *Journal of Southern History,* LXXXIII (February 2017), 37–68, contains a good overview of the relevant literature and discusses the phenomenon of white women's nursing the people they enslaved. In the French Enlightenment context, see Jean Mainil, "Allaitement et contamination: Naissance de la Mère-Nourrice dans le discours médical sous les Lumières," *L'esprit créateur,* XXXVII, no. 3 (Fall 1997), 14–24.

Chapter Five

1. Félix d'Azara, *Essais sur l'histoire naturelle des quadrupèdes de la province du Paraguay . . . ,* trans. M. L. E. Moreau-Saint-Méry, 2 vols. (Paris, 1801), II, 257–263 (hereafter cited as *Essais*). Apparently, Moreau's monkeys created havoc at home—escaping onto the roof, stealing food, and throwing things. Faquin learned how to untie himself and had free rein of the household. On his and Faquin's reconciliation after a week's separation, Moreau wrote, "He jumped on my shoulder, passed his clinging tail around my neck,

placed one of his hands on each cheek, and began to moan and shed tears, staring intently at me. I consoled him as best as I could, and out of the recognition that his expressive affection inspired in me, I promised him a hundred times, almost involuntarily, never to abandon him again" (Il me sauta sur l'épaule, me passa autour du cou sa queue prenante, me plaça une de ses mains sur chaque joue, et se mit à gémir et à répandre des larmes, en me fixant attentivement. Je le consolai de mon mieux, et dans l'espèce de reconnaissance que m'inspirait son expressive affection, je lui promis cent fois, et presque involontairement, de ne le plus abandonner) (ibid., II, 258). Who was master of whom? Did Moreau's servants intentionally kill the monkey by luring him with poisoned pudding? This is pure conjecture; the enslaved had to take care of him, and perhaps they were happy to get him out of the way. Many thanks to Anna Brickhouse for her very helpful comments on this chapter.

2. Ibid., II, 262. Of the regional animal trade, Moreau wrote, "It is there [in the market for whites] that every Sunday . . . one sees displayed . . . all kinds of dry goods and edibles brought from France; scrap metal, pottery, earthenware, haberdashery, etc. One can find jewels, shoes, hats, parrots, monkeys, and almost everything that one can buy in Cap Français" (C'est là [le marché aux Blancs] que chaque dimanche . . . on voit étaler . . . toutes sortes de marchandise sèches et de comestibles apportés de France; ferrailles, poteries, fayancerie, merceries, etc. On y trouve des bijoux, des souliers, des chapeaux, des perroquets, des singes, et presque tout ce qu'on peut acheter au Cap). See Médéric Louis Élie Moreau de Saint-Méry, *La description topographique, physique, civile, politique et historique de la partie française de l'isle Saint-Domingue . . .*, ed. Blanche Maurel and Étienne Taillemite, new ed., 3 vols. (Saint-Denis, France, 2004), I, 316 (hereafter cited as *Description de la partie française de l'isle Saint-Domingue*).

3. Moreau ushered *Essais* into production, and it was available for sale throughout Europe, including Holland, Denmark, Germany, England, Poland, Switzerland, Russia, Sweden, Spain, and multiple cities in France.

4. Elizabeth Alexander, "The Venus Hottentot," in Alexander, *The Venus Hottentot* (Charlottesville, Va., 1990), 3–7. The poem may also be viewed through the Poetry Foundation, https://www.poetryfoundation.org/poems/52111/the-venus-hottentot. For more on Baartman, see Clifton Crais and Pamela Scully's biography *Sara Baartman and the Hottentot Venus: A Ghost Story and a Biography* (Princeton, N.J., 2009). Georges Cuvier argued that there were "three" distinct varieties of human beings. "The Negro race," he wrote, "is marked by a black complexion, crisped or woolly hair, compressed cranium, and a flat nose. The projection of the lower parts of the face, and the thick lips, evidently approximate it to the monkey tribe: the hordes of which it consists have always remained in the most complete state of utter barbarism." See Cuvier, "Varieties of the Human Species," in Cuvier, *The Animal Kingdom Arranged in Conformity with Its Organization . . . The Crustacea, Arachnides, and Insecta, by P. A. Latreille . . .*, trans. H. M'Murtrie, I (New York, 1831), 52, also reprinted in Emmanuel Chukwudi Eze, ed., *Race and the Enlightenment: A Reader* (Malden, Mass., 1997), 104–105. There is extensive work on Baartman, including fictional renditions of her life and art installations. For a discussion of some of these art pieces, see Kayleigh Perkov, "To Know a Hottentot Venus Feminist: Feminist Epistemology and the Artworks Surrounding Sarah Bartman," July 16, 2015, *Aleph*,

http://aleph.humanities.ucla.edu/2015/07/26/to-know-a-hottentot-venus-feminist-feminist
-epistemology-and-the-artworks-surrounding-sarah-bartman/.

5. A summary of Cuvier's report of his dissection explains that he categorized Baartman "with numerous species of monkey since her ears [were] small and weakly formed, as with the orangutan, and she frequently [jutted] her lip outwards in a like manner; likewise, her skull resemble[d] a monkey's more than any other he [had] examined. Even her vivacity [was] translated into rapid and unexpected movements like those of a monkey." See Sadiah Qureshi, "Displaying Sara Baartman, The 'Hottentot Venus,'" *History of Science,* XLII (2004), 233–257, esp. 242.

6. [Pompée-Valentin], Baron de Vastey, *The Colonial System Unveiled,* ed. and trans. Chris Bongie (Liverpool, U.K., 2014), 103; [Pompée-Valentin], Baron de Vastey, *Le système colonial dévoilé* (Cap Haitien, 1814), 31.

7. For more on José Nicolás de Azara, see his obituary by [Alexandre-Maurice Blanc Hauterive, Jean-François de Bourgoing, and Charles-Maurice de Talleyrand-Périgord], *Notice historique sur le chevalier Don Joseph-Nicolas d'Azara, arragonais; Ambassadeur d'Espagne à Paris, mort dans cette ville le 5 pluviose an XII* (n.p., [1804]). In the translator's preface to *Essais,* Moreau commented on José Nicolás de Azara's love for France, stating that "in his sentiments, in his thoughts, Monsieur Azara confuses France with Spain, Spain with France; proof of this is everywhere, even in the fact, so simple in itself, of the priority of the publication of these essays granted to France and the French language" (dans ses sentimens, dans ses pensées, M. le bailli d'Azara confound la France avec l'Espagne, l'Espagne avec la France; que la prevue s'en trouve par-tout, même dans le fait si simple en soi de la priorité de la publication de ces essais accordée à la France et à la langue française) (*Essais,* I, xxxvi). Moreau published *Essais* with Charles Pougens, himself a famous high-end bookshop owner, printer, and translator in Paris. In addition to *Essais,* Moreau claimed to be working on and about to publish a translation of Félix de Azara's "Descripción histórica, phísica, política, y geográfica de la provincia del Paraguay . . . ," what he called "an unedited description of Paraguay" (une description inédite de Paraguay) in two volumes, in octavo format, although he never seems to have published it (*Note des travaux du c[itoy]en Moreau-St.-Méry* [Paris, 1799], 7; *Essais,* I, viii, x). This beautifully handwritten manuscript, dated 1793, is still in the French archives at the Service historique de la Défense at the Château de Vincennes, cataloged as Manuscript 120. I suspect it might have been acquired from an unknown donor at the same time as Moreau's manuscript translation of Abbad y Lasierra's work on Puerto Rico, "Histoire geographique, civile et politique de l'isle de St. Jean-Baptiste de Porto-Rico" (Manuscript 116), also at the Service historique de la Défense, Château de Vincennes. More than two hundred years later, a Spanish edition of Azara's "Descripción" was published based on a manuscript copy in Madrid as Félix de Azara, *Descripción histórica, física, política y geográfica de la provincia del Paraguay: El manuscrito de Madrid, 1793,* ed. Herib Caballero Campos and Dario Solís (Asunción, Paraguay, 2016). Moreau outlined the contents of several of Félix de Azara's manuscripts given to him by José Nicolás de Azara. As the titles were adapted in subsequent French and Spanish editions and translations, it is not completely clear which ones Moreau had access to. Charles A. Walckenaer, who worked on an 1809 French edition of Azara's works, "published based on the author's manuscripts" (publiées d'après les

manuscrits de l'auteur), also seems to have been working with multiple manuscripts, and parts of Azara's "Descripción," above, were included. See Félix de Azara, *Voyages dans l'Amérique méridionale . . .* , ed. Walckenaer, 4 vols. (Paris, 1809). For listings of Moreau's extensive collection of natural histories and travel narratives, see [Moreau de Saint-Méry], *Catalogue of Books, Stationary* [sic]*, Engravings, Mathematical Instruments, Maps, Charts, and Other Goods of Moreau de St. Mery, and Co's. Store, No. 84, South Front-Street, Corner of Walnut* (Philadelphia, 1795).

8. Moreau de Saint-Méry, *Voyage aux États-Unis de l'Amérique, 1793–1798,* ed. Stewart L. Mims (New Haven, Conn., 1913), 400. For plans to transfer the Louisiana Territory back to France from Spain, see the Third Treaty of San Idelfonso, Oct. 1, 1800. Talleyrand was also interested in expanding the borders of French Guiana into Brazil. Félix de Azara had been in Paraguay actively surveying territory contested between the Spanish and Portuguese. He left voluminous correspondence about his long mission there, including maps. For more on this, see chapter 3 of Karen Stolley's work on Azara in Stolley, *Domesticating Empire: Enlightenment in Spanish America* (Nashville, Tenn., 2013); and Jeffrey Alan Erbig, Jr., *Where Caciques and Mapmakers Met: Border Making in Eighteenth-Century South America* (Chapel Hill, N.C., 2020).

9. Christopher P. Iannini, *Fatal Revolutions: Natural History, West Indian Slavery, and the Routes of American Literature* (Williamsburg, Va., and Chapel Hill, N.C, 2012), 15. Iannini continues, "By the end of the [eighteenth] century," natural history "served as the lingua franca of letters, art, and politics in Europe and the Americas. . . . Science traveled primarily along trade routes . . . and with the growth of the triangle trade those routes invariably converged in the sugar islands" (19). His ultimate conclusion is that "natural history is the eighteenth-century genre (or incipient genre) most directly engaged with problems of slavery and finance in its full circumatlantic dimensions" (40). For a detailed assessment of late-eighteenth- and early-nineteenth century debates among prominent intellectuals on both sides of the Atlantic about whether the Americas were allegedly inferior to the Old World, see, for example, Antonello Gerbi, *The Dispute of the New World: The History of a Polemic, 1750–1900,* trans. Jeremy Moyle (Pittsburgh, Pa., 2010).

10. Moreau de Saint-Méry, "Discours préliminaire," in Moreau de Saint-Méry, *Loix et constitutions des colonies françaises de l'Amérique sous le vent . . .* , 6 vols. (Paris, [1784–1790]), I, xv; Jorge Cañizares-Esguerra, *How to Write the History of the New World: Histories, Epistemologies, and Identities in the Eighteenth-Century Atlantic World* (Stanford, Calif., 2001), esp. chap. 4 (204–265). There is an enormous body of scholarship about natural history as a genre and its relationship to science, institution building, and knowledge production. For example, see E. C. Spary's *Utopia's Garden: French National History from Old Regime to Revolution* (Chicago, 2000); and Daniela Bleichmar and Paula De Vos's work, including articles collected in Bleichmar et al., eds., *Science in the Spanish and Portuguese Empires, 1500–1800* (Stanford, Calif., 2009). The special issue "The New Natural History," *Early American Literature,* LIV (2019), includes a very helpful collection of essays, especially Juliane Braun, "Bioprospecting Breadfruit: Imperial Botany, Transoceanic Relations, and the Politics of Translation," 643–671. For some of Moreau's essays on natural history, see his contributions to *Mémoires d'agriculture, d'économie rurale et domestique* published by the Société royale d'agriculture de Paris, including "Procédé pour faire le vin

d'orange," I (Winter, 1789), 29–32; and "Observations sur la culture de la canne à sucre dans les Antilles et plus particulièrement de celle d'Otaïti," I (1799), 277–290. He worked as a corresponding member of the society and later as a local member, contributing pieces between 1788 and 1798.

11. Moreau published *Description topographique et politique de la partie espagnole de l'isle Saint-Domingue* in Philadelphia in 1796. It was translated as *A Topographical and Political Description of the Spanish Part of Saint-Domingo . . .* (1796) by the famed British propagandist William Cobbett, who was also living in Philadelphia at the time. The work followed the format of much natural history, containing a wealth of information about Spanish settlement, local customs, and Moreau's claim to have found the remains of Christopher Columbus in Santo Domingo's cathedral. It documents Moreau's belief in the importance of the neighboring part of the island to the French side—as a market for cattle, a dangerous asylum for runaway enslaved people, and a potential area of agricultural development. The Spanish ceded Santo Domingo to the French as part of the 1795 Treaty of Basel, timing that Moreau believed made his production of the book all the more relevant. For a discussion of the publication, see Maria Cristina Fumagalli, "Landscaping Hispaniola: Moreau de Saint-Méry's Border Politics," *New West Indian Guide / Nieuwe West-Indische Gids,* LXXXV (2011), 169–190. Moreau's translation of Andreas Everardus van Braam Houckgeest's account of his journey to meet the Chinese emperor Qianlong was published in Philadelphia in 1797 and 1798 (*Voyage de l'ambassade de la Compagnie des Indes orientales hollandaises, vers l'empereur de la Chine, dans les années 1794 et 1795 . . . Le tout tiré du journal d'André Everard van Braam Houckgeest . . . ,* 2 vols.). For his reference to a publication on Jamaica, see Moreau's *Note des travaux du c[itoy]en Moreau-St.-Méry,* 7. This manuscript on Jamaica is not extant, but it appears he was working with William Beckford's *A Descriptive Account of the Island of Jamaica* (1790), an account of a so-called moderate slaveowner's experience managing his enslaved workers on his estates. Beckford invited his friend George Robertson, the painter, to join him in Jamaica, and Robertson produced many famous landscapes of the island, some depicting the enslaved. Moreau also would have been familiar with the work of Edward Long and Bryan Edwards, who wrote what would become canonical descriptions of the island in the 1770s and 1790s. He sold the latter's work in his bookstore. See [Moreau de Saint-Méry], *Catalogue of Books,* 9. For his work on Ouaire, see Moreau de Saint-Méry, "Observations sur le Royaume de Ouaire, à la Côte-d'Or en Afrique," in *Mémoires du Musée de Paris,* Belles lettres et arts, no. 1 (Paris, 1785), 58–59. Additionally, Moreau wrote many works on Italy. For example, see M. L. E. Moreau de Saint-Méry, *Historique états de parme, 1749–1808,* ed. Carla Corradi Martini (Parma, Italy, 2003).

12. Moreau's manuscript copy of *Essais* is dated 1800 (Archives nationales d'outre-mer, Aix-en-Provence, France [ANOM], Collection Moreau de Saint-Méry [Ser. F3], 118). See Francisco de Goya, *Retrato de Félix de Azara,* 1805, oil on canvas, Museo Goya: Colección Ibercajan–Museo Camó Aznar, Zaragoza, Spain. There is a large bibliography on Azara's work. For instance, see publications by Enrique Álvarez López, including "Félix de Azara, precursor de Darwin," *Revista de Occidente,* XLIII (1934), 149–166.

13. For more on Spanish and Spanish American natural history operations, see Daniela Bleichmar's elegant discussion of overseas expeditions and the competition and

communication networks that existed between naturalists and patrons in Spain and the West Indies, Chile, Peru, New Granada, New Spain, and the Philippines, particularly her elaboration of the workings of "visual epistemology" in Bleichmar, *Visible Empire: Botanical Expeditions and Visual Culture in the Hispanic Enlightenment* (Chicago, 2012), 21 ("visual epistemology"). Both the manuscript and print editions of *Essais* include a letter from Cuvier, the comte de Lacépède, and Richard, then employed by the Institut national des sciences et arts, stating the value of the publication. Moreau spent time with many renowned naturalists during these years, including the ornithologist Louis Jean Pierre Vieillot, who had been his companion on the fraught, disease-ridden boat trip from Philadelphia to France in 1798, and the entomology specialist Palisot de Beauvois. Two of Vieillot's daughters died from fever while on board. "What a scene! Where to flee! Death horribly was everywhere in the narrow confines in which we were imprisoned." See Kenneth Roberts and Anna M. Roberts, eds. and trans., *Moreau de Saint Méry's American Journey [1793–1798]* (New York, 1947), 365–366 (quotation on 366). Palisot de Beauvois is another interesting character. He traveled with the ship captain and slave trader Jean-François Landolphe to the Warri Kingdom, came down with yellow fever while there, and ended up on a ship to Saint-Domingue, where he had family. He continued his study of insects in Saint-Domingue and eventually made his way to Philadelphia, where he joined Moreau as a member of the American Philosophical Society. Moreau's association with Beauvois and Landolphe provides a clear example of the intersections of natural history, slavery, and intellectual societies. See A[mbrose]-M[arie]-F[rançois]-J[oseph] Palisot de Beauvois, *Insectes recueillis en Afrique et en Amérique, dans les royaumes d'Oware et de Benin, a Saint-Domingue et dans les États-Unis, pendant les années 1786–1797* (Paris, 1805).

14. *Note des travaux du c[itoy]en Moreau-St.-Méry,* 7; Moreau de Saint-Méry, *Danse . . .* (Philadelphia, 1796). Originally published in Madrid in 1788, Abbad y Lasierra's work was reissued in 1866 with extensive annotations by the abolitionist and public intellectual José Julián Acosta y Calbo, who claimed to have found a copy as a young man in the Cuban literatus Domingo del Monte's Madrid library. See Iñigo Abbad y Lasierra, *Historia geográfica, civil y natural de la Isla de San Juan Bautista de Puerto-Rico,* [ed.] Jose Julian de Acosta y Calbo, new ed. (Puerto Rico, 1866). Moreau's fascination with the text is further indication of its hemispheric American importance.

15. *Essais,* I, lxviii, lxxix.

16. Ibid., I, 206n, 266, 282, II, 81, 320n.

17. Ibid., I, 152.

18. Ibid., I, xxix–xxx, xlviii–xlix. Although Moreau did not subscribe to Buffon's belief in the degeneration of American species, he had great admiration for him. He believed that Buffon's prose "renders sensible to vulgar minds the most hidden secrets of this vast universe. By adopting him as a worthy painter, nature lends him her colors; pictures, both the most sublime and the most endearing, are born under his brushes; the man least disposed to give in to enthusiasm cannot defend himself from a kind of rapture" (rend sensibles pour les esprits vulgaires les secrets les plus cachés de ce vaste univers. En l'adoptant comme un peintre digne d'elle, la nature lui prête ses couleurs; les tableaux tout-à-la-fois les plus sublimes et les plus attachans, naissent sous ses pinceaux: l'homme le moins disposé à céder à l'enthousiasme, ne peut se défendre d'une sorte de ravissement)

(ibid., I, xix–xx). This admiration led him to feel discomfort at Azara's critques of Buffon: "I will nevertheless go so far as to confess that I have not always found myself indifferent to what the author has said about Buffon. A feeling that is perhaps national pride . . . even made me regret that the reproaches of the Spanish naturalist were so frequent, and I avow, without shame, too often well-founded, although there were also many that lack solidity" (J'irai néanmoins jusqu'à confesser que je ne me suis pas toujours trouvé indifférent à ce que l'auteur a dit du Buffon. Un sentiment qui est peut-être de la fierté nationale . . . m'a même fait regretter que les reproches du naturaliste espagnol fussent aussi fréquens, et, je l'avoue sans honte, trop souvent fondés, quoiqu'il y en ait aussi beaucoup que manquent de solidité) (ibid., I, xviii–xix). For more on Azara and his work with the Real Gabinete, see Helen Cowie, "A Creole in Paris and a Spaniard in Paraguay: Geographies of Natural History in the Hispanic World (1750–1808)," *Journal of Latin American Geography*, X, no. 1 (2011), 175–197.

19. On Moreau's Latin proficiency, see M. Fournier-Pescay, *Discours prononcé aux obsèques de M. Moreau de Saint-Méry, le 30 janvier 1819* ([Paris], 1819), 3–4. For more on translation theories in the eighteenth century and the move toward French as a lingua franca, see Fania Oz-Salzberger, "Translation," in Alan Charles Kors, ed., *Oxford Encyclopedia of the Enlightenment,* IV (Oxford, 2003), 181–188.

20. *Essais,* I, xxvii; Oz-Salzberger, "Translation," in Kors, ed., *Oxford Encyclopedia of the Enlightenment,* IV, 183. Jennifer Marie Forsythe's excellent work on Inca Garcilaso de la Vega's *La Florida del Inca* considers these shifts in eighteenth-century translational practices. See Forsythe, *"La Florida del Inca* and the Florida of the Others: The Multilingual Afterlives of Garcilaso's Florida" (Ph.D. diss., University of California Los Angeles, 2019).

21. Susan Bassnett and Harish Trivedi, "Introduction: Of Colonies, Cannibals, and Vernaculars," in Bassnett and Trivedi, eds., *Post-Colonial Translation: Theory and Practice* (London, 1999), 6. The volume coedited by Doris Y. Kadish and Françoise Massardier-Kenney, *Translating Slavery,* I, *Gender and Race in French Abolitionist Writing, 1780–1830,* 2d ed., rev. (Kent, Ohio, 2009), contains several pieces that describe in detail the interconnectedness of race, gender, and translation practices around the issue of slavery; for Berman's position on translation, see 75.

22. *Essais,* I, viii. Moreau described both the *soumis* (conquered) tribes of the area, including the Guaraní and those never conquered by the Spanish, the "*non-soumis.*" He was clear about choosing to translate *"barbare"* as such. For his explanation of the use of these terms, see *Essais,* I, lxx–lxxi. For a helpful discussion of Guaraní, see Yliana Rodriguez, "Spanish-Guarani Diglossia in Colonial Paraguay: A Language Undertaking," in Brigette Weber, ed., *The Linguistic Heritage of Colonial Practice* (Berlin, 2019).

23. *Essais,* I, li, II, 74. For examples of how Indigenous knowledge was brought into European natural history as a valuable source of information, see Gordon M. Sayre's excellent article *"Michipichik* and the Walrus: Anishinaabe Natural History in the Seventeenth-Century Work of Louis Nicolas," *Journal for Early Modern Cultural Studies,* XVII, no. 4 (Fall 2017), 21–48. There are exceptions in Azara's work to his general unwillingness to incorporate Indigenous knowledge into his own beliefs, though nowhere near in complexity to the melding of ideas that Sayre describes in Nicolas's work. For example, Azara took exception to the German naturalist Georg Marcgrave's name for the peccary *(pécari).* He

preferred the Guaraní name *Caaigouara,* noting that "one should say *Caaigouara*" (l'on doit dire *Caaigouara*), since "*Caaigoua* means *small mountain,* and *ra* means *imitation* or *resemblance;* and the Pécari has nothing that can reveal an idea of its resemblance more than of its back as the top of a mountain" (*Caaigoua* signifie *mont,* et *ra* signifie *imitation, ressemblance;* or, le Pécari n'a rien qui puisse réveiller une idée de ressemblance, si ce n'est celle de son dos avec la cime d'une montagne) (*Essais,* I, 36).

24. Moreau explained thusly why he chose to include this appendix: "That is how, after demonstrating to myself that it was necessary to adopt a constant and uniform pronunciation of the Guaraní words, I passed their absolute value into our language, and I believed, besides, that I should provide an alphabetical list of these words that appear in the work, with their pronunciation well figured and clearly indicated. Buffon voiced . . . his opinion on the advantages of this uniformity of pronunciation; and this idea helped me make up my mind" (C'est ainsi qu'après m'être démontré à moi-même qu'il fallait adopter une prononciation constante et uniforme des mots Guaranis, j'ai fait passer dans notre langue leur valeur absolue, et que j'ai cru devoir donner en outre une liste alphabétique de ces mots qui se présentent dans l'ouvrage, avec leur prononciation bien figurée, et clairement indiquée. Buffon a exprimé . . . son opinion sur les avantages de cette uniformité de prononciation; et cette idée a achevé de me décider). See *Essais,* I, xxviii.

25. Sean P. Harvey, *Native Tongues: Colonialism and Race from Encounter to the Reservation* (Cambridge, Mass., 2015), 5, 19–20, 139; P[ierre François Xavier] de Charlevoix, *Journal of a Voyage to North-America . . . ,* I (London, 1761), 299; John Heckewelder to Peter S. DuPonceau, July 24, 1818, in "A Correspondence between the Rev. John Heckewelder, of Bethlehem, and Peter S. DuPonceau, Esq. . . . ," *Transactions of the Historical and Literary Committee of the American Philosophical Society,* I (Philadelphia, 1818), 396. See also Feliciano Pacheco, AL Central Residences, Vice-Province 1660, Huai'an, July 19, 1661, BAJA 49-V-14:704r, quoted in Liam Matthew Brockey, *Journey to the East: The Jesuit Mission to China, 1579–1724* (Cambridge, Mass., 2007), 245 ("language"); and Th[omas] Herbert, *A Relation of Some Yeares Travaile . . . into Afrique and the Greater Asia . . .* (London, 1634), 16 ("Apes"). In a Latin American context, Azara and many of his predecessors and contemporaries attempted to learn Indigenous languages. From Jesuits who compiled extensive vocabularies in the sixteenth and seventeenth centuries to natural historians in the eighteenth and nineteenth centuries, those who acquired knowledge of local languages had many strategic reasons to do so. Londa Schiebinger writes of how "La Condamine, Pouppé-Desports, and Alexander Humboldt (1769–1859) were all keenly interested in local languages. La Condamine spoke what he called 'the Peruvian language' and even owned a 1614 'quichoa' (Quechua) dictionary. . . . Humboldt, who traveled extensively in present-day Venezuela and Colombia, prepared a dictionary of the Chaymas language that consisted of only about 140 words." See Schiebinger, "Prospecting for Drugs: European Naturalists in the West Indies," in Schiebinger and Claudia Swan, eds., *Colonial Botany: Science, Commerce, and Politics in the Early Modern World* (Philadelphia, 2005), 127–128. Language learning was part of a natural historian's toolbox, and some were more proficient at their studies than others.

26. Azara, *Voyages dans l'Amérique méridionale,* ed. Walckenaer, II, 58; *Essais,* I, lvii ("l'orthographe *Guaranique*"), 35 ("prononcent le *z*"), 253 ("*Sarigoué*"). There are many

indications in Azara's published work that he had learned grammatical rules of Guaraní and that he used them regularly. For example, he noted that adding a *y* made a word diminutive. See *Essais,* I, 107. He also noted that many Spaniards living in the region had acquired the language, especially those born to Guaraní mothers, and that Guaraní became their dominant language (ibid., 107–108). Azara's comments about the supposed linguistic poverty of Guaraní ignore, as Sean P. Harvey has observed, that "travelers, traders, and others did not always realize that they were taking down or learning languages that had been dumbed down, both for their own benefit and to allow Indians to preserve a desirable cultural distance. This led to dismissive appraisals of a given language's worth, and by the mid-eighteenth century, the learned reinforced such views." See Harvey, *Native Tongues,* 26. Azara claimed to have learned multiple Indigenous languages, although some scholars have doubted how proficient he might have been. When describing the language of the Pampas tribe, for example, Azara stated that it "has no nasal or guttural sound" (il n'a aucun son nasal, ni gutturale) and could be "written with the letters of our alphabet" (qu'on pourrait l'écrire avec les lettres de notre alphabet). He said that this group was "less silent than other nations, and their voices more sonorous and full" (moins silencieux que les autres nations, est que leur voix et plus sonore et plus pleine) (Azara, *Voyages dans l'Amérique méridionale,* ed. Walckenaer, II, 41).

27. Azara, *Voyages dans l'Amérique méridionale,* ed. Walckenaer, II, 58. For Moreau's citation of Garcilaso de la Vega, see his manuscript copy of *Essais* in ANOM, F3, 118 and 119, and *Essais,* I, 10. Moreau also cites European naturalists and all their names for the mborebi. For his large personal collection of scholarship on Latin America, see *Catalogue des livres et manuscrits de la bibliothèque de feu M. Moreau de Saint-Méry, . . . dont la vente se fera le mercredi 15 décembre 1819 . . .* ([Paris], 1819), items 1137, 776, 778, 1137. For early Jesuit grammars and catechisms, see, for example, Antonio Ruiz [de Montoya], *Tesoro de la lengua Guarani* (Madrid, 1639), published in Paris and Leipzig in 1876. Ruiz's publication was an eight-hundred-plus-page listing of Guaraní words, sample phrases, detailed explanations about parts of speech such as particles, and relevant Spanish translations.

28. *Essais,* I, lix, lxvii.

29. El Inca Garcilaso de la Vega, *Comentarios reales de los incas,* ed. Miró Quesada Sosa, I (Caracas, 1985), 15, translated in Anna Brickhouse, *The Unsettlement of America: Translation, Interpretation, and the Story of Don Luis de Velasco, 1560–1945* (New York, 2015), 35–36. Brickhouse quotes Margarita Zamora, *Language, Authority, and Indigenous History in the "Comentarios reales de los incas"* (Cambridge, U.K., 2005), 63, 67.

30. Stolley, *Domesticating Empire,* 2.

31. For examples of Azara's noting that people were giving him information about animals, and a reference to his enslaved man Francisco, see *Essais,* I, 74 ("m'a dit," "m'ont dit"), 349 ("m'ont dit"), II, 102 ("Mon nègre Francisque"). Azara echoed Moreau in his commentary about how the people he enslaved cared for him so much that they did not want their freedom, also suggesting that slavery as it was practiced in Paraguay was much less difficult for the enslaved than it was for people in other parts of the Americas. He wrote, "None of mine [enslaved people] wish to accept freedom except by force" (Aucun des miens ne voulut l'accepter que par force). See Azara, *Voyages dans l'Amérique méridionale,* ed. Walckenaer, II, 270.

32. For a discussion of Azara as an "isolated Spanish genius," see Barbara G. Beddall, "'Un Naturalista Original': Don Félix de Azara, 1746–1821," *Journal of the History of Biology,* VIII (1975), 15–66; and Beddall, "The Isolated Spanish Genius—Myth or Reality? Félix de Azara and the Birds of Paraguay," *Journal of the History of Biology,* XVI (1983), 225–258. For more on how British naturalists made use of the knowledge of their informants, see Kathleen S. Murphy, "Translating the Vernacular: Indigenous and African Knowledge in the Eighteenth-Century British Atlantic," *Atlantic Studies,* VIII (2011), 29–48. On the Jesuit reductions, Miguel de Asúa writes: "By the first decade of the eighteenth century, 100,000 Guaraní, 150 Jesuits and 1300 black slaves lived in the missions. The Jesuits purchased black slaves from the English South Sea Company in Buenos Aires. In 1767 there were a total of 3164 slaves working for the Society of Jesus in Paraguay: 1043 in Córdoba, 381 in Buenos Aires and 570 in Asunción." His study on Jesuit knowledge production in the region was extremely helpful as I researched this chapter. See Asúa, *Science in the Vanished Arcadia: Knowledge of Nature in the Jesuit Missions of Paraguay and Río de la Plata* (Leiden, Netherlands, 2014), 17, citing Nicholas P. Cushner, *Jesuit Ranches and the Agrarian Development of Colonial Argentina, 1650–1767* (Albany, N.Y., 1983), 99–113. Asúa also notes, "The fact remains that despite Azara's priority claims, more than a century before he began his researches, Jesuit authors had created a kaleidoscopic and richly textured image of the landscape, peoples and creatures of those lands" (27). He asserts that Azara had little respect for this work. The research of scholars, including Susan Scott Parrish, *American Curiosity: Cultures of Natural History in the Colonial British Atlantic World* (Williamsburg, Va., and Chapel Hill, N.C., 2006), Caroline Winterer, *American Enlightenments: Pursuing Happiness in the Age of Reason* (New Haven, Conn., 2016), and Londa Schiebinger, *Secret Cures of Slaves: People, Plants, and Medicine in the Eighteenth-Century Atlantic World* (Stanford, Calif., 2017), has done much to elucidate the networks of informants, many Black and Indigenous, who facilitated the work of prominent European and American naturalists.

33. Beddall, "Isolated Spanish Genius," *Journal of the History of Biology,* XVI (1983), 233 ("animals"), cited in Stolley, *Domesticating Empire,* who calls him an "Aragonese Doctor Doolittle" (209 n. 62); Azara, *Voyages dans l'Amérique méridionale,* ed. Walckenaer, I, xxvi–xxvii ("climat brulant"), II, 59 ("mediocre"), 261 ("gens de couleur"), 263 (mulâtre, métis), 268 ("connaisseurs"). As with *Essais,* or *Apuntamientos para la historia natural de los quadrúpedos del Paragüay y Rio de la Plata,* multiple editions of Azara's work were published in Spanish and French. In North America, as was the case in all colonial contexts, men also sought to develop these relationships with Native women to develop their linguistic skills. Sean P. Harvey writes: "Men from Canada to Carolina frequently sought to form close relationships with women who would live with them, dress pelts and skins, provide valuable kinship connections, and teach them Native words and ways. The surveyor John Lawson rarely found British traders 'without an *Indian* Female for his Bed[-]fellow,' archly reporting that this 'Correspondence makes them learn the *Indian* Tongue much the sooner.'" See Harvey, *Native Tongues,* 24. See also Hugh Talmage Lefler, ed., *A New Voyage to Carolina by John Lawson* (Chapel Hill, N.C., 1967), 35–36.

34. Elizabeth Polcha, "Voyeur in the Torrid Zone: John Gabriel Stedman's *Narrative of*

a Five Years Expedition against the Revolted Negroes of Surinam, 1773–1838," Early American Literature, LIV (2019), 675–676. As Sharon Block writes in her work on sexual assault in colonial North America, "Men's racial and class identities largely determined whether they could coerce sex undetected and unpunished, just as women's identities determined their vulnerability to men's sexual force. Such identities did not exist independent of life experiences but could be generated through these very sexual interactions. Elite white masculinity did not just allow powerful men to possibly avoid criminal prosecution for rape; it also helped such men reshape coercion into the appearance of consent before, during, and after a sexual attack." The "appearance" of consent existed on a spectrum that also included the display of public sexualized violence as a means of asserting control in the communities in which Azara traveled. There is an extensive bibliography on sexual violence in the colonial context. See Block, *Rape and Sexual Power in Early America* (Williamsburg, Va., and Chapel Hill, N.C., 2006), 4. See also Anne McClintock, *Imperial Leather: Race, Gender, and Sexuality in the Colonial Conquest* (New York, 1995); and Ann Laura Stoler, *Carnal Knowledge and Imperial Power: Race and the Intimate in Colonial Rule* (Berkeley, Calif., 2002).

35. Moreau de Saint-Méry, *Description de la partie française de l'isle Saint-Domingue,* I, 104–105; Rebecca Earle, "The Pleasures of Taxonomy: Casta Paintings, Classification, and Colonialism," *William and Mary Quarterly,* 3d Ser., LXXIII (2016), 427–466.

36. Gayatri Chakravorty Spivak, "The Politics of Translation," in Michèle Barrett and Anne Phillips, eds., *Destabilizing Theory: Contemporary Feminist Debates* (Stanford, Calif., 1992), 181; Pete Sigal, Zeb Tortorici, and Neil L. Whitehead, eds., *Ethnopornography: Sexuality, Colonialism, and Archival Knowledge* (Durham, N.C., 2020), 1–2.

37. *Essais,* II, 262–263.

38. Many thanks to the sociologist and poet Elias Caurey for the translation from Spanish into Bolivian Guaraní. Thanks also to Bret Gustafson and Nancy Postero for putting us into contact.

39. *Note des travaux du c[itoy]en Moreau-St.-Méry,* 7; Iñigo Abbad y Lasierra, "Histoire geographique, civile et politique de l'isle de St. Jean-Baptiste de Porto-Rico," trans. Moreau de Saint-Méry, Manuscript 116, Service historique de la Défense, Château de Vincennes.

40. Moreau de Saint-Méry, *Description de la partie française de l'isle Saint-Domingue,* I, 63; [Richard de Tussac], *Cri des colons contre un ouvrage de M. L'Evèque et Senateur Gregoire . . .* (Paris, 1810), 292, cited in Laurent Dubois, David Garner, and Mary Caton Lingold, "The Haitian Banza," Banjology, https://sites.duke.edu/banjology/the-banjo -in-haiti/the-haitian-banza/. In his aforementioned publication on the Warri Kingdom in West Africa, Moreau wrote about the importance of dance, music, and feasting to funerary traditions. He mentioned that "a drum, banzas, triangular cymbals and scrapers, mingle their discordant and monotonous sounds" (un tambour, des banzas, des cymballes triangulaires et des échalettes, mêlent leurs sons discordans et monotones). He added a footnote to his descriptions of African performative mourning rituals that noted similar traditions in the French Caribbean, saying, "The custom of rejoicing on the occasion of funerals is common to several peoples of Africa. They brought it to the French West Indies, and notably to Saint-Domingue, where the death of a Black person usually brings a meal that follows dancing" (L'usage de se réjouir à l'occasion des funérailles est commun à

plusieurs peoples d'Afrique. Ils l'ont apporté dans les Antilles Françaises, et notamment à Saint-Domingue, où la mort d'un Nègre amène ordinairement un repas que suit la danse). We have seen that Moreau paid for these festivities when Castor, a man he enslaved, passed away. See Moreau de Saint-Méry, "Observations sur le Royaume de Ouaire," in *Mémoires du Musée de Paris,* 58–59.

41. See Santa Arias, "Looking to the Southeast Antilles: Iñigo Abbad y Lasierra's Geopolitical Thought in His *Historia geográfica, civil y natural de la Isla de San Juan Bautista de Puerto Rico* (1788)," *Colonial Latin American Review,* XXIV (2015), 17–35 (quotation on 18). Santa Arias shares my interest in how interisland travel, in this case Abbad y Lasierra's trips to Trinidad and Martinique, helped inform the pan-Caribbean interests of Moreau and Abbad y Lasierra. For more on hispanophone Caribbean natural history and its connections to costumbrista literature from the 1830s through the early twentieth century, see Daylet Domínguez, "Cuadros de costumbres en Cuba y Puerto Rico: De la historia natural y la literatura de viajes a las ciencias sociales," *Revista hispánica moderna,* LXIX (2016), 133–149.

42. Abbad y Lasierra, "Histoire geographique, civile et politique de l'isle de St. Jean-Baptiste de Porto-Rico," trans. Moreau de Saint-Méry, Manuscript 116, Service historique de la Défense, Château de Vincennes. In the 1797 Battle of San Juan, a French visitor to Puerto Rico, the naturalist André Ledru, in service to the Paris Natural History Museum, wrote a memoir of the fight against the British. The manuscript, "Relation . . . ," is folded into the back of Moreau's volume on Puerto Rico, with a note from the author in 1807 verifying it was written in 1798.

43. This burial site supposedly held the remains of twenty-four Spaniards, killed by the local Taino and interred according to their customs. See Moreau de Saint-Méry, *Description de la partie française de l'isle Saint-Domingue,* I, 95, 212–215.

44. Moreau de Saint-Méry, *Description de la partie française de l'isle Saint-Domingue,* III, 1407. On the human remains collected by the Cercle des Philadelphes, see the entry for "Caraïbes and *crâne*" in Chapter 1.

45. Moreau de Saint-Méry, *Description de la partie française de l'isle Saint-Domingue,* I, 94–95. Joan [Colin] Dayan memorably writes about Moreau's racial taxonomies: "Stranger than any supernatural fiction, and surely one of the most remarkable legalistic fantasies of the New World, the radical irrationality of Moreau's method demonstrates to what lengths the imagination can go if driven by racial prejudice. The figures of blackness imagined by the white colonialist exposed how unnatural were the attempts to sustain 'natural' distinctions between races of men." See Dayan, "Codes of Law and Bodies of Color," *New Literary History,* XXVI (1995), 300.

Chapter Six

1. [Louis Narcisse] Baudry des Lozières, *Second voyage à la Louisiane, faisant suite au premier de l'auteur de 1794 à 1798 . . . ,* 2 vols. (Paris, 1803), II, 115. The "Dictionnaire ou Vocabulaire Congo" appears as an appendix in the second volume (72–146). Though eighteenth-century French sources spelled Congo with a *C,* I have opted to use the more modern Kongo. Kikongo is itself an umbrella name for a large cluster of Bantu family

languages in West Central Africa. For a very helpful overview of the mobilization of
Kongo in Africa and the Americas, see Wyatt MacGaffey, "Constructing a Kongo Identity: Scholarship and Mythopoesis," *Comparative Studies in Society and History,* LVIII
(2016), 159–180. Much excellent linguistic work has been done on Kikongo languages.
For an overview, see Gilles-Maurice de Schryver et al., "Introducing a State-of-the-Art
Phylogenetic Classification of the Kikongo Language Cluster," *Africana Linguistica,* XXI
(2015), 87–163; and Koen Bostoen and Schryver, "Seventeenth-Century Kikongo Is Not
the Ancestor of Present-Day Kikongo," in Bostoen and Inge Brinkman, eds., *The Kongo
Kingdom: The Origins, Dynamics, and Cosmopolitan Culture of an African Polity* (Cambridge, 2018), 60–102.

2. Linda M. Heywood, ed., *Central Africans and Cultural Transformations in the American Diaspora* (New York, 2002), 41. See also John K. Thornton, "'I Am the Subject of
the King of Congo': African Political Ideology and the Haitian Revolution," *Journal of
World History,* IV (1993), 185. He cites David Geggus's work on plantation inventories to
say that in the 1780s the "'Congos' made up 60 percent of the slaves in the North Province, where the revolution began, and about the same percentage in the south" (ibid., 185,
185n). For information on the Kongolese population in North America, see Winifred
Kellersberger Vass, *The Bantu Speaking Heritage of the United States* (Los Angeles, 1979);
and Michael A. Gomez, *Exchanging Our Country Marks: The Transformation of African
Identities in the Colonial and Antebellum South* (Chapel Hill, N.C., 1998). Gomez in-
corporates the work of Gwendolyn Midlo Hall, Philip D. Curtin, Peter H. Wood, and
Paul Lovejoy on demographics. On the Kongolese Atlantic, see the essays in Heywood,
ed., *Central Africans and Cultural Transformations,* esp. Hein Vanhee, "Central African
Popular Christianity and the Making of Haitian Vodou Religion," 243–264, and Terry
Rey, "Kongolese Catholic Influences on Haitian Popular Catholicism: A Sociohistorical Exploration," 265–285; Heywood and Thornton, eds., *Central Africans, Atlantic Creoles, and the Foundation of the Americas, 1585–1660* (New York, 2007); Jason R. Young,
*Rituals of Resistance: African Atlantic Religion in Kongo and the Lowcountry South in
the Era of Slavery* (Baton Rouge, La., 2007); Maureen Warner-Lewis, *Central Africa in
the Caribbean: Transcending Time, Transforming Cultures* (Mona, Jamaica, 2002), esp.
chap. 11; James H. Sweet, *Recreating Africa: Culture, Kinship, and Religion in the African-
Portuguese World, 1441–1770* (Chapel Hill, N.C., 2003). Christina Frances Mobley uses a
historical linguistics approach to examine Baudry's vocabulary as a principal source for the
word lists she generates to evaluate the geographic origins of Kongolese enslaved people in
Saint-Domingue and the continued importance of their cultural forms on the island. See
Mobley, "The Kongolese Atlantic: Central African Slavery and Culture from Mayombe
to Haiti" (Ph.D. diss., Duke University, 2015). Historical linguistics methodologies have
a tremendous amount to teach us about the colonial Americas through expert analysis
of African language sources. The study of words allows discussions about place of origin,
migration, how people viewed their surroundings, and why they might have chosen to
act in certain ways. See Kathryn M. de Luna, "Sounding the African Atlantic," *William
and Mary Quarterly,* 3d Ser., LXXVIII (2021), 581–616, for an example of how historical
figures such as Makandal can be reevaluated through an analysis of naming practices and

what these practices demonstrate about the intellectual and social practices of his enslaved community. Her close reading of the morphology of his name allows her to make a deeply nuanced and evocative "set of arguments about the mechanisms by which the world is made right," according to Makandal's peers (598).

3. More than fifteen years ago, Robin D. G. Kelley remarked that he was "intrigued by recent discussions of how 'globalization' has pushed United States scholars to think beyond the nation-state, develop 'transnational' and international approaches, and reconsider 'diaspora' as an analytical framework," but "Black studies, Chicano/a studies, and Asian American studies were diasporic from their inception" (Kelley, "'But a Local Phase of a World Problem': Black History's Global Vision, 1883–1950," in "The Nation and Beyond: Transnational Perspectives on United States History; A Special Issue," *Journal of American History,* LXXXVI [1999], 1045). See also Donald Pease, "Introduction: Re-mapping the Transnational Turn," in Winfried Fluck, Pease, and John Carlos Rowe, eds., *Re-framing the Transnational Turn in American Studies* (Hanover, N.H., 2011), 1–46.

4. L[ou]is-N[arci]sse B[audr]y Deslozières, *Les égaremens du nigrophilisme* (Paris, 1802), 4; Baudry des Lozières, *Second voyage à la Louisiane,* I, 185. For one example of Baudry serving as Moreau's power of attorney, see the manumission act for Angélique and her two children, "Acte de liberté," Mar. 17, 1783, Archives nationales d'outre-mer, Aix-en-Provence, Notariat Saint-Domingue, 542, Grimperel, acting notary. A number of advertisements in the *Affiches américaines* announced that Baudry would be acting as Moreau's representative in Saint-Domingue while the latter was abroad. On the Cercle des Philadelphes, see James E. McClellan III, *Colonialism and Science: Saint Domingue in the Old Regime* (Baltimore, 1992), esp. part 3; Albert Depréaux, "Le commandant des Lozières et la phalange de Crête-dragons," *Revue de l'histoire des colonies françaises,* XVII, no. 1 (1924), 41.

5. Baudry des Lozières, *Second voyage à la Louisiane,* I, iii (dedication), II, 73; B[audr]y Deslozières, *Les égaremens du nigrophilisme,* iii, 3 ("périraient de faim"), 4 ("odieux"), 17 ("barbarians"), 28 ("libérateurs"), 60 ("que par le nom"). A close colleague of Baudry's reports that, when Baudry was asked to legally represent the interests of wealthy "*mulâtres* and free Blacks" before the National Assembly, he replied, "I am white, and I stick to the cause of the whites. . . . I want the best for you, but I also wish for you to stay in the place that nature and social customs indicate." G[abriel] C[hastenet-]d'Esterre, *Précis historique sur le régiment de Crête, dragons; suivi d'une notice sur la vie militaire, politique et privée de M. Baudry-Deslozières, colonel-inspecteur dudit régiment,* 3d ed. ([Paris?], 1804), 311. For a truly nauseating summary of Baudry's politics, in particular his thoughts about life on the African continent and enslaved Africans when they first arrived in the colonies and their subsequent "acclimation," see *Les égaremens du nigrophilisme,* 28–38.

6. Madame Catherine Baudry des Lozières to Moreau de Saint-Méry, Feb. 20, 1789, in Moreau de Saint-Méry, *Mémoire justificatif* ([Paris, 1790]), 114; Ada Ferrer, *Freedom's Mirror: Cuba and Haiti in the Age of Revolution* (New York, 2014), 1. Baudry claimed that his properties in Saint-Domingue were valued at 19.500,00 and 1.280,00 French francs (10 percent of the estimated value of the properties in 1789) when he requested indemnification for his lost estate according to 1826 French law. See Ministère des finances, *État*

détaillé des liquidations opérées . . . par la Commission chargée de répartir l'indemnité at-
tribuée aux anciens colons de Saint-Domingue, en exécution de la loi du 30 avril 1826, etc.
(Paris, 1828), microfilm, I, 260–261, 274–275. Bibliographic information on the indemnity
claimed by Baudry appears courtesy of Oliver Gliech, www.domingino.de.

7. B[audr]y Deslozières, *Les égaremens du nigrophilisme,* ix–x; Depréaux, "Le commandant des Lozières," *Revue de l'histoire des colonies françaises,* XVII, no. 1 (1924), 32. Baudry
noted that his former enslaved workers saved his wife and daughter on several occasions
and that a Black family, the Lafleurs, hid them for three days in the forest from a group of
petits blancs (Baudry des Lozières, *Second voyage à la Louisiane,* I, 395).

8. Kenneth Roberts and Anna M. Roberts, eds. and trans., *Moreau de Saint Méry's
American Journey [1793–1798]* (Garden City, N.Y., 1947), 233, 255. For more on Moreau's
time in Philadelphia, see Chapter 3.

9. Though Baudry's work on Louisiana is not canonical—as Charlevoix's, Dumont
de Montigny's, and Le Page du Pratz's works on Louisiana have become—it was read by
European and North American audiences in his lifetime. For example, the book was re-
viewed in England and Scotland, and Thomas Jefferson had a copy of the *Second voyage*
in his Monticello library. See "Books on American Geography in Thomas Jefferson's Library," accessed Dec. 4, 2016, https://www.monticello.org/site/jefferson/books-american
-geography-thomas-jeffersons-library. Baudry's discussions of the 1729 Natchez uprising
against the French and the 1768 revolt against Spain continued to be cited by chronicles
of Louisiana, such as Charles Gayarré's *History of Louisiana: The Spanish Domination*
(New York, 1854) and many twentieth- and twenty-first-century studies. For more on
connections between Louisiana and war in Saint-Domingue, see the classic collection
Carl A. Brasseaux and Glenn R. Conrad, eds., *The Road to Louisiana: The Saint-Domingue
Refugees, 1792–1809,* trans. David Cheramie (Lafayette, La., 1992); and the short piece by
Paul Lachance, "An Empire Gone Awry: Why Napoleon Sold Louisiana," *Humanities,*
XXIII, no. 6 (November 2002), 17–19. The volume by Peter J. Kastor and François Weil,
eds., *Empires of the Imagination: Transatlantic Histories of the Louisiana Purchase* (Charlottesville, Va., 2009), likewise highlights the many ties between Saint-Domingue and
Louisiana. For continued efforts to return Saint-Domingue to French control after 1804,
see Jean-François Brière, *Haïti et la France, 1804–1848: Le rêve brisé* (Paris, 2008). Kongolese men and women did come in large numbers to the United States well into the nineteenth century. Baudry's book would thus conceivably still have been of use, if only to
inhabitants of another nation.

10. The literature documenting linguistics and its connection to colonial and nationalist
projects is vast. See Julie Tetel Andresen, *Linguistics in America, 1769–1924: A Critical
History* (London, 1990); Jill Lepore, *A Is for American: Letters and Other Characters in the
Newly United States* (New York, 2002); Sean P. Harvey, *Native Tongues: Colonialism and
Race from Encounter to Reservation* (Cambridge, Mass., 2015); Peter Thompson, "'Judi-
cious Neology': The Imperative of Paternalism in Thomas Jefferson's Linguistic Studies,"
Early American Studies, I (2003), 187–224; and Joseph Errington, *Linguistics in a Colonial
World: A Story of Language, Meaning, and Power* (Malden, Mass., 2007). Johannes Fabi-
an's work on Swahili phrase books is helpful in a later British colonial context; see Fabian,

Language and Colonial Power: The Appropriation of Swahili in the Former Belgian Congo, 1880–1938 (1986; rpt. Berkeley, Calif., 1991). Likewise, much of the study of language use in colonial and postcolonial contexts concentrates on the violence that was done to colonized peoples who had to learn their oppressors' languages.

11. Baudry des Lozières, *Second voyage à la Louisiane,* II, 72–73.

12. Ibid., II, 72 ("Ces malheureux esclaves"), 74 ("est encore d'une grande utilité"), 111 *(es-tu aveugle?),* 121 *(dyssenterie),* 124 *(ton estomach),* 128 *(hernie),* 136 *(as-tu mal aux oreilles).*

13. Ibid., II, 1, 74. Extensive work has been done on how the expertise of the enslaved was put to use in colonial contexts. See Clay Risen, "Jack Daniel's Embraces a Hidden Ingredient: Help from a Slave," *New York Times,* June 25, 2016, https://www.nytimes.com/2016/06/26/dining/jack-daniels-whiskey-nearis-green-slave.html?_r=0, for a recently publicized example of how the enslaved's intellectual knowledge was mobilized in North American businesses; and Jean-Baptiste Lautard, *Histoire de l'Académie de Marseille, depuis sa fondation en 1726 jusqu'en 1826* (Marseille, France, 1829), 116.

14. McClellan, *Colonialism and Science,* 48–49, 52 (McClellan notes that "percentages of whites and free people of color [mulatto and black] in the colony . . . were very small in comparison, at 6 percent and 5 percent respectively" [48]); Carolyn E. Fick, *The Making of Haiti: The Saint-Domingue Revolution from Below* (Knoxville, Tenn., 1990), 59; Médéric Louis Élie Moreau de Saint-Méry, *La description topographique, physique, civile, politique et historique de la partie française de l'isle Saint-Domingue . . . ,* ed. Blanche Maurel and Étienne Taillemite, new ed., 3 vols. (Saint-Denis, France, 2004) (hereafter cited as *Description de la partie française de l'isle Saint-Domingue),* I, 53; and see Linda M. Heywood's table "Slaves Boarded from Central Africa, by Decades," in Heywood, ed., *Central Africans and Cultural Transformations,* 64–65.

15. For more on the Kongolese Atlantic, see note 2.

16. Mobley, "Kongolese Atlantic," 212 (quotation). Many thanks to Elisabeth Boyi and John Thornton for their generosity answering questions about several examples from Baudry's "Vocabulaire" (personal correspondence, Sept. 11, 2014, and June 15 and 18, 2016). Thornton's work on Palo Mayombe in Cuba mentions that Lydia Cabrera and Fernando Ortiz located Kikongo sources while doing their ethnographic research; see Cabrera and Ortiz, "The Kingdom of Kongo and Palo Mayombe: Reflections on an African-American Religion," *Slavery and Abolition,* XXXVII (2016), 1–22, esp. 14, and nn. 94, 95; L[ouis-Marie-Joseph O'Hier] de Grandpré, *Voyage à la côte occidentale d'Afrique: Fait dans les années 1786 et 1787* (Paris, 1801).

17. Important historiography about colonial and revolutionary Saint-Domingue continues to view the island as bilingual. In McClellan's *Colonialism and Science,* he states, "Saint Domingue was a bilingual colony, with French and Creole spoken. French ruled as the language of government. Whites spoke French, as did the rest of the population to varying degrees. . . . All Creoles—that is, all persons born in Saint Domingue, black, white, and otherwise—could speak Creole. Slaves spoke Creole exclusively among themselves" (54). I think it unlikely that the "rest" of the population spoke some degree of French, and given the dominance of Kongolese enslaved people, it is highly unlikely that they spoke only Kreyòl among themselves. In Jeremy D. Popkin's *You Are All Free: The*

Haitian Revolution and the Abolition of Slavery (Cambridge, 2010), when discussing the French commissioners' Kreyòl language decrees, he states that they "had it translated into Creole, the language of the colony's black population" (143). This statement implies that it was the principal, even only, language spoken by Blacks (and that it wasn't also spoken by whites). In a later book, Popkin suggests, "These new arrivals could hardly have mastered Creole, let alone French, before the start of the slave uprising in 1791." His comments acknowledge that French and Haitian Kreyòl were not mastered by all speakers and that French language declarations might not have been as influential on the trajectory of the revolution as previously thought. He stops short, however, of suggesting that the enslaved would have had other lingua francas (*A Concise History of the Haitian Revolution* [Malden, Mass., 2012], 30).

18. Jean-François and Biassou to Commissioners, Dec. 17, 1791, Archives nationales de France, section D–XXV, carton 1, dossier 4, doc. 10, quoted in Thornton, "I Am the Subject," *Journal of World History,* IV (1993), 202, 204; Jean-Jacques Dessalines, proclamation, rpt. in [James Barskett], *History of the Island of St. Domingo, from Its First Discovery by Columbus to the Present Period* (1818; rpt. Westport, Conn., 1971), 178.

19. Gomez, *Exchanging Our Country Marks,* 154–155.

20. Scholarship on Native American languages has been particularly helpful as I have worked on this chapter. In his preface to *The Language Encounter in the Americas, 1492–1800: A Collection of Essays,* Norman Fiering writes: "The burden of overcoming language barriers was a problem faced by all peoples of the New World in the early modern era: African slaves and native peoples in the Lower Mississippi Valley; Jesuit missionaries and Huron-speaking peoples in New France; Spanish conquistadors and the Aztec rulers. All of these groups confronted America's complex linguistic environment, and all of them had to devise ways of transcending that environment—a problem that sometimes arose with life or death implications." More scholarship documenting linguistic work in African languages in the Americas would be a welcome addition to the field. See Edward G. Gray and Fiering, eds., *The Language Encounter in the Americas, 1492–1800: A Collection of Essays* (New York, 2000), vii–viii.

21. Research has examined the vocabularies of Native American languages in North America compiled by missionaries and traders from the seventeenth century on. It would be interesting to know whether Baudry read them, especially the Jesuit tracts. Laura J. Murray, "Vocabularies of Native American Languages: A Literary and Historical Approach to an Elusive Genre," *American Quarterly,* LIII (2001), 590–623, esp. 596–597, is particularly helpful. Brett Rushforth, *Bonds of Alliance: Indigenous and Atlantic Slaveries in New France* (Williamsburg, Va., and Chapel Hill, N.C., 2012) is fascinating both as a methodological approach and for the content it reveals; see esp. chap. 1 on how to use Jesuit dictionaries to build a sense of what slavery might have looked like from within Sioux communities. For other parts of the Americas, see Olabiyi Yai, "Texts of Enslavement: Fon and Yoruba Vocabularies from Eighteenth- and Nineteenth-Century Brazil," in Paul Lovejoy, ed., *Identity in the Shadow of Slavery* (New York, 2009), 102–112; Baudry des Lozières, *Second voyage à la Louisiane,* II, 111 *(as-tu de l'appétit?),* 115 *(fils de femme débauchée),* 131 *(que tu es laid!).*

22. Baudry des Lozières, *Second voyage à la Louisiane,* II, 108 *(achever),* 111 *(allez achever votre ouvrage),* 135 *(nous, nous sommes bons).*

23. Ibid., 113 *(blanc),* 123 *(esclave),* 128 *(habitation),* 129 *(indienne),* 132 *(maître, maîtresse),* 137 *(mon pays, ton pays, pays des blancs, pays des nègres),* 143 *(le sucre).*

24. Ibid., 105 ("un caractère doux"), 106 ("recherchés," "répandent la joie"), 109 *(allumer),* 111 *(assiette),* 119 *(l'enfant crie),* 120 *(chercher l'eau),* 123 *(essuyer),* 125 *(frotter),* 131 *(linge).*

25. Ibid., 108 *(agenouiller),* 109 *(aimer),* 112 *(baiser),* 115 *(balaye),* 117 *(chatouiller),* 122 *(dépêche-toi),* 123 *(embrasser),* 124 *(allez chercher).*

26. Ibid., 111 *(m'aimes-tu?),* 120 *(allez-vous coucher),* 131 *(votre lait est bon),* 136 *(oui monsieur, ouvre ta bouche),* 143 *(ne sales pas).* The scholarship on gender, reproduction, and sexual abuse in slave societies is extensive and includes the work of Jennifer Morgan, Bernard Moitt, Brenda E. Stevenson, Sasha Turner, Diana Paton, Marisa J. Fuentes, and Jessica Marie Johnson. Daina Ramey Berry and Leslie M. Harris, eds., *Sexuality and Slavery: Reclaiming Intimate Histories in the Americas* (Athens, Ga., 2018) provides an excellent selection of essays.

27. Baudry des Lozières, *Second voyage à la Louisiane,* II, 112 *(baiser),* 122 *(va te déshabiller),* 123 *(embrasser),* 127 *(es-tu grosse?),* 145 *(as-tu mal aux testicules?);* Wilma King, "'Prematurely Knowing of Evil Things': The Sexual Abuse of African American Girls and Young Women in Slavery and Freedom," *Journal of African American History,* XCIX (2014), 174, 176; Moreau, *Description de la partie française de l'isle Saint-Domingue,* I, 107. Thomas Jefferson's comments are illustrative as they pertain to pregnancy and sexualized labor. He wrote to his manager, "I consider a woman who brings a child every two years as more profitable than the best man on the farm. . . . What she produces is an addition to capital" (quoted in Wilma King, "'Suffer with Them till Death': Slave Women and Their Children in Nineteenth-Century America," in David Barry Gaspar and Darlene Clark Hine, eds., *More than Chattel: Black Women and Slavery in the Americas* [Bloomington, Ind., 1996], 147). For an overview of how slavery and sexual violence affected Black men, see Thomas A. Foster, "The Sexual Abuse of Black Men under American Slavery," *Journal of the History of Sexuality,* XX (2011), 445–464.

28. Baudry des Lozières, *Second voyage à la Louisiane,* II, 115 *(n'doki),* 128 *(vonda montou),* 130 *(tu es empoisonneur),* 132 *(mentir),* 135 *(quel navire),* 145 *(si tu ne travailles pas),* 146 *(voleur).* The formation of kinship networks out of a shared common experience of the Middle Passage has been studied in various imperial contexts. See, for example, Walter Hawthorne's "'Being Now, as It Were, One Family': Shipmate Bonding on the Slave Vessel *Emilia,* in Rio de Janeiro and throughout the Atlantic World," *Luso-Brazilian Review,* XLV, no. 1 (June 2008), 53–77.

29. Rick Dyson, "The Haitian Revolution," in Junius P. Rodriguez, ed., *Encyclopedia of Slave Resistance and Rebellion,* I (Westport, Conn., 2007), 229; Baudry des Lozières, *Second voyage à la Louisiane,* II, 108 ("Chaque cahute"), 125 *(fouet),* 126 *(prends garde),* 137 *(peur),* 138 *(pleurer),* 139 *(ne pleurez pas).*

30. Baudry des Lozières, *Second voyage à la Louisiane,* II, 75 ("séduisante"); B[audr]y Deslozières, *Les égaremens du nigrophilisme,* 16.

31. Gomez, *Exchanging Our Country Marks,* 170–171.

32. De Luna, "Sounding the African Atlantic," *WMQ,* 3d Ser., LXXVIII (2021), 585; James Sweet, "Research Note: New Perspectives on Kongo in Revolutionary Haiti," *Americas,* LXXIV (2017), 83–97, esp. 87, 90, 91–92. In another example, his close reading of *m'poutou* is suggestive of the work that historical linguistic approaches will continue to bring to our understanding of the Haitian Revolution and colonial Saint-Domingue more generally. He writes that Baudry's "entry for 'France' is translated into Kikongo as *m'poutou.* We know that the term *m'poutou* is a corruption of 'Portugal,' a reference to the first European colonists to arrive in central Africa in the fifteenth century. For Kongolese speakers, all of Europe became *m'poutou,* regardless of national distinction. Hence, Baudry's interpretation of France as *m'poutou* is technically correct, but the translation of France as Portugal (or Europe) reveals the ways that African homogenization of Europe elided difference in much the same way that the term 'Africa' did for Europeans. For Kongolese in St. Domingue, France and Portugal remained interchangeable as the imaginary collective homeland of all white people *(mondélé),* calling into question African understandings of the existence of 'France,' let alone the distinct principles of its revolution and their supposed influence on the Haitian uprising" (86). Sweet is also interested in how Kikongo worldviews were adopted by French colonial masters. I appreciate conversations with Kathryn de Luna about the root *-pIka* and thank her for referring me to the invaluable work of Marcos Abreu Leitão de Almeida, "Speaking of Slavery: Slaving Strategies and Moral Imaginations in the Lower Congo (Early Times to the Late 19th Century)" (Ph.D. diss., Northwestern University, 2020).

33. B[audr]y, Deslozières, *Les égaremens du nigrophilisme,* 16 ("l'interrogation"); Baudry des Lozières, *Second voyage à la Louisiane,* II, 109 *(antropophage),* 119 *(comment nommez-vous telle chose),* 124 *(entends-tu, as-tu entendu).* Many thanks to Elisabeth Boyi for noting errors in his terms. See also de Luna, "Sounding the African Atlantic," *WMQ,* 3d Ser., LXXVIII (2021), 615.

34. Baudry also had an interest in North American Indigenous languages. His "Deux vocabulaires de sauvages" is shorter than the Kikongo vocabulary, but it includes a word list, a few phrases, and translations of a "chanson sauvage." There is little about these two tribes specifically in either of his *Voyages à la Louisiane,* given the volumes' focus on the Lower Mississippi Valley, and it is unclear whether he actually met any of these speakers, which forces one to wonder how he was familiar with pronunciation (*Voyage à la Louisiane, et sur le continent de l'Amérique septentrionale* . . . [Paris, 1802], 348, 349). Michael Aubin confirms, "There is good reason to be skeptical of Baudry's implication that he bases it largely on his personal experiences with Ojibwa speakers." See "A Look at the Ojibwa Vocabulary of Baudry Des Lozières," in William Cowan, ed., *Actes du vingt-cinquième congrès des Algonquinistes* (Ottawa, 1994), 11.

35. Baudry des Lozières, *Second voyage à la Louisiane,* II, 107. For a detailed presentation of these dictionaries compiled by French, Italian, Portuguese, and Spanish authors with particular focus on missionary linguistic competence, see Jean de Dieu Nsondé's excellent *Langues, culture et histoire Koongo aux XVIIe et XVIIIe siècles: À travers les documents linguistiques* (Paris, 1995). I have determined that one of Nsondé's anonymous sources,

held as an undated manuscript in the Bibliothèque nationale de France (BnF), appears to be Baudry's "Vocabulaire." Although not an exact copy, Baudry's published version is undeniably based on the same text, as the content and order of presentation are nearly identical. A handwriting comparison between this manuscript and Baudry's other work is inconclusive, although I am more inclined to say it is not Baudry's handwriting. I am thus unsure whether the copy in the BnF is Baudry's own manuscript or he plagiarized large parts of it and took credit for being the author. See "Dictionnaire Congo," Département des manuscrits, Côte Africain 5, BnF. This uncertainty makes me reluctant to share Sweet's belief: "That Baudry could recall such an extensive vocabulary ten years after leaving St. Domingue highlights just how conversant he was in Kikongo. Indeed, one wonders if Kikongo was much more than a simple 'leisure' activity for Baudry; it appears that it might have been a lingua franca" (Sweet, "Research Note," *Americas*, LXXIV [2017], 86). I do not think that Baudry personally knew as much Kikongo as the "Vocabulaire" suggests.

36. This same Landolphe was involved in French republican naval battles in the Caribbean, specifically Guadeloupe. For more on Landolphe, see Anne Pérotin-Dumon, *La ville aux Iles, la ville dans l'île: Basse-Terre et Pointe-à-Pitre, Guadeloupe, 1650–1820* (Paris, 2000), 233. Imagining Landolphe, an accomplished transatlantic slave trader, working as a *corsair de la liberté* is further proof of the brilliance of Alejo Carpentier's *El siglo de las luces* (Mexico City, 1965), which used historical sources to undergird his fictional account of how the French Revolution played out in the Caribbean—particularly the contradictions of "radical" revolutionaries actively involved in the slave trade. For more on Boudacan, see his entry in Chapter 1.

37. For more on Jean Gabriel Dentu, who also incidentally published Azara's 1809 work *Voyages dans l'Amérique méridionale,* with notes by Georges Cuvier, see the conclusion of Carla Hesse, *Publishing and Cultural Politics in Revolutionary Paris, 1789–1810* (Berkeley, Calif., 1991), 240–249. Grandpré's vocabulary is not alphabetically ordered, but the Kongolese word is listed first, with the French translation to the right (Grandpré, *Voyage à la côte occidentale d'Afrique,* 159). For more on the presence of women in the Middle Passage, see Jennifer L. Morgan, "Accounting for 'The Most Excruciating Torment': Gender, Slavery, and Trans-Atlantic Passages," *History of the Present,* VI (2016), 184–207.

38. Christopher L. Miller, *The French Atlantic Triangle: Literature and Culture of the Slave Trade* (Durham, N.C., 2008); [Jean Antoine Brûletout de] Préfontaine, *Maison rustique, à l'usage des habitans de la partie de la France équinoxiale, connue sous le nom de Cayenne* (Paris, 1763); S. J. Ducoeurjoly, *Manuel des habitans de Saint-Domingue: Contenant un précis de l'histoire de cette île, depuis sa découverte . . .* (Paris, 1802). *DeBow's Review* was published from 1846 to 1884. Work in management and business studies discusses slavery as a quintessentially modern institution. For work on planter manuals, see Caitlin C. Rosenthal, "From Memory to Mastery: Accounting for Control in America, 1750–1880," *Enterprise and Society,* XIV (2013), 732–748; and Bill Cooke, "The Denial of Slavery in Management Studies," *Journal of Management Studies,* XL (2003), 1895–1918. See also [Moreau de Saint-Méry], *Catalogue of Books, Stationary* [sic], *Engravings, Mathematical Instruments, Maps, Charts, and Other Goods of Moreau de St. Mery, and Co's. Store, No. 84, South Front-Street, Corner of Walnut* (Philadelphia, 1795); and *Catalogue*

des livres et manuscrits de la bibliothèque de feu M. Moreau de Saint-Méry, . . . dont la vente se fera le mercredi 15 décembre 1819 (Paris, 1819). Many thanks to Chris Hodson for drawing my attention to Préfontaine's work.

39. Baudry des Lozières, *Second voyage à la Louisiane,* I, iii, II, 116, 122.

40. See "Art. VII. *Second Voyage à la Louisiane,* faisant suite au premier de l'auteur," *Edinburgh Review, or Critical Journal,* III, no. 5, 2d ed. (October 1803–January 1804), 81; and "Art. V. *Second Voyage a la Louisiane . . . ," Monthly Review; or Literary Journal,* XLII (1803), appendix, 483. Mills's work *The Racial Contract* (Ithaca, N.Y., 1999), 18, is quoted in John Ernest, *Liberation Historiography: African American Writers and the Challenge of History, 1794–1861* (Chapel Hill, N.C., 2004), 3.

41. Marlene L. Daut, *Tropics of Haiti: Race and the Literary History of the Haitian Revolution in the Atlantic World, 1789–1865* (Liverpool, U.K., 2015); Craig Womack, *Red on Red: Native American Literary Separatism* (Minneapolis, 1999), 2, quoted in Birgit Brander Rasmussen, *Queequeg's Coffin: Indigenous Literacies and Early American Literature* (Durham, N.C., 2012), 5.

Chapter Seven

1. I am reminded of Edwin Abbott Abbott's *Flatland: A Romance of Many Dimensions* (London, 1884), in which allegories of worlds of knowledge exist without being easily apprehended when one- and two-dimensional figures (lines, squares) attempt to understand each other and then a third dimension (spheres).

2. See Wyatt MacGaffey, "Dialogues of the Deaf: Europeans on the Atlantic Coast of Africa," in Stuart B. Schwartz, ed., *Implicit Understandings: Observing, Reporting, and Reflecting on the Encounters between Europeans and Other Peoples in the Early Modern Era* (Cambridge, 1994), 249–267.

3. These words appear in Table 1, Chapter 6, and in some of the close readings of particular phrases. I provide a visual "key" at the end of the chapter that includes some of the words from [Louis Narcisse] Baudry de Lozières's "Dictionnaire ou Vocabulaire Congo," in Baudry des Lozières, *Second voyage à la Louisiane, faisant suite au premier de l'auteur de 1794 à 1798 . . . ,* 2 vols. (Paris, 1803), II, 108–146.

4. See debates about "dragon creole" in Martinique and Guadeloupe in the 1970s and 1980s, centered around the Université des Antilles Schoelcher campus's Creole Institute (GEREC) publications. For a summary of these debates, see chapter 5 of Shireen K. Lewis, *Race, Culture, and Identity: Francophone West African and Caribbean Literature and Theory from Négritude to Créolité* (Lanham, Md., 2006). Similar discussions have occurred about models for writing other oral languages, including North American Indigenous ones. Discussions about how to write and compile dictionaries of Kikongo cluster languages literally go back centuries; see Jasper De Kind, Gilles-Maurice de Schryver, and Koen Bostoen, "Pushing Back the Origin of Bantu Lexicography: The *Vocabularium Congense* of 1652, 1928, 2012," *Lexikos,* XXII (2012), 159–194.

5. Robert Bringhurst, *The Elements of Typographic Style,* 3d ed. (Point Roberts, Wash., 2004), 17. This attempt to capture sound on the page obviously has a long history, from

Language poets to more contemporary work such as M. NourbeSe Philip and Setaey Adamu Boateng's masterful *Zong!* (Middletown, Conn., 2008). Ana-Maurine Lara's *Kohnjehr Woman* (Washington, D.C., 2017) creates a thought-provoking portrait of "Shee," an African woman from "Sandoman," her thoughts captured in what Lara describes to a reader thusly: "The voice of Shee, the kohnjehr woman, is connected to your own. Her words are intended to be read out loud, to pass through your body, to invoke. They are not a dialect. They are the sounds of a broken tongue" (opening note).

6. Félix d'Azara, *Essais sur l'histoire naturelle des quadrupèdes de la province du Paraguay . . .* , trans. M. L. E. Moreau-Saint-Méry, 2 vols. (Paris, 1801), I, lix, lxii; Moreau de Saint-Méry, "Observations sur le Royaume de Ouaire, à la Cote-d'Or en Afrique," *Mémoires du Musée de Paris,* Belles lettres et arts, no. 1 (Paris, 1785), 44; [Louis Narcisse] B[audry] D[eslozières], *Voyage à la Louisiane, et sur le continent de l'Amérique septentrionale . . .* (Paris, 1802), 348.

7. See Anna Brickhouse's discussion of how Indigenous knowledge circuits come to life when evaluating "unsuccessful" or "motivated mistranslation" incidents as a strategic process of unsettlement in *The Unsettlement of America: Translation, Interpretation, and the Story of Don Luis de Velasco, 1560–1945* (New York, 2015). It is helpful to imagine the Kikongo-speaking sources for Baudry's project deliberately misleading him.

8. "Esclaves en maronage," *Supplément aux Affiches américains* (Cap Français, Saint-Domingue), Aug. 4, 1784, [4].

9. G[abriel] C[hastenet-]d'Esterre, *Précis historique sur le régiment de Crête, dragons; suivi d'une notice sur la vie militaire, politique et privée de M. Baudry-Deslozières, colonel-inspecteur dudit régiment,* 3d ed. ([Paris?], 1804), 293 (Crete, Mount Ida), 299 ("toute nue"), 300 ("fameaux jardins," "couvre son habitation").

10. Ibid., 289 ("son gérant"), 302 ("50 . . . *bossals*"); Madame Catherine Baudry des Lozières to Moreau de Saint-Méry, Feb. 20, 1789, in Moreau de Saint-Méry, *Mémoire justificatif* ([Paris, 1790]), 114.

11. [Chastenet-]d'Esterre, *Précis historique,* 293; see also an advertisement placed in multiple editions by Baudry's neighbor, M. Morel, a businessman in Port-au-Prince, "A Vendre," *Affiches américaines,* May 13, 1790, [3]; and "A Vendre," *Supplément aux Affiches américains,* May 20, 1790, [3].

12. For more on *vika* and *mvika,* see my discussion in Chapter 6 as it relates to close readings of Kikongo words in James Sweet's and Kathryn M. de Luna's work on Baudry's "Vocabulaire"; see Sweet, "Research Note: New Perspectives on Kongo in Revolutionary Haiti," *Americas,* LXXIV (2017), 83–97; de Luna, "Sounding the African Atlantic," *William and Mary Quarterly,* 3d Ser., LXXVIII (2021), 581–616.

13. See the advertisements for Thérèse and Magdeleine under "Esclave *[sic]* en marronage," *Gazette de Saint-Domingue,* May 18, 1791. For a discussion of the Nago designation in the context of other labels used to identify geographic and ethnic groups in Africa, see Alison Zinna, Deborah Jenson, and Laurent Dubois, "Nation," in *Haitian Marronnage: Voyages and Resistance,* https://sites.duke.edu/marronnagevoyages/nations/.

14. Advertisements in *Affiches américaines* also include reproductions of brands that appeared upside down on people's bodies when seen by another person. See, for example,

the description of Marie and how her inverted brand was reproduced in "Esclaves marrons entrés à la geôle," June 24, 1790, [1]. See Katrina H. B. Keefer's discussion of the history and mechanical business of branding in "Marked by Fire: Brands, Slavery, and Identity," *Slavery and Abolition,* XL (2019), 659–681; and see the unattributed "History of Scarification in Africa," in *Hadithi Africa,* https://hadithi.africa/the-history-of-scarification-in-africa/. For a useful discussion of scarification practices in the nineteenth century, see Olatunji Ojo, "Beyond Diversity: Women, Scarification, and Yoruba Identity," *History in Africa,* XXXV (2008), 347–374. For a more general discussion of bodily marking practices, see Enid Schildkrout, "Inscribing the Body," *Annual Review of Anthropology,* XXXIII (2004), 319–344. Yoruba was originally written in the Ajami script. It was later codified with a Latin alphabet, a process begun in the mid-nineteenth century and elaborated by the Anglican bishop Ajayi Crowther. See Olúṣẹ̀yẹ Adéṣọlá, "Language: Standardization and Literacy," in Tóyìn Fálọlá and Akíntúndé Akínyẹmí, eds., *Encyclopedia of the Yorùbá* (Bloomington, Ind., 2016), 194–195.

15. In her historically grounded novel *The Infamous Rosalie / Rosalie L'Infâme,* Haitian writer Évelyne Trouillot imagines such a process. The protagonist's grandmother describes her branding: "TR, the initials of the slave ship, the only letters I ever learned, were from the ship that brought me here. *The Rosalie.* Your eyes tell me that you would have wanted me to learn other letters. . . . For me it's too late: the alphabet will always embody the character of hell." See Évelyne Trouillot, *The Infamous Rosalie,* trans. M. A. Salvodon (Lincoln, Neb., 2013), 80, quoted in Alyssa Goldstein Sepinwall, "If This Is a Woman: Evelyne Trouillot's *The Infamous Rosalie* and the Lost Stories of New-World Slavery," *Fiction and Film for French Historians,* V, no. 4 (February 2015), https://h-france.net/fffh/classics/if-this-is-a-woman-evelyne-trouillots-the-infamous-rosalie-and-the-lost-stories-of-new-world-slavery/.

16. "Esclaves en maronage," *Supplément aux Affiches américaines,* May 14, 1783, [4], June 25, 1783, [2], Aug. 4, 1784, [4]; "Nègres Marons," *Affiches américaines,* June 18, 1783, [2] (more than two hundred men, women, and children identified as "Congo" were publicly claimed as maroons in the 1783 announcements in this paper alone); Jean-Baptiste Labat, *Nouveau voyage aux isles de l'Amérique, contenant l'histoire naturelle de ces pays, l'origine, les moeurs, la religion et le gouvernement des habitans anciens et modernes,* 6 vols. (Paris, 1722), V, 255–256, quoted in Katherine Dauge-Roth, *Signing the Body: Marks on Skin in Early Modern France* (London, 2019), 220. It is impossible to think of Labat's comments apart from Hortense J. Spillers's discussion of seeing flesh as a "primary narrative." She writes, "These undecipherable markings on the captive body render a kind of hieroglyphics of the flesh whose severe disjunctures come to be hidden to the cultural seeing by skin color. We might well ask if this phenomenon of marking and branding actually 'transfers' from one generation to another." See Spillers, "Mama's Baby, Papa's Maybe: An American Grammar Book," *Diacritics,* XVII, no. 2 (Summer 1987), 64–81 (quotation on 67).

17. "Esclaves en maronage," *Supplément aux Affiches américaines,* Aug. 4, 1784, [4].

18. For inspiration, I have used descriptions in [Pompée-Valentin], Baron de Vastey, *The Colonial System Unveiled,* ed. and trans. Chris Bongie (Liverpool, U.K., 2014); and

Médéric Louis Élie Moreau de Saint-Méry, *La description topographique, physique, civile, politique et historique de la partie française de l'isle Saint-Domingue . . .*, ed. Blanche Maurel and Étienne Taillemite, new ed., 3 vols. (Saint-Denis, France, 2004) (see esp. I, 236 for an example). Moreau's work is a source for much scholarship on maroon communities. For more recent work on these communities in Saint-Domingue and Santo Domingo, see Johnhenry Gonzalez's *Maroon Nation: A History of Revolutionary Haiti* (New Haven, Conn., 2019); Jean Fouchard's work, including the classic *Les marrons de la liberté* (Paris, 1972); Erica Johnson Edwards's three-part series "Unclaimed Runaways and the Power Struggles of Colonial Haiti" (2020), posted to https://ageofrevolutions.com/2020/07/06 /unclaimed-runaways-and-the-power-struggles-of-colonial-haiti-part-i-legislating-negres -epaves/; and Charlton W. Yingling's "Maroons of Santo Domingo in the Age of Revolutions: Adaptation and Evasion, 1783–1800," *History Workshop Journal*, no. 79 (2015), 25–51.

19. "Esclaves en maronage," *Supplément aux Affiches américaines*, Oct. 16, 1782, [2], Mar. 26, 1783, [4], Oct. 27, 1784, [8]. An enslaved man named Colin, branded and wearing "a ball and chain" (un nabot au pied) also escaped from Curet, perhaps the same surgeon in Le Cap. See ibid., Jan. 3, 1778, [4].

20. Saidiya Hartman, *Wayward Lives, Beautiful Experiments: Intimate Histories of Social Upheaval* (New York, 2019), 228.

21. SJ Zhang is also working on the historical figure of Rosette in her work on women maroons in the extended Americas. I appreciate our conversations. Thanks to Sarah Eyerly for our discussion about the possibility of trepanning. I also thank P. Gabrielle Foreman for encouraging me to consider Rosette's story alongside that of Harriet Tubman, who suffered a traumatic brain injury when she was hit on the head by an overseer. This injury, and the lifetime of sudden deep sleep–trancelike spells that it occasioned, led to her visions, which she believed were premonitions from God.

22. Philip and Boateng, *Zong!;* Kyle Baker, *Nat Turner* (New York, 2015). On adapting novels about slavery to graphic form (color choices, what passages to include, etc.), see a discussion between John Jennings and Damian Duffy about working on Octavia Butler's work at http:// www.comicosity.com/anatomy-of-a-panel-john-jennings-damian-duffy-and-parable-of-the -sower/. Many thanks to Shelley Streeby for our conversations about these trends. Her work in *Radical Sensations: World Movements, Violence, and Visual Culture* (Durham, N.C., 2013) was also very helpful for how I thought about the importance of visual culture. For context on these discussions, see Stephen Best, "Neither Lost nor Found: Slavery and the Visual Archive," *Representations*, CXIII, no. 1 (Winter 2011), 150–163. He claims: "However exhaustive one's catalog of the visual archive of slavery, it will always be lacking in works by slaves themselves. There are no visual equivalents of *Incidents in the Life of a Slave Girl*. When it comes to the representation of the inner life of the enslaved, few of our sources are visual in nature. For slaves are not the subject of the visual imagination, they are its object. Slavery in the slaves' visual imagination remains foreclosed as a site of critical and historical inquiry—an absent cause only to be approached by way of historical metalepsis" (151).

23. Although the wooden locks Moreau described in such detail have long since disintegrated, his explanation and visualization of their use is yet another example of why his

research has been an invaluable primary source for modern-day scholars. He asserts, "Now [in the 1780s when he published this piece] only the enslaved and poor people of color use them" (maintenant les seuls esclaves ou les gens de couleur pauvres en font usage). See Moreau de Saint-Méry, "Note sur les serrures de bois, dont les nègres se servent aux Antilles," *Mémoires d'agriculture, d'économie rurale et domestique,* I (Winter 1789), 20–24, with an additional appendix in the same volume, "Additions à la note sur les serrures de bois …," xxvii–xxxvi. The appendix provided a detailed explanation of the drawings (ibid., 21, 23). Patricia Samford maintains that locks were rarely found in African American archaeological sites, further evidence of how Moreau's work enables a host of discussions about quotidian life for the enslaved (Samford, "The Archaeology of African-American Slavery and Material Culture," *WMQ,* 3d Ser., LIII [1996], 87–114, esp. 110).

Chapter Eight

1. Moreau de Saint-Méry, "Discours préliminaire," in Moreau de Saint-Méry, *Loix et constitutions des colonies françaises de l'Amérique sous le vent …,* 6 vols. (Paris, [1784–1790]), I, xxv.

2. See, for example, William Max Nelson, "The Atlantic Enlightenment," in D'Maris Coffman, Adrian Leonard, and William O'Reilly, eds., *The Atlantic World* (London, 2015), 655–656.

3. Ferdinando Cossetti, "Progetto di arco di trionfo dedicato a Moreau de Saint-Méry," [1802], Archivio di Stato di Parma, Raccolta Mappe e Disegni, vol. IX, no. 45, vol. 12, nn. 54a–b, reproduced as figure 117 in [Marzio Dall'Acqua], *L'ossessione della memoria: Parma settecentesca nei disegni del Conte Alessandro Sanseverini* (Parma, Italy, 1997), 153 n. 129; William Cobbett, trans., *A Topographical and Political Description of the Spanish Part of Saint-Domingo …,* 2 vols. (Philadelphia, 1798), I, 7 (quotation), 212–213; M[édéric] L[ouis] É[lie] Moreau de Saint-Méry, *Description topographique et politique de la partie espagnole de l'isle Saint-Domingue …* (Philadelphia, 1796), I, 7.

4. Eve Gerber, "African American History Books Recommended by Imani Perry," *Five Books* (blog), https://fivebooks.com/best-books/african-american-history-imani-perry/; Kim F. Hall, "I Can't Love This the Way You Want Me To: Archival Blackness," *Postmedieval,* XI (2020), 171–179 (quotation on 171). Thanks to Sarah Knott for sharing this piece. As Nathalie Pierre put it when we conversed about this project, would we rely on Jeff Bezos to write a history of those who worked in his multibillion-dollar Amazon empire? Would he be an accurate chronicler of their thoughts, motivations, and politics? The idea is laughable.

5. Aménaïde Dall'Asta's memorial is in the "Cippo Famiglia Conti Dall'Asta" in the Cimitero della Villetta in Parma, Italy. Interestingly, Aménaïde's son Eduardo / Edouard, the future Count Dall'Asta, legally added Moreau de Saint-Méry to his own name as an adult. I am curious about the name Maria in the inscription. Aménaïde is listed in official documents from her childhood as Jeanne-Louise, although she seems to have gone by Aménaïde most of her life. Her biological mother was named Marie-Louise. Could she have added Maria to her name to honor her biological mother?

6. Lists of names provide a powerful visual strategy for engaging an audience and commemorating the named. See how museums have done this to great effect, for example, in the installation *Paradox of Liberty: Slavery at Jefferson's Monticello,* a traveling exhibit at Richmond's Black History Museum and Cultural Center of Virginia. A statue of Jefferson is placed in front of 607 names of the enslaved who worked for him. The May 24, 2020, issue of the *New York Times* printed a sobering COVID-19 memorial of the one hundred thousand lives lost to the disease (Dan Barry, "U.S. Deaths Near 100,000, an Incalculable Loss"). This number, now years old, grew exponentially. The loss is still incalculable. Politics of memorialization are alive and well in current debates about Confederate, colonialist monuments. See, for example, Marlene L. Daut's piece on Thomas Jefferson's statue in Paris's seventh arrondissement, "Tear Down That Statue, Mr. Macron!" in June 2020, which sparked controversy on H-Net, France (see History News Network, Columbian College of Arts and Sciences, George Washington University, https://historynewsnetwork.org/article/175963). For more on the relationships between monuments and slavery, see Celeste-Marie Bernier and Judie Newman, "Public Art, Artefacts, and Atlantic Slavery: Introduction," *Slavery and Abolition,* XXIX (2008), 135–150.

7. [Pompée-Valentin], Baron de Vastey, *The Colonial System Unveiled,* ed. and trans. Chris Bongie (Liverpool, U.K., 2014), 108.

8. See "Répertoire des notions coloniales; par ordre alphabétique," Archives nationales d'outre-mer, Aix-en-Provence, France (ANOM), Collection Moreau de Saint-Méry (Ser. F3), 74, s.v. "bibliothèque."

9. Moreau de Saint-Méry, *Voyage aux États-Unis de l'Amérique, 1793–1798,* ed. Stewart L. Mims (New Haven, Conn., 1913), 1; Kenneth Roberts and Anna M. Roberts, eds. and trans., *Moreau de Saint Méry's American Journey [1793–1798]* (New York, 1947), 16–17.

10. Jennifer L. Morgan, *Laboring Women: Reproduction and Gender in New World Slavery* (Philadelphia, Pa., 2004), 199.

11. Anna Brickhouse, "Mistranslation, Unsettlement, La Navidad," *PMLA,* CXXVIII (2013), 938–946.

12. Médéric Louis Élie Moreau de Saint-Méry, *La Description topographique, physique, civile, politique et historique de la partie française de l'isle Saint-Domingue . . . ,* ed. Blanche Maurel and Étienne Taillemite, new ed., 3 vols. (Saint-Denis, France, 2004), 56 (hereafter cited as *Description de la partie française de l'isle Saint-Domingue*).

13. "Répertoire des notions colonials; par ordre alphabétique," ANOM, F3, 73, s.v. "arsenic." The fear of poisoning was rife in Caribbean colonies. These fears reached their apogee in Saint-Domingue during what sources of the time described as Makandal's 1750s poison campaign.

14. Moreau wrote, "The formation of these mountains . . . and the neighboring Spanish part of the island, . . . all of these things make these regions the preferred asylum for runaway Blacks" (La conformation de ces montagnes . . . et le voisinage de la Partie espagnole, . . . tout dispose ces lieux pour être l'asyle préféré des nègres fugitifs). "The area of Trou," Moreau continued, "has suffered from long vexations caused by the Black Polydor at the head of a band of armed Blacks, who were finally destroyed by the union of local inhabitants. The fright that Polydor spread with his atrocities was so great that his destruction

was considered a service to the colony; and the Black man named Laurent, called Cézar, who went in search of Polydor alongside his master M.   Nautel, cornered this criminal in the savanna that has kept his name, where he preferred to be killed *[as opposed to surrendering]*" (La dépendance du Trou a dû les longues vexations que lui fit souffrir le nègre Polydor à la tête d'une bande de nègres armés, qui fut enfin détruite par la réunion des habitans du lieu et des environs. L'effroi qu'avait répandu Polydor par ses atrocités était si grand, que sa destruction fut considérée comme un service rendu à toute la Colonie; et le nègre Laurent, dit Cézar, qui concourut avec M. Natuel son maître, à arrêter ce scélérat dans la savane qui a gardé son nom, où il fut tué [*plutôt que de se rendre*]). See Moreau de Saint-Méry, *Description de la partie française de l'isle Saint-Domingue,* 183.

15. Nineteenth-century history writing, particularly about the French Revolution, includes the strong narrative presence of the writer serving as a guide to the reader. See David A. Bell, "Tocqueville, Napoleon, and History-Writing in a Democratic Age," *Tocqueville Review,* XLII, no. 2 (2021), 43–55. The "Materiali per la biografia di M. Moreau de Saint-Méry" is housed in the Dono Monza collection, folder 6, Archivio di Stato, Parma, Italy.

16. Marian Bantjes, "Intricate Beauty by Design," filmed February 2010, TED video, 2:29, 7:19, https://www.ted.com/talks/marian_bantjes_intricate_beauty_by_design/transcript ?language=en.

17. Annette Gordon-Reed, *The Hemingses of Monticello: An American Family* (New York, 2008), 15–16.

18. Saidiya Hartman, *Wayward Lives, Beautiful Experiments: Intimate Histories of Social Upheaval* (New York, 2019), xiv.

BIBLIOGRAPHY

Selected Manuscript and Print Sources Written, Edited, Translated, or Printed by Moreau de Saint-Méry

Bordes, J. Marie de. *Défense des colons de Saint-Domingue; ou, Examen rapide de la nouvelle Déclaration des droits de l'homme, en ce qu'elle à particulièrement de relatif aux colonies*. [Philadelphia: Moreau de Saint-Méry], 1796.

Carra, Emilia. *Gli inediti di Moreau de Saint-Méry a Parma*. Parma, Italy, 1955.

La Rochefoucauld-Liancourt, [François-Alexandre-Frédéric]. *Des prisons de Philadelphie*. Philadelphia: Moreau de Saint-Méry, 1796.

———. *On the Prisons of Philadelphia*. Philadelphia: Moreau de Saint-Méry, 1796.

Moreau de Saint-Méry, Médéric Louis Élie. "Additions à la note sur les serrures de bois. . . ." *Mémoires d'agriculture, d'économie rurale et domestique*, I (Winter 1789), xxvii–xxxvi.

———. *Catalogue of Books, Stationary* [sic], *Engravings, Mathematical Instruments, Maps, Charts, and Other Goods of Moreau de St. Mery, and Co.'s Store, No. 84, South Front-Street, Corner of Walnut*. Philadelphia: Moreau de Saint-Méry, 1795.

———. *A Civilization That Perished: The Last Years of White Colonial Rule in Haiti. . . .* Edited and translated by Ivor D. Spencer. Lanham, Md., 1985.

———. *Considérations présentées aux vrais amis du repos et du bonheur de la France: À l'occasion des nouveaux mouvemens de quelques soi-disant Amis-des-noirs*. Paris, 1791.

———. Correspondence with Giambattista Bodoni. Fondo Moreau de Saint-Méry. Biblioteca Palatina, Parma, Italy.

———. *Courrier de la France et des colonies*. Edited by Louis Gateau. Philadelphia: Moreau de Saint-Méry, 1795–1796.

———. *Danse: Article extrait d'un ouvrage de M. L. E. Moreau de Saint-Méry; ayant pour titre: "Répertoire des notions coloniales; par ordre alphabétique."* Philadelphia: Moreau de Saint-Méry, 1796.

———. *De la danse. . . .* Parma, Italy, 1801 and 1803.

———. "Description topographique, physique, civile, politique et historique de la partie française de l'isle Saint-Domingue." Unpublished manuscript. Archives nationales d'outre-mer, Aix-en-Provence, France (ANOM). Collection Moreau de Saint-Méry. Series F3, 96–101.

———. *Description topographique, physique, civile, politique et historique de la partie française de l'isle Saint-Domingue. . . .* 2 vols. Philadelphia: Moreau de Saint-Méry, 1797–1798.

———. *Description topographique, physique, civile, politique et historique de la partie française de l'isle Saint-Domingue*. Edited by Blanche Maurel and Étienne Taillemite. 3 vols. Paris, 1958.

———. *La description topographique, physique, civile, politique et historique de la partie française de l'isle Saint-Domingue. . . .* Edited by Blanche Maurel and Étienne Taillemite. New ed. 3 vols. Saint-Denis, France, 2004.

———. "Description topographique et politique de la partie espagnole de l'isle Saint-Domingue. . . ." Unpublished manuscript. ANOM. Collection Moreau de Saint-Méry. Series F3, 102–105.

———. *Description topographique et politique de la partie espagnole de l'isle Saint-Domingue. . . .* 2 vols. Philadelphia: Moreau de Saint-Méry, 1796.

———. *Discours sur l'utilité du musée établi à Paris: Prononcé dans sa séance publique du 1er décembre 1784.* Parma, Italy, 1805.

———, ed. and trans. "Essais sur l'histoire naturelle des quadrupèdes . . . de la province du Paraguay." By Félix de Azara. Unpublished manuscript. ANOM. Collection Moreau de Saint-Méry. Series F3, 118–119.

———, ed. and trans. *Essais sur l'histoire naturelle des quadrupèdes de la province du Paraguay. . . .* By Félix d'Azara. 2 vols. Paris, 1801.

———. *Essai sur la manière d'améliorer l'éducation des chevaux en Amérique.* Philadelphia: Moreau de Saint-Méry, 1795.

———. *An Essay on the Manner of Improving the Breed of Horses in America.* Philadelphia: Moreau de Saint-Méry, 1795.

———. Family Correspondence. 1806–1813. Fondo Carte Moreau de Saint-Méry, Dono Monza, Archivio di Stato di Parma, Italy.

———. *Fragment sur les moeurs de Saint-Domingue.* [Port-au-Prince, Saint-Domingue, 1788].

———. *General View or Abstract of the Arts and Sciences, Adapted to the Capacity of Youth.* Translated by Michael Fortune. Philadelphia: Moreau de Saint-Méry, 1797.

———. "Histoire géographique, civile et politique de l'isle de St. Jean-Baptiste de Porto-Rico." Unpublished manuscript translation of Iñigo Abbad y Lasierra, *Historia geográfica, civil y natural de la Isla de San Juan Bautista de Puerto Rico.* MS 116. Service historique de la Défense, Château de Vincennes.

———. *Historique: Etats de Parme, 1749–1808.* Edited by Carla Corradi Martini. Parma, Italy, 2003.

———. *Idée générale ou abrégé des sciences et des arts à l'usage de la jeunesse.* Edited from the work of M[ichael] Forney. Philadelphia: Moreau de Saint-Méry, 1796.

———. "Journal de Moreau de Saint-Méry." 5 vols. Transcribed by A. Saccò, I (1801–1802), G. Quaquarelli, II (1803–1804), G. Tambini, III (1805), D. Faidherbe, IV (1806), and S. Zanardi, V (1807), under the supervision of Carminella Biondi (theses, Università degli studi di Parma, 1980–1986), from the manuscript "Journal de ma vie," in Fondo Carte Moreau de Saint-Méry, Dono Monza, Archivio di Stato di Parma, Italy.

———. *Loix et constitutions des colonies françaises de l'Amérique sous le vent. . . .* 6 vols. Paris, [1784–1790].

———. *Mémoire justificatif.* [Paris, 1790].

———. "Mémoire sur la patate." *Mémoires d'agriculture,* I (Winter 1789), 43–57.

————. "Mémoire sur une espèce de coton, nommé à Saint-Domingue *Coton de Soie,* ou *Coton de Sainte-Marthe.*" Paris, 1790.

————. "Moreau de Saint-Méry: Correspondance à sa famille, 1808–1809." Transcribed by Cecilia Paini, under the supervision of Carminella Biondi (thesis, Università degli studi di Parma, 1986–1987), from the manuscript letters in Fondo Carte Moreau de Saint-Méry, Dono Monza, Archivio di Stato di Parma, Italy.

————. *Moreau de Saint Méry's American Journey [1793–1798].* Edited and translated by Kenneth Roberts and Anna M. Roberts. Garden City, N.Y., 1947.

————. *Note des travaux du c[itoy]en Moreau-St.-Méry.* Paris, 1799.

————. "Note sur les serrures de bois, dont les nègres se servent aux Antilles." *Mémoires d'agriculture,* I (Winter 1789), 20–24.

————. *Observations d'un habitant des colonies, sur le mémoire en faveur des gens de couleur, ou sang-mêlés, de St-Domingue et des autres isles françaises de l'Amérique.* Paris, 1789.

————. "Observations sur la culture de la canne à sucre dans les Antilles et plus particulièrement de celle d'Otaïti." *Mémoires d'agriculture,* I (Winter 1789), 277–290.

————. "Observations sur le Royaume de Ouaire, à la Côte-d'Or en Afrique." In *Mémoires du Musée de Paris,* Belles lettres et arts, no. 1 (Paris, 1785), 43–72.

————. "Observations sur les animaux utiles aux colonies françaises, considérés dans leur rapport avec l'economie rurale et domestique de ces mêmes colonies." *Mémoires d'agriculture,* I (Winter 1789), 83–136.

————. *Opinion de M. Moreau de Saint-Méry, député de la Martinique à l'Assemblée nationale: Sur les dangers de la division du ministère de la marine et des colonies.* Paris, 1790.

————. "Procédé pour faire le vin d'orange." *Mémoires d'agriculture,* I (Winter 1789), 29–32.

————. "Répertoire des notions coloniales; par ordre alphabétique." Unpublished manuscript. ANOM. Collection Moreau de Saint-Méry. Series F3, 73–78.

————. *A Topographical and Political Description of the Spanish Part of Saint-Domingo.* . . . Translated by William Cobbett. 2 vols. Philadelphia: Moreau de Saint-Méry, 1798.

————. "Voyage aux États-Unis de l'Amérique, 1793–1798." Unpublished manuscript. ANOM. Collection Moreau de Saint-Méry. Series F3, 123.

————. *Voyage aux États-Unis de l'Amérique, 1793–1798.* Edited by Stewart L. Mims. New Haven, Conn., 1913.

————. *Voyage aux États-Unis de l'Amérique, 1793–1798.* Edited by Monique Pouliquen. New ed. Saint-Denis, France, 2007.

————, ed. and trans. "Voyage de l'ambassade de la Compagnie des Indes orientales hollandaises, vers l'empereur de la Chine, en 1794–1795." By A. E. van Braam Houckgeest. Unpublished manuscript. ANOM. Collection Moreau de Saint-Méry. Series F3, 110–111.

————, ed. and trans. *Voyage de l'ambassade de la Compagnie des Indes orientales hollandaises, vers l'empereur de la Chine, dans les années 1794 et 1795.* . . . *Le tout tiré du*

Journal d'André Everard Van Braam Houckgeest. . . . 2 vols. Philadelphia: Moreau de
   Saint-Méry, 1797–1798.
Priestley, Joseph. *Réflexions sur la doctrine du phlogistique et la décomposition de l'eau.*
   Translated by P. A. Adet. Philadelphia: Moreau de Saint-Méry, 1797.
Tanguy de La Boissière, C[laude] C[orentin]. *Observations on the Dispatch Written the
   16th. January 1797, by Mr. Pickering, Secretary of State of the United States of America,
   to Mr. Pinkney, Minister Plenipotentiary of the United States near the French Republic.*
   Translated by Samuel Chandler. Philadelphia: Moreau de Saint-Méry, 1797.
———. *Observations sur la dépêche écrite le 16 janvier 1797 par M. Pickering, secrétaire
   d'État des États-Unis de l'Amérique, à M. Pinkney, ministre plénipotentiaire des États-
   Unis près la République française.* Philadelphia: Moreau de Saint-Méry, 1797.

Periodical Sources

Affiches américaines
Aurora General Advertiser (Philadelphia)
Bristol Courier (Philadelphia)
City Gazette, or the Daily Advertiser (Charleston, S.C.)
Claypoole's American Daily Advertiser (Philadelphia)
Columbian Herald, or the Independent Courier of North-America (Charleston, S.C.)
Courrier de la France et des colonies (Philadelphia)
Courrier français (Philadelphia)
Edinburgh Review, or Critical Journal
Gazette de Saint-Domingue
Gazzetta di Parma
Jamaica Mercury (Kingston)
Journal des révolutions (Philadelphia)
Mémoires d'agriculture, d'économie rurale et domestique
Monthly Review; or Literary Journal
New York Times
Le Patriote français
Pennsylvania Packet, and Daily Advertiser (Philadelphia)
La petite revue hebdomadaire (Port-au-Prince, Haiti)
Philadelphia Inquirer
South-Carolina Gazette, and Public Advertiser (Charleston, S.C.)

Additional Manuscript Sources

Archives nationales d'outre-mer (ANOM), Aix-en-Provence, France. Collection Moreau
   de Saint-Méry. Series F3, 1–287. Microfilm, 247 MIOM.
ANOM. Collection Moreau de Saint-Méry. Series F3, Atlas Moreau de Saint-Méry,
   288–297.
ANOM. Notariat répertoires des doubles minutes Saint-Domingue, 25, 114, 116, 130, 131.
ANOM. Notariat Saint-Domingue, 360, 526, 542, 861, 869, 870.

Azara, Félix de. "Descripción histórica, phísica, política, y geográfica de la provincia del Paraguay." 1793. MS 120. Service historique de la Défense, Château de Vincennes.

"Dictionnaire Congo." Département des manuscrits, Côte Africain 5. Bibliothèque nationale de France (BnF).

"Diplomi accademi." Fondo Carte Moreau de Saint-Méry, Dono Monza, box 6, Materiali per la biografia di M. Moreau de Saint-Méry. Archivio di Stato di Parma, Italy.

Papiers de Louis-Narcisse Baudry des Lozières. BnF.

Published Print and Visual Sources

Abbad y Lasierra, Iñigo. *Historia geográfica, civil y natural de la isla de San Juan Bautista de Puerto-Rico*. Edited by Jose Julian de Acosta y Calbo. New ed. Puerto Rico, 1866.

Abbott, Edwin Abbott. *Flatland: A Romance of Many Dimensions*. London, 1884.

Adéṣọlá, Olúṣẹ̀yẹ. "Language: Standardization and Literacy." In Tóyìn Fálọlá and Akíntúndé Akínyẹmí, eds., *Encyclopedia of the Yorúbá*, 194–195. Bloomington, Ind., 2016.

Aldama, Frederick Luis. "Anatomy of a Panel: John Jennings, Damian Duffy, and *Parable of the Sower*." *Comicosity*, February 26, 2020. https://www.comicosity.com/anatomy-of-a-panel-john-jennings-damian-duffy-and-parable-of-the-sower/.

Aldridge, A[lfred] Owen. *The Dragon and the Eagle: The Presence of China in the American Enlightenment*. Detroit, 1993.

Alexander, Elizabeth. "The Venus Hottentot." *Poetry Foundation*. https://www.poetryfoundation.org/poems/52111/the-venus-hottentot.

Alexander, Leslie M. *Fear of a Black Republic: Haiti and the Birth of Black Internationalism in the United States*. Champaign, Ill., 2023.

Aljoe, Nicole N. *Creole Testimonies: Slave Narratives from the British West Indies, 1709–1838*. New York, 2012.

Allegri Tassoni, Giuseppina. "Un tableau retrouvé de Girolamo Mazzola Bedoli." *Aurea Parma*, XL, fasc. 4 (1956), 265–283.

Allewaert, Monique. *Ariel's Ecology: Plantations, Personhood, and Colonialism in the American Tropics*. Minneapolis, 2013.

Almeida, Marcos Abreu Leitão de. "Speaking of Slavery: Slaving Strategies and Moral Imaginations in the Lower Congo (Early Times to the Late 19th Century)." Ph.D. diss., Northwestern University, 2020.

Andresen, Julie Tetel. *Linguistics in America, 1769–1924: A Critical History*. London, 1990.

Arias, Santa. "Looking to the Southeast Antilles: Iñigo Abbad y Lasierra's Geopolitical Thought in His *Historia geográfica, civil y natural de la Isla de San Juan Bautista de Puerto Rico* (1788)." *Colonial Latin American Review*, XXIV (2015), 17–35.

Arthaud, [Charles]. *Recherches sur la constitution des naturels du pays, sur leurs arts, leur industrie, et les moyens de leur subsistance*. Cap Français, Saint-Domingue, 1786.

Asúa, Miguel de. *Science in the Vanished Arcadia: Knowledge of Nature in the Jesuit Missions of Paraguay and Río de la Plata*. Leiden, Netherlands, 2014.

Aubert, Guillaume. "'The Blood of France': Race and Purity of Blood in the French Atlantic World." *William and Mary Quarterly,* 3d Ser., LXI (2004), 439–478.

Aubin, Michael. "A Look at the Ojibwa Vocabulary of Baudry Des Lozières." In William Cowan, ed., *Actes du vingt-cinquième congrès des Algonquinistes,* 1–12. Ottawa, Ont., 1994.

Azara, Félix de. *Apuntamientos para la historia de los quadrúpedos del Paragüay y Rio de la Plata.* Madrid, 1802.

———. *Descripción histórica, física, política y geográfica de la provincia del Paraguay: El manuscrito de Madrid, 1793.* Edited and transcribed by Herib Caballero Campos and Dario Solís. Asunción, Paraguay, 2016.

———. *Voyages dans l'Amérique méridionale. . . .* Edited by Charles A. Walckenaer. 4 vols. Paris, 1809.

Bagneris, Mia L. *Colouring the Caribbean: Race and the Art of Agostino Brunias.* Manchester, U.K., 2018.

Baker, Kyle. *Nat Turner.* New York, 2015.

Baker, Philip. "Assessing the African Contribution to French-Based Creoles." In Salikoko S. Mufwene, ed., with the assistance of Nancy Condon, *Africanisms in Afro-American Language Varieties,* 123–155. Athens, Ga., 1993.

Ball, Erica L., Tatiana Seijas, and Terri L. Snyder, eds. *As If She Were Free: A Collective Biography of Women and Emancipation in the Americas.* Cambridge, 2020.

Bandau, Anja. "The Narrations of the Destruction of Saint-Domingue in the Late 18th Century and Their Reinterpretations after the Bicentennial of the Haitian Revolution." *L'ordinaire des Amériques,* no. 215 (2013). https://doi.org/10.4000/orda.688.

Banks, Kenneth J. *Chasing Empire across the Sea: Communications and the State in the French Atlantic, 1713–1763.* Montreal, Que., 2014.

Banner, Lois W. "Biography as History." *American Historical Review,* CXIV (2009), 579–586.

Baptist, Edward E. *The Half Has Never Been Told: Slavery and the Making of American Capitalism.* New York, 2014.

Barbier, Frédéric, Sabine Juratic, and Annick Mellerio. *Dictionnaire des imprimeurs, libraires et gens du livre à Paris, 1701–1789, A–C.* Geneva, Switzerland, 2007.

Barnesley, Edward R. "History of China's Retreat." *Bristol Courier,* May 9–11, 1933.

Barry, Dan. "U.S. Deaths Near 100,000, an Incalculable Loss." *New York Times,* May 24, 2020. https://www.nytimes.com/interactive/2020/05/24/us/us-coronavirus-deaths-100000.html.

[Barskett, James]. *History of the Island of St. Domingo, from Its First Discovery by Columbus to the Present Period.* 1818. Rpt. Westport, Conn., 1971.

Barthelemy, Gérard. "Tentatives de description de l'Afrique et des Africains à partir des Amériques à la fin du XVIIIe siècle." In Taffin, ed., *Moreau de Saint-Méry,* 147–158.

Bassnett, Susan, and Harish Trivedi, eds. *Post-Colonial Translation: Theory and Practice.* London, 1999.

Baudry des Lozières, Louis Narcisse. *Les égaremens du nigrophilisme.* Paris, 1802.

———. *Second voyage à la Louisiane, faisant suite au premier de l'auteur de 1794 à 1798. . . .* 2 vols. Paris, 1803.

———. *Voyage à la Louisiane, et sur le continent de l'Amérique septentrionale. . . .* [Paris, 1802].

Beauvois, A[mbrose]-M[arie]-F[rançois]-J[oseph] Palisot de. *Insectes recueillis en Afrique et en Amérique, dans les royaumes d'Oware et de Benin, a Saint-Domingue et dans les États-Unis, pendant les années 1786–1797.* Paris, 1805.

Beckles, Hilary McD. *Centering Woman: Gender Discourses in Caribbean Slave Society.* Kingston, Jamaica, 1999.

Bédarida, Henri. *A l'apogée de la puissance bourbonienne: Parme dans la politique française au XVIIIe siècle.* Paris, 1930.

Beddall, Barbara G. "The Isolated Spanish Genius—Myth or Reality? Félix de Azara and the Birds of Paraguay." *Journal of the History of Biology,* XVI (1983), 225–258.

———. "'Un Naturalista Original': Don Félix de Azara, 1746–1821." *Journal of the History of Biology,* VIII (1975), 15–66.

Belaubre, Christophe, Jordana Dym, and John Savage, eds. *Napoleon's Atlantic: The Impact of the Napoleonic Empire in the Atlantic World.* Leiden, Netherlands, 2010.

Bell, David A. "Tocqueville, Napoleon, and History-Writing in a Democratic Age." *Tocqueville Review / La revue Tocqueville,* XLII, no. 2 (2021), 43–55.

———. "What We've Lost with the Demise of Print Encyclopedias." *New Republic,* Mar. 19, 2012. https://newrepublic.com/article/101795/encyclopedia-britannica -publish-information.

Bellagamba, Alice, Sandra E. Greene, and Martin A. Klein, eds. *African Voices on Slavery and the Slave Trade.* Vol. I, *The Sources.* New York, 2013.

———. *African Voices on Slavery and the Slave Trade.* Vol. II, *Essays on Sources and Methods.* Cambridge, 2016.

Belleau, Jean-Philippe E. "Love in the Time of Hierarchy: Ethnographic Voices in 18th-Century Haiti." In Larry Wolff and Marco Cipolloni, eds., *The Anthropology of the Enlightenment,* 209–238. Stanford, Calif., 2007.

Belmonte Postigo, José Luis. "Bajo el negro velo de la ilegalidad: Un análisis del mercado de esclavos dominicano, 1746–1821." *Nuevo mundo, mundos nuevos,* July 7, 2016. http://journals.openedition.org/nuevomundo/69478.

Bénot, Yves. *La démence coloniale sous Napoléon: Essai.* Paris, 1992.

Bénot, Yves, and Marcel Dorigny, eds. *1802, le rétablissement de l'esclavage dans les colonies françaises . . . aux origines d'Haïti.* Paris, 2003.

Benson, LeGrace. "A Queen in Diaspora: The Sorrowful Exile of Queen Marie-Louise Christophe (1778, Ouanaminth, Haiti–March 11, 1851, Pisa, Italy)." *Journal of Haitian Studies,* XX, no. 2 (Fall 2014), 90–101.

Berlin, Ira, and Philip D. Morgan, eds. *Cultivation and Culture: Labor and the Shaping of Slave Life in the Americas.* Charlottesville, Va., 1993.

Bernier, Celeste-Marie, and Hannah Durkin, eds. *Visualising Slavery: Art across the African Diaspora.* Liverpool, U.K., 2016.

Bernier, Celeste-Marie, and Judie Newman. "Public Art, Artefacts, and Atlantic Slavery: Introduction." *Slavery and Abolition,* XXIX (2008), 135–150.

Berry, Daina Ramey. *The Price for Their Pound of Flesh: The Value of the Enslaved, from Womb to Grave, in the Building of a Nation.* Boston, 2017.

Berry, Daina Ramey, and Leslie M. Harris, eds. *Sexuality and Slavery: Reclaiming Inti-mate Histories in the Americas.* Athens, Ga., 2018.

Best, Stephen. "Neither Lost nor Found: Slavery and the Visual Archive." *Representa-tions,* CXIII, no. 1 (Winter 2011), 150–163.

———. *None Like Us: Blackness, Belonging, Aesthetic Life.* Durham, N.C., 2018.

Bialuschewski, Arne, and Lindford D. Fisher, eds. "Native American Slavery in the Sev-enteenth Century." Special issue of *Ethnohistory,* LXIV (2017).

Bibliothèque Moreau de Saint-Méry. 275 vols. Bibliothèque nationale de France (BnF).

Birch, William Russell. *China Retreat Pennsyla. the Seat of Mr. Manigault.* [Bristol, Pennsylvania]. 1809. 1 print: engraving, hand-colored mounted on paper; 16 × 20 cm (6 × 7.75 in). The Library Company of Philadelphia. https://digital.librarycompany .org/islandora/object/islandora%3A323587.

———. *Van Brant's* [sic] *Place on the Delaware River.* Circa 1808. 1 drawing: watercolor; 15 × 20 cm (5.5 × 7.5 in). The Library Company of Philadelphia. https://digital.library company.org/islandora/object/Islandora%3A13387?solr_nav%5Bid%5D=6582a23eba 75b0d0789a&solr_nav%5Bpage%5D=0&solr_nav%5Boffset%5D=0.

Bleichmar, Daniela. *Visible Empire: Botanical Expeditions and Visual Culture in the His-panic Enlightenment.* Chicago, 2012.

Bleichmar, Daniela, Paula De Vos, Kristin Huffine, and Kevin Sheehan, eds. *Science in the Spanish and Portuguese Empires, 1500–1800.* Stanford, Calif., 2009.

Block, Sharon. *Rape and Sexual Power in Early America.* Williamsburg, Va., and Chapel Hill, N.C., 2006.

Bodoni, G[iambattista]. *Autobiografia di G. B. Bodoni in 200 lettere inedite all'incisore Francesco Rosaspina.* Edited by Luigi Servolini. Parma, Italy, 1958.

Boidin, Capucine, and Angélica Otazú Melgarejo. "Toward a Guarani Semantic His-tory: Political Vocabulary in Guarani (Sixteenth to Nineteenth Centuries)." In Alan Durston and Bruce Mannheim, eds., *Indigenous Languages, Politics, and Authority in Latin America: Historical and Ethnographic Perspectives,* 125–160. Notre Dame, Ind., 2018.

Bongie, Chris. *Friends and Enemies: The Scribal Politics of Post/Colonial Literature.* Liverpool, U.K., 2008.

"Book Printing Lingo: What Is the Spine of a Book?" Formax Printing Solutions. https://www.formaxprinting.com/blog/2013/01/book-printing-lingo-what-is-the -spine-of-a-book.

Bostoen, Koen, and Gilles-Maurice de Schryver. "Seventeenth-Century Kikongo Is Not the Ancestor of Present-Day Kikongo." In Bostoen and Inge Brinkman, eds., *The Kongo Kingdom: The Origins, Dynamics, and Cosmopolitan Culture of an African Polity,* 60–102. Cambridge, 2018.

Boulle, Pierre H., and Sue Peabody. *Le droit des noirs en France au temps de l'esclavage: Textes choisis et commentés.* Paris, 2014.

Bowyer, William. *The Origin of Printing: In Two Essays. . . .* London, 1774.

Bradford, Thomas. *Bradford's Catalogue of Books and Stationary* [sic]*, Wholesale and Retail, for 1796. . . .* Philadelphia, 1796.

Brasseaux, Carl A., and Glenn R. Conrad, eds. *The Road to Louisiana: The Saint-Domingue Refugees, 1792–1809.* Translated by David Cheramie. Lafayette, La., 1992.

Braun, Juliane. "Bioprospecting Breadfruit: Imperial Botany, Transoceanic Relations, and the Politics of Translation." In "The New Natural History." Special issue of *Early American Literature,* LIV (2019), 643–671.

Breen, T. H. "The Meaning of 'Likeness': American Portrait Painting in an Eighteenth-Century Consumer Society." *Word and Image,* VI (1990), 325–350.

Brickhouse, Anna. "Mistranslation, Unsettlement, La Navidad." *PMLA,* CXXVIII (2013), 938–946.

———. *The Unsettlement of America: Translation, Interpretation, and the Story of Don Luis de Velasco, 1560–1945.* New York, 2015.

Brière, Jean-François. *Haïti et la France, 1804–1848: Le rêve brisé.* Paris, 2008.

Brigham, Clarence S. *Cabon's History of Haiti Journalism.* Worcester, Mass., 1940. Orig. publ. as Adolphe Cabon, "Un siècle et demi de journalisme en Haïti." *La petite revue hebdomadaire* (Port-au-Prince, Haiti), Apr. 12 –Nov. 14, 1919.

Bringhurst, Robert. *The Elements of Typographic Style.* 3d ed. Point Roberts, Wash., 2004.

Brockey, Liam Matthew. *Journey to the East: The Jesuit Mission to China, 1579–1724.* Cambridge, Mass., 2007.

Brody, Jennifer DeVere. *Punctuation: Art, Politics, and Play.* Durham, N.C., 2008.

Brown, Laurence. "Visions of Violence in the Haitian Revolution." *Atlantic Studies,* XIII (2016), 144–164.

Brown, Vincent. *The Reaper's Garden: Death and Power in the World of Atlantic Slavery.* Cambridge, Mass., 2010.

[Brûletout de] Préfontaine, [Jean Antoine]. *Maison rustique, à l'usage des habitans de la partie de la France équinoxiale, connue sous le nom de Cayenne.* Paris, 1763.

Brunazzi Celaschi, Luisella. "La storia dell'Università di Parma negli scritti e nell'azione politica di Moreau de Saint-Méry." *Studi parmensi,* XXIV (1979), 67–112.

Burnard, Trevor, and John Garrigus. *The Plantation Machine: Atlantic Capitalism in French Saint-Domingue and British Jamaica.* Philadelphia, 2016.

Bush, Barbara. "'Sable Venus,' 'She Devil,' or 'Drudge'? British Slavery and the 'Fabulous Fiction' of Black Women's Identities, c. 1650–1838." *Women's History Review,* IX (2000), 761–789.

———. "White 'Ladies,' Coloured 'Favourites,' and Black 'Wenches': Some Considerations on Sex, Race, and Class Factors in Social Relations in White Creole Society in the British Caribbean." *Slavery and Abolition,* II (1981), 245–262.

[Callières de l'Etang, Pierre Jean Georges]. *Chanson sur la prise des Invalides et de la Bastille, les lundi 13 et mardi 14 juillet 1789. . . .* [Paris], 1789.

Camier, Bernard. "Jalons pour une histoire de la représentation des noirs à travers la musique en France et dans ses colonies (1750–1820)." Colloque pluridisciplinaire, February 27–28, March 1–2, 2013, Université des Antilles et de la Guyane.

———. "Moreau de Saint-Méry et la musique coloniale des Antilles françaises au XVIIIe siècle." In Taffin, ed., *Moreau de Saint-Méry,* 173–187.

Camier, Bernard, and Laurent Dubois. "Voltaire et Zaïre; ou, Le théâtre des Lumières dans l'aire atlantique française." *Revue d'histoire moderne et contemporaine,* LIV, no. 4 (October–December 2007), 39–69.

Camus, A. G. *Histoire et procédés du polytypage et de la stéréotypie.* Paris, [1801].

Camus, Michel. "Une fille naturelle de Moreau de Saint-Méry?" *Généalogie et historie de la Caribe,* no. 93 (May 1997), 1960.

———. "Une fille naturelle de Moreau de Saint-Méry à Saint-Domingue." *Revue de la Société haïtienne d'histoire et de geographie,* XLVI, no. 162 (March 1989), 51–52.

Cañizares-Esguerra, Jorge. *How to Write the History of the New World: Histories, Epistemologies, and Identities in the Eighteenth-Century Atlantic World.* Stanford, Calif., 2001.

———. "Nation and Nature: Natural History and the Fashioning of Creole National Identity in Late Colonial Spanish America." Conference Paper. XX International Congress of the Latin American Studies Association, Apr. 17–19, 1997, Guadalajara, Mexico.

Cañizares-Esguerra, Jorge, Matt D. Childs, and James Sidbury, eds. *The Black Urban Atlantic in the Age of the Slave Trade.* Philadelphia, 2013.

Carey, Daniel, and Lynn Festa, eds. *The Postcolonial Enlightenment: Eighteenth-Century Colonialism and Postcolonial Theory.* New York, 2015.

Carey, Mathew. *Mathew Carey's Catalogue of Books, Etc. for Sale, on the Most Reasonable Terms at No. 118, Market-Street, Near Fourth-Street, Philadelphia.* Philadelphia, 1794.

Carlyle, Thomas. *The French Revolution: A History,* I. [Paris, 1837].

Carpenter, Charles H., Jr. "The Chinese Collection of A. E. van Braam Houckgeest." *Antiques,* CV (1974), 338–347.

Carpentier, Alejo. *The Kingdom of This World.* Translated by Harriet de Onís. New York, 1970.

———. *El reino de est mundo.* 6th ed. Mexico City, 1991.

———. *El siglo de las luces.* Mexico City, 1965.

Casimir, Jean. *The Haitians: A Decolonial History.* Translated by Laurent Dubois. Chapel Hill, N.C., 2020.

Casper, Scott E. *Constructing American Lives: Biography and Culture in Nineteenth-Century America.* Chapel Hill, N.C., 1999.

Casper, Scott E., Joanne D. Chaison, and Jeffrey D. Groves, eds. *Perspectives on American Book History: Artifacts and Commentary.* Amherst, Mass., 2002.

Castera, Justin Emmanuel. *Bref coup d'oeil sur les origins de la presse haïtienne (1764–1850).* Port-au-Prince, Haiti, 1986.

Castiglia, Christopher, and Julia Stern. Introduction to "Interiority in Early American Literature." Special issue of *Early American Literature,* XXXVII (2002), 1–7.

Catalogue des livres et manuscrits de la bibliothèque de feu M. Moreau de Saint-Méry, . . . dont la vente se fera le mercredi 15 décembre 1819. . . . [Paris], 1819.

Charlevoix, P[ierre François Xavier] de. *Journal of a Voyage to North-America, . . .* I. London, 1761.

Charpentier de Cossigny, [Joseph-François]. *Voyage à Canton, capitale de la province de ce nom, à la Chine. . . .* Paris, 1799.

Chartier, Roger. *The Cultural Uses of Print in Early Modern France.* Translated by Lydia G. Cochrane. Princeton, N.J., 2014.

Charton, Louis. *Observation de M. Charton à la motion de M. Moreau de Saint-Méry.* Paris, 1789.

C[hastenet-]d'Esterre, G[abriel]. *Précis historique sur le régiment de Crête, dragons; suivi d'une notice sur la vie militaire, politique et privée de M. Baudry-Deslozières, colonel-inspecteur dudit régiment.* 3d ed. [Paris?] 1804.

Chu, Petra ten-Doesschate, and Jennifer Milam, eds. *Beyond Chinoiserie: Artistic Exchange between China and the West during the Late Qing Dynasty (1796–1911).* Leiden, Netherlands, 2019.

Cioccolo, Floriana. "Artiste a Parma e a Milano: La creatività femminile fra obbligo pedagogico e veto istituzionale." *Memorie della accademia delle scienze di Torino,* XXIV (2000), 325–363.

Clark, Emily. *The Strange History of the American Quadroon: Free Women of Color in the Revolutionary Atlantic World.* Chapel Hill, N.C., 2013.

Clark, Fiona. "'Read All about It': Science, Translation, Adaptation, and Confrontation in the *Gazeta de literatura de México,* 1788–1795." In Bleichmar, De Vos, Huffine, and Sheehan, eds., *Science in the Spanish and Portuguese Empires,* 147–177.

Clavigero, Francesco Saverio. *Storia antica del Messico. . . .* 4 vols. Cesena, Italy, 1780–1781.

Cleland, T. M. *Giambattista Bodoni of Parma.* Boston, 1916.

Clover, David. "The British Abolitionist Movement and Print Culture: James Phillips, Activist, Printer and Bookseller." Paper given at the Society for Caribbean Studies (U.K.) Annual Conference, 2013, Warwick University, Coventry, U.K.

Coates, Ta-Nehisi. "The Case for Reparations." *Atlantic,* June 2014, 54–71. https://www.theatlantic.com/magazine/archive/2014/06/the-case-for-reparations/361631/.

Cohen, Lara Langer, and Jordan Alexander Stein, eds. *Early African American Print Culture.* Philadelphia, 2012.

Colwill, Elizabeth. "Sex, Savagery, and Slavery in the Shaping of the French Body Politic." In Sara E. Melzer and Kathryn Norberg, eds., *From the Royal to the Republican Body: Incorporating the Political in Seventeenth- and Eighteenth-Century France,* 198–223. Berkeley, Calif., 1998.

Cooke, Bill. "The Denial of Slavery in Management Studies." *Journal of Management Studies,* XL (2003), 1895–1918.

Copeland, Huey, and Krista Thompson. "Perpetual Returns: New World Slavery and the Matter of the Visual." Special issue of *Representations,* CXIII, no. 1 (Winter 2011), 1–15.

"A Correspondence between the Rev. John Heckewelder, of Bethlehem, and Peter S. DuPonceau, Esq. . . ." *Transactions of the Historical and Literary Committee of the American Philosophical Society,* I. Philadelphia, 1818.

Cosentino, Donald J., ed. *Sacred Arts of Haitian Vodou.* Exhibition Catalog. Los Angeles, 1995.

Courbe, Wilbrode Magloire Nicolas, and Charles Toussaint Labadye. *Médéric Louis*

Élie Moreau de St. Méry: Présid[en]t des elect[eur]s de Paris au mois de j[uil]let. . . . BnF, 1789. https://purl.stanford.edu/sw430xf3001.

Cowie, Helen. "A Creole in Paris and a Spaniard in Paraguay: Geographies of Natural History in the Hispanic World (1750–1808)." *Journal of Latin American Geography,* X, no. 1 (2011), 175–197. https://muse.jhu.edu/article/424448.

Cowling, Camillia, Maria Helena Pereira Toledo Machado, Diana Paton, and Emily West. "Mothering Slaves: Comparative Perspectives on Motherhood, Childlessness, and the Care of Children in Atlantic Slave Societies." *Slavery and Abolition,* XXXVIII (2017), 223–231.

Crais, Clifton, and Pamela Scully. *Sara Baartman and the Hottentot Venus: A Ghost Story and a Biography.* Princeton, N.J., 2009.

Cross, Elizabeth. "The Last French East India Company in the Revolutionary Atlantic." *William and Mary Quarterly,* 3d Ser., LXXVII (2020), 613–640.

Curran, Andrew S. *The Anatomy of Blackness: Science and Slavery in an Age of Enlightenment.* Baltimore, 2011.

———. "Rethinking Race History: The Role of the Albino in the French Enlightenment Life Sciences." *History and Theory,* XLVIII (2009), 151–179.

Cushner, Nicholas P. *Jesuit Ranches and the Agrarian Development of Colonial Argentina, 1650–1767.* Albany, N.Y., 1983.

Cuvier, Georges. *The Animal Kingdom Arranged in Conformity with Its Organization.* . . . Translated by H[enry] M[c]Murtrie, I. New York, 1831.

[Dall'Acqua, Marzio]. *L'ossessione della memoria: Parma settecentesca nei disegni del Conte Alessandro Sanseverini.* Parma, Italy, 1997.

Darnton, Robert. *The Business of Enlightenment: A Publishing History of the Encyclopédie, 1775–1800.* 1979. Rpt. Cambridge, Mass., 2012.

———. *The Forbidden Best-Sellers of Pre-revolutionary France.* New York, 1996.

———. "What Is the History of Books?" *Daedalus,* CXI, no. 3 (Summer 1982), 65–83.

Dauge-Roth, Katherine. *Signing the Body: Marks on Skin in Early Modern France.* London, 2019.

Daunou, [Pierre-Claude-François]. *Analyse des opinions diverses sur l'origine de l'imprimerie.* Paris, [1802].

Daut, Marlene L. *Baron de Vastey and the Origins of Black Atlantic Humanism.* New York, 2017.

———. "Tear Down That Statue, Mr. Macron!" History News Network. https://historynewsnetwork.org/article/175963.

———. *Tropics of Haiti: Race and the Literary History of the Haitian Revolution in the Atlantic World, 1789–1865.* Liverpool, U.K., 2015.

Daut, Marlene L., Grégory Pierrot, and Marion C. Rohrleitner, eds. and trans. *Haitian Revolutionary Fictions: An Anthology.* Charlottesville, Va., 2022.

Davis, David Brion. *The Problem of Slavery in the Age of Revolution, 1770–1823.* 2d ed. New York, 1999.

Davis, Donald G., Jr., and John Mark Tucker, eds. *American Library History: A Comprehensive Guide to the Literature.* Santa Barbara, Calif., 1989.

Davis, Kiersten Larsen. "Secondhand Chinoiserie and the Confucian Revolutionary:

Colonial America's Decorative Arts 'After the Chinese Taste.'" Ph.D. diss., Brigham Young University, 2008.

Dawdy, Shannon Lee. "Proper Caresses and Prudent Distance: A How-To Manual from Colonial Louisiana." In Ann Laura Stoler, ed., *Haunted by Empire: Geographies of Intimacy in North American History,* 140–162. Durham, N.C., 2006.

Dayan, Joan [Colin]. "Codes of Law and Bodies of Color." *New Literary History,* XXVI (1995), 283–308.

———. *Haiti, History, and the Gods.* Berkeley, Calif., 1998.

Debbasch, Yvan. *Couleur et liberté: Le jeu du critère ethnique dans un ordre juridique esclavagiste. . . .* Paris, 1967.

Debien, Gabriel. *Les colons de Saint-Domingue et la Révolution: Essai sur le Club Massiac (août 1789–août 1792).* Paris, 1953.

"Declaration of Independence: Thomas Jefferson's Draft with Congress's Changes (July 4, 1776)." In Thomas Jefferson, *Notes on the State of Virginia.* Edited by David Waldstreicher, 47–53. Boston, 2002.

DeLombard, Jeannine Marie. *Slavery on Trial: Law, Abolitionism, and Print Culture.* Chapel Hill, N.C., 2007.

de Luna, Kathryn M. "Sounding the African Atlantic." *William and Mary Quarterly,* 3d Ser., LXXVIII (2021), 581–616.

Dépréaux, Albert. "Le commandant Baudry des Lozières et la phalange de Crête-dragons." *Revue de l'histoire des colonies françaises,* XVII, no. 1 (1924), 1–42.

Dessalines, Jean Jacques. "Proclamation of Dessalines." In [James Barskett], *History of the Island of St. Domingo, from Its First Discovery by Columbus to the Present Period,* 178–179. 1818. Rpt. Westport, Conn., 1971.

DeWispelare, Daniel. "Introduction: Multiplicity and Relation; Toward an Anglophone Eighteenth Century." In *Multilingual Subjects: On Standard English, Its Speakers, and Others in the Long Eighteenth Century,* 1–24. Philadelphia, 2017.

Dillon, Elizabeth Maddock. *"Translatio Studii* and the Poetics of the Digital Archive: Early American Literature, Caribbean Assemblages, and Freedom Dreams." *American Literary History,* XXIX (2017), 248–266.

Dinius, Marcy J. "'Look!! Look!!! At This!!!!': The Radical Typography of David Walker's *Appeal.*" *PMLA,* CXXVI (2011), 55–72.

Dobie, Madeleine. *Trading Places: Colonization and Slavery in Eighteenth-Century French Culture.* Ithaca, N.Y., 2010.

Domínguez, Daylet. "Cuadros de costumbres en Cuba y Puerto Rico: De la historia natural y la literatura de viajes a las ciencias sociales." *Revista hispánica moderna,* LXIX (2016), 133–149.

Dorigny, Marcel, Dominique Rogers, and Étienne Taillemite. *Des constitutions à la description de Saint-Domingue: La colonie française en Haïti vue par Moreau de St-Méry.* [Fort-de-France?], Martinique, 2004.

Dubois, Laurent. *Avengers of the New World: The Story of the Haitian Revolution.* Cambridge, Mass., 2004.

———. "An Enslaved Enlightenment: Rethinking the Intellectual History of the French Atlantic." *Social History,* XXXI (2006), 1–14.

Dubois, Laurent, David Garner, and Mary Caton Lingold. "The Haitian Banza." *Banjology.* https://sites.duke.edu/banjology/the-banjo-in-haiti/the-haitian-banza/.

Dubois, Laurent, and John D. Garrigus. *Slave Revolution in the Caribbean, 1789–1804: A Brief History with Documents,* 18–22, 78–82. New York, 2006.

Duchet, Michèle. *Anthropologie et histoire au siècle des Lumières: Buffon, Voltaire, Rousseau, Helvétius, Diderot.* Paris, 1971.

Ducoeurjoly, S. J. *Manuel des habitans de Saint-Domingue: Contenant un précis de l'histoire de cette île, depuis sa découverte. . . .* Paris, 1802.

Dumas, Paula E. *Proslavery Britain: Fighting for Slavery in an Era of Abolition.* Houndmills, Basingstoke, U.K., 2016.

Dun, James Alexander. "'What Avenues of Commerce, Will You, Americans, Not Explore!': Commercial Philadelphia's Vantage onto the Early Haitian Revolution." *William and Mary Quarterly,* 3d Ser., LXII (2005), 473–504.

Duval-Carrié, Edouard. *Colons et châtiments.* 2004. Painting; sequined versions by Sylva Joseph.

[Duval de Sanadon, David]. *Discours sur l'esclavage des nègres, et sur l'idée de leur affranchissement dans les colonies; par un colon de Saint-Domingue.* Amsterdam and Paris, 1786.

————. *Réclamations et observations des colons, sur l'idée de l'abolition de la traite et de l'affranchissement des nègres.* Paris, 1789.

Duyvendak, J. J. L. "The Last Dutch Embassy to the Chinese Court (1794–1795)." *T'oung Pao,* 2d Ser., XXXIV (1938), 1–137.

————. "Supplementary Documents on the Last Dutch Embassy to the Chinese Court." *T'oung Pao,* 2d Ser., XXXV (1940), 329–353.

Dyson, Rick. "The Haitian Revolution." In Junius P. Rodriguez, ed., *Encyclopedia of Slave Resistance and Rebellion,* I, 227–233. Westport, Conn., 2007.

Earle, Rebecca. "The Pleasures of Taxonomy: Casta Paintings, Classification, and Colonialism." *William and Mary Quarterly,* 3d Ser., LXXIII (2016), 427–466.

Early Proceedings of the American Philosophical Society for the Promotion of Useful Knowledge, Compiled by One of the Secretaries, from the Manuscript Minutes of Its Meetings from 1744 to 1838. Philadelphia, 1884.

Edinburgh Review, or Critical Journal. Unsigned review of *Second voyage à la Louisiane: Faisant suite au premier de l'auteur,* by Louis Narcisse Baudry des Lozières, III, no. 5 (October 1803–January 1804), 81–90.

Edwards, Erica Johnson. "Unclaimed Runaways and the Power Struggles of Colonial Haiti." *Age of Revolutions,* July 6, 2020. https://ageofrevolutions.com/2020/07/06/unclaimed-runaways-and-the-power-struggles-of-colonial-haiti-part-i-legislating-negres-epaves/.

Ehret, Christopher. *History and the Testimony of Language.* Berkeley, Calif., 2011.

Elicona, Anthony Louis. *Un colonial sous la Révolution en France et en Amérique: Moreau de Saint-Méry.* Paris, 1934.

Ellwood, Scott. "One Dynasty, Three Names." *Grolier Club,* May 24, 2019. https://grolierclub.wordpress.com/2019/05/24/one-dynasty-three-names/.

Erben, Patrick M. *A Harmony of the Spirits: Translation and the Language of Community in Early Pennsylvania.* Williamsburg, Va., and Chapel Hill, N.C., 2012.

Erbig, Jeffrey Alan, Jr. *Where Caciques and Mapmakers Met: Border Making in Eighteenth-Century South America.* Chapel Hill, N.C., 2020.

Ernest, John. *Liberation Historiography: African American Writers and the Challenge of History, 1794–1861.* Chapel Hill, N.C., 2004.

Errington, Joseph. *Linguistics in a Colonial World: A Story of Language, Meaning, and Power.* Malden, Mass., 2007.

Ethiop [William J. Wilson]. "Afric-American Picture Gallery." *Anglo-African Magazine,* I (1859), 52–324: 52–55, 87–90, 100–103, 173–177, 216–219, 243–247, 321–324.

Eze, Emmanuel Chukwudi, ed. *Race and the Enlightenment: A Reader.* Malden, Mass., 1997.

Fabella, Yvonne. "'An Empire Founded on Libertinage': The Mulâtresse and Colonial Anxiety in Saint Domingue." In Nora E. Jaffary, ed., *Gender, Race, and Religion in the Colonization of the Americas,* 109–124. Aldershot, U.K., 2007.

———. "Redeeming the 'Character of the Creoles': Whiteness, Gender, and Creolization in Pre-revolutionary Saint Domingue." *Journal of Historical Sociology,* XXIII (2010), 40–72.

Fabian, Johannes. *Language and Colonial Power: The Appropriation of Swahili in the Former Belgian Congo, 1880–1938.* 1986. Rpt. Berkeley, Calif., 1991.

Faÿ, Bernard. *La Franc-maçonnerie et la révolution intellectuelle du XVIIIe siècle.* Paris, 1942.

Ferguson, Robert A. *The American Enlightenment, 1750–1820.* Cambridge, Mass., 1997.

Ferrer, Ada. *Freedom's Mirror: Cuba and Haiti in the Age of Revolution.* New York, 2014.

Ferrer, Ada, Matt D. Childs, Linda Rodriguez, Kris Minhae Choe, Eric Anderson, Sibylle M. Fischer, Anges Lugo-Ortiz, Stephan Palmié, and Jorge Pavez-Ojeda. *Digital Aponte.* https://aponte.hosting.nyu.edu/.

Fick, Carolyn E. *The Making of Haiti: The Saint-Domingue Revolution from Below.* Knoxville, Tenn., 1990.

Fiering, Norman. Preface to Edward G. Gray and Fiering, eds., *The Language Encounter in the Americas, 1492–1800: A Collection of Essays,* vii–viii. New York, 2000.

Figueroa, Marcelo Fabián. "Félix de Azara and the Birds of Paraguay: Making Inventories and Taxonomies at the Boundaries of the Spanish Empire, 1784–1802." In Patrick Manning and Daniel Rood, eds., *Global Scientific Practice in an Age of Revolutions, 1750–1850,* 147–162. Pittsburgh, 2016.

Fildes, Valerie A. *Wet Nursing: A History from Antiquity to the Present.* Oxford, 1988.

Finley, Alexandra J. *An Intimate Economy: Enslaved Women, Work, and America's Domestic Slave Trade.* Chapel Hill, N.C., 2020.

Finseth, Ian Frederick. *Shades of Green: Visions of Nature in the Literature of American Slavery, 1770–1860.* Athens, Ga., 2009.

Fischer, Sibylle. "Bolívar in Haiti: Republicanism in the Revolutionary Atlantic." In Carla Calargé, Raphael Dalleo, Luis Duno-Gottberg, and Clevis Headley, eds., *Haiti and the Americas,* 25–53. Jackson, Miss., 2013.

Fleming, Crystal Marie. *Resurrecting Slavery: Racial Legacies and White Supremacy in France*. Philadelphia, 2017.

Foreman, P. Gabrielle. "A Riff, a Call, and a Response: Reframing the Problem That Led to Our Being Tokens in Ethnic and Gender Studies; or, Where Are We Going Anyway and with Whom Will We Travel?" *Legacy,* XXX (2013), 306–322.

Forsythe, Jennifer Marie. *"La Florida del Inca* and the Florida of the Others: The Multilingual Afterlives of Garcilaso's Florida." Ph.D. diss., University of California Los Angeles, 2019.

Forte, Maximillian C., ed. *Indigenous Resurgence in the Contemporary Caribbean: Amerindian Survival and Revival*. New York, 2006.

Foster, Thomas A., ed. *Long before Stonewall: Histories of Same-Sex Sexuality in Early America*. New York, 2007.

———. "The Sexual Abuse of Black Men under American Slavery." *Journal of the History of Sexuality,* XX (2011), 445–464.

Fouchard, Jean. "Les joies de la lecture à Saint-Domingue." *Revue d'histoire des colonies,* XLI (1954), 103–111.

———. *Les marrons de la liberté*. Paris, 1972.

Fournier, Pierre-Simon, le Jeune. *Manuel typographique, utile aux gens de lettres, et à ceux qui exercent les différents parties de l'Art de l'Imprimerie,* II. Paris, 1766.

———. *Traités historiques et critiques sur l'origine et les progrès de l'imprimerie*. Paris, 1763.

Fournier-Pescay, [François]. *Discours prononcé aux obsèques de M. Moreau de Saint-Méry, le 30 janvier 1819*. Paris, 1819.

Frank, Caroline. *Objectifying China, Imagining America: Chinese Commodities in Early America*. Chicago, 2011.

Frostin, Charles. *Les révoltes blanches à Saint-Domingue aux XVIIe et XVIIIe siècles: Haïti avant 1789*. Rennes, France, 1975.

Fry, Edmund, and Isaac Steele. *Specimen of Metal Cast Ornaments, Curiously Adjusted to Paper. . . .* London, 1793.

Fuentes, Marisa J. *Dispossessed Lives: Enslaved Women, Violence, and the Archive*. Philadelphia, 2016.

Fumagalli, Maria Cristina. "Landscaping Hispaniola: Moreau de Saint-Méry's Border Politics." *New West Indian Guide / Nieuwe West-Indische Gids,* LXXXV (2011), 169–190.

Furstenberg, François. *When the United States Spoke French: Five Refugees Who Shaped a Nation*. New York, 2014.

Garraway, Doris. *The Libertine Colony: Creolization in the Early French Caribbean*. Durham, N.C., 2005.

Garrigus, John D. *Before Haiti: Race and Citizenship in French Saint-Domingue*. New York, 2006.

———. "Moreau de Saint-Méry et le patriotisme créole à Saint-Domingue." In Taffin, ed., *Moreau de Saint-Méry,* 65–76.

———. "Opportunist or Patriot? Julien Raimond (1744–1801) and the Haitian Revolution." *Slavery and Abolition,* XXVIII (2007), 1–21.

Gaspar, David Barry, and Darlene Clark Hine, eds. *More than Chattel: Black Women and Slavery in the Americas*. Bloomington, Ind., 1996.

Gaterau, [Louis]. *Réponse aux libelles séditieux publiés à Philadelphie contre les hommes de couleur de Saint Domingue*. Philadelphia, 1796.

Gauthier, Florence. *L'aristocratie de l'épiderme: Le combat de la Société des citoyens de couleur, 1789–1791*. Paris, 2007.

———. "Au coeur du *préjugé de couleur* dans la colonie de Saint-Domingue: Médéric Moreau de Saint Méry contre Julien Raimond, 1789–91." *Le canard republicain,* June 10, 2010. https://lecanardrépublicain.net/spip.php?article356.

Gayarré, Charles. *History of Louisiana: The Spanish Domination*. New York, 1854.

Geggus, David. "The French Slave Trade: An Overview." *William and Mary Quarterly,* 3d Ser., LVIII (2001), 119–138.

———. "Moreau de Saint-Méry et la Révolution de Saint-Domingue." In Taffin, ed., *Moreau de Saint-Méry,* 129–136.

———. "Print Culture and the Haitian Revolution: The Written and the Spoken Word." American Antiquarian Society, *Proceedings,* CXVI, pt. 2 (2006), 299–316.

———. "Racial Equality, Slavery, and Colonial Secession during the Constituent Assembly." *American Historical Review,* XCIV (1989), 1290–1308.

Gerber, Eve. "African American History Books Recommended by Imani Perry." *Five Books* (blog). https://fivebooks.com/best-books/african-american-history-imani-perry/.

Gerbi, Antonello. *The Dispute of the New World: The History of a Polemic, 1750–1900*. Translated by Jeremy Moyle. 1973. Rpt. Pittsburgh, 2010.

Gerbner, Katherine. "Antislavery in Print: The Germantown Protest, the 'Exhortation,' and the Seventeenth-Century Quaker Debate on Slavery." *Early American Studies,* IX (2011), 552–575.

Ghachem, Malick W. "Montesquieu in the Caribbean: The Colonial Enlightenment between Code Noir and Code Civil." *Historical Reflections / Réflexions historiques,* XXV (1999), 183–210.

———. *The Old Regime and the Haitian Revolution*. New York, 2012.

———. "Prosecuting Torture: The Strategic Ethics of Slavery in Pre-revolutionary Saint-Domingue (Haiti)." *Law and History Review,* XXIX (2011), 985–1029.

———. "The 'Trap' of Representation: Sovereignty, Slavery, and the Road to the Haitian Revolution." *Historical Reflections / Réflexions historiques,* XXIX (2003), 123–144.

Gibbs, Jenna M. *Performing the Temple of Liberty: Slavery, Theater, and Popular Culture in London and Philadelphia, 1760–1850*. Baltimore, 2011.

Gikandi, Simon. "Rethinking the Archive of Enslavement." *Early American Literature,* L (2015), 81–102.

———. *Slavery and the Culture of Taste*. Princeton, N.J., 2011.

Girard, Philippe R. "The Haitian Revolution, History's New Frontier: State of the Scholarship and Archival Sources." *Slavery and Abolition,* XXXIV (2013), 485–507.

Gliech, Oliver. "Bibliografien zu Geschichte, Politik und Gesellschaft." *Domingino-Verlag.* https://www.domingino.de/.

Glover, Kaiama L. "Exploiting the Undead: The Usefulness of the Zombie in Haitian Literature." *Journal of Haitian Studies,* XI, no. 2 (Fall 2005), 105–121.

Gomez, Michael A. "The Anguished Igbo Response to Enslavement in the Americas." In Carolyn A. Brown and Paul E. Lovejoy, eds., *Repercussions of the Atlantic Slave Trade: The Interior of the Bight of Biafra and the African Diaspora,* 103–118. Trenton, N.J., 2011.

———. *Exchanging Our Country Marks: The Transformation of African Identities in the Colonial and Antebellum South.* Chapel Hill, N.C., 1998.

Gómez, Pablo F. *The Experiential Caribbean: Creating Knowledge and Healing in the Early Modern Atlantic.* Chapel Hill, N.C., 2017.

Gonzalez, Johnhenry. *Maroon Nation: A History of Revolutionary Haiti.* New Haven, Conn., 2019.

Goodman, Dena. *The Republic of Letters: A Cultural History of the French Enlightenment.* Ithaca, N.Y., 1994.

Gordon, Leah. "The Caste Portraits." https://www.leahgordon.co.uk/index.php/project/caste/.

Gordon-Reed, Annette. *The Hemingses of Monticello: An American Family.* New York, 2008.

———. "Writing Early American Lives as Biography." *William and Mary Quarterly,* 3d Ser., LXXI (2014), 491–516.

Goya, Francisco de. *Retrato de Félix de Azara.* 1805. Oil on canvas. Museo Goya. https://museogoya.fundacionibercaja.es/obras/retrato-de-felix-de-azara.

Grandpré, L[ouis-Marie-Joseph O'Hier de]. *Voyage [à] la côte occidentale d'Afrique, fait dans les années 1786 et 1787.* Paris, 1801.

Grégoire, [Henri]. *Mémoire en faveur des gens de couleur ou sang-mêlés de St. Domingue, et des autres isles françaises de l'Amérique, adressé à l'Assemblée nationale.* Paris, 1789.

Griffiths, Antony. "Proofs in Eighteenth-Century French Printmaking." *Print Quarterly,* XXI (2004), 3–17.

Groce, George C., and David H. Wallace. *The New York Historical Society's Dictionary of Artists in America, 1564–1860.* New Haven, Conn., 1957.

Grohmann, Jean Godefroi. *Moeurs et coutumes des Chinois, et leurs costumes en couleur d'après les tableaux de Pu-Qùa, peintre à Canton pour servier de suite aux Voyages de Macartney et de Van Braam; 60 planches avec le texte français et allemande / Gebräuche und Kleidungen der Chinesen dargestellt in bunten Gemälden von dem Mahler Pu-Qúa in Canton als Zusatz zu Macartneys und Van Braams Reisen; 60 Kupfer mit Erklärung in deutscher und französischer Sprache herausgegeben.* Leipzig, Germany, 1800.

Gross, Robert A., and Mary Kelley, eds. *An Extensive Republic: Print, Culture, and Society in the New Nation, 1790–1840.* Vol. II of *History of the Book in America.* Chapel Hill, N.C., 2010.

Guterl, Matthew Pratt. *American Mediterranean: Southern Slaveholders in the Age of Emancipation.* Cambridge, Mass., 2008.

Haddad, John Rogers. *The Romance of China: Excursions to China in U.S. Culture, 1776–1876.* New York, 2008.

Hall, Kim F. "I Can't Love This the Way You Want Me To: Archival Blackness." *Postmedieval,* XI (2020), 171–179.

Hannah-Jones, Nikole, et al. *The 1619 Project: New York Times Magazine.* August 14, 2019.

Hardwick, Julie, Sarah M. S. Pearsall, and Karin Wulf. "Centering Families in Atlantic Histories." Special issue of *William and Mary Quarterly,* 3d Ser., LXX (2013), 205–224.

Harsanyi, Doina Pasca. *Lessons from America: Liberal French Nobles in Exile, 1793–1798.* University Park, Pa., 2010.

———. "Sidestepping a Historical Wave: A Cancelled Revolution in Northern Italy, 1796–1797." *Napoleonica,* XXXVII (2020), 2–24.

Hartman, Saidiya. *Lose Your Mother: A Journey along the Atlantic Slave Route.* New York, 2007.

———. "Venus in Two Acts." *Small Axe,* XII, no. 2 (June 2008), 1–14.

———. *Wayward Lives, Beautiful Experiments: Intimate Histories of Social Upheaval.* New York, 2019.

Harvey, Sean P. *Native Tongues: Colonialism and Race from Encounter to the Reservation.* Cambridge, Mass., 2015.

Hawthorne, Walter. "'Being Now, as It Were, One Family': Shipmate Bonding on the Slave Vessel *Emilia,* in Rio de Janeiro and throughout the Atlantic World." *Luso-Brazilian Review,* XLV, no. 1 (June 2008), 53–77.

Hazaël-Massieux, Marie-Christine. *Textes anciens en créole Français de la Caraïbe: Histoire et analyse.* Paris, 2008.

Hazan, Éric. *A People's History of the French Revolution.* Translated by David Fernbach. London, 2014.

Hébert, Catherine. "The French Element in Pennsylvania in the 1790s: The Francophone Immigrants' Impact." *Pennsylvania Magazine of History and Biography,* CVIII (1984), 45–69.

———. "French Publications in Philadelphia in the Age of the French Revolution: A Bibliographical Essay." *Pennsylvania History,* LVIII (1991), 37–61.

Helton, Laura, Justin Leroy, Max A. Mishler, Samantha Seeley, and Shauna Sweeney. "The Question of Recovery: Slavery, Freedom, and the Archive." Special issue of *Social Text,* XXXIII, no. 4 (125) (December 2015), 1–18.

Herbert, Th[omas]. *A Relation of Some Yeares Travaile . . . into Afrique and the Greater Asia. . . .* London, 1634.

Hesse, Carla. *Publishing and Cultural Politics in Revolutionary Paris, 1789–1810.* Berkeley, Calif., 1991.

Hevia, James L. *Cherishing Men from Afar: Qing Guest Ritual and the Macartney Embassy of 1793.* Durham, N.C., 1995.

Heywood, Linda M., ed. *Central Africans and Cultural Transformations in the American Diaspora.* New York, 2002.

Heywood, Linda M., and John K. Thornton, eds. *Central Africans, Atlantic Creoles, and the Foundation of the Americas, 1585–1660.* New York, 2007.

Hibbard, Allen. "Biographer and Subject: A Tale of Two Narratives." *Journal of the South Central,* XXIII, no. 3 (Fall 2006), 19–36.

H[illiard] d'[Auberteuil], [Michel-René]. *Considérations sur l'état present de la colonie française de Saint-Domingue: Ouvrage politique et législatif; presenté au minister de la marine,* I. Paris, 1776.

"The History of Scarification in Africa." *Hadithi Africa.* https://hadithi.africa/the -history-of-scarification-in-africa/.

Hugo, Victor. "Talleyrand" (1838). In Hugo, *Things Seen (Choses vues),* I. New York, 1887.

Hunt, Lynn, ed. *The Invention of Pornography: Obscenity and the Origins of Modernity, 1500–1800.* Princeton, N.J., 1993.

Huyghues-Belrose, Vincent. "Moreau de Saint-Méry, arpenteur créole de Saint-Domingue." In Taffin, ed., *Moreau de Saint-Méry,* 9–23.

Iannini, Christopher P. *Fatal Revolutions: Natural History, West Indian Slavery, and the Routes of American Literature.* Williamsburg, Va., and Chapel Hill, N.C., 2012.

[Isabey, Jean Baptiste]. *Ritratto dell'amministratore general degli Stati di Parma, Piacenza e Guastella Médéric Louis-Elie Moreau de Saint-Méry.* Charcoal drawing. No date. Glauco Lombardi Museum. Parma, Italy.

Jackson, Shona N. *Creole Indigeneity: Between Myth and Nation in the Caribbean.* Minneapolis, 2012.

Jean-Charles, Régine Michelle. "*Memwa se paswa:* Sifting the Slave Past in Haiti." In Soyica Diggs Colbert, Robert J. Patterson, and Aida Levy-Hussen, eds., *The Psychic Hold of Slavery: Legacies in American Expressive Culture,* 86–106. New Brunswick, N.J., 2016.

Jennings, Lawrence C. *French Anti-slavery: The Movement for the Abolition of Slavery in France, 1802–1848.* Cambridge, 2000.

———. "The Interaction of French and British Antislavery, 1789–1848." *Proceedings of the Fifteenth Meeting of the French Colonial Historical Society, . . .* XV (1992), 81–91.

Jenson, Deborah. *Beyond the Slave Narrative: Politics, Sex, and Manuscripts in the Haitian Revolution.* Liverpool, U.K., 2011.

———. "Jean-Jacques Dessalines and the African Character of the Haitian Revolution." *William and Mary Quarterly,* 3d Ser., LXIX (2012), 615–638.

Johnson, Jessica Marie. *Wicked Flesh: Black Women, Intimacy, and Freedom in the Atlantic World.* Philadelphia, 2020.

Johnson, Sara E. *The Fear of French Negroes: Transcolonial Collaboration in the Revolutionary Americas.* Berkeley, Calif., 2012.

———. "'He Was a Lion, and He Would Destroy Much': A Speculative School of Revolutionary Politics." *Small Axe,* XXIII, no. 1 (March 2019), 195–207.

———. "Moreau de Saint-Méry: Itinerant Bibliophile." *Library and Information History,* XXXI (2015), 171–197.

———. "'You Should Give Them Blacks to Eat': Waging Inter-American Wars of Torture and Terror." *American Quarterly,* LXI (2009), 65–92.

Jordan, June. "The Difficult Miracle of Black Poetry in America: Or Something Like a Sonnet for Phillis Wheatley." In *Some of Us Did Not Die: New and Selected Essays of June Jordan,* 174–186. New York, 2003.

Joseph-Gabriel, Annette K. "Creolizing Freedom: French-Creole Translations of

Liberty and Equality in the Haitian Revolution." *Slavery and Abolition,* XXXVI (2015), 111–123.

Josephson, Nancy. "Artists on Artists: Nancy Josephson on Haitian Sequin Artists." In "The Americas Issue: Tribute to Haiti." Special issue of *Bomb,* no. 90 (Winter 2004 / 2005), 14–17.

Jung, Moon-Ho. *Coolies and Cane: Race, Labor, and Sugar in the Age of Emancipation.* Baltimore, 2006.

Kadish, Doris Y., and Deborah Jenson, eds. *Poetry of Haitian Independence.* New Haven, Conn., 2015.

Kadish, Doris Y., and Françoise Massardier-Kenney, eds. *Translating Slavery,* I, *Gender and Race in French Abolitionist Writing, 1780–1830.* 2d ed., rev. Kent, Ohio, 2009.

———. *Translating Slavery,* II, *Ourika and Its Progeny.* Kent, Ohio, 2010.

Kastor, Peter J., and François Weil, eds. *Empires of the Imagination: Transatlantic Histories of the Louisiana Purchase.* Charlottesville, Va., 2009.

Kazanjian, David. *The Brink of Freedom: Improvising Life in the Nineteenth-Century Atlantic World.* Durham, N.C., 2016.

———. "Freedom's Surprise: Two Paths through Slavery's Archives." *History of the Present,* VI (2016), 133–145.

———. "Scenes of Speculation." *Social Text,* XXXIII, no. 4 (125) (December 2015), 77–84.

Keefer, Katrina H. B. "Marked by Fire: Brands, Slavery, and Identity." *Slavery and Abolition,* XL (2019), 659–681.

Kelley, Robin D. G. "'But a Local Phase of a World Problem': Black History's Global Vision, 1883–1950." In "The Nation and Beyond: Transnational Perspectives on United States History." Special issue of *Journal of American History,* LXXXVI (1999), 1045–1077.

Kelly, Catherine E. *Republic of Taste: Art, Politics, and Everyday Life in Early America.* Philadelphia, 2016.

Kendi, Ibram X., and Keisha N. Blain, eds. *Four Hundred Souls: A Community History of African America, 1619–2019.* New York, 2021.

Kent, Henry W. "Chez Moreau de Saint-Méry, Philadelphie . . . with a List of Imprints Enlarged by George Parker Winship." In *Bibliographical Essays: A Tribute to Wilberforce Eames,* 67–78. Cambridge, Mass., 1924.

———. "Encore Moreau de Saint-Méry." In [Deoch Fulton], ed., *Bookmen's Holiday: Notes and Studies Written and Gathered in Tribute to Harry Miller Lydenberg,* 239–247. New York, 1943.

———. "Van Braam Houckgeest, an Early American Collector." American Antiquarian Society, *Proceedings,* XL, pt. 2 (1930), 159–174.

Kind, Jasper De, Gilles-Maurice de Schryver, and Koen Bostoen. "Pushing Back the Origin of Bantu Lexicography: The *Vocabularium Congense* of 1652, 1928, 2012." *Lexikos,* XXII (2012), 159–194.

King, Stewart R. *Blue Coat or Powdered Wig: Free People of Color in Pre-revolutionary Saint Domingue.* Athens, Ga., 2001.

King, Wilma. "'Prematurely Knowing of Evil Things': The Sexual Abuse of African American Girls and Young Women in Slavery and Freedom." *Journal of African American History,* XCIX (2014), 173–196.

———. "Suffer with Them till Death: Slave Women and Their Children in Nineteenth-Century America." In Gaspar and Hine, eds., *More than Chattel,* 147–168.

Klooster, Wim. *Revolutions in the Atlantic World: A Comparative History.* New ed. New York, 2018.

Klooster, Wim, and Gert Oostindie. *Realm between Empires: The Second Dutch Atlantic, 1680–1815.* Ithaca, N.Y., 2018.

Knott, Sarah. *Mother Is a Verb: An Unconventional History.* New York, 2019.

———. "Narrating the Age of Revolution." *William and Mary Quarterly,* 3d Ser., LXXIII (2016), 3–36.

———. *Sensibility and the American Revolution.* Williamsburg, Va., and Chapel Hill, N.C., 2009.

Knott, Sarah, and Barbara Taylor, eds. *Women, Gender, and Enlightenment.* Basingstoke, U.K., 2005.

Koon, Yeewan. "Narrating the City: Pu Qua and the Depiction of Street Life in Canton." In Petra ten-Doesschate Chu and Ning Ding, with Lidy Jane Chu, eds., *Qing Encounters: Artistic Exchanges between China and the West,* 217–231. Los Angeles, 2015.

Korhonen, Kuisma, ed. *Tropes for the Past: Hayden White and the History / Literature Debate.* Amsterdam, 2006.

LaBan, Craig. "George Washington's Enslaved Chef, Who Cooked in Philadelphia, Disappears from Painting, but May Have Reappeared in New York." *Philadelphia Inquirer,* Mar. 1, 2019. https://www.inquirer.com/food/craig-laban/george-washington-slave-chef-cook-hercules-gilbert-stuart-painting-wrong-20190301.html.

Labat, Jean-Baptiste. *Nouveau voyage aux isles de l'Amérique, contenant l'histoire naturelle de ces pays, l'origine, les moeurs, la religion et le gouvernement des habitans anciens et modernes.* 6 vols. V. Paris, 1722.

Lachance, Paul. "An Empire Gone Awry: Why Napoleon Sold Louisiana." *Humanities-Washington,* XXIII, no. 6 (November 2002), 17–19.

Lafuente, Antonio. "Enlightenment in an Imperial Context: Local Science in the Late-Eighteenth-Century Hispanic World." *Osiris,* 2d ed., XV (2000), 155–173.

Lai, Walton Look. *Indentured Labor, Caribbean Sugar: Chinese and Indian Migrants to the British West Indies, 1838–1918.* Baltimore, 1993.

L'Aîné, Ostervald. *Ritratto de Moreau de Saint-Méry.* No date. Etching with pointillé, watercolor. Parma, Italy, private collection.

Lara, Ana-Maurine. *Kohnjehr Woman.* Washington, D.C., 2017.

Lasagni, Roberto. *Dizionario biografico dei parmigiani,* III. Parma, Italy, 1999.

Lautard, Jean-Baptiste. *Histoire de l'Académie de Marseille, depuis sa fondation en 1726 jusqu'en 1826.* Marseille, France, 1829.

Lawson, Alexander. *Anatomy of a Typeface.* Boston, 1990.

Lazo, Rodrigo. *Letters from Filadelfia: Early Latino Literature and the Trans-American Elite.* Charlottesville, Va., 2020.

[Leclerc, Georges-Louis], comte de Buffon. *Histoire naturelle, générale et particulière, servant de suite à l'histoire naturelle de l'homme.* Paris, 1777.

Lee, Jean Gordon. *Philadelphians and the China Trade, 1784–1844.* Philadelphia, [1984].

Lefler, Hugh Talmage, ed. *A New Voyage to Carolina by John Lawson.* Chapel Hill, N.C., 1967.

Lepore, Jill. *A Is for American: Letters and Other Characters in the Newly United States.* New York, 2002.

——. *Book of Ages: The Life and Opinions of Jane Franklin.* New York, 2013.

——. "Historians Who Love Too Much: Reflections on Microhistory and Biography." *Journal of American History,* LXXXVIII (2001), 129–144.

Leumas, Emilie. "Ties That Bind: The Family, Social, and Business Associations of the Insurrectionists of 1768." *Louisiana History,* XLVII (2006), 183–202.

Levander, Caroline F., and Robert S. Levine, eds. *Hemispheric American Studies.* New Brunswick, N.J., 2008.

Lewis, Elizabeth Franklin, Mónica Bolufer Peruga, and Catherine M. Jaffe, eds. *The Routledge Companion to the Hispanic Enlightenment.* London, 2019.

Lewis, Shireen K. *Race, Culture, and Identity: Francophone West African and Caribbean Literature and Theory from Négritude to Créolité.* Lanham, Md., 2006.

Lindsay, Lisa A., and John Wood Sweet, eds. *Biography and the Black Atlantic.* Philadelphia, 2014.

Loehr, George R. "A. E. van Braam Houckgeest: The First American at the Court of China." *Princeton University Library Chronicle,* XV (1954), 179–193.

López, Enrique Álvarez. "Félix de Azara, precursor de Darwin." *Revista de Occidente,* XLIII (1934), 149–166.

López, Kathleen. *Chinese Cubans: A Transnational History.* Chapel Hill, N.C., 2013.

Lorde, Audre. "The Master's Tools Will Never Dismantle the Master's House." In *Sister Outsider: Essays and Speeches.* Berkeley, Calif., 1984.

Loughran, Trish. *The Republic in Print: Print Culture in the Age of U.S. Nation Building, 1770–1870.* New York, 2009.

Lowe, Lisa. "History Hesitant." *Social Text,* XXXIII, no. 4 (125) (December 2015), 85–107.

——. *The Intimacies of Four Continents.* Durham, N.C., 2015.

Lugo-Ortiz, Agnes, and Angela Rosenthal, eds. *Slave Portraiture in the Atlantic World.* New York, 2013.

Lyons, Clare A. "Mapping an Atlantic Sexual Culture: Homoeroticism in Eighteenth-Century Philadelphia." In Foster, ed., *Long before Stonewall,* 164–203.

MacGaffey, Wyatt. "Constructing a Kongo Identity: Scholarship and Mythopoesis." *Comparative Studies in Society and History,* LVIII (2016), 159–180.

——. "Dialogues of the Deaf: Europeans on the Atlantic Coast of Africa." In Stuart B. Schwartz, ed., *Implicit Understandings: Observing, Reporting, and Reflecting on the Encounters between Europeans and Other Peoples in the Early Modern Era,* 249–267. Cambridge, 1994.

Mainil, Jean. "Allaitement et contamination: Naissance de la Mère-Nourrice dans le discours médical sous les Lumières." *L'Esprit Créateur,* XXXVII, no. 3 (Fall 1997), 14–24.

Mallipeddi, Ramesh. *Spectacular Suffering: Witnessing Slavery in the Eighteenth-Century British Atlantic.* Charlottesville, Va., 2016.

Martini, Carla Corradi. "Aspetti inediti di vita parmigiana negli scritti di Moreau de Saint-Méry." *Aurea Parma,* LXIV, fasc. 2 (1980), 137–142.

————. "L'epoca di Du Tillot nel giudizio di Moreau de Saint-Méry." *Aurea Parma,* LXXXIII, fasc. 1 (1999), 409–428.

————. "Misoginia di Moreau de Saint-Méry nella ricostruzione dei costume parmi-giani di fine settecento." In *Francia e Italia nel XVIII secolo: Immagini e pregiudizi reciproci / France et Italie au XVIIIe siècle: Images et préjugés réciproques.* V Colloquio italo-francese, Torino, 1994, 263–274. Alessandria, Italy, 1995.

————. "Un monument à la gloire de Parme: La Description de Moreau de Saint-Méry." In Christine Peyrard, Francis Pomponi, and Michel Vovelle, eds., *L'administration napoléonienne en Europe: Adhésions et résistances,* 17–34. Aix-en-Provence, 2008.

Mason, George Henry. *The Costume of China, Illustrated by Sixty Engravings: With Ex-planations in English and French.* London, 1800.

McClellan, James E., III. *Colonialism and Science: Saint Domingue in the Old Regime.* Baltimore, 1992.

McClellan, James E., III, and François Regourd. *The Colonial Machine: French Science and Overseas Expansion in the Old Regime.* Turnhout, Belgium, 2011.

————. "Moreau de Saint-Méry et la machine coloniale." In Taffin, ed., *Moreau de Saint-Méry,* 25–38.

McClintock, Anne. *Imperial Leather: Race, Gender, and Sexuality in the Colonial Con-test.* New York, 1995.

McKittrick, Katherine. *Dear Science and Other Stories.* Durham, N.C., 2021.

Meadows, R. Darrell. "Engineering Exile: Social Networks and the French Atlantic Community, 1789–1809." *French Historical Studies,* XXIII (2000), 67–102.

"Médéric Louis Elie Moreau de Saint-Mery." *Geneanet.* https://gw.geneanet.org/pierfit ?n=moreau+de+saint+mery&oc=&p=mederic+louis+elie.

Michaud, Louis Gabriel. *Biographie des hommes vivants; ou, Histoire par ordre alpha-bétique de la vie publique de tous les hommes qui se sont fait remarquer par leurs actions ou leurs écrits.* Paris, 1818.

Miles, Ellen G., ed. *The Portrait in Eighteenth-Century America.* Newark, Del., 1993.

Miller, Christopher L. *The French Atlantic Triangle: Literature and Culture of the Slave Trade.* Durham, N.C., 2008.

Miller, Joseph C. "Central Africa during the Era of the Slave Trade, c. 1490s–1850s." In Linda M. Heywood, ed., *Central Africans and Cultural Transformations in the Ameri-can Diaspora,* 21–70. New York, 2001.

Miller, Paul B. *Elusive Origins: The Enlightenment in the Modern Caribbean Historical Imagination.* Charlottesville, Va., 2010.

Ministère des finances. *État détaillé des liquidations opérées . . . par la Commission chargée de répartir l'indemnité attribuée aux anciens colons de Saint-Domingue, en exécution de la loi du 30 avril 1826, etc.* Paris, 1828.

Mitchell, W. J. T. *Picture Theory: Essays on Verbal and Visual Representation*. Chicago, 1994.

Mobley, Christina Frances. "The Kongolese Atlantic: Central African Slavery and Culture from Mayombe to Haiti." Ph.D. diss., Duke University, 2015.

Molineux, Catherine. *Faces of Perfect Ebony: Encountering Atlantic Slavery in Imperial Britain*. Cambridge, Mass., 2012.

Monneron, Pierre. *Sur les gens de couleur: Observations sur une lettre de M. Moreau de Saint-Méry, député de la Martinique à l'Assemblée nationale.* . . . Paris, 1791.

Monthly Review; or Literary Journal. Unsigned review of *Second voyage à la Louisiane: Faisant suite au premier de l'auteur*, by Louis-Narcisse Baudry des Lozières. Art. V (1803), appendix, 479–483.

Moore, Lara Jennifer. *Restoring Order: The Ecole des Chartes and the Organization of Archives and Libraries in France, 1820–1870*. Duluth, Minn., 2008.

Moreau de Saint-Méry, Aménaïde. *Conte Moreau de Saint-Méry*. Circa 1800–1805. Galleria Nazionale, Parma, Italy.

Morgan, Edmund S. "Slavery and Freedom: The American Paradox." *Journal of American History*, LIX (1972), 5–29.

Morgan, Jennifer L. "Accounting for 'The Most Excruciating Torment': Gender, Slavery, and Trans-Atlantic Passages." *History of the Present*, VI (2016), 184–207.

———. *Laboring Women: Reproduction and Gender in New World Slavery*. Philadelphia, 2004.

———. *Reckoning with Slavery: Gender, Kinship, and Capitalism in the Early Black Atlantic*. Durham, N.C., 2021.

Morgan, Philip D. "Life in the New World." In *Captive Passage: The Transatlantic Slave Trade and the Making of the Americas*. Washington, D.C., and Newport News, Va., 2002.

Morrison, Toni. *A Mercy*. New York, 2008.

———. *Playing in the Dark: Whiteness and the Literary Imagination*. Cambridge, Mass., 1992.

Murphy, Kathleen S. "Translating the Vernacular: Indigenous and African Knowledge in the Eighteenth-Century British Atlantic." *Atlantic Studies*, VIII (2011), 29–48.

Murray, Laura J. "Vocabularies of Native American Languages: A Literary and Historical Approach to an Elusive Genre." *American Quarterly*, LIII (2001), 590–623.

Nash, Gary B. *Forging Freedom: The Formation of Philadelphia's Black Community, 1720–1840*. Cambridge, Mass., 1991.

Nelson, William Max. "The Atlantic Enlightenment." In D'Maris Coffman, Adrian Leonard, and William O'Reilly, eds., *The Atlantic World*, 650–666. London, 2015.

———. "Making Men: Enlightenment Ideas of Racial Engineering." *American Historical Review*, CXV (2010), 1364–1394.

Nicolson, Père. *Essai sur l'histoire naturelle de l'isle de Saint-Domingue, avec des figures en taille-douce*. Paris, 1776.

Niemcewicz, Julian Ursyn. *Under Their Vine and Fig Tree: Travels through America in 1797–1799, 1805 with Some Further Account of Life in New Jersey*. Edited and translated by Metchie J. E. Budka. Newark, N.J., 1965.

Noël, Érick, ed. *Dictionnaire des gens de couleur dans la France moderne: Paris et son basin; Entrée par localités et par année (fin XVe siècle–1792), Paris suivi des provinces classées alphabétiquement,* I. Geneva, 2011.

Norton, Marcy. "The Chicken or the *Iegue:* Human-Animal Relationships and the Columbian Exchange." *American Historical Review,* CXX (2015), 28–60.

Nsondé, Jean de Dieu. *Langues, culture et histoire Koongo aux XVIIe et XVIIIe siècles: À travers les documents linguistiques.* Paris, 1995.

Ogle, Gene E. "'The Eternal Power of Reason' and 'The Superiority of Whites': Hilliard d'Auberteuil's Colonial Enlightenment." *French Colonial History,* III (2003), 35–50.

Ojo, Olatunji. "Beyond Diversity: Women, Scarification, and Yoruba Identity." *History in Africa,* XXXV (2008), 347–374.

Oz-Salzberger, Fania. "Translation." In Alan Charles Kors, ed., *Oxford Encyclopedia of the Enlightenment,* IV, 181–188. Oxford, 2003.

Palmer, Jennifer L. *Intimate Bonds: Family and Slavery in the French Atlantic.* Philadelphia, 2016.

Palmié, Stephan. "Conventionalization, Distortion, and Plagiarism in the Historiography of Afro-Caribbean Religion in New Orleans." In Wolfgang Binder, ed., *Creoles and Cajuns: French Louisiana—La Louisiane française,* 315–344. Frankfurt, Germany, 1998.

Paquette, Gabriel, ed. *Enlightened Reform in Southern Europe and Its Atlantic Colonies, c. 1750–1830.* London, 2009.

Parrish, Susan Scott. *American Curiosity: Cultures of Natural History in the Colonial British Atlantic World.* Williamsburg, Va., and Chapel Hill, N.C., 2006.

———. "Diasporic African Sources of Enlightenment Knowledge." In James Delbourgo and Nicholas Dew, eds., *Science and Empire in the Atlantic World,* 281–310. London, 2008.

Pasley, Jeffrey L. *"The Tyranny of Printers": Newspaper Politics in the Early American Republic.* Charlottesville, Va., 2002.

Paton, Diana. "Maternal Struggles and the Politics of Childlessness under Pronatalist Caribbean Slavery." *Slavery and Abolition,* XXXVIII (2017), 251–268.

———. "Telling Stories about Slavery (Review)." *History Workshop Journal,* LIX (2005), 251–262.

Peabody, Sue. *Madeleine's Children: Family, Freedom, Secrets, and Lies in France's Indian Ocean Colonies.* New York, 2017.

———. "Microhistory, Biography, Fiction: The Politics of Narrating the Lives of People under Slavery." *Transatlantica,* II (2012), 1–19.

———. "Reading and Writing Historical Fiction." *Iowa Journal of Literary Studies,* X (1989), 29–39.

———. *"There Are No Slaves in France": The Political Culture of Race and Slavery in the Ancien Régime.* New York, 1996.

Peabody, Sue, and Tyler Stovall, eds. *The Color of Liberty: Histories of Race in France.* Durham, N.C., 2003.

Pease, Donald. "Introduction: Re-mapping the Transnational Turn." In Winfried Fluck, Pease, and John Carlos Rowe, eds., *Re-framing the Transnational Turn in American Studies,* 1–46. Hanover, N.H., 2011.

Perkov, Kayleigh. "To Know a Hottentot Venus Feminist: Feminist Epistemology and the Artworks Surrounding Sarah Bartman." *Aleph,* July 26, 2015. http://aleph .humanities.ucla.edu/2015/07/26/to-know-a-hottentot-venus-feminist-feminist -epistemology-and-the-artworks-surrounding-sarah-bartman/.

Pérotin-Dumon, Anne. *La ville aux Iles, la ville dans l'île: Basse-Terre et Pointe-à-Pitre, Guadeloupe, 1650–1820.* Paris, 2000.

Peyrard, Christine, Francis Pomponi, and Michel Vovelle, eds. *L'administration napoléonienne en Europe: Adhésions et résistances.* Aix-en-Provence, France, 2008.

Philip, M. NourbeSe, and Setaey Adamu Boateng. *Zong!* Middletown, Conn., 2008.

Phillips, Dana. *The Truth of Ecology: Nature, Culture, and Literature in America.* New York, 2003.

Plaisir, Marielle. Variation on *Aponte Lámina 23.* In *The Book of Life.* 2017. Inks, gold pigment, and pencil on 350g paper, 20 × 15 in. *Visionary Aponte: Art and Black Freedom* exhibit, Little Haiti Cultural Center, New York University, and Duke University, 2017–2018.

Polcha, Elizabeth. "Voyeur in the Torrid Zone: John Gabriel Stedman's *Narrative of a Five Years Expedition against the Revolted Negroes of Surinam, 1773–1838.*" *Early American Literature,* LIV (2019), 673–710.

Ponce, Nicolas. *Les illustres français; ou, Tableaux historiques des grands hommes de la France....* Paris, [1790–1816].

———. *Recueil de vues des lieux principaux de la colonie française de Saint-Domingue.* Paris, 1791.

Pons, Bruno. "Les cadres français du XVIIIe siècle et leurs ornements." *Revue de l'art,* LXXVI (1987), 41–50.

Popkin, Jeremy D. "A Colonial Media Revolution: The Press in Saint-Domingue, 1789– 1793." *Americas,* LXXV (2018), 3–25.

———. *A Concise History of the Haitian Revolution.* [Malden, Mass., 2012].

———. *You Are All Free: The Haitian Revolution and the Abolition of Slavery.* Cambridge, 2010.

Putnam, Lara. "To Study the Fragments / Whole: Microhistory and the Atlantic World." *Journal of Social History,* XXXIX (2006), 615–630.

Quinlan, Sean. "Colonial Bodies, Hygiene, and Abolitionist Politics in Eighteenth-Century France." *History Workshop Journal,* no. 42 (Autumn 1996), 106–125.

Quintero Saravia, Gonzalo M. *Bernardo de Gálvez: Spanish Hero of the American Revolution.* Chapel Hill, N.C., 2018.

Qureshi, Sadiah. "Displaying Sara Baartman, the 'Hottentot Venus.'" *History of Science,* XLII (2004), 233–257.

Raddin, George Gates, Jr. *An Early New York Library of Fiction: With a Checklist of the Fiction in H. Caritat's Circulating Library, No. 1 City Hotel, Broadway, New York, 1804.* New York, 1940.

———. *Hocquet Caritat and the Early New York Literary Scene*. Dover, N.J., 1953.

Raimond, Julien. *Observations adressées à l'Assemblée nationale, par un député des colons américains*. [Paris?], 1789.

———. *Observations sur l'origine et les progrés du préjugé des colons blancs contre les hommes de couleur*. Paris, 1791.

———. *Réponse aux considérations de M. Moreau, dit Saint-Méry, député à l'Assemblée nationale, sur les colonies; par M. Raymond, citoyen de couleur de Saint-Domingue*. Paris, 1791.

Rasmussen, Birgit Brander. *Queequeg's Coffin: Indigenous Literacies and Early American Literature*. Durham, N.C., 2012.

Rediker, Marcus. "The Art of History: The Poetics of History from Below." *Perspectives on History*, September 1, 2010. https://www.historians.org/publications-and -directories/perspectives-on-history/september-2010/the-poetics-of-history-from -below.

Regis, Pamela. *Describing Early America: Bartram, Jefferson, Crèvecoeur, and the Influence of Natural History*. Philadelphia, 1999.

Reid-Maroney, Nina. *Philadelphia's Enlightenment, 1740–1800: Kingdom of Christ, Empire of Reason*. Westport, Conn., 2001.

Reinhardt, Catherine A. *Claims to Memory: Beyond Slavery and Emancipation in the French Caribbean*. New York, 2006.

Reséndez, Andrés. *The Other Slavery: The Uncovered Story of Indian Enslavement in America*. Boston, 2016.

Ricken, Ulrich. *Linguistics, Anthropology, and Philosophy in the French Enlightenment: A Contribution to the History of the Relationship between Language Theory and Ideology*. London, 2014.

Risen, Clay. "Jack Daniel's Embraces a Hidden Ingredient: Help from a Slave." *New York Times*, June 25, 2016, A4. https://www.nytimes.com/2016/06/26/dining /jack-daniels-whiskey-nearis-green-slave.html?_r=0.

Rivett, Sarah. "Learning to Write Algonquian Letters: The Indigenous Place of Language Philosophy in the Seventeenth-Century Atlantic World." *William and Mary Quarterly*, 3d Ser., LXXI (2014), 549–588.

Robins, Nick. *The Corporation That Changed the World: How the East India Company Shaped the Modern Multinational*. 2d ed. London, 2012.

Rodriguez, Yliana. "Spanish-Guarani Diglossia in Colonial Paraguay: A Language Undertaking." In Brigitte Weber, ed., *The Linguistic Heritage of Colonial Practice*, 153–168. Berlin, 2019.

Rogers, Dominique. "Entre 'Lumières' et préjugés: Moreau de Saint-Méry et les libres de couleur de la partie française de Saint-Domingue." In Taffin, ed., *Moreau de Saint-Méry*, 77–94.

———. "Les Libres de couleur dans les capitales de Saint-Domingue: Fortune, mentalités et intégration à la fin de l'Ancien Régime (1776–1789)." Ph.D. diss., Université Michel de Montaigne-Bordeaux III, 2001.

———. "Réussir dans un monde d'hommes: Les stratégies des femmes de couleur du Cap-Français." *Journal of Haitian Studies*, IX, no. 1 (Spring 2003), 40–51.

Rogers, Dominique, and Stewart King. "Housekeepers, Merchants, Rentières: Free
    Women of Color in the Port Cities of Colonial Saint-Domingue, 1750–1790." In
    Douglas Catterall and Jodi Campbell, eds., *Women in Port: Gendering Communities,
    Economies, and Social Networks in Atlantic Port Cities, 1500–1800,* 357–398. Leiden,
    Netherlands, 2012.

Rosengarten, Joseph G. "Moreau de Saint Mery and His French Friends in the American
    Philosophical Society." American Philosophical Society, *Proceedings,* L (1911), 168–178.

Rosenthal, Caitlin C. "From Memory to Mastery: Accounting for Control in America,
    1750–1880." *Enterprise and Society,* XIV (2013), 732–748.

Rossignol, Bernadette, and Philippe Rossignol. "Moreau de Saint-Méry," *Généalogie et
    Histoire de la Caraïbe,* no. 171 (June 2002), 4221.

Ruiz [de Montoya], Antonio. *Tesoro de la lengua Guarani.* Madrid, 1639.

Rushforth, Brett. *Bonds of Alliance: Indigenous and Atlantic Slaveries in New France.*
    Williamsburg, Va., and Chapel Hill, N.C., 2012.

Saillant, John. "The Black Body Erotic and the Republican Body Politic, 1790–1820."
    In Foster, ed., *Long before Stonewall,* 303–330.

Sala-Molins, Louis. *Le code noir; ou, Le calvaire de Canaan.* Paris, 1987.

———. *Dark Side of the Light: Slavery and the French Enlightenment.* Minneapolis,
    2006.

Samford, Patricia. "The Archaeology of African-American Slavery and Material Cul-
    ture." *William and Mary Quarterly,* 3d Ser., LIII (1996), 87–114.

Saunders, Patricia. "Defending the Dead, Confronting the Archive: A Conversation
    with M. NourbeSe Philip." *Small Axe,* XII, no. 2 (June 2008), 63–79.

Sayre, Gordon M. *Les Sauvages Américains: Representations of Native Americans in
    French and English Colonial Literature.* Chapel Hill, N.C., 1997.

———. "*Michipichik* and the Walrus: Anishinaabe Natural History in the Seventeenth-
    Century Work of Louis Nicolas." *Journal for Early Modern Cultural Studies,* XVII,
    no. 4 (Fall 2017), 21–48.

———. "'Take My Scalp, Please!': Colonial Mimesis and the French Origins of the
    Mississippi Tall Tale." In Matt Cohen and Jeffrey Glover, eds., *Colonial Mediascapes:
    Sensory Worlds of the Early Americas,* 203–229. Lincoln, Neb., 2014.

Schama, Simon. *Patriots and Liberators: Revolution in the Netherlands, 1780–1813.* New
    York, 1977.

Schiebinger, Londa, and Claudia Swan, eds. *Colonial Botany: Science, Commerce, and
    Politics in the Early Modern World.* Philadelphia, 2005.

Schildkrout, Enid. "Inscribing the Body." *Annual Review of Anthropology,* XXXIII
    (2004), 319–344.

Schinz, Albert. "La librairie française en Amérique au temps de Washington." *Revue
    d'histoire littéraire de la France,* XXIV (1917), 568–584.

Schryver, Gilles-Maurice de, Rebecca Grollemund, Simon Branford, and Koen Bostoen.
    "Introducing a State-of-the-Art Phylogenetic Classification of the Kikongo Language
    Cluster." *Africana Linguistica,* XXI (2015), 87–163.

Scott, David. "Antinomies of Slavery, Enlightenment, and Universal History." *Small
    Axe,* XIV, no. 3 (November 2010), 152–162.

———. *Conscripts of Modernity: The Tragedy of Colonial Enlightenment.* Durham, N.C., 2004.

———. *Omens of Adversity: Tragedy, Time, Memory, Justice.* Durham, N.C., 2014.

Scott, Rebecca J., and Jean M. Hébrard. *Freedom Papers: An Atlantic Odyssey in the Age of Emancipation.* Cambridge, Mass., 2012.

Scruggs, John, performer. "Little Old Log Cabin in the Lane." In *Times Ain't Like They Used to Be: Early American Rural and Popular American Music, 1928–1935.* Produced by Sherwin Dunner and Richard Nevins. Shanachie Entertainment, 2000. Videodisc (DVD), circa 70 min.

Seeber, Edward Derbyshire. *Anti-Slavery Opinion in France during the Second Half of the Eighteenth Century.* Baltimore, 1937.

Sellwood, Jane. "Brooke, Frances Moore." In William H. New, ed., *Encyclopedia of Literature in Canada,* 156–158. Toronto, 2002.

Semley, Lorelle. *To Be Free and French: Citizenship in France's Atlantic Empire.* Cambridge, 2017.

Sepinwall, Alyssa Goldstein. "If This Is a Woman: Evelyne Trouillot's *The Infamous Rosalie* and the Lost Stories of New-World Slavery." *Fiction and Film for French Historians,* V, no. 4 (February 2015). https://h-france.net/fffh/classics/if-this-is-a-woman-evelyne-trouillots-the-infamous-rosalie-and-the-lost-stories-of-new-world-slavery/.

———. "Whiteness, Gender, and Slavery in Enlightenment Le Havre: Marie Le Masson Le Golft's Self-Fashioning as a *Femme des Lettres*." *Journal of the Western Society for French History,* XLVIII (2022), 25–27.

Shapiro, Stephen. "In a French Position: Radical Pornography and Homoerotic Society in Charles Brockden Brown's *Ormond or the Secret Witness*." In Foster, ed., *Long before Stonewall,* 357–383.

Sharpe, Christina E. *In the Wake: On Blackness and Being.* Durham, N.C., 2016.

Sharples, James. *Médéric-Louis-Élie Moreau de Saint-Méry.* 1798. Pastel and black chalk (or black pastel) on toned (now oxidized) wove paper. 9 7/16 × 7 1/4 in. (24 × 18.4 cm). The Metropolitan Museum of Art. https://www.metmuseum.org/art/collection/search/12563.

Shelford, April G. "Pascal in Jamaica: Or, The French Enlightenment in Translation." *Proceedings of the Western Society for French History,* XXXVI (2008), 53–74.

Shields, David S., et al. *Liberty! Égalité! ¡Independencia!: Print Culture, Enlightenment, and Revolutions in the Americas, 1776–1838.* Worcester, Mass., 2007.

Sidbury, James. *Becoming African in America: Race and Nation in the Early Black Atlantic.* New York, 2007.

Sigal, Pete, Zeb Tortorici, and Neil L. Whitehead, eds. *Ethno-pornography: Sexuality, Colonialism, and Archival Knowledge.* Durham, N.C., 2020.

Silvestre, [Augustin-François de]. *Discours prononcé le 30 janvier 1819, lors de l'inhumation de M. Moreau de Saint-Méry, membre de la Société.* [Paris], 1819.

Simonin, Anne, and Elisabeth Liris. "François-Jean Baudouin Itinéraire (1759–1835)." *Décrets et Lois 1789–1795: Collection Baudouin.* http://archives-web.univ-paris1.fr/collection-baudouin/f-j-baudouin/itineraire-de-vie-1759-1835/index.html.

Slauter, Eric. "History, Literature, and the Atlantic World." *William and Mary Quarterly,* 3d Ser., LVI (2008), 153–186.

Sloan, Phillip R. "Natural History." In Knud Haakonssen, ed., *The Cambridge History of Eighteenth-Century Philosophy,* II, 903–938. New York, 2006.

Smallwood, Stephanie E. "The Politics of the Archive and History's Accountability to the Enslaved." *History of the Present,* VI, no. 2 (Fall 2016), 117–132.

———. *Saltwater Slavery: A Middle Passage from Africa to American Diaspora.* Cambridge, Mass., 2007.

Smiley, Michelle. "Daguerreotypes and Humbugs: Pwan-Ye-Koo, Racial Science, and the Circulation of Ethnographic Images around 1850." *Panorama: Journal of the Association of Historians of American Art,* VI, no. 2 (Fall 2020). https://doi.org/10.24926/24716839.10895.

Smith, John. *The Printer's Grammar: Containing a Concise History of the Origin of Printing. . . .* London, 1787.

Smith, Matthew J. *Liberty, Fraternity, Exile: Haiti and Jamaica after Emancipation.* Chapel Hill, N.C., 2014.

Snyder, Terri L. *The Power to Die: Slavery and Suicide in British North America.* Chicago, 2015.

Socolow, Susan M. "Economic Roles of the Free Women of Color of Cap Français." In Gaspar and Hine, eds., *More than Chattel,* 279–297.

Spary, E. C. *Utopia's Garden: French Natural History from Old Regime to Revolution.* Chicago, 2000.

Spillers, Hortense J. "Mama's Baby, Papa's Maybe: An American Grammar Book." *Diacritics,* XVII, no. 2 (Summer 1987), 64–81.

Spires, Derrick R. *The Practice of Citizenship: Black Politics and Print Culture in the Early United States.* Philadelphia, 2019.

Spivak, Gayatri Chakravorty. "The Politics of Translation." In Michèle Barrett and Anne Phillips, eds., *Destabilizing Theory: Contemporary Feminist Debates,* 179–200. Stanford, Calif., 1992.

Stedman, J[ohn] G[abriel]. *Narrative, of a Five Years' Expedition, against the Revolted Negroes of Surinam, in Guiana, on the Wild Coast of South America; from the Year 1772, to 1777. . . .* 2 vols. London, 1796.

St. George, Robert Blair, ed. *Possible Pasts: Becoming Colonial in Early America.* Ithaca, N.Y., 2000.

Stitt, Jocelyn Fenton. *Dreams of Archives Unfolded: Absence and Caribbean Life Writing.* New Brunswick, N.J., 2021.

Stoler, Ann Laura. *Carnal Knowledge and Imperial Power: Race and the Intimate in Colonial Rule.* Berkeley, Calif., 2002.

Stolley, Karen. *Domesticating Empire: Enlightenment in Spanish America.* Nashville, Tenn., 2013.

Streeby, Shelley. *Radical Sensations: World Movements, Violence, and Visual Culture.* Durham, N.C., 2013.

Sullivan, Edward J., ed. *Continental Shifts: The Art of Edouard Duval Carrié.* Miami, 2007.

Sweet, James H. *Recreating Africa: Culture, Kinship, and Religion in the African-Portuguese World, 1441–1770.* Chapel Hill, N.C., 2003.

———. "Reimagining the African-Atlantic Archive: Method, Concept, Epistemology, Ontology." *Journal of African History,* LV (2014), 147–159.

———. "Research Note: New Perspectives on Kongo in Revolutionary Haiti." *Americas,* LXXIV (2017), 83–97.

Syrett, Harold C., ed. *The Papers of Alexander Hamilton.* Vol. XVII, *August 1794–December 1794.* New York, 1972.

Taber, Robert D., and Charlton W. Yingling. "Networks, Tastes, and Labor in Free Communities of Color: Transforming the Revolutionary Caribbean." *Atlantic Studies,* XIV (2017), 263–274.

Taffin, Dominique, ed. *Moreau de Saint-Méry; ou, Les ambiguïtés d'un créole des Lumières. . . .* [Fort-de-France], Martinique, 2006.

Taillemite, Étienne. "Moreau de Saint-Méry." In Médéric Louis Élie Moreau de Saint-Méry, *La description topographique, physique, civile, politique et historique de la partie française de l'isle Saint-Domingue. . . .* Edited by Blanche Maurel and Taillemite. New ed. 3 vols. I, vii–xxxvi. Saint-Denis, France, 2004.

Tardieu, Patrick D. "Pierre Roux et Lémery Imprimeurs de Saint-Domingue à Haïti." *Revue de la Société haïtienne d'histoire et de géographie,* LXXIX, no. 218 (April 2004), 1–30.

Taylor, Alan. *American Revolutions: A Continental History, 1750–1804.* New York, 2016.

Thompson, Peter. "'Judicious Neology': The Imperative of Paternalism in Thomas Jefferson's Linguistic Studies." *Early American Studies,* I (2003), 187–224.

Thornton, John. "African Soldiers in the Haitian Revolution." In Laurent Dubois and Julius S. Scott, eds., *Origins of the Black Atlantic: Rewriting Histories,* 195–213. New York, 2010. Originally published in *Journal of Caribbean History,* XXV (1991), 58–80.

———. *A Cultural History of the Atlantic World, 1250–1820.* Cambridge, 2012.

———. "'I Am the Subject of the King of Congo': African Political Ideology in the Haitian Revolution." *Journal of World History,* IV (1993), 181–214.

———. "The Kingdom of Kongo and Palo Mayombe: Reflections on an African-American Religion." *Slavery and Abolition,* XXXVII (2016), 1–22.

Tricoire, Damien, ed. *Enlightened Colonialism: Civilization Narratives and Imperial Politics in the Age of Reason.* Cham, Switzerland, 2017.

Trouillot, Évelyne. *The Infamous Rosalie / Rosalie L'infâme.* Translated by M. A. Salvodon. Lincoln, Neb., 2013.

Trouillot, Michel-Rolph. *Silencing the Past: Power and the Production of History.* Boston, 1995.

Trumbull, John. *George Washington and William Lee.* 1780. Oil on canvas. 36 × 28 in. (91.4 × 71.1 cm). The Metropolitan Museum of Art. https://www.metmuseum.org/art/collection/search/12822.

Turner, Sasha. *Contested Bodies: Pregnancy, Childrearing, and Slavery in Jamaica.* Philadelphia, 2017.

———. "The Nameless and the Forgotten: Maternal Grief, Sacred Protection, and the Archive of Slavery." Special issue of *Slavery and Abolition,* XXXVIII (2017), 232–250.

[Tussac, François Richard de]. *Cri des colons contre un ouvrage de M. L'Evêque et Sénateur Grégoire.... Paris, 1810.*

Ulysse, Gina Athena. *Why Haiti Needs New Narratives: A Post-Quake Chronicle.* Middletown, Conn., 2015.

van Braam [Houckgeest], André Everard. *An Authentic Account of the Embassy of the Dutch East-India Company, to the Court of the Emperor of China, in the Years 1794 and 1795....* London, 1798.

Van Winkle Keller, Kate. *Dance and Its Music in America, 1528–1789.* Hillsdale, N.Y., 2007.

Vass, Winifred Kellersberger. *The Bantu Speaking Heritage of the United States.* Los Angeles, 1979.

Vastey, [Pompée-Valentin], Baron de. *The Colonial System Unveiled.* Edited and translated by Chris Bongie. Liverpool, U.K., 2014.

———. *Le système colonial dévoilé.* [Cap Haitien], Haiti, 1814.

Vélez, María Teresa. *Drumming for the Gods: The Life and Times of Felipe García Villamil, Santero, Palero, and Abakuá.* Philadelphia, 2000.

Wagner, Muriel. "Eerie Tales Surround History of Croydon's 'China Hall': Old Mansion Rumored as Former Slave Market." *Bristol Daily Courier,* Sept. 20, 1956.

Walters, Wendy W. *Archives of the Black Atlantic: Reading between Literature and History.* New York, 2013.

———. "'One of Dese Mornings, Bright and Fair, / Take My Wings and Cleave de Air': The Legend of the Flying Africans and Diasporic Consciousness." *MELUS,* XXII, no. 3 (Fall 1997), 3–29.

Warner-Lewis, Maureen. *Central Africa in the Caribbean: Transcending Time, Transforming Cultures.* Mona, Jamaica, 2002.

Watson, Tim. *Caribbean Culture and British Fiction in the Atlantic World, 1770–1870.* Cambridge, 2008.

Weaver, Karol K. *Medical Revolutionaries: The Enslaved Healers of Eighteenth-Century Saint Domingue.* Urbana, Ill., 2006.

Webber, Mabel L. "Marriage and Death Notices from the South Carolina Weekly Gazette." *South Carolina Historical and Genealogical Magazine,* II (1918), 109–110, and XIX (1918), 137.

West, Emily, and R. J. Knight. "Mothers' Milk: Slavery, Wet-Nursing, and Black and White Women in the Antebellum South." *Journal of Southern History,* LXXXIII (2017), 37–68.

White, Ashli. *Encountering Revolution: Haiti and the Making of the Early Republic.* Baltimore, 2010.

White, Hayden. *The Fiction of Narrative: Essays on History, Literature, and Theory, 1957–2007.* Baltimore, 2010.

White, Sophie. *Voices of the Enslaved: Love, Labor, and Longing in French Louisiana.* Williamsburg, Va., and Chapel Hill, N.C., 2019.

Wills, John E., Jr. *Pepper, Guns, and Parleys: The Dutch East India Company and China, 1662–1681.* Los Angeles, 2005.

Wilson, Ivy G. *Specters of Democracy: Blackness and the Aesthetics of Politics in the Antebellum U.S.* New York, 2011.

———. "The Writing on the Wall: Revolutionary Aesthetics and Interior Spaces." In Cindy Weinstein and Christopher Looby, eds., *American Literature's Aesthetic Dimensions,* 56–72. New York, 2012.

Winterer, Caroline. *American Enlightenments: Pursuing Happiness in the Age of Reason.* New Haven, Conn., 2016.

Wolff, Lesley A., Michael D. Carrasco, and Paul B. Niell. "Rituals of Refinement: Edouard Duval-Carrié's Historical Pursuits." In *Decolonizing Refinement: Contemporary Pursuits in the Art of Edouard Duval-Carrié.* Florida State University Museum of Fine Arts Exhibition Catalog, Tallahassee, 2018.

Womack, Craig. *Red on Red: Native American Literary Separatism.* Minneapolis, 1999.

Wong, Edlie L. *Neither Fugitive nor Free: Atlantic Slavery, Freedom Suits, and the Legal Culture of Travel.* New York, 2009.

Wood, Laurie M. *Archipelago of Justice: Law in France's Early Modern Empire.* New Haven, Conn., 2020.

Wood, Marcus. *Black Milk: Imagining Slavery in the Visual Cultures of Brazil and America.* Oxford, 2013.

Wood, Peter H. *Strange New Land: Africans in Colonial America.* New York, 2003.

Wroth, Lawrence C. *The Colonial Printer.* 1931. Rpt. New York, 1994.

Yai, Olabiyi. "Texts of Enslavement: Fon and Yoruba Vocabularies from Eighteenth- and Nineteenth-Century Brazil." In Paul Lovejoy, ed., *Identity in the Shadow of Slavery,* 102–112. New York, 2009.

Yang, Chi-ming. *Performing China: Virtue, Commerce, and Orientalism in Eighteenth-Century England, 1660–1760.* Baltimore, 2011.

Yingling, Charlton W. "The Maroons of Santo Domingo in the Age of Revolutions: Adaptation and Evasion, 1783–1800." *History Workshop Journal,* no. 79 (2015), 25–51.

Young, Jason R. "All God's Children Had Wings: The Flying African in History, Literature, and Lore." *Journal of Africana Religions,* V (2017), 50–70.

———. *Rituals of Resistance: African Atlantic Religion in Kongo and the Lowcountry South in the Era of Slavery.* Baton Rouge, La., 2007.

Zamora, Margarita. *Language, Authority, and Indigenous History in the "Comentarios reales de los incas."* Cambridge, 2005.

Zavitz, Erin. "Revolutionary Narrations: Early Haitian Historiography and the Challenge of Writing Counter-History." *Atlantic Studies,* XIV (2017), 336–353.

Zinna, Alison, Deborah Jenson, and Laurent Dubois. "Nation." *Haitian Marronage: Voyages and Resistance.* https://sites.duke.edu/marronnagevoyages/nations/.

INDEX

Page numbers in italics refer to illustrations.

212–213; and natural history, 163–164, 166, 170–171, 174
Boudacan-Marc (prince of the Warri Kingdom), 23, 41–43, 211
Boutin, Pierre-Louis, 47
Brazil, 167, 173, 197
Brissot de Warville, Jacques-Pierre, 140
Brunias, Agostino, 19, 65–69, 72, 80, 86
Buffon, Georges-Louis Leclerc, comte de, 164–166, 169

Canada, 7, 43, 170, 184
Canga, 246
Caribbean: Moreau and, 1–2, 5, 9–12, 42, 118, 155, 235–236, 246; French, 3, 103, 235; revolutions in, 14, 54, 89, 106, 128; artistic portrayals of (artists), 19, 63–65, 69, 84, 86, 89, 118; hispanophone, 20, 155; and Kreyòl, 23, 36, 44–47; Aménaïde in, 26–29; in literature, 40–41, 59, 189, 192, 194, 212, 214; and slavery (enslaved people), 40–41, 76–79, 125, 140, 142, 145, 182; and Africa (Africans), 54, 56, 121–122; and printing, 90, 99, 103, 109; and language, 108, 180–181; and the United States, 129, 131; and natural history, 159–162; and law, 179; and Indigenous peoples, 184
Caribs, 23, 43–44, 184–185, 212
Carpentier, Alejo, 86
Castellanos, Juan, 184
Castor, 15–16, 36, 49–50
Castration, 58–59
Catherine (woman forced to work as an enslaved laborer for the Milhet–Baudry des Lozières family), 131–132
Catherine (woman purchased in Saint-Domingue by Gálvez), 32
Cayenne, 97, 165, 212, 259
Cercle des Philadelphes, 12, 43–44, 108, 133, 184, 190, 196
Charlevoix, Pierre François Xavier de, 169–170

Charton, Louis, 92, 99
Children: Moreau as biological father of, 3; in Moreau's household, 4, 19, 50, 62, 91, 114, 132, 137; and ethics of writing about slavery, 8; Moreau's grandchildren, 28, 76–77; white, 38; and childcare workers, 40, 80–82, 202; and Moreau's taxonomy, 44; death of, 72; as print laborers, 111; and albinism, 163; and puberty, 177; and language, 199–200, 215, 222. See also Angélique (Mirza); Moreau de Saint-Méry, Jeanne-Louise (Aménaïde; Contessa Dall'Asta); Négresses; Wet nurses (nourrices)
China, 87–126; in Moreau's scholarship, 5, 10, 20; and printing, 11, 64, 89–90, 103–104, 161, 163; and labor, 11, 109–113, 116–118, 122–126; Qing, 20, 89, 104, 110; and Emperor Qianlong, 89, 113; diplomatic missions to, 89, 121; and trade relationships with early United States, 90, 104; and Van Braam's "Chinese Retreat" (la retraite chinoise), 90, 113, 115, 117, 122; and adaptation of Van Braam–Moreau title page, 104–106; bridges of, 104, 108, 110–112; Macao, 109, 113; and material culture, 115–116, 244; Mandarin, 116, 120–121; and slavery, 119–120; and gom-gom, 121, 182
Choctaw, 16, 128
Clavigiero, Francisco, 169
Clavijo y Fajardo, José, 165–166
Club Massaic, 12, 91, 98, 142, 262n. 27, 283n. 7
Coercion: sexual, 20, 155, 174–176, 188, 203, 211; and slavery, 128, 177–178, 221
Coffee, 14, 93, 114, 182, 192, 213, 220–221, 224, 244, 252
Colons: European, 14; in Saint-Domingue, 73, 89, 93–94, 99, 101, 139, 225, 236; American, 101, 140, 144
Columbus, Christopher, 3, 184